THE CAMBRIDGE HISTORY OF ARABIC LITERATURE

MODERN ARABIC LITERATURE

WITHDRAWN
UTSA LIBRARIES

MODERN ARABIC LITERATURE

EDITED BY
M. M. BADAWI
Fellow of St Antony's College, Oxford

CAMBRIDGE UNIVERSITY PRESS
Cambridge, New York, Melbourne, Madrid, Cape Town, Singapore, São Paulo

Cambridge University Press
The Edinburgh Building, Cambridge CB2 2RU, UK

Published in the United States of America by Cambridge University Press, New York

www.cambridge.org
Information on this title: www.cambridge.org/9780521331975

© Cambridge University Press 1992

This publication is in copyright. Subject to statutory exception
and to the provisions of relevant collective licensing agreements,
no reproduction of any part may take place without
the written permission of Cambridge University Press.

First published 1992
Reprinted 1997
Hardback version transferred to digital printing 2006
Digitally printed first paperback version 2006

A catalogue record for this publication is available from the British Library

Library of Congress Cataloguing in Publication data

Modern Arabic literature/edited by M. M. Badawī.
p. cm. – (The Cambridge History of Arabic literature)
Includes bibliographical references and index.
ISBN 0-521-33197-8 (hardback)
1. Arabic literature – 20th century – History and criticism.
I. Badawī, Muḥammad Muṣṭafā. II. Series.
PJ7538.M58 1992
892'.7095 – dc20 91-41007-CIP

ISBN-13 978-0-521-33197-5 hardback
ISBN-10 0-521-33197-8 hardback

ISBN-13 978-0-521-02853-0 paperback
ISBN-10 0-521-02853-1 paperback

Library
University of Texas
at San Antonio

CONTENTS

EDITORIAL NOTE

A consolidated bibliography for the whole of this volume would have been too cumbersome to handle and its usefulness would have been somewhat limited. It was decided therefore to have separate bibliographies for individual chapters even at the risk of some repetition. In conformity with the other volumes of the *Cambridge History of Arabic Literature* contributors have been asked, mainly for reasons of space, to reduce their footnotes as far as possible to the bare minimum and to confine their bibliographies to the more important works, although obviously some have found it easier to comply with this request than others and, indeed, in a number of chapters footnotes have been omitted altogether to make room for text. An exception to this rule has been made in the case of the last two chapters dealing with 'Poetry in the vernacular' and 'Arab women writers', respectively, as these are relatively unknown fields and it was felt that a fuller list of references might be of some help to scholars wishing to carry out further investigations in them. Because of the proliferation of studies of modern Arabic literature in French, German, Italian, Spanish, Russian, and even Dutch and Polish, bibliographies have in general been confined to works in the English language. Since the Short Story has emerged as a major genre in modern Arabic literature, enjoying perhaps greater popularity with writers and readers alike than other genres, more space has been allotted to it in the bibliography to give the reader some idea of its size and scope.

I should like to thank all the staff at the Cambridge University Press who have helped in the production of this volume, especially Dr Katharina Brett. I am also grateful to Mrs Barbara Hird for compiling the index.

CHRONOLOGICAL TABLE OF EVENTS

1787	Death of Muhammad ibn Abd al-Wahhab, founder of the Wahhabi Movement in Arabia.
1798	Bonaparte's campaign in Egypt.
1801	French troops evacuate Egypt.
1805	Muhammad Ali becomes effective ruler of Egypt.
1806	Wahhabi forces led by Muhammad al-Saud occupy Mecca, in rebellion against the Ottoman Sultan.
1811	Muhammad Ali wipes out the Mamelukes.
1818	Ibrahim, son of Muhammad Ali, defeats the Wahhabis in Hijaz on behalf of the Ottoman Sultan.
1820s	British pacts with the Gulf Arab Sheiks.
1822	Muhammad Ali's Arabic printing press.
1830	French occupy Algeria.
1831–40	Egyptian occupation of Syria.
1832	Ibrahim defeats the Turks near Konya.
1833	Peace of Kutahya.
1839	British occupation of Aden.
	Turko–Egyptian war.
1840	London conference to settle Egyptian–Turkish relations.
1848	Muhammad Ali dies and is succeeded by Abbas (–1854).
1851–67	Alexandria–Cairo–Suez Railway built.
1860	Construction of the Suez Canal begun. Egyptians occupy Sudan.
	Civil war in Lebanon.
	Persecution of Christians in Damascus.
1861	Creation of autonomous Lebanon.
1863–80	Ismail Pasha of Egypt; in 1866 assumes the title Khedive.
1869	Suez Canal opened.
1875	Mixed Courts introduced in Egypt.
	Ismail sells his Suez shares to Britain.
1880–92	Tawfiq, Khedive of Egypt.
1881	French occupy Tunisia.
1882	Urabi rebellion against Khedive Tawfiq.

	British occupy Egypt, after defeating Urabi at Tall al-Kabir.
1883	Mahdi drives Egyptians out of Sudan.
1885	Khartoum attacked; Gordon killed. Mahdi dies and is succeeded by his Khalifah Abdullahi Abu Bakr.
1896	Kitchener defeats Mahdists at Umm Durman. Khalifah slain.
1901–	Ibn Saud begins reconquest of Najd.
1906	The Dinshaway affair. Cromer's resignation.
1908	Revolution of the Young Turks.
1911–12	Italy captures Libya.
1914	Turkey in World War I. Abbas II deposed and Husayn Kamil made Sultan of Egypt by the British. Egypt declared a British Protectorate.
1916	Arab revolt in Hijaz.
1917	Balfour Declaration issued promising a Jewish National Home in Palestine.
	British take Baghdad. Conquest of Palestine. Fuad Sultan of Egypt.
1918	Arab Hashemite forces occupy Damascus.
	End of Ottoman rule in Arab lands.
1919	Egyptian revolution against the British, led by Saad Zaghlul, head of the Wafd.
1920	French mandates established for Syria and Lebanon, and British for Palestine, Transjordan and Iraq.
	Nationalist revolt in Iraq.
	Arab rising in Palestine.
1924	Abolition of the Ottoman Caliphate by Atatürk.
1924–25	Ibn Saud conquers Hijaz.
1925	Nationalist revolt in Syria.
1932	Saudi Arabian Kingdom proclaimed by Ibn Saud.
	End of British Mandate in Iraq.
1936	Anglo-Egyptian treaty, recognizing independence of Egypt.
1945	League of Arab States created.
1946	Britain recognizes independence of Transjordan, which becomes a monarchy.
	Syria and Lebanon become independent republics after the end of the Mandate.
1948	End of mandate for Palestine, establishment of State of Israel.
	Arab–Jewish war.
1949	First of various *coups d'état* in Syria.
	Assassination of Hasan al-Banna (b. 1906), founder of the Muslim Brotherhood (1928).
1951	Libya becomes an independent Kingdom.

1952	Egyptian army revolution, abdication of King Farouk.
1953	Egypt becomes a Republic.
	Husayn ibn Talal becomes King of Jordan.
1954	Colonel Gamal Abd al-Nasser becomes President of Egypt.
1955	British evacuation of Suez Canal zone. Baghdad Pact signed with Iraq and Jordan.
1956	Sudan, Tunisia and Morocco become independent.
	Nasser nationalizes Suez Canal. Israeli invasion of Sinai and Anglo-French expedition in Suez. British/French forces withdrawn in 1956, and Israeli in 1957.
1957	Tunisia becomes a Republic, with Bourguiba as President.
1958	Egypt and Syria form United Arab Republic.
	Revolution in Iraq, which becomes a Republic with Abdul Karim Kassem as President.
1960	Mauritania becomes independent.
1961	Kuwait becomes independent.
	Syria secedes from the United Arab Republic. Egypt adopts Arab socialism.
1962	Algeria becomes independent after a prolonged and bloody war of independence.
	Republican revolution in Yemen. Royalist–Republican civil war.
1962–67	Egyptian forces fight on the side of the revolutionaries.
1963	Baathist revolution in Syria.
1967	Arab–Israeli war (June War). Israeli occupation of West Bank and Gaza.
1968	Republic of South Yemen.
1969	King Idris of Libya ousted by young army officers, led by Colonel Muammar Qaddafi.
	Yasser Arafat becomes Chairman of Palestine Liberation Organization.
1970	Nasser dies and is succeeded by Anwar Sadat.
1971	General Hafez Asad becomes President of Syrian Arab Republic.
	Qatar and Bahrain become independent.
	Formation of Union of Arab Emirates (Abu Dhabi, Ajman, Dubai, Fujaira, Ras al-Khaima, Sharja and Umm al-Quwain).
1973	Arab–Israeli war (October War). Egyptian forces storm the Bar-lev line and cross the Suez canal.
	Emergence of oil as powerful weapon used by the Arab oil states.

1975–	Lebanese civil war.
1977	President Sadat visits Jerusalem and addresses the Israeli Knesset.
1978–79	Iranian revolution led by Ayatollah Khomeini, overthrow of Shah.
1978	Sadat signs the Camp David accord with Israel.
1979	Sadat signs the Israeli–Egyptian Peace Treaty. Egypt isolated and expelled from the Arab League. Saddam Husayn takes over as President of Iraq.
1979–88	Iraq–Iran war.
1981	President Sadat assassinated by Muslim fundamentalists and is succeeded by Husni Mubarak.
1982–84	Israeli invasion of Lebanon to crush the Palestinian Liberation Organisation led by Yasser Arafat.
1987–	Palestinian *intifada*: uprising of Palestinian Arabs in territories occupied by Israel.
1989	(May) Egypt readmitted to the Arab League. (December) Syria restores diplomatic relations with Egypt.
1990	(May) Republic of Yemen formed by the union of the Yemen Arab Republic (North Yemen) and People's Democratic Republic of Yemen (South Yemen).
1990	(August) occupation and annexation of Kuwait by Saddam Husayn's Iraqi troops.
1991	(March) expulsion of Iraqi soldiers from Kuwait by Allied forces of the United Nations.

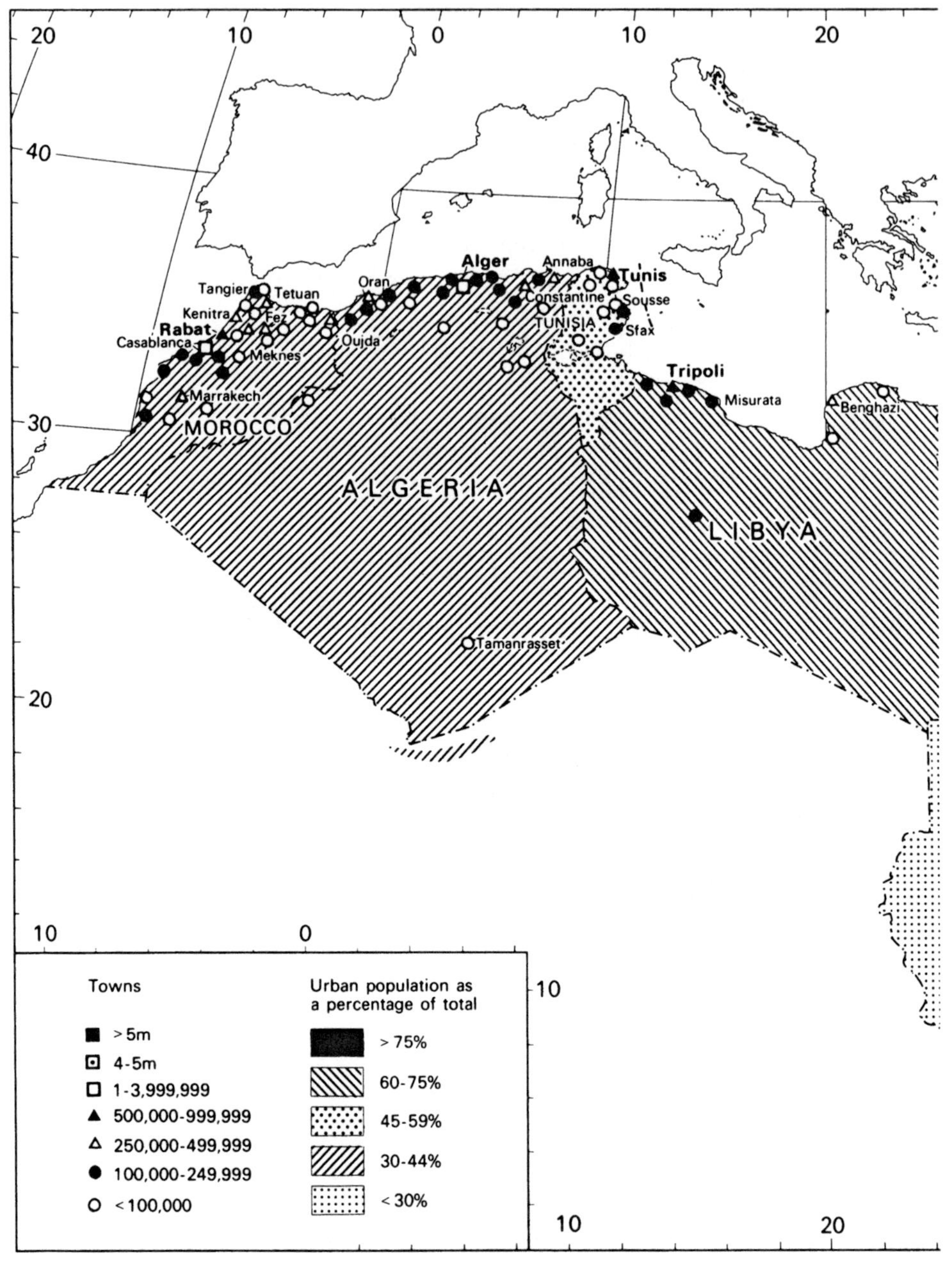

MAP OF THE ARAB WORLD
(Source: *The Cambridge Atlas of the Middle East and North Africa*, 1987)

Population figures in the Arab World (1989)
(Source: *Encyclopaedia Britannica* 1990 *Book of the year*)

Algeria 24,579,000
Bahrain 488,500
Egypt 51,748,000
Iraq 17,215,000
Jordan 3,059,000
Kuwait 2,048,000
Lebanon 2,897,000
Libya 4,080,000
Morocco 24,530,000

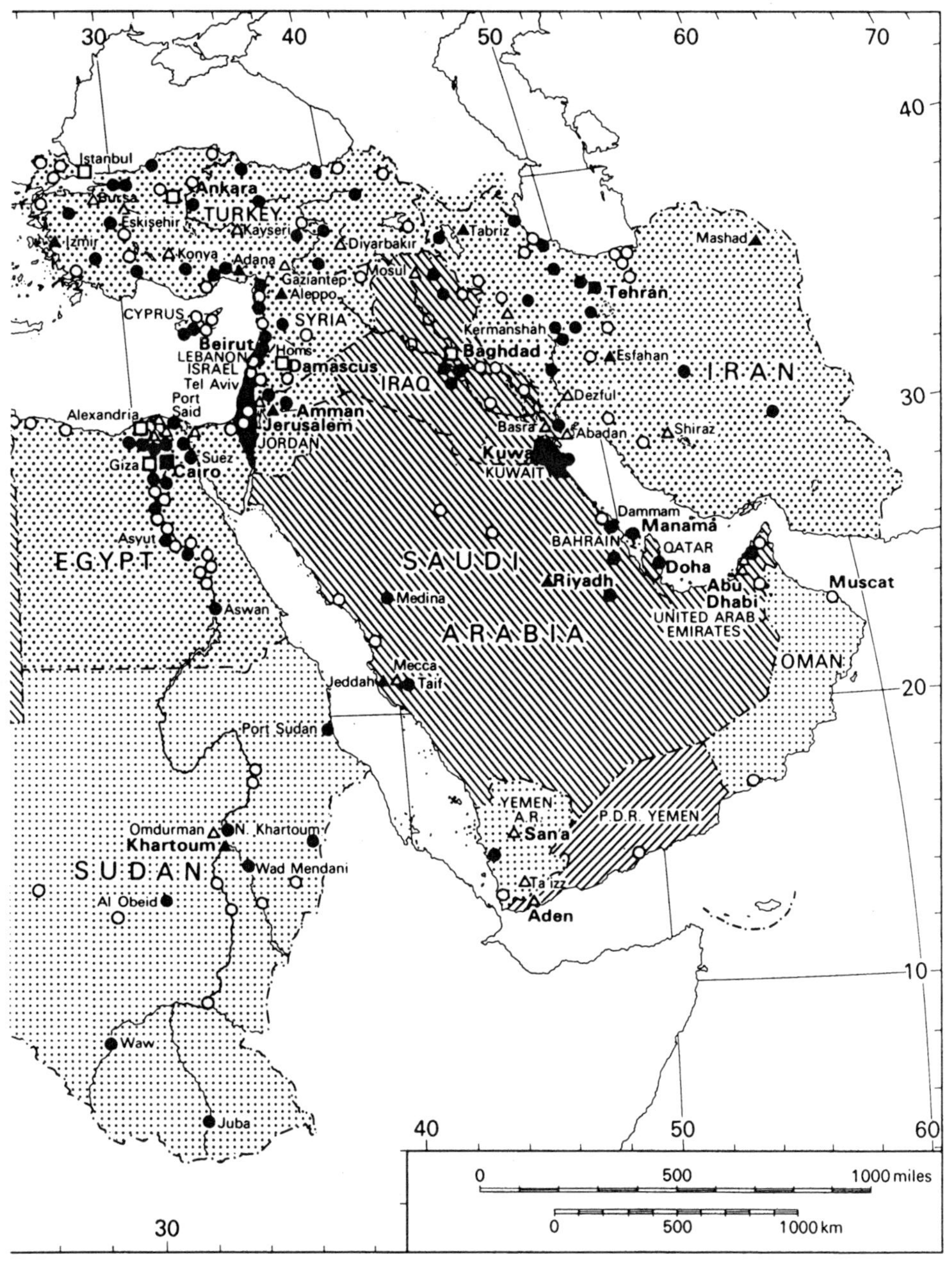

Oman 1,422,000
Qatar 427,000
Saudi Arabia 13,592,000

Sudan 27,268,000
Syria 11,719,000
Tunisia 7,973,000
United Arab Emirates
1,827,000

*Yemen Arab Republic
8,834,000
*People's Democratic
Republic of Yemen
2,406,000

*Both republics united in 1990 and called Republic of Yemen

CHAPTER 1

INTRODUCTION

I THE BACKGROUND

The Nahḍah

Compared with earlier periods of Arabic literature the Modern period, often referred to in Arabic as *al-Nahḍah* (= renaissance), requires an approach that is at once simpler and more complicated. While Classical Arabic literature can safely be regarded as fundamentally a continuum, Modern literature constitutes in certain important respects an entirely new departure, even though its break with the Classical has sometimes been exaggerated, for despite its borrowing of European forms such as drama and the novel, Modern literature never really completely severed its link with its past. The *Nahḍah* was in fact a product of a fruitful meeting of two forces: the indigenous tradition, and the imported western forms. Moreover, the change from the past was an extremely slow and gradual process. However, because of the profound influence exercised by western literature on the *Nahḍah*, it seems more natural to divide its treatment into chapters on poetry, the novel, short story, drama and literary criticism, much as one might do in a traditional survey of a western literature. But it would be wrong to be blind to the continuities in Arabic literature, Classical and Modern: continuities that have determined the manner of the Arabs' apprehension and hence adaptation of the imported genres. Equally, we would be guilty of distortion if we ignored the various important issues that seem to be peculiar to Modern Arabic literature, or at least to distinguish it from the literature of the west. By modern Arabic literature, it must be pointed out, is meant literature written exclusively in the Arabic language. The peculiarly modern phenomenon of Arab authors expressing themselves in their creative writing in a European language, be it in French or English, is no doubt both fascinating and important, and merits serious study for literary and extra-literary considerations, but strictly speaking it does not belong to *Arabic* literature and as such it had to be excluded from this survey. There is so much that has been and is being written in Arabic throughout the Arab world, which stretches from the Atlantic Ocean to the

(Persian) Gulf and from the Northern Mediterranean to the heart of Africa, that in such a vast and fast-growing field the following treatment must perforce be rigorously selective.

Modern Arabic literature is obviously the literature of the modern Arab world, and this is generally assumed to begin with the French campaign in Egypt in 1798. The date is significant, for it marks the dramatic opening of the Arab world, which was then part of the Ottoman Empire, to the west, ultimately with momentous consequences for its political, economic, social and cultural development. For various reasons the modern renaissance of Arabic literature began to make itself felt in Egypt and Syria (which then included Lebanon), from which it spread slowly to the rest of the Arab world.

The Ottoman period

The Arabs had started their steady decline early in the sixteenth century with the rise to power of the Ottoman Turks who imposed their rule over virtually the whole of the Arab world: the Turks conquered Syria in 1516, Egypt in 1517, Algiers in 1516, Tripoli in 1555, Tunis in 1574, and established their rule in Iraq in 1639 and subsequently in Yemen and Hejaz. Only Central Arabia (Nejd) and Morocco remained independent of the Ottomans. Apart from North Africa, the conquered Arab territories continued to be governed, albeit in some cases nominally, by the Ottomans until early in the twentieth century.

The Arab territories were divided into provinces, each governed by an Ottoman pacha, a ruler responsible directly to the Sultan in Constantinople, with the help of officials, tax collectors and *Sharīʿah* judges, all appointed by the central government, officially for one year only in order to ensure their obedience. Local elements such as ulema or notables were also made use of and gradually these often assumed considerable power, as in the case of Egypt where the Mamelukes regained effective control, with the Ottoman Pacha acting as the nominal governor. The vast majority of the Arabs were illiterate peasants bound to their village communities and families and engaged in a subsistence type of agriculture, though of course they had to pay the heavy taxes imposed upon them by the tax farmers. The rest of the Arabs, who lived in urban centres and enjoyed greater prestige and privileges, were largely craftsmen loosely organized and often affiliated to mystical orders of brotherhood together with merchants and ulema. Alike in town and in country an Arab then belonged to a cohesive body from which he seemed to derive some security. The phenomena of the landless peasant and the urban lumpen proletariate, which provide the themes of much twentieth-century Arabic literature, were clearly not known prior to modern times.

With the weakening of the Ottoman Empire in the eighteenth century, the subject peoples suffered from an increasingly heavy burden of taxation, oppression by corrupt officials and tax farmers, insecurity caused by the local rulers' bloody struggles for power as well as periodic raids by Beduin tribesmen. Yet they continued to form an integrated society with commonly held views and assumptions about this world and the hereafter. They may have resented much of the ill-treatment they received at the hands of their Turkish rulers and the rapacious and bloodthirsty warring Mameluke Beys. Nevertheless, in the days prior to nationalism the Arabs felt strongly that they all constituted the Muslim *Ummah*, the Community of Believers, and that as defenders of the sacred law of *Sharīᶜah* the Ottoman rulers had the right to be obeyed. Moreover, they lived in seemingly total cultural isolation from the west, smugly convinced of the superiority of the Muslim civilization.

The ulema, the guardians of the faith, were held in respect by the Ottoman rulers, yet because Turkish was the official language of the Empire, Arabic culture generally suffered for lack of sufficient patronage. In fact, the Ottoman period marks the nadir of Arabic literature. Although historians of literature may have exaggerated the decline, there is no doubt that the period is characterized by the absence of creativity and loss of vigour. It is usually described as the age of commentaries and compendia because a considerable portion of the output of writers and scholars consisted of commentaries on texts, and even commentaries on commentaries. By the time we reach the eighteenth century we find that prose writers and poets had become equally enamoured of an excessively ornate, artificial type of style in which more attention is given to manner than to matter. Their work generally lacked seriousness, while those who cared for the content of their writing tended to employ an undistinguished prose which was devoid of literary merit. In creative writing the themes were conventional: *maqāmah* – like prose epistles, pious verses in praise of the Prophet, popular sufi or ascetic poems, empty panegyrics addressed to local notables, celebrations of trivial social occasions and numerous lifeless and passionless love poems. With very few exceptions, such as the Egyptian Ḥasan Badrī al-Ḥijāzī (d. 1718) and the Syrian ᶜAbd al-Ghanī al-Nābulsī (d. 1731), the imagery poets used was stock in trade and the language cliché-ridden: in short, it was a literature of an exhausted, inward-looking culture, albeit a complacent and perfectly self-satisfied one.

The French Campaign

Out of this complacency Arabic culture was rudely awakened when Bonaparte invaded Egypt in 1798. The extent of the shock suffered by the inhabitants can be gauged from the way the distinguished Egyptian historian ʿAbd al-Raḥmān al-Jabartī (1756–1825) opened his account of the year of the invasion, which he witnessed, in his chronicle *ʿAjāʾib al-āthār fīʾl tarājim waʾl-akhbār*: he regarded it as the year of the ultimate catastrophe, of the disastrous reversal of the natural order of things. Bonaparte, whose expedition in this strategically important country was an episode in the history of Anglo-French rivalry in imperial expansion which was designed to cut off Britain's route to India, made an announcement to the Egyptian people in which he posed as a champion of Islam and a liberator of Egypt from the tyrannical rule of the Mamelukes. Whatever they thought about this specious claim, the easy victory achieved by the French forces over the Mameluke army shocked Muslims out of their complacency, bringing home to them the enormous superiority, efficiency and military might of the west.

Bonaparte brought with him a team of French experts, scientists and scholars who undertook a thorough and systematic survey of Egypt and its resources: they conducted scientific experiments in the *Institut d'Egypte*, founded for that purpose, and published their findings in a newly established French language periodical. Bonaparte invited the chief ulema and notables, whom he regarded as leaders of the Egyptian people, to form an Administrative Council to participate in the French-controlled government of Egypt and in the promulgation of the legislation necessary for his proposed reforms in landownership and taxation, amongst other things. He had brought with him from the Vatican an Arabic language press, the very first Arabic printing press to enter Egypt, for the publication of French proclamations in Arabic.

The response of the Egyptians to the French was understandably a mixed one. They obviously admired their efficiency and organization, and their diligence in the construction of roads and factories. The educated among them, such as al-Jabartī and Ḥasan al-ʿAṭṭār, the teacher of al-Ṭahṭāwī, who had the chance to visit the *Institut*, were impressed by its library and by some of the scientific experiments which they watched in something like uncomprehending wonder, and they were intrigued by the manners and ways of the French such as their dramatic entertainments. No doubt Egyptians were relieved to be rid of the Mamelukes who had been thoroughly discredited by their ignominious defeat at the hands of the French. On the other hand, despite being given the chance of the experience of limited representative government, the Egyptians felt humiliated at being ruled by the infidel French whose revolutionary doctrines the Ottoman government had thoroughly condemned. They were critical of the behaviour of the French forces and what they regarded as the immorality of French women, and were alarmed at the dangerous example they had set to some of their own Muslim women. Moreover, when in response to the blockade imposed upon them by the Anglo-Ottoman fleets in the Mediterranean the French forces of occupation had to resort to harsh measures of taxation, the Egyptian people, led by the Azhar, rebelled and the rebellion was ruthlessly put down by the French troops some of whom committed scandalous atrocities.

Although the French expedition is generally judged as a military failure for the French, its significance for Egypt (and the Arab world) cannot be exaggerated, and that is in spite of claims made by some revisionist historians. True, the occupation lasted only three years, the Egyptians' exposure to western learning and science, as well as representative self-government, was too brief to be meaningful, but the campaign brought to an end the isolation of the Arab world from the west. It signalled the beginning of a process of western expansion and colonization, which in the course of time resulted in practically the entire Arab world falling under the domination of western powers, notably France and Britain. France invaded Algeria in 1830, Britain occupied Aden in 1839, France occupied Tunisia in 1881, Britain Egypt in 1882, Italy seized Libya in 1911–12, and in 1920 France acquired mandates over Syria and Lebanon, while the mandates for Palestine, Transjordan and Iraq went to Britain. Even Morocco, which had retained its independence for a long time, fell prey to the ambitions of France and Spain which in 1904 concluded a secret agreement that divided Morocco into two spheres of influence between them, and in 1912 Morocco was declared a French protectorate. Britain imposed her authority upon the Arab rulers of the small Persian Gulf states by means of treaties which go as far back as the 1820s. The bloody and unequal encounter with the west which varied in ferocity and violence from one Arab country to another and according to whether the colonizer was France, Britain or Italy, had such a profound and traumatic effect upon the Arab imagination, even though it was sometimes latent and slow to reveal itself, that to this day the East/West opposition has remained one of the leading motifs in Arabic literature. In their search for identity, Arab writers have for many generations often tried to define themselves in relation to the other, the other being in most cases the European.

Likewise, the nationalist struggle for independence became a permanent, indeed at times obsessive preoccupation for writers for many years: the end of the mandate in Iraq came only in 1932, the Anglo-Egyptian treaty which gave Egypt her relative independence was concluded in 1936, the mandate for Syria and Lebanon came to an end in 1941. In 1946 Transjordan attained her independence, Libya in 1951, Sudan, Tunisia and Morocco in 1956, Kuwait in 1961, while Algeria achieved hers after a prolonged and bloody struggle as late as 1962. In 1948 the mandate for Palestine came to an end, and the state of Israel was established. Even after the Arab states formally attained their independence, they remained within the spheres of influence of western powers for a long time, in fact until Jamāl ᶜAbd al-Nāṣir appeared on the scene after the Egyptian Army Revolution of 1952, which in its turn helped to push Arabic literature in other directions.

The rise of Muhammad Ali

The whole course of modern Arabic literature might have been entirely different if it had not been for one indirect result of the French campaign. This was the emergence of Muhammad Ali, the Albanian officer who came to Egypt with the Ottoman forces to help drive out the French and who, in the confusion that followed the departure of the French, managed, through sheer genius, machiavellian intrigues and utter ruthlessness to fill the void and become, in 1805, the ruler of Egypt (1805–1848). He created a dynasty which ruled Egypt until its last descendant, King Farouk, was forced to abdicate by the revolutionary junta led by Nāṣir. Inspired by the example of the Ottoman Sultan Selim III, the ambitious Muhammad Ali launched a more successful and comprehensive programme of military reform along the lines of the superior and well-organized western armies of which he had first-hand experience. To this end he employed all the available resources in Egypt, and in so doing he altered the economic, political and social structure of the country. After he had got rid of the Mameluke adversaries in a notorious massacre, he destroyed the forces that had helped him to attain power, including the class of Azhar ulema, who were shorn of their economic and political influence. He imposed state ownership of land, abolished the old system of tax farming and had the monopoly of trade. By introducing intensive cotton cultivation in the 1820s and improving irrigation, transport and marketing, he laid the foundation of modern Egyptian economy: through the export of cotton Egyptian agriculture became integrated into the international economy. This he achieved with the help of European experts, technicians and officers, who enabled him to create an army and a navy strong enough to wage successful wars in other Arab countries and even to pose a threat to the authority of the Ottoman Sultan himself. When the Sultan refused his request to grant the governorship of Syria to his son Ibrahim as a reward for his assistance during the Greek rebellion, the armies of Muhammad Ali occupied Syria and threatened Istanbul. The threat was ultimately averted through the interference of the allied European powers whose policy it was to try to protect the weak Ottoman Empire from total collapse. As a result of the 1841 Treaty of London, signed by England, Austria, Prussia and Russia, Muhammad Ali was forced to return Syria to the Sultan and to limit his army to 18,000 men in return for hereditary right to the rule of Egypt under the suzerainty of the Sultan. Muhammad Ali recompensed his functionaries and members of his own family by giving them land to develop, thus gradually creating a new feudal structure, which was to replace the old landed class of Mamelukes and others and which in the course of time and under his successors increased immeasurably the gap between the rich and the poor.

Modernization of education

Muhammad Ali imported not only western technicians and military advisors, but also western forms of education, and sent local Arabs on educational missions to the west (mainly to France), to learn the secret of its military supremacy. In 1816 he started a process of superimposing upon the country a western type of educational system which had very little in common with the traditional religious Azhar system. He set up a number of modern technological and military schools in which modern sciences and European languages were taught and in which some of the teachers were Italian, French and later English. Despite his shrewdness and practical intelligence, Muhammad Ali was not an educated man with any interest in European culture: his aim was strictly limited to what was conducive to the building up of a powerful régime with a strong army. The members of his educational missions in Europe were all technically army officers, with specific ranks; they had to follow an army discipline and were not even allowed to make a tour of the countries in which they were studying. Nevertheless, it was impossible for these young men to keep interest in western technology in the long run entirely separate from interest in some of the cultural values underlying that technology. Furthermore, the setting up of a new secular system of education, different from the traditional theocentric one, a system which produced men who were to occupy important posts in the government, was bound to result eventually in the weakening of the authority of traditional values. Arab Muslim society therefore ceased to be the 'closed' culture it had been for so long. After the frustration of his military ambitions, Muhammad Ali lost interest in his educational programme, which was also neglected by his successor who was not noted for his sympathy towards the west. The modern technological schools were closed and so was the School of Languages. However, when Muhammad Ali's grandson Ismail came to the throne (1863–1879), he pursued the policy of modernizing education with remarkable zeal, and did so on a much larger scale than his grandfather, reorganizing the entire system of public education. In the course of time western culture and western languages were to play an ever-increasing role in the cultural make-up of the Arab world. Another important development is that because secular education did not grow slowly and gradually out of the indigenous traditional religious system of al-Azhar, but was instead imposed upon it from above, a cultural dichotomy or polarity ensued with grave psychological consequences, which had already worried the religious reformer Muḥammad ʿAbduh (1849–1905), and which are still visible today.

Arabic printing press, birth of translation movement and journalism

Muhammad Ali needed books and manuals for his modern schools and the army, so he ordered an Arabic printing press: in fact the very first educational mission member to be sent to Europe went to Italy to study printing (in 1809). This press (set up in Bulaq in 1822) was not the first to be found in the Arab world: even before Bonaparte brought with him an Arabic press to publish his proclamations in Egypt, as early as 1706 the Maronite priests had their own press in Aleppo for the purpose of printing Christian texts. This was followed by others in Shuwayr (1734) and Beirut (1753). Muhammad Ali's press, later to be known as the Government Press, was to play an important cultural role in the Arab Muslim world: it printed translations of European works, at first scientific and technological, but later literary translations as well as Arabic classics such as the work of Ibn Khaldūn, which became more freely available than they used to be when they were accessible only in the form of expensive manuscripts copied out by hand. Likewise the press printed the very first periodical, an official gazette, *al-Waqāʾiʿ al-Miṣriyyah* (1828). This marked the birth of journalism, which was to become a potent factor in the development not only of modern Arab thought, society and politics, but also of modern Arabic literature. Together with translations of scientific works, journalism helped to change gradually the style of Arabic prose, ridding it of excessive rhetorical devices, making it a simpler and fitter vehicle for conveying ideas.

The editing of the official gazette was assigned to the distinguished

Rifā'ah Rāfi' al-Ṭahṭāwī (1801–1873), who is generally regarded as the father of modern Arab thought. An Azharite by training, he was sent in 1826 to France, on the recommendation of his teacher Shaykh Ḥasan al'Aṭṭār, as an Imam to the large batch of mission students. But he spent his five years in Paris learning French and studying various aspects of French culture, and on his return to Egypt he published in 1834 his observations and impressions of his trip, in a book which became very well known and was translated into Turkish: *Takhlīṣ al-ibrīz ilā talkhīṣ bārīz*. In it as well as in his numerous other writings, particularly *Manāhij al-albāb al-miṣriyyah* (1869), he expressed his respect for the rationality and the good organization of social and political institutions of the west, and the civic virtues such as the love of the fatherland (*al-waṭan*), qualities which he advocated as necessary for the betterment of Islamic society in Egypt. Al-Ṭahṭāwī was also appointed director of one of the important modern schools founded by Muhammad Ali in 1835, the Cairo School of Languages for the teaching of Italian, French and English, which produced a number of distinguished translators and writers. A Translation Bureau was set up in 1841. This marks the beginning of a significant translation movement, which at first was limited to technological and military books (graduates of the School of Languages are said to have translated some two thousand works from European languages), but in the course of time included literary and historical writings, so that during the last two decades of the nineteenth century literary works alone formed no less than one third of the total output of translations.

Muhammad Ali's various projects resulted in a remarkable rise in the number of Europeans residing in Egypt, and hence in the spread of European schools as well as missionary activity. His liberal attitude towards Europeans made the decade of Egyptian occupation of Syria (1831–1840) one of crucial importance in its cultural history: it resulted in a dramatic increase in French, British and American missionary and educational activities. These culminated in the Americans founding a college in 1847 which became the American College in 1866, later to be named the American University of Beirut, the Jesuits transferring their College (the University of St Joseph) to Beirut in 1874. Missionary schools for girls were also opened. The graduates of these western institutions were naturally more receptive to western ideas, with the result that they played a pioneering role in westernization. Coming after the earlier generation of Nāṣīf al-Yāzijī (1800–1871), who were among the first Christian writers to develop a keen and serious interest in Arabic language and literature, these younger Christians were eager to experiment in new forms hitherto unknown in the Arabic literary heritage. Whole families, such as those of al-

Yāzijī, al-Bustānī and al-Naqqāsh, became associated with these new forms, together with translations and adaptations, as well as serious journalism of a general cultural and literary type. Mārūn al-Naqqāsh, for example, wrote the first play in Arabic (1847) and was followed by his nephew, Salīm al-Naqqāsh. Salīm al-Bustānī was the author of the first novel (in 1870), Buṭrus al-Bustānī (1819–1883), who probably translated *Robinson Crusoe*, wrote the first Arabic encyclopaedia. Sulaymān al-Bustānī produced his verse translation of Homer's *Iliad* (1904), a *tour de force*, accompanied by a lengthy introduction which includes a comparative study of Greek and Arabic poetry. In 1861 Fāris al-Shidyāq launched the important newspaper *al-Jawāʾib* (in Constantinople), which was read throughout the Arab world and continued to appear until 1884. Yaʿqūb Ṣarrūf and Fāris Nimr founded their epoch-making cultural periodical *al-Muqtaṭaf* in Beirut in 1876, which gave the Arab reader much information about western thought, science and technology (in 1885 it was transferred to Egypt where it continued to appear until 1952). The prolific Jurjī Zaydān, among his various activities in Cairo, published the monthly cultural periodical *al-Hilāl* (begun in 1892) which still appears to this day.

Ismail and westernization

As a result of the religious conflicts and disturbances in Syria in the wake of the enforced evacuation of the Egyptian troops, which culminated in the massacre of 1860 and the harsh rule of the Ottomans, many Syrians left their country; some went to America and were eventually to make a significant contribution to Arabic writing, known as the literature of *al-Mahjar* (the Emigrants or Expatriates). Others went to Egypt, lured by the reports of the munificence of Khedive Ismail (1863–1879). Ismail had been educated in France, and despite his foolish extravagances, which brought financial ruin to Egypt and which in turn led to European interference in the government of the country and ultimately to British occupation in 1882, he showed remarkable interest in promoting culture. Unlike Muhammad Ali, who cared only for the technological type of school immediately relevant to the needs of his army, Ismail was genuinely interested in popular education (including education of girls), which was organized by his able minister of education ʿAlī Mubārak (1824–1893), an engineer who was himself a product of the new secular school system. By the 1860s Arabic had replaced Turkish as the official language of Egypt. Ismail also allowed a large number of Christian missions to establish schools, where many Egyptian children, girls as well as boys, received their education in a European language, mainly French. In 1872 he established Dār al-ʿUlūm (The

Teachers' Training College), which aimed at combining traditional Islamic Arabic culture with western learning. He founded learned societies, a museum and an observatory, and patronized exploration, scholarly research and the arts. In 1870 he set up Dār al-Kutub (The National Library). He founded the Opera House in Cairo, which was opened in 1869 with a performance of *Rigoletto*, as part of the extravagant celebrations of the opening of the Suez Canal. He encouraged (for a while) the first Egyptian dramatist Yaᶜqūb Ṣannūᶜ, as well as visiting theatrical troupes from Syria. He gave financial aid to Buṭrus al-Bustānī to enable him to work on his Arabic Encyclopaedia. Ismail was intent on making Egypt, as it were, part of Europe. European methods of administration and finance were followed and legal codes were translated. Even European dress was adopted by Egyptian civil servants and members of the professions. Under his rule many of the major topographical changes in Cairo took place, his inspiration being Baron Haussmann's elegant city of Paris; over a hundred European schools were opened, the number of Europeans residing in Egypt rose from a few thousand in 1860 to over a hundred thousand in 1876. In short, the course of westernization was assured.

Westernization and Islam

Westernization, however, was problematic in a Muslim country; not even Ismail himself was prepared to shed some of his 'oriental' ways such as, for instance, polygamy, an attack on which seems to have been the reason why the dramatist Ṣannūᶜ incurred his displeasure and was ordered to close down his theatre. The key issue that preoccupied the minds of Arab intellectuals was how to westernize or modernize while remaining Muslims. The problem, of course, did not arise in the case of Christian Arabs, some of whom, like al-Shidyāq, adopted an anti-clerical stance or even advocated secularization, like Shiblī Shumayyil (1860–1917) and Faraḥ Anṭūn (1874–1922), who believed in the need to separate secular and religious powers. The need for modernization, however, was keenly felt by all when the superiority of the west was a fact that could no longer be ignored. It would, of course, be wrong to assume that the revival of religious thought and the reconsideration of the fundamentals of Islam came only as a result of the encounter with the west: already in the eighteenth century an indigenous puritan movement of religious reform arose in Arabia, led by Muḥammad ibn ᶜAbd al-Wahhāb (1703–1787), who preached a return to pristine Islam unencumbered by the saint worship and superstitious accretions that had developed across the centuries, and who had the support of Ibn Saud, the founder of what became Saudi Arabia. But

Wahhabism was essentially an inward- or backward-looking movement, unlike the nineteenth-century forward-looking religious reform movement in Egypt and Syria, the two leading intellectual centres of the *Nahḍah*, which was promoted by the desire to catch up with the modern world. The members of what Albert Hourani called the first generation of modern thinkers (up to 1870), that of al-Ṭahṭāwī of Egypt and Khayr al-Dīn of Tunisia (1810–89), were impressed by what they saw in Europe, which for them stood for material progress and science rather than the political power and aggressive expansion of which later generations were made painfully aware. Their problem was how to reconcile reason and the rationalism of the French Enlightenment with *Sharīʿah*, the divine law of Islam, how to reconcile the needs of the *Ummah*, the Community of Muslims, with those of the *waṭan*, the nation, including the adoption of the political institutions of the west, generally regarded as the source of its strength.

For the subsequent generation the situation had changed radically. It was no longer a question of Islam trying to copy or catch up with the west, but one of survival, of fighting against external danger. As Hourani put it (in the Introduction to the 1983 edition of his *Arabic Thought in the Liberal Age of 1789–1939*), 'Europe had become the adversary as well as the model' for

> its armies were present in Egypt, Algeria and Tunisia, and its political influence was growing throughout the Ottoman Empire; its schools were forming students whose processes of thought and view of the world were far from those of their parents; the cities were being remade on a European model, and the familiar signs of urban life were being replaced by others.

The main problem for Muslim thinkers such as the Messianic and controversial Jamāl al-Dīn al-Afghānī (1839–1897), who lived in Egypt from 1871 until his expulsion in 1879 by Khedive Tawfīq for fear of his revolutionary views, and al-Afghānī's most influential disciple Muḥammad ʿAbduh (1849–1905), became not so much how to convince their contemporaries to adopt western institutions without losing their Muslim identity, as 'to reinterpret Islam so as to make it compatible with living in the modern world, and even a source of strength in it, and to convince those formed in a new mould that they could still hold on to something from their own past'. Al-Afghānī preached the need to revitalize Islam, to oppose the autocratic government of Muslim despots, to limit absolute rule by constitutions, to unite the Muslims so that they could fight against European intervention. His lectures on Islamic thought and philosophy were well attended by the young intellectuals of Cairo, who were spellbound by his rhetoric and who welcomed his rejection of *taqlīd* (blind imitation of traditional thinking), his advocacy of the need to exercise *ijtihād* (individual judgement) and above all his insistence that Egyptians should endeavour to achieve national unity in order to fight British occupation. Muḥammad ʿAbduh was more moderate than Afghānī, his position was one of eclecticism with a strong rationalist Muʿtazilite component. He held that Islam was never opposed to science or rational enquiry, that a distinction must be drawn between the permanent core of Islam, namely its simple doctrines, and its inessential elements, which may be changed according to individual judgement. To this school of thought belonged the Islamic reformer and modernizer Qāsim Amīn (1865–1908), who in his books *Taḥrīr al-marʾah* ('The emancipation of woman', 1899) and *al- Marʾah al-jadīdah* ('The new woman', 1901) argued, against much conservative opposition in Egypt, that the emancipation of women, which was essential to the revival of Muslims, is in no way against Islamic doctrine.

The defence of Islam in the writings of these thinkers must also be seen against the background of western attacks on this religion in the latter part of the nineteenth century by people as different as the French philosopher and philologist Ernest Renan, and the British Consul-General of Egypt, Lord Cromer, as well as by many orientalists, who maintained that Islam actually hindered progress. The younger generation of writers and littérateurs who had been profoundly influenced by Muḥammad ʿAbduh continued this Islamic apologetic tradition, especially as after the abolition of the Ottoman Caliphate by Atatürk in 1924 it was felt in some quarters that Islam was in grave danger. In Egypt Ṭāhā Ḥusayn (1889–1973), Muḥammad Ḥusayn Haykal (1888–1956) and ʿAbbās Maḥmūd al-ʿAqqād (1889–1964), and even Tawfīq al-Ḥakīm (1898–1987), tried to defend Islam or to make it more relevant to the problems of contemporary Egyptian society, by treating themes from Islamic history from certain angles or by writing a large number of Islamic biographies, including that of the Prophet Muhammad, or else by pointing out that Classical Arabic, the language of the Koran, is no obstacle to progress. Seen in this context, it is not surprising that the very writers who were enthusiastic about western literature and thought and were anxious to introduce these to the modern Arab reader, devoted so much of their energy to writing about Islam. It was not, as it has been put, simply a question of these writers, who had once espoused the cause of westernization, becoming subsequently disillusioned with the west, turning their backs on it and returning to their Islamic roots: this would be crude oversimplification. For instance, Ṭāhā Ḥusayn wrote his book on 'The future of culture in Egypt', *Mustaqbal al-thaqāfah fī Miṣr* (published 1938), in which he argued that Egypt was part of the Mediterranean civilization, at the same time as his religious books *ʿAlā hāmish al-sīrah* (1937–43). Indeed he went on to edit his distinguished cultural periodical *al-Kātib al-Miṣrī* (1945–48), which published serious articles on leading modern writers and poets of the west.

However, in the course of the century many changes took place. These included the growth of nationalist feeling, be it religious, territorial, ethnic or linguistic, the emergence of, and subsequent disillusionment with, political parties, the failure of the liberal democratic experiment in Egypt, and the deterioration of the economic situation as a result first of the Depression, then of the inflation brought about by World War II, the alarming rate of population growth, the gaping gulf separating the urban and rural poor from the greedy and often corrupt rich, and the emergence of the lumpenproletariat as a result of the mass migration of destitute peasants to the overcrowded cities in search of employment. Many people were driven therefore to the Islamic fundamentalist position of the Muslim Brothers started in 1928 by Ḥasan al-Bannā (d. 1949), a follower of ᶜAbduh's disciple and biographer Rashīd Riḍā, while others turned to an equally extreme leftist position. After the war, the loss of Palestine and the creation of Israel in 1948 enforced both Islamic fundamentalism and Arab nationalism of the secular variety, and indirectly led to the Egyptian army revolution of 1952, which under the spreading influence of Nasserism was followed by a series of army coups in other newly independent Arab states. New régimes arose whose ideals were often a mixture of Arab nationalism and socialism. Among the important changes mention must be made of the significant growth of the middle classes leading to some monarchies and feudal or semi-feudal ruling houses being ousted by the middle class or lower middle class, usually army officers, who assumed power and ruled in the name of the people. This was accompanied by the spread of education and the decrease of illiteracy, and the rise in importance of the position of women, especially in socialist régimes. The constant pursuit of the ideal of Arab unity, prompted by the awareness of the Israeli threat, has been frustrated by interminable inter-state strife, fed by differences and contradictions between the political systems of these states, and their polarization as they were caught up in the Cold War between Russia and America, the two superpowers which since the 1950s have gradually replaced Britain and France as the dominant foreign forces in the region. Other developments include not only the sufferings of the Palestinian diaspora and the victims of the long-drawn-out Arab–Israeli conflict as well as the tragic Lebanese civil war, but also the dramatic rise in importance of the role of oil in the economy and position of some of the states in the region and subsequent migration of labour from the poor to the richer Arab states. Added to that is the phenomenon of the exiled and self-exiled intellectuals fleeing from hostile authoritarian governments.

These developments are reflected in the literature of the time. To take but one example, one comes across the serious and indeed at times tragic struggle of the individual against coercive authority – initially foreign under western occupation, and subsequently native, tyranny – often of the military rule variety in the wake of national liberation. Such a struggle provides one of the most recurrent and haunting themes, the authors' passionate cry for freedom under authoritarian rule is an assertion of the democratic rights of the individual in a modern state, those rights which ironically enough are sometimes suppressed by the authorities in their very endeavour to achieve modernization.

New conception of literature, new reading public

For literature to reflect such developments a radical change had to take place in modern Arabic writings in the conception of literature and the function of the writer. The mediaeval view which had dominated until well into the nineteenth century and which regarded writing as either morally and spiritually edifying or else entertaining through mastery of language and verbal skill, gradually gave way to the attitude that literature should reflect and indeed change social reality. The patron prince or ruler who encouraged poets to flock to his court to sing of his achievements and immortalize his name in memorable *qaṣīdas*, formal sonorous odes, was being replaced by a middle-class reading public, educated in secular and not theocentric schools, who as a result of the introduction of printing had access to printed books and did not rely on a few copied manuscripts, and who were wooed not through oral recitation or declamation but by the pages of newspapers and magazines. Admittedly in a society where the degree of illiteracy was extremely high, the size of the reading public was initially very small, but their number grew rapidly with the spread of popular education. (In Egypt the illiteracy rate dropped from 92.7 per cent in 1907 to 70.3 per cent of the population in 1960.) Gone therefore was the poet craftsman who offered his panegyrical verse to the highest bidder; in his place came the 'inspired' poet, the man of feeling who valued sincerity or the campaigner who had strong views about wider issues, particularly the ills of his society. The traditional prose writer who sought to entertain the privileged learned minority by drawing, but not too heavily, on diverse aspects of knowledge (*al-akhdh min kull fann bi ṭaraf*) or who embroidered his epistles to fellow writers or his *maqāmahs* (narratives of sorts in rhyming prose) with all kinds of figures of speech (*badīʿ*), in the most artificial manner imaginable, gave way to the concerned essayist or journalist burning with reforming zeal in matters intellectual, religious, social and political, no less than in language and literature. Whatever might be the attitude to the mimetic view of literature nowadays in the era of Post-structuralism and Deconstruction, it is the emergence of literature as a *mimesis*, as an imitation of life, that signalled the arrival of modern Arabic literature on the scene. Instead of the ideal types provided in traditional mediaeval literature, presented in the most elaborate language ('what oft was thought but ne'er so well express'd'), concrete observable reality became the subject-matter of writers, particularly in the newly imported forms of drama and fiction.

Three periods of development of modern Arabic literature

The history of modern Arabic literature could be divided into three main periods: the first from 1834 to 1914, which may be termed the Age of Translations and Adaptations as well as Neo-classicism; the second is the inter-war period, which may be described as the Age of Romanticism and Nationalism; the third is from the end of World War II to the present: it embraces a wide variety of schools, approaches and styles, but may conveniently be called the Age of Conflicting Ideologies.

1. Translations, adaptations and Neo-classicism

The year 1834 is an important landmark, because it marks the publication of al-Ṭahṭāwī's account of his trip to France, *Takhlīṣ al-ibrīz ilā talkhīṣ Bārīz*. The book contains specimens of al-Ṭahṭāwī's translations of French verse, perhaps the first to be undertaken in Arabic. Although they are of an indifferent quality and are much more adaptations than translations, nevertheless they are important insofar as they signal the very beginning of the process of introduction to, and assimilation of, western literature. In his account al-Ṭahṭāwī also tells us that during his mission in Paris he read works by Racine, Voltaire, Rousseau and Montesquieu, amongst other things. It is true that his major literary translation of Fénélon's *Télémaque* was to appear much later (1867); nevertheless it was during his stay in Paris that he studied the art of translation, what he called *Fann al-tarjamah*, and according to him he translated twelve works (obviously technological and historical rather than literary). After his return he occupied the position of head of the newly created Translation Bureau which produced a large number of distinguished translators of literature. In 1835 the anonymous translation of *Robinson Crusoe* was published in Malta.

Equally 1914 is an appropriate date to end this first period, for around that date significant works appeared in which Arab authors seemed to go beyond the stage of translation or adaptation, revealing their mastery or near-mastery of the imported literary forms, namely Haykal's novel *Zaynab* and Ibrāhīm Ramzī's comedy *Dukhūl al-ḥammām* (Admission to the Baths) and his historical drama *Abṭāl al-Manṣūrah* (The Heroes of Mansurah).

This early period witnessed the emergence of the Arabic printing press, which not only made more available the Arabic classics to which authors turned for inspiration in an attempt to assert their identity in the face of external danger, but also produced an increasing number of governmental and, more importantly for our purpose, non-govermental periodicals of a general cultural nature in which early translations, adaptations and imitations of western fiction were published. They catered for a new type of reader, the product of missionary institutions in Syria or Ismail's new, more secular type of school, a reader who was not deeply grounded in the Arabic classics but who sought entertainment in a simpler and more direct Arabic style than that provided in the traditional *maqāmah*. The newspapers provided a forum for political activists and religious and social reformers, resulting in the birth and development of the modern Essay from the rather crude and informative attempts in official and semi-governmental periodicals made by the pioneer generation of al-Ṭahṭāwī, to the more powerful and impassioned work of politically committed Egyptian and Syrian essayists, mostly the disciples of al-Afghānī, who published their articles in, for example, *al-Ahrām*. Under the influence of Muḥammad ʿAbduh they sought to express their views in a less ornate style, a sinewy prose, relatively free from the artificialities of *badīʿ*. These include Adīb Isḥāq, Salīm al-Naqqāsh, ʿAbdallah Nadīm, Muḥammad ʿUthmān Jalāl, Muḥammad ʿAbduh himself, Ibrāhīm al-Muwayliḥī and ʿAbd al-Raḥmān al-Kawākibī. Their work was further developed under British occupation by ʿAlī Yūsuf in the conservative *al-Mu'ayyad*, Muṣṭafā Kāmil in *al-Liwāʾ*, the organ of the Nationalist Party, and particularly Ahmād Luṭfī al-Sayyid (1872–1963) in *al-Jarīdah*, the mouthpiece of the *Ummah* Party which represented the more liberal Arab intellectuals and stood for intelligent westernization, rationality and the scientific attitude in education and social reform. Luṭfī al-Sayyid's thoughtful essays, in which he stated his responsible and enlightened secular, liberal and patriotic position, earned him the title of *Ustādh al-jīl* (the Master/Mentor of the generation) and through *al-Jarīdah* many of the leading writers and essayists found their way to the public: ʿAbd al-Raḥmān Shukrī, ʿAbd al-ʿAzīz al-Bishrī, Ibrāhīm Ramzī, Muḥammad al-Sibāʿī, ʿAbd al-Ḥamīd Ḥamdī, Muḥammad Ḥusayn Haykal, Ṭāhā Ḥusayn, al-Māzinī, al-ʿAqqād, Muṣṭafā ʿAbd al-Rāziq and Salāmah Mūsā, as well as women essayists like Labībah Hāshim, Nabawiyyah Mūsā and Malak Ḥifnī Nāṣif. In the hands of some of these writers, particularly al-Māzinī and Ṭāhā Ḥusayn, it can be said that the essay had attained its most elegant form.

During this period a close connection between journalism and serious literature was established to the extent that towards the end of it we find not only *qaṣīdas* by the major poets and short stories, but whole novels, such as Jurjī Zaydān's, appearing (serially) in the papers. In fact this connection was only strengthened in later periods: leading novelists and even literary critics (such as Ṭāhā Ḥusayn) first published their works in newspapers. Even today Najīb Maḥfūẓ's novels first appear in instalments in *al-Ahrām* and the literary page of a newspaper is still regarded as one of its distinguishing features and a valuable asset. No doubt this is also due to the fact that it has been extremely difficult for a modern Arab writer to live on the royalties of his books alone, hence the need to have another regular job which often tends to be journalism, something that suits newspaper proprietors because having a distinguished author on their staff increases the circulation of their papers. However, this close link between literature and journalism proved to be a mixed blessing, for while on the whole it helped to raise the standard of journalistic writing, often it contributed to the superficiality of some of the literature published.

2. *Romanticism and nationalism*

It is not surprising that the period between the two world wars was the Age of Romanticism and Nationalism. The Great War resulted in the dissolution of the Ottoman Empire and the placing of its remaining Arab provinces under British and French mandate. Egypt, already under British occupation, was declared a Protectorate in 1914. The strength of nationalist feeling erupted in a series of major revolts first in Egypt (1919), then in Iraq (1920) and Syria (1925). The search for specifically Egyptian literature and for the Egyptian identity was a slogan of many authors in Egypt, especially a group of young men associated with what became known as *al-Madrasah al-Ḥadīthah* (The New School), such as Maḥmūd Ṭahir Lāshīn and the Taymūr brothers (Muḥammad and Maḥmūd) who later distinguished themselves both in fiction and in drama. Related to this is the call for the use of the Egyptian colloquial at least in dialogue. The emphasis on the Pharaonic past of Egypt by writers such as Haykal and al-Ḥakīm is paralleled by the need to relate to the Phoenician civilization expressed by Saᶜīd ᶜAql in Lebanon.

This is the period in which Arab countries tried to shake off foreign domination and attain statehood. In Egypt, attempts were made by, for example, Ṭalᶜat Ḥarb to establish national industry and banking. The desire to achieve progress and modernity (which meant westernization) was keenly felt, and this entailed a critical and at times rejectionist stance to traditional values. In the wake of Kamal Atatürk's abolition of the caliphate in Istanbul in 1924, two famous debates took place as a result of the publication of two revolutionary books: ʿAlī ʿAbd al-Rāziq's *al-Islam wa uṣūl al-ḥukm* ('Islam and the principles of government', 1925), in which he argued that the caliphate is not an integral part of Islam, and Ṭāḥā Ḥusayn's *Fiʿl Shiʿr al-jāhilī* ('On Pre-Islamic poetry', 1926) which cast doubt on the authenticity of Pre-Islamic poetry and the historical veracity of certain allusions in the Koran. The former caused its author to be expelled from the body of ulema, while the latter cost Ṭāḥā Ḥusayn his job and brought about calls for his trial and imprisonment. In literary criticism several iconoclastic works appeared such as the Egyptians al-ʿAqqād and al-Māzinī's *al-Dīwān* (1921) and the Mahjari Mikhā'īl Nuʿaymah's *al-Ghirbāl* (1923), and the Tunisian al-Shābbī's *al-Khayāl al-shiʿrī ʿind al-ʿArab* ('The Arab poetic imagination', 1929). Other considerations apart, it was quite natural for Arab writers, particularly poets, to turn for their inspiration to European Romanticism, which was a literature of revolt. Unlike classicism which, with its stress on polish and good form, is an expression of a fairly stable culture in which there is common agreement on fundamental issues, Romanticism is a product of a society which is at odds with itself and in which the individual questions the relevance of traditional values. As I have tried to show in my *Critical introduction to modern Arabic poetry* (1975), since the traditional Arab conception of literature shares many of the fundamental assumptions of European classicism, it was understandable that when the desire to break with their past and enter the modern world was genuinely felt, Arab writers found in European Romanticism, which was professedly anti-classical, the assumptions and ideals which seemed to them to fulfil adequately their own needs. It must be emphasized however, that the Arab Romantics, whether in the Arab East or in the Americas, were not simply imitating western postures. The heightened sense of individuality, the agonizing feeling of social and cultural change, the political malaise, the occasional awareness of loss of direction and of being strangers in an unfamiliar universe, were in one way or another facts of Arab existence for some time. Nor were the Arab Romantics mere dreamers inhabiting an ivory tower: many were politically committed nationalists, and they were keenly aware of the ills of their society.

The role of journalism grew more important during this period as a result of the rise of political parties in Egypt which tried to enlist the help of distinguished writers in their partisan daily or weekly newspapers: such as *al-Siyāsah al-Usbūʿiyyah* which published Ṭāḥā Ḥusayn, al-Bishrī and Muḥammad Ḥusayn Haykal, and *al-Balāgh al-Usbūʿī* in which al-ʿAqqād's articles appeared. Literary periodicals (long- and short-lived) also appeared, such as Abū Shādī's *Apollo* (1932–1934), Aḥmad Ḥasan al-Zayyāt's *al-Risālah* (1933–1952) and Aḥmad Amīn's *al-Thaqāfah* (1939–

1952), all of which appeared in Cairo. In Damascus *al-Rābiṭah al-Adabiyyah* (1921–1922) was published, while Beirut saw *al-Amālī* (1938–1941), *al-Makshūf* (1936–1947) and *al-Adīb* (1942–), among others.

3. Recoil from Romanticism and rise of conflicting ideologies

After the Second World War Arabic literature, indeed the whole of the Arab world, entered a new phase. While Romanticism was discredited, political commitment increased and competition grew fierce between clashing loyalties and ideologies, against a background of internal and external changes.

In the aftermath of the war Britain and France ceased to be the dominant foreign powers in the area; their roles were gradually assumed, albeit in a different form, by America and the Soviet Union which, unlike Britain and France, were not simply two rival superpowers with imperialist ambitions, but stood for opposite ideologies. This no doubt contributed to the polarization of the Arab states and of intellectuals within the same state. But what proved to be the most important single external development for the Arab world was obviously the creation of Israel in 1948 and the series of Arab–Israeli wars which ensued and which generally ended in frustration and bitter disappointment and helped to determine Arab attitudes to the outside world. The impact of this upon Arabic literature, both prose and poetry, has been overwhelming.

The Second World War accelerated the process of independence of Arab states and the League of Arab States was formed in 1945. Some of the energy of resistance against the external enemy was therefore directed at the enemy within: war was waged on the privileged communities and feudal rich who had collaborated with the foreign occupier, or the ruling élites who, in the opinion of the people, were guilty of corruption and mismanagement. This corruption and mismanagement was glaringly evident in the disastrous defeat of the Arab armies in the first Arab–Israeli war of 1948, in which some Arab troops were fighting with defective arms supplied to them by their own government. In Egypt the disillusionment with the short-lived democratic experiment and with the performance of political parties coincided with the rapid growth of an educated urban middle class suffering from the result of inflation caused by the war and the inevitable profiteering that ensued. The gap between the rich and the poor, particularly the masses of the destitute who migrated from the countryside in search of a meagre living in overcrowded cities, became wider than ever, thus giving rise to popular movements and mass demonstrations in which students (and workers) figured prominently. With the failure of the liberal democratic experiment, the populace looked for salvation either to the extreme Right (Muslim Brotherhood) or to the extreme Left (Marxism).

The need for literature to promote socialist values was reiterated by the radical Egyptian thinker Salāmah Mūsā (1887–1958), who fell under the influence of the Fabian Society and who continued the tradition of the early Lebanese secularizers such as Shiblī Shumayyil. In 1929 he published his progressive review *al-Majallah al-Jadīdah*, which advocated the adoption of the scientific attitude to life and society and demanded that literature should be written for the people about the problems of the people and in a language that the people could understand. Salāmah Mūsā's ideas found response in many distinguished critics and writers such as Luwīs ʿAwaḍ and Najīb Maḥfūẓ. Other leftist magazines appeared in the Arab world, for example *al-Ṭalīʿah* (1935) in Damascus and *al-Ṭarīq* (1941) in Beirut. Marxist ideas were propagated by ʿUmar Fākhūrī in Damascus and Raʾīf Khūrī (1912–1967) in Lebanon. During the war years young intellectuals from Egypt and other Arab countries became increasingly interested in Marxist philosophy as favourable information about the Soviet régime became more available in the cultural centres of the Middle East, since Russia was one of the allies. Influenced by Marxist English literary criticism, Luwīs ʿAwaḍ (1914–90) published his Marxist interpretation of leading English writers in his articles in Ṭaḥa Ḥusayn's distinguished review *al-Kātib al-Miṣrī* (1945). In 1945 the more influential critic Muḥammad Mandūr (1907–1965) gave up his academic career to engage in active leftist politics, and after the 1952 revolution became editor of the Arabic Soviet cultural periodical *al-Sharq*, supporting the cause of socialist realism, at least in a moderate form. A stream of novels of angry social protest began to pour out in 1944: heavily documented works which describe in great detail the misery and deprivation of Egyptian urban life, adding social injustice and class struggle to national independence as political themes. The pursuit of social realism in fiction was not confined to the younger generation of ʿĀdil Kāmil and Najīb Maḥfūẓ, but can be found in the work of the older generation of Yaḥyā Ḥaqqī and Ṭaḥā Ḥusayn in Egypt.

The early 1950s witnessed the eruption of noisy debates about commitment in literature, in which leading critics and writers, young and old alike, took part. The Arabic word for commitment, *iltizām*, obviously a translation of Jean-Paul Sartre's *engagement* used in his articles first published in *Les Temps Modernes*, later collected in his *Qu'est ce que la littérature* (1948), became an essential part of the vocabulary of literary criticism soon after its first appearance on the literary scene around 1950. Its meaning was diffuse, to be sure: sometimes it meant the adoption of a Marxist stand, at other times an existentialist position, but at all times it denoted at least a certain measure of nationalism, Arab or otherwise. In other words, it emphasized the need for a writer to have a message. This need was explicitly expressed in the manifesto-like editorial note to the first volume of Suhayl Idrīs' Beirut monthly periodical *al-Ādāb* (January 1953), which, more than any other, helped to determine the course of modern Arabic literature by publication both of creative work and of criticism and evaluation of contemporary literature. In August 1954 one contributor to the *Ādāb* wrote that 'the idea of committed literature dominates the Arab world now'. In the same year a controversy arose in Cairo newspapers about the relation of form and content in literature, in which the older generation of Ṭāhā Ḥusayn and al-ᶜAqqād were vehemently opposed by the younger Maḥmūd Amīn al-ᶜĀlim and ᶜAbd al-ᶜAẓīm Anīs who later published their Marxist contribution in Beirut (1955) in an influential book *Fī'l-Thaqāfah al-Miṣriyyah* ('On Egyptian culture') with an introduction by the distinguished Lebanese Marxist critic Ḥusayn Muruwwah, the author of *Qaḍāyā adabiyyah* ('Literary issues', 1956). In 1955 a celebrated formal debate was held in Beirut between Ṭāhā Ḥusayn and Raʾīf Khūrī on the subject 'Does the writer write for the élite or for the general public?' The debate was really about the issue of commitment and the text was published in full in *al-Ādāb* (May 1955).

Against this background the recoil from Romanticism in modern Arabic literature must be seen. The reaction was prompted by a growing painful awareness of the harsh political and social realities of the Arab world, an awareness that was later reinforced by subsequent developments ranging from the horrors of Arab–Israeli wars, the plight of the Palestinians, oppressive Arab régimes, the Iran–Iraq war, to inter-Arab strife and the civil war in the Lebanon. The early success of the 1952 army revolution and the rise of Nasserism gave a boost to Arab nationalism and created a mood of euphoria and optimism. One expression of this nationalistic pride and self-confidence was the hectic search for autonomous or indigenous Arab art forms, such as the specifically Arab or Egyptian or Moroccan theatre, which swept all over the Arab countries. Optimism, however, turned into bitterness when the dream of Arab unity was shattered, civil liberties were crushed by totalitarian régimes, and the Arabs suffered the disastrous defeat of 1967. Despite the disillusionment and set-backs the search continues in some quarters for cultural autonomy, for independent narrative and dramatic art forms, for authentic Arab or more specifically Islamic values. This is undertaken even by those who, like Ḥasan Ḥanafī, themselves received western intellectual or philosophical training and therefore employ western categories in their search and in their rejection of the west, a rejection which may in some measure be explained by the generally unsympathetic if not at times downright hostile attitude adopted towards the Arabs in their various conflicts by the western powers, in particular by the United States. Indeed the limited Arab victory of 1973, revealed in the destruction of the Bar Lev line and the crossing of the Suez Canal, may have restored some of the Arab dignity, but it coincided with the rise of Islamic fundamentalism, which may not be unrelated to this search for total cultural independence by more moderate Arab or Muslim intellectuals. Yet it is a mark of the complexity of the current Arab cultural scene that several Arab intellectuals have at the same time not been immune to the allure of the latest western fashions of Structuralism, Post-structuralism and Deconstruction.

Obviously the dates suggested here for the three periods of development of modern Arabic literature do not constitute sharp lines of demarcation, since there is considerable overlap between the periods. Furthermore, although nearly every Arab state at present boasts one or more practically identical-looking glossy cultural or literary reviews, not all the Arab states have developed at the same rate: for instance, the states of North Africa and the Arabian Peninsula began to make their distinct literary contribution only some time after the Second World War. However, it is to be hoped that these dates are useful pointers. But before the proper survey of modern Arabic literature begins, it may be helpful to provide a discussion of the translations and adaptations, which is the subject of the next section of this Introduction.

2 TRANSLATIONS AND ADAPTATIONS 1834–1914

Between the time when Arabic-speaking peoples acquainted themselves with Greek thought and the beginning of their modern renaissance, not one of their scholars or men of letters is known to have mastered any European language.[1] The contrast with the period we are considering could scarcely be greater.

The emulation of the west

What happened was that the ascendancy gradually acquired by European powers, and demonstrated in many ways but perhaps most glaringly on the battlefield, forced the Arab intellectual élites out of their illusions of self-sufficiency and redirected their energies towards far-reaching reforms for which acquaintance with the achievements of 'the west' has been and to a large extent remains essential.

[1] On how limited the interest of Muslims in Europe was, see Bernard Lewis, *The Middle East and the west*, Bloomington, 1964; also his *Islam in history*, London, 1973, especially pp. 92–114.

It was natural that the need should first have been felt at the heart of the Ottoman Empire, and in the eighteenth century military and administrative reforms were initiated there that were bound to widen in scope and to percolate to the Arab provinces. The stimulation, however, came more directly and dramatically to the Arabs with the Bonaparte expedition to Egypt in 1798, especially as the French came not only with an army using the latest technology then available, but also with teams of translators and scientists who were enormously active during their short stay in the area.

How deep and lasting a mark the French left is a matter of some debate.[2] Certainly their initiatives were meant to benefit them, not their temporary subjects; by the latter they were resented and at best imperfectly understood. Nevertheless, to a leavening of open-minded men they had given a glimpse of a way of thinking and acting that bore the stamp of power and seemed to promise all manner of worldly benefits. It is no accident that the next ruler of Egypt, Muhammad Ali, set about creating an army on the French model, and he brought about far-reaching changes which he perceived to be necessary to such an army. Besides, the association of western ways with power and success first demonstrated by Bonaparte's forces were all too soon to be confirmed, as virtually every part of the Arab world fell under the sway of one western European nation or another.

In fact, western models have played so prominent a part in almost every aspect of the Arab *Nahḍah* that one needs to guard against the assumption that the relationship was merely one of tutelage. It is worth recalling that 'westernization' was a direction taken by local élites even before they had to bend to lasting foreign rule; that the driving force behind it was never submission but the desire for emulation as the surest means of self-assertion; that 'the west', adopted as an example, viewed as monolithic and often idealized, was an abstraction tinged by Arab perceptions of their needs and aspirations; that the imitation was intended to be selective, even though accompanied by grave miscalculations about what was jeopardized by the choices; and that the progress achieved was seldom on an even front.

This last point bears a little elaboration. The most immediately impressive feature of modern western civilization is its technological attainments, and men of will and action – like Muhammad Ali – were quick to see the benefits they would reap from adopting and imitating them. Appreciation of the intellectual curiosity that informs them came later, and acceptance of the philosophic and aesthetic values that are part of the same package later still. At the same time, each act of accreditation of a foreign-inspired innovation facilitated the next, and by a process not of careful sifting but of validation by association, the civilization that had produced

[2] J. Brugman, *An introduction to the history of modern Arabic literature in Egypt*, Leiden, 1984; pp. 10–11.

such clearly beneficial inventions as the steam engine and wireless telegraphy came to be looked upon as holding the answers to virtually every problem of modern life.[3]

By the end of the nineteenth century a new educated élite had come into being in the leading Arab countries that did not so much assert as take for granted the overall superiority of the west in almost every aspect other than revealed religion. Here – as one of countless examples – is the way Jurjī Zaydān (1861–1914) introduces a comparison between 'European and Oriental writers', specifically in connection with their influence on public affairs:[4]

> It may occur to you on reading this title that there is no comparison between the two groups. You may say, 'What is there to link the outstanding writers of Europe, the tips of whose pens determine the politics of their country, with the writers of the East who cut no thread and knot together no rope?' I do not deny this, for I am not unaware of the immense disparity there is between the two countries in degrees of civilization, nor are we ignorant of the high status enjoyed by European writers who hold the reins of government either directly by occupying high positions, or else indirectly by the views they propagate among the leading parties. They are indeed the leaders of thought, the luminaries of civilization, the advisers of the State.

What strikes me most forcibly in this is that he speaks not of different civilizations, but of degrees of attainment in what he takes to be one civilization.

This bespeaks a momentum of change of which many activities were a part. To pick translation out of these is necessary for purposes of analysis, but it is arbitrary, and would be a distortion if not accompanied by a reminder that it was intimately linked with the spread of printing and of journalism, to say nothing of a radical redirection of the priorities of writers and readers alike.

Sources of energy

Thanks largely to the work initiated by Jāk Tājir who as Librarian to the King of Egypt had access to first-hand material, we are well-informed about who the early translators were and what they translated.[5] Rather than reel off names and titles available elsewhere, let me therefore point out what seem to me the main bursts of energy that I detect in the movement.

[3] For a fuller exposition of the process, see my 'The assumptions and aspirations of Egyptian modernists', in *Islam: past influence and present challenge*, ed. Alford T. Welch and P. Cachia, Edinburgh, 1979, pp. 210–35.

[4] 'Kuttāb Ūrubbā wa Kuttāb al-Sharq', *al-Hilāl*, VIII, 8 (15 January 1900), p. 230.

[5] *Ḥarakat al-tarjamah bi Miṣr khilāl al qarn al-tāsiʿ ʿashar*, Cairo [c. 1945]. See also Jamāl ad-Dīn al-Shayyāl, *Tārīkh al-tarjamah fi Miṣr fi ʿahd al-ḥamlah al-faransiyyah*, Cairo, 1950, and *Tārīkh al-tarjamah wa ḥarakat al-thaqāfah fī ʿasr Muḥammad ʿAlī*, Cairo, 1951.

Governmental initiative

We need to acknowledge that the first impulse was given by the ruler of Egypt, Muhammad Ali, whose interest was almost entirely in the technology needed by his army. He took advantage of previous efforts, reprinting twenty of the technical translations made in Turkey from about 1780 onward,[6] and attracting to his service at least one of the Syrian Christian translators who had worked for the French, Father Rufāʾīl Zākhūr Rāhib (d. 1831).[7] But with characteristic energy and single-mindedness, he was to carry the movement a great deal further forward.[8] The lessons taught by foreign experts in his schools were translated on the spot, and some after revision were printed for wider diffusion. He demanded of students sent abroad that they translate the texts they used. Between 1809 and 1816 he had an agent scouring Italy and France for more books. And in 1835, he founded a School of Languages that improved the quality of the work produced and ensured its continuity and extension, governmental initiatives never ceasing to play an important part in the movement.

His and his immediate successors' right-hand man in the most onerous of these ventures was Rifāʿah Rāfiʿ al-Ṭahṭāwī (1801–73), who has good claims to be considered not only a translator and administrator of prodigious energy, but also the leading intellectual figure of his age.

Needless to say, literary texts had no place in these early efforts, but new ideas were being disseminated and Arabic was being forced into new moulds in order to express them; in time the combination was profoundly to affect linguistic habits.

The Christian contribution

To the stream thus started, a sizeable tributary came from Christian missionary work. Christian Arabs – mainly Syrians – were in fact to make disproportionately large contributions to several aspects of the *Nahḍah* in its early stages, if only because (at a time when group loyalties were formed on religious rather than national or ethnic axes) they found it easier than did the Muslims to accept ideas originating in, or transmitted by, Christian Europe. The transmission was facilitated when the Anglican Church Missionary Society, established in Malta, began printing Arabic texts for

[6] J. Heyworth-Dunne, 'Printing and Translation under Muhammad Ali', *Journal of the Royal Asiatic Society* (July 1940), p. 336.

[7] Matti I. Moosa, 'Early 19th-century Printing and Translation', *Islamic Quarterly*, XIV, 4 (Oct.–Dec. 1970), pp. 207–9.

[8] See Heyworth-Dunne, 'Printing', especially pp. 341–2, 332–3.

diffusion in the Arab world from 1825 onward. It was soon joined by the American Presbyterian Mission, which then transferred its activities to the Lebanon in 1834. When this provoked a riposte from the Jesuits, more was done for cultural stimulation than for Christian witness.

Of direct relevance here is that rival translations of the Bible were undertaken. Until then, the only parts of the Bible that had been printed in Arabic were the Gospels, produced by the Medici Oriental Press in 1591[9] but apparently not in wide circulation at the time with which we are concerned, and the Psalms, printed in Rome as early as 1614.[10] In the new undertaking, alongside western scholars, some of the foremost Arab writers of the period were engaged, namely Fāris (later Aḥmad Fāris) al-Shidyāq (1804–87), Buṭrus al-Bustānī (1819–83) and Nāṣīf al-Yāzijī (1800–71).

In addition, a number of Protestant hymns came into use in Arabic translations which are of little distinction in themselves, but which can be seen to have affected the diction and – in secularized form – the notions of some later poets, mainly Syro-Americans.[11]

Evidently these Christian translations were intended for a restricted public, but the training provided by such extensive labours in collaboration with western Arabists was invaluable. Besides, some cross-fertilization between Christian and Muslim communities was inevitable, especially as new bridges were built between them to some extent by freemasonry in the 1860s,[12] and later and on a larger scale by common national aspirations.

Individual efforts

Probably the most significant surge forward occurred when individuals, no longer waiting for the promptings either of the state or of foreign missionaries but directly addressing a new kind of readership, turned their hands to the translation or adaptation of texts for their literary or entertainment value alone.

The first such effort on record (if we except Rufāʾīl Zākhūr Rāhib's *Fables* of La Fontaine, produced in France, and an anonymous *Robinson Crusoe*, printed in Malta[13]) is Ṭahṭāwī's translation of Fénelon's *Télémaque*, not surprisingly the result of a period of retrenchment in governmental activity under ʿAbbās, when Ṭahṭāwī was reduced to the headmastership of a primary school in the Sudan.

9 Robert Jones, 'Arabic publications of the Medici Oriental Press, 1584–1614', paper presented to the *BRISMES/MESA* International Conference, 9 July 1986.

10 Mārūn ʿAbbūd, *Ṣaqr Lubnān*, Beirut, 1950, pp. 49–50.

11 Shmuel Moreh, *Modern Arabic poetry 1800–1970*, Leiden, 1976, pp. 24–32.

12 Moreh, *Modern Arabic poetry*, pp. 98–101.

13 Moosa, 'Early 19th century printing', pp. 210–11.

This appears to have been a somewhat isolated pioneering attempt, but it was not long before the movement gathered strength. Muḥammad Yūsuf Najm[14] mentions some seventy French works of fiction translated in Egypt between 1870 and 1914. Some English and Scottish ones also (notably by Sir Walter Scott) began to appear after the British had made their presence directly felt.

The mushroom growth of non-governmental journalism – beginning with *Ḥadīqat al-Akhbār* founded in Beirut in 1858, but finding its greatest scope in Egypt thereafter – gave a great fillip to this development.[15] Short stories in particular found a ready outlet in journals and even in newspapers, but many novels also first appeared in serialised form in this ephemeral medium, or as special numbers of a periodical.

Understandably, literary histories make much of the masterpieces that then became known to an Arabic-reading public. The bulk of what was translated, however, was not of such a high calibre. It consisted mostly of sensationalist material – thrillers, spy and later detective stories, and 'penny dreadfuls'. The reason is not far to seek: in a genre so new to the Arabs, taste was as yet unformed, and swung to the extreme opposite of the formal, diction-conscious literature previously held in honour. Thus a novel that created enough of a stir in 1880 to attract the attention even of Muḥammad ʿAbduh (1849–1905) was the now forgotten Pierre Zaccone's *La Vengeance*, translated by Adīb Isḥāq (1856–1885) and Salīm al-Naqqāsh (d. 1884).[16]

The theatre also has some claim to pioneering efforts in this field, for the very first Arabic play produced in European style, Mārūn al-Naqqāsh's (1817–1855) *al-Bakhīl* staged in Beirut late in 1847, is broadly based on Molière's *l'Avare*, and direct translations were soon to follow. Throughout the period under review, however, the live theatre was mostly in the hands of actor-managers whose interest was overwhelmingly in the performances, so that the translations, adaptations or original works which they wrote themselves or commissioned were hardly ever printed in their time, and therefore reached only their own patrons.

It was someone unconnected with any of the acting companies who was first to contribute substantially to written drama. This was a pupil of Ṭahṭāwī, Muḥammad ʿUthmān Jalāl (1829–1894) who, in addition to his onerous activities in government service as an official translator, as a judge, and at one time as a Cabinet minister, gave Arabs versions of at least one novel and (in verse) of the fables of La Fontaine, but whose heart appears to have been in the theatre. It is not clear whether it is to him we owe a volume

[14] *al-Qiṣṣah fī 'l-adab al-ʿarabī l-ḥadīth*, pp. 13–21.

[15] Henri Pérès, 'Le roman, le conte, et la nouvelle dans la littérature Arabe moderne', *Annales de l'Institut d'Études Orientales*, Tome III, Année 1937, pp. 266–337, lists one journal after another that included translated narratives.

[16] Pérès, 'Le roman', p. 267.

of plays translated from the Italian under the title of *Alʿāb al-Tiyātrāt* advertised in *Wādī' l-Nīl*, IV, 58 (11 November 1870), the novelty of which is stressed in the notice, which is headed: 'A literary innovation and a work of Arabization, or the introduction of a new form of authorship in the Arabic language'.[17] What is certain is that he paid particular attention to the French classical theatre, translating five plays by Molière and three by Racine. A remarkable feature of his work is that – even though not concerned with the box-office – he went further than most writers for the theatre in that he chose colloquial verse for the rendering of even the loftiest of tragedies.

Apart from such verse plays (including several of Shakespeare's[18]), the church hymns mentioned earlier, and the monumental but isolated translation of the Iliad by Sulaymān al-Bustānī (1856–1925) in 1904, poetry did not arouse nearly so much interest among the translators as did the other genres. There are some notable approaches to European lyric poetry, such as Aḥmad Shawqī's (1868–1932) translation (now lost) of Lamartine's 'Le Lac', made while he was a student in France between 1887 and 1891, but this does not seem to have made a profound impression even on his own poetry. As for the English Romantics, it was not until the appearance of the Dīwān school early in the twentieth century that they received much attention, and this mostly in journals. A book on Byron containing seven translations was published by Muḥammad al-Sibāʿī in 1912, but the most ample and authoritative translations of English poems were by ʿAbbās Maḥmūd al-ʿAqqād (1889–1964), whose poems were not collected in book form until 1929.[19]

It is tempting to relate this phenomenon to the general observation that the concrete products of the west had more immediate appeal than the abstract, but the simpler explanation is that the narrative and theatrical genres were totally new to high Arabic literature, so that the only models to be followed were foreign ones, whereas poets had in their own culture a rich treasury to draw on.

That the public's interest in western perceptions was constantly widening and deepening is indicated when translators on their own initiative went beyond texts that may be held to have entertainment value to thought-provoking, philosophical ones. An important pioneer in this line was Fatḥī Zaghlūl (d. 1914), who translated several of Jeremy Bentham's

[17] 'Bidʿah adabiyyah wa qiṭʿah taʿrībiyyah aw idkhāl uslūb jadīd min at-ta'līf fī 'l-lughah al-ʿarabiyyah', quoted in Yūsuf Rāmītsh, *Usrat al-Muwaylihī wa atharuhā fī' l-adab al-ʿarabī*, Cairo [1980], p. 153.

[18] See the chapter 'The Arabs and Shakespeare', in M. M. Badawi, *Modern Arabic literature and the west*, London, 1985.

[19] See Muḥammad ʿAbdul-Ḥai, 'A Bibliography of Arabic Translations of English and American Poetry (1830–1970)', *Journal of Arabic Literature*, VII (1976), pp. 120–150.

books – the earliest in 1888 – as well as sociological works by Gustave Le Bon and one by E. Desmoulins entitled *À quoi tient la superiorité des Anglo-Saxons*.[20] The significance of this last choice in British-occupied territory is self-evident. No less evident is the fact that such initiatives were quick to multiply.

Difficulties encountered

The energy and initiative displayed by Arab translators is all the more impressive as they have had to face peculiar problems in addition to those familiar to any of us who have ventured into this field, perhaps with the comfortable assumption that fluency in two languages is all that is required. Shidyāq, one of the pioneers, expressed himself in verse on the subject[21]:

> He who has missed out on translation knows not what travail is:
> None but the warrior is scorched by the fire of war!
> I find a thousand notions for which there is none akin
> Amongst us, and a thousand with none appropriate;
> And a thousand terms with no equivalent.
> I find disjunction for junction, though junction is needed.
> And terseness of style when the context calls for
> Elaboration, if the purpose is to be attained.

Obviously the most basic difficulty was the absence of a technical vocabulary, not only in the new sciences but also in the new literary genres. In discussing novels in 1881, Muḥammad ʿAbduh had no word for the new genre other than a coinage from the French, *rūmāniyyāt*,[22] and for several decades thereafter *riwāyah* often did duty for both a novel and a play.

A revealing example of the pressure under which an Arab intellectual had to function, of the ingenuity he displayed and of the way that disparate endeavours supported one another, is Shidyāq's fumbling for an Arabic rendition of 'socialist'. This was when, as editor of *al-Jawāʾib* and no doubt as rushed for time as most editors are, he had to comment on the activities of various left-wing groups in Europe, such as the French *communards*; he resorted to various circumlocutions such as *al-ṣushyālīst al-qāʾilīn bi 'l-ishtirāk fī 'l-amlāk* before finally coining *ishtirākī*, to which he was led by his own earlier translation of 'The Acts of the Apostles' 4:32.[23]

The challenge was compounded by the Arabs' long-established reverence for their language as both the medium of revelation and the repository of past glories. Because the issue has long been played out, it is easy to lose

[20] Jāk Tājir, *Ḥarakat al-tarjamah*, pp. 127–8.

[21] Quoted in ʿImād al-Ṣulḥ, *Aḥmad Fāris al-Shidyāq: Āthāruh wa ʿaṣruh*, Beirut, 1980, p. 144.

[22] Pérès, 'Le roman', p. 267.

[23] On Shidyāq's labours as a translator, see ʿImād al-Ṣulḥ, *Aḥmad Fāris al-Shidyāq*, pp. 144–165.

sight of the fact that there was a substantial body of conservatives to whom it was dogma that Arabic was perfect and complete and who – mainly between 1910 and 1925 – engaged the modernists in heated polemics,[24] contending that only ignorance of its treasures made it necessary for them to add loan words or even new coinages to it.

Furthermore, Shidyāq's hint in the verse I have quoted at the difficulty of deciding what had to be abridged and what was to be elaborated shows that, from the start, Arab translators did not view their task as one of slavish transposition, but rather of adaptation to the needs of a new public. When working on the Bible, Shidyāq did not hide his impatience with his English collaborators over their excursions into etymology to decide the precise meaning of a word and their suspicion of stylistic flourishes suggestive of the Qurʾān.

At the very least, the choice of the material and the style in which it was rendered were reflections of prevailing standards. Thus in the translations produced in the nineteenth century, even when the story-line was fairly faithfully maintained, elaborately rhyming titles bear witness to the persistence of the stylistic preferences of previous centuries. A good illustration is *Paul et Virginie*, the climax of which has the heroine on a ship that is foundering within sight of shore, but refusing the chance of being saved by a sailor because she literally would rather die than take off her voluminous skirts; this was translated three times, and in Muḥammad ʿUthmān Jalāl's version[25] it becomes *al-Amānī wa 'l-Minnah fī Ḥadīth Qabūl wa Ward Jannah.* Not only are the protagonists given names that are phonetically close to the originals yet recognizably Arabic (although not without some strain), but the text is in rhymed prose throughout and studded with verses and philosophical reflections.

Muḥammad ʿUthmān Jalāl did the same with the plays. A detailed comparison of his *al-Shaykh Matlūf* with the first scene of Molière's *Tartuffe*[26] shows that, having converted the characters to Islam, he then toned down both the criticism of the man of religion and expressions of children's rebellion against their parents, to say nothing of other arbitrary changes, all at some cost to the characterization and the dramatic effect.

At the other end of the spectrum are adaptations so free that a later critic[27] was to say that most of the writers of the first quarter of the twentieth century were 'creators when translating, and translators when creating'.

24 For an echo of this controversy, see Ṭāhā Ḥusayn, *Ḥadīth al-Arbiʿāʾ*, vol. II, Cairo, 1937, pp. 327–9.

25 See H. A. R. Gibb, 'Studies in contemporary Arabic literature', *Bulletin of the School of Oriental Studies*, V, Pt 3, pp. 1–2.

26 In Shimon Ballas, 'Iṭlālah ʿalā Manhaj Muḥammad ʿUthmān Jalāl fī l-tarjamah', *al-Karmil*, 6 (1985), pp. 7–36.

27 Ḥabīb Zaḥlāwī, 'Kitābān wa Kātibān', *al-Risālah*, xvii, 821 (28 March 1949), pp. 379–81.

This is well exemplified by Muṣṭafā Luṭfī al-Manfalūṭī (1876–1924), who 'translated' several French novels although he knew no French. I have even been told that – at least at the height of the Romantic wave in the twenties and thirties of this century – hopeful young writers used to submit to journals effusions of their own labelled 'free translations', in the belief that the prestige of things western was such that they stood a better chance of having them published than if they presented them as original works.

Two of the terms used in this process were *taʿrīb* and *tamṣīr*, literally 'Arabization' and 'Egyptianization'. These are not always used in a precise sense (for example, Muḥammad ʿUthmān Jalāl's use of *taʿrīb* for rendering into the colloquial is peculiar to him), but both imply a good deal more than mere translation into standard Arabic or into Egyptian colloquial. Especially in the theatre, what was involved was nothing less than the transposition of the plot to an Arab or Egyptian milieu, and that in turn entailed making the characters behave in accordance with locally acceptable customs. On the practices that took shape at about the time of the first World War, we have the personal testimony of the main architect of modern Arab drama, Tawfīq al-Ḥakīm (1898–1987):[28]

The 'Egyptianized' foreign play used to be described as *iqtibās* [literally, 'lighting a piece of wood from a fire', hence 'acquisition' or 'adoption'], just as a foreign novel freely translated (as was done by al-Manfalūṭī) was described as 'Arabization' – i.e. 'Arabization' [was the term used] in [fictional] literature, and 'Egyptianization' in the theatre. The word *iqtibās* was not used in its strict linguistic sense. In common usage, it meant that the play was neither pure creation nor pure translation. It consisted rather of transferring the topic from one milieu to another, changing the foreign characters into Egyptians or Orientals . . .

Amongst us, theatrical *iqtibās* . . . amounted almost to semi-authorship especially in those long departed days when we used to write before women abandoned the veil. At that time, in our sex-segregated society, we had to alter the social relations that existed among men and women in an integrated one; so if we wanted to adapt a play in which a man met a woman, we got into all sorts of complications . . . It was impossible to make the wife of So-and-So 'display herself' in front of the husband of Such-and-Such. We used to get round this in various ways, making this woman the paternal or maternal cousin of that man, and so on, so that men and women in all the plays of that period were related . . . The alteration of social relations in accordance with the demands of our milieu in turn necessitated changes in the dialogue, the characterization and some of the situations of the play, adding up to considerable departures from the original . . . These activities were tantamount to a school for the training of playwrights, giving the opportunity to such of them as wished to spread their wings in the future to fly solo . . .

None of us allowed himself to write the word *taʾlīf* ['authorship'] unless that was what had actually taken place, or if his inventiveness and effort had reached the point of creative writing. If the play was translated, then the name of the foreign

[28] *Sijn al-ʿumr*, Cairo, 1988, pp. 194–6.

author was mentioned in all advertisements, no matter how valuable the contribution of the translator or 'Arabizer' was . . . But if this was not practicable – because the play had been so changed that it had become something else – then it was enough to say, '*iqtibās* from the pen of So-and-So'. It so happened that ᶜAbbās ᶜAllām wanted to get rid of this word *iqtibās* that had become customary, so he adopted – and perhaps he was the first to do so – that obscure, ambiguous formula when used by itself: 'from the pen of . . .' . . . This practice spread among all writers until it came to seem natural.

A small factor in the equation, but one usually overlooked, is that inherited Arab notions of plagiarism are not identical with western ones, or are at least more elaborately graded, the concern with choice diction being such that only word for word reproduction is condemned outright. The liberties taken by such as al-Manfalūṭī did give rise to some debate at the time, but in terms of what they contributed or failed to contribute to Arab readers, not out of an obligation of faithfulness to the originals. A view closer to that prevailing in the west was bound to develop in time.

Indeed many Arab translators impress us as much with their selfless devotion as with their energy. Those who assume an immediate economic motivation behind every initiative would find it hard to explain Muḥammad ᶜUthmān Jalāl's persistence in the use of the colloquial, for he could find no patronage for his first book and had to publish it at his own expense, and even the most celebrated of his plays, the adaptation of *Tartuffe*, was never staged in his lifetime.[29] Much is owed to the determination or out-and-out idiosyncrasies of some men of learning. A French–Arabic dictionary that deserves to be better known is that of Mohammad El-Naggary Bey,[30] a judge who – besides giving special attention to legal terms – was so fond of La Fontaine that under such words as 'loup' or 'renard' he reproduces the whole of the relevant fables with Arabic verse translations, most signed by the same Muḥammad ᶜUthmān Jalāl. Mīkhāʾīl Nuᶜaymah's (1889–1988) *cri de coeur* has often been repeated:[31]

We are in a stage of our literary and social evolution in which many spiritual needs have awakened – needs which we did not feel before our contact with the West. As we have not the pens or the brains that can fulfil those needs, let us then translate! And let us honour the translators because they are the mediators between us and the larger human family.

In trumpeting his call, he was unnecessarily and unjustly derogatory towards his contemporaries' creative powers, but he was also putting into

29 Ballas, 'Muḥammad ᶜUthmān Jalāl', pp. 8, 13.

30 *Dictionnaire français-arabe*, 2 vols, Alexandria, 1903, 1905.

31 Taher Khemiri and Georg Kampffmeyer, *Leaders in contemporary Arabic literature*, Pt 1, Leipzig, 1930, p. 31, translating from *al-Ghirbāl*, p. 127; see also M. M. Badawi, *A critical introduction to modern Arabic poetry*, Cambridge, 1975, p. 182.

words the broad concern with culture evinced by those already engaged in the task he advocated.

The stimulation of creativity

One more aspect of our question deserves consideration. We all know that a shelf laden with books is no guarantee that the owner is a well-read man. How much of the translators' sizeable output was in constant currency, impinging upon young minds and helping in their formation?[32]

Once again, we have cause to be grateful to Tawfīq al-Ḥakīm, the city-bred son of a judge, for his candid account of the effect some foreign works had upon him in a period extending roughly from 1910 to 1918, when he was still a schoolboy.[33] After recalling his delight at his mother's recounting of folk tales, he writes:

There began to appear on the market European narratives translated by the Syrians who were good at languages and had been educated in the missionary schools. My mother became fond of these too, and re-told them to us as she had done with previous ones . . .

My pride at passing the primary school certificate at the first attempt had the effect of making me irresponsible, lax, contemptuous, and neglectful [of my studies] – this is to say nothing of the lack of constraint I experienced as my parents were away from time to time, and the existence of the 'American Cosmograph' [showing] episodes of the adventure serials that entranced me: after the Zigomar serial came the episodes of Fantomas! Add to all this the Rocambole novels which were available for hire in bookshops . . . I had only to pay five piastres a month to become a member, and I could then hire and read the twenty parts of a long story like Rocambole, or the collected works of Alexandre Dumas père.

I remember that I bought out of my pocket money a book newly translated into Arabic: it was by the English philosopher Spencer, on ethics, and I felt proud to be reading philosophy, although I do not now believe that I understood anything worth mentioning in this book or its likes. Our knowledge of English was not such as to enable us to read English philosophical books, and even if it had been, we would not have found the wherewithal in our pockets. As for the Arab philosophers, such as al-Ghazali, Averroes and Avicenna, no one ever directed us to them . . .

The only [literary] translations that had appeared then were the first part of Hugo's *Les Misérables* translated by Ḥāfiẓ Ibrāhīm in grand Arabic style which we used actually to intone. Then there appeared a poor translation of Tolstoy's *Anna Karenina* which was incapable of suggesting to us that it was of lasting literary quality. It is true that Fatḥī Zaghlūl had translated something by Montesquieu, perhaps *L'Esprit des Lois*, and my father had many copies of this which he was to distribute, but that book did not attract me at the time . . .

What I was really eager to read at that age was the plays which we used to see at

[32] For a present-day critic's estimate of the most significant translations. See Luwīs ʿAwaḍ, 'Maskh al-Kāʾināt', *Ahrām*, 24 November 1972, p. 7.

[33] *Sijn al-ʿumr*, pp. 79, 114–15, 132–7.

the Opera House and other theatres, . . . but despite long searches I found only a few, poorly printed, such as *Buridan*, *The Martyrs of Love* [i.e. *Romeo and Juliet*] with all its poetry, *Othello*, and then *Louis XI* with which I was greatly delighted, memorizing from it the entire part of Louis. But I did not find *Hamlet* although I was eager to read it as it had been staged in Arabic, nor did I find a single one of the Molière plays which ʿUthmān Jalāl had translated into colloquial verse.

This may be compared with the books that another eminent writer of about the same age, Ṭāhā Ḥusayn (1889–1973), remembers as having been on sale in the shops of provincial towns. These were mainly devotional works and hagiographies, books of magic, and some folk tales, with not a single translation among them.[34]

The contrast is striking. And yet even Tawfīq al-Ḥakīm's list is not particularly impressive, nor did the difference ensure that he should become a man of wider culture than his more humbly born contemporary. Even more decisive were their temperaments, their consciously made choices, their mastery of languages giving them direct access to other literatures. Indeed Ṭāhā Ḥusayn was to comment on one of his own translations:[35]

The aim of those who transpose poetry from one language to another is not to convey to their readers a true picture of it. The aim must be to give their readers an inkling of it, and to lead those who have the time and the resources to get to know it, and to drink of it at the source.

At a time when elements of two cultures were meeting, vying, clashing or intermingling, translation was a revealing index of new directions and new priorities, as well as an important channel for the diffusion of new information and new perceptions; but it was only one of a complex of interacting forces produced by and producing change.

[34] *al-Ayyām*, I, tr. as *An Egyptian childhood* by E. H. Paxton, London, 1981, p. 50.
[35] *Suḥuf mukhtārah min al-shiʿr al-tamthīlī ʿind al-Yūnān*, Cairo 1920, p. 50

CHAPTER 2

THE NEO-CLASSICAL ARABIC POETS

1 INTRODUCTION

The emergence of Neo-classical poetry in modern Arabic literature in the nineteenth century was not the outcome of the sudden incursion of a new literary model upon the established system of literature. Neither was it the product of a literary grouping around an innovative poet (or group of poets) endowed with revolutionary zeal. Quite the contrary. Its development was quiet, involving no visible upheavals. The main trend of this school (if school it was) was to go back to an old, venerable model, and to relive the glorious experience of ancient poets. The model is, of course, that of medieval Arabic poetry at its peak, as represented by the spirited bards of the *Jāhilī* (Pre-Islamic) and early Islamic periods and, more emphatically, by the great urbane poets of the heyday of Abbasid creativity: al-Mutanabbī, al-Buḥturī, Abū Tammām, Abū 'l-ʿAlaʾ al-Maʿarrī and al-Sharīf al-Raḍiyy.

In point of fact, modern neo-classical poetry does not constitute a phase of literature that can be sharply separated from its immediate ancestry. Arab poets, writing in traditional fashions, never ceased operating in the Arabic-speaking regions. Even in the darkest of times, for example between the fourteenth and nineteenth centuries, the production of poetry in *fuṣḥā* (= literary Arabic) and according to the traditional metres continued. Admittedly, this was generally dull poetry of uninspired literary quality and recondite language. It was composed by imitative versifiers who very rarely employed it as a means of expressing fresh human experience. The bulk of late medieval *dīwāns* (collections of verse) are replete with rhetorical devices and puns. Rather than addressing the major issues of life and society, these works dabbled in trifling matters; and rather than demonstrating individual poetic voice, the late medieval poet was prized for his ability to display a variety of imitations, verbal tricks and chronograms. The public for whom these poems were meant was, as a rule, a select group of ulema and privileged *literati* who saw the poet as an entertainer and boon-companion. The poet was in the main a reciter of his own poetry, since the printing press was not in general use in Arab lands before the nineteenth century, and a reading public in the proper sense was virtually non-existent owing to the paucity of general education among the masses.

With the rejuvenation of cultural life in Lebanon, Egypt and other Arab regions in the course of the last century, the awareness that something was radically wrong with poetry – and with literary life as a whole – began to dawn upon authors and readers alike. The exposure to European literature, directly or through translations, posed a great challenge to Arab authors. The spread of popular education, the advent of printing and the emergence of the mass press all created a set of new cultural realities and, above all, a reading public of growing numbers and of a new social background. Some basic assumptions in the realm of literature had, therefore, to be reassessed, and certain practices had to be changed to cope with the new realities.

Prose was quick to respond. In the second half of the nineteenth century it was already undergoing radical changes through the adoption of new literary and journalistic genres and through the coining of new words and phrases suited for the needs of modern life. Medieval prose, along with its rhymes, parallelism and *hendiadis*, was giving way to a new pliable style, accessible to the common reader. Toward the end of the last century the prose style of many modern Arab writers had little in it that resembled late medieval prose (which, like poetry, was recondite and burdened with verbal acrobatics). Poetry, however, was unable to forsake its ancient moorings. Fourteen centuries of continuous tradition was at stake. It was doubly difficult for Arabic poets to adopt 'imported' literary models and concepts since that would have involved a violation of the very paradigm of cultural values. Poetry in its traditional forms and language was enshrined in the history of Arab-Islamic civilization, invoking its finest hours. Furthermore, the 'Arab ear' was so accustomed to the rhythms of that poetry, so entranced by it, that any experimentation that affected the inherited rhythmic structure was bound to alienate the reading (or auditive) public.

Therefore, instead of adopting a new set of operative principles, Arabic poetry in the nineteenth century opted for a 'return to the sources', and set out to bridge the gap of long centuries of immobility. The aim of the neo-classical poets was to produce verses which were reminiscent in their 'masculinity' and lucidity of al-Mutanabbī and his peers, and to refrain as much as possible from the trivial pursuits that characterized the poetry of the 'period of decline'. The idea of a radical undermining of the norms of classical poetry was not entertained by any major poet or critic of the early *Nahḍah* (Renaissance). Such notions as deviating from the stylistic norms of medieval poetry or reforming the old metrical system were hardly ever treated seriously, and it was only in the second half of this century that they gained popularity. Admittedly, poets sometimes expressed a desire to diverge from the accepted poetic practices. One such expression is the famous statement of Aḥmad Shawqī, in his introduction to the first volume of *al-Shawqiyyāt* (1898), concerning his efforts to introduce new features into his poetry. Shawqī asserts that he had to employ devious means in order to make these poems palatable to his editors and mentors. But what was the nature of these innovations? Judging by the poetry he published at that early stage of his career, it is possible to assume that in spite of his familiarity with French literature, Shawqī never intended to effect a far-reaching change in the structure of the poem or in its language. The poetic text that he provides in his introduction to illustrate his point is highly indicative of a neo-classical rather than a modernizing bent. Instead of opening his panegyric with a *nasīb* section bewailing the deserted campsite of the beloved, as in *Jāhilī* poems, he produces an amorous prelude reminiscent of Abbasid or Andalusian love poetry.

The impact of western poetic concepts on nineteenth-century Arabic poetry was negligible. Translations from European poetry into Arabic were few and far between. This fact is noteworthy in view of the profusion of translated western prose (fiction, drama, history and so on) in Egypt and Lebanon in the second half of the nineteenth century. Although some of these translators (such as Najīb al-Ḥaddād [1867–1899], a Lebanese who settled in Egypt) were themselves poets, it was only on rare occasions that they translated poetry into Arabic.[1] Admittedly, western plays in verse were translated into Arabic, but this activity was totally divorced, at least in the minds of Arab authors and readers, from the world of the 'poem' although it stimulated the rise of a local verse drama (whose most prominent practitioner in the first decades of our century was Aḥmad Shawqī).

It is of interest to note that those poets and intellectuals who were very much at home with European literature never dared, in the early stages of *Nahḍah*, to urge Arabic poetry to expose itself to the influence of western poetic concepts. Najīb al-Ḥaddād once again comes to mind in this context. His work as a whole testifies to an impressive familiarity with western poetry, old and new. This familiarity is well represented by his famous article 'A comparison between Arabic and European poetry', which constitutes a systematic and illuminating analysis of the distinctive qualities of each, touching upon issues of themes, prosody, language and imagery. However, in the conclusion of his article he has these things to say:

[1] The remarkable translation of the *Iliad* by Sulaymān al-Bustānī (1856–1925) into versified Arabic was published in Cairo in 1904.

To sum up: they [the Europeans] have excelled over us in certain things, while we excelled over them in many things. Our poetry embraces the best qualities of theirs, while their poetry embraces none of ours. This is undoubtedly due to the superior nature of the Arabic language. No other language possesses the richness of its lexicon, the abundance of its expressive devices or the grandeur of its eloquence. The Europeans themselves have described it as 'the most perfect language in the world'. This acknowledgment suffices to demonstrate its superiority over all languages, as well as the superiority of our poetry over all others.[2]

The adherence to tradition, however, was less binding when it came to the subject matter of poetic expression. True, here too the early poets and critics did not explicitly advocate a change in the topics of poetry although some of them, including Maḥmūd Sāmī al-Bārūdī, one of the earliest and greatest of the neo-classicists, occasionally hinted at the need for change. Al-Bārūdī expressed, in his introduction to his *dīwān* as well as in some of his poems, a new attitude concerning the function of poetry and the subject-matter on which it draws.[3] However, al-Bārūdī and other poets went on composing poetry according to the traditional *aghrāḍ* (normative thematic types). The poets' exposure to the winds of change in the modern Arab world, as well as the changing nature of their audience (readers of mass circulating papers and printed *dīwāns* as opposed to listeners at private or public gatherings), brought about a greater awareness on their part that it was their duty to reflect 'modern' topics without deserting the traditional modes of expression. In the year 1900 the Lebanese-Egyptian poet Khalīl Muṭrān (who was not himself a neo-classicist in the strict sense of this term) expressed this awareness as follows:

The [classical] Arab way (*khiṭṭa*) in poetry should not necessarily be our own. The Arabs lived in their own age, and we live in ours. They had their manners, mores and sciences, and we have ours. It is imperative, therefore, that our poetry should reflect our own conceptions and feelings rather than those of the ancients. However the expression of these should conform to the same set of formal and verbal modes as theirs.[4]

This is one of the most lucid expressions of what may be described as the implicit ideology of modern Arabic neo-classical poetry: to be traditional in form and contemporary in content; to express the outlook and concerns of our age while adhering to the compositional principles of another. Indeed, neo-classical poets went a long way in ridding themselves of trifling concerns and grappling with current issues. But the distinction between

2 See Muṣṭafā Luṭfī al-Manfalūṭī (ed.), *Mukhtārāt al-Manfalūṭī*, Cairo, n.d., p. 138.

3 See M. M. Badawi, 'Al-Bārūdī: precursor of the modern Arabic poetic revival', *Die Welt des Islams* n.s., XII (1969), pp. 232–4.

4 *Al-Majallah al-Miṣriyyah*, July 1900, p. 85; quoted in Adunīs (ʿAlī Aḥmad Saʿīd), *Al-Thābit wa'l-mutaḥawwil*, III, Beirut, 1978, p. 94.

'form' and 'content' inherent in the above formulation and in many similar ones was an impracticable course of action, for the old prosodic and stylistic constraints were very often detrimental to the poet's desire to be 'contemporary'. On the other hand, the classical model itself has not remained untouched, as we shall see, in the course of the last hundred years. Some of the basic medieval Arabic poetic norms underwent gradual but important changes at the hands of the major neo-classical poets.

The main epoch of Arabic neo-classical poetry spans the last third of the nineteenth century and the first third of the twentieth. The year 1932 marks the death of two of Egypt's foremost neo-classical poets, Shawqī and Ḥāfiẓ Ibrāhīm, and at least in that country it signifies the end of an era. As we shall presently see, the neo-classical type continued to live after that date, and many important poets who write in that style are active in several Arab countries up to this day. However, a new type of poetry, commonly referred to as Post-classical or 'Romantic', which had its beginnings in the first and second decades of our century, occupied a central position in the world of poetry in the 1930s and 1940s, and rendered the neo-classical type outmoded. After the rise of the romantic type and even before that, we find many poets vacillating between the norms of classical and post-classical poetry.

The question now arises as to what corpus falls into the category of neo-classical poetry. The primary distinctive feature of that poetry as represented by its major practitioners may be summed up as follows:

1. The poems of the neo-classical poets are composed in the traditional metres of classical Arabic poetry, with minor derivative metres. As a rule, they are monorhyming.

2. Neo-classical poets continue to use the classical *aghrāḍ* (thematic types), and most of their *dīwāns* are arranged accordingly. These *aghrāḍ* often impose a pre-determined structure, and sometimes affect the choice of metres.

3. The poems are frequently impersonal, and the poet's experience is hidden beneath layers of convention. Sections of these poems which sometimes impress their reader as 'confessional' often turn out to be genre-bound rather than spontaneous.

4. The neo-classical language is essentially dependent on that of mediaeval Arab poetry, especially that of the Abbasid period. Not only the lexical inventory but the choice of figurative language is derivative in this fashion. The invocation of classical place-names, images and personages is a major feature in the art of most representative neo-classical poets.

It is to be emphasized that not all these features function equally prominently in the works of the different poets who belong to this trend.

Some have little recourse to the traditional *aghrāḍ* (for example Jamīl Ṣidqī al-Zahāwī); others are less attuned to the language of classical poetry, drawing heavily on the modern prose style and occasionally on the vernacular (for example Aḥmad al-Ṣāfī al-Najafī). Moreover, there are poets who, though employing classical *aghrāḍ* and language, display in some of their poems a sensitivity and structure which render their poetry in part romantic rather than strictly neo-classical. A case in point is Khalīl Muṭrān (1872–1949), one of the most distinguished Arab poets of this century, whose poetry betrays neo-classical features but also certain elements that stand in stark contrast to the spirit of classicism. Finally, we find today a great number of poets who employ the neo-classical model only in a fraction of their poetry (mainly in poems meant to be recited at public gatherings) while the bulk of their poetry is of a blatantly post-classical, even modernistic, nature.

The major neo-classical poets have received their due share of critical appraisal in the last fifty years or so. However, Arab critics and scholars have so far not reached an accepted term by which to designate this poetic school. Several terms are in use for this purpose, two of which are fairly common: *shiʿr al-ʾIḥyāʾ* (the poetry of revival) and *al-madrasah al-taqlīdiyyah/al-ittibāʿiyyah* (the traditional/classical school). In recent years one frequently comes across the term *al-shiʿr al-ʿamūdī* (poetry based on the norms of medieval poetics). Other current terms are *al-shiʿr al-turāthī* (poetry pertaining to the heritage), *madrasat al-Bārūdī wa-Shawqī* (the school of al-Bārūdī and Shawqī); and, finally, *al-madrasah al-klāsīkiyyah al-jadīdah* (the neo-classical school).

2. HISTORY

It is possible to discern three stages in the history of modern neo-classical poetry. The first begins at the middle of the nineteenth century and ends at its end, with the appearance of the fully developed poetry of Shawqī. During this period the late-medieval poetic paradigm was still paramount, but poets in Lebanon and Egypt were gradually deviating from it. These poets, Christian and Muslim, were, consciously or unconsciously, aiming for the restoration of the radiant classical model and were following in its footsteps. They had no ambition to evolve a new poetic tradition unknown to the Arabs; neither were they purposely trying to transform old concepts and practices to suit their time.

The second stage spans the first thirty or so years of the twentieth century, a period in which Shawqī was the dominant figure, with other Egyptian poets (Ḥāfiẓ Ibrāhīm, Ismaʿīl Ṣabrī) as cohorts. It was during this period that the distinctive features of what might be termed 'high neo-classical poetry' took shape, and new centres of the poetry of revival, as it is sometimes called by Arab authors, came to the fore, notably in Iraq and Syria. Unlike the first period, however, the age of Shawqī was already witness to the rise of more audacious trends in Arabic poetry and criticism which at times were blatantly anti-classical. The appearance of such proto-romantic or romantic figures as Muṭrān and Shukrī in Egypt, as well as Gibrān and Nuʿaymah in the American offshoot of the Lebanese centre (*al-Mahjar*, that is, parts of America to which some Arab writers emigrated), had a considerable, if unacknowledged, influence on the ways of the neo-classical school during its 'golden age' and thereafter. It is conceivable that the advent of a wave of militant anti-neo-classical criticism (as in the early writings of al-ʿAqqād in Egypt and Nuʿaymah in *al-Mahjar*) might paradoxically have forced the neo-classicists to entrench in the traditional modes rather than demonstrate a greater measure of modernity. The dialectic of literary evolution, however, teaches us that a dynamic literary movement (and the neo-classical school was definitely dynamic at that stage) can under no circumstances be effectively insulated from innovative trends and, indeed, from interacting with its very rivals. Consequently, we witness a variety of new features – conceptual, thematic and stylistic – gradually percolating through the thick layers of convention, rendering the neo-classical poetic text at once 'restorative' and 'relevant'.

The third stage, which carries us down to the present day, is characterized by the virtual stagnation of the poetic model, although several neo-classical poets of merit did make their debut after, or shortly before, the death of Shawqī.

Early neo-classicism

It is a platitude to say that modern Arabic poetry, like modern Arabic literature in general, was set in motion by the social, political and cultural developments which swept the Arab world during the nineteenth century. Literary history, however, is called upon to pay special attention to those factors within the literary system and in its vicinity which contributed to the rise of a new breed of literature. One such factor is, without doubt, the repercussions caused by the coming of the printing press. All the different types of literary production were affected. Texts of medieval literature were being printed by this fledgling industry, thus becoming accessible to wide circles of readers. The reading public itself was not only growing in numbers but also exhibiting new literary predilections, different from those of the lucky few who had been the main connoisseurs of literature in pre-modern times.

Within the literary system itself a realignment of the constituent elements was taking place. A new kind of prose was emerging which was simpler than that of the past, introducing its ever-widening public to a range of new, dynamic genres: the novel and the short story, the magazine article and the feuilleton, a variety of historical and biographical writings of remarkable lucidity. Poetry thus found itself confronting an aggressive contender that was threatening to dislodge it from the supreme status that it had enjoyed throughout previous ages.

Therefore, Arab writers of traditional training who had the opportunity to obtain a glimpse of European culture were quick to recognize that poetry had to be invigorated if it was to stand up to the challenge. Complacency had to be left behind, and the trivial preoccupations of the pre-modern poets had to be replaced by more serious concerns. The increasing availability of the printed *dīwāns* of ancient Arabic poetry familiarized the reading public, as well as the poets, with the masterpieces of the golden age of that poetry; and it was in these masterpieces that the neo-classical poets found their inspiration as well as their operative models.

Lebanon was evidently the first country in which the old corpus was emulated. The new wave of poets came mainly from amongst the court poets whom rulers, princes and church prelates employed in their service. In the early decades of the nineteenth century, the court of Bashīr al-Shihābī was the scene of much poetic activity. In that court, poets of some note, such as Nīqūlā al-Turk (1763–1828) and Buṭrus Karāmah (1774–1851), continued to write in accordance with the late medieval style, and a great many of their poems consisted of elaborations of older poems (*tashṭīr* and *takhmīs*). But it was in the selfsame court that one of the precursors of neo-classicism rose to prominence. Nāṣīf al-Yāzijī (1800–1871) was a scholar and poet, steeped in classical Arabic lore. After leaving the court he participated in the new translation of the Bible into Arabic. His many books on grammar and rhetoric attest to his great erudition in the traditional branches of knowledge. His interest in Abbasid poetry is reflected in his edition of the *dīwān* of al-Mutanabbī. His own poetry, though not demonstrably free of artifice and trivial concerns, rises high above that of his immediate predecessors in the richness and lucidity of its language. At times, his panegyrics addressed to Prince Bashīr are truly reminiscent of those of al-Mutanabbī and al-Sharīf al-Raḍiyy, and the last poem he wrote, lamenting the death of his son Ḥabīb, is in its sincerity and simplicity far superior to the elegies of the late medieval versifiers.

In emulating the style of the great Abbasid poets, al-Yāzijī showed the way out of the stagnation and immobility in which Arabic poetry had languished for centuries. Many of his followers, including his sons Khalīl and Ibrāhīm, were later to emerge as notable participants in the development of neo-classical poetry. His daughter, Wardah al-Yāzijī (1838–1924), along with the Egyptian poetess ʿĀʾishah al-Taymūriyyah (1840–1902), was among the first Arab women in modern times to write and publish poetry.[5]

Many of the Lebanese writers and poets emigrated to Egypt in the second half of the nineteenth century, and left their mark on the development of modern Arabic literature and journalism in that country rather than in the country of their origin. Others emigrated to far-off places, including the New World, where they maintained their loyalty to Arabic language and literature for a long period. It was from amongst these emigrants that the first anti-classical revolution emanated in the early decades of our century under the leadership of Gibrān Khalīl Gibrān (Jibrān).

Closely related to the Lebanese centre (Beirut and its environs) were the other centres of traditional learning in greater Syria, including Damascus and Aleppo. In some of these centres poetry was slowly breaking loose from its medieval fetters. Although no major neo-classical poet arose in these centres in the nineteenth century, we do find in Aleppo a number of groupings or families of writers who made their contribution to modern Arabic literature. One such family is that of al-Marrāsh. Two brothers, ʿAbd Allāh and Faransīs, as well as their sister Mariyāna, were among the earliest Arabs of those regions to evince a modernizing spirit. Faransīs Marrāsh (1836–1873) studied in Aleppo and in Paris. His poetry book, *Mirʾāt al-Ḥasnāʾ* ('The beautiful maiden's mirror', 1872), is a curious mixture of classicism of language and modernity of outlook. In his introduction to this book, he rejects the traditional poetic *aghrāḍ*, notably the panegyrics and the lampoons. Indeed, his poetry is free of the conventional amatory preludes and word jugglery. His sister Mariyāna al-Marrāsh (1848–1919) was equally at home with the poetry of Ibn al-Fāriḍ, the medieval Sufi poet, and with Lamartine; but her own poetry, published in her collection *Bint Fikr* ('Daughter of thought', 1893), was of a distinctly traditional bent.

The hotbed of neo-classical poetry, however, was Egypt. As in Lebanon and Syria, the mid-nineteenth century witnessed a flurry of poetic and other literary activity in that country. But the leading poets of that period (Ismāʿīl al-Khashshāb and ʿAlī Abū' l-Naṣr, among others) were not far removed from the practices of their predecessors, and their poetry, though plentiful, had little in it that was original.

[5] Wardah al-Yāzijī, *Ḥadīqat al-ward*, Beirut, n.d. [1867]; ʿĀʾishah al-Taymūriyyah, *Ḥilyat al-ṭirāz*, Cairo, n.d. [1885].

It was in the person of Maḥmūd Sāmī al-Bārūdī (1839–1904) that modern Arabic literature found its first great poet. He was born into a Circassian family of generals and courtiers, and was educated by private tutors in his family's mansion in Cairo, as well as in the military academy. He was thus saved from the old curriculum that was pursued in al-Azhar and similar religious institutions, where most of al-Bārūdī's contemporaries were trained. His fondness for the poetry of the mediaeval Golden Age was so great that he took pains to put together a colossal anthology of that poetry which after his death was published in four volumes as *Mukhtārāt al-Bārūdī* (1909). His selections reveal his enchantment with the beauty of these poems, a predilection that distinguished him from other anthologists of his age (including al-Yāzijī) whose interest in classical poetry was by and large scholastic and philological.

Al-Bārūdī's poetic talent manifested itself early in his youth and accompanied him throughout his eventful life. He was a warrior, participating in the wars of the Crimea and Crete under the Ottoman banner; a courtier and ambassador; and a statesman who at different times assumed the ministries of education and of war and, for a short while, the prime-ministership of his country. His involvement in the ʿUrābī revolt brought his towering career to an abrupt end, and his punishment was a seventeen-year exile on the island of Ceylon. He died in Cairo four years after his return from banishment.

The poetry of al-Bārūdī is traditional in language and highly conventional in structure and themes, but his models were the Abbasid rather than the late-medieval poets. Furthermore, his own personality and life-experience were capable of defying the old conventions and coming to the surface in all their clarity. His *dīwān*, also published posthumously, contains some of the first manifestations of the grand style that was to become the hallmark of the neo-classical school in its heyday. His poems are not marred by an excessive recourse to medieval tropes and verbal affectations. Several of them also exhibit new thematic bearings, expressing the poet's pride in his country (he was probably the first poet to write extensively about the Pharaonic monuments and their historical significance) and, later on, his predicament in prison and in exile. Some of his more audacious political poems were apparently suppressed by the editors of his *dīwān*, surfacing fifty years after his death.[6]

Al-Bārūdī's exceptional poetic talent made him the pillar of neo-classical poetry in the last century. Yet al-Bārūdī is as good a proof as any that individual talent in isolation cannot flourish or generate a new literary

[6] See ʿAlī Muḥammad al-Ḥadīdī, *Maḥmūd Sāmī al-Bārūdī shāʿir al-Nahḍah*, second ed., Cairo, 1969; Badawi, ʿAl-Bārūdī'.

movement. Only in a period in which the whole literary system is undergoing a major upheaval is such a talent liable to come to fruition and exert a significant impact on the literary sensitivity of the age. Al-Bārūdī emerged upon the literary scene at a time when classical literary works were being edited and published through the burgeoning printing industry. New institutions of learning were being set up, and a fairly new literary curriculum, somewhat more attentive to the 'literariness' of the classical texts, was being introduced. Finally, a new type of literary scholarship was taking its first hesitant steps. Most of the new writers on literary matters were Lebanese *literati* who had settled in Egypt, but some Egyptian Muslims were also in evidence. Shaykh Ḥusayn al-Marṣafī was by far the most proficient literary scholar of the day. In his lectures delivered at *Dār al-ᶜUlūm* (later published under the title *al-Wasīlah al-adabiyyah* ['The literary organon'], 1874), al-Marṣafī devoted many pages to the poetry of al-Bārūdī.[7] Quoting some of al-Bārūdī's poems, he compared them, sometimes favourably, with the mediaeval poems upon which they were modelled. He also quoted with lavish praise poems in which al-Bārūdī described his experience on the battlefield, making much of the fact that they emanated from first-hand encounters with war rather than from a prior literary model.

Admittedly, al-Marṣafī in his lectures did not advocate a new poetic concept, but his clear partiality for the classical masterpieces was instrumental in showing the way to 'the roots' and encouraging the fledgling poets of his time to follow the example of the grand old poets. His tribute to the poetry of al-Bārūdī was an added incentive to the young poet to pursue his own bent. In comparing al-Bārūdī to the great poets of the Golden Age (Abū Nuwās, Abū Firās, al-Sharīf al-Raḍiyy), al-Marṣafī, in effect, canonized him, thus causing his poetic lead to serve as an inspiration to a new generation of poets.

In addition to Egypt, Lebanon and Syria, Iraq is also a region that deserves mention in this cursory survey of the early stages of neo-classicism. This is so mainly because that country was to become a very important centre in the subsequent history of Arabic poetry. In the nineteenth century, however, very few innovative poets were active in the major seats of traditional learning in Mesopotamia: Baghdad, Najaf and Mosul. Families of poets composing in the stilted style of the 'period of decline' predominated in these cities. Some of these poets wrote copiously on didactic, religious and casual topics. The city of Najaf, the stronghold of Shīᶜī learning in Iraq, was especially well known for the versificatory aptitude of its learned men, young and old. But in the nineteenth century

[7] Ḥusayn al-Marṣafī, *Al-Wasīlah al-adabiyyah*, II, Cairo, 1292 A.H., pp. 474–502.

there was little to stimulate a cultural resurgence that would effect a rejuvenation of literature. The poetry of ʿAbd al-Ghaffār al-Akhras (1805–1873), Ḥaydar al-Ḥillī (1831–1887) and Muḥammad Saʿīd al-Ḥabbūbī (1849–1916) was therefore only vaguely suggestive of the surge of poetic creativity that was to sweep the country in coming decades.

The heyday of neo-classicism

As we shall see in our discussion of themes and types, it was only when the classical *aghrāḍ* were transformed and augmented that neo-classical poetry reached its full maturity, which enabled it to retain its central position in the literary system for many years. These developments happened principally in the post-Bārūdī period, their main scenes of action being Egypt and Iraq. There is little doubt, however, that the outstanding figure in this period was an Egyptian poet, Aḥmad Shawqī (1868–1932).

Shawqī was born into a family of courtiers, and grew up in the vicinity of the Khedive's palace. In his early years Egypt was undergoing one of its most dynamic periods under the Khedive Ismāʿīl, and the modern school system was becoming increasingly predominant. Shawqī was educated in one of Cairo's newly established schools, and upon graduating from the School of Law, he was sent by the court to study in France. Soon after his return to Egypt he became the Khedive's court poet (*shāʿir al-amīr*). As such he was required to produce a number of panegyrics addressed to the ruler every year (for example on the occasions of Islamic feasts and official ceremonies). In 1915, however, he was forced to leave his country and spend four years as a political exile in Spain. The last thirteen years of his life in Cairo were among his most fecund. During this period he was a 'free poet', unattached to the court, attaining near-unanimous acclaim as 'the prince of poets' (*amīr al-shuʿarāʾ*).

Shawqī's output was prodigious, and although a sizable portion was devoted to panegyrics and elegies, he was a versatile poet who contributed to the development of many old and new poetic types. His poetry demonstrates a stupendous command of language and a captivating sonority. In his poetic diction and techniques he depended heavily on the Abbasid masters, but he was also capable of deviating from classical conventions and exploring new poetic modes and genres.

Although Shawqī was recognized in his lifetime as the greatest poet of his day, he was not immune to harsh criticism. Early in his poetic career, he was censured by Muḥammad al-Muwayliḥī for transgressing the classical poetic norms. Many years later, when he had become an imposing literary figure, he was harshly attacked by several modern-minded critics, notably

ʿAbbās Maḥmūd al-ʿAqqād and, to a lesser degree, Ṭāhā Ḥusayn. The young critics accused his poetry, among other things, of imitativeness and lack of coherence. These attacks, far from shattering the poet, seem to have emboldened him and, at the same time, led him to seek ways and means to improve and diversify his poetic output. Indeed, it was through his interaction with the changing modes of literary expression that he was able to establish the dominant paradigm of neo-classical poetry.

Muḥammad Ḥāfiẓ Ibrāhīm (1871–1932), the second pillar of neo-classical poetry in Egypt in this century, was an avowed follower of al-Bārūdī and al-Marṣafī. Although he was not a court poet, he was nevertheless as avid a panegyrist as Shawqī. However, his poetry often reflected the political and social aspirations of his people, a quality that earned him such titles as 'the poet of the Nile' and 'the poet of the people'.

Ḥāfiẓ Ibrāhīm was less of an innovator than Shawqī, and his poetry lacked the sense of composition and sonority that characterize the latter's verses. The literary rivalry between these two, sometimes covert, sometimes overt, was in itself a factor that contributed not only to enhancing the fecundity of the poets themselves, but also to the emergence of a lively literary life in Egypt. The young Egyptians were then divided into two camps: the admirers of Shawqī and the admirers of Ḥāfiẓ Ibrāhīm. Aḥmad Amīn, in his introduction to the latter's *dīwān*, remarks, however, that 'those who favoured Ḥāfiẓ Ibrāhīm did so because his poetry nourished their hearts, their patriotism; while those who favoured Shawqī did so for his art and imagination'.[8]

Iraq produced its own variety of neo-classicism. At the turn of the century, it was shedding its immobility and joining the ranks of the *Nahḍah*. It was soon to claim a leading position in modern Arabic poetry, a claim based on the Abbasid precedent. In the Shīʿī centres of Najaf, Kaẓimayn and Ḥillah, a great many new poets were making their debuts. Many of these were inspired by the great Shīʿī poets of the Abbasid period, notably al-Sharīf al-Raḍiyy. Among the newcomers of this period we find such Shīʿī poets as ʿAbd al-Muḥsin al-Kāẓimī (1865–1935), who settled in Egypt, Muḥammad Riẓā al-Shabībī (1888–1965), and ʿAlī al-Sharqī (1892–1962). Their poetry moved progressively away from the realm of religion to embrace national and social causes. This trend culminated in the poetry of Muḥammad Mahdī al-Jawāhirī (b.1900), a Najaf-born poet of a distinct classical aptitude, who was in later years to become the grand bard of political and social revolution in his country.

It was in Baghdad, however, that the Iraqi neo-classical school

[8] *Dīwān Ḥāfiẓ Ibrāhīm*, I, p. ẓ. For full details of this and other references, see the Bibliographical Notes for this chapter.

developed its distinctive features. Maʿrūf al-Ruṣāfī (1875–1945) was a poet with a truly innovative penchant. Although his classical training is well reflected in most of his poetry he was not shackled by classical conventions. He experimented with a variety of poetic techniques, at times willingly giving up classical grandiloquence in favour of a simple, near-modern language. His *dīwān* includes very few panegyrics and conventional elegies. It is significant that, unlike many of his Egyptian or Lebanese contemporaries, al-Ruṣāfī did not master a European language, and his only glimpse of western literature was attained through Turkish translations. His interest in the welfare of his country and its people was matched only by his passion for modern concepts and inventions. The ideas of national independence, social justice, the liberation of Muslim women, democracy and progress run through his poetry in all its stages. It is possible to contend that his poetic gift was inferior to that of Shawqī, but he was more modern by far in his worldview and more open to new poetic trends. His most productive period spanned the first thirty years of this century, after which the flow of his creativity abated somewhat. In his last years he lived in seclusion, away from the literary limelight. His poetry as a whole presents a unique brand of neo-classicism marked by a great readiness to incorporate new ideas and techniques.

Al-Ruṣāfī's contemporary and countryman, Jamīl Ṣidqī al-Zahāwī (1863–1936), was also a prolific poet, fired by the ambitions and concerns of the modern world. His poetry was so replete with scientific and social ideas that his concern for the poeticality of his poems was often meagre. Many of these poems, both long and short, are tantamount to versified didactic or polemical tracts. Al-Zahāwī devoted several poems to such unusual topics as the theories of relativity and gravity. His expression of some atheistic (or pantheistic) notions stands in sharp contrast to the practices of many of his contemporaries, who wrote religious poetry, whether out of sincere devotion or in response to social pressure.

Late neo-classicism

It is essential to reiterate at this juncture that during the 1920s, the finest hour of Arab neo-classicism, anti-classical tendencies were already making inroads on the literary system. By the early 1930s, the Arab romantic school had established itself not only in *al-Mahjar* but also in the Egyptian centre. The emergent romantic model (in concept, language and prosodic preferences) came to occupy a central position in modern Arabic poetry. The deaths in 1932 of Shawqī and Ḥāfiẓ Ibrāhīm marked the end of the supremacy of their school. Egyptian poets who went on pursuing the neo-classical path were regarded by several critics as remnants of the past and, indeed, their poetry was at times epigonic. In Iraq, however, the neo-classical model reigned supreme until the late 1940s, when a sudden upsurge of post-romantic poetry burst into being. Al-Jawāhirī continued, however, to enjoy respect and popularity as the 'last neo-classicist'.

In Syria and Lebanon neo-classicism yielded many interesting late-comers, including the Lebanese Bishārah al-Khūrī (1890–1968) and the Syrians Muḥammad al-Bizm (1887–1955) and Shafīq Jabrī (1898–1980). A belated burst of neo-classicism took place, surprisingly enough, in the South American extension of the Syrian–Lebanese centre (mainly in Brazil). In the Maghrib, too, neo-classicism was on the rise in the 1930s and 1940s. The Moroccan ᶜAllāl al-Fāsī (b. 1910), the Algerian Muḥammad al-Khalīfah al-ᶜĪd (b. 1904) and the Tunisian Aḥmad Khayr al-Dīn (1906–1967), adopted the neo-classical model and employed it in the struggle for national independence. In recent years, however, a new breed of Maghribi poets has come to the fore, exhibiting not only non-classical predilections but, at times, true modernistic zeal.

Finally, in several states of the Arabian peninsula and the Gulf, neo-classical poets of note did not appear before the 1940s and 1950s. In these countries, neo-classicism seems to be still on the rise. This is the reverse of what we find in the older literary centres and, in fact, in the rest of the Arab world, where neo-classical poetry is now composed, by and large, by marginal poets.

3. THEMES AND TYPES

It would be extremely difficult to pinpoint one major thematic axis around which neo-classical poetry revolves. Like mediaeval Arabic poetry, it deals with a variety of traditional thematic types (*aghrāḍ*); in addition it was called upon to address a host of new situations and topics related to contemporary life.

One of the main characteristics of Arabic poetry, classical or neo-classical, is that it is outwardly oriented and highly declamatory in its cadence. As such, it is hardly attuned to intimate discourse, and the poet's personality tends to hide behind a thick veil of 'objectivity'. Nevertheless, several neo-classical poets (for example al-Bārūdī in Egypt and al-Jawāhirī in Iraq) were at times successful in injecting into their poetry a distinctly individual tone and in making it a vehicle for expressing their own experience.

As we shall presently see, the major thematic types of mediaeval Arabic poetry continued to function prominently in the works of the neo-classicists, and their *dīwāns* are often divided into *abwāb* (sections), each devoted to one of these thematic types. Yet in its entirety, neo-classical poetry was in no way divorced from the realities of its time and place. Poets in the last hundred years have been quick to respond to the dramatic events and developments taking place in the Arab world – so much so, in fact, that their poetry can be seen as a vivid mirror of these events. The old Arabic dictum to the effect that 'poetry is the annals of the Arabs' (*al-shiʿru dīwānu'l-ʿarab*) has never been so true in the history of Arabic literature as it was in the heyday of neo-classical poetry (in subsequent decades this function has largely been relegated to other literary genres, notably the novel). Poetry aptly recorded the major upheavals that beset the region in recent times: the dismemberment of the Ottoman Empire; the encroachment of western imperialism; the struggle for independence, unity and democracy. It potently reflected the tensions between traditional Islamic values and those promulgated through the impact of the west. It addressed such critical issues facing modern Arab society as the position of women and the 'ignominious triad' of ignorance, poverty and disease which was the lot of large sections of Arab societies. The contemporary realities were, therefore, forcefully mirrored by the neo-classicists, and the imprint of modern concepts and technologies was equally prominently, if somewhat naively, reflected in the *dīwāns* of Shawqī, al-Ruṣāfī, al-Zahāwī and several others.

These poets, however, were not merely objective witnesses of their times, and it would be grossly incorrect to treat their poetry as raw material for historians. To be sure, they saw themselves as active participants in the shaping of realities. The poets juxtaposed the dismal picture of the present with the glorious days of mediaeval Arab civilization, and viewed the subjugation of the Islamic world to the west as particularly offensive in relation to the supremacy of Islam in the past. The tradition of classical Arabic poetry to which they were totally devoted now made it possible for them to serve as eloquent spokesmen of their nations. Poetry, composed in the past predominantly in the service of rulers and patrons, was now increasingly addressed to 'the people', and the voice of the poet, now wrathful, now sagacious, played an important role in rousing the masses to action. This is particularly true in the case of the political struggles in Egypt, Iraq and Syria around the year 1920, during which poets of the neo-classical school spoke out at the tops of their voices.

This transformation, however, did not occur as the result of a radical departure from the traditional thematic types of Arabic poetry. Rather it was carried out within the framework of the old *aghrāḍ*, although these *aghrāḍ* underwent certain functional, if not formal, mutations. The following sketch of the changes that took place in some of the major thematic types is meant to illustrate these mutations but also to underline the persistence of basic traditional features in the work of the major neoclassicists. Further, we shall dwell upon certain thematic types that are not necessarily the descendants of classical models.

Traditional thematic types

a. Madīḥ (panegyric)

The *dīwāns* of Shawqī, Ḥafiẓ Ibrāhīm, Ṣabrī, al-Jārim, al-Kaẓimī and others are replete with panegyrics. Shawqī, for instance, was for a good part of his career a court poet. The four volumes of his collected poetry, *al-Shawqiyyāt*, contain as many as thirty courtly panegyrics, and in the two volumes of his 'additional' poetry, edited by Muḥammad Ṣabrī, there are a further thirty-seven such poems. Several other poems of praise were produced by the poet in honour of eminent people in Egypt and abroad. Ḥāfiẓ Ibrāhīm, who was not a court poet, shows a similar predilection for panegyrics.[9]

Although these poems are composed in accordance with the conventions and language of traditional *madīḥ*, certain new features creep in, as we shall see in our discussion of the structure of one of Shawqī's panegyrics. In time, the need to write panegyrics lessened. Shawqī himself was in the last two decades of his life addressing his poems to the 'general public' rather than to the Egyptian khedive or the Ottoman sultan. Certain traditional features of *madīḥ* poetry endured but were used to serve different functions, notably in poems written for important public occasions (*munāsabāt*). The structure of a typical *madīḥ* consists of an amorous prelude, followed by *waṣf* (for example journey to the *mamdūḥ* or natural scenes), and ending with praise and/or congratulations. Several poets in this century used this structure for composing poems meant to be recited at important political or cultural gatherings. In the early 1940s, for instance, an all-Arab medical convention took place in Lebanon. ʿAlī al-Jārim (1881–1949) was delegated by the Egyptian government to recite a long poem that he had composed specially for that occasion. This poem[10] consists of seventy-two lines (*abyāt*; sing. *bayt*), and is divided into several 'movements', very much in the tradition of *madīḥ*. Appropriately enough, it opens with an amorous prelude (thirteen lines), after which comes the reference to the journey (seven lines), this time a train ride (probably from Cairo to Alexandria en route to Beirut). The third and longest section (thirty-nine lines) praises Lebanon, the host

[9] A new edition of his *dīwān*, published in Cairo in 1956–7 (edited by Aḥmad Amīn and others), eliminates the panegyrics addressed to the Khedive (later King) and his family. Nevertheless, a great number of poems appear in this edition that were written in honour of dignitaries who did not belong to the royal family.

[10] ʿAlī al-Jārim, *Dīwān al-Jārim*, Cairo, 1968, pp. 481–7.

country: its natural beauty, its marvellous people, its glorious history. The fourth section (eighteen lines) lauds the medical profession, with special reference to Arab physicians, who are called upon to use good Arabic rather than a dialect or a foreign language in their professional dealings (al-Jārim was an eminent member of the Arabic Language Academy). This section obviously contains the gist of the whole *qaṣīdah*, but the poem does not end until the poet has devoted an additional section, consisting of five lines, to praising the president and prime minister of Lebanon, as well as the king of Egypt.

In spite of its final section, which can be described as *madīḥ* in the traditional sense, the main concern of the poet is with a public affair (the conference) and with expression of admiration for Lebanon. Other poets, especially in more recent years, drop the praise section altogether but adhere, in one way or another, to the classical structure of *madīḥ* in the poetry of *munāsabāt*. The old structure, together with the concomitant lofty language and long metres, seems best suited to these important occasions and is therefore appropriated to commemorate them.

b. Rithāʾ (elegy)

Elegies constitute a major genre in classical Arabic poetry, and they are equally prominent in the *dīwāns* of the neo-classicists. One of the volumes of Shawqī's collected poems, *al-Shawqiyyāt*, is devoted entirely to *rithāʾ*; in other words, one quarter of his 'authorized' poetry consists of elegies. This fact does not testify to an especially mournful or macabre disposition on the part of the poet. It is in keeping with the traditions and functions of classical Arabic poetry. The same applies to Ḥāfiẓ Ibrāhīm, in whose *dīwān* again as much as one quarter of the text consists of *rithāʾ* (the second half of the second volume in the 1956 edition of the poet's *dīwān*).

These elegies are not normally intimate in tone, and it is only on rare occasions that the poet laments the death of a dear friend or relative. Elegiac sections of a more personal nature are sometimes interpolated in poems which do not necessarily belong to the *rithāʾ* mode. An example of this usage is al-Bārūdī's lamentation of the death of dear people in the folds of his poem *ayna ayyāmu ladhdhatī wa-shabābī*,[11] which was written during the poet's long exile in Ceylon, and which structurally belongs to the *fakhr* and *zuhd* modes. The bulk of neo-classical *rithāʾ* poems were written upon the deaths of prominent figures (royalty, political leaders, eminent authors and journalists). Some fifty of Shawqī's elegies lament the death of such personalities, while only two or three concern members of his family.[12] In

11 *Dīwān al-Bārūdī*, I, pp. 104–7; this poem is discussed below.

12 See Antoine Boudot-Lamotte, *Aḥmad Šawqi: l'homme et l'oeuvre*, Damascus, 1977, pp. 158–62.

the *dīwān* of Ḥāfiẓ Ibrāhīm we find forty-five elegies, none of which concerns a family member or a friend who is not a public figure.

As a rule, the neo-classical elegies conform to the classical structure of *rithāʾ*. The first section of a typical elegy is an apostrophe to the deceased or, alternatively, meditations on life and death. The second and main part is an enumeration of the virtues of the deceased and a summary or his or her noble deeds. In time, however, a new thematic ingredient became increasingly prominent in neo-classical *rithāʾ*. This ingredient concerns the social and political causes which the deceased championed in his lifetime. Elegies written by Shawqī in the last two decades of his life were far more outspoken politically than his previous poetry. His *rithāʾ* of Musṭafā Kāmil, written in 1908 shortly after the death of the young Egyptian nationalist leader, was a typical classical elegy.[13] Sixteen years later, however, he wrote another poem in memory of Kāmil that was strikingly different in its thematic structure from the first. This poem (*ilāma'l-khulfu baynakumū ilāmā*), is in essence an appeal to the nation and its leaders to unite in their struggle against the British, and a diatribe against those politicians whose devotion to national causes falls far short of that of the late Muṣṭafā Kāmil. The following lines, in which the poet apostrophizes Kāmil, will illustrate Shawqī's new type of discourse:

shahīda l-ḥaqqi qum tarahu yatīman
bi-arḍin ḍuyyiʿat fīhā l-yatāmā
aqāma ʿalā l-shifāhī bihā gharīban
wa-marra ʿalā l-qulūbi famā aqāmā.[14]

(You, who died in the cause of justice, rise and see: it [justice] is orphaned in a land where orphans are deserted./In it [=this land] it [justice] rested on the lips [of leaders], out of place, and crossed their hearts but found no abode there.)

These lines, declamatory though they are, and burdened as they are with traditional embellishments (note, for instance, the rhetorical pattern called *rad al-ʿajuz ʿalā al-ṣadr* in the second *bayt*), nevertheless constitute an audacious departure from the modes of early neo-classical *rithāʾ*. It might be argued that what enabled Shawqī to adopt such a new mode of expression was the fact that in the 1920s he had ceased being a court poet. But this kind of reasoning is insufficient given that the same kind of innovation was at that time infiltrating the elegies of several other neo-classical poets. Elegies by such poets as al-Ruṣāfī and al-Jawāhirī are highly indicative of the change in the social function of *rithāʾ*. In the 1940s and 1950s the latter poet composed some of his most blatantly political poems within the framework of *rithāʾ*. One such poem is his "ʿAdnān al-Mālikī' (1956), in which he

[13] *Al-Shawqiyyāt*, III, pp. 157–160. [14] *Al-Shawqiyyāt*, I, p. 223.

elegized a Syrian national figure who was assassinated by his political rivals.[15] This politicizing trend is best exemplified in the poems in which he mourned his young brother Jaᶜfar, who was killed in 1948 by police bullets in the course of a political demonstration:

a-taᶜlamu am anta lā taᶜlamū
biʾanna jirāḥaʾl-ḍaḥāyā famū
famun laysa ka-ʾl-muddaᶜī qawlatan
wa-laysa ka-ʾākhara yastarḥimū
yaṣīḥu ᶜalāʾl-mudqiᶜīnaʾl-jiyāᶜi
arīqū dimāʾakumū tuṭᶜamū.[16]

(Do you know that the wounds of those victims are a mouth?/A mouth that is neither making undue claims, nor asking for mercy./It is bellowing out at the poverty-stricken, at the starving: If you let your blood flow [in struggle], you will have ample food to eat.)

c. Other aghrāḍ

Almost all the other traditional thematic types are also available in the *dīwāns* of the neo-classicists, although to a lesser degree. In most of these *aghrāḍ* it is possible to notice the same kind of gradual transformations in typology and function.

One such type is *hijāʾ* ('lampoons'), which gradually changes from a personally-oriented type to one with modern political substance. A case in point is Shawqī's scathing poem written upon the departure of Lord Cromer from Egypt in 1907,[17] likewise the many political satires scattered in the *diwans* of al-Ruṣāfī, ᶜAlī al-Ghāyātī and others.

The type known as *fakhr* ('self-glorification') is also in evidence in these *dīwāns*. Once again, however, the *fakhr* is gradually being transformed from private self-praise in matters of *ḥasab/nasab* ('noble ancestry') to a medium whereby political struggle is glorified. Many of al-Bārūdī's poems (or sections of poems) provide the most luminous examples in modern times of the traditional concept of *fakhr* although some of his later poems, written during his exile, exhibit rudiments of the 'modern' function. Al-Jawāhirī represents this latter function in its full amplitude. His poem 'To Dr Hāshim al-Witrī', written in 1949, includes a long section that stylistically falls within the mode of *fakhr*. It speaks of the poet's steadfastness in the face of oppression and temptations, but it constitutes in effect a condemnation of the rulers of his country as well as of their British 'overlords'. The predicament of the poet and his family is viewed in the context of the sufferings of the people of Iraq. However, the poet is

[15] *Dīwān al-Jawāhirī*, pp. 259–266. [16] *Dīwān al-Jawāhirī*, p. 139.
[17] Opening with *ayyāmukum am ᶜahdu Ismāᶜīlā* (*al-Shawqiyyāt*, I, pp. 173–6).

confident that his poetry will eventually prevail, incurring devastation and damnation on 'the tyrants'.[18]

Finally, the type known as *waṣf* (description), which was developed particularly in the Abbasid period, is also worth consideration in its neo-classical configuration. The typical form of this type is shorter than the *qaṣīdah*, and its main use in the classical period was in the description of natural scenes. Some modern critics have maintained that nature in classical Arabic poetry is 'static'.[19] Neo-classical poets often use the *waṣf* sub-genre in much the same manner as their mediaeval predecessors. In their *waṣf* pieces we find very little interaction between nature and the poet. It is therefore understandable that Muṭrān's poem 'al-Masāʾ' ('Evening'), written in 1902, is often treated by Arab critics as the harbinger of a new poetic mode precisely because it brings out such an interaction.[20]

Muṭrān's example, however, had little effect on the neo-classical poets, whose poetry, as a rule, retained a static quality in their descriptions of nature. Yet the *waṣf* type in their poetry was expanded beyond natural scenes to include the description of modern inventions. This new feature in neo-classical poetry deserves more than a passing reference if only by virtue of its sheer abundance. The treatment of new technologies and devices was felt by these poets to provide the 'modern' ingredient necessary to balance their dependence on medieval poetic modes, and thus to fulfil the implied formula of 'new wine in old vessels'. Some poets, like al-Zahāwī of Iraq, went to the extreme of packing whole *dīwāns* with 'scientific' poetry; but modern technologies also figure prominently in the works of the major neo-classicists, including Shawqī, Ḥāfiẓ Ibrāhīm and al-Ruṣāfī. Their 'technological' poems are often studded with modern terms (including borrowings from European languages) denoting modern devices and inventions: electricity, the zeppelin, the train, the streetcar, the aeroplane, the radio, the telegraph, the telescope, the telephone and so on. The last two devices even serve al-Ruṣāfī as a 'vehicle' for conveying a spiritual tenor in one of his poems where sleep is described as 'a telephone by which we hear the transcendental, and a telescope to [observe] the spiritual' (*tilifūnun bihī ilā 'l-ghaybi nusghī wa-tiliskụpunā ilā'l-arwāḥī*).[21] At times the neo-classical poet is tempted to compare these inventions favourably with the primitive means that characterized the life of the ancient Arabs, as in another of al-Ruṣāfī's poems:

[18] *Dīwān al-Jawāhirī*, p. 468.

[19] G. von Grunebaum, 'The response to nature in Arabic poetry', *Journal of Near Eastern Studies*, IV (1945), pp. 137–51.

[20] Adūnīs, *Al-Thābit wa'l mutaḥawwil*, p. 96; M. M. Badawi, *A critical introduction to modern Arabic poetry*, Cambridge, 1975, p. 73.

[21] *Dīwān al-Ruṣāfī*, p. 203.

taʿālayta yā ʿaṣra l-bukhāri mufaḍḍalan
ʿalā kulli ʿaṣrin qad qaḍā ahluhu naḥbā
fakam ẓaharat li'l-ʿilmi fīka maʿājiẓun
bihā ʾāmana'l-sayfu 'l-ladhī kadhdhaba'l-kutbā[22]

(Glory to you, the age of steam [-engine]. You are far superior to all the bygone ages whose people are dead and buried./Science has exhibited such miracles, that even the sword that [in the past] used to give the lie to the books, now would believe in them.)

These lines, naive though they are, represent a stance common to many of the neo-classicists. On the one hand, the poet is repudiating the past and glorifying the present (and the future). On the other, the poet's allusion to Abū Tammām's famous hemistich *al-sayfu aṣdaqu anbāʾan mina'l-kutubī* ('The sword is more truthful than the books [for example of astrology]') is a potent reminder that the poet is still working within the tradition of classical Arabic poetry, which provides him with his point of departure even in a technologically oriented poem. This standpoint is even more forcefully brought into relief in another poem by al-Ruṣāfī entitled 'Safar fī l-Tumbīl' ('A car ride'), in which he compares the modern vehicle in which he is riding with the lumbering camels of the ancient Arabian poets al-Nābighah, Labīd, Ṭarafah and others.[23] It is significant that in the *dīwāns* of al-Ruṣāfī and his contemporaries these and similar poems are grouped in the sections entitled *waṣf* or *waṣfiyyāt*, which also include poems describing natural phenomena.

d. *Muʿāraḍāt*

In the above discussion of the different 'inherited' types of poetry, special emphasis was laid on the new functions, thematic and/or generic, that they have acquired with time. However, the neo-classical poets were by no means consciously abandoning the ancient modes of poetic composition. Their adherence to the core structure and language of medieval Arabic poetry was an act of identification with, indeed devotion to, their classical predecessors. Nowhere is this devotion more evident than in those of their poems that deliberately and openly imitate ancient ones. This type is called *muʿāraḍah* (pl. *muʿāraḍāt*), a term used for a poem identical in its metre and rhyme (and often in its thematic substance) with a classical model.

To be sure, the impact of the mediaeval prototype on a modern *muʿāradah* is not confined to metre–rhyme–topic. The echoes of the prototype are evident in the overall language of the *muʿāradah*, and the medieval poet's set of collocations surface in the lines of his imitator. These echoes are

22 *Dīwān al-Ruṣāfī*, p. 217.
23 *Dīwān al-Ruṣāfī*, pp. 221–2.

particularly noticeable in the vicinity of the rhyme words; and since nearly all the poems in question are monorhyming, the cumulative effect of these echoes is overwhelming in the *muʿāraḍāt*. The modern poet, far from trying to obliterate the palimpsest, uses a variety of devices to acknowledge his borrowing. One such device is to mention the name of the mediaeval poet in one or more of the lines of the imitation.[24] Another method is to quote verbatim famous collocations, hemistiches or lines from the prototype, at times enclosing them in quotation marks.

The topics of these *muʿāraḍāt* vary. They include all the different *aghrāḍ* of classical poetry, ranging from religious poetry (for example Shawqī's famous 'Nahj al-Burdah', dealing with the mission of the Prophet Muhammad and based on a poem by the late mediaeval poet al-Būṣīrī), to amorous poetry. A very popular love poem from the late Middle Ages that served as a prototype for very many modern poets is one by the thirteenth-century poet al-Ḥuṣrī al-Qayrawānī, whose opening words are *yā laylu, 'l-ṣabbu matā ghaduhu* (which can be loosely translated as, 'O night, the suffering lover is anxiously awaiting the daybreak'). An anthology published in Baghdad in 1961 comprises no less than eighty-six *muʿāraḍāt* written (mostly by neo-classical poets) in imitation of al-Ḥuṣrī's prototype.[25] Aḥmad Shawqī figures prominently among the imitators of that poem, and his *muʿāraḍah*, opening with the words *muḍnāka jafāhu marqaduhū*, achieved great popularity in the Arab world thanks to the music and voice of the Egyptian singer Muḥammad ʿAbd al-Wahhāb. Another notable *muʿāraḍah* by Shawqī is his imitation of a poem by the Andalusian poet Ibn Zaydūn (rhyme *-īna*).[26] Shawqī wrote this poem during his involuntary exile in Spain at the time of the First World War. In it, he expresses his longing for Egypt, but the Andalusian setting of Ibn Zaydūn's poem is skilfully exploited by Shawqī to evoke the land of his exile.

The extent of *muʿāraḍāt*, acknowledged and unacknowledged, in the *dīwāns* of the neo-classical poets is truly astounding. A recent study identifies no less than fifty fully fledged *muʿāraḍāt* in the poetry of Shawqī.[27] Most of these are long poems, which add up to a substantial portion of his entire output. Other neo-classical poets do not lag far behind.

Some of these *muʿāraḍāt*, particularly in the *dīwāns* of lesser poets, are nothing but pale imitations of old masterpieces. However, in the hands of poets of great talent even a *muʿāraḍah* breathes the spirit of creativity, as in the poems composed by al-Bārūdī in imitation of such great Abbasid poets

[24] See, for instance, Shawqī's poem 'Nahj al-Burdah' (*al-Shawqiyyāt*, I, pp. 190 ff.), where in line 100 the author of the original 'al-Burdah', al-Buṣīrī, is specified; and two lines later there is an explicit reference to *muʿāraḍah*.

[25] Muḥammad ʿAlī Ḥasan (ed.), *Dīwān Yā laylu'l-ṣabbu*, Baghdad, 1961.

[26] *Al-Shawqiyyāt*, II, pp. 103–7.

[27] Ibrāhīm ʿAwaḍayn, *Al-Muʿāraḍah fī shiʿr Shawqī*, Cairo, 1982.

as al-Sharīf al-Raḍiyy, Abū Nuwās and Abū Firās al-Ḥamdānī. It was none other than the classically minded al-Marṣafī who in the early 1870s discussed some of these *muʿāraḍāt* by al-Bārūdī, finding them equal if not superior to their classical prototypes in matters of compositional coherence and originality of trope.[28]

By their very nature, however, the intentional *muʿāraḍāt* represent an activity that is hardly open to innovation; and in the poems written by the neo-classicists in this fashion, the traditional elements are preserved without significant functional transformations.

New departures

So far only those thematic types that have their roots in the classical heritage have been discussed. Other traditional *aghrāḍ* that persisted in the poetry of the neo-classicists include *ghazal* (love poems), *ḥikmah* (wise and philosophical reflections), and *zuhd* (poems of asceticism), as well as lesser types such as casual and humorous pieces and, at times, even chronograms.

But in the *dīwāns* of neo-classical poets we also find new thematic types that are not necessarily dependent on traditional models. Most notable in this context are the poems devoted in their entirety to social and political issues. Other new types include narrative and historical poems as well as patriotic anthems and poems designed for children.

a. Social poetry

The new ideas of solidarity with the poor and the oppressed, whether in their philanthropic or radical manifestations, were quick to generate a new thematic focus in the works of the neo-classicists. Ḥāfiẓ Ibrāhīm in Egypt and al-Ruṣāfī in Iraq were among the first to depict in their poetry the predicament of the wretched on earth, to identify with them and to demand that their societies rescue them from their misery. Al-Jawāhirī went one step further in preaching social change not through charitable measures but by means of a social revolution led by the oppressed masses. But the philanthropic type is by far the most dominant in the poetry of the neo-classicists.

The philanthropic ideal appears, for instance, in the series of poems written by al-Ruṣāfī on the fate of the poor widows and orphans who are often encountered in the streets of Baghdad. One of the most popular of these poems is 'The breast-feeding widow' ('Al-Armalah al murḍiʿah').[29] In this poem not only the theme is uncharacteristic of classical Arabic poetry,

[28] *Al-Wasīlah al-adabiyyah*, pp. 474 ff.; especially pp. 483, 489 and 492.
[29] *Dīwān al-Ruṣāfī*, pp. 217–19.

but some of the compositional principles as well. The poem has a narrative structure: the poet comes across a poverty-stricken widow seated on a pavement with her infant child, barefoot and in tatters. She is weeping and lamenting her dead husband who left her and her infant in destitution. The poet is deeply moved. He approaches the widow to express his sincere sympathy not only by word of mouth but also by a generous donation. The widow bursts into tears of gratitude, saying 'if your act of sympathy were to become widespread, no creature would stray in the wilderness of poverty'. Variations on the theme of this poem, with the same semi-narrative composition, occur repeatedly in the *dīwān* of al-Ruṣāfī,[30] as well as in the works of other poets who followed in his footsteps.

b. Political poems

In our discussion of such thematic types as the elegy, the lampoon and even the panegyric, we were able to discern a growing politicization of certain *aghrāḍ*. But the political themes are not only a subsidiary activity in the *dīwāns* of the neo-classicists. With the increasing participation of the 'man in the street' in political activities, and with the growth of national consciousness throughout the Arab world, the poets were called upon to address these issues. The Dinshaway affair in Egypt[31] (1906) caused great indignation against the British among the Egyptian masses, and every important poet in that country wrote one or more poems on the event. Ḥāfiẓ Ibrāhīm was among the most outspoken, but even Shawqī, the court poet, came out with his own, somewhat belated, poem. Another famous political poem was written by Shawqī in the wake of the French bombardment of Damascus in 1926. In this poem, entitled 'The calamity of Damascus' ('Nakbat Dimashq'),[32] a new style of political poetry is discernible. Words and phrases drawn from the modern political vocabulary, such as *al-shuʿūb* ('the peoples') or *al-ḥuriyyah al-ḥamrāʾ* ('red liberty') make an appearance in this and other poems of the 1920s.

Another poet who became a political herald of his nation is al-Jawāhirī, whose *dīwān* is packed with political poems written between the 1920s and 1970s. Like his social poetry, these poems are exceedingly inflammatory, fraught with revolutionary pathos. During the Second World War al-Jawāhirī became strongly sympathetic to communism, and his long, enthusiastic poems on the battles of Stalingrad and Sevastopol are two

30 For example *Dīwān al-Ruṣāfī*, pp. 52–6 ('Umm al-yatīm'); pp. 74–80 ('al-Yatīm fī 'l-ʿīd'); pp. 223–5 ('Min Waylāt al-ḥarb'); pp. 279–82 ('Umm al-ṭifl fī mashhad al-ḥarīq').

31 A fight broke out between three British officers who were shooting birds and the villagers of Dinshaway in Upper Egypt resulting in one officer's death. The government under Cromer immediately retaliated by publicly executing four villagers, flogging and imprisoning three and sentencing two to life imprisonment.

32 *Al-Shawqiyyāt*, II, pp. 73–6.

among many that reflect his new outlook. In 1948, during the anti-British *wathbah* (popular uprising), al-Jawāhirī assumed the role of revolutionary prophet, his poems becoming the gospel of the Baghdad masses.

The political poetry of Shawqī and al-Jawāhirī retained the elaborate classical style of their authors. Other poets, however, were less scrupulous about the elegance of political poetry. In seeking to address 'the masses', they gradually eliminated many of the verbal conventions that are the distinctive feature of classical poetry, while frequently giving structure and form less than their due. A poem entitled 'A demonstration' ('Muẓāharah')[33] by the Egyptian Muḥammad al-Asmar (1900–1956), written in the aftermath of a bloody political demonstration, illustrates this pedestrian approach. It consists of a concatenation of political clichés, mingled with hackneyed collocations culled from the mediaeval repertoire. 'It is a sin', the poet tells us, 'that we sleep while the blood of good, innocent people is flowing'. Further, we hear that 'no nation attains its freedom without struggle'. The poem contains hardly any reflection of the poet's special vision of the tragic event, nor does its use of metaphor convey a personal style.

This kind of prose-like political poetry is not confined to minor poets. It is widespread in the *dīwāns* of the major neo-classicists as well. The *dīwān* of al-Ruṣāfī, for instance, contains an abundance of such poems. In a poem entitled 'The East awakening' (Nahḍat al-Sharq')[34] we read such statements as:

> I discern in the East, after a long slumber, an ambitious awakening . . . In Egypt institutions of learning have been set up, based on analysis, research and critical enquiry. They employ the methods of experimentation to reach the core of useful knowledge . . . In India there is a movement of political liberation, a non-violent movement led by Gandhi . . . Ours is a time in which every nation is awakening politically, and at long last the Kurds are also in rebellion.

These lines are tantamount to an 'editorial in rhyme and metre'. Al-Ruṣāfī was not unaware of this prosaic quality, and in one of his poems he proudly admits that '[my] verses are so lucid that their audience mistakes them for prose'.[35]

The 'article in verse' is no less prominent in the *dīwāns* of another Iraqi poet, al-Ṣāfī al-Najafī, as well as in the poetry of politically inclined poets in Egypt (for example ʿAlī al-Ghāyātī), Syria (for example Khayr al-Dīn al-Ziraklī) and other Arab countries. These poems frequently employ a logical flow of ideas, but apart from rhyme and metre there is little in them that reads as poetry. However, the very emergence of this thematic type

[33] Muḥammad al-Asmar, *Dīwān al-Asmar*, Cairo, n.d., p. 97. [34] *Dīwān al-Ruṣāfī*, p. 271.
[35] *Dīwān al-Ruṣāfī*, p. 67.

demonstrates conclusively that the neo-classical poets were not circumscribed by the traditional *aghrāḍ*.

c. Narrative and historical poems

Medieval Arabic literature has little to offer in the way of narrative poetry, especially long epic pieces. Admittedly, there are long poems on a variety of religious and didactic topics, prominent among which is the *Alfiyyah* of Ibn Mālik (thirteenth century), a systematic excursus on Arabic grammar. However, these poems were normally written in the form of *urjūzah* (*rajaz* metre, with rhyming couplets rather than monorhyme). In the Arabic literary system the *urjūzah* type was relegated to the periphery, and its form was regarded as essentially sub-canonical, that is, unsuitable for high-brow poetry.

In contradistinction, the neo-classical poets developed a tradition of writing long poems that were not necessarily didactic. At times they were ambitious enough to attempt epic poetry. In order to underline the 'canonicity' of these poems, their authors often resorted to the monorhyming scheme characteristic of the *qaṣīdah*, and the metres they chose were the long, respectable ones rather than the *rajaz*.

One of the earliest of these attempts was Shawqī's poems entitled 'The major events in the Nile valley' ('Kibār al-ḥawādith fī wādī al-Nīl'),[36] recited at the International Congress of Orientalists that convened in Geneva in 1884. This is a long monorhyming poem (320 lines in *khafīf* metre, rhyme *-āʾū*), narrating the eventful history of Egypt from the early Pharaonic days up to the present. The poet's admiration for the achievements of Pharaonic civilization is matched in the poem only by his pride in the great light that Islam brought to his country. Egypt is also seen as the cradle of monotheism, the land that embraced the young Moses and the infant Jesus. But Egypt also witnessed a succession of calamities caused mainly by foreign invaders (such as the Hyksos, the Persians and the Romans). Some critics maintain that Shawqī's poem was modelled on Victor Hugo's *Légende des siècles*.[37] This might be true as regards the actual idea of writing a 'survey' of national history, but the spirit and language of Shawqī's poem do not betray the impact of a non-Arabic model. In many senses, this poem is one of the outstanding products of early neo-classicism, combining the grandeur of the old style with the spirit of patriotism and *Nahḍah*.

Shawqī wrote several long poems on the history of Islam and its Prophet (for example, 'Al-Hamziyyah al-Nabawiyyah' and 'Nahj al-burdah'); on ʿAbd al-Raḥmān I, the first Umayyad monarch of Muslim Spain ('Ṣaqr

[36] *Al-Shawqiyyāt*, I, pp. 17–33.

[37] Shawqī Ḍayf, *Shawqī shāʿir al-ʿaṣr al-ḥadīth*, Cairo, 1953, p. 97.

Quraysh'); on the Ottoman–Greek war ('Ṣadā al-ḥarb') and other subjects. The last two poems present some interesting innovations in their form and conception. 'Ṣaqr Quraysh' is written in the strophic form of *muwashshaḥ*, a form that is linked to the cultural history of Muslim Spain and thus highly appropriate in a poem relating to the history of that country. Indeed, the poem's subtitle is 'An Andalusian *muwashshaḥ*'.[38] The other poem, 'Ṣadā al-ḥarb'[39] (consisting of 264 monorhyming lines in *al-ṭawīl* metre, rhyme *-a/i/ ubū*), is divided into sections, each of which has its own subtitle (for example 'The feats of the soldiers at the border', 'The invincibility of the Ottoman shores', 'Zaynab the volunteer in action', 'The dreams of the Greeks'). These new features indicate a clear awareness on the poet's part that a new sub-genre, formally distinguished from the *qaṣīdah* or the *waṣf* poem (*qiṭʿah*), was being attempted.

Shawqī was apparently not the first neo-classical poet to experiment with long poems on historical or religious topics. In the 1870s a Syrian poet, Jibrāʾīl al-Dallāl (1836–1892), produced a long poem, also with subtitles, entitled 'al-ʿArsh wa'l-haykal' ('The throne and the temple'), which in its subject matter and underlying philosophy clearly reflects the anti-clerical writings of Voltaire.[40] It was Shawqī's experiments, however, notably his Islamic poems, which engendered a trend among his contemporaries and successors to produce long narrative poems on the history of Islam. Among these, mention should be made of *Majd al-Islām* ('The glory of Islam', subtitled 'The Islamic Iliad') by the Egyptian poet Aḥmad Muḥarram (1877–1945),[41] which consists of some 6,000 lines; and *ʿĪd al-Ghadīr* (subtitled 'The first Arabic epos') by the Lebanese poet Būlus Salāmah (1902–1979), consisting of 5,000 lines. As late as the 1970s we find an Egyptian poet, Kāmil Amīn, undertaking a series of colossal Islamic 'epics' of 10,000 or more lines each, composed in a somewhat diluted neo-classical style (*Malḥamat ʿAyn Jālūt*, 1975; *Al-Malḥamah al-Muḥammadiyyah*, 1979).

d. 'Marginal' types

Whereas the innovations discussed above were treated by their authors as belonging to the canon of poetry, a few other new types were also used by the neo-classicists that were viewed as less than canonical and were often excluded from the representative *dīwāns* of these poets. One such type that appealed to poets around the turn of the century is versified fables. The translation by Muḥammad ʿUthmān Jalāl of La Fontaine's fables in 1870 in

[38] *Al-Shawqiyyāt*, II, pp. 170 ff. [39] *Al-Shawqiyyāt*, I, pp. 42–58.

[40] Excerpts from this poem can be found in Sāmī al-Kayyālī, *Al-Adab al-ʿArabī al-muʿāṣir fī Sūriyā*, second edn, Cairo, 1968, pp. 65–71.

[41] On Muḥarram's 'Iliad' see M. M. Badawi, *Modern Arabic literature and the west*, London, 1985, p. 49.

fuṣḥā (literary Arabic), and *ᶜāmmiyyah* (colloquial Arabic) was probably among the factors that prompted other poets to produce their own fables composed in exemplary *fuṣḥā*. Shawqī was particularly fond of this genre, and a posthumous volume of his *al-Shawqiyyāt* (vol. 4) includes some sixty short fables in verse. Thirty-six of these fables have the 'non-canonical' *rajaz* metre, and in most of them rhyming couplets rather than monorhymes are employed.

Another type is *anāshīd* (sing. *nashīd*), that is, short march-like poems composed to be sung or recited on patriotic or communal occasions. This type has its beginnings in the works of such early modern authors as Rifāᶜah Rāfiᶜ al-Ṭahṭāwī, who early in the nineteenth century wrote anthems and school-poems in emulation of similar poems in French (al-Ṭahṭāwī also translated the Marseillaise into Arabic verse[42]). Most of the *anāshīd* of the neo-classicists use a 'European' strophic scheme, which historically preceded the adoption of strophic poetry by romantic Arab poets in the inter-war period.

A third kind of 'marginal' neo-classical poetry consists of poems written for children. These poems were produced at the request of educational institutions and were usually published in anthologies meant for very young students. Although many of these verses became extremely popular throughout the Arab world, their authors rarely included them in their *dīwāns*.

Despite their 'lowly' status, these types of poetry are of special interest in the history of neo-classical poetry. This is so because their authors generally avoided the use of recondite words and classical clichés. They strove to concoct a poetic language accessible to the young and the uninitiated and, at times, to reproduce the rhythms and spirit of the spoken language within the bounds of *fuṣḥā*. Thus, these 'marginal' verses represent a far-reaching departure from the tenets of classicism. A close study of their language may show that they were instrumental in the rise, several decades later, of a new, non-classical poetic language in modern Arabic literature.

e. Verse drama

Reference should also be made to the fact that some neo-classical poets engaged in writing verse drama, a genre totally unknown to their predecessors. This was due, at least in part, to the growing popularity, in the last decades of the nineteenth century, of theatrical troupes. Many of these troupes were staging semi-operatic plays, whose texts combined prose and poetry. Although Egypt was teeming with such dramatic activity

[42] This translation can be found in *al-Hilāl*, January 1918, p. 325.

at the turn of the century, the beginnings of Arabic drama, including versified plays, are to be found in Lebanon. As early as 1876 we find a play by Khalīl al-Yāzijī entitled *al-Murūʾah waʾl-wafāʾ* ('Valour and fidelity')[43] written entirely in verse. This play, which deals with the manners and customs of pre-Islamic Arabs, is noteworthy in that its verses and even its hemistiches are often divided between two or more speakers. This practice facilitated the use of classical Arabic verse on stage and was to become the hallmark of the verse dramas of Shawqī and his followers. Lebanese authors who settled in Egypt, notably Najīb al-Ḥaddād, used a similar technique in their translations or adaptations of western poetic dramas into Arabic: for example, Haddad's version of Shakespeare's *Romeo and Juliet*, which in its Arabic rendering bears the title 'Shuhadāʾ al-gharām' ('The martyrs of love').

But the culmination of the neo-classical verse drama is the five versified plays written by Shawqī in the last two decades of his life. In fact, he had made an attempt to write a verse play as early as 1893, when he published the first version of his *ʿAlī Bek al-Kabīr*; however, he completely revised this play, republishing it in 1932 under the same title.

A full discussion of verse drama does not fall within the purview of this chapter. The above reference is designed to serve as another reminder of the diversity of the poetic discourse of the neo-classicists. The work of these poets was by no means restricted to imitative *qaṣīdas* and traditional *aghrāḍ*. Their staunch adherence to medieval models mellowed with time, and several innovations, some far-reaching, percolated into their literary universe.

4. STRUCTURE

Contrary to a widely held view, the neo-classical *qaṣīdah* is not devoid of structure. This untenable impression was probably created through the repeated contention of literary critics that the poems of the neo-classicists suffered from incoherence and disjointedness (*tahāfut, tafakkuk*).[44] The harshest of these diatribes was promulgated in 1921 by ʿAbbās Maḥmūd al-ʿAqqād in his analysis of Shawqī's poem in memory of Musṭafā Kāmil. Not only did al-ʿAqqād accuse the poet of triviality and lack of a coherent idea, but he also claimed that the order of the poem's lines was haphazard, that they could easily be reshuffled without changing the poem's general

43 Second edition, Cairo, 1902. On this play see Muḥammad Yūsuf Najm, *Al-Masraḥiyyah fī 'l-adab al Arabī al-ḥadīth*, Beirut, 1956, pp. 294–8.

44 See: S. Moreh, 'The neoclassical *qaṣīda*: modern poets and critics', in G. von Grunebaum, (ed.), *Arabic poetry: theory and development*, Wiesbaden, 1973, pp. 155–79.

'meaning'. Indeed he took trouble to re-arrange the lines according to his own scheme to prove that the poem lacked unity and structure.[45]

This kind of contention is given some credibility by the repeated affirmation of medieval Arab critics that the single line (*bayt*) should be self-contained, and that enjambment should be avoided. As late as the 1870s, we find Ḥusayn al-Marṣafī defining the poem as an 'eloquent text, based on tropes and descriptions [*awṣāf*], divided into separate units sharing a single rhyme and a single metre, each of these units being thematically independent from what precedes and follows it, adhering to the poetic norms of the Arabs'.[46]

This and other similar pronouncements, whether they are intended to be descriptive or prescriptive, are not substantiated by modern research. It has been amply demonstrated by recent studies that the *bayt* in classical Arabic poetry is 'far from being the isolated, self-contained unit it is usually said to be. Despite the rule prohibiting enjambment, verses are often connected by their syntax.'[47]

But not only groups of lines frequently share a common theme in classical (and neo-classical) poetry. The poem itself usually has an overall structure; although this is, to be sure, a highly conventional structure, determined to a great extent by the thematic type of the poem rather than by the free interplay of the elements of the individual poem.

What characterizes the neo-classical poem, however, is that even when the poet is elaborating on a single topic, he does not treat the whole text of his poem as a single unit of signification. To him it is a concatenation of fairly independent subunits, linked by an underlying conventional scheme. There is no need for the poet to provide an overt linkage between these subunits because he can count on the 'literary competence' of his readers (or listeners), who are at home with the inventory of conventional structures. In fact, far from trying to stitch these subunits together by means of local 'shifters', the poet sometimes underlines their separateness by inserting a verse of *ḥikmah* (gnome, that is, a line in which a general observation or a piece of advice is encapsulated) at the end of a subunit. The practice of linking the main part of the panegyric with the preceding subsection by means of the contrivance known as *takhalluṣ* has itself become so conventionalized that when it is used by a poet like Shawqī (as we shall see in the following pages), it is not meant to enhance the unity of the poem. Rather, it is used as yet another trope, designed to exhibit the poet's dexterity and his adherence to a hallowed convention.

45 ʿAbbās Maḥmūd al-ʿAqqād and Ibrāhīm ʿAbd al-Qādir al-Māzinī, *Al-Dīwān: kitāb fī'l-naqd wa'l-adab*, Cairo, 1921, pp. 47–54. 46 *Al-Wasīlah al-adabiyyah*, II, p. 468.

47 Raymond P. Scheindlin, *Form and structure in the poetry of al-Muʿtamid ibn ʿAbbad*, Leiden, 1974, p. 108.

At times, however, the poet may follow a single logical line throughout his poem. This is true particularly with regard to the poetic type referred to earlier as 'article in verse'. The unity in this type of poetry is very similar to what we find in discursive writing, and the dynamic of 'poetic unity' is therefore only marginally, if at all, activated.

The language of neo-classical poetry is very infrequently employed as an element contributing to structural unity. This is so because the neo-classical poem as a whole is not usually an intra-textual web, based on the interaction of the small units of the poem itself.[48] A typical neo-classical poem is, rather, a succession of inter-textual references, constantly and deliberately alluding to the language of specific medieval texts (poetic, religious, historical). Admittedly, the poet's preferences, reflected in his selection from the large repository of these texts, are instrumental in creating an 'individual style', distinguishable from the style of other poets. But the particular stylistic predilections of the poet are not in themselves a determinant factor in what is known as 'organic unity'.

In the following, the thematic structure of five poems will be briefly discussed by way of illustrating their 'unity through diversity'. The first of these poems conforms to one of the traditional thematic types (*madīḥ*); three of the four other poems are not easily definable in terms of the classical *aghrāḍ*, although poems II, III and IV exhibit the traditional sense of structure. Finally a poem belonging to the 'article in verse' type will also be discussed.

I. Praise of the Khedive by Ahmad Shawqī[49]

This untitled poem was originally published in the Cairene journal *al-Wāʿiẓ* on 4 March 1904 on the religious occasion of *al-ʿĪd al-Kabīr* ('The Major Festival', that is, the sacrificial feast on the tenth of the Muslim month Dhu'l-Ḥijjah). It consists of thirty-six lines, fittingly composed in the stately metre *al-ṭawīl*. Its rhyme is *-īrū*.

As is customary in many medieval panegyrics, this poem consists of two distinct parts: the traditional *nasīb* ('amatory prelude'), and the actual praise of the khedive. These parts are appropriately linked by means of *takhalluṣ*, which occurs in line twenty-five. A closer look at the thematic structure of the poem, however, reveals a larger number of 'movements'. Furthermore, its overall thematics, though in keeping with medieval practices, have an added element which is markedly contemporary. The following sections and subsections can be discerned:

[48] Cf. M. M. Badawi's analysis of Shawqī's poem 'al-Hilāl' (*Journal of Arabic Literature*, II [1971], pp. 127–35), in which he points out intra-textual interactions.

[49] *Al-Shawqiyyāt al-majhūlah*, II, pp. 5–6.

A. The prelude (lines 1–24). This section consists of three subsections:

A-a. The *Nasīb* (lines 1–11). Although the poem was written for a festive occasion, it opens with a sorrowful complaint:

shujūnī wa-in janna al-ẓalāmu kathīrū
yu'allibuhā ʿādī l-hawā wa-yuthīrū

(When darkness descends, my sorrows are great,
agitated by the ferocity of love.)

The poet goes on to describe the pangs of love which render his night sleepless, wine being unable to assuage his sorrows.

A-b. The apostrophe to the dove (lines 12–19). Like the poet, the dove on the tree branch is tormented by an unfulfilled love and crushed by separation (*bayn*) from the beloved. The poet confesses to the bird that the virtue of forbearance has deserted him.

A-c. *Fakhr* (lines 20–4). The poet now asserts that in spite of this weakness on his part, he is of a lofty nature: strong in the face of calamity and kind to others. The linkage between A-b and A-c is implicitly provided by the word *ṣabr* ('forbearance', 'steadfastness'), appearing in line 19.

B. The praise (lines 25–36). Line 25 is in the nature of a 'shifter'. It explains that it is only through praising the khedive, the illustrious scion of Muhammad Ali, that the poet recovers his noble self.

B-a. (lines 25–31). The khedive is praised in the traditional manner: the sun is envious of his light; he is noble and pious; he has the ability to accomplish those things for which his subjects (*raʿāyā*) are aspiring (and which, the poet asserts, other peoples have already achieved) because he is both brave and wise.

B-b. (lines 32–6). A plea on behalf of the people: the khedive's grandfather, Muhammad Ali, has shown the East the path to progress, and it is therefore inconceivable that another nation (obviously Japan) is achieving glory while Egypt is not. Ambition and education are the tools to attaining progress and national revival.

The final subsection of the poem is somewhat at variance with its other parts. It expresses a demand that the khedive take concrete steps toward modernizing and strengthening Egypt. The impact of the Japanese performance at Port Arthur is evident (the poem was published only a few weeks after the event, and Shawqī was not alone, as we shall see, in calling for emulation of the Japanese example). Further, line 30, which foreshadows the final segment, hints at another demand on the khedive: that he allow a measure of parliamentary democracy, as in other progressive nations.

In other words, the thematic structure of this poem, though conforming to the basic conventions of *madīḥ*, is not compatible in all its parts with medieval panegyric. The modern theme crops up toward the end of the poem and lends it a dimension that is anything but medieval.

It is worth noting that a few weeks after the publication of this poem in *al-Wāʿiẓ*, Ḥāfiẓ Ibrāhīm (who was not a court poet) published in the same journal a panegyric to the khedive on the occasion of the Muslim new year, which is not only a *muʿāraḍah* of Shawqī's poem in matters of metre and rhyme, but also opens with *nasīb* and ends with a mention of Japan's feat.[50]

II. 'Tutankhamen' by Aḥmad Shawqī[51]

This is one of several poems of Shawqī which have the name Tutankhamen (*tūt ʿankh āmūn*) in their titles. However this poem, written around 1923, is not devoted in its entirety to that Pharaoh, for it ends with praise of the incumbent monarch of Egypt, King Fouad I.

The poem consists of ninety-four lines composed in *al-wāfir* metre, its rhyme being *ī/ūna*. It is divided into six sections, separated in the *dīwān* by asterisks. This division represents the actual thematic subunits of the poem, which indeed comprises six such units:

A. Rumination (lines 1–7). The poet addresses the sun ('the sister of Joshua'), the supreme witness to the history of mankind amid all its vicissitudes.

B. History (lines 8–33). Tutankhamen signifies the glory of ancient Egyptian civilization. This civilization is unfairly accused of being repressive, even though the history of western Christendom is also replete with violent excesses.

C. The discovery of the grave (lines 34–47). The poet addresses Lord Caernarvon, who is lauded for unearthing the grave of Tutankhamen and its treasures. If he has been maligned by some Egyptians, it is only because they are apprehensive lest their national monuments be plundered by foreigners.

D. The Valley of the Kings (lines 48–64). It was in this site that the grave of Tutankhamen was discovered. The discovery was so astounding that it reverberated in the corridors of the Geneva Conference, although the powers attending the conference did not treat Egypt's national aspirations favourably.

50 *Dīwān Ḥāfiẓ Ibrāhīm*, I, pp. 26–8. This poem, along with other panegyrics addressed to the line of Muhammad Ali, was expurgated from the seventh edition (Cairo, 1955) of the *Dīwān*. On the impact of the Port Arthur affair see also *Dīwān al-Ruṣāfī*, pp. 345–7.

51 *Al-Shawqiyyāt* I, pp. 266–74; originally published in *Majallat Sarkīs*, January 1923. For a discussion of this poem see Boudot-Lamotte, *Aḥmad Šawqi*, pp. 80–4.

E. Reflections on Tutankhamen (lines 65–80). These concern the ancient Egyptians' views of life, death and resurrection.

F. Praise to King Fouad (lines 81–94). Unlike the Pharaohs, Fouad's is a constitutional monarchy. The modern monarch is urged to guide the misguided and cure the ailments of his nation.

The poet thus moves back and forth between the distant past and the immediate present. Sections B, D and E are concerned in the main with Tutankhamen and the Pharaonic civilization; sections C and F deal with contemporary issues; while section A is in the nature of metaphysical reflection. Of these six sections, only two consecutive sections (E and F) are explicitly joined. This is achieved by means of the contrivance of *takhalluṣ* (lines 81–2) in which the poet declares:

zamānu 'l-fardi yā firʿawnu wallā
wa-dālat dawlatu 'l-mutajabbirīnā
wa-aṣbaḥati 'l-ruʿātu bikulli arḍin
ʿalā ḥukmi 'l-raʿiyyati nāzilīnā

(Pharaoh, the age of absolute rulers is a thing of the past, and fortune has turned against oppressors./In our time the shepherds everywhere abide by the opinion of their flock.)

This statement allows the poet to set about praising the benevolent king of 'our time'; his praise runs for the last twelve lines of the poem.[52] The words of this 'shifter', however, are somewhat out of step with the rest of the poem, since in section B the poet has to all intents and purposes cleared Pharaonic Egypt of undue tyranny. Sections D and E can be seen as dealing with related topics (the discovery of the remains of Tutankhamen/ his concepts of life and death), although the last four lines of section D tangentially address a current issue (the conference in Geneva), thus undermining the linkage between these two sections. The other sections are manifestly independent of each other; and it is significant that three sections – A, C and E – are rounded off with gnomic lines (lines 7, 47 and 70), a fact that emphasizes their discreteness rather than their interdependence.

Although the poem in its entirety can be regarded as a panegyric, it is not composed in accordance with the traditional conventions of *madīḥ*. The poet might still justify the poem's structure in traditional terminology, for example that the last segment is its *bayt al-qaṣīd* (the essence of the poem, appearing towards its end); however, the fact that he elected to give it the title 'Tutankhamen' rather than 'In praise of Fouad' is significant. The vision of ancient Egypt dominates the poem, and when the present scene is

52 These twelve final lines are omitted without due notice from the editions of *al-Shawqiyyāt* published in Egypt after the 1952 revolution. Thus, the two lines quoted above lose their connective function, becoming the concluding lines of the entire poem, which renders them preposterously improper.

alluded to, it is somehow linked to the past. In other words, the overall thematic tenor of the poem may be construed as 'the fate of Egypt, past and present, seen in the light of the recent archaeological finds'. This scheme allows the poet to ramble from past to present, archaeology to politics, pride to hope. The inclusion of the final section praising King Fouad can also be justified: he is the heir to the ancient Pharaohs, yet a more equitable monarch even so. As to the first section invoking the sun, this can be seen as an appropriate 'grand opening' to a poem about the fate of a nation.

III. *Ayna ayyāmu ladhdhatī by al-Bārūdī*[53]

This is a poem with a 'personal' rather than a 'public' theme. Like all al-Bārūdī's poems, it has no title, but the poet (or the editor of his *dīwān*) provides it with the following preface: 'Written in Ceylon, expressing the poet's yearning for Egypt and lamenting the death of his friends Shaykh Ḥusayn al-Marṣafī and ᶜAbd Allāh Fikrī'. Indeed these two topics play a major part in the poem, but we shall presently see that the poem encompasses other matters as well.

The poem is relatively short, consisting of thirty-four lines in *al-khafīf* metre, their rhyme being *-ābī*. It has at least three distinct subunits although in the printed *dīwān* there are no breaks between these sections:

A. Remembering bygone youth (lines 1–13). This section opens with the words 'Where are the happy days of my youth?', and goes on to reminisce about those memorable days in Cairo.

B. Old age and the death of dear ones (lines 14–26). This section commences with an apostrophe to two unspecified companions:

yā nadīmayya fī Sarandība kuffā
ᶜan malāmī wa-khalliyānī li-mā-bī

(My two companions in Ceylon, stop reproaching me, and leave me to myself.)

Although this line is reminiscent of the conventional appeal to two unspecified companions used by Arab poets since pre-Islamic times, the mention of the place of action, Ceylon, lends it a measure of spontaneity and credibility. The following eleven lines are devoted to two types of lamentation:

B-a. Lamenting old age (lines 15–20). In contrast to the vivacious youth portrayed in section A, this subsection describes the lamentable situation in which the poet finds himself in his exile. Old age is taking its toll on him. His body is enfeebled, his sight dimmed.

B-b. Death of the beloved ones (lines 20–6). News of the deaths of his

[53] *Dīwān al-Bārūdī*, I, pp. 104–7.

relatives and friends in Egypt reaches the poet in rapid succession: his parents, his wife and finally his two unforgettable friends, Ḥusayn and ʿAbd Allāh.

C. *Fakhr* (lines 27–34). The poet is much maligned, but he is composed. He has stopped mingling with people and heeding their envious words and deeds. He is fully aware of all that is happening around him although he feigns ignorance. Age is his guide to wisdom and steadfastness in facing calamity. This is a subdued *fakhr*, different from al-Bārūdī's youthful *fakhr* poems. Whereas in the earlier poems the praise was directed to the poet's ancestry or to his courage and noble deeds, the object of the *fakhr* in these lines is moral courage in times of distress. This tallies with the grim tone of the entire poem. But while the first two major sections blend, creating a logical as well as emotional continuum (how pleasant was youth in Egypt; how sad it is now, away from home, when old age is creeping, dear ones are dying!), the final section, with its *fakhr*-like style, is somewhat detrimental to the unity of the poem. Furthermore, at several points in the poem the poet stops the flow of his memories and lamentations to insert a gnome or a general reflection. Such gnomes occur in lines 4 ('A sensitive man may forget everything, save for the joyous days of his youth'), 12 ('Only a man of honour is mindful of the obligations of old friendship'), 25 ('Men of high renown leave behind them a repute that gives pride to their ancestors') and 34 ('Man is a figure destined to perish; the end of construction signals the beginning of destruction').

In spite of these deviations from the poem's overreaching spirit, it is possible to say that this poem is far more coherent in theme, mood and form than the preceding two poems, or, for that matter, all the other neo-classical poems discussed in this chapter. Its segments are not disparate, and its adherence to traditional modes of poetic expression does not prevent it from pursuing its own internal logic or from reflecting a coherent human experience.

IV. 'In the Train' (fī 'l-qiṭār) by al-Ruṣāfī[54]

This is a thirty-six line poem composed in *al-ṭawīl* metre, rhyming *vcbā*. Below its title we find the following short explanation: 'Written when the poet took the train from Constantinople to Salonika in 1908' – an explanation which, as it turns out, is essential for understanding the relation between the constitutent parts of the poem. The poem has three sections separated from each other by means of asterisks:

A. Nostalgia and sadness (lines 1–10). The opening line of the poem is:

[54] *Dīwān al-Ruṣāfī*, pp. 215–7.

tadhakkartu fī awṭāniya l-ʾahla wa-l-ṣahbā
fa-arslatu damʿan fāḍa wābiluhu sakbā

(I remembered my family and friends in my homeland and my tears gushed like a torrent.)

The poet also remembers certain calamities which Fate (*al-dahr*) had inflicted upon him. He explains, though, that he is normally a composed and enduring man. Only when he is nostalgic or when the strings of his heart are strummed by sorrow does he allow his tears to flow. In short, this section begins and ends with the notion of nostalgia. The reader is thus encouraged to believe that he is reading a confessional poem. However, the subsequent sections belie these anticipations, and the entire poem develops in conformity with the multi-purpose structure so typical of classical poetry. Moreover, the first section itself is not devoid of classical conventions and notions, notably the need for the poet to explain his 'weakness' as an aberration. This apology is performed, here as in other poems, by means of a *fakhr*-like interpolation, which is hardly in keeping with the sad mood of the section.

B. The train in motion (lines 11–27). This section opens with *wāw rubba*, a conjunction marking in classical poetry the beginning of a new sub-topic:

wa-qāṭiratin tarmī l-faḍā bi-dukhānihā
wa tamlaʾu ṣadra l-arḍi fī sayrihā ruʿbā

(Here is a train, hurling its smoke against the sky, filling the earth with fear as it moves along.)

The subsequent lines are a marvellous example of neo-classical 'technological' poetry, in which the poet describes new inventions with enthusiasm and awe. The train is quick, undaunted by nightfall or the coming of a storm. Nothing stands in its way as it darts, whistling, ever ready to move ahead. Except for the last three lines, which tell us that the train travelled the distance between Constantinople and Salonika overnight, the descriptions in this section are impersonal. Moreover, the vivacity that permeates the entire section is incompatible with the morose spirit of section A, nor does the poem provide any explanation for this sudden change of mood.

C. Science and the Orient (lines 28–36). This section opens with laudatory lines addressed to science, among whose achievements are electricity and the steam engine. The Orient, however, is afflicted by ignorance. It is imperative that it adopt science and progress.

Each of the poem's three sections is self-contained.[55] Without the

[55] The second section, describing the train, with the exception of its three last lines, was separated from the poem and included in elementary school readers in several Arab countries.

introductory remark, the reader would be at a loss to establish any continuity or linkage among the three sections. In spite of its 'modern' subject matter (inventions, science, progress), the poem is highly traditional in structure. As is the case with most poems based on traditional models, the thematic substance of this poem may be summarized in one or two sentences, viz: 'While I was riding a train and admiring modern science for creating it, nostalgia hit me; upon remembering my country, I also remembered its scientific backwardness'. However, this thematic summary is not fulfilled by the words of the text, neither does its temporal arrangement agree with the order of the poem's sections. Without the 'literary competence' which the reader of classical Arabic poetry is supposed to have, and without the prose note below the title, the poem would strike its reader as a conglomeration of three disparate poetic texts, loosely joined by means of a monorhyme and a monometre.

V. 'Hailing the Muslim Year' (taḥiyyat al-ᶜām al-hijrī) by Ḥāfiẓ Ibrāhīm[56]

This poem, first published in January 1909, consists of sixty-five lines in *al-ṭawīl* metre, rhyming *a/i/urū*. It provides a survey of the events that took place during the preceding year throughout the Muslim world. The printed text is continuous, that is there are no breaks between its segments.

Appropriately, the poem opens on a religious note since the event that marks the beginning of the Muslim calendar is Muḥammad's emigration (*hijrah*) from Mecca to Medina in A.D. 622. Lines 1–8, therefore, recall the day on which the Prophet departed from Mecca, surrounded by the angels of God. Lines 9–13 comment in general terms on the quality of the year that has just ended. It was a blessed year for the world of Islam, and although thousands of people perished, millions were born. The Muslim world is witnessing a great awakening.

Lines 14–39 sum up the events in several Muslim regions: Turkey (15–20) – the constitutionalists made a breakthrough; Iran (21–7) – the wicked Shah is still at the helm, but the masses are demanding their rights; Morocco (28–31) – the hedonistic sultan ᶜAbd al-ᶜAzīz abdicated in favour of his brother; Afghanistan (32–4) – foreign powers (Russia and Britain) were successfully fended off; India (35–6) – science and progress are under way. Events in Java, Algiers and Tunisia are also mentioned in lines 37, 38 and 39 respectively.

The rest of the poem focuses on Egypt. In lines 40–7 the poet states that the days of slumber are gone, and a new spirit has animated the Egyptian nation. In lines 48–57 the poet appeals to the young people of his country to

[56] *Dīwān Ḥāfiẓ Ibrāhīm*, II, pp. 37–42.

exhibit leadership, wisdom and resolution, qualities that are much needed for building a happy homeland (each of the first seven lines of this segment opens with the identical apostrophe *rijāla 'l-ghadi 'l-maʾmūli*, 'Men of the coveted morrow'). Lines 58–61 address those Egyptians who are demanding a constitution. The poet is supportive of their struggle, but he warns them against excessive actions that may jeopardize its outcome. Finally, lines 62–3 strike another optimistic note: it is to be hoped that the Egyptians will accomplish their aspirations in the new year as the Turks did in the year past. The last two lines customarily laud the khedive.

It is possible, therefore, to distinguish three parts in the poem: the prelude; the world of Islam; Egypt. However, these parts are not disjointed, as in the other poems considered here, for the overall design of the poem encompasses its different segments in a continuum. Furthermore, there is a clear thematic kernel informing the entire poem: the world of Islam has enjoyed a benign year; let us, therefore, be hopeful.

Although unity of theme and structure exist in this poem, its unity is not of a kind that one would look for in poetry. The four preceding poems have at least the traditional sense of structure to support their poeticality. Ḥāfiẓ Ibrāhīm's poem, on the other hand, relies solely on discursive flow to sustain its structure. Without the rhyme and metre and without the traditional poetic clichés dispersed throughout its lines, the poem would be nothing but an article recording and commenting on a set of events. Indeed, the language of the poem sometimes comes very close to that of a medieval chronicle. This is particularly evident in the segments about the different Muslim countries. Most of these segments open with the formulas *wa-fīhi*/*fa-fīhi* ('in it', that is in the year under review).[57] This formula is customary in the writing of late medieval Arab chroniclers, notably in the annals of al-Jabartī, the Egyptian historian who recorded the French occupation of his country.

5. POETIC LANGUAGE

One of the most salient characteristics of the modern neo-classical poem is its exacting language, which demands of its reader a measure of familiarity with the language and conventions of medieval Arabic poetry. Often a modern *qaṣīdah* is modelled on an older one, and a reader who is unaware of the medieval prototype is bound to miss many of its intricacies. Moreover, a typical neo-classical poem is, as we have seen, a highly intertextual discourse that alludes to a variety of prior texts. Only a reader sufficiently versed in the medieval heritage is likely fully to grasp the nuances of a modern *qaṣīdah*.

[57] Lines 13, 28, 35, 37 and 40.

To be sure, the neo-classical poets were keenly aware that the new reading public lacked the traditional literary competence of the *literati* of past generations; and some took great pains to avoid the use of too many recondite words and phrases. However, as the very structure of the monorhyming *qaṣīdah* made it impossible for them fully to realise this goal, the poets resorted to different means to make their poetry comprehensible to the average reader: they furnished their *dīwāns* with annotations elucidating difficult words, collocations and even whole poetic lines. Thus, many *dīwāns* of the neo-classical poets, adorned as they are with footnotes, resemble in format scholarly editions of medieval texts rather than books of modern poetry. Some of the glosses provided in the footnotes by the poets themselves are not only useful for deciphering unfamiliar words but are indicative of the poets' own interpretations of certain ambiguous texts. However, not all these glosses are the work of the poets themselves; rather, they are the work of language experts, written during the lifetime of the poet or posthumously. Often these latter annotations, copious though they are, fail to discuss the words of the poem in their specific context; they engage instead in learned but irrelevant discussions. A case in point is Shaykh al-Manṣūrī's ponderous set of annotations to the first edition of *Dīwān al-Bārūdī* (1914–5).

Nor is the impact of the classical language necessarily more conspicuous in the *qaṣīdas* of the early neo-classicists than in those of their successors. Shawqī's language is no less dependent on the medieval repertoire than al-Bārūdī's; and al-Jawāhirī's classicism is decidedly more pronounced than that of al-Ruṣāfī or al-Zahāwī. The old, Bedouin element is detectable not only in the *qaṣīdas* of such poets as the Egyptian Muḥammad ʿAbd al-Muṭṭalib (1871–1931), who consciously injects desert-ridden usages into his works, but also in the poems of such urbane poets as Bishārah al-Khūrī and ʿAlī al-Jārim. The *jāhilī* poetic language which obtained in most of the poetry of the Islamic era is inevitable in any poetic discourse pertaining to the classical model.

Words and allusions

In all literatures there exists a poetic diction, different from the 'standard' language. This is doubly true of the language of neo-classical poetry because its poetic diction is not that of contemporary literature but decidedly that of ancient times. The craft of neo-classical poetry demands from the poet not only mastery of the classical language but also a memory crowded with medieval poetic texts. Neo-classical poets often tell us how in their youth they memorized entire *dīwāns* of medieval Arab poets, usually on the advice of their teachers or of older poets. The memorized poems are supposed to enhance the poet's competence (*malakah*), but in effect they serve as a reservoir from which he actively borrows throughout his literary career. These borrowings are not confined to words and collocations but also include syntactic structures that encompass entire lines or hemistiches and tally with the prosodic patterns of the different Arabic metres.

The dependence of the poet on classical models, however, goes beyond borrowing lexical and syntactic items. The very employment of these borrowings is, in fact, determined by their use by earlier poets. In a simile, for instance, the poet is encouraged to use a medieval 'vehicle' rather than constructing his own by drawing on his life-experience or imagination. In the poem 'The breast-feeding widow', al-Ruṣāfī describes the effect of malnutrition on his protagonist by saying *wa-ṣfarra ka'l-warsi min jūʿin muḥayyāha*[58] ('hunger made her face as yellow as *wars*'). Now, the word *wars* is an old word, defined by classical dictionaries as 'a kind of yellow plant of Yemen used as liniment or yellow dye'. The word is not in use in contemporary Arabic, at least not in the poet's native speech. The poet therefore relies in his simile on an item drawn from the old literary vocabulary. To be sure, the vehicle of the simile seems to be borrowed directly from a line of the famous *sīniyyah* poem by al-Buḥturī:[59]

fi-khḍirārin mina'l-libāsi ʿalā aṣfara
yakhtālu fī ṣabīghati warsī

(Robed in green over yellow (= gold), proudly flaunting the dye of the *wars*.)

The intertextual quality of neo-classical poetry is not confined to the borrowing of words, collocations and metaphors. The neo-classical poet is deemed competent, above all, when he succeeds in establishing a direct link between what he is saying in his poetic line and what has been said in a well-known medieval poem. Thus a medieval situation is *embedded* in his own poem. In a poem addressed to King Faisal I of Iraq, Aḥmad Shawqī apostrophizes a sailboat floating down the river Tigris as follows:

qif tamahhal wa-khudh amānan li-qalbī
min ʿuyūni'l-mahā warāʾa l-sawādī[60]

(Halt, stay a while, and seek refuge for my heart from the eyes of antelopes behind the lands of Sawad.)

The use of antelopes as an allusion to charming maidens recurs abundantly in medieval and late medieval Arabic poetry, and the notion (*maʿnā*) that

[58] *Dīwān al-Ruṣāfī*, p. 217.
[59] See A. J. Arberry, *Arabic poetry: a primer for students*, Cambridge, 1965, pp. 73–81, where this poem appears side by side with its English translation.
[60] *Al-Shawqiyyāt*, IV, p. 88.

their eyes pose an emotional threat, from which the poet seeks refuge (*amān*), is also a common cliché. To talk of this kind of borrowing in terms of intertextuality is therefore to commit overkill. However, there is more to the above line than hackneyed metaphor. It alludes to a famous *bayt* by the ninth-century Baghdadi poet ʿAlī Ibn al-Jahm:

ʿuyūnu l-mahā bayna l-ruṣāfati wa'l-jisrī
jalabna'l-hawā min ḥaythu adrī wa-lā adrī[61]

(The eyes of antelopes between al-Ruṣāfah and al-Jisr conjured love from all around.)

In order fully to comprehend Shawqī's dependence on Ibn al-Jahm here, it is important to know that al-Ruṣāfah and al-Jisr ('The bridge') are the names of places in Baghdad on the banks of the Tigris. In the context of a eulogy directed to the king of contemporary Iraq, there is no better way of praising the king's capital than by invoking a classical reference to it. By alluding to the line of the old poet extolling the beauty of Baghdad and its maidens, Shawqī achieves the same result through a shortcut. An added effect achieved by the oblique reference to the ancient poet of Baghdad is to evoke the glorious cultural and political past of that city. It would be safe to say that the skilful embedding of old texts in new poems is one of the most significant techniques in the verbal art of the neo-classical poets.

Old rhetorical devices

In contradistinction to their immediate predecessors, major neo-classical poets after al-Bārūdī tried to avoid excessive recourse to verbal tricks and old, deserted words. In the pre-modern 'age of decline', one of the most consuming preoccupations of poets was the mastery of unfamiliar language and the exhibition of their linguistic skills through a variety of rhetorical devices. Thus, for example, a poet would be highly esteemed for producing a poem in which all the words are composed of three letters, or a poem in which all the letters are without diacritical points (*ʿāṭil*), or a poem whose very language illustrates all the traditional tropes and juggleries. Especially excessive were the devices of paronomasia (*jinās*) and antithesis (*ṭibāq*), as well as certain special rhythmical arrangements of words and collocations in the poetic line (for example *tarṣīʿ*, *muqābalah*, *muwāzanah* and *radd al-ʿajuz ʿalā 'l-ṣadr*).

Admittedly, in the *dīwāns* of the neo-classical poets one finds all these devices, but their incidence in the poems is far less. Moreover, these devices

[61] *Dīwān ʿAlī b. al-Jahm*, ed. Khalīl Mardam, Damascus 1949, p. 141.

are sometimes used functionally, that is, to support the meaning of the lines in which they appear. One of these devices, however, remains particularly prominent in these *dīwāns*: paronomasia. In an amorous poem by Ismāʿīl Ṣabrī, for instance, we find the following lines:

wa-ilā matā dhā'l-ṣaddu ʿan muḍnā'l-hawā
ʿūdī li-yūriqa bi'l-tawāṣuli ʿūdī
wa-staʾnifī mawṣūla ʿāʾ idi ʾunsinā
fa'l-qurbu ʿīdī wa'l-buʿādu waʿīdī[62]

(How much longer will you shun your suffering lover? *Come back* to me and our reunion will turn verdant the twig that I am. Resume our *old* intimacy as before; for togetherness is my *celebration*, and separation is my *threat*.)

In these two lines there are five words derived from roots that consist of combinations of the consonants *ʿ-w(y)-d*. This is clearly designed to be an exercise in linguistic dexterity, a display of verbal acrobatics that is its own raison d'être, fulfilling no semantic or alliterative function that would enhance the meaning of the poetic text. It is therefore very much in keeping with the practices of late medieval poets.

Many other poets exercise paronomasia in a more functional manner. In a poem that Shawqī addressed to the squabbling political leaders of his country we find the following line:

tarāmaytum fa-qāla'l-nāsu qawmun
ilā'l-khudhlāni amruhumu tarāmā[63]

(*You attacked each other*, and people said: This is a nation whose fortunes have *come to nought*.)

This line utilizes not only paronomasia (*tarāmytum*, *tarāmā*) but also the device known as *radd al-ʿajuz ʿalā 'l-ṣadr* (that is, a line that begins and ends with the same expression), which we have already encountered in a previous section. In this instance, these devices serve a real rhetorical purpose. Both of the words derived from the root *r-m-y* indicate central themes around which the line, and the entire poem, revolve: the political infighting and the fate of Egypt. The juxtaposition of these two words, as well as giving them prominent positions in the line, effectively accentuates the idea. It is worth adding, however, that two lines later Shawqī produces another wordplay based on the root *r-m-y*:

idhā kāna'l-rumātu rumāta sūʾin
aḥallū ghayra marmāha l-sihāmā

(When the marksmen are incompetent their arrows hit the wrong targets.)

[62] Ismāʿīl Ṣabrī, *Dīwān*, ed. Aḥmad al-Zayn, Cairo, 1938, p. 2.

[63] *Al-Shawqiyyāt*, I, p. 221.

Here, the three words derived from the above root (the first two mean 'marksman', the third 'target') are hardly functional, and the purpose of the pun is to adorn the poem with yet another embellishment. To be sure, the whole line is in the nature of a gnome designed to serve as a conventional 'breathing space' between topical subsections.

New lexical items

Neo-classical poetry, then, was unable to rid itself of many of the rhetorical features that characterized the verbal craft of the late medieval poets. Some of these inherited practices were considered by modern critics, indeed by some of the poets themselves, as being unsuitable for modern times. But the loyalty to the classical model, including its late medieval manifestations, was overpowering.

Side by side with these old elements, however, the impact of modern life and language became increasingly tangible in the *diwans* of the neo-classicists. Poets differ as to the degree of their readiness to incorporate in their poems newly coined words (for example, *rajᶜiyy* = reactionary) or old Arabic words that were invested with new meaning (for instance, *ḍamīr* = conscience; *jāmiᶜah* = university). The same applies to their receptivity to modern phraseology and syntactic structures or, for that matter, to European words that are used in modern Arabic (for instance, parliament, democracy, microbe). As noted earlier, certain poets were particularly fond of European words denoting modern technological and scientific features because they felt that such unmistakably modern words provided their poetry with the coveted 'modern content'. But many other poets were loath to employ foreign words lest they blemish the purity of their language. Shawqī took a middle course between these two opposing approaches. He was sparing in his use of foreign words, particularly the more technological vocabulary. However, he did not hesitate to incorporate foreign names and, at times, foreign words, into his major poems. This is particularly true of his humorous or 'light' poetry, but we also come across such usages in his most 'respectable' poems. In his poem 'Tutankhamen', for instance, we find the name Caernarvon. This name acquires a doubly conspicuous effect in the line in which it occurs, because the poet uses it as a rhyme-word, with the added long *a* vowel at its end, as demanded by the poem's prosodic structure (the hemistiches in question being *furūᶜu'l-majdi min karnārifūnā*). Another striking example of Shawqī's employment of a foreign word occurs in the scathing poem he wrote upon the departure of Lord Cromer from Egypt in 1907. The word 'football' appears, again as a rhyme-word with the added long *a* affixed at its end:

hal min nadāka ʿalā'l-madārisi annahā
tadharu'l-ʿulūma wa-taʾkhdhu'l-futbūlā[64]

(Is it a mark of your generosity that schools are forsaking learning in favour of football?)

Finally, it is possible to find in the poetry of some neo-classicists (particularly late ones such as Bishārah al-Khūrī and al-Jawāhirī) certain collocations that are reminiscent of the language of the Arab romantic school, which in its turn reflect a European concept of poetic language. Such collocations are *aṣaṭīru 'l-hawā* (myths of love), *naghmatu'l-ḥuzn* (the melody of grief), *lahību'l-ḥayāt* (the flame of life). But these usages are few and far between; and when they do occur, they are often flanked by the vocabulary and imagery of medieval poetry. Furthermore, the language of neo-classical poetry is predominantly denotative rather than connotative, and the semantic interaction of a word in a poem is confined, as a rule, within the bounds of the *bayt* or, at best, within a subsection of the poem. Very rarely does a word interact with the language of the entire poem to yield a new, condensed and suggestive semantic content. The suggestiveness of a word in a neo-classic poem is more often than not identical with what we find in the language of classical poetry. Thus the word *al-zamān*, literally meaning 'time', would normally suggest 'fate, fortune, destiny' as in classical poetry. It would rarely connote an individualized sense of time, conveyed through the dynamics of an individual poem.

Neo-classical poets, therefore, were unable, indeed unwilling, to produce a new language of poetic expression, although the fingerprints of modern Arabic language are sometimes visible on the surface of their poems. It was only with the rise of a new concept of poetry in the interwar period, embodied in the *al-Mahjar* group and, later, in the Egyptian romantic school, that a new poetic language came to the fore.

[64] *Al-Shawqiyyāt*, I, p. 174.

CHAPTER 3

THE ROMANTIC POETS

It is not accidental that the rise of Romantic poetry coincided with a period of convulsive change which was to shape the lives of many Arab countries for most of the twentieth century. As a result of the First World War, the Ottoman Empire, which had been the most successful political system in the history of Islam, no longer existed. What had been the Arab provinces of the Empire in Egypt and the Levant became new nation-states in the course of the 1920s. In spite of these new political forms, Anglo-French domination of the Nile Valley and the Levant remained very much in place, as in 1922 the League of Nations approved the mandate system for Syria, Lebanon, and Palestine with Transjordan. Although both Egypt and Iraq were declared sovereign independent states, these new versions of national independence were harshly circumscribed by the continuing reality of European power, while in North Africa the French colonial system had a depressingly permanent air. Yet in spite of all these deceptions these were heady days in Cairo, Damascus and Baghdad. The final downfall of the Ottoman system gave great new impetus to the forces of Arab nationalism, which had to some extent been held in check during the war years, and the appearance of these new national political forms was accompanied by waves of strong, sincere emotions on the part of Arab populations and their leaders. On occasion, these forces of patriotic emotion and the resistance they encountered from one or other of the western powers, developed into full-scale revolution, as was the case in Egypt in 1919 and Iraq in 1920.

The brave new world of the Arab nation-states that emerged from the aftermath of World War I was the culmination of political and intellectual activities which extended well back into the nineteenth century. Literature had not been slow to play its part in the challenges posed by the technology and the social and political theories which came from western Europe. Originally inspired by translations and adaptations from English and French literature, the new genres of the novel, the drama and the short story were well established in Arabic literature in the early decades of the twentieth century, with Egyptian writers blazing the trail of innovation. But these dramatic formal transformations in Arabic prose were not matched by similar developments in poetic form. The prosody and form of the *qaṣīdah* as written so impressively by the neo-classical poets were still in their essentials the same as those used by Imruʾl-Qays some thirteen centuries earlier. Since pre-Islamic times, poetry had been the supreme Arab art and was one of the few weapons of pride and distinction that the Arabs could use with self-esteem in the face of the apparent omnipotence of western Europe. Although a number of romantic poets were to experiment with form and prosody and called enthusiastically for change and innovation in literature, the greater part of the poetry produced before World War II retained the familiar monorhyme and metrical systems: in the case of modern Arabic poetry the wealth of the tradition was both a source of inspiration and a factor which inhibited too rapid change. Yet while the external façade of Arabic poetry evolved only gradually rather than dramatically between 1910 and 1940, it is to the credit of the romantic poets that in this period they achieved nothing less than a revolution in the language of poetry and in general poetic sensibility. The truly radical changes in poetic form were only to occur in the late 1940s when romanticism had lost its relevance as a mode of expression in modern Arabic literature.

The major contribution of the neo-classical poets lay in their rediscovery and their recreation of the quality and the dignity of classical Arabic verse, but they were also harbingers of the new spirit which was to reach its fullest expression in the romantics. What marks off the neo-classical poets from their romantic successors is a crucial difference in degree of individual involvement and intensity in their respective poetic expressions. Even on the notable occasions when al-Bārūdī and Shawqī are at their most introspective and subjective, they write easily and masterfully within a long tradition of poetry; they are comfortable within its conventions and are not in a state of tension or potential revolt against them. The mission of the neo-classical poets was to revive and regenerate old forms and language in poetry. Their romantic counterparts sought to break the old moulds of thought and practice, and to transform poetic diction: in the former task they were at best only partially successful, but their achievements in the latter were nothing short of remarkable. The neo-classical poets were essentially conservative in their relation to the Arabic literary tradition. The romantics called for change, reform, renewal (*tajdīd*) and, occasionally, iconoclasm. In the final analysis, the neo-classical poets looked to the masters of classical Arabic as the yardstick by which their own talents should be measured. The vision of the romantic poets was firmly directed towards western Europe, in common with their contemporaries in the *avant garde* of political and intellectual activity. The single most significant message to emerge from the new European-derived liberal wisdom was that of the sanctity of the individual: any individual, whether humble or great, male or female, could and should expect to play a part in the destiny of the community. Whatever the realities of the situation in the different Arab countries, this was a powerful idea which generated great new excitements and ecstasies, as well as confusion, bewilderment and ultimate disillusionment.

KHALĪL MUṬRĀN (1872–1949)

Khalīl Muṭrān was a typical member of that flowering of the intellectual and artistic life of Syria and Lebanon, many of whom in the late nineteenth century abandoned their homeland because of a combination of economic hardship and the political persecution they suffered at the hands of the Ottoman Turkish authorities. After two hectic years in Paris where he broadened his knowledge of French literature and was active in émigré political circles opposed to the rule of the Sultan ʿAbd al-Ḥamīd, in 1892 Muṭrān followed in the footsteps of a number of eminent Syrian and Lebanese men of letters and settled in Egypt, where he remained until his death in 1949. Not surprisingly it was as a journalist that he first rose to prominence, working for *al-Ahrām* for almost ten years. In 1900 he started producing his own twice-monthly periodical called *al-Majallah al-Miṣriyyah*, and in 1902 a daily paper, *al-Jawāʾib al-Miṣriyyah*. If one glances through the pages of his periodical one can form an impression of the sort of man Muṭrān must have been, with his great energy and his all-embracing intellectual and scientific interests: every issue of the periodical was divided into sections on literature, politics, economics, agriculture, questions of public health and so forth. It was a truly polymathic production in keeping with the needs of the time, when the small numbers of intellectuals felt an urgent need to inform and educate their fellow citizens. The literary sections occupied an important place, and his own poems appeared alongside those of his colleagues and friends Aḥmad Shawqī and Ḥāfiẓ Ibrāhīm.

Muṭrān displayed a lively interest in literary innovation and experimentation, most of which was inspired by the French cultural scene. One of his early articles, ‘A new style in French poetry’, discusses a series of poems by the Italian futurist writer Marinetti, which were published in French in *La revue blanche* (July 1901) and in which Muṭrān sees certain of the virtues possessed by the best Arabic poetry, with one important exception:

The lines and their meanings are all linked one to another throughout the whole poem, all leading to a single end. This is quite unlike the manner of our own compositions both new and old, apart from the efforts made by the owner of this periodical [Muṭrān himself] to create a method which departs from the traditional . . .[1]

The other significant point at which Muṭrān reveals himself to be interested in breaking the moulds of old poetic theory comes in the preface that he wrote to his first published volume of verse, *Dīwān al-Khalīl* (Cairo, 1908). He is weary of the rigidity that stifles so much of contemporary poetry: the patterns woven by so many pens on white sheets of paper are like the prints made by feet wandering over a trackless desert. Now he wants to write poetry in his own fashion, to relieve his soul when in solitude, and the demands of metre and rhyme will not sway him from his objective. Both in his preface and in the article on Marinetti's poetry, Muṭrān emphasizes the importance of the structural unity of the poem more clearly and unequivocally than any of his contemporaries or predecessors. He also places the individual in a position of primacy vis-à-vis the time-honoured rules according to which poetry had been composed since pre-Islamic days. The rhetoric of poetry will henceforth serve the emotions and the soul of the individual artist, and it is the firm declaration of belief in this principle that sets Muṭrān apart from his neo-classical contemporaries and makes him the genuine precursor of romantic poetry proper. But theory alone would not be sufficient to entitle him to this distinction without the solid evidence of his verse, which in fact demonstrates both the originality and the essentially transitional nature of his contribution.

An initial examination of his earliest work written in the 1890s indicates that his poetry is an intriguing combination of that very traditional style of which he complains in his preface, and something fresher and more original: 'My full moon and that in the sky' ('*Badrī wa badru'l-samā*ʾ', 1894) is based on the old clichéd comparison of the poet's beloved and the full moon, which is surrounded by clouds like slave girls. Yet these rather hackneyed artificial images occur alongside lines in which nature is endowed with a spirit of its own to express all the bitter-sweet passions of the lover who is doomed to unhappiness:

> In the air is a longing, a sighing of love,
> In the water a moaning from which melts the stone,
> In the breeze is a murmur which rolls o'er the meadows,
> The flowers have fragrance which tells of their thoughts.[2]

In a similar fashion 'Death of the two loved ones' ('*Wafāt ʿazīzayn*', 1897) at first sight appears to be a traditional elegy or *rithā*ʾ written by the poet on the untimely deaths of his relative Yūsuf Muṭrān and his wife. He laments

[1] *al-Majallah al-miṣriyyah*, 15 August 1901.
[2] Khalīl Muṭrān, *Dīwān al-Khalīl*, (2nd edition), Cairo, 1949, I, p. 24.

the harshness of fate as he narrates the story of the two deaths, making much of the innocence and goodness of the victims, but there is an important difference that distinguishes the poem from the familiar model of the *rithāʾ*: the poet is not performing for a group of relatives or for a circle of mourners; on the contrary, he is alone in a meadow, in the tranquillity and beauty of which he seeks relief from his overwhelming grief. This is not part of the public ritual which redeems some of the grief occasioned by a bereavement, but is a retreat into nature on the part of a stricken individual:

> I walk by night in the slumbering meadow, as it takes
> pleasure in the comforting gloom,
> Each time I approach with heart lamenting, my tears
> fall limpid as its waters while it smiles.
> Comfort I seek there from a disaster, which advancing
> time leaves undiminished . . .
> Meadow be a haven for my heart, a refuge from the clinging sorrow.[3]

This strong identification of the poet's inner turmoil with the surrounding natural scenery reaches a peak of intensity in 'Evening' ('*al-Masāʾ*'), written in Alexandria in 1902. Once again the first impressions of the poem reveal little out of the ordinary as the poet suffers the debilitating physical effects of the pangs of unrequited love, a theme as old as Arabic poetry itself. It is only as the poem moves into the final three sections that the poet's personality begins to inspire and to dominate the language and the imagery. As he contemplates the setting sun, he sees reflections of his own predicament: it is a struggle between night and day not unlike that within himself; the bright certainty of the light becomes shot through with gloomy shafts of doubt as the visible tangible world is blotted out. The rays of light which play over dark hills and through clouds form glistening effects similar to the light reflected in his own tears. The whole of creation weeps with him as he watches this symbol of the ebbing of his own life and vigour:

> As if the last tear in creation had joined with
> the last of my tears to mourn me.
> As though I had known the passing of my day, and
> seen my own twilight reflected.[4]

This is the type of poem which makes Muṭrān such a key figure of transition in the development of modern Arabic poetry. Other examples which illustrate similar features include 'The weeping lion' ('*al-Asad al-bākī*') 'Reproach' ('*ʿitāb*') and 'Solitude in the desert' ('*al-ʿuzlah fī l-ṣaḥrāʾ*'). Although it would be wrong to suggest that they represent dramatic breaks with tradition, the dominant impression that emerges from them is of a poet

[3] Khalīl Muṭrān, *Dīwān*, I, pp. 66–7. [4] Khalīl Muṭrān, *Dīwān*, I, p. 146.

who is frequently alone with his thoughts and emotions, expressing them intimately and directly in language marked by its simplicity and lack of straining for rhetorical effect.

On occasion Muṭrān attempts to put into practice his own calls for innovation in the form and content of Arabic poetry: 'Flower scent' ('*Nafḥat al-zahr*', 1905) is composed in both *ramal* and *kāmil* metre, and in one section of the poem the first half of each line is in *ramal* and the second half in *kāmil*. He describes one of the elegies composed on his former teacher Ibrāhīm al-Yāzijī as a 'prose poem': it consists of rhythmic prose which employs both assonance and reiteration, although it is not *sajʿ* and it is devoid of any rhyme or metrical scheme. However, these are isolated experiments which he does not repeat and are worthy of mention only for their curiosity value. A much more significant and lasting contribution to the future of Arabic poetry was Muṭrān's taste for dramatic narrative verse, one of the clearest instances of how he introduced a European poetic genre into Arabic with striking success. His historical narrative about the two Napoleons, '1806–1870', was written when he was only sixteen, and this was only the first of a number of remarkable poems of this type, some of which reveal the poet's passionate commitment to oppose despotism in all its forms. Poems such as 'Nero', 'The great wall of China' and 'The death of Buzurjumuhr' are virtual allegories which comment obliquely on contemporary tyrannies in the Arab world. 'The martyred child' ('*al-Janīn al-shahīd*') is a sharp indictment of the combined effects of poverty and urban exploitation on an innocent country girl, while 'A cup of coffee' ('*Finjān qahwah*') is a tragic romantic drama of unfulfilled love, full of incident, remarkable description, striking atmospheric background and lively effective dialogue between the characters. Although there had always been narrative elements in pre-modern Arabic poetry, they were usually subordinate to the basic themes of *madīḥ* or *tafākhur*, and were used as devices to praise the deeds of patrons or to sing the poet's own qualities and achievements. In these compositions by Muṭrān, the narrative became the total form of the poem, which was often of considerable length ('Nero' consists of 327 lines).

In many ways Muṭrān did fulfil the claims he made in the preface to his first *dīwān*: in wanting to write poetry that was relevant to his own time he demonstrated constantly his concern with freedom and liberty, on both a national and an individual level. The force and vitality of his personality burgeon through the normally traditional framework of his compositions as he writes simply and directly about his own emotional predicaments. Yet in his work there is a constant and unresolved tension between the poet who writes 'to relieve my soul in solitude' and the poet who was the friend and contemporary of Ḥāfiẓ and Shawqī. For every poem of profound personal introspection such as 'Evening', there are numerous other pieces of *madīḥ* and *rithāʾ* and poems for every possible social and political occasion. For every narrative poem such as 'A cup of coffee' or 'The martyred child', which explore new themes and imaginative possibilities, there are many pieces which go to the opposite extreme in conventionality. Nor was this tension resolved at a later stage in his career: all the signs of Muṭrān the innovator can be found in the first volume of his poems published in 1908. The three subsequent volumes of his *Dīwān* do not go beyond the significant achievements of the 1908 edition. Nonetheless, he fulfilled the wish expressed in the preface to that first *dīwān*: he prepared the ground so that poets in his own time and after him might attain the objectives to which he showed the way.

THE DĪWĀN POETS

Khalīl Muṭrān's considerable poetic talents worked largely within the parameters of neo-classical poetry, albeit in a state of creative tension. Although in his writings about poetry he expressed impatience with the restrictions imposed by the classical structures of poetic form, on the whole his voice was balanced and restrained, leaving the evidence of certain significant areas of his poetry to point the way to future developments. A very different impact was made by three Egyptians of a slightly younger generation: ʿAbd al-Raḥmān Shukrī (1886–1958), Ibrāhīm ʿAbd al-Qādir al-Māzinī (1890–1949) and ʿAbbās Maḥmūd al-ʿAqqād (1889–1964). They rose to literary prominence during the second decade of this century at a time when crucial transitions were taking place in the political and cultural life of Egypt. They were typical representatives of the new Egyptians who came into their own after the First World War as citizens of the new nation-state. Both Shukrī and al-Māzinī were products of the secular schools that had been established in Egypt in the late nineteenth century, and both were graduates of the Teachers' Training College in Cairo. Al-ʿAqqād, a native of Aswan, did not complete secondary school, but came to Cairo and began to make his living as a journalist and schoolteacher. After the war he and al-Māzinī became full-time journalists and writers, and were active supporters of the Wafd party. Shukrī's career was somewhat different: he spent the period 1909–1912 in England at Sheffield University, and on his return to Egypt he remained in the service of the Ministry of Education until his retirement in 1944, without ever involving himself in public life in the manner of al-Māzinī and al-ʿAqqād.

All three took it upon themselves to inaugurate a new departure. Deeply influenced by English lyrical poetry, they became passionate advocates of the romantic imagination in Arabic verse, and attacked loudly and bitterly the type of work written by the neo-classical poets, especially the master practitioner of that style, Aḥmad Shawqī. The book that gives them their name as a group is 'The *Dīwān*: a book on criticism and literature' (*al-Dīwān, kitāb fī'l-naqd wa'l-adab*), published in two volumes in Cairo in 1921, although by that date a bitter quarrel had arisen between Shukrī and al-Māzinī so the book appeared only under the joint authorship of al-ᶜAqqād and al-Māzinī. Al-ᶜAqqād led the attack on Aḥmad Shawqī, the figurehead of the generation of neo-classical poets which he and his colleagues were determined to discredit. His most frequent method of attacking Shawqī was to take lines at random and, without making any allowance for Shawqī's use of conceit or poetic licence, he would force the lines to literal interpretations never intended by the poet, and expose them to scorn and ridicule. This is obviously not a work of careful critical method, but more a book of violent reaction against traditional ways of thinking. It is thus reminiscent of other books of the same period such as Ṭāhā Ḥusayn's book on pre-Islamic poetry or ᶜAlī ᶜAbd al-Rāziq's 'Islam and the principles of government'. Like them it contains a mixture of some items of value and progress and others which demonstrate a certain lack of equilibrium; nor is it free of that personal invective which was a mark of many so-called 'critical' articles written in newspapers and periodicals at that time. But it would be a mistake to imply that the book is devoid of sound literary criticism: al-ᶜAqqād's critique of Shawqī's elegy on ᶜUthmān Ghālib does indeed expose the extent to which Shawqī's language could be strained and conceited so as to test the credence of the reader, while al-Māzinī's analysis of the bombastic prose style of al-Manfalūṭī is probably the best piece of applied criticism in the whole book. The co-authors of *al-Dīwān* had some very genuine points to make in their criticisms of those who dominated the literary tastes of the time, Shawqī and al-Manfalūṭī in particular, and on occasion they expressed themselves cogently and to good effect. But too often the valuable points made in the book are obscured by passages that are both extreme and misguided, which concentrate more on the personality of the author who is being criticized than on the text of his work.

al-Māzinī and al-ᶜAqqād

Both al-Māzinī and al-ᶜAqqād owe their reputations to activities strictly outside the realm of poetry, although their onslaught in *al-Dīwān* did much to shake the foundations of the imposing neo-classical edifice. In the case of al-Māzinī, he has just one short *dīwān* in two volumes, published in Cairo in

1913 and 1917, but thereafter he turned away from poetry, and apart from his career in politics and journalism, he became one of the most important pioneers in the development of the modern Egyptian novel. When he wrote the preface to al-ᶜAqqād's four-volume *dīwān* in 1928, al-Māzinī makes the following highly unfavourable comparison between his own verse and that of his colleague:

> I applied this standard to myself and concluded that there is no merit in the poetry which I composed, that Egyptian literature is not enhanced by it, and that the loss of it would not be detrimental, so I ceased versifying, and stayed my hand from composing poetry.[5]

In spite of this discouraging condemnation from the author himself, al-Māzinī's verse is of a certain historical interest in that it demonstrates clearly the twin sources of inspiration for the *Dīwān* group: English lyrical poetry and certain poets from the ᶜAbbāsid period. One of the books with which both al-Māzinī and Shukrī had become familiar at college in Cairo was *The golden treasury*, the anthology of English lyrical poetry selected and arranged by Francis Palgrave and first published in 1861, covering the period from Shakespeare to the mid nineteenth century. No one was more enthusiastic than al-Māzinī for the melancholic musings of Edmund Waller or Robert Burns on the transient nature of life. It is noticeable that he chooses to explain the more obscure or archaic items of vocabulary in his poetry by references to Abbāsid poets, with Ibn al-Rūmī being a particular favourite. In the final analysis one has to agree that al-Māzinī's poetry does not rise to great heights, yet there are occasions when the strength of his feelings overrides the obvious derivations of theme and style, and when his direct uncomplicated language is charged with powerful emotion to impressive effect.

Although al-ᶜAqqād was a much more prolific poet than al-Māzinī, once again it is not primarily because of his verse that he is remembered. After his audacious attack on the literary establishment in *al-Dīwān*, he remained a controversial figure for most of his life, but he is a figure of great historical value because his writings give clear indications of the ideas and literary trends fashionable in Egypt in the early decades of the twentieth century. He called constantly for a poetry of the individual and the emotions which would be a more authentic literary experience than the verse of the neo-classicists. He proclaimed Hazlitt – the champion of the imagination and the passions – as the *imām* of the new school of literature, and quotes the names of Wordsworth, Byron and Shelley as great influences on his generation. He produced no fewer than eight volumes of poetry, of which

5 ᶜAbbās Maḥmūd al-ᶜAqqād, *Dīwān al-ᶜAqqād*, Aswān, 1967, preface, p. 14.

the first collection published in 1928 is the most significant: it is in four sections and covers the period from 1916. In one of the brief prefaces written by al-ʿAqqād himself, he calls for a literature of nature as opposed to the literature of the intellect and reason, very much after the manner of Wordsworth and Hazlitt. But the contents of this *dīwān* suggest that al-ʿAqqād was more consistent in the theory than in the practice of poetry: he is certainly capable of producing highly competent verse of lyrical subjectivity in line with the principles that he advocates, but he is equally prone to producing work that is both prosaic and uninspired. The impact of the English romantics is clearly detectable in poems such as 'Autumn' ('*al-Kharīf*'), 'Reflections on sunset' ('*Sawāniḥ al-ghurūb*') and 'Onset of winter' ('*Qudūm al-shitāʾ*'), and it is worth adding that the language of these poems is of a simplicity and lack of pretension of which Wordsworth himself would have approved, far removed from the tradition-laden rhetoric of neo-classical poetry. One of the best examples of this new language of poetry in action is 'Elegy on a little girl' ('*Rithāʾ ṭiflah*'), in which the beauty and innocence of the child accentuate the tragedy of her untimely death. The poet is able to recapture her happy image only in dreams which are dispelled by the light of the morning:

> Make merry in our hearts, and laugh in our souls,
> But when the morning shines, go back; hurry on before it.
> How harsh for little ones is the prison of the tomb.[6]

In common with al-Māzinī, al-ʿAqqād reveals that Abbāsid poets such as Ibn al-Rūmī, Ibn al-Fāriḍ and Abū'l-ʿAlāʾ al-Maʿarrī were important models for him, forming an intriguing combination of inspirational sources with the English lyrical poets.

The subsequent volumes of verse that appeared after 1928 add little to the story of al-ʿAqqād as a poet, although some of the prefaces are of interest for the light they shed on literary debates and the general development of literary thought in this period. In his introduction to 'The wayfarer' ('*ʿĀbir sabīl*', 1937) he calls for a greatly increased variety in 'poetic subjects', in tastes and imaginations. He makes a plea for the inclusion of simple everyday subjects in the register of poetry, rather after the manner of Wordsworth in *Preface to the lyrical ballads*, and he claims to treat such subjects in this, his latest collection. While these ideas may sound superfluous and irrelevant to the modern ear, in the 1930s such a message was worth proclaiming: in the recent past Arabic poetry had certainly suffered from a surfeit of linguistic ornament and artificial styles, while much of the new romantic poetry had a tendency to concentrate on the

[6] al-ʿAqqād, *Dīwān*, p. 57.

more ethereal realms of the romantic imagination. Al-ᶜAqqād made lasting contributions to the theory and criticism of the new poetry, and it is for this that he will be remembered rather than for his own verse.

ᶜAbd al-Raḥmān Shukrī

The fact that ᶜAbd al-Raḥmān Shukrī maintained a much lower profile than either al-ᶜAqqād or al-Māzinī was responsible for the partial neglect of his true significance, for of the three members of the *Dīwān* group he is by far the most gifted and innovative poet. After the bitter personal attack against him which al-Māzinī had published in the 1921 *al-Dīwān*, Shukrī faded quietly from the scene, apart from occasional poems and articles published in newspapers and periodicals. Later in the 1930s al-Māzinī admitted how wrong he had been to attack Shukrī: he acknowledged the debt he owed to him as one who had opened his eyes to European literature, and to English literature in particular. Al-Māzinī confessed that during the early formative period of his life Shukrī was something of a master to him in these important new fields.

Shukrī was at the height of his creative powers between the years 1909–1919: his first volume of verse appeared in 1909 just before his departure for England and the second section appeared in 1913 after his return. The third, fourth, fifth and sixth sections of his collected works all appeared between the years 1915 and 1918, and it is in the prefaces to these sections that Shukrī reveals the depth of his knowledge of poetry and criticism in eighteenth- and nineteenth-century England, and the extent to which he felt able to adapt many of these ideas to literature in Egypt. He complains strongly of the lifeless artificial nature of contemporary Arabic poetry, and scorns the age-old imagery current in amatory verse which still centred round the moon, the branch of the willow, the hill in the desert, the pearl, the grape and the eyes of the wild cow. His complaints are in the language and terms of Hazlitt or Keats, Coleridge or Wordsworth: throughout the prefaces to the third and fourth sections Shukrī insists on the vital role of the imagination and the passions (*al-khayāl wa'l-ᶜawāṭif*), and he extends the meaning of *ᶜāṭifah* to include emotional polarities such as love–hate, hope–despair, jealousy–remorse, bravery–cowardice. In what seems to be a direct paraphrase from Hazlitt's *Lectures on the English poets*, he speaks of poetry as the language of passions, the imagination and good taste, and at one point he repeats the Coleridgean distinction between the superior faculty of the imagination (*al-takhayyul*) and the not so elevated faculty of fancy (*al-tawahhum*) in poetry. Other familiar ideas from the romantic tradition include the poet as a person of special vision capable of glimpsing immortality, the need for simple everyday language in poetry, and the insistence on the primacy of beauty in all things.

The first two sections of Shukrī's complete works are, not unexpectedly, the most traditional in style and theme, in which frequent signs of the language and imagery of classical Abbāsid poetry loom large. They also contain elegies on figures such as Qāsim Amīn, Muṣṭafā Kāmil and Muḥammad ʿAbduh, which are competent poems but which would hardly distinguish Shukrī from his neo-classical contemporaries. With the 1913 volume a distinctive development becomes apparent: his earlier classical fortitude in the face of the pangs of unrequited love now becomes transformed into a desperate pattern of striving and aspiration, accompanied by inevitable despair. He is frustrated by man's impotence to escape from destiny, and weeps not from pain but from man's degradation in the face of his fate. Such distress on occasion inspires him to Promethean heights as he imagines the benevolent effects he might have on mankind if only he had divine powers. He would rule over mankind, and would dispense justice, love, compassion and good, gentle government:

Love and I will be immortal, each of us with energy drunk, having the strength of armies.
She is my mate, and creation a new born child; she is my boon companion, my happiness, my partner.
Oh beauty of life! Who taught lovers the taste of dark red lips and the kissing of bosoms?
Oh beauty of life! Who taught the poet how to sing of love and to weave his verse?[7]

Shukrī searches for love and beauty with a religious fervour, and the ethereal plane of his quest is reflected in such titles as 'The poet and the vision of perfection' ('*al-Shāʿir wa ṣūrat al-kamāl*'), or 'Beauty and worship' ('*al-Jamāl wa'l-ʿibādah*'). His vision of love is very much a double-edged experience: for him it has a spiritual role to satisfy the soul and a baser physical side to satisfy the body. His deep-rooted sense of the ambiguity of love is compounded by strong hints of misogyny, revealed in a line where he likens the kiss of a woman to the sting of a scorpion, or in poems such as 'The deceitful beauty' ('*al-Ḥasnāʾ al-ghādirah*') or 'The kiss of the treacherous wife' ('*Qublat al-zawjah al-khāʾinah*'). Yet still at this stage, in spite of the dark hints, the dominant image of Shukrī is of the young poet setting out bravely and determinedly in an age of change and flux, with his hopes and ideals as yet only slightly contaminated by doubt and disappointment.

7 From the poem 'Would I were a God' ('*Laytanī kuntu ilāhan*'), *Dīwān ʿAbd al-Raḥmān Shukrī* (ed. Niqūlā Yūsif), Alexandria, 1960, p. 126.

With volume three of the complete works there is a dramatic change: Shukrī was a vigorous advocate of the primacy of the imagination and the passions in the voice and terms of Hazlitt, and he seized on the violent emotional contrasts described by Hazlitt and became obsessed with polarities of feeling. Henceforth, Shukrī concentrated with single-minded consistency on his own emotional psyche and produced verse of the deepest introspection. The greater part of his work now takes on something of the manic–depressive: throughout the remainder of his poetry it is rare to find a moment of pure joy which is not spoiled by some cloud of sadness, and it is usually the dark side which triumphs, as the unrelieved pain of unhappiness in love leads Shukrī to dwell more and more on the perfidy of men and the deceit of life:

Life is a wolf with bloody chops, and fatal tooth and claw.
But it's also like wine which is sweet to drink, though it deadens the mind and thought.[8]

The constant cycle of aspiration and frustration had two major effects on his work. The former spurred him on to what he himself described as a 'madness' of passion and anguish, and it was poems such as 'Consolation of madness' ('*Sulwān al-junūn*') which provided al-Māzinī with the ammunition for the personal attacks calling Shukrī's sanity into question. The other effect of his constant failure in love was to turn him away from the physical to the spiritual side of the division he himself had established. Similarly the imperfections and perfidy of the human condition also drove him to aspire towards mysterious realms of the spiritual, to dreams of divine bliss and paradise.

Two short prose works published by Shukrī in 1916 are worthy of mention in that they are largely prose versions of much of what one encounters in his verse: 'Book of confession' (*Kitāb al-iʿtirāf*) and 'Book of the fruits' (*Kitāb al-thamarāt*) record the thoughts and feelings of a young Egyptian coping with the problems of living at that time. The youth is prone to grandiose hopes and dreams, but a certain incapacity prevents him from putting them into effect. He is full of excitement about the future, but also given to pessimism because of the long ages of tyranny which his country has endured. Above all he is prey to doubt and bewilderment, caught between two stools of the old and the new, not knowing what are the sound bases on which to plan his future development. There is much in these two brief works which provides the key to Shukrī's personality, as well as giving a searching indication of the mentality of his whole generation. There is a general lack of variety in all his doleful introspection

[8] Shukrī, *Dīwān*, p. 213. From the poem 'Between life and death' ('*Bayna 'l-ḥayāh wa'l-mawt*').

which reminds one of the consistent gloom and endurance of Abbāsid poets such as ʿAbbās b. al-Aḥnaf or Abū'l-ʿAtāhiyah. Yet Shukrī was of the utmost importance for the introduction of ideas from English literature into the development of modern Arabic poetry, and his was a vital contribution to the lyrical poetry of personal meditation in Arabic. With his hopes and aspirations, and his ultimate despair, he represents the voice and experience of his generation, which saw many frustrations in social and political spheres. Unlike both of his former colleagues, al-ʿAqqād and al-Māzinī, Shukrī remained a prisoner of his own particular psychological crisis, and did not overcome it as they did by a sense of humour or ridicule, or by immersing himself in the social and political issues of the time.

THE MAHJAR POETS

In the section on Khalīl Muṭrān, reference was made to the Syrians and Lebanese who emigrated in substantial numbers during the late nineteenth century. Most of them were Christians like Muṭrān himself, and like him some of the most important and influential lived and worked in Egypt. Many of these emigrants came from the mission schools in Lebanon and were looked upon favourably by the British authorities in Egypt and the Sudan, for whom their knowledge of Arabic and usually also English or French was of great benefit. By far the greater number, however, went to North or South America, or to Australia or West Africa, and they established thriving merchant communities in major cities such as New York, Rio de Janeiro and San Paulo. These migrations were not without far-reaching cultural effects, because the material wealth sent back to their villages and families by those emigrants who prospered was often accompanied by new ideas and attitudes. By a happy chance, during the first two decades of this century there came together in New York a group of these Syrian and Lebanese exiles who had a general interest in literature and in poetry in particular. By cooperating and helping each other in their work and ideas, they were able to form a coherent group with common characteristics, and some of them had the talent to produce work of a quality and originality which became a vital stage in the development of romantic poetry in Arabic.

These writers were initially brought together through the journalism of the Arabic-speaking community in New York, and by one literary monthly magazine in particular, 'The Arts' (*al-Funūn*), edited by Nasīb ʿArīḍah. Its publication was rarely free of problems caused by financial difficulties, and it appeared only sporadically between 1913 and 1918 when it disappeared, having produced only twenty-nine numbers in all. Another important outlet for the *mahjar* writers was the twice-weekly paper *al-Sāʾiḥ* which had been established in New York in 1912 by ʿAbd al-Masīḥ Ḥaddād. After the collapse of *al-Funūn*, the writers decided to organize themselves into a group in order to preserve themselves as a literary movement, and this led to the formation of 'The Pen Association' ('*al-Rābiṭah al-Qalamiyyah*') in 1920: Jibrān Khalīl Jibrān was the first president and Mīkhāʾīl Nuʿaymah became the secretary. *Al-Sāʾiḥ* took the place of *al-Funūn* as the medium through which their works and ideas would appear, and it was hoped that a special edition would be produced at the beginning of each year dedicated to the group. Thus it was that the first genuine literary school in modern Arabic was created, without whose ideas and works the development of romantic poetry inside the Arab world would certainly have been the poorer.

Jibrān Khalīl Jibrān (1883–1931)

Jibrān Khalīl Jibrān played a crucial role in the lives of the 'Pen Association' poets in North America, not so much because of his talent as a poet, which was unremarkable, but because of his intellectual leadership and the strong impact of his rebellious romantic personality on other members of the group who were more talented as poets. He provided ideas, inspiration, encouragement and general education for those of his colleagues who did not possess his range of knowledge and experience. Although Jibrān is probably the most widely known Arab author outside the Arab world, this is because of the books he wrote in English such as *The prophet*, *Jesus son of man*, *The wanderer* and *Sand and foam*, books which have enjoyed a wide readership, particularly in America. Yet despite the great popular appeal of these books in English, they have not had any durable effect on serious literary activities in the west, and by far his most significant contribution to literature has been within the Arab world and from his work written originally in Arabic, in New York in the early years of this century. It is in these early prose works that one finds most of the themes and ideas that the 'Pen Association' poets found so inspirational.

Jibrān was fiercely anti-clerical, and championed the cause of simple virtuous people who in his eyes were victimized by the hierarchies and institutions of the Maronite church. This is the theme of 'John the madman' ('*Yūḥannā 'l-majnūn*') from the collection of short stories 'Brides of the meadows' (*ʿArāʾis al-murūj*) which first appeared in America in 1906: John the shepherd boy is portrayed in a highly idealized, romantic manner, and the rural scenes serve as a celebration of the pastoral idyll. 'Khalīl the unbeliever' ('*Khalīl al-kāfir*'), from 'Rebellious spirits' (*al-Arwāḥ al-*

mutamarridah, New York, 1908) is modelled on precisely the same pattern, and in both cases individuals possessing natural wisdom and virtue, untouched by the institutions and bonds of sophisticated society, become outcast figures and lonely voices in the wilderness. This type of theme is developed further in 'Rebellious spirits' as Jibrān rails against civilized society and its systems of laws which so often become instruments of injustice and oppression rather than the guarantee of individual rights and liberties. In this context he finds much to say on the unhappiness suffered by women in his native land, who were forced to marry those chosen for them by their parents or guardians. The collection of articles 'A tear and a smile' (*Dam*ᶜ*ah wa ibtisāmah*) was first published in book form in 1914 by the editor of *al-Funūn*, Nasīb ᶜArīḍah, and the by now familiar Jibranian *idées fixes* are expressed with even greater force: foremost among these is the vision of corruption and unhappiness which civilized society brought to men whom the author imagines to be innocent and virtuous in their natural pastoral states. Needless to say, the city, which is the highest form of the civilized condition, is the source of most of the evil and unhappiness:

> 'Why do you lament, oh pure stream?' and it replied: 'Because I am going against my will to the city where men despise me and exchange me for the juice of the vine, and make use of me to transport their filth. How should I not lament when soon my purity will become filth and my clearness squalor?'[9]

The saving graces in which Jibrān puts his faith are his belief in the primitive goodness and unspoilt innocence of man, the peace and purity of nature which seems to represent all that men should be or once were, a Keatsian idea of beauty, and love which is not inhibited by man-made laws, manners and customs. Two further Jibranian themes are worthy of mention because of their importance for his colleagues. One is the neo-Platonic idea that the soul has a separate existence above the impurity and adulteration of the body, a conception of duality which was to be often repeated by other poets of the *mahjar* group. The other is the typical romantic view of the poet as a prophet-like figure, an enlightened individual who is not in harmony with the rest of society which is incapable of his vision and insight. Thus the role of the despised and rejected individual is transferred to the poet who sees more clearly and deeply than other men, and who is in consequence misunderstood and persecuted.

The only work of any length written by Jibrān in rhyme and metre was 'The processions' ('*al-Mawākib*', New York, 1919). This poem is less than inspired and is merely a repetition in verse form of much of what the author had said previously in his more original and attractive prose works. It does,

[9] From 'Lamentation in the meadow' ('*Manāḥah fī 'l-ḥaql*'), *al-Majmū*'*ah al-kāmilah li mu*'*allfāt Jibrān Khalīl Jibrān*, Beirut, 1959, p. 283.

however, have a certain structural interest in that it consists of two voices each with its own metre (*basīṭ* and *ramal*), and it proceeds from stanza to stanza in the form of a dialogue. In this, as in other of Jibrān's writings, one can see an uneasy amalgam of various strands of western thought which often lacks depth and subtlety. His obsession with the lack of liberty and the evil and corruption of life in civilized society echoes the writings of Rousseau, particularly when this is contrasted with an ideal life in the purity of nature as portrayed through the *ghāb* (forest). With his view of the poet as one who is gifted with a special insight and vision, almost approaching prophecy, and one who is scorned by the generality of uncomprehending society, Jibrān identifies closely with the career and works of William Blake: the similarity between them extends to Jibrān's talent with the artist's brush as well as the pen. Another clearly traceable influence is that of Nietzsche, for although Jibrān was not acquainted with the majority of his work, *Also sprach Zarathustra* excited him a great deal. Clearly Jibrān was alienated from his society in Lebanon, and existence did not become any easier for him in America. One is grateful for the attractiveness and originality of his early Arabic prose and for the social comment that much of it contains. However, one has to conclude that his work often descends to the level of an unsubtle primitivism with a vaguely defined role of primacy for the heart and emotions; the escapism of a rootless and rather unbalanced individual which is not always made more palatable by a great literary talent.

Mīkhāʾīl Nuʿaymah (1889–1988)

Khalīl Jibrān was the President of the 'Pen Association' and a somewhat extrovert head of the whole northern *mahjar* movement. The Secretary was Mīkhāʾīl Nuʿaymah, whose great value lay in the fact that he was an able critic and theoretician of literature, and at the same time was able to illustrate his ideas in his own poetry. Unlike Muṭrān, the 'Dīwān' poets and Jibrān, who drew much of their inspiration from French and English literature of the eighteenth and nineteenth centuries, Nuʿaymah's initial window upon the wider world of western culture came via Russian literature: he was a pupil in the Russian primary school at his birthplace, Baskinta, before moving on to the Russian Teachers' Training College in Nazareth. From there he went to Russia in 1906, where until 1911 he attended an Orthodox seminary in Poltava in the Ukraine. This was a vital stage in his formative years when he became acquainted with the theatre, opera, ballet, and of course the masterpieces of Russian literature. Because of his increasingly strong anti-clericalism, he left the seminary under something of a cloud, and in 1912 followed the well-trodden path to the New World where he joined the family of his elder brother in the state of Washington. After graduating from the University of Seattle in 1916, he was persuaded to go to New York by the editor of *al-Funūn*, Nasīb ʿArīḍah, who had been a fellow-student at the Russian College in Nazareth. From then on, most of his energies were centred round *al-Funūn* and *al-Sāʾiḥ* and the group of writers who made up the 'Pen Association' when it was created in 1920.

Apart from the intrinsic achievements of the *mahjar* writers as romantic poets, one of their most important functions was to stimulate interest in and awareness of what they were doing inside the Arab world itself. A collection of twenty-two of Nuʿaymah's critical articles first appeared in book form in Egypt in 1923 under the title 'The sieve' (*al-Ghirbāl*). If the notorious *Dīwān* on literature and criticism was the literary manifesto of al-ʿAqqād and al-Māzinī and their supporters, 'The sieve' occupies a similar position for the northern *mahjar* group. Appropriately the first edition of 'The sieve' has a preface written by al-ʿAqqād. Nuʿaymah has his own radical version of the theme which in theory had also preoccupied Khalīl Muṭrān, namely how to introduce greater freedom for the expression of subjective emotions into the complex and rigid systems of traditional Arabic prosody:

> Neither the metres nor the rhymes are necessary elements of poetry, just as temples and rites are not strictly necessary to prayers and worship. There is many a piece of prose which is beautifully composed and musical to the ear which contains more elements of poetry than a *qaṣīdah* of a hundred rhyming lines.[10]

Nuʿaymah obviously believes that by concentrating too much on the mechanics and intricacies of prosody, the poet may be distracted from more important considerations: the soul which can produce only correct metres and resounding rhymes is barren, but sooner or later it must flourish and discover thoughts and emotions as well as rhyme and metre. Even more radically, Nuʿaymah extends the same logic to the hallowed domain of the Arabic language itself, which he sees as a living organism, constantly changing and developing. One should not consider the rules of language as being in any way immutable or sacred:

> What is the eternal law which links your tongue with that of a Bedouin who lived thousands of years before you, and which does not link you with the tongue of a contemporary poet?[11]

It is interesting to note that this was too much even for the iconoclastic al-ʿAqqād, who in the preface to 'The sieve' took Nuʿaymah severely to task

[10] Mikhāʾīl Nuʿaymah, *al-Ghirbāl*, Beirut, 1964, p. 116.
[11] Nuʿaymah, *al-Ghirbāl*, p. 98.

for not having sufficient concern for the rules and correctness of Arabic grammar and syntax. In fact the difference between the two of them was one of priorities: at no point does Nuᶜaymah actually advocate the incorrect use of grammar and syntax, but for him the primacy of the voice of individual subjectivity in poetry was paramount, and for the sake of this cardinal principle he was prepared to tolerate occasional irregularities in the use of language. This point he reinforces further in the chapter 'The pivot of literature' ('*Miḥwar al-adab*'), where he states that the man who deserves to be called a writer is the one who derives the content of his message directly from his heart, and the prime function of literature is to act as a message which passes from the soul of the writer to the soul of the reader. Like Verlaine in his plea for musicality in poetry, for the sake of lyrical subjectivity Nuᶜaymah is willing to countenance departures from the normal rules. Language and prosody are systems which must serve the individual creative writer and not inhibit his artistic liberty. It is sentiments such as these from Jibrān or Nuᶜaymah that represent the voice of genuine romantic rebellion in Arabic literature.

Nuᶜaymah was not a prolific poet, having only one small volume of verse entitled 'Whispering eyelids' (*Hams al-jufūn*), and of the contents only some thirty poems were original Arabic works, the remainder having been translated into Arabic after having been written in English. All the Arabic poems were written between 1917 and 1928, and one of the earliest of these, 'The frozen river' ('*al-Nahr al-mutajammid*'), dated 1917, is an Arabic version of a poem that Nuᶜaymah wrote originally in Russian. If one comes to 'Whispering eyelids' after reading Muṭrān or even the 'Dīwān' poets, one is immediately struck by the lack of complexity in the language, there being an almost total absence of the *recherché* and the obscure in his vocabulary. It is a poetic language of artful simplicity and directness, and has a quiet contemplative tone which is able to achieve great intensity of feeling without loud rhetorical effects. Qualities such as these were greatly admired by the Egyptian critic Muḥammad Mandūr, and this new, restrained, intimate language of poetry led him to coin the term *al-adab al-mahmūs*, 'the quiet voice in literature', recognizing that this *mahjar* verse was a definite new departure in Arabic poetry generally and in romantic poetry in particular. One of Nuᶜaymah's poems which Mandūr rightly singled out for particular attention is 'My friend' ('*Akhī*', 1917), a rare example of an Arabic poem which is both a war poem and a patriotic piece, and which is quite devoid of any loud tone of declamation or strained rhetorical effect. Written in 1917, this fine poem was at least a generation ahead of its time. Another point on which Nuᶜaymah insisted at length in 'The sieve' was the importance of music and rhythm in poetry. While at one level this may seem to be stating the obvious, there are several examples in his work where the rhythm and movement of the poem become integral parts of its overall unity, essential elements which blend with the different moods and varying levels of intensity. 'Sound of bells' ('*Ṣadā 'l-ajrās*'), 'Autumn leaves' ('*Awrāq al-kharīf*', 1921) and 'Song of the winds' ('*Tarnīmat al-riyāḥ*', 1923) all illustrate these particular skills at work.

The dominant impression left by Nuᶜaymah's small corpus of verse is of a quiet, introspective personality preoccupied with inner problems of the spirit and the emotions. These are expressed in a language which is deceptively simple and without linguistic pretension. True to his own theories, he makes the conflicts within his troubled self the basic theme and justification for his poetry. His work is by no means of even and sustained quality, but some of the examples referred to above rank with the best efforts of romantic lyrical poetry in Arabic. The fact that he was able to express precise ideas on how such poetry should be written and was also able to demonstrate some of these in some of his own work, lent him great significance amongst his colleagues both in the *mahjar* and inside the Arab world.

Īlyā Abū Māḍī (1889–1957)

In flamboyant terms the critic Lūwīs ᶜAwaḍ speaks of Jibrān as the high priest of the *mahjar* movement, Nuᶜaymah as its lawgiver and philosopher, and Īlyā Abū Māḍī as the one who provided the musical expression: in other words, Abū Māḍī was the most prolific poet of the whole movement, and the most gifted. Born in Lebanon in 1889, he had little formal education and spent the years 1900–1911 in Alexandria in apparently humble circumstances, before travelling on to the United States in 1911. He went to Cincinatti before moving to New York in 1916 where he joined the group of writers around *al-Funūn*, playing an active role as poet, general writer and journalist. In 1929 he began to edit his own periodical, *al-Samīr*, which was of a lighter, more popular nature than *al-Funūn* had been, aimed probably at a wider reading public. The information on the years Abū Māḍī spent in Alexandria is sketchy in the extreme, but shortly before he left for America, when he was about twenty years old, his first *dīwān* was published (in 1911), entitled 'Remembrance of the past' (*Tadhkār al-māḍī*). On the whole there is little in these youthful efforts to suggest that their author was subsequently to become one of the major poets in modern Arabic: most of them are heavy, moralistic compositions, strongly didactic in tone, and more concerned with the moral fibre of society and man's shortcomings than with giving expression to the poet's deep personal emotions. The second section of this *dīwān* is much the most interesting: it consists of poetic narratives, a type of composition which was still very much in its infancy in Arabic at this time, and one of the most original aspects of the work of Khalīl Muṭrān. There is no evidence of any direct contact between the youthful, inexperienced Abū Māḍī in Alexandria, and Muṭrān who was one of the more eminent poets and journalists working in Cairo. However, Abū Māḍī could certainly have known Muṭrān's work from newspapers and periodicals or from Muṭrān's first *dīwān* published in Cairo in 1908. There is no doubt that even at this early stage, Abū Māḍī displayed a certain talent for this dramatic narrative poetry, which was an unusual style for a young poet to cultivate in Egypt at that time.

The difference between 'Rembrance of the past' and the second *dīwān* of Abū Māḍī, which appeared in New York in 1919, is indicative of a poet who has both made great technical progress and widened the limits of his own experience of life. His contact with the other members of the *mahjar* group is clearly visible at this stage, demonstrating the value such a cohesive group could have. The preface to the 1919 collection was written by Jibrān, who presents the by now familiar thoughts on the special gifts of the poet who, by his unique powers of thought and imagination, rises above the world of ordinary mortals. In his poem 'The poet' ('*al-Shāʿir*'), Abū Māḍī prefers to dwell on the problems and suffering that beset him, but this piece also illustrates what became a frequent feature of his work, developed from his taste for the dramatic narrative: the poem is in the form of a dialogue between the poet and a female companion who urges him to describe the nature and function of his art and personality. This he struggles to do, fearful that she will turn away and leave him. The dialogue and the contrived situation between the two characters create a poem which is more stimulating and gripping than a work which merely speculates in the abstract on the elusive nature of the poet:

> If he laments, the spirits are in his tears; if he
> sings, love is in his strains.
> He weeps with the exiled for his homeland; he joins
> the grief-stricken in his tears . . .
> He is one who lives for others, while those who
> misunderstand think he lives for himself.[12]

Abū Māḍī's enthusiasm for narrative verse continues in this second *dīwān* with 'The rose seller' ('*Bāʾiʿat al-wurūd*'), which is reminiscent of Muṭrān's 'The martyred child', but even so, this collection remains something of a transitional stage between the conventional neo-classical and genuine romantic poetry. Yet even when Abū Māḍī uses the traditional language

[12] *Īlyā Abū Māḍī, shāʿir al-mahjar al-akbar* (Damascus, 1963 edition of complete works, with study by Zuhayr Mīrzā), p. 437.

and imagery of classical Arabic poetry, there is a refreshing simplicity and conversational tone which remove any barrier to the direct communication of his inner feelings. The love poem 'As for me' ('*Ammā anā*') is frankly sensual and explicit in the manner of old Arabic amatory verse, but the impression it leaves is of a poet who writes to relieve and express his emotions, not one who is constrained uneasily to write in accordance with a certain tradition:

When birds suffer thirst and are worn out by it, they fall to the rivers from high
in the sky.
As for me, if I thirst, I thirst most of all for the crimson of her lips . . .
People seek incense in the hills amongst roses and the breezes of the east wind.
As for me, sweeter than the scent of incense is the fragrance of her breasts.[13]

Unlike Nuᶜaymah and Jibrān, Abū Māḍī did not have any deep knowledge of literature in languages other than Arabic, and it was natural that he should use the language and imagery familiar to him from his own heritage as he began to develop new styles and modes of expression. Even at the height of his most romantic phase, of all the *mahjar* writers he was the least prone to experimentation with prosody, and his preferred form remained the *qaṣīdah*-type composition with monorhyme. Also he never became strictly limited to the tortured confines of his own personal world but retained a healthy sense of the reality of the lives and sufferings of others. The poem 'A nation is dying while you play' ('*Ummatun tafnā wa antum talᶜabūn*') shows the profoundest concern for the hardships experienced by his countrymen during the First World War:

Many a tiny one like the chicks of the sand grouse, perish from severe famine.
Their sinews are weak when it attacks; and hunger will destroy the strength of
lions.
Have you seen a necklace when it comes apart? Thus are the tears on their
cheeks.
Their spirits have run away like water
Through grief; God, what a cruel fate![14]

With his third volume of verse, 'The streams' (*al-Jadāwil*), published in New York in 1927, Abū Māḍī reached the peak of his achievement as a romantic poet. In the short preface to the first edition written by Mīkhāᵓīl Nuᶜaymah, he says that now he feels a definite spiritual link between himself and the author which he had not felt about the first two volumes of Abū Māḍī's work. The poet himself wrote a brief introduction in verse in which reflections of some of the ideas from 'The sieve' are clearly visible, but it is the first poem in the collection, 'The phoenix' ('*al-ᶜAnqāᵓ*'), which provides

[13] *Abū Māḍī* (1963 complete works), p. 478.
[14] *Abū Māḍī* (1963 complete works), p. 699.

conclusive evidence of Abū Māḍī's new departure: this poem is a long statement of doubt, urgent aspiration, mystery and constant searching. The strange legendary bird is a symbol for something people seek but which constantly eludes them. No precise information is offered about the identity of the object of the search, which is indicated only by the feminine pronoun: it may be beauty, happiness or truth; it may be the poet's soul or a manifestation of God's presence; or it may be linked with his beloved who is no longer with him. The extent of the poet's search assumes cosmic proportions as he ranges far and wide in his anxiety:

I sought her in the bosom of the dawn and in the gloom; even unto the stars I stretched my hands.
Lo, they both are in confusion at a perplexed, enfeebled lover.
Lo, the stars tremble in the broad heavens either from knowledge or ignorance.[15]

Most of the poem proceeds in this atmosphere of vagueness, mystery and trembling uncertainty. Only at the final moment when all seems lost and the poet's spirit dissolves into tears of grief does he get a glimpse of what he has been looking for, but there is no joy in the prospect and it profits him little finally to realize that the object of his search lay within himself all the time:

Grief pressed my spirit, and it flowed out in tears. Then I glimpsed it and touched it in my tears.
I realized when the knowledge was in vain, that what I had lost was within me![16]

Such expressions of extreme individual malaise which flourished in pained atmospheres of vagueness and perplexity became one of the hallmarks of this *mahjar* poetry, and of romantic poetry in general. The most lengthy and detailed expression of the painful mysteries which beset him is Abū Māḍī's poem 'Mysteries' ('*al-Ṭalāsim*'), the whole object of which is to give vent to a long series of statements of confusion and metaphysical doubt, without offering any solutions or evidence of deep thought about the problems raised. The poem as a whole lacks discipline and sustained imaginative power in its choice of detail and situation, but because it is a virtual manifesto in verse of the major themes that appealed to the *mahjar* writers and indeed to their whole generation, it has enjoyed great popularity. Artistically much more convincing is 'Evening' ('*al-Masāʾ*'): although the general theme is by now more than familiar – confusion and deep unease about questions of youth, love, old age and death – Abū Māḍī uses his favourite device of addressing questions directly to a female companion, in

[15] *Abū Māḍī* (1963 complete works), p. 512. [16] *Abū Māḍī* (1963 complete works), p. 514.

this case a girl named Salma, thus avoiding the abstract, rather mechanical posturings of 'Mysteries'. The language of the poem is subtle and allusive, creating powerful atmospheric effects, and altogether this short piece is of much greater poetic worth than the rather rambling, undisciplined queries of 'Mysteries':

> The clouds range over the wide heavens, as though in fright,
> The sun appears behind them, pallid round the brow,
> The sea is calm, silent, with the meekness of piety,
> But your eyes are bewildered on the far horizon.
>   Salma – of what do you think?
>   Salma – of what do you dream?[17]

One of the great strengths of Abū Māḍī is that, for all his flights of bewildered metaphysical fancy, he retains a sense of bitter realism and depth of perception that is rare, both amongst the *mahjar* writers and in romantic poetry in the Arab world. In the final analysis, he was never quite able to accept the self-righteous, splendid isolation of the poet's role as expounded by Jibrān and others. On the face of it, 'In the desert' ('*Fī'l-qafr*') is a typical flight from a civilized society which is full of corruption and unhappiness. The desert becomes a substitute for the Jibranian ideal of *al-ghāb*, the forest of ideal purity and goodness, and this refuge is an enormous temptation for the poet, but with rare honesty he concludes that it is futile to try to escape from people and all their shortcomings: after all, he is one of them and they are all in some sense part of him. The depth of Abū Māḍī's social conscience emerges in 'The pauper' ('*al-Faqīr*'): he recognizes that in the face of such wretchedness there can be no luxury of melancholic star-gazing, neither will the darkness be any source of comfort to one with the pauper's problems. Even to grieve for his condition is almost an act of futility.

'The streams' represents the high point of Abū Māḍī's poetic development, beyond which he did not progress in his subsequent work: 'The thickets' (*al-Khamāʾil*) appeared in 1940, and there was one more posthumous *dīwān* published in 1960, 'Gold and dust' (*Tibr wa turāb*). In 'The thickets' poems of an 'occasional' nature begin to reappear, and in the posthumous volume most of the material is of this type: poems for special occasions, people and places, and elegies for friends and colleagues. Abū Māḍī's career is a fascinating development from unremarkable neo-classical verse to some of the peaks of achievement in romantic poetry. His work also has that extra dimension of imaginative power which on occasion takes it beyond the limits of the romantic experience, and lends it a permanent value which transcends the style of his immediate generation.

[17] *Abū Māḍī* (1963 complete works), p. 784.

Nasīb ʿArīḍah, Rashīd Ayyūb and Nadrah Ḥaddād

The dominating influences of Jibrān and Nuʿaymah led to their ideas on literature being adopted by other members of the group with an unusual frequency and consistency, to the extent that one can think of the *mahjar* writers as being the first genuine school or movement in modern Arabic literature. The degree to which this was so can be gauged from the work of Nasīb ʿArīḍah, Rashīd Ayyūb and Nadrah Ḥaddād. ʿArīḍah (1887–1946) had been the earliest friend and colleague of Nuʿaymah, as they had both attended the Russian Teachers' Training College in Nazareth: he emigrated to New York in 1905 and in 1912 he founded the Atlantic Press which was to produce *al-Funūn*. Although he is not so well known for his own works as Jibrān, Nuʿaymah or Abū Māḍī, to him must go much of the credit for struggling to keep *al-Funūn* going during its sporadic career in which it was beset by financial crises. He is the author of one volume of verse, 'Perplexed spirits' (*al-Arwāḥ al-ḥāʾirah*), which was published in New York in 1946, the year of his death, although most of the poems had been composed between 1912 and the late 1920s. ʿArīḍah identified strongly with the Jibranian vision of the poet suffering in splendid isolation in an uncomprehending world, and a general air of gloom and pessimism pervades the whole of his poetry. In common with the other *mahjar* writers he feels keenly the reality of being cut off from his native country in an unsympathetic environment. Sometimes this is expressed as nostalgia (see 'The basket of fruit' ('*Sallat fawākih*')), but on other occasions he is moved to frustration and anger by the spectacle of weakness and degradation presented by the inhabitants of Syria and Lebanon in the First World War:

> Wrap them in a shroud! Bury them! Put them into the deep tomb's abyss!
> Pass on. Do not mourn them. They are a dead people who will not wake.[18]

These lines, taken from 'The end' ('*al-Nihāyah*'), are (in their Arabic original) a good illustration of the prosodic style of much *mahjar* verse, demonstrating a preference for the shorter, simple metres and stanzaic forms. The metre is *ramal* and the poem consists of couplets with three feet in the first hemistich and two in the second, but for effect the poet breaks up the lines and keeps the first three words of each couplet separate. This is an excellent example of how the *mahjar* poets continued to use regular rhyme and metre but took ever greater liberties with the classical *qaṣīdah* form, using lines of irregular length and occasionally varying the metres within individual poems.

One device by which ʿArīḍah breaks the generally unrelieved cycle of

[18] Nasīb ʿArīḍah, *al-Arwāḥ al-ḥāʾirah*, New York, 1946, pp. 65–7.

gloom and anguish in his verse is to commune with his soul in Jibranian fashion, and to rise above mundane, earthly troubles. His piece 'Oh soul' ('*Yā nafs*') is his most complete version of this idea, and this poem was analyzed by Muḥammad Mandūr alongside Nuᶜaymah's 'My friend' in the article in which Mandūr demonstrates some of the most appealing features of *mahjar* poetry. Along with Abū Māḍī and Nuᶜaymah, ᶜArīḍah makes his own contribution to the poetry of introspective malaise and perplexity with pieces such as 'Why' ('*Limādhā*') and 'The rider's return' ('*ᶜAwdat al-fāris*'), but in the end his poetic vision remains locked in gloom and pessimism. It is this rather than a lack of talent which leaves one with a certain feeling of dissatisfaction: although his poems of painful quest and mystical longing are moving and attractive, he does not progress beyond them. The egocentric concentration on his own tortured personality did not serve to deepen his general perception, but rather kept him going round in the same mysterious circles.

Rashīd Ayyūb (1881–1941) was a native of Mīkhā'īl Nuᶜaymah's village, Baskinta, who emigrated to North America by way first of Paris and Manchester. His three volumes of poetry were all published in New York, where he died in 1941, and the critics Iḥsān ᶜAbbās and Yūsuf Najm remark on the 'bewitching effect' Jibrān had on his work. Ayyūb's first *dīwān*, al-Ayyūbiyyāt (1916), represents very much a transitional stage between social and 'occasional' poetry and the more subjective romantic themes which dominated his work at a later stage. 'Songs of the dervish' ('*Aghānī al-darwīsh*', 1928) sees him developing his own version of the Jibranian poet who is a stranger in the world and in society. For Ayyūb, the dervish or wandering mystic becomes the symbol of the poet who is a person of mystery possessed of special secrets unknown to others. This solitude is a state which is positively desired and cultivated: 'I am not of them' ('*Lastu minhum*') states an open preference for an ivory-tower existence which leads to narcissism and delusion. Although the poet insists that his sadness for the people who revile him is greater than the pleasure he takes in his superiority over them, he concentrates too much on this pleasure to make the claim convincing:

> I went on, with poetry as my custom and the house of inspiration my shelter.
> If the night darkens, I whisper; or if the dawn breaks, I sing.
> Nay, by the goddess of my verse, my abode is like the garden of Eden.[19]

Ayyūb's general inclination for the grand romantic state of solitude is also expressed in a withdrawal from all materialistic concerns, and a flight into

[19] Rashīd Ayyūb, *Aghānī 'l-Darwīsh*, Beirut, 1959, pp. 66–7.

the simple, pristine innocence of nature. *Al-dunyā* (normal earthly life) is the world of wealth and ordinary mortals which the poet tends to shun, not infrequently from the heights of alcoholic intoxication (see the poem '*Hiya 'l-dunyā*'). The poet is obviously identifying with certain aspects of the Sufi tradition, and this type of escapism into mystical intoxication is continued in the final *dīwān* 'Such is life' (*Hiya 'l-dunyā*, 1942), a volume which confirms the impression that Rashīd Ayyūb was very much an extension of the ideas and personality of Jibrān.

The poetry of Nadrah Ḥaddād (1887–1950) conforms to a very similar pattern: he produced one collection, 'Autumn leaves' (*Awrāq al-kharīf*), which was published in New York in 1941. The opening poem 'Go with me' ('*Sir maᶜī*') is an invitation which had been extended by most of his colleagues, namely to forget all about life in the real world with its unending burdens and materialistic values. He reproduces the familiar *mahjar* themes of belief in the primitive goodness of nature, the dual existence of the body and the soul, and the special characteristics of the poet. One of the drawbacks in his work is that it contains a pronounced didactic, 'holier-than-thou' strain as he inveighs against the vainglory of the world and the obsession of men with getting and spending. His poem 'He who sees yet is blind' ('*al-Baṣīr al-aᶜmā*') brings together a number of subjects dear to Ḥaddād's colleagues: perplexed queries about the meaning of life, nostalgia for Syria and Lebanon, and a strong sense of alienation. The piece is almost a paradigm for much of the poetry of the northern *mahjar*, and indicates the extent to which Nadrah Ḥaddād was a faithful member of the group, his role ultimately being more one of imitation than emulation.

It should be mentioned at this point that the *mahjar* poets based in New York had their counterparts in Latin America, although the poetic achievements of this southern *mahjar* were neither as dramatic nor as radical as those of the northern group. The Arab poets in Latin America did not form a genuine literary movement or school in the same way as did the members of the 'Pen Association' in Brooklyn, but the most significant of them did congregate in San Paulo in Brazil where, in 1933, they formed their own literary association called *al-ᶜUṣbah al-Andalusiyyah*. The most widely known poet of the group was Rashīd Salīm al-Khūrī (1887–1984), known as *al-shāᶜir al-qarawī* – the country poet – and who is celebrated in the Arab world for his political poetry and the enthusiasm with which he espoused the cause of Arab nationalism, especially in his *dīwān* 'The tempests' (*al-Aᶜāṣīr*, San Paulo, 1933). The work of Ilyās Ḥabīb Farḥāt

(1893–1977) shows a more marked resemblance to the work of the Arab poets of New York, especially in his *dīwān* entitled 'Dreams of the shepherd' (*Aḥlām al-rāʿī*): this was written in Brazil during 1933–4 and consists of six sections of idyllic pastoral verse, in which Jibranian themes are particularly strong, such as the contrast between the imagined purity of nature and the evil and corruption of the man-made world. Fawzī al-Maʿlūf (b. 1899) died prematurely in 1930 and is remembered chiefly as a result of his poem 'On the carpet of the wind' (*ʿalā bisāṭ al-rīḥ*, Rio de Janeiro, 1929). This is a long composition divided into some fourteen sections, in the course of which one meets many familiar *mahjar* themes. In the fourth section the poet is transported into the air, not by a flight of the imagination but by a strange flying machine: he makes the mistake of being too explicit about his means of transport to the realms of the stars and the spirits, and this rather weakens the effect of the poem as a whole. Nevertheless, there are moving and impressive sections when the poet enjoys a brief ecstatic union with his spirit, although it is difficult for the poem as a whole to recover from some of its more ludicrous effects.

There are two sides to the lasting significance of the poetry of the *mahjar*, especially that produced by the poets of the 'Pen Association'. First, it represents some of the finest romantic poetry written in Arabic. The fact that these poets were removed from immediate contact with their own societies meant that they were less inhibited by the dominant canons of literary taste that prevailed in Damascus, Beirut or Cairo. Hence they were freer to be more adventurous and innovative and this was the secret of much of their success: the language of poetry which flowed from their pens was a genuine new departure, as was recognized by Muḥammad Mandūr, although some of their irregularities in this context offended purists like al-ʿAqqād. The themes on which they wrote such as the duality of body and soul, the poet-prophet of grandiose isolation, or simply bewildered subjective malaise, changed the face of Arabic poetry during the period between the two world wars. With their preference for short simple metres and stanzaic forms, and their willingness to experiment with lines of irregular length, they paved the way for the formal revolutions that were to occur after World War II. Second, and even more crucial than the intrinsic value of their work, was the fact that their achievements did not pass unnoticed inside the Arab world. Had the opposite been true, much of their value as a literary movement would have been lost, for theirs was a pocket of immigrant culture which could not establish fruitful contacts with the surrounding English–American scene, and within a generation in America it was doomed to extinction. As it happened, much of their poetry and many of their theories did not remain cut off from the Arab world, where they had a catalytic effect of great importance for the subsequent development of romantic verse.

AḤMAD ZAKĪ ABŪ SHĀDĪ AND THE 'APOLLO' POETS

In September 1932, fourteen years after *al-Funūn* ceased publication in New York, there appeared in Egypt the first periodical in the Arab world to be devoted entirely to literature and the arts: this was the *Apollo* review which was published every month for the next two years until its closure in 1934. Al-ᶜAqqād complained bitterly about the adoption of such a 'western' title for a publication devoted to Arabic literature, but in the first issue he was politely but firmly put in his place by the editor and founder Aḥmad Zakī Abū Shādī (1892–1955). Also in 1932 the 'Apollo society' was formed, to improve and promote the cause of literature, and to help and increase cooperation between Arab writers both inside and outside Egypt. The whole spirit of the 'Apollo society' was quite unlike the movement represented by the 'Dīwān' poets who had become notorious for their biting critical dissociation from Shawqī and the neo-classical mode; nor did it resemble the 'Pen Association' in New York in that it was not a definite literary school of clearly defined characteristics which can be traced from author to author. In fact the 'Apollo society' was marked by a catholicity of literary tastes and types: its first president was Aḥmad Shawqī, and when he died in 1932 he was succeeded by Khalīl Muṭrān, while the general secretary was Abū Shādī himself. The creation of the society was a clear attempt to bridge the factionalism and quarrels which bedevilled the political and cultural life of newly independent Egypt, and despite the broad range of its membership 'Apollo' became the natural centre of attraction for some of the most significant Arab romantic poets. Khalīl Muṭrān was especially revered by the 'Apollo' group and was recognized as the key figure, which he undoubtedly was, with generous tributes being paid to his innovative work by Abū Shādī and other associates.

Aḥmad Zakī Abū Shādī was a man of such amazing output and varied talents that concise evaluations will rarely do him justice. On completing his secondary education in 1911 he entered the School of Medicine in Cairo, but remained there for only a short time. This was a time of poor health and emotional crisis: he was deeply affected by an unsuccessful love affair when the woman of his affections married another man, but the effects of this trauma remained with him long afterwards. This woman appears in his poetry under the name 'Zaynab', which is the title of one of his collections published in 1924, and she remained one of his most consistent sources of inspiration throughout his career. Between 1912–22 he pursued his medical studies in England, and developed the varied list of his consuming passions – literature, painting and bee-keeping. After his return in 1922 he became one of the most gifted members of the new Egyptian intelligentsia, achieving distinction in literature and in scientific and academic life: he was the moving spirit behind a number of scientific and agricultural societies, and was appointed to the Chair of Bacteriology at the University of Alexandria in 1942. The combination of the death of his wife and a disillusioned feeling that his own society did not really accord him proper recognition led to his emigration to the United States in 1946. Apart from forming the 'Apollo society' and editing the review, he was the author of some nineteen collections of verse, several scripts intended as operas, plus a number of translations and literary studies.

His earliest major *dīwān*, 'Dewdrops of dawn' (*Andāʾ al-fajr*), was first published in 1910 and reprinted in 1934 with some late additions which were obviously not included in the original edition. The dedication dated July 1934 is to the woman Zaynab who became the *leitmotiv* of so much of his poetry:

Twenty-five years have passed away, and still the flame of my love leaps and flickers.
I still remain that maddened youth, with pounding heart.
Memories of love and its frenzied visions parade before me sleeping and awake.
She is part of me, so how can I forsake her? Oh welcome to imagination, by which I hold and touch.[20]

Of particular interest in this *dīwān* is the contrast between amatory verse such as 'First love' ('*al-Ḥubb al-awwal*'), 'Time of passion' ("*ʿAhd al-ṣabābah*') and 'After separation' ('*Baʿda 'l-firāq*'), poems which are laden with traditional cliché-ridden lines about unrequited love, and the short lyrical pieces which are notable for their uncomplicated language and are vibrant with powerful emotion. Typical of these are 'Daughters of autumn' ('*Banāt al-kharīf*'), 'Inspired by rain' ('*Waḥy al-maṭar*') and 'Adoration' ("*ʿIbādāt*'):

What ails my eye that it weeps for joy when we meet?
Is it because of joy or rather for dread that my dream will be shattered?
I have a hope which is undying, yet a hope which does not shine.
Like a troubled bewildered man, I take flight in the refuge of the visions of the mind.[21]

Such themes were continued in *Zaynab* (1924), the first *dīwān* Abū Shādī published after his return from England and which he subtitled 'Breaths of lyrical poetry chosen from the verse of youth'. Through this love poetry he

[20] A.Z. Abū Shādī, *Andāʾ al-fajr*, Cairo, 1934, p. 5.

[21] Abū Shādī, *Andāʾ al-fajr*, p. 63.

made a particularly important contribution to the more general development of the romantic movement. To be sure, a great deal of amatory poetry had been written previously by Muṭrān and the 'Dīwān' poets but, with the exception of some of Shukrī's work, this was an area in which Arabic poetry was not yet distinguished by any great originality. The theme of unrequited love predominated and it did so in a manner which rarely departed from the pattern of the rhetoric of old Arabic amatory verse. Unrequited love was also the basis of most of Abū Shādī's love poetry, but through his simple and relatively unaffected poetic diction, and the intense and subtle analysis of all the finer shades of his emotional states, he created a genuine new departure, putting aside the conventional imagery associated with this age-old theme. It is striking that in a number of the 'Zaynab' poems, he invests his beloved with strongly spiritual qualities as his feelings rise to heights of platonic intensity:

Be, oh my angel, an ideal of purity which brings me close to your God . . .
My feelings, my passion, my all, are pledged to that which is most perfect and beautiful in you.[22]

Obviously this is more reminiscent of the spiritual love associated with the romantic poetry of western Europe rather than with the mainstream, highly sensual Arabic amatory verse, but on occasions Abū Shādī achieves a splendid fusion of the ethereal and the physical, so combining the best of both traditions.

Throughout his career, Abū Shādī continued to produce this love poetry which is one of the most satisfying aspects of his work, but it represents only a small portion of his overall output as a poet. A major problem in dealing with him is that most of his omnivorous interests are present in the vast corpus of his poetry. 'Poems on Egypt' (*Miṣriyyāt*), also published in 1924, celebrates the author's romantic patriotism and his veneration of Saᶜad Zaghlūl, and remind the reader of his profound commitment to social and political issues. Although Abū Shādī's lasting contribution was to the development of romantic poetry both in his own work and in the inspiration and encouragement he gave to others, he also played to the full the traditional role of the poet in this cultural milieu: thus in the *dīwān* 'Moans and reverberations' (*Anīn wa ranīn*, 1925) he frequently appears as a social versifier, with pieces written in honour of friends and those whom he admires; there is an exchange of correspondence in verse between him and his friend and mentor Khalīl Muṭrān, as well as a number of 'occasional' poems. Being one of the great polymaths of his age, in common with other noted intellectuals of his generation, Abū Shādī took seriously his role as

[22] A.Z. Abū Shādī, *Zaynab*, Cairo, 1924, p. 16.

educator of friends, associates and the literate public at large: many of his *dīwāns* are much more than collections of poetry, also containing numerous articles and critical commentary on poetry, literature and a wide range of cultural topics in which the fine arts were usually accorded a prominent place. He rarely lost an opportunity to inform, and to stimulate debate and discussion, to the extent that some of his *dīwāns* look more like literary and cultural reviews than volumes of poetry. The *Apollo* magazine which he started in 1932 was more or less a monthly continuation of the type of publication he had already produced in his own books of verse.

The huge tome 'The weeping twilight' (*al-Shafaq al-bākī*, 1926–7) runs to some 1,336 pages and sheds some light on why Abū Shādī apparently felt it necessary to treat such large numbers of themes and topics in his verse, ludicrous though many of them now appear. Man of letters and scientist as he was, Abū Shādī was more aware than most of the sheer complexities faced by a twentieth-century society seeking dramatic transformation and change as was the case with Egypt. Yet it seems he wanted to see poetry continue the role it had always played in pre-modern society, as a sort of 'public register' of Arab life, even though his was a society in the throes of modernization. The neo-classical poets had already tried to cope with a range of thematic demands which was too great for their medium to handle, while at the same time the Arabic language and literature found new scope in journalism, novels, short stories and plays. In spite of this, Abū Shādī continued to insist on poetry as the public register of Arab life: perhaps he saw it as a means of fusing together such disparate pursuits as science, philosophy and literature, and thought that he could break down the barriers of the alienating specializations which are a necessary feature of modern life. He himself was a lively example of modern Egyptian renaissance man as bacteriologist, painter, poet and bee-keeper, and he strove to make his poetry a medium through which such different figures could communicate. Throughout 'The weeping twilight' there are manifestoes in verse on all manner of subjects: literature, art, social problems, science and religion, alongside the romantic pieces of intimate love poetry or meditative verses in which he communes with nature. Many of his *dīwāns* present a similar mixture of romantic poetry of considerable quality and originality which is often almost lost amidst numerous passages of 'verse journalism' which are no more felicitous than they had been when produced by Aḥmad Shawqī or Ḥāfiẓ Ibrāhīm.

The early years of the 1930s when the 'Apollo society' was formed and the monthly review began its publication, coincided with a period of astonishing productivity on the part of Abū Shādī the poet, as no fewer than five major *dīwāns* appeared between 1931 and 1935. Collections such as

'Rays and shadows' (*Ashi*^{cc} *ah wa ẓilāl*, 1931) or 'Spring phantoms' (*Aṭyāf al-rabī*^{c}, 1933) are eloquent testimony to the enormous breadth of their author's cultural learning and his desire to disseminate this culture as widely as possible. 'Rays and shadows' demonstrates one of his favourite techniques in that the book is full of reproductions of paintings, most of them European but including some by Egyptian contemporaries, and Abū Shādī provides poems on the subjects treated in the canvasses. Most of the *dīwāns* from this period are lavishly illustrated with themes from classical mythology, Biblical stories, Ancient Egyptian motifs, western art and a certain number of contemporary Egyptian paintings. The nude female form was one of the most popular subjects of these illustrations, being presented with a frequency and frankness that were astonishing for this time and context. Whilst the quality of the poetry during these years was highly uneven, these volumes are a tribute to the great cultural adventure and voyage of broadminded liberal discovery which the 'Apollo' movement undoubtedly was. It was inevitable that Abū Shādī and his group would arouse the ire and enmity of the more conservative and prejudiced sections of his society, which were unable to stomach the broad-minded revolutionary nature of his general artistic endeavour: in December 1934 the *Apollo* review ceased publication because of lack of financial backing and political pressure. Unlike most of the leading intellectuals of his generation, Abū Shādī eschewed active involvement in politics and strove to avoid the polemical factionalism which at the time bedevilled the discourse of literary criticism in Egypt. In one of the last numbers of *Apollo* to appear he wrote:

> Perhaps one of the most important principles that *Apollo* has promoted is freedom from the rivalry for the leading positions in poetry which youth used to worship, and the spreading of the spirit of truth and personal respect amongst that youth which is the hope of the present and the future, and on which we depend for the continuation of the Renaissance.[23]

Following the disappearance of the *Apollo* magazine, the previous vast output of Abū Shādī's verse was drastically curtailed, and the last twenty years of his life are represented by only two *dīwāns* in Arabic, 'Return of the shepherd' (^{c}*Awdat al-rā*^{c}*ī*), published privately in Alexandria in 1942, and 'From the heavens' (*Min al-samā*$^{\supset}$), which was published in New York in 1949. Not surprisingly, the poems written prior to his emigration in 1946 are clouded by a sense of rejection and disappointment at the lack of fulfilment of his hopes and the lack of appreciation accorded him inside Egypt. Because the corpus of his poetry was so vast and extremely uneven

[23] *Apollo*, September 1934.

in type and quality, it is not always easy to focus clearly on the important contributions that he made to the general development of romantic verse, especially in his love poetry and nature poetry. But although he suffered great personal disappointment, his achievement in creating the 'Apollo society' and its periodical had an importance out of all proportion to their brief existence. Through the spirit of *Apollo*, something of Abū Shādī's own magnanimity, liberal nature and all-embracing cultural tastes were introduced into Arabic literature and society, and a great impetus was lent to the romantic movement as a whole.

Ibrāhīm Nāgī (Najī) (1898–1953) and ʿAlī Maḥmūd Ṭāhā (1902–1949)

One of the lasting contributions which Abū Shādī made to Egyptian culture was the encouragement and patronage which he and the 'Apollo society' afforded to previously unrecognized poets. In the preface to 'Spring phantoms', tribute is paid to this fact by Ibrāhīm Nāgī, the vice-president of the 'Apollo society' and one of the most impressive of Abū Shādī's Egyptian disciples. He was born into a relatively comfortable and cultured family, and is said to have been familiar with English, French and German literature, although the predominant influence which appears in his work is that of nineteenth-century French romantic poetry. He qualified as a doctor, graduating from the School of Medicine in Cairo in 1923. He was the author of three volumes of verse, the first of which appeared in 1934, the last year of publication of *Apollo*. This was 'Behind the clouds' (*Warāʾ al-ghamām*) and is the most impressive of the three. The second collection was 'Nights of Cairo' (*Layālī 'l-Qāhirah*), the title being derived from a series of poems in the book which were almost certainly inspired by *Les Nuits* of Alfred de Musset. These poems were composed during the war in 1944, but they appeared in a *dīwān* with this title in 1951, along with other poems. The third volume is a posthumous collection, 'The wounded bird' (*al-Ṭāʾir al-jarīḥ*), published in 1957.

Largely through the work of Abū Shādī, the romantic love poem came into its own in modern Arabic, for although this had been an important theme in the poetry of both Muṭrān and the 'Dīwān' poets, it was by no means the most convincing part of their work. With the romantic poets of the 'Apollo' group, amatory poetry reached new heights of frankness combined with subtlety of expression, and in the case of Nāgī, his love poetry is certainly the outstanding element in his work; in this respect he forms an interesting contrast with many of his contemporaries in Egypt and beyond. One result of the romantic reaction against the classical conventions that prevailed in old Arabic amatory verse was a tendency towards idealization, or something akin to the European tradition of confusing the human and the divine in the transmuting experience of love. This was certainly true of much *mahjar* poetry, and was also a feature of romantic poetry inside the Arab world. But while it is not totally absent from Nāgī's work, for him the significant experiences in love were anything but disembodied, ethereal and non-human. His love poems are indeed full of frustration and lack of fulfilment, but the fact that he was usually dissatisfied in love did not lead him to seek consolation in the realms of the spirit. His work is warm and human with strong strains of that sensuality found in so many of his classical predecessors.

Nāgī's love poetry can be divided into two broad categories: there are numerous short pieces which concentrate on reproducing some moment of joyful, amorous dalliance or which describe some aspect of the pleasurable physical experiences of love. Then there are the longer works in which his love is situated in the wider, less happy context of the personal problems which beset the romantic poet: he grows old and his youthful pleasures become a thing of the past, like a mirage in which he can no longer believe. He is powerless against the advances of time and fate, which change him and his beloved beyond all recognition and destroy the joy they shared. Generally the mood of this second category is one of gentle melancholy and pessimistic longing. His short love lyrics are usually no more than six or seven lines in length, but many are masterpieces of complex suggestion and expression: 'Analysis of a kiss' ('*Taḥlīl qublah*') compresses all the implied questions and conflicting emotions aroused when two lovers meet after a long absence:

My mouth spreads the secret of passion to one who is kissed; I am generous in spirit with it, not withholding.
If you are in doubt, ask the kiss which divulged every hidden secret:
The secret talk of passion, the renewal of trust; the dispersal of fancies, the dispelling of suspicions.
The complaints of burning passion, and violent illness; sleepless eyelids and the enduring of years.[24]

A notable feature of the longer, more complex poems in which the pleasures of love are often engulfed by the attendant problems of the romantic poet, is that Nāgī uses themes and imagery which have their roots in the classical Arab heritage. Desert scenery is an important source of inspiration for him as he adapts traditional motifs with great skill to satisfy the modern mentality. His well-known poem, 'The return' ('*al-ᶜAwdah*') combines strong echoes of classical Arabic with the spirit of modern

[24] *Dīwān Nāgī* (edited by Aḥmad Rāmī, Ṣāliḥ Jawdat, Aḥmad ᶜAbd al-Maqṣūd Haykal and Muḥammad Nāgī), Cairo, 1961, p. 321.

romanticism: the poet revisits a house which had belonged to friends of his and in which he had enjoyed love, beauty and happiness. He laments the fact that all has been changed by the ravages of time, not in the terms of the old Arab poets who bemoaned the passing of former joys over the ruins of some encampment, but more after the manner of Lamartine in poems such as *Le lac* or *Milly ou La terre natale*:

Oh woe for what time has done to us. And are you then this frowning ruin?
And I this ghost with downcast head? How harsh is the duress we have endured.
Where is the group, where the chatter? Where your happy people? and my friends?
Wherever I turn my gaze, tears leap to my eye, and it mists over . . .
You are my abode, but I am an outcast, banished for ever in the world of my distress.
If I return, then I return to quiet communion; and then depart when my glass is empty.[25]

Titles such as 'Separation' ('*al-Firāq*') and 'Standing by a house' ('*Waqfah ʿalā dār*') both evoke echoes of the classical tradition of amatory poetry, and even more so Nāgī's poem 'The ruins' ('*al-Aṭlāl*'), but the similarity to classical poetry ends with the title: this is a long lament in simple, moving language, not over the ruins of the site of some former adventure, but over the symbolic ruins of his love affair with a woman who deceived him and left him desolate:

I have seen creation as a narrow tomb, in which reigned silence and despair.
My eye saw the deceptions of love, as flimsy as spiders' webs.
You used to lament for me and know my pain, if ever a silent statue could lament for tears.
At your feet a world ends. At your door hopes die.[26]

Nāgī's familiarity with some nineteenth-century French poets is obvious from the pages of his collected works: there are attractive translations from both Lamartine and de Musset, and he also published a book on Baudelaire with translations of selected poems from *Les Fleurs du Mal*. But in his own work the effects of Lamartine and de Musset are by far the most dominant, particularly in the numerous poems of unrelieved nostalgia in which he reflects on man's transience and impotence in the face of time and fate ('Thoughts of sunset' ('*Khawāṭir al-ghurūb*'), 'Rock of the rendezvous' ('*Ṣakhrat al-multaqā*'), 'Complaints of time' ('*Shakwā 'l-zaman*')). The series of poems 'Nights of Cairo', the conception of which seems to derive directly from de Musset, are described as records of the poet's impressions and experiences in World War II when the depression and fears of the times

[25] *Dīwān Nāgī*, pp. 39–40. [26] *Dīwān Nāgī*, pp. 344–5.

were reflected in the mood of the people. For Nāgī, the night and darkness are potent and omnipresent sources of inspiration and occur throughout his work with the same frequency as the desert motifs. In true romantic fashion, it inspires in him reactions of the deepest gloom and pessimism ('In the gloom' ('*Fī 'l-ẓalām*')), or else it is a refuge and haven in which he can seek solace from his suffering and hide from the perfidy of men ('The nights' ('*al-Layālī*')). Although in the final analysis there is a certain lack of variety in the thematic and emotional range of Nāgī's work, his verse presents some of the finest examples of Arabic romantic poetry at the height of its development. With his particular gift for fusing traditional Arabic themes and sources of imagery with the romantic sensibility derived from western Europe, he was a fine vindication of the 'Apollo' vision of the modern Arab renaissance poet.

The work of ʿAlī Maḥmūd Ṭāhā is a fine illustration of how effective the example of Abū Shādī had been, and it is also a culmination of some of the most typical features of romantic poetry in Arabic. Ṭāhā's most important *dīwān* 'The lost mariner' (*al-Mallāḥ al-tāʾih*, 1934) has the following few lines of dedication:

> To those who are attracted by the longing for the unknown,
> To those lost upon the sea of life,
> To the explorers of the deserted shore,
> I dedicate this *dīwān*.[27]

This prepares the reader for the poetry of romantic introspection which had been developed to such a high degree by the *mahjar*, expressions of extreme individual malaise which concentrate on perplexity, bewilderment and general estrangement from the rest of society. In the case of ʿAlī Maḥmūd Ṭāhā, this is combined with a powerful spirit of rebellious adventure and exciting sensuality. His language consists of suggestion, allusion and the ethereal, rather than the concrete and the explicit, and it is a marvellous creation of that sense of musical delight in Arabic verse which has been rivalled by only a few other poets, such as Aḥmad Shawqī or Nizār Qabbānī, in the twentieth century.

Like Ibrāhīm Nāgī, Ṭāhā was born into comfortable family circumstances and his writings show him to have been familiar with both English and French literature. His professional career was also non-literary, and he graduated as a construction engineer in 1924. His poetry is much more varied than that of Nāgī and is not confined to subjective lyrical pieces. 'Spirits and ghosts' (*Arwāḥ wa ashbāḥ*, 1942) is a long poetic drama in which

[27] ʿAlī Maḥmūd Ṭāhā, *al-Mallāḥ al-tāʾih*, Cairo, 1941, Dedication.

the characters and themes are taken from Greek legend and the Old Testament in a manner characteristic of the 'Apollo' members' wide-ranging cultural enthusiasms. 'Song of the four winds' (*Ughniyat al-riyāḥ al-arbaᶜ*, 1943) is also a poetic drama containing certain sections which are designed to be sung, strongly reminiscent of Abū Shādī's attempts to produce poetic librettos for operas, and which was inspired by a French translation of a pharaonic song. After Abū Shādī himself, Ṭāhā is the most complete representative of all that 'Apollo' stood for: his sources of cultural inspiration were anything but parochial, he was attracted by artistic experimentation and innovation, and he sought to widen the scope of conventions in life and art. His enthusiasm for European culture and society was a great source of liberation to him, and is constantly present in most of his work: large numbers of his poems are recollections of scenes of his travels in Europe, and in his book 'Vagrant spirits' (*Arwāḥ shāridah*, 1941) there are articles on Verlaine and Baudelaire, and a series of translations from Shelley, John Masefield, Osbert Sitwell and de Vigny. These are followed by prose passages recalling his memories and impressions of travels in Europe, containing much the same type of material as many of his poems. The *avant garde* nature of his life and literature attracted the attention of critics such as Ṭāhā Ḥusayn and Muḥammad Mandūr. Ṭāhā Ḥusayn in particular expressed a marked preference for his work over that of his colleague Ibrāhīm Nāgī, and Mandūr seems to regard him as the epitome of all that 'Apollo' stood for. While the range of Ṭāhā's work as a whole is undoubtedly greater than that of Nāgī, within the strictly limited realm of romantic lyrical verse it is not in fact markedly superior, although in its general choice of theme and diction there are significant differences.

If desert imagery was one of the recurrent motifs in the work of Ibrāhīm Nāgī, for ᶜAlī Maḥmūd Ṭāhā it is the sea which provides his inspiration more than any other natural phenomenon. In 'The lost mariner' he finds a suitable setting to describe the confused turmoil of his own thoughts and emotions in the tumult and swiftly changing moods of the sea. In such poems as 'To the sea' ('*Ilā 'l-baḥr*'), 'The lost mariner' ('*al-Mallāḥ al-tāʾih*') and 'On the white rock' ('ᶜ*alā 'l-ṣakhrah al-bayḍāʾ*'), the writer concentrates on reproducing moods and hints of visions which are only vaguely formulated in his mind:

I am alone, thirsting in your flowing depths, drowned in my bewilderment and doubt.
I look at the distant shore with an eye which sheds continuous tears in the gloom.[28]

[28] Ṭāhā, *al-Mallāḥ al-tāʾih*, from the poem 'To the sea', pp. 176–7.

The concept of the 'unknown shore' or the 'distant shore' seems to represent an unattainable goal to which Ṭāhā constantly aspires:

I heard the roar of the sea around me, and there surged within me the emotions of a turbulent heart of foaming depth.
I stood filling my thoughts with them, as though my mind swam to the shore of the unknown.[29]

The theme of lonely isolation exemplified above was of course commonplace in the register of romantic expression, for the *mahjar* poets had developed it to a particular pitch of intensity. 'The outcast' ('*al-Ṭarīd*') presents some of Ṭāhā's strongest feelings of alienation, but this piece is interesting in that it is more than usually explicit about the causes of his distress. The familiar figure of bewildered perplexity wanders around as though a voice is summoning him to the 'unknown shore', and when asked to explain his distressed condition, he replies:[30]

I summoned to freedom of thought a people whose culture was a false sort of knowledge.

However, this call to freedom of thought and expression was not heeded, and this left the poet bitter and frustrated. One of the motives for his constant search was to find a place where his advice and example would be appreciated, and where he himself would not feel restrained by his immediate environment. This frustration with the constraints imposed by the parochial elements in his society and culture was certainly echoed by Abū Shādī in poems such as 'The *muʾadhdhin*' and 'Our environment' ('*Bīʾatunā*') in his *dīwān* 'Rays and shadows' (pp. 36 and 42), and of course these were the problems which the 'Apollo society' ultimately was unable to overcome.

As an individual ʿAlī Maḥmūd Ṭāhā found considerable liberation in the frequent trips to Europe which he began to make from 1938 onwards, and which he celebrates in his second *dīwān* 'Nights of the lost mariner' (*Layālī 'l-mallāḥ al-tāʾih*, 1940). The descriptions of Venice, Lake Como, Zurich and the Rhine are very different from the highly suggestive, evocative scenes of the melancholy seas, lakes and valleys of his first *dīwān*. There the poet used those natural backgrounds to touch off anguished expressions of his suffering in love and in life, but the portraits of Europe serve as attractive impressionistic scenes of pursuits of pleasure which are relatively uncomplicated by any ambiguous feelings of guilt or remorse. One result of the new mood of liberated hedonism is that Ṭāhā begins to write love poetry of powerful exciting sensuality: the spirit of the poem 'The amorous

[29] Ṭāhā, *al-Mallāḥ al-tāʾih*, from the poem 'On the white rock', p. 57.
[30] Ṭāhā, *al-Mallāḥ al-tāʾih*, p. 187.

moon' (*'al-Qamar al-ʿāshiq'*) would have been quite familiar to many poets in classical Arabic, but its language is exclusively of the twentieth century:

> When the thin light of the moon wanders around the balcony,
> And shimmers over you like a dream or the ray of a thought,
> Whilst you are on the bed of purity like a slumbering lily,
> Then hold your naked body, and guard that beauty . . .
> I am jealous, I am jealous, if it kisses this mouth or enfolds it,
> And softly envelops the bosom, and clasps the supple body.
> Its light has a heart, and its charm has an eye,
> Which hunts the virgin ripple from its depths by night.[31]

Some of Ṭāhā's shorter amatory pieces can be compared with the brief love-lyrics of Ibrāhīm Nāgī and are equally concrete and immediate, leaving little scope for vague suggestive effect or mystery to tease the imagination (see 'Dream of a night' (*'Ḥulm laylah'*) or 'She' (*'Hiya'*)). They often occur in an atmosphere of alcoholic intoxication, a trend which is emphasized even more in 'Flowers and wine' (*Zahr wa khamr*, 1943), the *dīwān* which appeared after Ṭāhā had written his studies on European poets ('Vagrant spirits') and the dramatic narrative 'Spirits and ghosts'. This collection develops further the trend of carefree hedonism which became apparent in 'Nights of the lost mariner': showing all his talents for brilliant impressionistic description, Ṭāhā creates vivid scenes of night-long revels in taverns with wine, dancing girls and drinking companions. Both 'Nights of the lost mariner' and 'Flowers and wine' leave a dominant image of a man revelling in his pleasures and passions in scenes of unrestrained hedonism, but with 'The return of passion' (*al-Shawq al-ʿāʾid*, 1945) this obsessive concentration on the heat of the moment becomes tempered by retrospective reflection which is inevitably melancholic in its undertones. 'Question and answer' (*'Suʾāl wa jawāb'*) introduces a sense of reckoning for this life of pleasure: a woman companion interrogates the poet about his past loves and he is moved to give some explanation for his previous conduct and his present state:

> A heart which was wretched, and had lost its way in the world, enticed me to delights.
> I return as you see addicted to a glass; I have a thirst the fire of which is unquenched . . .
> She said: 'What is your life?' and I said: 'A dream of passions which I prefer to prolong.
> My life is a story which began with a glass to which I sang, and a beautiful woman.'[32]

[31] ʿAlī Maḥmūd Ṭāhā, *Layālī 'l-mallāḥ al-tāʾih*, Cairo, 1943, pp. 10–11.
[32] Quoted in Suhayl Ayyūb, *ʿAlī Maḥmūd Ṭāhā, shiʿr wa dirāsah*, Damascus, 1962, pp. 441–2.

The poet's own comments on the nature of his career in love and in art are supported by the vast majority of his lyrical poems, and the example of his life and work struck many chords amongst his contemporaries in Egypt and elsewhere. His bohemian attitude to the prevailing manners and customs of his own milieu, his enthusiasm for all aspects of the good life in Europe and the exciting sensuality of his love poetry found an avid public in Near and Middle Eastern societies where sexual repression remained a constant factor in the lives of young people. All this and the magical musicality of his verse combined to make him the major cult figure in Arabic poetry in the inter-war period.

Ilyās Abū Shabakah (1903–47)

While some of the most dramatic contributions to the development of romantic poetry were made by the *mahjar* poets in New York and subsequently by the 'Apollo group' in Egypt, other poets in Syria and Lebanon such as ᶜUmar Abū Rīshah, Ṣalāḥ Labakī and Bishārah al-Khūrī were also establishing high reputations as proponents of the new style of lyrical verse. Of all the Syrian and Lebanese poets who were active in their native countries, Ilyās Abū Shabakah is outstanding for the range and variety of his work: in a manner reminiscent of Īlyā Abū Māḍī or ᶜAbd al-Raḥmān Shukrī, one can trace his evolution from beginnings which have strong echoes of the classical Arabic tradition to a creative flowering of great originality and individuality. Abū Shabakah was actually born in the USA of Christian Lebanese parents, but while in his infancy his parents returned to Lebanon where he spent most of the rest of his life. He had a full and varied career as a teacher, writer, journalist and translator, and he was an ardent francophile, an enthusiasm that was already evident in his first *dīwān* of poetry, 'The lyre' (*al-Qīthārah*, 1926), although at this stage this took the form of translations rather than having a discernible impact on his own creative work. 'The lyre' is the longest of his *dīwāns*, and gives clear indications of the young poet's debt to the classical tradition. It is dedicated to the spirit of his father who was murdered when Abū Shabakah was only ten, and indeed there is little in the book about the joys of life: the dominant strains are of melancholy and pessimism, and there is a constant impression of a young man who is under the influence of a sage who is older, wiser and sadder than himself:

How many princes and kings have gone, swallowed up by darkness and tombs?
While the blind al-Maᶜarrī still is alive, and the blind al-Maᶜarrī was poor.[33]

[33] Ilyās Abū Shabakah, *al-Qīthārah*, Beirut, 1926, p. 5.

Throughout this collection there is a general air of world-weary pessimism strongly reminiscent of the great blind poet of the tenth century (see 'Song of glory' ('*Ughniyat al-majd*'), 'Song of death' ('*Ughniyat al-mawt*') or 'Above the cemetery' ('*Fawqa 'l-maqbarah*')), all of which seems to lay a premature burden on the shoulders of the youthful poet. Apart from ponderous speculations about the lack of virtue in the world, there are poems on political issues, the main theme of which is the lack of freedom and liberty in Lebanon, and love poems which tend to emphasize the deceit and disappointment which can play a large part in such experiences. Once again there is a strong sense of an older person talking through Abū Shabakah, warning him of the pitfalls of love in a clear tone of misogyny:

> Beware of love! In love there is evil, a melting fire in the heart.
> If there is a deceitful heart in men, then the hearts of women are more so.[34]

At this stage, the poet seems able to accept the pains of love and life in the hope of God's mercy and the ultimate release of death. The same melancholic philosophy informs his earliest attempt at narrative poetry, 'The silent invalid' (*al-Marīḍ al-ṣāmit*, 1928), a tragic tale of two lovers whose affair is brought to an end by the premature death from tuberculosis of the young man.

The next phase in Abū Shabakah's work is represented by the two volumes, 'Serpents of Paradise' (*Afāʿī 'l-firdaws*, 1938), which contains thirteen poems written between 1928 and the date of publication, and the narrative poem 'Olga' (*Ghalwāʾ*), which was written between 1926 and 1932. The preface to 'Serpents of paradise' places the author firmly in the ranks of the romantics in terms of his beliefs on the nature of poetry and the creative process. The theories of the *mahjar* poets are echoed in his remarks on the primacy of inspiration and the role of the soul: inspiration is one of the conditions of the soul when it is in direct contact with a supernatural power, and the poet becomes the medium for this supernatural power, just as the prophets were. Thus this supernatural power is not cut off from man but is the essence of his soul. In the creative process, visible phenomena of the world fuse with this essence, while all the senses share in the process. The major influence under which a poet falls is that of his soul, and the soul is a power that cannot be apprehended by definition. Second only to the importance of inspiration via the soul is nature: this is the proper spatial environment for the poet, and his feelings are formed according to what he sees there. Abū Shabakah makes a strong attack on Paul Valéry for denying the value of inspiration in the creative process, and dismisses Valéry's insistence that the art and craft of the poet reduce him to the level of a

34 Abū Shabakah, *al-Qīthārah*, p. 35.

carpenter or a smith, who is the one who acts, not the one who is acted upon, by other forces. The preface is a typical romantic reaction to the rational theoretical view of poetry represented by Valéry: it is the reaction of one for whom the expression of immediate feeling and emotion in poetry is the prime consideration, an expression which should be as far as possible unhindered by anything outside those feelings.

The transition from 'The lyre' to 'Serpents of Paradise' and 'Olga' is both shocking and dramatic. The naive puritanical morality which had sustained him during his juvenile years was no match for the complexes and pressures which gripped him as he sought to cope with the effects of an affair with a married woman, during his long engagement to Olga, the fiancée who lent her name to the narrative poem. A sense of sin and spiritual debasement surrounds his inability to control the animal passions of sexual lust, and this dominates most of the thirteen poems. Biblical subjects such as Sodom illustrate the depravity of mankind, and the story of Samson and Delilah (strongly reminiscent of de Vigny's poem on the same subject) provides ambiguous images of strength and degradation, nobility and treachery, as the night of death follows the morning of love, and the soft space between Delilah's breasts leads Samson to the abyss of his doom:

The flame died in the master of the forest, the victorious prince of the caverns.
And the great one, the great one, is weakened by a female, and is led like the lowly, the lowly!
Flatter him, for in the rays of your eyes is the morning of love and the night of the tombs.
On your beautiful lips are fruits which concealed the lust of death in their juice.
Flatter him, for between your breasts the abyss of death yawned on the comfortable bed.[35]

There could be no greater contrast than that which exists between this phase of Abū Shabakah's work and the tendency to idealize both women and the experience of love which was typical of many of the other Arab romantics. For them love was usually a holy, mystical experience of a particularly elevating kind, while for Abū Shabakah the animality of sexual passion drags him down to the very dregs of sinful existence ('In the temple of lusts' ('*Fī haykal al-shahawāt*'), 'Red lust' ('*al-Shahwah al-ḥamrā*ʾ')). The colour red creates potent associations with evil, derived from the heat of passion, the red of wine, or the burning of his lust which tortures him like a flame. His work is possessed of sinister depths which go far beyond the happy hedonism of ʿAlī Maḥmūd Ṭāhā: 'Filth' ('*al-Qādhūrah*') is frightening in the strength of its horrific visions. As the poet awakes from dreaming of a world of enchantment and delight, he looks at the world of real life:

35 Ilyās Abū Shabakah, *Afāʿī 'l-firdaws*, Beirut, 1948, p. 22.

I wandered in a flood of night, whilst obscenity dinned round about, and filth fumed and foamed.
There is a simmering in the boiling mire, and a lather; as though men were a sighing bog.
I thrust my glance into the solid gloom, with a rasp of lashes in each of my eyes . . .
Filthy things walk joyfully through life, singing; and the echoes of the tombs call back.
They are the people of the world, stuffed phantoms. I wept for them in my hell, and they made merry.[36]

A notable feature of these poems of surrealistic horror is that the poet does not stand apart in splendid isolation; there is no suggestion of moralizing or withdrawal from this world of sin. In contrast to the ivory-tower speculation about the evils of man and civilization typical of the *mahjar* poets or of ʿAbd al-Raḥmān Shukrī, Abū Shabakah himself is part of the degradation and corruption. The scenes of defilement cause him to despair on his own account as well as for others.

The narrative poem 'Olga' was written between 1926 and 1932 when Abū Shabakah was also producing some of the most powerful poems in 'Serpents of paradise'. It was inspired by the poet's fiancée, Olga, to whom he had a long engagement of some ten years before they were finally able to marry, and once again it is a poem obsessed by the ambiguities and duality of love. The action is divided into four sections which alternate subtly between the world of reality and the dreams and imaginations of Ghalwāʾ and Shafīq, who falls in love with her. The poem proceeds through the psychological crises and illness of Ghalwāʾ, who struggles to reconcile her sense of female sexuality and lust with her undoubted aspiration to purity and virtue. It ends with a scene of redemption in which the lovers are united and Ghalwāʾ finally comes to terms with both her sexuality and her desire to live a life of virtue. This is probably the most accomplished and original narrative poem of the whole romantic period; with its concentration on the painful awareness of the latent power of evil in love, it is a fascinating complement to 'Serpents of paradise'.

The scene of redemption which forms the finale of 'Olga' is an apt symbol for the later stages of Abū Shabakah's career, represented by a further narrative poem 'To eternity' (*Ilā 'l-abad*, 1944), and the *dīwāns* 'The melodies' (*al-Alḥān*, 1941) and 'Call of the heart' (*Nidāʾ al-qalb*, 1944). One other volume, 'From the gods above' (*Min ṣaʿīd al-ālihah*) was published posthumously in 1959, and consists entirely of elegies written on other poets. After the trials and the tortures of his journeys through the worlds of sin and vice, Abū Shabakah emerges with his faith and belief in love intact.

36 Abū Shabakah, *Afāʿī ʾl-firdaws*, pp. 26–7.

Nature now reverts to its former benign self and becomes once again the source of joy and solace; on occasion the poet seems to find something of the peace of God in the harmony and repose afforded by nature. Although sadness and the pains of love are in no sense absent from these later *dīwāns*, the poet now believes much more in its saving grace than did the man who wrote about Delilah's perfidy and the destructive forces of animal passion. Nevertheless it is to 'Serpents of paradise' and 'Olga' that Abū Shabakah owes the major part of his reputation: he represented a quite new experience for modern Arabic poetry as he wrestled with the problems posed by his physical lusts and his conscience in the face of sin, identifying fully with the evil and suffering around him. One senses in 'Serpents of paradise' a strong influence from Baudelaire and *Les Fleurs du Mal*, as Abū Shabakah explored ruthlessly and honestly the conflicts within himself between good and evil, not trying to set himself apart from the enquiry. In spite of the reconciliations evident in his later works, for his whole generation he was the embodiment of the *poète maudit*.

Abū 'l-Qāsim al-Shābbī (1909–1934)

An important achievement of the 'Apollo society' and its periodical was that their influence was not restricted to Egyptian literature and Egypt, and Abū Shādī's call for cooperation between Arab writers from other countries meant more than paying lip-service to a principle. One of the most outstanding contributors to *Apollo* from outside Egypt was the Tunisian poet Abū 'l-Qāsim al-Shābbī: the first direct reference to him in the periodical appeared in March 1933 with a review by Mukhtār al-Wakīl of al-Shābbī's printed lecture 'The poetic imagination and the Arabs' (*al-Khayāl al-shiᶜrī ᶜinda 'l-ᶜarab*, Tunis, 1929); and in the April 1933 number, two of al-Shābbī's poems were published, 'Prayers in the temple of love' ('*Ṣalawāt fī haykal al-ḥubb*') and 'Happiness' ('*al-Saᶜādah*'). There is a brief foreword to Abū Shādī's *dīwān* 'The fountain' (*al-Yanbūᶜ*) written by al-Shābbī, full of his admiration for and appreciation of the founder of *Apollo*. In his work there are clear signs of influence from both *mahjar* literature and the 'Apollo' group, and although some of his themes are clearly derivative from these sources, this pales into insignificance before his own great poetic talents. Al-Shābbī had a traditional Islamic upbringing and education at the Zaytounah mosque-university in Tunis, where he gained a thorough training in the classical Arabic language and literature. During his brief life he learned no foreign language, but he came to know other literatures through translations and was obviously well aware of the latest literary developments in Egypt and the *mahjar*. He died tragically young in 1934 of heart disease, having that same year begun to prepare for publication his single *dīwān* 'Songs of life' (*Aghānī 'l-ḥayāh*). The book was to have been published in Egypt, but his death intervened before work on the text was completed, and it was not finally published until 1955, when it came out in Tunis. Although this is the only volume by al-Shābbī, its quality is such as to make it something of a climax in the romantic poetry of the Arab world.

The themes of al-Shābbī's *dīwān* revolve consistently around the stuff of romantic lyrical verse: he concentrates deeply on the intimate problems of his own existence, his dissatisfaction and suffering in life, his loves, and the questions posed by death. Yet he rises above the limits of his own personality with visions of a rebirth or a redemption after life and death, and this he expresses frequently through the symbol of a new dawn breaking: thus in his imagination he tries to pass beyond the finite limits of his own person to grasp something which is more ideal and eternal, of which life on earth is a most imperfect imitation. Constant features of his poetry are images of light and darkness usually derived from the night and the dawn, expressed through language of a rare musicality in which the sound effects are an essential contribution to the overall artistic impact:

Oh night. You are a pleasant melody amongst the lamentation on the lips of time.
The song of the silence which trembles in your sluggish, spacious bosom
Makes the soul in the gentleness of desires hear the echo of truth and enchanting beauty.[37]

Although certain of his poems express visions of unrelieved melancholia ('Sad evening' ('*al-Masāʾ al-ḥazīn*'), 'In the gloom' ('*Fī 'l-Ẓalām*'), 'Oh night' ('*Ayyuhā 'l-layl*')), it is much more frequent to find the pure joyful dawn breaking over the dark brooding night, a symbol of a new start after the trials of life. 'New morning' ('*al-Ṣabāḥ al-jadīd*') is the epitome of his brief but glowing vision of the dawn of life after death. Written in 1933 when he was in the grip of his fatal illness, the poignancy of the vision in relation to his own situation is greatly increased. The poem is also an excellent illustration of how al-Shābbī took great care with the overall construction and development of even relatively short pieces, moving as it does from its hushed beginning to a final joyous crescendo:

From behind the clouds and the surge of the waters
I am called by the Morning and the Spring of life . . .
Farewell! Farewell! Oh mountains of trouble.
Oh mists of grief. Oh valleys of hell.[38]

The new morning is nothing less than a resurrection: pain has been buried in the valleys of death and his tears have been scattered to the winds of non-

[37] Abū'l-Qāsim al-Shābbī, *Aghānī 'l-ḥayāh*, Tunis, 1966, p. 75.
[38] al-Shābbī, *Aghānī 'l-ḥayāh*, p. 236.

existence. On occasion the symbol of the morning inspired the poet to intoxicating dream-like visions: 'Memory of a morning' ('*Dhikrā ṣabāḥ*') creates the image of a beautiful angelic figure singing with the birds through the morning mists, her long black tresses dancing in the breeze. He begs the tresses to enfold him for only thus when he is caught up by the vision of beauty and love can he feel free as a poet and an artist:

Shackle me in these locks, which are loose in the temptation of langorous coquetry.
Shackle my thoughts oh chains of love, and the dreams of my erring heart.
Shackle me with all the fragrance within you, and holy mysterious enchantment.
Shackle me, for the artist finds his freedom in the likes of these fetters.[39]

Of all the romantic poets, al-Shābbī's love poems are the most strongly spiritual and platonic, love being an emotion which enables him on earth to experience something approaching the ideal purity of Divinity. The tortured sensuality of Ilyās Abū Shabakah or the happy hedonism of ʿAlī Maḥmūd Ṭāhā form a complete contrast with the ethereal visions of al-Shābbī's female ideal. In fact the manner in which he portrays women is a direct result of his rebellion against certain aspects of his culture and society, and in particular their attitude to women in literature and in life. In 1929 he published his only critical essay, 'The poetic imagination and the Arabs', which had been delivered some time previously as an impassioned lecture to a somewhat shell-shocked audience in the Khaldūniyyah Institute. It was a bitter and undoubtedly extreme attack on indigenous Arab-Islamic culture:[40]

The attitude of Arabic literature to woman is base and ignoble and sinks to the lowest depths of materialism. It only sees in woman a body to be desired and one of the basest pleasures in life to be enjoyed . . . (p. 72)

Have you ever heard anyone among them [i.e. the Arab poets] talk about woman, who is the altar of love in this universe, in the way a devout worshipper talks about the house of God?

(p. 91; translation by M.M. Badawi)

So al-Shābbī reacted against the heavily physical conventions of the traditional Arab portrayal of woman's attributes with an excess of platonic spiritualism, and in this he was accompanied by many of his contemporaries. He took as his model and inspiration the highly idealized spiritual representations of love and woman which had been characteristic of European literature in its more intensely romantic phases. True to his

[39] al-Shābbī, *Aghānī 'l-ḥayāh*, p. 231.

[40] Quoted in M. M. Badawi: 'Convention and revolt in modern Arabic poetry' in *Arabic poetry, theory and development*, ed. G. E. von Grunebaum, Wiesbaden, 1973, p. 196.

word, he produced 'Prayers in the temple of love': here he gives free rein to his desire to elevate woman to a plane of ethereal adoration, as he would see it to compensate for centuries of degradation at the hands of Arab-Islamic tradition. The poem builds up from a beginning of quiet wonderment to a climax of adoration, as the repetitious rhythms of the lines produce an effect of religious incantation:

You . . . You are life in its heavenly holiness, in its unique pleasant enchantment.
You . . . You are life in the delicacy of the dawn, in the splendour of the new-born spring.
You . . . You are life at all times in a new freshness of youth.
You . . . You are life. In you and in your eyes are signs of its spreading magic.[41]

The poems about death which al-Shābbī wrote towards the end of his life stand in poignant relation to his own tragic situation, as he was increasingly dogged by his fatal disease ('Story of the cemetery' ('*Ḥadīth al-maqbarah*'), 'In the shadow of the valley of death' ('*Fī ẓill wādī 'l-mawt*')); ultimately he puts behind him all the sufferings and the painful mysteries he has endured in life and adopts a positive Promethean attitude to death in 'Song of the Colossus' ('*Nashīd al-jabbār*', 1933), written less than a year before he died. Death now holds no fear for him, and in what remains of his life, he will concentrate on the realms of the spirit and the emotions which are the poet's proper concern. The body is hastening towards physical destruction, but the disease can never fetter his proud spirit:

Despite the disease and my enemies, I shall live on like the eagle above the lofty summit,
Looking at the illuminating sun, mocking the clouds, the rains and the hurricanes,
Not beholding the despairing shadow, and not seeing what lies in the bottom of the black abyss.[42]

One of the great strengths of al-Shābbī's work is that while at one level it is intensely personal and subjective, it also has a strong element of external validity which applies to his whole society. There is a constant transition in his poetry from the mimetic to the symbolic. During the 1920s, the grip of the French Protectorate over Tunisia seemed depressingly permanent, and political opposition was both embryonic and ineffectual. The career of al-Shābbī, wracked as it was by physical and spiritual crises, can be seen as a symbol of the wider sufferings of the majority of his contemporaries. The body politic was in a palsied state, just as his own body was stricken with heart disease, yet small groups of activists still had faith and visions which

[41] al-Shābbī, *Aghānī 'l-ḥayāh*, p. 185. [42] al-Shābbī, *Aghānī 'l-ḥayāh*, p. 256.

transcended their reality just as al-Shābbī put his trust in resurrections and new dawns. His identification with the struggles of the Tunisian people is at its most obvious in one of his best-loved poems "Will to live' (*'Irādat al-ḥayāh'*) in which the characters are the elemental forces of nature: after a long winter in which the seeds remain locked beneath layers of fog, ice and clay, when even the sky seems to be extinguished, the earth is finally riven by the life, power and light of spring. The awakening seeds are blessed for their constant faith and they inherit the earth and the heavens. This is a poem which looks ahead to the works of the 1950s when poets used myths of fertility rites as symbols for the death and resurrection of their societies. Although his mode of expression was that of the romantic poet, al-Shābbī was an impassioned prophet of eschatalogical vision who foreshadowed the Tammūz poets of a later generation.

By no means all the romantic poets of note have been covered in detail in this brief survey: like al-Shābbī, there were other figures such as the Sudanese al-Tījānī Yūsuf Bashīr (1912–1937) and the Egyptian Muḥammad ᶜAbd al-Muᶜṭī al-Hamsharī (1908–1938) who had similarly brief Keats-like lives of remarkable creative brilliance, although they did not quite scale the same heights as their Tunisian contemporary. The Syrian ᶜUmar Abū Rīshah (b. 1910) retained strong links with the classical tradition and was in many ways the most politicized of all the romantics. His poem 'The eagle' (*'al-Nisr'*) was recognized throughout the Arab world as one of the most powerful artistic expressions of the difficult course of Syrian, and Arab, nationalism. Although romantic poetry was still being produced in the 1950s by poets such as Ṣāliḥ Jawdat and Maḥmūd Ḥasan Ismāᶜīl, by then it had become increasingly irrelevant in artistic terms. It belonged properly to that inter-war period of soaring aspiration when the countries of the Levant and the Nile Valley were gripped by the heady excitements of the possibilities that seemed to be offered to the new generation of Arab nation-states. In the event, the hopes and expectations of both societies and individuals were in many cases transformed to frustration and disillusion as the dreams of the 1920s became the nightmare of the 1930s and 1940s. Since the Second World War, there has been a tendency by poets and critics alike to undervalue the achievements of the romantic movement: partly it has been discredited by its association with those political systems and attitudes of mind which have gained little credit in the history of the modern Arab world; partly it has been damned by the faint praise of subsequent generations of poets who reacted strongly against it in their own work and who shared the tendency of many *avant garde* movements to deny their debts to their immediate predecessors. The fact remains that the romantic movement was the first wave of a genuinely modern sensibility which revolutionized the development of modern Arabic poetry and literature in general: it introduced a vital phase of flexibility and experimentation into both form and metre which prepared the way for the prosodic transformations of the late 1940s and early 1950s, and it created nothing less than a new language of poetry in Arabic. It is true that at its worst it indulged in language and concepts which created a delibeiate cult of the vague and the nebulous, and which seemed to thrive in an atmosphere of shallow sentimentalism and facile escapism. At its best, in the hands of its major practitioners such as Īlyā Abū Māḍī, ʿAbd al-Raḥmān Shukrī, Ilyās Abū Shabakah or Abū'l-Qāsim al-Shābbī, it created moving artistic expressions of the ecstasies and the painful dilemmas which held both individuals and whole societies in thrall.

CHAPTER 4

MODERNIST POETRY IN ARABIC

Arab poetic modernity resulted from two major forces: the influence of the western modernist movement and of the other major experiments that preceded or accompanied it, and the state of Arabic poetry itself at the mid-point of the twentieth century, which responded to intrinsic needs for a change towards a more 'modern' apprehension of experience, aesthetic and otherwise. Major poetic change in any language is never wholly a matter of intention; neither the result of sheer conscious adoption, nor the following of fashion. The success of a major poetic change in any direction, no matter how drastic, proves not simply that genius and cogent talents lie behind it, but also the important fact that poetry at the time was, if not absolutely and specifically in need of the kind of change in question, at least potentially receptive to it. The second of these factors, the intrinsic need for change, will be in evidence throughout this essay. However, the first factor, the influence of western modernism on the Arab movement, needs more explicit consideration before we continue further.

There is a clear ambiguity in Arab writings between 'modern' and 'modernism', which is a term applied to a specific movement in art and literature in the west. Western 'modernism' took place within a certain period of time (c. 1910–1930) and was consequential on modern developments in the west, often a protest against them.

Western modernism itself never attained a clear definition. However, there are certain tendencies and concepts that seem to sum up the general movement. Some of these were adopted, consciously or unconsciously, by some contemporary Arab poets, while others did not come to have any connection with the Arab movement, for reasons that I shall attempt to demonstrate in due course. However, before describing western modernism, I would hasten to point out a basic difference between the western movement and its poets, and the Arab movement and its poets. It must be remembered that the western poets were the immediate heirs of many great ideas and transformations which took place over a considerable time as a result of such major developments as the industrial revolution, the rise of technology, the spread of education and the circulation of many new ideas concerning man and his place in the universe. Western apprehension of all the changes that have taken place in the intellectual and material realms developed in a natural and gradual fashion, and the reaction to all this as expressed in art was congruent with the level of progress and the established presence of new concepts at the time. Indeed, it was this general cultural achievement, with its wealth of variety and nuances, its contradictions and uncertainties, its many highly multilayered interpretations of man and his universe, and its general ferment of intellectual investigation and controversy, that initially gave rise to the modernist movement. The greater stress in the western movement on the aesthetic aspects of modernism reflected the fact that the attitude towards man and his universe, embodying the newly acquired knowledge and discoveries in the fields of science and technology as well as in the humanities, and assimilating them as part of the cognitive wealth of the times, was not too much in question among the modernists themselves.

With the Arab movement, on the other hand, this was not the case, and the need for a modernized *outlook* free of medieval tendencies was imperative. The Arabs at the beginning of this century had just emerged from an almost medieval mode of life in the nineteenth century informed by a corresponding *Weltanschauung* governing mores, attitudes, and life in general. One of the basic prerequisites for any successful modern movement in Arabic was an *attitudinal* transformation away from this *Weltanschauung*, parallel to the aesthetic change in form, diction and metaphor.

WESTERN MODERNISM

Several cultural events, regarded as 'the intellectual basis of Modernism', took place in Europe prior to the rise of the movement, which did much to shape the modernist tendency by completely contradicting prior beliefs and concepts and introducing new interpretations of art, history and human experience.

Among the figures who contributed to this changed sensibility was Sir James Frazer. In *The Golden Bough* (1890) he wrote about the presence of archetypal rhythms in human life, in particular the rhythms of the birth and rebirth of the gods, proclaiming the capacity of myth to re-establish links with primal sources of experience in a world controlled by 'functional rationality'. The idea of death and rebirth, in Lionel Trilling's words, 'captivated the literary mind' of Europe, and Frazer's work led to 'extreme mental states, rapture, ecstasy, and transcendence'.[1] Darwin's concept of the origin of species challenged the very foundation of religious belief. Freud became, in Auden's words, 'a whole climate of opinion', and his description of the ineluctable conflict between nature and culture gave rise to the discomfort of civilization, the idea of the damage done to the life of the instinct. Marx exposed the exploitative nature of capitalist society and showed how it transformed 'personal worth into exchange value'. Nietzsche, who, for example, emphasized Dionysiac energy and rapture which civilized life tried to tame, who declared that God was dead, and who announced the concept of the Superman, had the most profound influence on western thought and literature. All these thinkers sought to disestablish communal reality, destroying at once the certainties of traditional culture and thus challenging the state of European civilization. This pervasive challenge to civilization lies at the very heart of western modernism.

European modernism was not a logical development, but an abrupt break with tradition. As it decomposed old frames of reference, violated expected continuities and broke away from familiar functions of language and conventions of form, it administered a 'shock' to literary sensibility which often involved a bleak outlook on history.[2] Trilling identifies it as 'the disenchantment of our culture with culture itself'.[3] Modernist literature occurred during large-scale industrialism and is, therefore, a literature of the city, where nature is largely abandoned and space is urban. The city is often seen by the poet as the ogre, the centre of corruption, injustice and crime. It became the specific milieu of this century and was described in antipathetic terms as the swarming, petrified, industrial wasteland of spleen and boredom. Western modernism is also linked with technology, the greatest product of the city which inspired not only the subject-matter and outlook, but the very aesthetic of the work: its form, style and diction.

The modernist movement is not only divorced from artistic tradition, but also from humanism. It is elitist and focuses on 'select' individuals who are capable of pure aesthetic experience, as opposed to those whom Ortega y Gasset calls 'the vulgar'.[4] It produces therefore a dehumanised art which has cut itself off from the natural relationship with reality, and would have no direct connection with the social or political world, but finds its expression primarily in the aesthetics of the work of art where 'the forms of

[1] 'On the modern element in modern literature', in *Beyond culture, essays in literature and learning*, London, 1966, republished in *The idea of the modern*, ed. Irving Howe, New York, 1967.

[2] See Malcolm Bradbury and James McFarlane, *Modernism, 1930–1980*, London, 1987, pp. 26, 30, *et passim*.

[3] Bradbury and McFarlane, *Modernism*, p. 82.

[4] See his original article, 'The dehumanisation of art', in *The dehumanisation of art and other essays*, London, 1972, reprinted in *The idea of the modern*, ed. Irving Howe, pp. 83–96.

the visible world . . . are treated solely as aesthetic necessities'. Thus recognizable human forms are 'no longer dependent on their specifically human expressiveness'. These features apply especially to painting and the plastic arts. In poetry, they appear primarily as a highly adventurous use of metaphor. 'The "substance" of the poem is no longer the reality which the metaphor expresses, but the metaphor itself crystallized into a curious linguistic world "distinct from human flora and fauna".' Realistic literature uses metaphor as decoration for the content of the poem, but modernist literature tends to 'realize the metaphor, to make it *res poetica*'.[5] The image became not only difficult, but often witty and hard, and modernist poetry is often derisive, negative and ironic. It breaks away from familiar functions of language and conventions of form. In a mechanistic, urban and middle-class order language has become cerebralized. The industrial order, mass democracy, the concept of efficiency, 'have destroyed the still point within the spirit', for technological society has demanded that people cultivate the conscious powers of their mind and will in order to deal with the linguistic anarchy created by the new age. Thus modern poetry is permeated by a sense of homelessness. The god, to use Pound's phrase, is locked inside the stone.[6]

Because the real world is felt to be fallen and suspect, the task of the modernist poet is to create a new language for poetry, redeemed and visionary. The poet

> abstracts words from their conventionalized place in speech and recombines them in such a way that their forgotten secondary potential – connotative properties, rhythmic and aural possibilities, similarities with other words, forgotten meanings – becomes primary. The traditional role of the adjective becomes suspect; the modern poet becomes disposed to use it not so much to describe the surface 'look' or 'feel' of a noun as to bring out its latent metaphorical dimensions . . . [liberating] the repressed expressive energies of language.[7]

Modernist literature reflects 'a prevailing, dominant or authentically contemporary view of the world by those artists who have most successfully intuited the quality of the human experience peculiar to their day'.[8] The importance of 'attitude' and 'sensibility' has been particularly stressed by Stephen Spender as an element of major importance in deciding whether a poet or writer is in fact modernist or not. In his article 'Moderns and contemporaries', Spender speaks of a new direction of sensibility away from the powers of the 'conscious ego', which is conditioned by the values of the modern age and has severed its communication with the values of the

[5] 'The dehumanisation of art', p. 90.
[6] See Richard Sheppard, 'The crisis of language', in Bradbury and McFarlane, *Modernism*, pp. 325–9.
[7] 'The crisis of language', p. 329.
[8] Wylie Sypher, *Rococo to Cubism in art and literature*, New York, 1960, p. xix.

past. It is not subject matter itself which is the determinant, but rather the attitude of the poet towards his subject. Unlike the non-modern poets and writers, who are in control of their world, the modern poets and writers are acted upon by their world.[9]

The end of the nineteenth century and the beginning of the twentieth witnessed a number of literary movements and trends. Some, such as symbolism, preceded the modernist movement, anticipating its great preoccupation with diction and obliquity. Others, such as imagism, futurism, vorticism, dadaism and surrealism, were either part of the broader modernist movement or had pronounced affinities with some of its manifestations. All these experiments stood in opposition to naturalism and romanticism, and to direct representation and the direct use of language.

ARAB POETIC MODERNITY

I. The Background

A. Romanticism

'Modern' poetry in contemporary Arabic was achieved only after decades of experimentation crowded with poetic experience on the levels of both theory and practice. Poetry moved from one major school to another in an instinctive attempt to transcend the centuries of stagnation which had led to the hackneyed and benighted verse of the nineteenth century. The discussion of the Arab literary renaissance in modern times belongs elsewhere in this volume. However, a brief summary of the neo-classical movement which dominated poetic creativity from the last decade of the nineteenth century through to the 1920s, and has never really died out, must be attempted.

Neo-classical poets – the greatest among whom was Aḥmad Shawqī – instinctively went back to their roots, taking for their models poetry from the vast wealth of classical Arabic literature; for what was urgently needed at that time was for poetry to acquire a new vigour and terseness of expression. Moreover, involvement with classical references was in harmony with the psychological situation of Arab authors at home. This is the period which preceded the age of protest and dissent. Poets were not yet

[9] See Spender's chapter, 'Moderns and contemporaries' in *The idea of the modern*, ed. Irving Howe, pp. 43–4, and see below p. 167. Other relevant works on western modernism include Marshall Berman, *All that is solid melts into air, the experience of modernity*, Penguin Books, 1988; D. W. Fokkema and Elrud Ibsch, *Modernist conjectures, a mainstream in European literature, 1910–1940*, London, 1987; Ihab Hassan, *The dismemberment of Orpheus, towards a postmodern literature*, 2nd edn, Wisconsin, 1982 and *The postmodern turn, essays in postmodern theory and culture*, Ohio, 1987; David Lodge, *The modes of modern writings*, Chicago, 1977; Renato Poggioli, *The theory of the avant-garde*, Cambridge, Ma. and London, 1968.

intellectually conscious of modern ideas of revolution and social struggle, and even when these ideas did begin to enter Arab consciousness, they addressed themselves to a stable and well-ordered universe where all evil came from the outside: colonialism, the encroachment of foreign cultures and capitalist interests. Neo-classical poets adopted the well-defined ethical, philosophical and aesthetic principles of their world. Their real achievement was to deliver the languid and moribund verse of the nineteenth century from its immense weaknesses and to imbue it with new strength of diction and form, securing for modern Arabic poetry a *well-rooted, robust basis* on which generations of avant-garde poets would operate. The task shouldered by the neo-classical poets should therefore be seen as a big step forward towards achieving modernity.

The drawbacks of neo-classicism lay in its sometimes excessive leaning towards rationality, objectivity and externality, its resort to rhetorical expressions and high tones, its rigidity of form and vision, and its inability to face the winds of change. As early as the second decade, avant-garde poets and critics, both in Egypt and in North America, began their direct attacks on neo-classicism. The émigré poets in America were led by Jibrān (Gibran Khalil Gibran), the poet who was the most influential of his generation in bringing about a revolution in both the outlook and the technique of poetry, reinforced by the critical writings (and to a lesser extent the verse) of Mīkhāʾīl Nuʿaymah and by the highly progressive and inspiring writings of Amīn al-Rayḥānī (1876–1940). The Egyptian school, on the other hand, known later as the '*Diwān*' group, through its vociferous attacks on the neo-classical school (and on all fossilized elements in poetry) aimed at revolutionizing the stable, well-ordered world of the neo-classical poets, and emphasized the subjective elements of experience. By the third decade a new group of young poets had risen to fame in Egypt, writing about individual longings and dreams, expressing a deep desire for freedom, and concentrating on personal experience and on the imaginative aspect of the poem. From America and Egypt the Arab romantic movement spread to other Arab countries wherever there were acute feelings of deprivation, or of a discrepancy between aspiration and reality, especially on the personal and social plane.

Although Arab romanticism enjoyed only a short span of life, it was a bold leap away from the neo-classical drawbacks and helped to emphasize the elements of emotion and imagination in the poem, thus making the poetic tools more malleable. It dislodged the neo-classical regard for the prevailing culture, and the alienation of the poet from society began in modern Arabic poetry. Most romantic poets at home reacted negatively to society's shortcomings and its repression of individual freedom and happiness, and sank into escapism and excesses of subjectivity, writing a poetry of spleen and introversion, full of langour, infinite discontent and endless regret, or, as in the case of Egypt's ᶜAlī Maḥmūd Ṭāhā, a poetry looking for the exotic and for joys and experiences as yet unattainable in their world.

Romantic weaknesses, however, quickly seeped into the poetry, and romanticism in the Arab world early embodied extreme sentimentalism, gloom, dilution, abstractionism and formlessness, which became the focus of the attack by poets of the fifties. Despite its boldness, good romantic poetry did not involve any adventurous innovations in form. Critics of the fifties, however, showed no awareness whatsoever of the role played by romanticism in revolutionizing poetry in ways which anticipated modernity; they wrote, in fact, as though modern poetry was a phenomenon which arose automatically, without having any real background in this century. They did not recognize that it was the outcome of an inner logic in the evolution of the poetic art, the result of major experiments (including, in large part, romanticism) which had, step by step, prepared the poetic tools for the advent of modernity.

There are, in fact, more points of connection between the two movements than most Arab writers on modernity have ever conceded. By relinquishing the hold on inherited values and traditions, and shifting away from society, by liberating the imagination, and freeing the poetic language from classical rigidity, pedantry, archaism and restraint, by giving great value to the subjective element of experience and the importance of vision in poetry, and by going into the self, romantics sowed the seeds of modernity.

B. *Symbolism*

An observer cannot fail to note the speed with which twentieth-century Arabic poetry developed into a modern art. Within a mere five decades or so, Arabic poetry had passed through almost all the phases of development which western poetry experienced over three centuries.

The neo-classicists had dominated the literary scene from the last decade of the nineteenth century and continued to do so throughout the first three decades of the twentieth, at least. The romantic movement began before neo-classicism had reached its maximum duration, with Jibrān rising to fame as early as the first decade of this century. By the second decade the romantic movement had already been launched in America and the Arab world, growing in the teeth of neo-classicism. By the third and fourth decades a number of different experiments in form, technique and orientation were taking place simultaneously. Among these the most important was symbolism.

The Arab symbolist trend, which reached its peak in the thirties with Saʿīd ʿAql's (b. 1912) publication of his long poem, ʿal-Majdaliyyahʾ in 1937, was based on nineteenth-century French symbolism. The western movement had its own philosophy and doctrine, and was propounded by great figures who dominated the poetic scene in France over many decades. The poets aspired to the ideal and the beautiful and proclaimed the dominance of intuitive perception, emphasizing a non-rational approach. They saw strangeness, obscurity and dream-like approaches as being valid for poetry, and believed in the correspondence of the senses and the evanescent and subjective mingling of sensations. They also saw a unity in the universe, which they tried to express in their work. They regarded language as a major element in poetry. They chose words both for their implicative meaning ('poetry should not inform but suggest and evoke,' Mallarmé said), and for their musical expressiveness. To the symbolists the music of words had an intrinsic meaning which intensified their implicative significance. The music of the single word must produce, together with the music of other words, a harmonious whole, a rhythmic unity that allows words 'to fly upon subtler wings'. They rejected the old bondage of rhetoric and exteriority, the moralizing theme and tone, and the concentration on the descriptive element, on the anecdote and on the appeal to the multitude.

The Arab symbolist experiment shared few of the causes that prompted the western symbolist movement. The very few Arab poets who tried their hand at this particular type of symbolism had nothing of the political disenchantment and the revulsion against bourgeois materalism and its cult of capitalist activity and success which characterized the influential French experiment. Behind the Arab experiment, one can discern, not a social or political, but an *artistic* impulse. It shows the great malleability that the poetic art had already acquired and the capacity it possessed to absorb radical change, particularly in language and style, and reflects the deep and active interest Arab poets have had throughout this century in western poetic techniques. This meant a continuous change of sensibility in Arab poets, and, eventually, in their audience. This pervasive acquisitional attitude, it must be remembered, was limited in any given period by the capacity of this sensibility to move further in directions unfamiliar in the traditional poetic heritage. The symbolist orientation in Arabic, however, is a special case, for the old poetry had seen a valuable and important experiment in a similar kind of symbolism in medieval times. The principle of the correspondence and the mingling of sensations and the unity of the universe were major elements in some *sufi* poetry. However, it is not certain whether Arab poets, such as Sa^{c}īd ^{c}Aql, who led the symbolist trend in Arabic, were acquainted with this old *Sufi* experiment.[10]

Sa^{c}īd ^{c}Aql's best verse contribution to symbolism was his long, majestic poem, 'al-Majdaliyyah', whose subject is the meeting of Christ and Mary Magdalene, which he prefaced with an introduction based on the writings of the French symbolists Mallarmé, Paul Valéry and Abbé H. Brémond. His later poetry, however, failed to attain even the laxer standards of symbolist writings, although he retained a select and gem-like language and an aesthetic decorum in most of his poems, which usually revolved around unrequited love and an unreachable beloved. Experiments by other poets writing in the same vein, such as Bishr Fāris (1907?–1963) in Egypt and Badī^{c} Ḥaqqī in Syria whose *dīwān, Siḥr*, appeared in 1953, had only a very modest effect.

Despite its limited scope, the symbolist experiment was able, particularly in the hands of ^{c}Aql, to inspire and even direct modern Arabic poetry in its *exploration of language*. However, the cult of the ideal and the beautiful, and the great value placed on the music of words, which were basic principles in ^{c}Aql's experiment, did not have any lasting influence. Following the 1948 Palestine tragedy, the whole world of both poet and audience crumbled as the debacle revealed how vastly and tragically unaware it was of contemporary evil. The Arab world was first plunged into deepening gloom, then, in the mid 1950s, experienced a resurgence of hope, and symbolism was not able to sustain its *Weltanschauung* of an ideal world for which the symbolist poet longed. The new situation involved attitudes which marked the end of the disengagement of the symbolists and heralded poetry's exit from the ivory tower. The way the symbolists explored the suggestive elements of language led to the birth of a symbolic (not symbolist) tendency which has now become a natural element in poetry. The poetry of the fifties needed to fuse the mistiness, mellowness and great pliability gained by the romantic experiment with the more sophisticated obliquity of symbolism in order to make an authentic advance towards modernity in poetry.

Symbolism, then, intensified the influence of the romantic revolution by its exploration of the great possibilities of language, by its rejection of formal literary and social authority and by its encouragement of originality and independence. Its abhorrence of the discursive, its interest in the subconscious, its exaltation of the dream, its inwardness, its connotative and subtle way of dealing with experience (combatting the high rhetoric,

[10] In his book, *al-Ramziyyah fī'l-shi^{c}r al-^{c}Arabī al-ḥadīth*, (1949) Anṭūn Ghaṭṭās Karam gave little significance to the *sufi* experiment.

directness and rationality of neo-classicism), its economy of language and its emotional restraint (both of which were reactions against romantic dilution and sentimentalism), brought Arabic poetry many steps nearer to the modernist situation.

C. Early experiments in form

It is now time to look at Arabic poetry before the 1950s from another angle. Throughout the half-century preceding the fifties, one can discern two activities taking place simultaneously. The first was the mainstream development discussed above. The second was more wayward and adventurous, and took place mainly on the sidelines, never entering mainstream poetry in any formal or recognized way, and never becoming a school or movement. It consisted of experiments in poetry, literature and art which were conducted by single individuals or particular circles, working outside the mainstream. They involved both form and language. It was that old intractable, two-hemistich monorhymed form of the inherited *qaṣīdah* which attracted the earliest experiments. Usually, though not always, it was poets who had been exposed to European verse, mainly English and French, who attempted these early radical experiments in form. None of them, however, was destined to greatness. The more gifted and permanently established poets experimented only mildly, trying their hands at stanzaic forms with varied rhymes and even sometimes varied lengths of verses, but always observing a fixed pattern that consistently recurred from stanza to stanza. These latter attempts had a good measure of success and represented a mild variation on the two-hemistich monorhymed form, but were limited in their possibilities, imposing certain restrictions on the tone and theme of the poem, and requiring them, usually, to be less weighty. Moreover, because they required a fixed pattern, they constricted the freedom of the poet. It was clear that the liberation of the old form – over fifteen centuries old and well entrenched in the memory of the race – had to find a new method which could allow the poet to express the fundamental, often tragic themes of modern Arab life without any loss of artistic effectiveness.

It is intriguing to note here that the revolutionary and successful experiments in the form of Arabic poetry which were attempted at the end of the forties by major poets were not the result of a creative radicalism on their part, but were the eventual outcome of a pervasive adventurism over three decades by minor poets, which gradually loosened the rigidity of poetic form, preparing it for the most radical and successful formal revolution in the history of Arabic poetry.

Several poets, including Jamīl Ṣidqī al-Zahāwī, ʿAbd al-Raḥmān Shukrī and Aḥmad Zakī Abū Shādī, attempted to discard rhyme altogether and write in blank verse. Abū Shādī, amongst others, also attempted what he called 'free versification', in which the poet did not stick to the same metre throughout the poem but changed it every verse or two, using several metres in the same poem. For artistic reasons, the experiments were a complete failure.[11] Poets continued to experiment, until eventually ᶜAlī Aḥmad Bākathīr of Hadramaut (1910–69), living in Egypt at the time, hit on the secret of freedom from the two-hemistich form. He was the first Arab poet to realise, as early as the mid 1930s, that for this form to be fractured the poet needed to break the pattern of symmetry and equal measures between one verse and another. It was the problem of symmetry and equilibrium that had to be overcome before any authentic change in the metrical and rhythmic patterns of the inherited Arabic form could be effected. This, Bākathīr achieved by making the single foot the metrical unit in the poem, not the verse or half verse, as is the case in the old form. The repetition of the single foot followed, not a fixed pattern, but the poet's own creative design. This was a momentous discovery which, in the hands of greater poets than Bākathīr, was to revolutionize the whole formal structure of Arabic poetry and open up the immensely rich potential of Arabic metrics, creating new metrical forms previously undreamed of.

Bākathīr himself was never given sufficient credit for his achievement. Avant-garde, adventurous and insightful, he possessed a talent neither great enough nor aggressive enough to push his major discovery in form to its furthest limits, particularly since he carried out his experiments in the dramatic medium, which was not a very popular form. His achievement remained totally obscure, and was only brought to the attention of the literary establishment when Nāzik al-Malāʾikah (b. 1923) claimed the whole discovery of free verse for herself. She had, in fact, been working with al-Sayyāb (1926–64) on free metrical constructions in the late forties, and the two had subsequently been linked as the initiators of the form. Irritated by her claim, al-Sayyāb announced Bākathīr's earlier experiment to the literary world.[12]

However, the whole of the Arab literary heartland (Egypt, Lebanon, Syria, Iraq, Palestine and, a little later, Jordan) was rife with experimentation. Gifted young poets could not avoid constant encounter with bold minor experiments which helped break their resistance to radical innovative techniques and weakened in them, however slightly, the old instinct of utter dedication to the regular rhythms of the two-hemistich mould.

[11] On these and the following experiments, see my book, *Trends and movements in modern Arabic poetry*, Vol. II, Leiden, 1977, pp. 536–56.

[12] In his preface to the 2nd edn of *Akhnātūn wa Nefertītī*, Bākathīr mentions al-Sayyāb's acknowledgement.

Moreover, the pervasive reading that young poets were doing in foreign poetries, both in the original languages and in Arabic translations, helped expose them to new and different poetic rhythms.

Another major experiment that had been going on since the turn of the century was that of poetry-in-prose, whose two early exponents were Jibrān and al-Rayḥānī in North America. Their experiments helped effect the gradual disintegration of traditional formal concepts in Arabic poetry.

Jibrān, whose attempts at verse were not particularly striking, was led by his artistic instinct to the right medium, prose. His poetry-in-prose was gripping enough to assure an immense influence over young Arab writers in the twenties and thirties. His experiment was initially offered to an audience devoted to the inherited, balanced metrics of Arabic poetry, and this would have created the greatest resistance were it not for the positive outlook Jibrān (and al-Rayḥānī) had towards their homeland. Jibrān was a literary genius, and was able, even through his poems-in-prose, to revolutionize Arabic poetry. He expressed his romantic rebellion against the social and religious practices of his time in a new diction and a captivating style which came to be known as the Jibranian style and diction. These two elements combined to produce those intoxicating, magical rhythms on which two generations of poets grew up. Through this uniqueness Jibrān laid one cornerstone for the modernist poetry of a much later period. However, prose was never taken seriously as a medium for poetry before the fifties. It was regarded by critics and audience alike as a marginal and inconsequential medium that could not touch the 'sacred' core of poetic form in Arabic.

D. *The surrealist experiment*

A third experiment from the thirties and forties in Egypt reflected the growing sophistication of the Arab creative talent early in the century. This is the surrealist activity among a number of Egyptian artists and writers who formed a group that preached revolutionary doctrines previously unheard of and forged direct links with the western surrealist and avant-garde movements.

Surrealism preached the destruction of existing reality so that it could be rebuilt, with its components reassembled in ways that could liberate it. The surrealists also rejected literature and art as expressions of reality. Eventually, they tried to find a balance between reality and surreality, between consciousness and subconsciousness, individual dreams and communal dreams, so that the salvation of all could be attained. Reason, which included memory, had to be banished, and the irrational was glorified. Logical thought, the surrealists maintained, could not comprehend the divine disorder which should replace sentiment. They only believed in disorder, as manifested in chance, the 'irrational, disorderly will of the universe'.

The international character of the surrealists is shown by their rejection of all deep-rooted emotions including love of home, family and country. Religion was also rejected, since belief in God involved a smug attitude that promised another fictive world as the focus of our longing for the infinite – a situation which deprived man of the liberty to investigate here in the present on earth. Surrealism, therefore, is mystical atheism. What the surrealists could not endure was the old way of looking at the world, in which light and darkness, the real and the imaginary, the past and the present, the living and the dead, were all regarded as contradictory entities. It is here, and in their interest in hysteria, dream, magic and the cult of the phantom, that the mystical essence of their creed is shown. Surrealism displayed acute antisocial attitudes and a will to destroy accepted values. Surrealists had a deep hatred for bourgeois society, for organized, well-established norms which halted creativity.

Surrealism was also a stylistic revolution. It fused poetry with prose, and it wanted literature to abandon its old involvement with semantic explication and the delineation of external reality. Rimbaud's deregulation of the senses remained a surrealist commitment, and to it was added the idea of automatic writing, in which there is no encroachment by the logical aspects of thinking. This showed in their choice of language and in the way their images were coined. The best image was that in which the relationship between the two agents of the image was remote; in fact, the remoter the better. They avoided natural, orderly images and, by using linguistic contradictions, expressed the disordinate as perceived by the irrational qualities of the mind.

In Beirut the poetic audience was intrigued by the new experiment of Saᶜīd ᶜAql and the symbolist gospel he preached, accepted the idea of poetic change, but took this no further than his experiment. Poets and critics made no significant links with the more radical fringe experiments then going on in Egypt, or, for that matter, with the radical experiment of Urkhān Muyassar (1911?–1965) in Syria in the mid 1940s.

It was in 1947 that Muyassar, great lover of literature, experimentalist and avant-garde writer, published, with ᶜAli al-Nāṣir, a small volume of surrealist poetry which he called *Siryāl*. Muyassar also wrote the introduction to this, which contained not only an explanation of the surrealist creed but some additional remarks reflecting an independent mind that did not rely wholly on western theory. In this volume of prose poems, the authors relied greatly on automatic writing, thus espousing one of the more extreme aspects of the surrealist creed.

Siryāl was the first attempt at surrealism in Arab countries east of the Mediterranean. However, surrealism and modernity in their real sense first manifested themselves in Egypt in the thirties, two decades before they were to materialize in Syria and Lebanon. 'The concept of Modernity was linked with the large group of foreign writers and artists who were either living in or visiting Egypt at the time, and who brought to both Cairo and Alexandria the more radical concepts of Surrealism and Trotskyism.'[13] 'Egypt in the thirties and forties,' says another writer, 'was more liberal intellectually and culturally, than it is now, in the eighties . . . and was part of the international cultural activity. The movement, for example, of the "Society of Art and Freedom" was part of world Surrealism at the end of its golden age.'[14] Another early manifestation was 'The Society of the Experimentalists' and 'The Effort Makers'. These were already fully active in the early thirties and had an avant-garde magazine, *Un Éffort*, in which they published their ideas and creative works.

Georges Hunein (Ḥunayn) (1914–1973) was perhaps the leading surrealist in Egypt in the thirties. In his work and that of other Egyptian writers and artists who called themselves surrealists, a radical political stance is tightly linked to a radical social, artistic and cultural outlook. It is particularly interesting to see how these writers, especially Hunein, were able to forge direct links with the western left and with major western writers such as André Breton, André Malraux, André Gide and others. This intercultural exchange has not been surpassed in quality, even in the contemporary period when communication and opportunity should have made possible the meeting of minds on a much larger scale.

Early avant-garde writings in Egypt were in French, which was also Hunein's first language, but he did publish some works in Arabic,[15] as did other poets such as Kāmil Zuhayrī, Ḥasan Tilmisānī and ᶜĀdil Amīn, as well as some fiction writers among the group.

In the pages of *Don Quichotte* the French language review which he helped found in Egypt in 1939, Hunein wrote his ideas on poetry:

> Poetry obeys certain magical, rhythmical and incantational laws, and . . . merges completely with a verbal ritual which gives birth to a special language, different from the ordinary language of the tribe or the city . . . It is the tool for the . . . challenge against universal forces such as death. The poet uses dream . . . against the poverty of reality . . . Modern poetry does not resort to the subconscious for its own sake, but in order to know ourselves, to discover all that is inside us.[16]

Hunein explained to his readers many aspects of modern poetry, bringing out the difference between modern poetic expressions and traditional ones.

13 ᶜIṣām Maḥfūẓ, *al-Suryāliyyah wa tafāᶜulātuhā al-ᶜarabiyyah*, Beirut, 1987, p. 50.

14 Samīr Gharīb, *al-Suryāliyyah fī Miṣr*, Cairo, 1986, p. 5.

15 Gharīb, *al-Suryāliyyah*, pp. 200–1.

16 Gharīb, *al-Suryāliyyah*, pp. 71–3.

In 1939 he wrote that the aim of the surrealists was not to change people's feelings, but to change society and reshape it.[17] In another place he wrote that 'Surrealism represents the most ambitious experiment of our times'.[18] Throughout World War II this avant-garde group continued to work and to announce its belief in freedom, progress and justice on earth. After the war, however, the notorious Ṣidqī Pasha, who persecuted all those who opposed him, dismantled the group. There is no doubt that this surrealist activity constituted the most extreme rejection of persistent classicism and realism in Egypt, a complete cultural revolution whose 'writers, poets and artists pierced the ceiling of their reality to the wider skies of Modernity'.[19] The criticism of religion was their greatest challenge.

Without ever becoming a complete and independent trend on its own, surrealism made a valuable contribution to Arabic poetry, especially during and after the 1960s, chiefly in the way poets treated diction and the poetic image. Great activity centred around the image, with the relationship between the image and its referent being made deliberately remote and poets competing vigorously in this area. The adventure with language and style became a very serious and creative undertaking, and both veered away from the direct and logical way in which the poetic phrase and vocabulary had been created in neo-classical and romantic poetry. A mild interest in dreams and visionary poetry, and also in the irrational, was displayed, and the prose medium became a recognized poetic form, employed by many of the avant-garde and acclaimed poets of the contemporary period.

II. The modernist period: 1948–

It is not always possible to assess the precise influences of an artistic activity on later generations of poets and refer them all to their rightful origins. However, forerunners herald changes, hold out examples of courage and adventure and, through their own changed sensibilities, anticipate imminent changes in later poets and readers.

The post-1948 generation of poets is now known as the 'generation of the pioneers'. They are also known as the 'generation of the catastrophe', referring to the Palestine catastrophe of 1948, which dealt a severe blow to the pride and aspirations of a whole generation of Arabs.

The 1948 Palestine debacle was instrumental in admitting radical change. The unanimous reaction of Arab poets all over the Arab world was one of anger, rejection, alienation and horror; an atmosphere of gloom and pessimism reigned, but it soon gave birth to feelings of challenge, to a

[17] Gharīb, *al-Suryāliyyah*, p. 19. [18] Gharīb, *al-Suryāliyyah*, p. 15.
[19] Maḥfūẓ, *al-Suryāliyyah*, p. 50.

rejection of old established ties with the inherited culture, and to a renunciation of loyalty to both the remote past, and the immediate past which had brought so much shame and frustration. A new courage was now born which would enable poets to find their own poetic style, free from the iron hold of old poetic traditions and concepts. With a background rich in experimental audacity, and with increased direct access to the most modern experiments in world poetry, the ground was now paved for the great poetic revolution of the fifties.

Broadly speaking, there have been three phases in the rich poetic activity since 1948. We can, however, only attempt a rough description of these, since it is impossible to give fixed labels or absolute definitions for them, or to discern clear boundaries between them. What we can recognize is not the beginning or end of these phases – these are always vague in any poetry – but rather their peaks, when their energy reached the maximum point of either creativity or chaos and new developments became necessary for healthy artistic growth.

The first is the pioneer phase, which occupies the fifties and most of the sixties; the second, which grew in the teeth of the first and out of its own exaggerations, is the chaotic phase of the seventies; and the third is the present ongoing phase in which a number of talented young poets are producing work of a high standard, equipped with fine modernist qualities free of those drawbacks which inevitably characterized the initial stages of such a revolutionary movement – the singing in unison, the fascination with styles and fashions *ad absurdum*, the occasional slight provincialism and naiveté, the pragmatism in modes and ideas and, above all, the lingering influences – even in some of the best pioneers, and particularly evident in tone and attitude – of previous periods and schools. The basic thrust of Arabic poetry since 1948 may then be seen as a great rolling wave, first a crest, then a trough, then a new crest. It is useful to think of all these phases as contingent on each other, the one issuing from the other as a natural outcome, without all the proclamations and announcements that accompany new schools and trends. This is because they all belong, symbiotically, to the same poetic modernity.

A. The first phase 1948–1967

This was the phase of the 'pioneers', which extended, approximately, up to the June War of 1967. The word 'pioneers' is, in fact, an understatement, for the group of highly gifted poets endowed with flair and courage, who came upon the scene in the fifties from many countries of the Arab world were movers and shakers who experimented briskly and aggressively with their poetic tools while, at the same time, trying to find their own poetic identities. They were able to introduce major concrete changes. Various obliquities were successfully incorporated, if sometimes with a measure of naive wonder. Myths taken from ancient Phoenician and Greek mythology, archetypes from history, especially from Arab history, folklore, proverbs and all kinds of allusions were explored with diligence and often with creativity. Treatment of time[20] and place became crucial and sophisticated. One of the finest achievements of modern poetry has been the successful use of spatial form. Time became compressed; poets, in dealing with major questions of freedom and struggle, and going beyond the personal into the far reaches of humanity, were able to wrench themselves free of the temporal and to identify contemporary personages and events with historical archetypes taken usually from Arab history. The pioneer poets studied Eliot well, particularly 'The waste land', and were influenced by this poem where, as Joseph Frank put it, 'the chief source of meaning is the sense of ironic dissimilarity and yet of profound human continuity between the modern protagonists and their long-dead (or only imaginary) exemplars'.[21] Modern Arab poets saw many contemporary figures as the bearers of continuous characteristics and attitudes particularly from Arab history, and in this way the poets have been able to transcend the limitations of history. Instead of treating time as a linear and flat progression, they treated it as a mythical permutation of past and present where all periods intermesh and interlock, juxtaposing past and present, merging periods and unifying human experience. History is brought alive in the present as a mythical motif of tragic immutability. Sequence is ignored, and only images of eternal repetition prevail. Begun in poetry, spatial form has later been adopted by novelists, and a mythical treatment of time has formed the kernel of some of the best creative works of modern Arabic literature. The city, one of the major modernist symbols, gained decisively in appeal. Other elements of the poem were also revolutionized. Form, diction and imagery underwent radical changes that transformed the whole concept of poetry and the whole approach to it.

1. Form as catalyst Form became a constant preoccupation, on both the artistic and the theoretical level. Even before the debacle, however, two experiments in poetic form appeared which heralded the free verse movement in the fifties. The first was al-Malāʾikah's poem 'Cholera', and the second was al-Sayyāb's volume, *Azhār dhābilah* ('Wilted flowers'), both of which appeared in 1947. I shall not reiterate the stale argument about which poet first produced a free verse poem. Neither did, as we have seen.

[20] See my study, 'Visions and attitudes in modern Arabic poetry: the treatment of time' in *Studies in modern Arabic literature*, ed. Robin Ostle, Warminster, 1975.

[21] *The widening gyre*, Bloomington and London, 1963, p. 58.

However, their attempts, certainly based on former experiments, assumed a more crucial role because they were better poets and produced their work with authority and a spirit of leadership, and because the atmosphere was now ripe, artistically and psychologically, for the kind of new experiment they offered.

It is possible to call the fifties 'the decade of constant discovery' in the field of poetry, with a steady and often dramatic development within a short span of time. The contrast between al-Sayyāb's *Azhār dhābilah*, and his great volume, *Unshūdat al-maṭar* ('Song of rain') in 1960, is a prime example, and there are many more. For example, al-Malāʾikah's critical introduction to her collection, *Shaẓāyā wa ramād* ('Ashes and shrapnel'), 1949, explaining the mechanism of free verse and detailing what she felt to be the technical reasons behind it, is naive and is dwarfed by her later writings at the end of the fifties on the same subject (published in her book, *Qaḍāyā 'l-shiʿr al-maʿāṣir*, ('Issues in contemporary poetry', 1962). Similarly, the pre-fifties poetry of Khalīl Ḥāwī (1922–82) and Yūsuf al-Khāl (1917–87) shows marked differences from their poetry written in the fifties. The poets demonstrated a sudden maturity and a firm grasp of their tools, effecting momentous innovations in all aspects of the Arabic poem, which eventually brought Arabic poetry to a level contemporaneous with world poetry.

The success of these early experiments in free verse opened a wide scope for further exploration into the great possibilities of Arabic metrics. The old form was now arrogantly discarded on the grounds of monotony, padding and rigidity – ignoring the great poetic monuments that made the Arab poetic heritage one of the finest artistic achievements of classical times. The essential concept of free verse is the reliance on the *free* repetition of the single foot in the poem, where the poet varies the number of feet in a single line according to need. This simple beginning of metrical deconstruction from the balanced, regular two-hemistich verse with its *fixed* number of feet in the line of poetry, was to lead to ever new forms and structures as poets grew in sophistication. It would also produce much chaotic work as less gifted poets came to feel lost in the freedom now allowed them. However, in the hands of the many gifted poets of this generation the new form was to give birth to a dynamic experimentation in other elements of the poem, such as language and imagery, and to allow the introduction of new elements such as myth and the historical archetype. Moreover, the new form would be free to call forth new thematic and attitudinal approaches and reflect a *Weltanschauung* full of new possibilities. Thus, the achievement of free verse would set the stage, quickly and decisively, for the birth of a modernist Arabic poetry of great universal worth.

In its initial stage, free verse quickly began to suffer from dilution, flabbiness, wordiness and a breathless musicality which made numerous poems sound indistinguishable from one another. Above all, the poetry of this early period was afflicted by the dominance of one fashionable metre after another, adopted simultaneously by many poets until aesthetic fatigue set in and another metre was taken up. This period was, indeed, marked by succeeding fashions in various aspects of the poem – a sign of youthful enthusiasm, but also of youthful naiveté and inexperience in the face of this unprecedented poetic revolution.

In those early years, the new form seemed to control the poet's creativity. A case in point is Khalīl Ḥāwī: though an unquestionably fine poet, his manipulation of metrical measures is breathless and long-winded. Much of the poetry of the period showed this gushing fluidity, without any saving grace of fluctuating measures or alternation between swelling and abating rhythms. This hazy situation did not, however, last much beyond the fifties. Even by the mid 1950s some edifices of noble rhythmical construction – particularly in the poetry of al-Sayyāb and, by the end of the decade, of the Syrian Adūnīs (ʿAlī Aḥmad Saʿīd; b. 1930) – were available to the new generation of poets. The metrical and rhythmic bases of such poems as al-Sayyāb's '*Fī 'l-Maghrib al-ʿArabī*' ('In the Arab Mahgreb'), '*Ughniyyah fī shahr Āb*' ('Song in the month of August') and '*Jaykūr wa'l-madīnah*' ('Jaykur and the city'), all written in the mid fifties, are organically linked with their thematic intentions: the ardent, quasi-heroic tones of the first, the ironic double meaning of the second and the tragic plea of the third, being in fact greatly enhanced by the particular rhythmic structure of the poems. Adūnīs's symphonic combinations in his long poem on 'The Eagle of Quraysh' and the self-sufficiency, terseness and compact perfection of his short poems in *Aghanī Mihyār al-Dimashqī* ('Songs of Mihyar, the Damascene'), similarly provide original models of metrical manipulation and skill.

The avant-garde movement of the early fifties was dominated by such figures as al-Sayyāb, al-Malāʾikah and ʿAbd al-Wahhāb al-Bayyātī (b. 1926), all from Iraq and all fine experimentalists with an outlook that was revolutionary, at the time, on poetry and society. Other poets would speedily rise to share the fame of these three young authors. During the fifties, it must be remembered, the poets who achieved the greatest fame and status were all *verse* poets. However, while the metrics of Arabic poetry, especially the six metres built on the repetition of the single foot with all their varied ramifications, were being explored passionately and creatively, and a few of them, such as the *rajaz* and the *khabab* (a shorter metre derived from *al-mutadārak*) were elevated from a rather obscure status in the old poetry to a status of crucial communicative and aesthetic value, another form was being tested with new seriousness. This was prose poetry and the prose poem. The segregation of verse and prose had been so complete in Arabic literature that the early mature and skilful experiments with poetry-in-prose in the fifties had been ignored by most, and despite the allure of Jibrān's prose poetry, this form was not considered as equivalent to verse. The whole poetry-in-prose output was vaguely regarded as a special, isolated genre, and was left alone by most aspiring poets. Yet it is important to remember at this stage that some very mature, avant-garde modernist experiments in prose poetry did in fact appear in the fifties, but were too early to attract much attention or to be recognized as true modernist experiments.

One of the foremost such experiments was that of the Palestinian poet, Tawfīq Ṣāyigh (1924–1971). He published his first volume of prose poetry, *Thalāthūn qaṣīdah* ('Thirty poems') in 1953, and this signalled the start of an original poetic career. Two more volumes appeared in subsequent years, *al-Qaṣīdah kāf* in 1960, and *Muʿallaqat Tawfīq Ṣayigh* ('Ode of Tawfiq Sayigh', 1963). However, despite its contribution to modernist poetry in Arabic, Ṣāyigh's work never, in his own lifetime, gained its rightful place in relation to the work of more vociferous poets then writing in verse.

Ṣāyigh's experiment merits further discussion here because it embodied some major modernist features early in the decade, proving that modernity had come early and naturally to western-educated poets in the Arab world. Together with al-Sayyāb's successful use of modernist techniques, it also proves what much contemporary writing on the subject ignores: that modernity in Arabic poetry, although helped and encouraged by the *Shiʿr* review which began publication in 1957, was not initiated by it, but had already firmly started before the establishment of this review.

It is clear that Ṣāyigh's need to express himself in prose (he never internalized Arabic metrics) facilitated his early arrival at a modernist expression which voiced his natural modernist affinities. His psychological make-up, his perfect urbanity, his fine poetic education and his passion for world literature all guaranteed him a modernist apprehension of experience. His treatment of language was revolutionary: hackeneyed vocabulary was discarded, and the idea of *poetic diction* was shunned. His language was very close to the contemporary language, although sometimes studded with unusual or antiquated words to give an impression of strangeness. His imagery was modern, a city man's imagery to be precise, with no hint of any provincialism or pastoral yearnings. However, his greatest achievement as a modernist lay in his tone and attitude – the two elements on which many claims of modernity in Arabic will founder. Ṣāyigh escaped the tenacious hold of the rhetorical, self-assertive tone of inherited poetry. An underlying, often witty irony pervades his poetry. This irony, seen even in his attitude to God and salvation, saves his often anguished poetry from gloom, as do the many witty expressions that provide moments of peace in an otherwise tragic oracle.

Ṣāyigh discarded all claims to heroism and the loud proclamations of self-importance or national defiance which are so widespread in modern Arabic poetry. In this general crisis, this era of failed endeavours, of world conspiracies, of destitution, of tragic duplicity and pervasive suffering and torture which has accompanied the political turmoil occurring since 1948, the poet recognizes himself as the '*victim*', not the 'hero',[22] of his times. It is this vision, found only rarely among this generation of pioneers, that will help decide how far a poet has absorbed modernity. Hermetic, private, alienated, sullen and shy of self-aggrandizement, Ṣāyigh showed admirable independence in an era of groupings, united fronts and literary cliques and fashions. From the fifties up to the beginning of the eighties, poets showed a preference for singing in unison; various fashions dominated particular periods, and were taken up by several leading poets at once. This points also to the 'learning' attitude of this period, and its pragmatic character.

Loner, victim and wanderer, Ṣāyigh wrote poetry which is a supreme example of an early modernity achieved because of the poet's particular qualities of vision and technique. Others achieved this either fully or in part, but several major poets, for all their skilful manipulation of their art and their deep modernist aspirations, revealed the defects of a sensibility not yet come to terms with the essential meaning of modernity.

Other experiments were carried out during the same period. A case in point is that of the Egyptian Muḥammad Muṣṭafā Badawī (b. 1925) who began experimenting in poetry in the mid 1940s. His first volume, *Rasāʾil min London* ('Letters from London', 1956), demonstrates an avant-garde spirit, a radical change in technique and outlook. His experiment is, as he says in his introduction to the volume, an attempt to use the Arabic metres 'nearest to the rhythms of prose and conversation, making the metre the framework of the poem'.

Besides Tawfīq Ṣāyigh's 'Thirty poems', the fifties saw the publication of several fine volumes of prose poetry. By 1959, the Syrian Muḥammad al-Māghūṭ's volume, *Ḥuzn fī ḍawʾi 'l-qamar* ('Sorrow in moonlight'), had appeared. It revolved around the poet's tragic experience as an outsider, a wanderer and a lost soul, and gave conclusive evidence of the potential and effectiveness of the form, and of its crucial relationship, not fully explored at the time, to poetic modernity, to the transformation of the traditional hero into victim and to the modernist abhorrence of assertiveness and pomp. In

[22] See below pp. 166ff.

the same year two other volumes appeared, the Palestinian Jabrā Ibrāhīm Jabrā's *Tammuz fī 'l-madīnah* ('Tammuz in the city'), and the Lebanese Unsī al-Ḥāj's *Lan* ('Never!'), the latter including an introduction by the author explaining the idea of a prose poem. The poetry of al-Ḥāj was based on a surrealist experience which was very difficult to apprehend at the time, but which seemed clearly suited to the form itself. It was followed in 1960 in Lebanon by Shawqī Abī Shaqrā's volume, *Khuṭuwāt al-malik* ('The king's footsteps'), which gave further strong confirmation of the potential of poetry-in-prose, then in 1962 by *Mawt al-ākharīn* ('The death of others'), by Riyāḍ al-Rayyis. All the volumes noted above were published by *Shiʿr*. By the end of the fifties, however, Adūnīs had already begun his magnificent experiments with the prose poem, and he also wrote about it at length, relying heavily on Suzanne Bernard's newly published book, *Le Poème en Prose de Baudelaire jusqu'à nos Jours* (Paris, 1960).[23] Other serious poets joined in the experiment, and by the end of the fifties both the prose poem and prose poetry came to be viewed, at least by avant-garde poets and critics, as legitimate forms to be freely used where the poet felt them to be appropriate.

There is a difference between prose poetry (*al-shiʿr al-manthūr*) and the prose poem (*Qaṣīdat al-nathr*) in the structure of the form itself. On the page, prose poetry looks like a free verse poem, with lines of varying length, and the reader usually tends to pause between one line and another. The prose poem, on the other hand, looks like a paragraph of prose. Neither, of course, uses metre, and there is usually no rhyme; indeed, the use of rhyme in non-metrical constructions is heavy-handed and creates an aura of artificiality. The readers of a prose poem pause only when there is a semantic necessity. Otherwise, they can read on at will, just as they would do when reading prose. Nevertheless, the prose poem differs from discursive prose in its density and tension, in its emotional base, in the type of its metaphoric representations and, quite importantly, in its rhythms. There is always a pronounced rhythm to both prose poetry and a prose poem which, in the hands of a gifted poet, can reach magical levels. There is certainly great effectiveness in the delicate, dreamlike rhythms of Abī Shaqrā's poetry, whether the form he uses is prose poetry or the prose poem. The tension and density of Unsī al-Ḥāj's poems, the double voice heard in them, the occasional anguish, the pervasive regret, once the domain of verse where the metrical rhythms carry echoes from centuries gone by, are a new and unforgettable experience for the sensitive reader, and can expand and modify his whole auditory sensibility. In the experiments of Adūnīs the prose poem has the feel of an established

[23] See his article, 'On the prose poem', *Shiʿr*, No. 14, Spring, 1960.

structure. Adūnīs continued to write his poetry in the two forms, sometimes alternating between metrical and prose constructions in the same poem, with powerful aesthetic effect.

There were several other individual explorations of the potential of the Arabic poem in the fifties, especially in prose poetry. They indicate how the tools of poetry were now ripe for extensive change. The period of the fifties sees the flowering of Arab genius everywhere. The mainstream movement itself was now rapidly emerging as a bold, dynamic, revolutionary and vigilantly creative one, ready to exploit the vast possibilities of poetry in almost all aspects of the poem. By the mid 1950s poetry had embarked on an irrevocable road towards a modernity that first took on the experiences of other literatures then, with ever increasing manipulative skill and acumen, quickly assumed its own identity.

The main thing, however, that militated against a prose medium for poetry was the immensely rich variety of Arabic metres, most of which had still not been explored to their full potential.

2. Early modernist features: myth, archetype and the city theme Form, however, was not the only element of the poem to undergo major transformation. Modernist activity in the pioneer period was complex and all inclusive. Most aspects of the Arabic poem were explored and underwent change. Poets were reading in modernist western poetry, especially Eliot's poetry but also that of Edith Sitwell, Lorca, Yeats and the French Moderns from Baudelaire through Rimbaud, Mallarmé and the surrealists, up to St John Perse. They were also reading avidly in western poetic criticism, some of which had accompanied the European modernist movement. By the mid fifties they felt that their tools were now malleable enough for as many modernist techniques as possible to be attempted.

This early phase is strongly indebted to al-Sayyāb's profound sensibility and poetic genius, as well as to his sharp instinct for the principles of poetic change and continuity. As mentioned above, he accomplished the first successful modernist experiments, introducing the fertility myth, the historical archetype and the theme of the city, and spearheading the movement in the fifties.

Al-Sayyāb's famous poem '*Unshūdat al-maṭar*' ('Song of rain') which in true Eliotian fashion, implicitly incorporated the Tammuzian fertility myth of resurrection through life-giving rain and the coming of spring after winter and death, was published in the *al-Ādāb* literary review in 1954. It heralded the intensive use of various fertility myths by such poets as the Lebanese poets Khalīl Ḥāwī, Yūsuf al-Khāl, and the Syrian Adūnīs, who used other Tammuzian symbols (Adonis, Baal), Biblical figures like

Lazarus (who was used by Ḥāwī) and the crucifixion symbol (used by al-Sayyāb himself), or other myths such as that of the Phoenix, employed by Adūnīs. The climate in the fifties was ripe for a new faith in the possibility of rebirth after the deadening blow dealt by the 1948 Palestine catastrophe, and a vision of hope and potency began to appear on the dark horizon of defeat, carrying the belief in the possibility of change and transcendence for the generation growing up in the havoc of a post-1948 Arab world. Khalīl Ḥāwī's moving poem '*al-Jisr*' ('The bridge'), written in the fifties and also published in *al-Ādāb*, and al-Sayyāb's 'Song of Rain' were testimonies to this faith in a better future for the younger generation which was, however, soon to face the still greater tragedy of the June 1967 War. But even before 1967 many poets experienced a loss of heart, particularly after the dissolution of the Union between Egypt and Syria, which dealt a severe blow to dreams of Arab unity.[24]

However, the fertility myths soon became obsolete. They were not myths rooted in the memory of the people, but had to be learned from books and could not, therefore, hold a lasting emotional content. The idea of resurrection after death fascinated poets to such a degree that they turned the symbol into a fashion, with all the dangerous monotony and tame familiarity that fashions can quickly produce. By the early sixties, the symbol was so exhausted that aesthetic fatigue had set in, augmented by the changed psychological atmosphere as the years passed and no glimpse of revival was seen. It was after that that the other mythic introduction, that of the historical archetype, presented itself as a welcome antidote. In 1956 al-Sayyāb had published, also in *al-Ādāb*, his great poem, 'In the Arab Maghreb' in praise of the Algerian Revolution raging during that time. It was dominated by the same theme of renewal and resurrection and contained powerful archetypal symbols taken from real historical figures: the Prophet Muḥammad and his group of valiant followers who had heralded the dawn of Arab civilization. When the glory of this civilization was spent because of inner weaknesses, with the death of resistance and valour, God and His Prophet died in the people, but now they are seen alive again in the Algerian mountains. It is a complex and moving poem which provides a successful early example of mythic time, of the recurrence of events particular to the race, recreating strong communal feelings that encompassed the whole Arab people and imparted a sense of unity. This use of the archetype was to gain greatly in popularity after the June War of 1967, but it often acquired certain sinister streaks.

Another supremely important introduction made by al-Sayyāb was the

24 See Khalīl Ḥāwī's subsequent poem, 'Lazarus, 1962', which was an ironic exploitation of the theme of resurrection, for Lazarus here rises from the dead but only as a man with a dead spirit.

theme of the city, to which he gave prominent contours and a tone of urgency. It is perhaps impossible to determine whether the use of the city by other poets, notably Ḥāwī in his important volume, *Nahr al-ramād* ('River of ashes', 1958), was inspired by al-Sayyāb's superior and tragic treatment of this theme. However, the city is an authentic modernist symbol and it is possible that poets arrived at it simultaneously. To the modernists, the city was the centre of coercive government establishment, with its brutal police force and its hordes of informers, and was the home of thousands of social outcasts living in sordid conditions that drove them to the limits of their endurance. In al-Sayyāb's poetry, the city was juxtaposed against the image of his village, Jaykūr, which, with its innocence, fertility and abundance stands in stark contrast to the barrenness and sordidness of the city where the poet has to reside. His early conversion to Marxism made him more keenly aware of the injustices that afflict so many of the city's inhabitants – the poor, the prostitutes, the downtrodden, the lost – and he established the city early as a well-perfected symbol of the greatest poignancy.

The city theme was particularly attractive to a number of poets forced to move to the city in search of knowledge or work, poets like Khalīl Ḥāwī, the Egyptian Aḥmad ʿAbd al-Muʿṭī Ḥijāzī (b. 1935), Adūnīs and Muḥammad al-Māghūṭ (b. 1934). A further poet, the Iraqi Buland al-Ḥaydarī (b. 1926), although a city man with urban ties and habits, nevertheless recognizes the city as a grinding human mill and rejects it. In most of this poetry the city is nameless, and is held as a symbol of all Arab cities, with no particular differentiating features. The greatest exception to this is Ḥāwī who names his cities. Beirut is the archetypal hybrid meeting-place of east and west, where everything is false and borrowed. On the other hand, Paris and London are symbols of western greed and aggressiveness. Unlike al-Sayyāb, who is a victim of the city, Ḥāwī stands outside all this evil, an angry sage who rejects both sides without allowing either to soil him. This is the eternal stance of the 'poet-hero' which we will encounter in the work of many poets of the age of the pioneers. And here again, al-Sayyāb confirms his deeper modernist vision, as he recognizes modern man as the victim and not the hero of modern civilization.

The treatment of the city was to continue in modern Arabic poetry, and reach global importance in Adūnīs's poem 'A grave for New York', the finest poem in modern Arabic to envelope an authentic global vision of great poignancy and effectiveness.[25]

3. The experiment of Shiʿr *review* Writers on Arab literary modernity do not usually give al-Sayyāb his rightful place as the *first major modernist* who

[25] See my *Modern Arabic poetry, an anthology*, New York, 1987, for an English version of a large selection from this poem, translated by Lena Jayyusi and Alan Brownjohn.

established, through a fine poetic contribution unrivalled in the fifties, some of the basic tenets of this important movement. Whether in form, or in the new and potent introduction of various obliquities – symbol, myth and the historical archetype – al-Sayyāb is the undisputed pioneer, with only Nāzik al-Malāʾikah sharing his pioneering efforts in form. However, the general trend, particularly in the eighties, has been to focus primarily on the work of the Lebanese poet, Yūsuf al-Khāl. Al-Khāl's significant services to Arab poetic modernity began in 1957 after a long sojourn abroad during which al-Sayyāb had already accomplished, almost singlehanded and without the backing of theories and manifestoes, some of the most crucial modernist innovations needed to transform the whole sensibility of the Arab poet to a new modernist outlook in both vision and technique. Al-Khāl's first modernist activity began in 1957 when he founded his review *Shiʿr*, dedicated to poetry. In the same period, he delivered a key lecture at al-Nudwah al-Lubnāniyyah entitled 'The future of Arabic poetry in Lebanon',[26] in which he gave the movement – which was already robustly in progress in the Arab world – the name of 'Modern Poetry' (*al-shiʿr al-ḥadīth*), hitherto known mainly as 'free verse' (*al-shiʿr al-ḥurr*), naively named after its most conspicuous characteristic. Al-Khāl detailed some of the essentials of the modern movement. All previous schools of poetry were rejected. The continuation of a poetic outlook and technique many centuries old was attacked. Poetry, he insisted, should be the expression of a truly lived experience where the major objective is humanity. It was not apparent at the time how squarely this creed was opposed to the great tendency in the western modernist movement towards the dehumanization of art, and how reminiscent it was of the ideas of that early romantic Arab critic, Mīkhāʾīl Nuʿaymah. Important to the modernist concept was al-Khāl's call for poets to *challenge the logic of traditional patterns*, and to forge real change in the old language and expressions which had become exhausted with use, a point which he took up with great seriousness in later writings. The image should be living and complex, and poets should not use direct similes, facile metaphors and abstractions. It is clear that this lecture is not exactly a *modernist* address, in the way modernism was understood in the west, and it fell short of al-Sayyāb's earlier contributions to the modernist field, a situation which has not been corrected since in later writings on modernism.

On the pages of *Shiʿr*, al-Khāl intermittently published some of his ideas on modernity which he eventually collected into a book entitled, *al-Ḥadāthah fī'l-shiʿr* ('Modernity in poetry', 1978). His greatest target remained 'language', which he found to be a major impediment to the

[26] *Shiʿr* quarterly, No. 2, Spring, 1957.

modernization of Arabic literature. There is no scope to discuss here his ideas on language, diglossia and the connection between a given situation and the creativity of poets. The Arab poetic language, however, was taking an unpredictable course at the time, as will be shown presently, a proof that theory was not the strongest factor in poetic developments in our century.

On the pages of *Shiʿr*, also, avant-garde poets and critics found an open platform for their creative experiments and literary ideas, as well as for the publication of many translations of modernist poetry from other languages, especially French and English. The review was a listening-post for all robust new experiments, and showed a great interest in emerging young talents. Al-Khāl also founded a publishing firm affiliated with the review in which some of the boldest avant-garde experiments in poetry and fiction were published. A ramification of the journal's activity was its Thursday evening circle, *Khamīs Majallat Shiʿr*, where al-Khāl had, at his home in Ras Beirut, a weekly open house for poets, critics and lovers of poetry. For several years (1957–64), the review continued its avant-garde message until it foundered on the rocks of Arab politics, judged, not by its avant-garde aesthetic message, but by the political views of its two editors, al-Khāl and Adūnīs, who had aligned, during a period of high Arab nationalist feelings, with separatist Lebanese and Syrian nationalism. The cessation of the review was a great loss for poetry, with repercussions in the seventies when chaos reigned in the poetic field and the services of a knowledgeable avant-garde review would have been invaluable. Although *Shiʿr* resumed publication in 1967 and continued for two further years, it had lost much of its punch and stamina.

The uniqueness of the review had attracted the attention of many, but not all, of the major poets writing at the time. Some of the most prominent among them had little to do with it. ʿAbd al-Wahhāb al-Bayyātī (b. 1926), the Syrian Nizār Qabbānī (b. 1923), and the foremost Egyptian poets Ṣalāḥ ʿAbd al-Ṣabūr (1931–81) and Aḥmad ʿAbd al-Muʿṭī Ḥijāzī (b. 1935), were not involved with the magazine's activity. The case of ʿAbd al-Ṣabūr is interesting here because he is one of the foremost modernists, and has probably absorbed modernity in all its aspects better than any other poet of his age.

Mention is here due to the *al-Ādāb* literary review, founded in 1953 by Suhayl Idrīs, a Lebanese Arab Nationalist and writer of fiction. Unlike *Shiʿr*, *al-Ādāb* was open to all genres of literature and to all available views on poetry, fiction and drama. It strongly supported the great thrust of literature toward change and innovation and encouraged all avant-garde experiments, greatly welcoming innovative techniques without, however, concentrating exclusively on avant-gardism. Moreover, it sided faithfully with the aspirations of the majority of Arabs at the time towards Arab nationalism and Arab unity, and, unlike *Shiʿr*, it had a wide circulation all over the Arab world.

4. Language, tone and attitude One of the major changes forged in the Arabic poem was the radicalizing of the language and imagery of poetry. The Arab poetic language has seen a tremendous development during this century. Change began first with the neo-classical poets, and was continued by the romantics, then the symbolists. Diction acquired strength, terseness and classical purity from the first; mellowness, mistiness, fervour and great malleability from the second; and allusiveness and economy from the third. The poets of the modern school were the heirs of all these achievements, as well as all the negative linguistic qualities which these schools introduced. They also had to wrestle with the many new concepts concerning the connection of diction to life and to the spoken language of the people, its intonations and rhythms, and its relationship to the inherited language of classical literature and the Quran, the richest source of linguistic strength and sublimity in Arabic.

T. S. Eliot has stated that poetry has primarily to do with the 'expression of feeling and emotion', adding that 'these . . . are best expressed in the common language of the people – that is, in the language common to all classes: the structure, the rhythm, the sound, the idiom of a language, express the personality of the people which speaks it'.[27] Stephen Spender asserts that 'the street speaks the idiom' which artists have to learn. It is an 'idiom of changed speech, vision and hearing'. He speaks of modernist artists 'inventing an idiom which responds to the tone of voice of contemporaries . . .: the rhythms of an altered contemporary tempo, the new voice of a humanity at times when the old social hierarchies are breaking down'.[28] There are witnesses to this dictum in the development of modern Arabic poetry, and yet there are stark contradictions too. A fine low-key language has been consistently employed by ʿAbd al-Wahhāb al-Bayyātī, with no pedantic hangovers from classical or neo-classical times and no adherence to the idea of 'diction' as radically *different* from the language of fine prose. His language, in fact, is a finely poeticized version of written Arabic, perhaps the most 'natural' in its development that can be found in these experiments, since it maintained the strength and lustre of what readers of the time would normally recognize as being fit for poetry, with a skilful approximation to the accepted language of good Arabic prose. Nizār Qabbānī's language is an elevated rendition of the way in

27 'The social function of poetry', *On poetry and poets*, London, 1957, p. 19.
28 'The modern as a vision of the whole', in *The idea of the modern*, ed. Irving Howe, pp. 50–51.

which urban Arabs speak, particularly in the area of greater Syria (a mode of speech not free of occasional heroics, male chauvinist exhortations and national indictments and self-assertiveness), with all the intonations and rhythms of everyday language and the warmth of actual human exchange. However, it was Ṣalāḥ ʿAbd al-Ṣabūr, Egypt's foremost poet until his premature death in 1981, who best conquered the powerful hold of classical poetry on the subconscious of poets. He wrote in a modern language, with not only a vocabulary, a syntax, intonations and rhythms that were part of the auditory consciousness of contemporary Arabs, but also with a new modernist spirit permeating the whole work where a noticeable but subtle dislocation of structures and a toning down of address are effected.

The pioneer generation (that of the fifties, sixties and part of the seventies in particular) mostly had strong linguistic roots. Al-Sayyāb's choice of the exact word, Khalīl Ḥāwī's crucial selection of words denoting extreme emotional states and serious intellectual challenges, Nāzik al-Malāʾikah's inventive vocabulary of ecstasy, ardour, suffering and beauty – other writers could be instanced – were all witnesses to the linguistic power and originality of this innovative generation. Their language was fresh and not adulterated by use but, on the whole, there was little approximation to the language and cadences of common speech. Although the use of symbols by many of these poets introduced some difficulty, poetry remained on the whole lucid at that time compared to later output.

It was through the work of Adūnīs that the 'great divide' in the language of modern poetry was established. The appearance of his volume, 'Songs of Mihyar, the Damascene', in 1961 and the subsequent ever-increasing complexity of his linguistic adventure were, despite their rich aesthetic attributes, an interference with the 'natural' course of linguistic development. His diction acted as a buffer against any introduction of colloquialisms, vulgarities and over-simplifications. At the same time, it also demonstrated a fascination with elevated obscurity which, in the hands of many others who embraced his method, proved completely unmanageable. However, the experiment touched a living chord in the hearts of Arabs whose love for the flourish and lustre of the inherited poetic language, with its refinements and rhetorical sway, its majestic address and dramatic appeal, remained as vibrant as ever.

Adūnīs achieved at the same time a firm continuity and a definite discontinuity with classical diction and style. No deformation was allowed, and no disintegration in the well-built edifice of language in its massive integrity and formidable command. But at the same time a completely new syntax, full of classical authority yet fresh and utterly original, was achieved. Despite its discordance with the inherited syntax, it remained in harmony with the nobility and rhetorical elevation which were central qualities of the classical Arab poetic language. The new venture was a great leap towards 'differentness', towards the repudiation of repetitive methods and styles, yet by no means a break with them.

ᶜAbd al-Ṣabūr's poetry, on the other hand, continued to develop and grow in richness of nuances, without ever experiencing any reversal in the level of language and tone achieved by him right from the beginning. He went against the instinctive, the expected and the treasured language of poetry. By cutting himself off from the 'primal source' of poetic diction and using more familiar words and phrases, he was abandoning all that was rooted in the Arabic poetic language. He wrestled with words and meanings, creating new paths and a new sensibility by raising the ordinary language, not to the level of the poetic language familiar to Arab lovers of poetry at the time, but to that of a poetic apprehension of experience possessing great poignancy; and he succeeded uniquely in this. ᶜAbd al-Ṣabūr's early writings in the fifties were received with suspicion, sometimes with ridicule. When in one of his early poems he said,

> I drank tea on the way
> and had my shoe mended

people sniggered. He was trying, while still at the beginning of his career and unsure of his methods, to bring poetry to the people through a natural feeling for their contemporary linguistic structures. But Arabs, so long used to classical elevation, could not accept the sight of their sumptuous poetic language being reduced to the apparent (though deceptive) mundaneness of daily urban life in Cairo.[29]

Given the spontaneous repugnance among the Arab audience of poetry at the mid century to any serious disintegration of the inherited edifice of the poetic language, it is easy to understand the greater appeal of the diction of Adūnīs, whose accomplishments in this area helped to lend an elevated aura to poetic language and to father a trend of high-level linguistic structures which many poets have followed. Adūnīs himself has become aware, *now*, of his firm classical affinities. In an essay written in 1984, in which he diametrically contradicts his earlier ideas on the Arabic language as well as those put forward by al-Khāl, he confirms this:

[29] It is interesting to read about the 'shock that awaited those who read Eliot's poems' when they first appeared. The reaction was not much different from, probably even greater than, the reaction to ᶜAbd al-Ṣabūr's early experiments. Eliot's poems, which contained 'casual and apparently random lines, conversations, odd juxtapositions, drops into triviality, lines about the smell of beer and steaks in passageways, were utterly unacceptable to established critics and poets'. Julian Symons, *Makers of the new, the revolution in literature 1912–1939*, London, 1987, p. 70. See also p. 112 for the way 'Prufrock' was ignored on its appearance.

Arab society and the Arabic language are not two fungal plants that have just mushroomed; they have a long and rich history. Since Arab Modernity can only be accomplished in them and through them, the knowledge of their history, its origins, development and problems, particularly what is related to the secrets and genius of the language, is an integral part of our knowledge of 'Modernity.' For the Arab poet, to be modern is to have his writing shine as if it were a flame rising from the fire of the old, and as if it was, at the same time, another fire.[30]

Is this true of modernist poetic language? And what are the secrets of the Arabic language; what is its particular genius which differentiates it so radically from other living languages? The poet does not explain this, but he hints that this 'particular genius' should prevent the modern poet from having any real linguistic ties with the language of daily Arabic speech which, he asserts in a sweeping denunciation, is 'stripped of questions and curiosity, and is [merely] concerned with direct, functional needs'. Unlike the English language, he asserts, Arabic has its own particular poetic qualities. It is true, he agrees, that the need for communication is becoming more and more pressing, but this need might lead the poet to see language merely as a means or a tool, which is a contradiction of what poetry and poetic language stand for. He explicitly rejects as being valid for Arabic Eliot's concept of the poetic language reverting to the language of daily speech in order to renew and modernize itself. What works for English, he asserts, does not work for Arabic.[31] It is clear here that he is applying Eliot's dictum literally to Arabic and finds it difficult to accept.

However, the point about Arabic poetic language is not that it should revert to the colloquial, but rather that it should move towards the written language of contemporary Arabs, the language used in written prose, in books, and even in newspapers, but elevated, charged and illuminated by the poet's creative genius. When English speakers allude to the language of daily speech, they are in fact speaking of a language that does not differ too much in its grammar and syntax from the language used in books and newspapers. The case with Arabic at the present time is different. Contemporary Arabic has a wide divergence between the language of daily speech and the contemporary written language, where the grammar and the very structure of words differ, mainly because of the end vowels that are still applied in written Arabic. However, what contemporary written Arabic has achieved has been a greater simplification and modernization, and a closer affinity than in classical Arabic with the rhythms, vocabulary and sentence structure of daily speech. In fact, there is a constant interaction between daily speech and written contemporary Arabic involving a continuous reciprocal exchange of vocabulary and grammatical and rhythmic structures.

30 *Fī 'l-shiʿriyyah al-ʿArabiyyah*, Beirut, 1984, pp. 111–12.

31 See 'The poetics of harmony' in, *Siyāsat al-shiʿr*, Beirut, 1985, pp. 131–2.

Adūnīs's idea of the 'genius' of the Arabic language and of the particular qualities which make it different from, say, the English language, is a new departure for him. He was certainly thinking along completely different lines in 1961 when he claimed that the Arabic language was not a language suited to express life, but was intellectual and cerebral, constituting primarily form and sound and, quoting Jacques Berque, he asserted that 'it descends on life and does not ascend from it'.[32] This same language became, in the 1980s, one with a special genius, and must therefore be allowed its very special attributes. It is interesting also to note that Adūnīs removed the above statement when he reprinted the same article in his volume *Ṣadmat al-ḥadāthah* ('The shock of modernity', 1978).

However, Adūnīs's writings during the *same* period, the early sixties, betray a hidden uncertainty, a struggle between the impressionable mind that quoted Berque and others, and the poet's inner knowledge of his own poetic mechanism and affinities. Speaking about poetic language, he says it needs to be unfamiliar, and to have a strangeness that is perplexing and even tiring. The poet is described as a 'horseman of language', a master of words who liberates them from their old implications and charges them with a new spirit. However, he describes this process as a kind of *return* to the *first* innocence of words, to their *original magic*. 'The poet,' he adds, 'should go down to the *roots* of language, exploding their unlimited potential through unlimited rhythms.'[33] And this is precisely what he did. This statement echoes André Breton's ideas in *The Disdainful Confession* (1924) that the modern poet should rediscover language and give it 'something fundamental' which has been lost to it. He 'abstracts' words from their conventionalized place in speech and recombines them in such a way that their forgotten secondary potential – connotative properties, rhythmic and aural possibilities, similarities with other words, forgotten meanings – becomes primary. It carries even greater reverberations from Heidegger's pervasive use of an unfamiliar and 'tiring' style and vocabulary, and his dictum on language: his intent on words containing 'the greatest charge of initial and valid human perception', his insistence on 'returning to the well-springs of language' in order to realise 'the authentic intentions of human discourse'; his use of words 'in their own, supposedly primal and radical sense'; and his assigning to German and Greek (as Adūnīs assigned to Arabic in the eighties) a pre-eminent status.[34]

But these ideas of the western writers cannot be applied to Arabic literally, as Arabic has its own different situation. The modernist

32 'Arabic poetry and the problem of innovation', a paper read at the Conference on Modern Arabic Literature, Rome, 1961, and published later in *Shiʿr*, No. 21, Winter, 1962.

33 *Zaman al-shiʿr*, Beirut, 1972, pp. 242–5.

34 George Steiner, *Heidegger*, Sussex, 1978, pp. 15–16. I am indebted to Dr Sadik Azm (Ṣādiq al-ʿAẓm) for drawing my attention to this connection between Adūnīs and Heidegger's ideas.

rediscovery of language is a rediscovery of the Arabic language's *modern* potential of connotative possibilities, forgotten meanings and latent metaphorical dimensions. The going back to *roots*, the return to *the first innocence of language, to its original magic* which Adūnīs proposes have different implications in Arabic, involving a kind of classical eloquence, rhetorical appeal and tonal elevation, well demonstrated in his poetry. Now, after years of experimentation, this poet eventually realised that the only language in which he could write was the terse, elevated language of classical Arabic poetry, exploded, modulated and revolutionized by him, but without any shedding of the aura of the old poetry and its rhetorical hold on readers, without, as he would now say, abandoning the particular 'genius' and the special qualities of the Arabic language. And a new rationale had to be invented asserting that *modernist* Arabic diction must perforce be this elevated rhetorical diction which has preserved the 'genius of Arabic'! His assertion, in 1977, that 'there is no trace of memory in my poetry in the cultural sense, neither on the level of the heritage nor on the personal level' is inaccurate.[35] He would say, in Wyndham Lewis's words, 'My mind is ahistoric, I would welcome the clean sweep', but his genuine wish was frustrated by his *rhétorique profonde* and his *déjà vu* vision of grandeur and self-aggrandisement, so well entrenched in the national memory that critics and readers did not recognize it as an aberration in a poet calling for modernity.

The linguistic homelessness of ᶜAbd al-Ṣabūr's poetry was, understandably, inconceivable to Adūnīs. The two men had a radically different poetic background and a diametrically opposed poetic outlook. Poetry in Egypt, the country which had been the centre of classical revival with the poetic achievement of al-Bārūdī and Shawqī, had also seen many experiments *away* from classicism, which were able to create a new poetic climate in Egypt more tolerant of linguistic simplifications away from classical attributes.

Such a situation could not have flourished at that time in the countries east of the Mediterranean. The Syrian neo-classical school was firmly entrenched, and there was a deep reverence for classical poetic virtues in all these countries, especially in Syria and Iraq, but also in Lebanon and Palestine. Poets in these countries were brought up in the strongest traditions of classical Arabic poetry, and although the literary field in Iraq saw the rise of that iconoclast, Jamīl Ṣidqī al-Zahāwī, whose uses of linguistic simplifications were as adventurous as his experiments in the field of ideas, he fathered no trend. The poetic language was raised to a new elevation by a great poet in Iraq, Muḥammad Mahdī al-Jawāhirī. His work had strong classical roots, nurtured in the Shiᶜah centres of learning in al-

[35] Interview with Nasīm Khūrī published in *Al-Mustaqbal* review, No. 38, 12 November 1977.

Najaf, and the popularity of his poetry, with its classical strength and beauty and its rhythmic sweep, shows yet again the strong affinities Arabs still feel with the classical mode of expression. None of the major poets who rose to fame at the time in those countries east of the Mediterranean showed the influence of linguistic simplifications. Adūnīs himself had the advantage of a very strong early poetic education. An Alawite educated until his early youth in the entrenched classicism of a religious Shiʿah community, he had early studied the great Shiʿah poets and the commanding and ever-fresh writings of ʿAlī ibn Abī Ṭālib, the head of the Shiʿah sect and a revered personality for all Muslims.

In a long essay which he wrote at the death of ʿAbd al-Ṣabūr, Adūnīs puts forth, through a maze of superfluous compliments, his negative opinion of ʿAbd al-Ṣabūr's poetic language and stance. Regarding language he says, 'We were absolutely at two opposite poles. I used to wonder when I read his work (as he might have perhaps wondered when he read mine) if it was necessary, in order to get rid of the traditional and inherited and assert a new poetic alternative, to use simple or simplified diction, or the language of daily speech?' He goes on to say that Arab life exhausts the poet, and so some poets use an exhausted language. 'In a crushed reality' poets sometimes look for similarities between the crushed soul of the poet and a crushed language. 'This is how, at the artistic level, such poets write with what I call a language below language, so that it can harmonize with this Arab life, which is below life.' He speaks here of his constant call to poets to 'explode' the traditional poetic language and says that many poets, including ʿAbd al-Ṣabūr, had misunderstood his call, for he had not meant by this the use of common structures in daily speech or any journalistic simplifications. This, he goes on to say, might tempt some people to think that they are innovating. What he meant, however, was the 'exploding' of the traditional poetic structure itself, the structure, for example, of its vision and logic. The problem is to shake the body of language, not simply to change the outer garment.[36]

In the same essay, Adūnīs alludes to ʿAbd al-Ṣabūr as a poet who preferred harmony to dissonance. He goes on to say, 'It seems to me that the problem of Arab society in general and of Arab culture in particular lies in the domination of what is prevalent over what is possible, of the tendency to compromise over the tendency to transcend'. Taken out of context, this is a true modernist stance, but in context it does grave injustice to ʿAbd al-Ṣabūr's whole poetic corpus, which harbours an authentic protest against

36 See 'The poetics of harmony', pp. 132–3. Was he implying that ʿAbd al-Ṣabūr heeded his words but misunderstood them? This sounds rather implausible in view of the fact that ʿAbd al-Ṣabūr, who was an independent poet, had started writing this kind of verse right from the beginning of his career in the mid fifties, before Adūnīs began writing critical theories about poetry.

the ills that hamper Arab life and the human condition in general. Adūnīs misunderstood the gentle but firm tones, the subtle rejections, the visionary but unheroic stance. A poet of loud tones, of strong manifestations of protest, negation, defiance and indictment, of passionate exhibitions of strength and potency, Adūnīs could not react favourably to ʿAbd al-Ṣabūr's more subdued tones and demure stance, which were the essence of the latter's modernity. It is the poets who see themselves as victims, not as heroes and conquerors, who will be able to employ lower tones or resort to ironic or comic modes. ʿAbd al-Ṣabūr resorted only occasionally to a comic expression of protest, which was a potent weapon in the hands of another modernist poet, Muḥammad al-Māghūṭ, but he employed in much of his poetry an underlying, often very subtle irony which was highly effective. However, irony's more modest and 'plebeian' tones and simpler language so far almost completely eluded Adūnīs and many other poets of his generation, who have also been wholly incapable of incorporating any saving humour into their work. This explains partly why Adūnīs's writings on ʿAbd al-Ṣabūr immediately after his death were so evasive in their praise.

Protest need not resort to loud terms, or adopt a heroic stance. By his very psychological and intellectual make-up – modest, gentle, idealistic, urbane and sophisticated – ʿAbd al-Ṣabūr was no heir to an inherited expression of heroics. He was a true child of the mid twentieth century with all its tragic destruction of individual heroism. Contemporary Arabic poetry has seen a pervasive continuity of heroic modes (which are almost non-existent in contemporary Arabic fiction – but then poetry has had a long history of these stances while fiction, a genre that has been developed only in this century as a *modern* experiment, does not), preserving a heroic tone rarely overcome in poetry before the eighties. Among his generation, ʿAbd al-Ṣabūr was the greatest exponent of this new, non-heroic attitude. Although the need for valiant self-sacrifice is still part of Arab resistance to the many aggressive forces, external and internal, that have ravaged the world around the poet, the tone of heroic resistance and virile defiance can contradict our sense of reality, and the nagging feeling that we have all become the *victims* of this unrelenting political malaise persists. Among the earlier poets of this period, ʿAbd al-Ṣabūr, and with him such poets as the Syrian Muḥammad al-Māghūṭ and, a little later, the Iraqi Saʿdī Yūsuf, (b. 1943), have cut the strings that might have tied them to the role of the ever-resistant hero, and have confessed in humble modernist terms their vulnerability and, indeed, the vulnerability of Arab life around them. The victim, which is the true identity of the hero in our times, can still resist, but he is not the inviolate and splendid hero of Ibrāhīm Ṭūqān's (1905–41) martyrs who face death unflinchingly, but rather the heroic victim who will let out a moan at the hour of death, and yet persist in defending his own dignity and honour, entering, in Raymond Williams' terms, 'the heroic deadlock in which men die still struggling to climb'.[37] The Palestinian poet Maḥmūd Darwīsh's (b. 1942) recent heroes are almost all of this kind.

The language, tone and attitude of poetry in this period were partly decided by the concept the poet had of himself and his role. In ʿAbd al-Ṣabūr's case, 'the hero defies an opposing world, full of lies and compromises and dead positions, only to find, as he struggles against it, that as a man he belongs to this world, and has its destructive forces in him'.[38] In his poetry, language undergoes a displacement from its inherited heights and ceases to be, in Richard Sheppard's words, 'the tool for asserting human lordship'.[39] As personified by Adūnīs, on the other hand, the poet is the 'heroic and liberating individual' with the power of the judge, who sees things from above and brings down his final indictment on a false and weak society. Stephen Spender gives a poignant interpretation of these two attitudes and their relationship to modernism. He speaks of those poets and writers who had the Voltairean 'I', that is 'the confidence that they stood outside a world of injustices and irrationality which they judged clearly with their powers of reason and imagination. They are not the product of the times that they deplored.' He goes on to explain that the Voltairean 'I' 'acts upon events', while the modern 'I' 'is acted upon by them'. The first tries to influence the world, the second, 'through receptiveness, suffering, passivity, *transforms* the world to which it is exposed' [italics mine]. Spender speaks of the Voltairean egoists whose belief is that they can deliver the world from evil, comparing them with the modernists (he mentions Rimbaud, Joyce, Proust and Eliot) who 'by allowing their sensibility to be acted upon by the modern experience as suffering, . . . will produce, partly as the result of unconscious processes, and partly through the exercise of critical consciousness, the idioms and forms of new art'.[40]

I have dwelt a little on this theme because it is essential for our understanding of contemporary Arab modernity. I also wanted to demonstrate how modern Ṣalāḥ ʿAbd al-Ṣabūr was and how greatly he was misunderstood. Adūnīs's labelling of his attitude towards the malaise of contemporary life around him as simply 'acquiescence' is a gross error of judgement. It does not recognize the modern consciousness of suffering as part of the modern sensibility, and does not realise the state of victimization to which the Arab malaise reduces the individual. This is strange coming from Adūnīs, for he is no stranger to this kind of suffering – although he

[37] *Modern tragedy*, Stanford, 1966, p. 100.
[38] Williams, *Modern tragedy*, p. 98.
[39] 'The crisis of language', p. 333.
[40] See 'Moderns and contemporaries', pp. 43–4.

tries to transcend it and mix it with a heroic streak so much a part of the inherited culture in which, despite his manifest conscious efforts to overcome it, he has somehow remained trapped. Adūnīs, however, is only partly 'Voltairean'. He hovers on the borderline between prophecy and tragic suffering, a Job-like prophet who is not averse to weeping as he indicts. He remains, nevertheless, outside the dungeons and never enters the soiled world of his contemporaries. This is why he misunderstood Ṣalāḥ ʿAbd al-Ṣabūr so completely.

The problem with most contemporary Arab poets (Adūnīs included) has been a *problem of tone and attitude*, because these have been the two major elements of the poem which, except rarely, were not much liberated before the eighties. Most pre-eighties poets almost never accepted a de-elevated, de-classed position for the poet.

What ʿAbd al-Ṣabūr achieved among his generation was a diverse manipulation of tone which placed him at the very heart of the modernist experiment. There were quite a few other poets who manipulated tone with flexibility, producing lower, more modernist expressions completely free of assertiveness and demonstrative heroics. Among these are Tawfīq Ṣāyigh, the new surrealists such as Unsī al-Ḥāj, Shawqī Abī Shaqrā and ʿIṣām Maḥfūẓ (b. 1939), and later Saʿdī Yūsuf. If a poet is proud enough not to acquiesce or surrender; and if he is modest enough (and realistic enough) not to believe he is the heroic redeemer and liberator of his times, the ultimate prophet and teacher; and if he can move from a tragic apprehension of the predicament that stifles his life (and everybody else's) to a position where he clearly sees the other, ironic face of tragedy; and finally, if he can achieve all this in a low, unassuming tone, then he has achieved genuine modernity.

In his poetry ʿAbd al-Ṣabūr never compromised, never accepted the prevalent. He wrote a poetry marked by a self-inversion of tradition and focusing on aspects of experience that have never occupied space in poetry before, probing deeply into the meaning of life and, in true modernist fashion, stripped of heroics, devoted to questions, completely free of absolutes, permeated, in its discovery of human frailty, by the two opposing streaks of the tragic and the ironic, with no real anchorage in which to rest, no feeling of security. It is, moreover, the poetry of a tormented soul, yet sparse in its overt emotions, employing rhythms that are alien to the strong, impassioned rhythms of inherited poetry, and a language so simplified that it defies one's expectations. His thematic range spans the cycle of life and death (*Ughniyyah lī'l-shitāʾ*, 'Winter song', *al-Shams wa 'l-marʾah*, 'The sun and the woman'), the warmth of love and the loneliness of its absence ('The gist of the story'), the disintegration of values

(*Ḥikāyat al-mughannī 'l-ḥazīn*, 'Story of the sad minstrel'), the *ennui* and disappointments of life (*Intiẓār al-layl wa 'l-nahār*, 'Expectations night and day'), and a wide range of communal preoccupations ('The return of the ugly face', *al-Nās fī bilādī*, 'The people of my country', *Hajama 'l-Tatār*, 'The Tartars' attack').

The term 'modern' must at once refer both to sensibility and to technique, to vision and to style, and no matter how modernist a poet's methods of writing are, it is always the way he looks at the world that will help decide how really 'modern' he is. Because of the immediate cultural background of the Arab world now, and the little time poets have had to undergo an authentic transformation towards a modern outlook on man and his universe, the insistence on sensibility and attitude when sizing up modernity in any experiment is of paramount importance.

Mention is here due of other successful experiments in the fifties and sixties which aimed at complexity and challenged the old order of words. The experiments with language of Unsī al-Ḥāj and Shawqī Abī Shaqrā and a few others were even more daring than those of Adūnīs but, being less rhetorical, were less attractive to the audience of poetry in the fifties and sixties. It took al-Ḥāj almost three decades to achieve the warm recognition which he now enjoys amongst the younger generation of poets. His poetry has gained greater simplicity, tenderness and a tone of deeper pathos, while Abī Shaqrā's continued to be complex but always touching in its tenderness and gentle tones. The influence of all these experiments must, however, be re-examined in future years, when there is a longer perspective from which to judge.

In the seventies, some very fine talents rose to fame writing a poetry of complex human situations in a language and style that were extremely difficult and often wayward, but were also deeply inspired and of a high artistic order. Outstanding among this group are the Iraqi, Ḥasab al-Shaykh Jaᶜfar (b. 1942), the Egyptian, Muḥammad ᶜAfīfī Maṭar (b. 1935) and the Syrian, Salīm Barakāt (b. 1951), though there are others too. During the seventies, these poets were leaders among the younger generation in this trend towards linguistic complexity and sophistication, but in the eighties only a few persisted in this method, as more and more poets found their way to an intermediate style of fine aesthetic expressiveness.

The second trend, the language of which stems from the written language of contemporary Arabic, culminated in the seventies in one of the finest experiments of modern Arabic poetry, that of Saᶜdī Yūsuf, whose regrettably slow rise to a position of poetic leadership was due to the unprecedented fascination felt by his generation of poets for the style and the linguistic and metaphorical practices of Adūnīs and others writing in the same vein. By the time Saᶜdī Yūsuf had succeeded in establishing his method, many talents had already been lost to poetry, talents whose artistic instincts were not strong enough to resist the weakening of their control over their language and metaphors.

5. Metaphor The difficulties surrounding the language of poetry in this period were augmented by the radical metaphorical adventure which accompanied it. The two experiments increased in complexity and sophistication with the years, but also developed many negative qualities.

In my critical history, *Trends and movements in modern Arabic poetry*, Vol. II, I discuss more fully than I can do here the metaphorical achievement of the pioneers. The experiments of this generation in the realm of the image liberated poetry from the abstractions and excesses of previous schools, and founded a more 'modern' basis for the image in Arabic. It was as if a vast new area of experimentation was suddenly made available to poets. A new fascination arose, a new feeling of liberation, of potency and audacity, of disalienation from the sanctimonious awe felt by poets towards radical experimentation in imagery, allowing a wide scope of new varieties of comparison. Poets were dominated by a deep wish to invent, to use their imagination and skill to their extreme. The best among them entered all realms of experience and were able to take advantage of the metaphorical power latent in all objects, finding fresh metaphorical equations for their new vision of the world. Old restrictions were now transcended and there seemed to be no end to inventiveness. Paradox, symbol and all kinds of obliquity were introduced with zeal and originality.

The attempts of al-Sayyāb became a major reference for the new imagery of modern poetry. A master of the metaphor, he could produce an immediate striking effect, exploring all kinds of kinetic, auditory, organic and visual imagery. However, his images were too crisp, clear and direct to serve maximally the *modernist* cause of poetry, and it is in his other contributions to the poem, discussed above, that his uncontested early lead in the modernist movement in Arabic is due. The poet who laid the cornerstone for the modernist treatment of the image in Arabic poetry, however, is Adūnīs.

What realm of the image was not attempted, renovated and exploded by Adūnīs? His is the unrivalled venture into this most intricate area of poetics, achieving complexity, originality and sophistication, and effecting a *mélange* between mysticism and surrealism. This is where this poet excels over anyone else, of his generation and of all generations. Of course, he tried to explode diction as much as he tried to explode the metaphor, and in one sense succeeded in that, but only to a certain degree. It is his imagery, however, which remains his greatest modernist achievement; his diction, despite its captivating beauty, remained alienated from a truly harmonious relationship with contemporary Arabic. It is often imperious and authoritative, retaining the loud tones and overbearing attitudes of classical times, albeit redeemed to a good degree by the poet's rejection of old associations and by his unfamiliar word combinations. Although, as we have seen, he writes pervasively on language, making it a central issue of the poetics he has been trying to expound, his remarks on the poetic image do not reach even partly the level of creativity he achieved in his actual treatment of the image, or show any real awareness of the crucial modernist experiment he carried out in the realm of the metaphor. He maintains that the image should be surprising, and that poets should use metaphors, not similes, a generally accepted modern premise voiced by many others. However, images, he asserts, are not the element which helps immortalize a poem. Writing before the seventies, the decade when poets, mainly under the influence of his own experiment, exaggerated their metaphorical adventure, making the image a central aim in the poem, he cautioned against allowing the images to dominate the poem totally, for 'the greatness and importance of the images are conditioned by their capacity to uncover the radiance of the poem's vision' or 'its poetic universe, with its relationship to man and the world'.[41]

Adūnīs's images are difficult and complex, self-conscious and often non-representational, reflecting, in true modernist fashion, a deep devotion to the aesthetics of the poem. They almost always contain an element of surprise, creating a completely unusual and unexpected atmosphere. They often form a central part of his poem. He culls them from all avenues of life and experience, treating the forms and shapes of the actual world around him as a means to satisfy the aesthetic necessities of his poem. This makes his experiment with metaphor a highly adventurous endeavour. In fact, the importance of his metaphorical inclusions sometimes transcends the vision and reality of the poem so that they form a world of their own. Although they usually inform his vision, they sometimes seem, in contradiction to what he says above, to have the purpose of simply realising themselves. Thus they are often alienated from direct reality. He seems, in fact, intent on 'deforming reality', as Ortega y Gasset would put it, on destroying the bridges and burning the ships 'that take us back to our daily world'. And it is a great achievement indeed to be able to 'construct something that is not a copy of "nature" and yet possesses substance of its own'. What Ortega further says about reality constantly waylaying the artist to prevent his

[41] *Zaman al-shiʿr*, pp. 231–2.

flight is also true, and it is certain that much artistic acumen is needed to effect the 'sublime escape'[42] which Adūnīs achieves through a metaphorical adventure that has preserved its aesthetic uniqueness despite the large following it attracted.

The most revolutionary aspect of Adūnīs's metaphorical adventure is the radicalization of the relationship between the image and its object. He coined many images of this sort in which there was often a remote relationship between these two agents, and imposed a new skill which younger poets strove, often beyond their talent and means, to achieve. His resort to paradox, although not as frequent, was also quite effective. However, most of his paradoxical formations were more of the directly verbal kind; he rarely wrote a whole poem built on paradox, as did poets like al-Malāʾikah and Tawfīq Ṣāyigh, for this kind of poetry is built on wit, and Adūnīs is more tragic and directly angry than witty.

'Modernity' as a subject of crucial importance was formally presented in the late seventies and early eighties by Adūnīs, but also by others. It quickly became an obsession, and the eighties saw an ardent involvement by poets, critics and readers alike with its nature, manifestations, conditions and 'crucial necessity'. It was treated not as a manifestation of artistic development that might or might not happen to a poetry, but as the ultimate goal, the 'be all and end all' of artistic progress, the sign of literary status and distinction. It became a fetish.

The campaign was more complex and sophisticated than the earlier writings in *Shiʿr*. With their crucial socio-political vision of liberation from traditions and established order, put forward at a time of great anger at military defeats, especially after the 1967 June War, Adūnīs's writings carried great attraction.

Adūnīs's two main essays, 'The shock of modernity' (1978) and 'The manifesto of modernity' (1980) best epitomize his ideas, but also reflect his serious contradictions. For lack of space, only a short outline is possible. The basic principles he asserts in the 1978 essay are that modernity is a timeless principle and happens when poets reject inherited models and assert individuality and uniqueness. But in Arabic culture Islam played a negative role, for it revolved around prophecy and dictated permanence of outlook and rigidity, emphasizing a constant reproduction of the old. This stood in opposition to western technology. For years Adūnīs had carried on a sustained attack on Islam, denigrating it as the greatest hindrance to creativity and hence to modernity.[43] This reductionist, idealistic tendency

[42] 'The dehumanisation of art', pp. 88–90.

[43] See *Mawāqif*, No. 6, 1969; and *Crisis in Arab thought*, essays presented at a conference in Kuwait, 1974, published by the Kuwaiti Ministry of Culture, 1974.

in him was further complicated by irreconcilible shifts in major attitudes and principles. For after the Islamic revolution in Iran in 1979, Islam suddenly became the prime mover of history and an awakening as bright as the sun.[44] This same attitude was repeated in his 'Manifesto'. Although here he again reasserts his refreshing call for a permanent revolt against the static in favour of individual uniqueness, he totally ignores his basic argument regarding the role religious authority played in stultifying Arabic culture. The most drastic notion he advances in his 'Manifesto' is the essentialist, Kipling-like opposition of East and West. At the level of creativity, he asserts, there is nothing which the West had not taken from the East; religion, philosophy, poetry, are all eastern. The speciality of the West is technology, a bastard, characterized by exploitation, domination, colonization and imperialism.

These assumptions by Adūnīs, laid out with eloquence and command, seem to presuppose, in a kind of reverse Orientalism,[45] the presence of natural attributes and divisions of functions between East and West, a kind of permanence in the qualities of nations and races, obviously untenable. However, contemporary avant-garde poetry seems to be taking some trends that are free of the conditions and ascriptions that have been laid down in the writings on modernity in general. It is as if Arabic poetry has now arrived at an artistic maturity that drives it on a course of its own, one of high aesthetic quality, the result, surely, of the numerous pervasive experiments that have been going on throughout the past decades, but a course that transcends contemporary theory and will itself dictate the birth of new theories to explain it.

B: *The Second Phase: The Seventies*

The general contradictions and the controversial nature of the ideas put forward by Adūnīs, al-Khāl and others on modernity produced an embarrassed and often erratic notion of the subject among readers even up to the end of the eighties. However, the basic insistence in these writings on creativity and uniqueness, and the persistent rejection of repetitiveness and rigid traditions, helped give young poets a new faith and self-confidence in their own possibilities, to enhance their courage to examine cultural strains and hindrances, and to inspire in them the audacity to create and experiment in areas hitherto treated with caution and often with conservative reverence. It was, however, Adūnīs's poetic experiment that influenced younger poets indelibly. The creative strangeness and artistic complexity of his poetry, and its loudly announced links with 'modernity', held an

44 'Thoughts on the Islamic Revolution in Iran', in *Al-Nahār al-ʿArabī wa 'l-dawlī*, Feb. 26, 1979.

45 See Sadik Azm, *Orientalism and orientalism in reverse, (al-Istishrāq wa 'l-istishrāq maʿkūsan)*, Beirut, 1981; and see M. J. Bārūt, 'The illusions of modernity', ('Awhām al-ḥadāthah') in *al-Nāqid* review, London, No. 10, April 1989, p. 23.

irrefutable attraction for the poets. The robust classical strength of his language, its sublime rhetoric, were rather intractable to many younger poets, but the audacity to radicalize linguistic structures and coin new vocabulary became a great preoccupation. However, the element which aroused the greatest incentive to experimentation among the poets of the sixties and seventies was Adūnīs's metaphorical adventure.

This metaphorical and linguistic approach, already established by the end of the sixties, was one of two major developments which took place simultaneously just before the beginning of the seventies. The second was the 1967 June War, with the enduring pain and frustration which losing this war generated among Arab poets and audience alike, and the resurgent wave of hope and pride which the rise of the Palestinian resistance at the end of the sixties created in the seventies. The natural tension between these two developments may account for the ensuing chaos of the decade.

Thus we had at once an aesthetic experiment being brought to a frenzy by the absolute fascination with it of a whole generation of younger poets, and a compulsive political involvement with resistance and heroic themes of courage and steadfastness. A deep commitment to aesthetics found itself, therefore, embracing an equally deep commitment to politics and life, with the two merging together into one unified experiment and experiencing, as a consequence, the pulls and strains of contradictory directions. There is no poet of importance (or otherwise, in fact), who has not been involved with the political situation in the Arab world in one way or another. The idea put forward by George Rylands that poetry is 'most simple when most terrible'[46] has been, therefore, radically contradicted by the poets of the seventies, for although the poetry of this decade revolved around terrible situations referring to war and defeat, to resistance and confrontation, to challenge and sacrifice, that is to clear human situations emotionally apprehended by all members of society, it aspired towards great complexity which, had it been artistically apt and mature, could anyway have been apprehended only by an elitist group of readers. As it was, much of it was apprehended by no one. The more inventive the metaphors, the richer the poem was thought to be. The result was that the fundamental aesthetic principle of economy often came to be overlooked as the poet, in a race against himself and others, crowded image after image, often unrelated and of the 'fire and water' type, into the poem, for the sheer purpose of inventiveness.

A whole generation of poets from Bahrain and Yemen to Morocco sank deeper and deeper into inventiveness for its own sake, unguided by any informed criticism that could help lead poets to a deeper insight into poetic

[46] *Words and poetry*, 2nd edn, 1928, p. 37.

methods and possibilities. This was augmented by the persistence of a high tone in poetry. Writing as they were on themes of resistance, anger and frustration, the achievement of lower rhythms and tones was, for most young poets, almost impossible at the time, and a loud, heroic tone together with pronounced rhythms dominated many poems. Much poetry was written that sounded like oratory in a foreign language. By the beginning of the eighties much pessimistic protest about the fate of Arabic poetry was being written all over the Arab world. Except for the work of a few poets, the major harm that befell poetry in general was that the uniqueness of the work vanished. There came to be a uniformity of style all over the Arab world, a series of highly energetic simulations and repetitions, so that it became very difficult to recognize any particular author or his local background. It was not only metaphor and vocabulary that became similar, but also themes and emphasis. Poetry was no longer held together by the internal strength of the poet's style, as was the case in the poetry of al-Sayyāb, al-Bayyātī, Ḥāwī, al-Malāʾikah and other earlier poets, but by the communal voice orchestrated in hundreds of poems and given validity by a deficient criticism trying to provide it with false modernist interpretations. However, amidst this anarchy, with its taste for the colossal and the extreme, an almost demonic energy for experimentation was generally displayed, a real line of creativity persisted, and several tendencies established themselves as positive modernist streaks. The best poetry came to be characterized by difficulty, novelty and sophistication, mixed with the notions of alienation and disintegration; and a sense of anguish, disorientation and nightmare dominated. Above all, the break with the past was quickly asserting its mark.

C. The Third Phase: The Eighties

It is now clear that the activity of the seventies was not foredoomed to sterility. It is true that by the beginning of the eighties a large amount of bad poetry had accumulated, but it turned out not to be a fungoid growth, not the beginning of decline as so often predicted.

Moreover, there were splendid and varied experiments in the seventies from which the later poets learned. Aside from the continued influence of al-Sayyāb, Ḥāwī and, above all, Adūnīs, whose poetry increased in sophistication and complexity, there were other poets whose kind of poetry is more deeply related to the best poetry of the eighties. First we have ʿAbd al-Ṣabūr's urbane and sensitive verse. One cannot overemphasise the importance of this poet's liberation, discussed above, from the non-modern concept of the poet as king, prophet and liberator, an attitude which was to establish itself decisively in the eighties. Then there is ʿAbd al-Wahhāb al-

Bayyātī's poetry with its lower tones and its deep interest in the plight and destiny of 'others'. However, Bayyātī's abiding faith in humanity had no aesthetically inferior relations to sloganism and didacticism, and his poetry developed constantly towards more complexity and deeper human implications. Another poet who superbly served the attitudinal element in poetry was Aḥmad ʿAbd al-Muʿṭī Ḥijāzī. He is almost unique among his generation (Tawfīq Ṣāyigh being an exception) in having been able to transcend the inherited self-glorification of poets and to admit, through a verse of candid confession, his own failings and limitations. It was only in the poetry of the eighties that this spirit of candour and modest appraisal of the human condition as it is exemplified by the poet himself finds an echo. Then there is Muḥammad al-Māghūṭ's poetry, with its modernist vision and its constant thrusts against contemporary political coercion and failure. His work is penetrated by a sense of anguish, where the poet stands terrorized, trembling with anger and fear, one of the victims of our epoch, whose greatest preoccupation is to avert the terror that can be imposed gratuitously upon him at any moment. It is also a truly modernist poetry in its language and style: derisive, ironic, negative and highly irreverent, using concrete, reverberating, witty images and similes to let out the most profound cry against contemporary horror and militarism. We have, too, Maḥmūd Darwīsh's mixture of agony and ecstasy, of pride and despair, of resistance and recognition of the dominating evil that foils heroism. A spokesman for his struggling people, he certainly cannot eliminate from his poetry the image of the resistant hero and the notions of valour and self-sacrifice that describe the strife of the hero towards freedom. Nevertheless, with his penetrating instinct as a great poet, he cannot but recognize the victim that lurks in the garb of the hero. Since the Tel al-Zaatar massacre of 1976, where fifteen thousand Palestinians, mainly civilians, were killed by the Lebanese Phalangist forces, and the ensuing catastrophes that befell the Palestinians thereafter – the exodus from Beirut following the Israeli invasion of 1982, and the Sabra and Shatila massacres in the same year – his voice has become impregnated with the proud sorrow of a spirit that knows that valour and the readiness to die for a great and just cause are no longer enough to redeem the hero in a contemporary world dominated by machine superiority and international power politics. The hero in his poetry is a man fighting to the limits of his capacity, striving and aspiring despite exile and defeat. Darwīsh's once triumphant and sometimes tragic hero has, therefore, finally become a heroic victim. It is this sensitive recognition that finally saves his verse, and sustains its inspirational power as it imbues it with a more modern spirit away from the loud bravado of all-potent heroics. And this has been a great gain for poetry because of the riches of his imagery, his profound originality and the depth and intensity of his ennobling vision. And then there is Saʿdī Yūsuf, indeed a poet of our times. His poetry became one of the cornerstones which has kept the new modern tradition healthy, and gifted young poets in the eighties were to follow his style more than that of any other. Characterized at the same time by simplicity and sophistication, directness and obliquity, it also has the necessary low tone and modern vision of the world at the end of the twentieth century. It is not clear if Saʿdī Yūsuf has been influenced by ʿAbd al-Ṣabūr, for their sensibility is somehow different. It is true that both poets have a sense of the tragic, are splendidly free of sentimentality, and see the universe as a place of constant struggle and disappointment, delineating a vision of a broken world full of victims and fallen heroes. It is true too that both poets often resort to the tragi-ironic mode. But while ʿAbd al-Ṣabūr elevated his theme to speak of great universals and of major national and human issues, Saʿdī Yūsuf often opted for the little things in life, announcing the rise of the 'little' man in an Arabic poetry accustomed for centuries to the celebration of the great and mighty. It is this kind of vision that has, finally, ushered in the true modern climate of Arabic poetry.

In their best work the younger poets of the eighties have confirmed the shift of sensibility that began in the fifties, and brought it to fulfilment. They were able to cut the umbilical cord that had linked them to the poetry of the pioneers and to show real independent creativity. The style which Adūnīs had established, and which was widely imitated in the sixties and seventies, proved to be less attractive to the new poets who, quite instinctively, chose a simpler style, nearer to the contemporary written, and, in quite a few experiments, the spoken language. The great exploration of the image in the seventies allowed gifted poets to find their way eventually to sound metaphorical representation, as fatigue with the undisciplined use of metaphor set in. The heroic mode and the vaunting spirit finally subsided. On the artistic level, the poetry of resistance and heroics reached saturation point, having by then exhausted all its technical resources, and repetition of the same attitudes, phrases and motifs made it artistically impossible to continue in this direction.

Related to this was the psychological climate of the period: the great spiritual fatigue felt regarding slogans, the increasingly heavy stamp of authority and of a coercive political order, and the continued external aggressions and global conspiracies against the poet's world, particularly in Palestine and Lebanon (Iraq at least was winning the war), all these were crushing the spirit of the individual. The poets of the fifties, sixties and the greater part of the seventies spoke to the world as prophets and leaders. They felt they could impose on their audience their visionary concept of a world in need of a saviour, whether this saviour was the leader born from the stock of the gods (Ḥāwī), the simple people triumphant at last and taking hold of their own destiny (Sayyāb and Bayyātī), or the poet himself perceiving, admonishing and guiding (Adūnīs and Qabbānī). There was, throughout the period before the eighties, greater faith in both the individual and the nation: in the two earlier decades, because the Palestine catastrophe was still new and had greater hopes of a solution, and because the national dream of Arab solidarity and perhaps even unity was still largely possible; and in the seventies, because of the active presence of the Palestinian resistance. The eighties had a different outlook. Repeated national disasters became unendurable psychologically, the curtailment of freedom had driven people into silence or exile, and an atmosphere of frustration and passive anger hung over the world of the poet.

The change in the best poetry of the eighties is dramatic. It is not at all the case that the new poets are introverted, individualistic, self-centred men and women. In fact, they are now more expansive and convincing, because they have been able to break free at last from the constrictions of an almost exclusive political preoccupation, yet without ever losing their concern for the increasing political dilemma of the Arab world. The political situation, particularly in its qualities of coercion and fragmentation, is very much a part of their experience, imposing itself quite often on their poetic vision. However, they view it now with the eyes of men and women who know their limitations and who have at last fully realised the dimensions of the conspiracy imposed upon their freedom; and whose concepts of themselves and of the role they can play as poets is diametrically changed. This is demonstrated eloquently in the works of contemporary Iraqi and Palestinian poets. Both groups have been engaged in a national strife, the first in a grinding war with Iran and the second in a protracted and soul-wrenching struggle with Israel for freedom and identity. In their work, both groups demonstrate the strongest belief in the necessity of solidarity and the glorious outcome of the struggle. However, even during the bloody Iraq–Iran war, Iraqi poetry was changing radically and we have sensitive poets like Yāsīn Ṭāhā Ḥāfiẓ (b. 1938), Sāmī Mahdī (b. 1940), and Ḥamīd Saᶜīd (b. 1941), all committed and highly placed government officials, abandoning the strident martial rhythms of war poetry even when writing about war. However, they also write about a hundred other preoccupations, personal and social, in the calm, low-toned, often private voice of the modern poet. As for the Palestinians, highly gifted poets in exile such as Aḥmad Daḥbūr (b. 1945), Khayrī Manṣūr (b. 1944), Murīd Barghūthī (b. 1946), Muḥammad al-Asᶜad (b. 1944) and several others are now writing a poetry whose modernist qualities help furnish proof that art has its own inner logic for growth.

It was *vision* and *tone* in poetry that underwent the greatest metamorphosis in this period. The moment the poet abandoned his vision of himself or another as hero and liberator, his tone and diction were bound to change. The defiant staccato rhythms, the devotional, solemn and fervid tone of the earlier periods, pregnant with loud proclamations of faith and the celebration of heroism, now abated. The clear-sighted vision the poet had of himself as hero and visionary shouldering the responsibility of the world gave way, in some, to a new ironic self-criticism, or to a calm contemplation of the kind of tragic experience which has afflicted the individual in the Arab world, changing him into the perpetual victim suffering fear and frustration from the total siege of his freedom, and the harsh entrenchment of autocracy and compliance. Much of what had always been prosaic was poeticized, and the trivial things of daily life were often used to expose a compromised, suffocating existence. A new loss of faith is detected at times, but is offered without the sonorous anger and terrorized screams of the older generation. Likewise, the severance of bonds with established sanctities is a noticeable phenomenon.

This transformation took place all over the Arab world from Bahrain to Morocco. The language of poetry has now become an accessible medium for the modern poet, who is revolutionizing it not by over-inventiveness and by exploding its classical potential, but by exploiting its contemporary power to convey poetic experience. This is clearly seen in the work of the Lebanese, ᶜAbbās Bayḍūn (b. 1939) or the Bahraini poet, Qāsim Ḥaddād (b. 1948), to mention but two examples.

Although none of the new poets has yet arrived at the level of the best poets among the generation of the pioneers, these new poets write a poetry which can boast of modernist qualities of a high order. The age is ripe with talent and poets show an instinctive knowledge of their art, of how poetry should be written in our times. There is every sign that the end of this century will prove as vigorous and artistically productive as the mid century has been.*

* Acknowledgement is gratefully made of the Rockefeller Residency Fellowship from the University of Michigan's Center for Near Eastern and North African Studies, which supported this research in 1987–88.

CHAPTER 5

THE BEGINNINGS OF THE ARABIC NOVEL

The beginnings of a fictional tradition in modern Arabic literature are part of the wider process of revival and cultural assimilation known in Arabic as *al-Nahḍah*. This process involved a creative fusion of two separate forces. One is the rediscovery of the treasures of the Arabic literary heritage and the emergence therefrom of a 'neo-classical' movement. The other is the translation of works of European fiction into Arabic, their adaptation and imitation, and the eventual appearance of an indigenous tradition of modern Arabic fiction. Not surprisingly, these two tendencies find themselves pitted against each other during the initial phases of development under the rubrics of 'traditional' and 'modern'.

In the case of fiction, such a 'revival' involved the investigation of the earlier tradition of Arabic prose in quest of precedents and models. To a western audience which has come to regard *The one thousand and one nights* as a great repository of tales, it may seem surprising that, in the process of re-examining the genres of prose writing, there was little recourse to this great collection; it was regarded as a repository of 'popular' culture and thus not part of the repertoire under consideration. However, a prose genre which had flourished within the thoroughly rhetoricized tradition of criticism during the preceding centuries was the *maqāmah*, the initiation of which is attributed to Badīᶜ al-zamān al-Hamadhānī (969–1008). Within the tradition of the *maqāmāt* we find a combination of aspects of the picaresque clearly evident in the relationship between the narrator and the 'hero' (in al-Hamadhānī's case, ᶜĪsā ibn Hishām and Abū 'l-Fatḥ al-Iskandarī, respectively) and their surroundings, and also in the virtuoso use of language within the framework of the ancient stylistic tradition of *sajᶜ*, usually translated as 'rhyming prose'. While the origins and generic purpose of the *maqāmah* tradition are still the subject of debate, it is hardly surprising that, when at the earliest stages of the *Nahḍah* literati began to investigate the treasures of the past, the *maqāmah* among prose writings was a particular focus of their attention. With its potential for both illustrating a renewed concern with language and providing a commentary on societal change the genre was to be an ideal vehicle for many littérateurs in various parts of the Arab world.

SYRIA AND LEBANON

In Lebanon, the Christian community had had long-established contacts with the Vatican (where there was a Maronite College). The name of Bishop Germanus Farḥāt (1670–1732), who wrote a wide variety of works including books of poetry and grammar, is often cited as a precursor of a revival of interest in the Arabic language. Among his successors, Buṭrus al-Bustānī (1819–83) became involved in a project undertaken by the Protestant churches to translate the Bible, and did a great deal to stimulate interest in the language itself. However, it was Nāṣīf al-Yāzijī (1800–71) who is credited with being the pioneer in the reinvestigation of the great works of Arabic literature from the past. He became acquainted with the tradition of the *maqāmāt* through a French edition of the collection of al-Ḥarīrī (1054–1122) and was inspired to produce a set of *maqāmāt* of his own, *Majmaᶜ al-baḥrayn* (1856). Another Lebanese author, Aḥmad Fāris al-Shidyāq (1804–87), was also much influenced by the classical tradition and the renewed interest in the history of the Arabic language when he came to write his famous work, *al- Sāq ᶜalā 'l-sāq fī-mā huwa 'l-Fāriyāq*. The puns and rhymes within the title and the extraordinary complexities of certain chapters of this book provide clear evidence of Shidyāq's interest in, and debt to, earlier examples of elaborate prose; indeed he states in the work's introduction that his purpose is 'to reveal peculiarities and rarities of language'. The 'hero', named al-Hāris ibn Hithām in a clear echo of the earlier *Maqāmah* tradition, takes the narrator on a trip which demonstrates the author's acquaintance with both the Mediterranean area and northen Europe, most specifically England. The autobiographical element, already evident in the title's use of the name 'Fāriyāq', a combination of the 'Fāri-' of Fāris and '-yāq' of Shidyāq, can also be clearly seen in the book's vigorous anti-clerical tone, a reflection of the fact that Aḥmad's own brother, Asᶜad, was killed on the orders of the Maronite Patriarch after converting to Protestantism. This same tone is also encountered in the works of Jibrān Khalīl Jibrān and Faraḥ Anṭūn to be discussed below.

Among pioneer figures in the development of modern Arabic fiction in the Syro-Lebanese region, mention must be made of Faransīs Marrāsh (d. 1873) and Salīm al-Bustānī (d. 1884). Born in Aleppo in 1836, Marrāsh also travelled to Paris, but ill-health forced him to return to Syria where he died at an early age. In 1865 he published in Aleppo a work entitled *Ghābat al-ḥaqq* ('The forest of truth'), a highly idealized, philosophical work, which is essentially an allegory about freedom. As one might expect in such a work, the 'characters' are in fact personifications of static qualities rather than dynamic agents of change. A second work by Marrāsh, *Durr al-ṣadaf fī gharā'ib al-ṣudaf* (Beirut, 1872), has a title in rhyming prose which not only tells us about the collection of coincidences which are incorporated within the work but also illustrates the author's debt to the earlier traditions of narrative through the use of framing techniques, the formalized rhyming prose style, and an abundance of moralistic sentiment. Salīm al-Bustānī, eldest son of Buṭrus al-Bustānī mentioned above, laid the groundwork for the emergence of the historical novel in a series of works published in the periodical *al-Jinān*. These novels began the crucial process of developing a reading public for the genre by combining elements of entertainment and instruction within a single work. In this case, episodes from Islamic history were combined with travel, love stories and adventure to form a thrilling montage which was to capture an ever-widening public for the genre. *Al-Huyām fī jinān al-Sham* ('Passion in Syrian gardens', 1870), for example, is set in the period of the Arab conquest of Syria soon after the death of Muhammad in 632.

Beginning in the 1850s the Syro-Lebanese region was torn apart by civil strife between different religious factions. Following a massacre of Christians in Damascus in 1860, large numbers of Syrian Christian families left the area. The effect of this large-scale emigration on both the region that they left behind and the countries to which they emigrated was considerable. For many of these families the destination was Egypt, but others were to travel much further afield, to the United States, to South America and to England.

EGYPT

The Christian families who settled in Egypt became part of a process of educational and cultural revival which had begun with the coming to power of Muhammad Ali. Much impressed by the equipment and military techniques of the French army, he determined to train an Egyptian army along similar lines. Beginning in the 1820s, he sent missions of young Egyptians to Europe, initially to Italy but later primarily to France. Rifāʿah Rāfiʿ al-Ṭahṭāwī (1801–73), a young Egyptian studying at al-Azhar in Cairo, was chosen as *imām* to accompany one of these early missions to Paris. He stayed in France for a period of five years and shortly after his return wrote *Takhlīṣ al-ibrīz ilā talkhīṣ Bārīz*, a description of life in France, including accounts of dress, food, government, laws and many other topics. However, while this work played a crucial role in increasing its readers' awareness of the changes in European society wrought by the industrial revolution and the resultant growth in urbanization, al-Ṭahṭāwī's most significant contributions to the development of modern Arabic fiction lie in other areas. In the first place, he was editor of the

Egyptian newspaper *al-Waqāʾiʿ al-Miṣriyyah*. While the function of this newspaper (which had been founded by Muhammad Ali in 1823) was to serve as the official gazette, it laid the foundations for the later emergence of a vigorous tradition of Egyptian journalism. In particular, the arrival of many Syro-Lebanese families in the 1870s and 1880s led to a rapid increase in the number and variety of newspapers. As newspapers and journals were founded to support particular political viewpoints and with specific audiences and purposes in mind, poems and works of fiction would be a regular feature of their columns (thus replicating the beginnings of the fictional tradition in Europe). Entire novels were published *seriatim* and were immensely popular. Among the earliest examples of these was the work of another member of the Bustānī family, Saʿīd (d. 1901). His *Dhāt al-khidr* ('Lady of the boudoir') was published in *al-Ahrām* in 1884 and shows all the complexities of plot and plethora of coincidence encountered in the works of Marrāsh and Salīm al-Bustānī mentioned earlier. It needs to be emphasized also that the press has continued to fulfil this 'previewing' role up to the present day. While publishing opportunities and circumstances vary in nature and scope from country to country, the Arab world's most illustrious novelist, Najīb Maḥfūẓ, continues to use the columns of the newspapers and journals of Cairo to introduce his new works to the public.

The second way in which al-Ṭahṭāwī was to make a contribution to the development of modern Arabic fiction in Egypt and beyond was through his role as a pioneer translator of European works. In 1835 Muhammad Ali established a School of Languages in Cairo, and al-Ṭahṭāwī was appointed as its director. The initial translation tasks were concerned with science and military strategy, but works of geography, history and philosophy were also included. Soon works of literature joined the list. After the death of Muhammad Ali, al-Ṭahṭāwī spent some time in virtual exile in the Sudan and occupied himself in part by translating Fénélon's *Les aventures de Télémaque*. Al-Ṭahṭāwī's famous pupil and collaborator, Muḥammad ʿUthmān Jalāl (1829–94), devoted the greater part of his energies to works of literature. Not only did he translate a large number of contributions to French literature, for example the plays of Molière and the fables of La Fontaine, but he also initiated a crucial intermediate process in the development of an indigenous tradition of modern fiction by 'egyptianizing' their contexts, thus paving the way for attempts at imitation and later the development of an indigenous generic tradition. With these translation activities underway, it is hardly surprising that by the 1870s and 1880s the adventure novels of Alexandre Dumas *père* and Jules Verne, early favourites for translation, were being rendered in Arabic. It is worth noting that these priorities in selection mirror very closely the parallel translation movement in Turkish where *Télémaque* was translated in 1859, Hugo's *Les misérables* in 1862 and Dumas's *The Count of Monte Cristo* in 1871.

Another important figure in the development of an incipient fictional tradition in Egypt was ᶜAlī Mubārak (1824–93). Selected to study in France in 1844, he returned to assume a number of military and technical posts before being appointed as Director of the National Library (*Dār al-kutub*) in 1870. Besides a multi-volume study of Egypt's topography, *al-Khiṭaṭ al-Tawfīqiyyah al-jadīdah* modelled on the earlier work of al-Maqrīzī (1346–1442), Mubārak also wrote *ᶜAlam al-dīn*, a voluminous further contribution to the literature of travel in Europe, running to over 1,400 pages. This book is also obviously inspired by the *maqāmah* tradition. An Englishman and an Egyptian first travel round Egypt and then proceed to Europe. Each chapter is called a *musāmarah* (evening chat), and there are elaborate descriptions of a wide variety of phenomena – marriage, railways, women, post, volcanoes and so on – with little attempt to link them into a coherent narrative structure. However, such novelistic criticism is obviously premature; the aim here is to provide instructive information, albeit with a thin veneer of fictionality.

Along with the increase in translation activity and in the availability of publication outlets through the press, there came the need to refine and simplify prevalent prose styles in order to produce a medium that was palatable to the ever-growing public for popular fiction. In this function Muṣṭafā Luṭfī al-Manfalūṭī (1876–1924) played a central role. Indeed his work may be seen as typical of the many contrasting forces at work in Egyptian intellectual life at this time. The patent inconsistencies in many of his political and cultural views has not endeared him to critics of later generations but it is perhaps the very candour, simplicity and idealism of his writings, and most especially his collection of vignettes entitled *al-Naẓarāt* (1910–21), which made him so popular at this time; in the new and powerful medium of the press, his straightforward style and uncomplex moral vision found a ready audience. Perhaps nothing can provide a more graphic illustration of the power and range of the translation movement mentioned above than the fact that al-Manfalūṭī, who apparently knew no European language himself, was able to take a whole series of works by Chateaubriand, Edmond Rostand (*Cyrano de Bergerac*), Dumas *fils* and others, and adapt them for publication as romantic tales in Arabic.

The analysis and criticism of society: Ḥadīth ᶜĪsā ibn Hishām

During the latter decades of the nineteenth century the pace of revival in Egypt quickened. The vigorous and expanding press tradition allowed for plentiful discussion of the various political positions which emerged following the British occupation. Opposition to the occupation was almost universal, but was multi-faceted. One of the most famous of these opponents was Jamāl al-dīn al-Asadābādī (usually known as 'al-Afghānī'; 1839–97). It is difficult to overestimate the effect that the teachings of Jamāl al-dīn and his famous Egyptian pupil, Muḥammad ᶜAbduh (1849–1905) had on an entire generation of writers in Egypt; a short list of intellectual 'disciples' would include Qāsim Amīn (1865–1908), who wrote in support of the cause of women, Ḥāfiẓ Ibrāhīm, (1871–1932) the 'poet of the Nile', Muṣṭafā Kāmil (1874–1908), a famous figure in the growth of Egyptian nationalism, and Muḥammad al-Muwayliḥī (1858–1930).

Al-Muwayliḥī's work, *Ḥadīth ᶜĪsā ibn Hishām*, has long been recognized as a significant contribution to the development of modern Arabic prose fiction. It was first published as a series of articles in *Miṣbāḥ al-sharq*, the newspaper of al-Muwayliḥī's father Ibrāhīm. The original articles were entitled '*Fatrah min al-zaman*' ('A period of time') and contained a great deal of political commentary and biting societal criticism which are not part of the work as currently available. In 1906 al-Muwayliḥī put most of his series of articles into book form. Episodes were edited, material was omitted (including most references to the British occupation, a subject with which the original episodes were filled), and new material was added. The book appeared in 1907, now called *Ḥadith ᶜĪsā ibn Hishām*.

Ḥadīth ᶜĪsā ibn Hishām is a major forward step in that, unlike its predecessors, it focuses its attention on Egyptian society during the author's own lifetime and subjects it to bitingly sarcastic criticism. A Minister of War from the time of Muhammad Ali, Aḥmad Pāshā al-Manīklī, is resurrected from his grave and meets up with ᶜĪsā ibn Hishām, a contemporary Egyptian whose name is identical with that of the narrator of the *maqāmāt* of al-Hamadhānī mentioned above. The two men travel around a Cairo which is in the process of being rapidly transformed into a cosmopolitan metropolis. Close to the beginning of the work the Pāshā is arrested for an assault on a donkeyman, and the reader is thus exposed to the chaotic legal system where a system of religious (Sharīᶜah) and secular courts (based on the French system) are operating under a British governmental administration. Closer to the end of the work, the figure of the *ᶜumdah* (village headman) and his two colleagues, the *khalīᶜ* (Playboy) and Merchant, provide some memorable moments of contrast between life in the countryside and the city, between the traditional tastes and values of the *ᶜumdah* and the westernized fads espoused by the Playboy. However, while the level of criticism implicit in the treatment of each societal group is constant, the chapters are nevertheless discrete entities with little to link them to other chapters apart from the presence of the narrator and his companion. Indeed, from the perspective of narrative structure, the work is very redolent of al-Hamadhānī's *maqāmāt*, the narrator of which provides al-Muwayliḥī's work with its title.

It seems clear then that, while al-Muwayliḥī was an astute and acerbic critic of his own society at the turn of the century, he had no intention of writing literature which would entertain in the same way that the adventure novels mentioned above were doing. Al-Muwayliḥī was not one to make concessions to any emerging audience for popular fiction. When we bear in mind his vitriolic reaction to attempts by the famous poet Aḥmad Shawqī to introduce new ideas about poetry into his collected works, we may be able to gauge his reaction to the kind of fiction which was becoming so popular.

Ḥadīth ᶜĪsā ibn Hishām thus fulfils a Janus-like function. By taking contemporary Egypt and its people as its subject-matter and scrutinizing both in an intense and often humorous manner, it represents a significant development over previous works which were set apart from the environment of their author in either place or time, or in both. On the other hand, al-Hamadhānī's narrator and the style of the *maqāmah* genre are revived to provide a superb and enduring example of neo-classical prose. Indeed the fate of al-Muwayliḥī's work may have been sealed in 1927 when it was chosen to be a set text in Egyptian schools. That rite of passage affirmed, as it were, the transformation of a lively and critical account of Egyptian society during 'a period of time' into a part of the canon of *maqāmāt*, an exercise in neo-classicism which, for all its relevance at one period, was soon to be overwhelmed by the emergence of the novel as a genre in Arabic literature.

It remains to be added that works with strong similarities to that of the *maqāmah* as revived in this creative manner by al-Muwayliḥī were to appear within both Egypt and other national traditions of Arabic fiction. In Egypt itself, al-Muwayliḥī's own father, Ibrāhīm (d. 1906), wrote a short essay in the genre entitled '*Mir'āt al-ᶜālam aw Ḥadīth Mūsā ibn ᶜIṣām*', which has never been published in book form. In 1906 the famous Egyptian poet, Ḥāfiẓ Ibrāhīm, a close friend of the al-Muwayliḥī family, published a work of his own, *Layālī Saṭīḥ* ('Nights of Saṭīḥ'). Ḥāfiẓ makes use of encounters between his narrator and a variety of inhabitants of Egypt to comment on a number of pressing issues of the time, including British rule of the Sudan, the presence of Syrian emigrés in Egypt, and the need for reform in women's rights. Muḥammad Luṭfī Jumᶜah's (1884–1953) book, *Layālī 'l-rūḥ al-ḥāᵓir* ('Nights of the perplexed Spirit', 1912) which is often cited in the current context, contains considerably less socio-political comment than the works mentioned thus far; while it makes use of similar scenarios and narrative devices, it is essentially a reflective and philosophical piece. Among authors from elsewhere in the Arab world whose works show signs of the influence of the classical or neo-classical *maqāmah* tradition, mention should be made of Sulaymān Fayḍī al-Mawṣilī in Iraq with his *Al-Riwāyah al-Īqāẓiyyah* ('The story of *Al-Īqāẓ*' – the name of Fayḍī's newspaper, 1919), ʿAlī al-Duʿājī in Tunis with his *Jawlah ḥawla ḥānāt al-baḥr al-abyaḍ al-mutawassiṭ* ('Trip around the bars of the Mediterranean', 1935), and in Morocco Muḥammad ibn ʿAbdallāh al-Muʾaqqit with his *Al-Riḥlah al-Marākushiyyah aw mirʾāt al-masāʾil al-waqtiyyah* ('Marrakesh journey or mirror of problems of the time', 1920s). While the dates of publication serve to illustrate the different time-frames for the development of modern fiction in the separate national literatures of the Arab world, all of these works can be regarded from the perspective of the 1980s as bridges between the narrative genres of Arabic classical prose and the emergence of a new entity which was to become the modern Arabic novel.

The historical novel: Jurjī Zaydān

Jurjī Zaydān (1861–1914), a Lebanese immigrant to Egypt, provides us with what is probably the best example of the way in which the press was to contribute to the development of an audience for the novel in the Arab world. After founding the magazine *al-Hilāl* in 1892, he proceeded to use it as a channel for the publication of a series of historical novels which brought this genre to new levels of sophistication and popularity; indeed they have remained in print ever since. In his study of the development of the novel in Egypt Ṭāhā Badr describes these works as being part entertainment and part educational, a verdict which aptly accounts for both their value in the development of the novel and their success. Zaydān was at pains to acquaint his generation with the history and literature of the Arabs, and used the historical novel to achieve his goals in a manner which is often compared with that of both Alexandre Dumas *père* and Sir Walter Scott. Avoiding some of the more improbable heroics of the adventure novels of earlier years, he chose a number of periods in Islamic history as time-frames for his novels. *Armanūsah al-Miṣriyyah* (1889) is concerned with the conquest of Egypt in 640; *Al-Ḥajjāj ibn Yūsuf* (1909) is about the famous governor of Iraq during the period of the Umayyad Caliphs; *Shajarat al-Durr* (1914) explores the reign of the famous queen of Egypt. *Istibdād al-Mamālīk* ('Mamluk tyranny', 1893) may serve as an illustration. The period is the eighteenth century, and the historical circumstances are the struggle for power between ʿAlī Bey, the ruler of Egypt, and his son-in-law,

Muḥammad Abū Dhahab. The action swings back and forth between Egypt and Syria. An Egyptian family, that of Sayyid ᶜAbd al-Raḥmān, finds itself caught up in the larger drama, as the father fights in the army in place of his son Ḥasan. Eventually Muḥammad Abū Dhahab emerges as victor, and all also turns out well for the family.

There can be little doubt that a principal cause of the continuing popularity of these novels has been the style in which they are written. By contrast with the elevated style of al-Muwayliḥī, for example, Zaydān set out to write his fiction in a style which would make his works accessible to a wide audience. The vocabulary is familiar, the sentence structure is simple and unburdened with complex imagery, and the narrative flows with an easy spontaneity, all of which earns the plaudits of a demanding critic such as Ṭāhā Ḥusayn.

BETWEEN EDUCATION AND ENTERTAINMENT

Other writers from Lebanon were to make use of the emerging press tradition in Egypt to contribute in significant ways to the development of an audience for modern Arabic fiction. Availing themselves of such publications as *al-Riwāyāt al-shahriyyah* ('Monthly novels'), Niqūlā Ḥaddād (c. 1872–1954) was to produce a whole series of works with titles such as *Ḥawwāʾ al-jadīdah* ('Modern Eve', 1906), *Asīrat al-ḥubb* ('Prisoner of love', n.d.) and *Fātinat al-Imperator* ('Enchantress of the emperor', 1922) which in their variety served as a valuable bridge between the prevailing taste for entertainment fiction and the gradual emergence of a tradition more closely focused on present reality. Yaᶜqūb Ṣarrūf (1852–1927), the founder of the journal *al-Muqtaṭaf*, and Faraḥ Anṭūn (1874–1922), the founder of the journal *al-Jāmiᶜah* and a renowned secularist, both wrote historical novels. Ṣarrūf's was entitled *Amīr Lubnān* ('Prince of Lebanon', 1907) and takes as its topic the history of his native land during the religious struggles of the 1850s and 1860s; Anṭūn delves further back into history in his novel, *Ūrishalīm al-jadīdah aw fatḥ al-ᶜArab bayt al-maqdis* ('New Jerusalem or the Arab conquest of the Holy City', 1904) which, as its title implies, is set during the Muslim conquest of Jerusalem in the seventh century A.D. However, in other works both Ṣarrūf and Anṭūn turned from the portrayal of the past to the present, albeit with a generous overlay of romance. In Ṣarrūf's novels *Fatāt Miṣr* (1905) and *Fatāt al-Fayyūm* (1908), the scene is set in his adopted country and among its Christian (Coptic) community. Anṭūn's other novels are a mirror of the various trends of his age: from the somewhat philosophical *al-ᶜIlm wa'l-dīn wa'l-māl* ('Science, religion and money', 1905) which, as the title implies, discusses the conflict of science and religion, to *al-Ḥubb ḥattā 'l-mawt* ('Love till death', 1898) and *al-Waḥsh, al-waḥsh, al-waḥsh* (1903), both of which treat the problems of Lebanese society confronted with returnees from the emigrant community in America.

A member of that very community, Jibrān Khalīl Jibrān (1883–1931), as well known for his publications in English as for those in Arabic, was another contributor to the development of romantic fiction in Arabic. While the abundance of epithets to be found in much of his fiction may not suit the tastes of today, there can be little doubt of his interest in developing a lucid and beautiful style in both his poetic and his prose writings. His works of fiction belong to the earlier part of his career and show a lively concern with some of the pressing societal issues of his time. *Al-Ajniḥah al-mutakassirah* ('Broken wings', 1908) and *al-Arwāḥ al-mutamarridah* ('Spirits rebellious', 1908) take up the cause of women's rights, of forced marriage and the question of the tyranny of the clergy, in a forthright manner which antedates more modern advocates of these causes by many decades. Jibrān is primarily remembered in the western world for the unique series of heavily allegorical and philosophical tales and aphorisms which are now most popular in their English versions, the principal amongst them being *The Prophet.* While Jibrān's own works of this type have maintained their appeal, they also may be seen as providing precedents for the writings of a number of other authors. In the late 1940s Mīkhā'īl Nuʿaymah (1889–1988), a close colleague of Jibrān, published a group of heavily philosophical tales in both English and Arabic although, in the case of at least one, *Mudhakkirāt al-arqash* (translated as *Memories of a vagrant soul*, 1952), we know that it was originally serialized at a much earlier date. These works have been characterized as 'really sermons based on the doctrine of metempsychosis and of the ultimate union of the human soul with its divine origin', and the resortings to the supernatural which are to be found in them, in the view of one critic, 'exercise beyond all legitimate limits the reader's willing suspension of disbelief'. (Muhammad Siddiq, *Al-ʿArabiyya*, Vol. 15 nos 1 and 2, 1982, p. 27) The work of the Tunisian writer Maḥmūd al-Masʿadī (b. 1911), *al-Sudd* ('The dam', written between 1939 and 1940 and published in 1955) appeared at a later date than the works of Jibrān and Nuʿaymah, but that seems merely a reflection of the varying chronological patterns of development in the Arab countries under review here. The structure and prevailing philosophical tone of al-Masʿadī's work have, from the outset, made it the object of considerable discussion regarding its generic purpose; it has been described as a play and as not falling 'into any of the recognized categories of literary form' (Robin Ostle, *Journal of Arabic Literature*, VIII (1977), p. 161). Given a warm reception by no less a figure than Ṭāhā Husayn, the work tells the story of Ghaylān and his female companion Maymūnah, who come to a valley where the people worship a goddess named Ṣāhabbāʾ. Ghaylān determines to change the way of life of this community by building a dam, but no sooner is the structure completed than it is destroyed by mysterious forces. Whatever the other qualities of the work, critical opinion is virtually unanimous in its esteem for the extreme elegance of its language, a factor which seems to have ensured it an enduring place in the history of modern Maghribī fiction.

The status of 'Zaynab' by Muḥammad Ḥusayn Haykal

A great deal of debate has surrounded the question as to which work represents the first 'real' novel in Arabic, ever since H. A. R. Gibb and others identified *Zaynab* by Muḥammad Ḥusayn Haykal (1888–1956) as occupying that position. While some critics would see *Zaynab* too as merely a step on the road to the appearance of the 'genuine' novel, more recently others have drawn attention to Maḥmūd Ṭāhir Ḥaqqī's (1884–1964) work *ʿAdhrāʾ Dinshawāy*, 1906 (translated as *The Maiden of Dinshway*, 1986) as at least a further intermediate step. This work by an Egyptian writer certainly places Egyptian characters into a contemporary Egyptian setting in both place and time, namely the events which ensued when, in reprisal for the death of a British soldier while shooting birds near an Egyptian village, the authorities passed sentences of execution on a number of the villagers. Here we have a contribution to fiction which manages to combine some of the elements mentioned earlier: the concern found in al-Muwayliḥī's work with the description and analysis of present-day Egypt (to which we might add the further similarity of publication in a newspaper, in this case Ḥaqqī's own *al-Minbar*) and from the tradition of the historical novel the introduction of a local love-story.

In view of recent research on the earlier periods in the development of modern Arabic fiction, and more specifically that written in Egypt, it is perhaps more useful to see *Zaynab* not so much as the first example of any particular category or quality of novel, but rather as an extremely important step in a continuing process. Without in any way diminishing the importance of Haykal's novel in the history of modern Arabic prose literature, we would suggest that a clearer historical perspective can be obtained by placing it in a broader generic context.

Zaynab was written while Haykal was in France and was published in Egypt in 1913 under the pseudonym '*Miṣrī fallāḥ*' ('a peasant-Egyptian'). Some argument has surrounded the fact that Haykal did not use his own name. His identity was certainly known to critics at the time, and it has recently been suggested that the purpose behind the use of a pseudonym was more concerned with the marketability of the book than with fear of whatever opprobrium may have been attached to the writing of fiction. Whatever the case may be, Haykal proceeds to place his readers firmly in the midst of the Egyptian countryside. Subtitling his book, '*Manāẓir wa-akhlāq rīfiyyah*' ('Rustic scenes and manners'), he depicts the Egyptian countryside in considerable detail and with not a little sentimentality which carries over into the portrayal of his characters. The plot once again has love as its primary focus. Ḥāmid is a student studying in Cairo who returns during his vacations to his parents' country estate. He maintains an epistolary relationship with his cousin, ᶜAzīzah, but she is married off to someone else. For a while, Ḥāmid turns his attention to Zaynab, a beautiful peasant girl who works on his father's lands, but eventually he returns in frustration to Cairo. Zaynab herself is in love with Ibrāhīm, another peasant worker, but she too is married off, to Ḥasan who, unlike Ibrāhīm, is able to afford the bride-price. Such is Ibrāhīm's poverty that he cannot afford the bribe necessary to avoid being drafted into the army. He is sent to the Sudan and is killed. Pining for her true love and clutching his handkerchief, Zaynab dies of tuberculosis.

In this work there is a heavy focus on local background. When we bear in mind the fact that Haykal was himself the son of a wealthy landowner and was writing about his homeland from a distance, this emphasis and the accompanying sentimentality become less surprising. Haykal also seems to follow or, in the case of the Arabic novel, even to establish, the trend whereby first novels tend to be heavily autobiographical; later works by Ibrāhīm al-Māzinī, Tawfīq al-Ḥakīm, ᶜAbbās Maḥmūd al-ᶜAqqād, Jabrā Ibrāhīm Jabrā and many others provide further evidence of this. When Ḥāmid writes a lengthy letter to his parents from Cairo expressing views on liberty and justice borrowed from John Stuart Mill and Herbert Spencer, he becomes the barely disguised voice of Haykal himself, a young man who had already been exposed to the ideas of such figures as Qāsim Amīn, the writer on women's rights mentioned earlier, and who was later to become one of the major intellectual figures in modern Egypt. With *Zaynab* we encounter a novel which places its characters into a fictional but authentic temporal and spatial context and then proceeds to explore some of the pressing social issues of the day. The resulting characters show obvious psychological flaws, but they *are* real Egyptian characters.

In this context, mention must also be made of the language or rather languages used in this work. Haykal followed the lead of earlier figures such as ᶜUthmān Jalāl, ᶜAbdallāh Nadīm (1854–96) and the dramatist Yaᶜqūb Ṣannūᵓ (1839–1912) by adopting the colloquial dialect as a literary medium and using it in the dialogue of his novel. The question of the literary value which is to be attached to the various registers of the Arabic language represents a matter of continuing debate among Arab littérateurs and critics, fired not only by the emotive issues of heritage and religion but also by the more practical aspects of localism and the ramifications of publics and publication. While *Zaynab* is too full of description to contain a great deal of dialogue, its attitude to this question of language usage is another factor contributing to the status of *Zaynab* as an important point of reference within the history of the modern Arabic novel.

CHAPTER 6

THE MATURE ARABIC NOVEL OUTSIDE EGYPT

THE EMERGENCE OF THE NOVEL: POLITICAL AND SOCIAL CONCERNS

My survey of the earliest stages in the development of the modern Arabic novel in the preceding chapter concluded with a brief discussion of Muḥammad Ḥusayn Haykal's novel, *Zaynab*. While this novel was much concerned, like many other examples of its own and earlier times, with romance, Haykal placed a set of Egyptian characters firmly into the present and proceeded to use them in a discussion of a societal problem which was of great interest to himself and to many other Egyptian intellectuals, namely the role of women in society. In the decades that have followed the publication of *Zaynab*, at the hands of some writers the novel continues its functions as both entertainer and educator. Novels of romance, designed to divert, continue to appear and have more recently provided ready material for both television and film. The tradition of the historical novel has also continued, particularly under the impetus of a growing sense of national pride fostered by Arab Nationalism but, in more recent times, the attention of novelists has tended to be more devoted to the events of the recent past and the lessons to be gleaned from them. However, as historical events bring about a process of change whereby the Arab world begins to challenge the hegemony of European colonialism and to play a much larger part in the course of its own destiny, so the novel, as reflector and even catalyst of change, assumes a more significant role. It is thus more than fitting that such a harbinger of change as *Zaynab* should be published in 1913, at the very moment when the colonial and other powers were making preparations for the most wasteful war ever fought in human terms, an event which led to vast changes throughout the Arab world.

The aftermath of the First World War can be seen in retrospect as sowing the seeds of many future problems. The successes of 'the Arab revolt' had raised among the Arab nations considerable hopes for independence when the fighting was over. Meanwhile, the Balfour Declaration of 1917, stating that a homeland for the Jewish people was a goal of the British

Government, laid the foundations for a whole series of misunderstandings and deceptions concerning the future of Palestine. All these hopes and expectations were dashed by the decision of the French and British to divide the former Ottoman dominions into 'protectorates'. Against such a background of foiled political aspirations, it is hardly surprising that there were wide-scale revolts aimed at the colonial power in both Egypt (1919), and Iraq (1920), but they were soon quashed. However, throughout the inter-war period the representatives of nationalism, both Arab as a whole and local, wrote copiously about national identity and discussed issues of independence and self-determination with their European colonizers.

In the realm of fiction, the need to develop and foster a sense of national identity and local pride based on a revival of the glorious past may help to explain the prevalence of historical novels in many countries of the region during the inter-war years. The Syrian novelist Maᶜrūf al-Arnāʾūṭ (d. 1947) published a series of four novels tracing early Islamic history, including one each on ᶜUmar, the second Caliph, and Ṭāriq ibn Ziyād, the hero of the conquest of Spain in the eighth century. Al-Bashīr Khurayyif, the Tunisian writer (b. 1917) uses his novel, *Barq al-layl* ('Night lightning', 1961), to portray life in his native country under Hafsid rule in the sixteenth century, although the inclusion of reference to the Spanish invasion in 1535 no doubt served to remind his readers of the realities of occupation in the twentieth century. However, while a number of Arab novelists continued to write historical works of fiction which would make their readers aware of glorious episodes from the past, the rapidly developing awareness among Arab intellectuals of the need for political and societal change led, almost inevitably, to a diminution in the role of the historical novel. Faced with the realities of colonial occupation, Arab novelists could find object lessons in the more immediate past. In Iraq, for example, Maḥmūd Aḥmad al-Sayyid (1903–37) used his novel *Jalāl Khālid* (1928) to portray some of the events during the Iraqi revolt of 1920 mentioned above. One decade later, Tawfīq Yūsuf ᶜAwwād (b. 1911) published his novel, *al-Raghīf* ('The loaf', 1939), in which the author gives graphic portrayals of Arab resistance to the Turks during the First World War. In still more recent times when history has been able to provide a regrettably rich repertoire of conflict in the Arab world (as will be discussed below), novelists have still occasionally turned to the earlier decades of this century for inspiration, as, for example, with the Syrian writer Fāris Zarzūr in his novels, *Lan tasquṭ al-madīnah* ('The city will not fall', 1969) set during the First World War, and *Ḥasan Jabal* (1969) which is a rather excessively documentary account of resistance to the French occupiers during the 1920s and 1930s.

The popularity of romantic fiction which was noted with regard to Egypt in the previous chapter is replicated within each of the local traditions under review here and often provides, as is the case with the status of *Zaynab* in the Egyptian tradition, a historical point of reference. The trend can be illustrated by a few examples culled from different national traditions and time periods, something which can serve as a demonstration of the way in which chronologies differ at this stage in the development of the novel genre. In 1947 the Algerian novelist Aḥmad Riḍā Ḥūḥū (1911–56) published *Ghādat Umm al-Qurā* ('The maid of the city', 1947), in which the topic is love and marriage and, in particular, the death of Zakiyyah, a young girl who is being forced into a marriage with a rich man when she is really in love with her cousin Jamīl. A larger number of Sudanese novelists have dealt with this same theme, among whom we would cite Badawī ʿAbd al-Qādir Khalīl with *Hā'im ʿalā 'l-arḍ aw rasāʾil al-ḥirmān* ('Roaming the earth or letters of deprivation', 1954) which, as the title suggests, makes heavy use of the epistolary mode, and Shākir Muṣṭafā with *Ḥattā taʿūd* ('Till she returns', 1959) in which the love affair of Maḥmūd and ʿAwāṭif is shattered when he marries a foreign woman and only returns to his real beloved as she lies dying.

Contacts with Europe and Europeans were among the principal sources of inspiration for Arab writers of fiction at the very earliest stages of the *Nahḍah*. As Arab nations continued to explore the nature of their own national identity and endeavoured in various ways to convince the western powers of their desire for independence, it is hardly surprising that the need to understand and assess the impact of European culture on Arab societies was reflected in a continuation and expansion of this type of fiction. Pioneers in the writing of the novel in three separate regions of the Arab world made encounters with the west the subject of their works. In Syria, Shakīb al-Jābirī (b. 1912) published *Naham* ('Greed', 1937), a novel set entirely in Germany with many German characters and scenes, which is widely acknowledged as a pioneer work within the Syrian novelistic tradition. In two later works, *Qadar yalhū* ('Fate at play', 1939) and *Qaws quzaḥ* ('Rainbow', 1946), al-Jābirī explores the relationship between an Arab student of medicine in Germany and Elsa, a poor German girl with whom he falls in love. In 1939, Dhū 'l-Nūn Ayyūb, the Iraqi novelist and short story writer, published *al-Duktūr Ibrāhīm* ('Dr Ibrahim'), a work which portrays the ruthless climb to power and influence of a young man who travels to Europe, and then returns to his homeland, only to consort with the foreigners who are occupying it until eventually he decides to leave in order to live in the west. As with so many of these early attempts at novel writing, the autobiographical element seems close to the surface here, in that the author wrote this novel following a decision by the Iraqi government to 'banish' him to Mawṣil after the publication of his collection of short stories entitled *Burj Bābil* ('The Tower of Babel', 1939).

During the inter-war period, the relationship between the Arab nations and the western powers (most especially Britain and France as the two 'protecting' powers) was one of suspicion and distrust. In Palestine the British became more and more bogged down in the political quagmire of their own making, and the few attempts at reconciling the unreconcilable merely antagonized both Arabs and Zionists. On the political front, both Egypt and Syria gained a degree of independence; the Saudi family's consolidation of its control in the Arabian peninsula was acknowledged by the western powers; and in Lebanon an agreement between Sunnis and Maronites in 1943 allowed for the emergence of a Lebanese state, albeit one based on a fragile balance, as subsequent events have shown all too clearly. However, for the majority of nations in the Arab world, the limited nature of the political gains during this period was abruptly underlined by the Second World War. Whatever gestures of 'independence' may have been granted were now abruptly swept aside as the armies of the Axis Powers and the Allies fought their way across North Africa, thus involving a large segment of the Arab world directly in the conflict and other parts indirectly through overt military occupation. At a later stage, when Arab nations had gained their independence and overthrown the various *anciens régimes*, several novelists in search of national heroes from the recent past were to make use of the restrictions placed on civil liberties as a result of these occupations and the popular resistance they aroused, as central themes in their works. The Syrian novelist Ḥannā Mīnah (b. 1924) sets his first two novels in this period: *Al-maṣābīḥ al-zurq* ('Blue lamps', 1954) is set in Ladhiqiyya and, with all the hyperbole of incipient social realism, recounts the tale of popular revolt against the French forces led by Muḥammad Ḥalabī, a local butcher. *Al-Shirāᶜ wa'l-ᶜāṣifah* ('The sail and the storm', 1966) contains less sloganeering than the previous novel and is again set on the coast of Syria where Abū Zuhdī al-Ṭurūsī, the hero of the novel, rescues a fisherman colleague during a storm but loses his own boat. Confined to the land for a while, he organizes popular opposition to the French before returning to his preferred environment in a new boat. The Iraqi novelist Ghāʾib Ṭuᶜmah Farmān (b. 1927) sets his novel *al-Nakhlah wa'l-jīrān* ('The palm-tree and the neighbours', 1966) during this same period, but his principal subject is the effect of wartime economy and the morals of the black market on all segments of the society.

Politics and society: the impetus for change

As an aftermath of the Second World War, there was talk on the international plane of the need to found a world organization devoted to the maintenance of peace, an entity which was later to be called the United Nations. Feelings in the Arab world, however, tended to be somewhat more sanguine. Along with the hopes for independence there was a growing resentment aimed not only at the colonial powers but also at many of the *anciens régimes* with their entrenched and often corrupt power structures. This was a volatile political and social mixture, as a number of uprisings and political assassinations during the period can demonstrate. On the political plane, the conduct of the Great Powers during the war had convinced even the most dogged pursuers of local national interests of the need to unite efforts and forces. The urgings of a number of advocates of Arab nationalism (such as Qusṭanṭīn Zurayq, Edmond Rabbath and Sāṭiᶜ al-Ḥuṣrī) were now to bear fruit in the establishment in Cairo in March 1945, of the Arab League, although in the view of one writer on the subject, Hishām Sharābī, it 'fell far short of the hopes and aspirations of most Arab nationalists'. In November 1947 a 'partition plan' was published for Palestine, and in April 1948 many villagers at Dayr Yāsīn were massacred by Zionists, provoking an exodus of many Palestinian families from the region; in May the state of Israel was proclaimed and the first of many conflicts between Arabs and Israelis took place. The events of 1948 were to have an impact far beyond the territory in dispute and, as we will see below, the plight of the Palestinian people has been one of the major focuses of Arab novelists. As the Moroccan historian-novelist ᶜAbdallāh al-ᶜArwī (Laroui) has noted, it is 'the Arab problem *par excellence*'.

During the 1950s and into the 1960s, the majority of countries within the Arab world witnessed enormous changes, both political and social. The long-sought independence was granted to several nations: Sudan, Tunisia and Morocco in 1956, Kuwait in 1961 and, after a protracted and vicious civil conflict beginning in 1954, Algeria became independent in 1962. Many countries went through the process of revolution, involving varying degrees of violence and social disruption; old political alignments were strengthened or abolished and new ones were created, not the least of which being the great experiment in Arab unity, the United Arab Republic of 1958–61; and in some countries there were recurring conflicts with segments of the population, such as the Kurds in Iraq and the peoples of the southern part of the Sudan.

With these and other events in mind and numerous forces for change at work, it is hardly surprising that, allowing for some chronological variation in different parts of the Arab world, the Arabic novel now enters a new, more committed phase of its development, one which makes full use of the work of pioneers in the genre to achieve a greater maturity.

PROMINENT THEMES OF THE ARABIC NOVEL IN RECENT DECADES

1 Conflict and confrontation

The fate of the Palestinian people

Arab novelists have had no shortage of conflicts and tensions, national and international, political and social, on which to base their works. Even so, writers from throughout the region have taken the continuing conflict with Israel over the status of the Palestinians as a major theme for their fictional works. The topic is many-sided: the series of military engagements which have taken place in 1948, 1956, 1967, 1973 and 1982; the activities of the 'freedom-fighters' or 'terrorists' (depending on point of view) on each side; the effects of the conflict on the peoples in neighbouring countries such as Lebanon, Syria and Jordan; and the life of the Palestinian communities, in Israel itself, in the occupied territories such as the West Bank and in various refugee camps. All these aspects have been explored in modern Arabic fiction and, while some works will, no doubt, prove to be of only temporary and occasional appeal, there are many others which are clearly destined to endure.

Three Palestinian writers have addressed themselves to the many phases and aspects of the recent history of their people, each in his own unique way: Ghassān Kanafānī (1936–72), Jabrā Ibrāhīm Jabrā (b. 1919) and Emīl Ḥabībī (b. 1921). All three have contributed in significant ways to the development of the Arabic novel. Commitment to the cause of the Palestinians and the name of Ghassān Kanafānī are closely linked, in that his early death was a result of a car-bomb in Beirut where he served as spokesman for the Popular Front for the Liberation of Palestine;. Kanafānī's fiction, in both novel and short story form, covers many aspects of Palestinian life. It has to be admitted that in some of these works the intensity of the commitment leads to an approach close to reportage, but it must be added that Kanafānī was a determined experimenter, most particularly in his novels, and that, if some of them may be less successful as works of fiction than others, they all manage to portray the agonies of deprivation and suffering in camps and the resulting frustration, anger and violence, with an unparalleled vividness. *Rijāl fī 'l-shams* (1963, English trans. *Men in the sun*, 1978) has long been regarded as a brilliant portrayal of Arab attitudes towards the Palestinians in the period before 1967. Three Palestinians of different generations endeavour to find work in Kuwait so that they can support their families. They have to be smuggled across the border and contract with various middlemen to reach their destination, being cheated at every turn. A water-tank lorry driver, Abū Khayzurān, rendered impotent by a previous war-wound, agrees to transport them, but at the crucial point, with the sun beating down, he is delayed at the border in a futile discussion about his purported girlfriend in Baṣrah. Rushing to cross the border and open the tank, he finds his three 'passengers' dead. He unloads the bodies at the closest municipal garbage dump, stripping their bodies of valuables as he does so. Why, he wonders, didn't they beat on the side of the tank? The symbolic message is devastating in its directness. In a later work, *Mā tabaqqā lakum* (1966, English trans. *What remains for you*, 1988), the symbolic aspect is handled with equal mastery, to which must be added an interesting linkage between character, time and style. At the beginning of this work about a family scattered by the events of 1948, the author explains that time and the desert join three characters as 'heroes of the novel'. Ḥāmid and Maryam, brother and sister, fight their separate battles, the former in an attempt to cross the desert in order to join his mother in Jordan, the latter to be rid of her treacherous husband Zakariyyā. The ticking of the clock on the wall and the pulses of the desert soil are used as symbols of the progress of the common struggle against enemies within and without. Kanafānī juxtaposes scenes from both venues, using different typefaces to indicate switches in character, time-frame and location. In this way, the exiled Palestinian family is shown to be united in its struggle, even though situations and dimensions may be different.

Jabrā Ibrāhīm Jabrā is one of the Arab world's most illustrious intellectual figures, a poet, translator (especially of Shakespeare) and critic of literature and art as well as a novelist. The characters who people his novels are drawn from intellectual circles: writers, artists, doctors, radical political thinkers and the like. Bearing in mind the breadth of Jabrā's background (one of his novels, *Hunters on a narrow street*, was written in English (London, 1960)), it is hardly surprising that these novels are full of discussions of works of literature, painting and philosophy, raising the question of readership which will be addressed below. In two recent works, *ʿĀlam bi-lā kharāʾiṭ* ('Mapless world', 1983) written with ʿAbd al-Raḥmān Munīf, and *al-Ghuraf al-ukhrā* ('The other rooms', 1986), Jabrā has addressed the problems of his contemporaries in more general terms; the latter work in particular is a nightmarish vision of a community which appears to exploit and thrive on anonymity. However, in earlier works Jabrā's focus was the fate of Palestinians in exile. This is seen clearly in *al-Safīnah* (1979, English trans. *The ship*, 1985) in which a group of acquaintances from different regions of the Middle East meet 'by chance' on a Mediterranean cruise ship. To the contemporary tragedy of Fāliḥ, the brilliant but cynical Baghdadi surgeon who commits suicide, is linked the story of Wadīᶜ ᶜAssāf, who longs to return to his native Palestine, the loss of which in 1948 is recounted in graphic detail; and of ᶜIṣām Salmān, the Iraqi intellectual, whose longstanding love for the beautiful Lumā, Fāliḥ's wife, has been blocked by traditional Arab 'tribalism'. In *al-Baḥth ᶜan Walīd Masᶜūd* ('In search of Walīd Masᶜūd', 1978) Jabrā makes use of another device to gather together a cross-section of Arab society around a Palestinian topic; in this case it is to hear a cassette-tape left in the car of Walīd Masᶜūd, a Palestinian intellectual, who has disappeared and perhaps has been killed. When confronted with the message on the tape, some of his male and female acquaintances recount in successive chapters the courses of their relationships with the missing 'hero'. The complexity of his lifestyle and the network of linkages with the fedayeen and intellectual circles provide a vivid picture of both the recent history of the Palestinian people and the tensions implicit in the search for solutions to its problems.

The focus of Emīl Ḥabībī's most notable fiction has been the life of Palestinians living, like himself, in Israel itself. While *Sudāsiyyat al-ayyām al-sittah* ('Sextet on the six days', 1969) recounts a set of stories of meetings between the Arab community in Israel and their relatives living elsewhere, his most famous work, *al-Waqāʾiᶜ al-gharībah fi-ikhtifāʾ Saᶜīd Abī 'l-naḥs al-mutashāʾil* (1974 and 1977, English trans. *The secret life of Saeed, the ill-fated pessoptimist*, 1982) describes with a generous overlay of sardonic and bitter-sweet humour the daily life of Arabs in Israel and particularly the absurdities faced by Saᶜīd who, desiring to cooperate with the Israelis, finds himself caught up in all manner of contradictions and bureaucratic nightmares. His only recourse is to 'pess-optimism'. The extraordinary elaborateness of the language of the title, the presence of a humorous anti-hero and the sense of parody which is thereby created, and the use of short chapters to recount episodes, all give Ḥabībī's work a refreshingly unique quality within the corpus of modern Arabic novels and at the same time link his work clearly with the classical tradition of the *maqāmah* genre which, as we suggested in the previous chapter, was also used to comment on and, by implication, criticize both customs and attitudes.

These three novelists focus in their works on the wider aspects of the Palestinian tragedy, although the periods of actual conflict are always present by implication. The different phases and aspects of this intractable situation have been treated in a number of ways by novelists throughout the Arab world. Some have treated part of the Palestinian community over a large period of time. In Nabīl Khụrī's *al-Raḥīl* ('The departure', 1969) we follow the moves of Abū ᶜAdnān from his home during the 1930s into exile in Bethlehem in 1948 and then again to a refugee camp in Jordan in 1967. Rashād Abū Shāwir uses his novel *al-ᶜUshshāq* ('The lovers', 1977) to give a picture of life in Jericho between the 1940s and 1967. The two major conflicts, that of 1948 (called *al-nakbah*, 'the disaster') and that of 1967 (*al-naksah*, 'the setback'), and their immediate consequences, have been the subject of a large number of works of fiction. For 1948, in addition to the works of Kanafānī and Jabrā already discussed, mention should be made of Yaḥyā Yakhluf's (b. 1944) *Tuffāḥ al-majānīn* ('Apples of the insane', n.d.), which adopts a deceptively childlike vision in its skilful recounting of the Arab defeat. For 1967 the list could be extremely long, but a representative group would include Nabīl Khūrī's *Ḥārat al-Naṣārā* (The Christian quarter', 1969), set in Jerusalem; Amīn Shinār's *al-Kābūs* ('The Nightmare', 1968), which uses a grandfather's memoirs as a vehicle for a more symbolic approach to the topic; ʿAbd al-Nabī Ḥijāzī's *Qārib al-zamān* ('The boat of time', 1970), set in the Syrian border town of Qunaytra, and ʿAbd al-Raḥmān Munīf's (b. 1933) *Ḥīna taraknā al-Jisr* ('When we abandoned the bridge', 1976). But among those who have used fiction as a means of depicting and commenting on these conflicts, particular mention must be made of two works by the Lebanese novelist-sociologist Ḥalīm Barakāt (b. 1933): *Sittat ayyām* ('Six days', 1961), and *ʿAwdat al-ṭāʾir ilā 'l-baḥr* ('The Flying Dutchman's return to the sea', 1969; English trans. *Days of dust*, 1974). The action of the first novel is placed during the events of 1948. The seaside town of Dayr al-Baḥr is under siege by Zionist forces, and through the eyes of the hero, Suhayl, the reader is introduced not only to the stages of the conflict and the final debacle but also to some of the social forces which have led to a sense of stagnation, a situation well symbolized by the village clock which has remained immobile for years. In the latter work, too, the analytical eye of Barakāt the sociologist is much in evidence; he himself has admitted that Ramzī, the hero who teaches in Beirut, can be translated as 'the symbol of me'. But what distinguishes this novel is the almost cinematic sweep with which the fighting is depicted in a large number of different venues, thus providing a devastatingly clear account of the rapidity with which events overwhelmed the Arabs: the false news accounts of victories, the napalming of civilians on the West Bank as they flee towards Jordan, the resignation of ʿAbd al-Nāṣir and the student riots demanding that he remain. The central chapters which illustrate the events of the six days with such immediacy and vividness are framed by two sections which describe Ramzī's visit to ʿAmmān in order to assess the human tragedy (during which telling use is made of a rewriting of the creation story in the Book of Genesis). This enclosure of the events of the conflict within an account of its aftermath turns this novel from being merely a highly realistic account of the events of the Six Day War itself into an important contribution to the analysis of the very bases of Arab societal values in general.

The impact of the June War on the entire Arab World was intense.

Novelists were, needless to say, a part of the process of self-analysis and criticism. Manṣūr, the history teacher who serves as the hero of ʿAbd al-Raḥmān Munīf's novel, *al-Ashjār wa ightiyāl Marzūq* ('The trees and Marzūq's assassination', 1973), explores the dimensions of this process of loss, recovery and self-criticism; he discovers that authorities continue to impose severe limits on the use of historical interpretation as a means of political and social protest. In the work of the Syrian novelist Mamdūḥ ʿUdwān (b. 1941), *al-Abtar* ('Flawed', 1970), the hero, Idrīs, has refused to leave Qunaytra unlike the rest of his fellow-villagers and stays to confront the Israeli forces. Such is the resistance of this sixty-year-old man to Israeli attempts at establishing a kibbutz that they eventually destroy his village and kill him. In *al-Ṣubār* (1976, English trans. *Wild thorns*, 1985), the Palestinian writer Saḥar Khalīfah (b. 1941) brings her hero, Usāmah, on a reverse journey from that of Kanafānī's trio in *Rijāl fī 'l-shams*: from a job in the Gulf back to the occupied West Bank. Commissioned by the Resistance to blow up the buses that carry workers into Israel each day, he is horrified to discover that his family, friends and childhood colleagues are adjusting to the realities of occupation. Stubbornly refusing to listen to the arguments of his friends and family, he proceeds with his plan. The workers who are killed by the resulting explosion are Arabs from his own town, and Usāmah and his Resistance colleagues are killed in the ensuing gunfight. Nor is that the end for, in accordance with policy, the Israeli forces proceed to evacuate the family home and blow it up.

Part of this process of self-examination and the search for alternatives was the emergence of the fedayeen, both as a means of countering the results of the defeat and as a mode of release for so much pent-up anger and frustration. In Jabrā's previously mentioned novel *al-Baḥth ʿan Walīd Masʿūd*, both Walīd and his son Marwān are closely involved with a guerrilla cell in both training and action. In Tawfīq Fayyāḍ's novel *Majmūʿat 778* ('778 Group', 1974), the action is carried into Israel itself where a group in ʿAkkā are goaded by the 1967 debacle and by contacts on the West Bank into conducting guerrilla activities. Their initial efforts end in failure because of poor information and supplies, leading in turn to telling comments on the lack of commitment and organization among the leadership on the West Bank which reflect very much the implications of Saḥar Khalīfa's novel just discussed. If Fayyāḍ's somewhat journalistic work focuses on a single group, Laylā ʿUsayrān (b. 1936) chooses three capital cities to provide a broader spatial background for her work *ʿAṣāfīr al-fajr* ('Dawn birds', 1968). A family living in Beirut is mystified by the disappearance of their son, Salmān, who has been studying in Germany. He has in fact joined a *fidā'ī* cell in Jerusalem. When he is wounded in action, he asks to return to his family in Beirut. Maryam, his sister, is delighted by his decision to abandon his studies in Europe and is further confirmed in her decision not to marry ᶜIṣām, a feckless Lebanese youth who refuses to become involved in the struggle. The third focus is on the city of ᶜAmmān where a doctor has to cope with the hopeless situation in the tent camps following the influx of a human flood of refugees.

Civil war in Lebanon

The modern histories of Lebanon and the Palestinians have, of course, been linked since 1948 and even before, but the uneasy *modus vivendi* between the many separate religious and ethnic communities which resulted from the creation of Lebanon as a nation-state, already strained by the influx of refugees from 1948, came under extreme stress during the post-1967 period. Raids across the border into Israel and resulting reprisals, as well as complex political alignments of a local and international nature all contributed to heightening tensions. It is difficult to pinpoint exactly when the civil war in Lebanon started, but by 1975 the fighting between the different communities was widespread; the conflict still continues as these words are being written. The presence of armed Palestinians in the country and the acts of reprisal which they brought forth from the Israelis have clearly been further contributors to the rising tensions and the ensuing chaos. In 1976, another chapter was written in the continuing Palestinian tragedy when refugees living in the Tell al-Zaᶜtar camp in Beirut were massacred by Christian forces. In 1982 the Israeli army entered Lebanon on yet another reprisal raid, but this time they headed north to Beirut itself. It was during their occupation of the city that another massacre of Palestinians occurred in the Sabra and Shatila refugee camps in South Beirut, an act of unbelievable barbarity even in this area inured to conflict.

The city of Beirut, one of the great cultural and commercial centres of the Middle East, has been transformed by this vortex of communal violence into a divided and shell-pocked city. And yet a number of novelists have managed to explore the manifold aspects of the conflict and its effects on society with a remarkable degree of creativity. Against this background the work of Tawfīq Yūsuf ᶜAwwād, *Ṭawāḥīn Bayrūt* ('The mills of Bayrut', 1972, English trans., *Death in Beirut*, 1976) in which he uses the arrival in Beirut from southern Lebanon of a Shiᶜite girl, Tamīmah, to expose factionalism and corruption in the wake of the 1967 War, becomes disarmingly prophetic. Ghādah al-Sammān's (b. 1942) work *Kawābīs Bayrut* ('Beirut nightmares', 1976), mixes reality and nightmarish fantasies in a recounting of the fighting in November 1975 around the hotels of Beirut, during which her protagonist is trapped with her cousin and uncle. With

Ḥanān al-Shaykh's *Ḥikāyat Zahrah* (1980, English trans. *The story of Zahra*, 1986), we have one of the most notable recent additions to modern Arabic fiction, both for the effective way in which a number of issues are presented to the reader and for the brilliant use of technique and style. Like ᶜAwwād's heroine Tamīmah, Zahrah is the daughter of a Shiᶜite family from southern Lebanon. The attitudes of both men and women within the family are not only vivid illustrations of the position of women within society but also, on a wider level, symbols of societal attitudes which have contributed to the making and continuation of the civil conflict. Fleeing from war-torn Lebanon and the sexual complexes which her attitude to her parents has engendered within her, Zahrah embarks on a marriage in Africa which is doomed to failure. Returning to Lebanon, she finds herself sucked into the war. Her suppressed sexuality finally finds expression at the hands of a sniper who is terrorizing the neighbourhood. However, within the twisted logic of war, their union cannot be allowed to become a creative entity; at the conclusion of the novel she herself is felled by one of his bullets. A more symbolic but equally successful novelistic treatment of Lebanese society is found in the works of Ilyās Khūrī. *Al-Jabal al-ṣaghīr* ('The small mountain', 1977, a name applied to Ashrafiyya, part of the Christian quarter of East Beirut) uses folktales and anecdotes as a framework for criticism of the Lebanese commercial ethic; the work seems to suggest that war will continue in the region until there is greater tolerance of diversity. Khūrī's second novel, *Abwāb al-madīnah* ('City gates', 1981) is even more symbolic. The hero, here simply known as 'the Man', seeks to gain admission to an anonymous city and, once admitted, wanders around in a confused daze. He meets a group of beautiful women, but his relationships with them are interrupted by hallucinations and amnesia; everything dissolves into a Kafkaesque incomprehensibility which aptly reflects the 'nightmare' of Lebanon.

2. *The Arab world and Europe: cultures in contact*

Throughout the lengthy process whereby the Arab nations demanded and eventually obtained independence from the colonial powers, a theme which was to provide a vehicle for the analysis of the often antagonistic and confrontational relationship between the cultures of the Arab world and the west was that of visits by Arabs, mostly as students, to different countries in Europe; a theme, it will be recalled, which inspired some of the earliest prose writings of the *Nahḍah* and which was later adopted by a number of pioneers of the novel. The example set by writers such as Tawfīq al-Ḥakīm in Egypt, Shakīb al-Jābirī in Syria and Dhū 'l-Nūn Ayyūb in Iraq, is replicated at a later date by novelists from other national traditions. In Morocco, for example, ᶜAbd al-Majīd ibn Jallūn (b. 1919) published his novel *Fī 'l-ṭufūlah* ('In childhood') in 1957. The distinct tendency towards the autobiographical is much in evidence here as in earlier works; indeed such is the attention to detailed descriptions of life in the English city of Manchester that, in spite of ibn Jallūn's efforts to lend his novel some degree of fictionality, it seems most closely related to a work of travel such as al-Ṭahṭāwī's *Takhlīṣ al-ibrīz* mentioned in the previous chapter. In Lebanon four years earlier, Suhayl Idrīs (b. 1923) had commenced publication of what has become one of the most influential literary journals in the Arab world, *al-Adāb*, which was to lay great stress on the need for commitment in literature. In the same year (1953), he himself published *al-Ḥayy al-Lātīnī* ('The Latin quarter'), a novel in which a more profound dimension was given to the general theme of cultural confrontation through the exploration of the sensual relationship between Arab men and European women and the many ways in which that could be used to reflect the larger issues of difference, both societal and political. The way in which the 'hero' of Idrīs's novel treats Jeanine Montreux, his French lover, is symbolic not only of the existentialist angst which is one of the author's favourite themes, but also, on a broader scale, of the almost wilful desire to misunderstand which seemed to characterize the attitude of both cultures towards each other during these decades.

The analysis of the tensions implicit in the process of communication and interchange during the post-colonial era reaches its highest point so far in *Mawsim al-hijrah ilā 'l-shamāl* (1966, English trans. *Season of migration to the north*, 1969) by the Sudanese writer, al-Ṭayyib Ṣāliḥ (b. 1929). In this work the Arab student visiting the west, Muṣṭafā Saᶜīd, comes from the south, from Africa, and not as a supplicant but in the role of avenger. Far from being overawed by western culture, he becomes part of it. Given a teaching post at a university and adopted by British society, he proceeds to exploit its hankering for exoticism through a series of destructive relationships with British women, culminating in the almost ritual murder of his wife, Jean Morris, whose sneering defiance he has failed to tame. Returning to his homeland seven years later, he encounters the narrator of the story who has also spent time in England. The novel unfolds through the intertwined stories of narrator and hero and, as a whole host of cultural complexes emerge, we are left with the tantalizing question as to whether the figure of Muṣṭafā Saᶜīd, presented to us by the narrator, may in fact be a part of the latter's own psyche. This novel, with its brilliant use of flashback as a means of framing the central narrative, its emphasis on the psychological aspects of character, and the authenticity of its portrait of the Sudanese village of

Wād Ḥāmid (where Ṣāliḥ sets his works of fiction), has already emerged as one of the most outstanding contributions to modern Arabic fiction.

In *al-Marʾah wa'l-wardah* ('The Woman and the rose', 1971) by the Moroccan writer Muḥammad Zifzāf (b. 1945), the use of this theme may be seen as coming full circle. The hero of the novel, Muḥammad, goes to France to corroborate his own sense of identity with European culture. From the perspective of the French underworld to which he attaches himself, his view becomes somewhat transformed, but the major purpose of the narrative is to present some telling comments on the lack of freedom in his own society.

3. After Independence

Once the nations of the Arab world had achieved their independence, the need to establish a sense of self-identity as a nation and, in some cases, to cement new alignments developed within the revolutionary process, was a primary stimulus in the emergence of a tradition of social-realist fiction which would trace the development of the independence movement and identify the social underpinnings upon which the new era would be built. Within this context highest prominence has long been given to the Egyptian novelist Najīb Maḥfūẓ (b. 1911), who wrote a series of works about his native land, and his native city, Cairo, during the 1940s and who, with *al-Thulāthiyyah* ('The trilogy', 1956–7), painted a vast landscape of a society undergoing the individual and collective turmoil of change during the period from 1917 to the 1940s. Maḥfūẓ's work stands virtually alone in the breadth of its scope, the painstaking detail of its attention to place and time, and the sophisticated way in which the portrayal of character reflects the generational clashes of the period. However, on a smaller scale a number of novelists throughout the Arab world addressed themselves to these themes within the context of their own society.

Analysis of the course of revolution and change

In those countries (like the Sudan, Algeria and Morocco) in which the granting of independence was in itself a major stimulus to the emergence of a novelistic tradition, it is not surprising to note that early novels concentrate on opposition to the occupying forces and the events leading up to the day itself; as, for example, in the Sudan, in *Min ajl Laylā* ('For Laylā's sake', 1960) by al-Sirr Ḥasan Faḍl and in *Liqāʾ ʿinda 'l-ghurūb* ('Meeting at sunset', 1963) by Amīn Muḥammad Zayn. In Morocco, ʿAbd al-Karīm Ghallāb (b. 1919) traces the resistance to the French, the class divisions within society, the separate educational systems and many other issues which were far from solved by the granting of independence. It is hardly surprising that one of the most vivid accounts of revolution and its aftermath in modern Arabic literature should come from the pen of an Algerian writer, that being the country which went through what was probably the most protracted and bitter of the wars of independence, between 1954 and 1962. In *al-Lāz* (the name of the hero, 1974), al-Ṭāhir Waṭṭār (b. 1936) broaches a problem which was typical of many post-revolutionary situations in the Arab world. Al-Lāz is the illegitimate son of Zaydān, a communist who operates a guerrilla cell in the mountains. Al-Lāz, who does not initially know who his father is, has been serving as an agent for the guerrillas in a French camp. He is betrayed and flees to his father's hideout, but discovers that, since his father has refused the demand of the Muslim members of the Nationalist Front (FLN) that he recant his Communist beliefs, he is about to die. Even after such a lengthy and bloody struggle for independence, there are still other scores to settle.

Other novelists place less emphasis on the struggle against the occupiers, and focus more on other aspects of the 'bad old days', most particularly on political corruption. Dhū 'l-Nūn Ayyūb has made this the focus of his novels, and in that he is followed by another Iraqi writer, Ghānim Dabbāgh (b. 1923), who in *Ḍajjah fī 'l-zuqāq* ('Din in the alley', 1975) uses his main character, Khalīl, to portray corruption in the petty bureaucracy in the provincial city of Mawṣil during the 'regime' of Nūrī Saᶜīd in the 1950s. On a much more ambitious scale, the Syrian writer Ṣidqī Ismāᶜīl (1924–72), uses *al-ᶜUṣāh* ('The rebels', 1964) to produce a study of political corruption in Syria from the turn of the century until 1948 and its effects on three generations of a prominent family in Aleppo. While the first generation is completely subservient to the Turkish regime, the second is drawn into the Nationalist cause against the French; the true import of the novel for both the present and the future, however, lies in the depiction of the third generation, which finds itself combating corruption and disillusion among fellow Syrians. In *al-Shams fī yawm ghāʾim* ('Sun on a cloudy day', 1973) Ḥannā Mīnah, whose earlier novels (noted above) depicted Syrian resistance with a vivid realism, also makes creative use of the period of the French occupation to illustrate the need for societal change. In this case, the son of an aristocratic family living on its past glories falls in love with a poor girl from whom he learns a particular folkloric dance. With the stage thus set using a rather obvious symbolism, the story proceeds with the hero rebelling against his own class background and the way in which poorer people are exploited.

Land and peasants: city and countryside

From a prolonged process of confrontation and even conflict with outside forces, the newly independent nations of the Arab world, several of which were faced with the challenge of implementing goals long espoused as part of the process of revolution, turned their attention to the enormous agenda of social reform which remained as a legacy from the earlier times. Bearing in mind that the exploitation of peasants and the land had been a common rallying-cry even before the advent of independence, it is hardly surprising that agricultural reform was one of the top priorities of the new generation of Arab governments and that the genre of the novel provided a fertile arena for a portrayal of the need for and implementation of such measures. Thus Dhū 'l-Nūn Ayyūb's novel, *al-Yad wa'l-arḍ wa'l-māʾ* ('Hand, earth and water', 1948), which had dealt with corruption and exploitation in the countryside of Iraq during the monarchy, anticipates the reforms initiated in several Arab countries. The laws passed in Egypt soon after the revolution are almost immediately reflected in the renowned novel by ʿAbd al-Raḥmān al-Sharqāwī, *al-Arḍ* ('The earth', 1954, trans. *Egyptian earth*, 1962), and the same pattern is repeated elsewhere. Two regions in which this topic is especially reflected in fiction are Algeria and Syria. Al-Ṭāhir Waṭṭār sets his novel, *al-Zilzāl* ('The earthquake', 1974) in the Algerian city of Constantine, significant not only because it is a centre of conservative religious belief but also because it gave its name to the last effort of the French before independence to reorganize Algerian agriculture. Shaykh ʿAbd al-Majīd Bū-Arwāḥ wanders around the various quarters of the city (which is itself built on an earthquake fault) repeating a phrase from the text of the Qurʾan about earthquakes. As he searches vainly for his relatives so that he can bequeathe to them portions of his land and thus avoid the strictures of the new Agricultural Reform Laws, the reader is presented through this shaykh's jaundiced eye with a most effective view of the changes which the revolution has brought about, all within a carefully crafted novelistic environment. This theme is taken up again by al-Waṭṭar in his second novel on al-Lāz, *al-Lāz, al-ʿishq wa'l-mawt fī 'l-zaman al-ḥarāshī* ('Al-Laz: Love and death in rough times', 1982). In Syria a number of writers of social-realist novels deal with the problems of the country's peasantry, although it has to be admitted that the results often tend to underline the frequently stated view that the expression of commitment to a cause does not guarantee a successful work of art or a positive critical response. Thus, Adīb Naḥawī applies himself to the topic of feudalism in *Matā yaʿūd al-maṭar* ('When the rain returns', 1958) and Fāris Zarzūr deals in *al-Ḥufāh* ('Without shoes', 1971) with the exploitation of migrant workers and in *al-Mudhnibūn* ('Sinners', 1974) with drought and extortion. ʿAbd al-Nabī Ḥijāzī produces in *al-Sindiyānah* ('The oak tree', 1971) a more subtle and carefully crafted piece of fiction about a village in the Syrian provinces in which the impact of crushing poverty is exploited by the Mukhtār to his own benefit.

In contemporary fiction, as in poetry, the city, and particularly the capital city, emerges in works such as these as 'a center of exploitation and misery, of social injustice and political intrigue' (to quote Salmā al-Jayyūsī), and that uneasy relationship provides modern Arabic fiction with a further extension of the countryside theme. In the Maghreb the transfer of the farming community to the city created social problems for each. Thus in ʿAbd al-Ḥamīd ibn Hadūqah's (b. 1929) early Algerian novel *Rīḥ al-janūb* ('South wind', 1971), the topic is not only the tension between city and village as reflected in the decision of Nafīsah, an eighteen-year-old girl, to go to the city to receive an education, but also the traditional attitudes forced upon her by a compulsory marriage to an older man. In a prize-winning novel, *al-Ṭayyibūn* ('The good folk', 1971), Mubārak Rabīʿ analyzes the nature of Moroccan society and illustrates the same tension, but within the context of the city. Here the land and those who live on it and by it are essentially pawns in the hands of landowners living far away. However, the novel which probably best conveys the remoteness and alien nature of the city within the life of those who work the land is ʿAbd al-Raḥmān Munīf's remarkable *al-Nihāyāt* ('Endings', 1978, trans. 1988) in which, against the graphic backdrop of the desert itself, the entire community of the village of al-Ṭība, and especially its eccentric hunting champion, ʿAssāf, struggle valiantly against the terrifying forces of nature. Token visits from family members living in the city, bringing promises of a new dam, are greeted with a cynicism born of neglect and both spatial and attitudinal distance.

The family in society: education

When we bear in mind the history of the novel as a genre in other cultures, it is hardly surprising that the period following independence and revolution in the Arab world should have seen the appearance of a large number of works concerning the most vital of societal institutions, the family, the unit which serves, in Lukacs's words, as 'a vehicle of the natural continuity of life'. As each society set out to establish its own political and social agenda, several novelists (especially during the 1950s) wrote works depicting the traditional points of tension within family life. Kawthar, the mother of an Aleppo family in Fāḍil al-Sibāʿī's (b. 1920) *Thumma azhara 'l-ḥuzn* ('Then sadness bloomed', 1963), struggles to maintain her household consisting of five daughters and a baby son after her husband dies (an echo, perhaps, of Maḥfūẓ's Samīrah in *Bidāyah wa-nihāyah* ('Beginning and end', 1951)). The period involved, 1958–61, is that of the United Arab Republic when Egypt and Syria were politically united, and emotional relationships and educational contacts involving members of the family reflect the complexities of the era. The mother meanwhile has to resist the advances of the polygamous al-Ḥājj Hilāl as she strives to maintain the educational progress and moral rectitude of her daughters. The consequences of the break-up of a family which Kawthar is at such pains to avoid are explored in a work by Ḥasīb Kayyālī, *Makātīb al-gharām* ('Love letters') in which, in a rather too obvious way, the sins of the parents (and particularly a profligate mother) are visited on their children.

The area where Kawthar's daughters in al-Sibāʿī's novel come most directly into contact with the forces of change is the educational system. In Morocco, both ʿAbd al-Karīm Ghallāb in *Dafannā 'l-māḍī* ('We have buried the past', 1966) and al-Bakrī Aḥmad al-Sibāʿī in *Bawtaqat al-ḥayāh* ('Life's crucible', 1966) point out the differences between traditional, mosque-based education and the new secular school system, an important and still-continuing point of debate in the Maghreb. In the eastern region, however, the primary focus in fiction was on the university level. The opportunities of a first generation to attend university brought about radical changes in both family and society as a whole. Sudanese novelists have tended to emphasize the direct role of students in fostering the developing goals of the revolution during the 1940s and 1950s, as, for example, in *Bidāyat al-rabīʿ* ('The beginning of spring', 1958) by Abū Bakr Khālid (1935–76) and *Liqāʾ ʿinda 'l-ghurūb* ('Encounter at sunset', 1963) by Amīn Muḥammad Zayn. In Syria the topic was the subject of two novels by Hānī al-Rāhib (b. 1939): *al-Mahzūmūn* ('The defeated', 1961) and *Sharkh fī tārīkh ṭawīl* ('Crack in a long history', 1969). Against the background of the society's attempts at identifying its future directions, these two works explore the attitudes of university students to politics, culture and sex and show clearly the sense of alienation which was frequently the consequence of such a radically transformed environment.

Educational opportunities and the changing attitudes which they brought about often led to severe clashes between the different generations within each family. The pain that such conflicts could cause is well captured in the title of a novel devoted to the topic, Walīd Midfaʿī's *Ghurabāʾ fī awṭāninā* ('Strangers in our own country', 1972) in which the sons of the family rebel against their domineering father and the daughter, Widād, refuses to contemplate an arranged marriage. A similar picture is created in the work of Suhayl Idrīs, *al-Khandaq al-ghamīq* ('The deep trench', 1958), in which older and more traditional values based on religion represented in the character of Fawzī, the father of the family, clash with the more secular values of Lebanese society as seen in the children; this is portrayed most vividly through the scorn with which the values they have learned at home are greeted by the children's peers.

From almost the outset, a particular focus of concern in the novelistic tradition in the Arab world has been the status of women: in Egypt in 1913 it was a major topic of Haykal's *Zaynab*, and later in chronology but at a similar incipient phase of development it was taken up by Aḥmad Riḍā Ḥūḥū in *Ghādat Umm al-qurā*. While the extent to which traditional attitudes to women have changed is open to debate, the topic of women's roles in society and of attitudes to them has become a prominent topic of Arabic fiction. Two early pioneers in the (relatively) bold expression of a woman's view of men were Laylā Baᶜalbakī (b. 1936) in *Anā aḥyā* ('I am alive', 1958) and *al-Ālihah 'l-mamsūkhah* ('Deformed deities', 1960), both of which paint a rather self-centred and pessimistic picture of the life of a young girl, and Colette Khūrī (b. 1937) in *Ayyām maᶜahu* ('Days with him', 1959) which emerges in a more positive light in that her heroine abandons her feckless lover. In other Arab societies women continue to fight for yet more basic rights, as is made clear by the protests of Nafīsah, the Algerian heroine of Ibn Hadūqah's novel *Rīḥ al-janūb* (South wind'), to her own mother:

> Tell my father that I will not get married; I won't stop my studies. I'm going back to Algiers, no matter what. I'm not going to put up with the humiliation you have to endure. You can be mother to someone else if you like, and he can be father to whomever he wishes. I won't allow this curse to get as far with me as it has with others. I am not a woman. Do you understand? I am not a woman. (pp. 88–89)

More recently, the voice of feminist writing has become more daring in its treatment not only of women's relationships with and their view of men, but also in their willingness to explore the more emotional and sensual aspects of their own self. This can be seen clearly through the works of such well-known political figures as Nawāl al-Saᶜdāwī in Egypt. The continuing social tragedy of Lebanon has provided the stimulus for a large number of women writers (of whom we have already mentioned Ghādah al-Sammān and Ḥanān al-Shaykh) who have addressed themselves to the fate of their country, pointing out with a fresh sense of élan and freedom, spawned in part perhaps by the very anarchy within which they created their works, the brutality and essential futility of the destructive urge which they witness all around them.

The individual and his identity: oppression and alienation

A number of critics who discuss writing by women use the image of the cage or prison to describe the lack of freedom which many women felt within the environment of traditional mores. Thus for women the family hierarchy came to represent in microcosm the very same restriction of liberty which was to be applied with regrettable regularity to members of the male population. In many Arab countries, the aftermath of independence brought an initial period of euphoria and expansion on the broader domestic and international front, followed on the individual level by a decade or more of repression and loss of civil liberties, a situation which was described by Arab novelists, often at considerable risk to themselves, in a number of works. In novels which deal with dissenters and rebels against the prevailing social and political order, prison is, more often than not, the resort. The Moroccan novelist ᶜAbd al-Karīm Ghallāb does at least set the hero of his early novel *Sabᶜat abwāb* ('Seven gates', 1965) within the nationalist struggle for independence and permits his cell-mates to recount tales of nationalist heroism. However, in a whole series of more recent works written across the breadth of the Arab world, the reader is presented with a horrific vision of a series of societies suppressing intellectual dissent and subjecting their populace to all manner of barbarous torture. Nabīl Sulaymān's *al-Sijn* ('Prison', n.d.), ᶜAbd al-Raḥmān al-Rubayᶜī's (b. 1939) *al-Washm* ('The tattoo', 1972), ᶜAbd al-Raḥmān Munīf's *Sharq al-Mutawassiṭ* ('East of the Mediterranean', 1977) – prefaced by the Declaration of Human Rights – and Ismāᶜīl Fahd Ismāᶜīl's (b. 1940) *al-Mustanqaᶜāt al-ḍawᵓiyyah* ('Light swamps', 1972) are the most critically acclaimed examples of this distressing illustration of the novel's ability, and indeed function, to portray all aspects of society.

While some of the heroes of these novels resist to the end, others succumb to the pressures of physical and psychological torture. Karīm al-Nāṣirī, the hero of al-Rubayᶜī's *al-Washm* is one such: after 'recanting' his past 'heresies', he is restored to society. However, he and others like him now become intellectual neuters; their only resort is a life of alienation and internal exile, itself the subject of Ismāᶜīl Fahd Ismāᶜīl's quartet of novels. While these 'activist' heroes may be reduced by the oppressive nature of the regime to a life of inactivity and detachment, other intellectuals find the complexities of modern life and the frustrations of unfulfilled political and personal hopes to be such that they choose alienation as a viable alternative, as an existentialist position. This too is reflected in a series of novels. Muṭāᶜ Ṣafadī (b. 1929), who in *Jīl al-qadar* ('Generation of fate', 1960) discusses alienation among students at the University of Damascus in the 1950s, turns in *Thāᵓir muḥtarif* ('Professional revolutionary', 1961) to the interaction between a group of revolutionaries and intellectuals. The principal character of the novel, Karīm, has participated in a number of revolutions, but is now tired of slogans and structures. The process of revolutionary change now operates on a more individual level; 'first and foremost it is the experience of the hero confronted by himself'.

The theme of exile, whether internal or external, is one to which many Arab novelists have resorted. For Emily Naṣrallāh (b. 1938), exile and absence in her early works, such as *Ṭuyūr Aylūl* ('September birds', 1962), implied a failure to reconcile the values of the city with those of the village and also the challenge for the community of facing the departure of its young folk to the *mahjar*, the community in the Americas. More recently, within the context of civil war and in such works as *Tilka 'l-dhikrayāt* ('Those memories', 1980), exile for Naṣrallāh has come to imply desertion of the homeland in a time of need. Ḥannā Mīnah's novel *al-Thalj ya'tī min al-nāfidhah* ('The snow comes through the window', 1969) also suggests, through the failures encountered by its principal character, Fayyāḍ, in his flight from Syria to Lebanon, that unforced exile from the homeland is meaningless escapism. On the level of personal alienation, perhaps the most disturbing vision is that of Jūrj Sālim, himself an eminent critic, in his novel with the significant title *Fī 'l-manfā* ('In exile', 1962). Using the devices of anonymity with skill, he manages to create an oppressively detached atmosphere very redolent of Kafka, not least via the use of an inquisitor.

The Moroccan author ʿAbdallāh al-ʿArwī (Laroui) (b. 1933) has written two novels, the first of which has a title which is of direct relevance to our current topic, *al-Ghurbah* ('Exile', 1971). In a work of considerable complexity, full of allusion, internal monologue and time switching, al-ʿArwī paints a picture of cultural fragmentation in post-independence Moroccan society. Through the despair of Shuʿayb, the ardent nationalist, at the current state of his country, and the failure of Idrīs and Maria to bring their relationship to fruition in a reconciliation of their attitudes to Europe, the reader is drawn to the conclusion that, during the post-colonial era, the interests of countries with close links to Europe cannot be well served by the attempt to develop alternative cultural models.

New experiments

The novel's most abiding feature has been its ability to describe change, and in some cases to promote it. The susceptibility of the genre itself to transformation has been an integral part of that process. While certain critics have long since forecast the 'death' of the novel, the term *le nouveau roman* has long been current within the French tradition in particular, but elsewhere as well. In recent years, a number of novelists in the Arab world have been prepared to experiment with the genre in radical ways. These authors seem to be reacting to the creative impulse in the way envisioned by the American novelist Joyce Carol Oates when she writes:

I anticipate novels that are in fact prose poems; and novels that are written for the ear . . . the freedom to attempt virtually anything within the elastic confines of the 'novel'. (*New York Times Book Review*, 5 April 1981, p. 11)

In a survey such as this, it is, of course, a very risky enterprise to attempt to identify which of these experiments will prove to have enduring merit, and so the authors and titles mentioned in the section that follows must be regarded simply as a sample culled from a list of works known to this writer.

The Syrian novelist Walīd Ikhlāṣī (b. 1935) may serve as a good example of this trend, and no more so than through the reaction of critics of which the following, by Muʾayyad al-Ṭalāl, may serve as an illustration:

The chief problem with Walīd Ikhlāṣī's novels is that they indulge in symbolism and imaginative fantasies to such an extent that some of them are impossible for the critic to analyse, let alone the ordinary reader! (*Al-Thawrah*, 15 June 1976)

While not all of Ikhlāṣī's fictional works (in both short story and novel form) fit this description, it is certainly true that in many of his novels there is no concern with creating a fictional world through any of the more traditional modes of coherence; instead the confusion and alienation of the modern world is established and illustrated through a fractured vision created through such devices as stream-of-consciousness, the absence of chronological logic, and often a chilling anonymity. His very first novel, *Shitāʾ al-baḥr al-yābis* ('Winter of the dry sea', 1964), tells five separate but synchronous tales in which events and characters appear in a bewildering blend of reality and dreams. In his third novel *Aḥzān al-ramād* ('Sorrows of ashes', 1975), Ikhlāṣī is again at pains to paint images and create atmosphere without providing descriptive details of character and place. Within this illogical and often surrealistic environment, the four segments, 'Introduction', 'He', 'She' and 'They', give a depressing picture of individual corruption and societal decay.

These same innovative tendencies are evident in the work of the Moroccan novelist Muḥammad ʿIzz al-dīn al-Tāzī (b. 1948), *Abrāj al-madīnah* ('City towers', 1978), in which, with the same 'neutral' environment and poetic style, the author portrays political and social oppression and criticizes the failure of the leftist political parties to offer valid alternatives. Even more extreme in its innovative techniques is *Zaman bayna 'l-wilādah wa'l-ḥulm* ('Time between birth and dream', 1976) by another Moroccan novelist, Aḥmad al-Middīnī (b. 1948). Critical reaction to this work has been much the same as that which greeted Ikhlāṣī's experiments. Al-Nassāj, for example, asks how it is possible to depict the reality of things through a chaos of writing, while al-Rubayʿī finds the novel lacking the basic underpinnings required by the genre. In a work in which time and place dissolve and there is no logical connection between sections, much emphasis is placed on the power and variation of language itself, including the incorporation into the text of extended sections of poetry and popular songs.

In *Barārī 'l-ḥummā* ('Fever prairies', 1985), the poet Ibrāhīm Naṣrallāh writes a novel in which reality and fantasy are blended in a language environment which mixes a wealth of metaphorical language with the tersest of dialogue and several poems. The heat implicit in the title can be seen as a reference to the setting, a remote village in the Empty Quarter region of Saudi Arabia, but it refers as much to the mental fever which possesses Muḥammad Ḥammād, the main character in the work, as his alienation from his surroundings intensifies, a process for which the author invokes, via a stream-of-consciousness, a nightmarish combination of hallucinations, visions, images and dreams.

In their rejection of the generic expectations for the more traditional novel, these novels may perhaps be said to require, within the context of the Arab world, something akin to Riffaterre's 'superreader'. It should immediately be emphasized that not all experiments in Arabic fiction follow such a radical path. Yūsuf Ḥabashī al-Ashqar, for example, has come to the novel after writing a number of increasingly innovative short-story collections. The description of the intricate web of characters found in *La tanbut judhụr fī 'l-samāʾ* ('Roots do not grow in heaven', 1971), for example, is intensified not only by the common expedient of time-switching, but also by taking the dramatic element in the novel, the dialogue, to what might be termed a logical conclusion: that of introducing a series of dramatic 'scenes' within the framework of the novel itself.

Discussion of innovative applications to the Arabic novel should not conclude without some mention of the creative experiments of the Egyptian Jamāl al-Ghīṭānī (b. 1945) and ʿAbd al-Raḥmān Munīf, involving the incorporation within their own fiction of either literary texts from other periods or imitations and pastiches of these, whether culled from historical sources or popular tales. Furthermore, in discussing the 'rhetoric of fiction', Emīl Ḥabībī's revival of the sardonic vision of the picaresque anti-hero in *al-Waqāʾiʿ al-gharībah* represents a refreshingly different approach to the question of narrative voice.

The novel: purpose and technique

In the wake of independence and revolution, many Arab nations looked forward to the future with an understandable sense of optimism and élan, and pursued a determined course of social change. In fictional terms, that was often translated into a school of social realism, the official orchestration of which was often scarcely concealed. Gradually, however, there developed alongside this tendency a more critical approach, one which was prepared to look beneath the surface of the official version of events and explore the many agonizing dilemmas of the society in general and the individual in particular. This tendency produces works of increasing psychological insight, as the manifold dimensions of alienation are explored. The process is often accompanied by a rich use of symbolism which, while often applied with great artistic skill, was often intended primarily as a means of obscuring from officialdom the unpalatability of the underlying message. At a conference in Morocco devoted to the Arabic novel (later published as Muḥammad Barrādah, *al-Riwāyah al-ᶜArabiyyah*, 1981) ᶜAbd al-Raḥmān Munīf, summarizes the role(s) which the novel has played and is playing in the region:

> The Arab world is going through a period of change, involving much insecurity, a historical stage replete with contradictions, dissension and struggle. All these things make the novel, as a mode of expression, more capable than any other genre of recording the inner dynamism involved; even perhaps of participating in the focusing of that dynamism in a particular direction. (p. 263)

Within the essentially 'epic' conception of novelistic purpose (the need being, to quote Lukacs, to discuss 'not a personal destiny but the destiny of a community'), the majority of the works cited above mostly employ an omniscient narrator who describes in chronological sequence a series of events affecting a group or community during a specified period of time and in a particular place; to use the terminology favoured by criticism of narrative, the aim is that of 'telling' rather than 'showing'. It has to be admitted that, in some of the works listed above, the societal agenda are presented in a forceful and concentrated fashion, often obscuring other aspects of the fictional art; the result is often close to reportage. Thus, while such works may play an important role at a certain point in time in a particular country, their impact remains ephemeral. However, the recent history of the Arabic novel can provide many examples of works in which the author not only places the 'destiny of the community' into a most successful piece of fiction but also experiments in interesting ways with different aspects of technique.

With regard to the treatment of place, for example, the city in the Arabic novel, as in other traditions, serves as the primary location. While in many works of fiction it serves as a nurturer to its inhabitants, this period in Middle Eastern history also shows it swallowing up the many 'outsiders' who venture inside its walls. It is also the place of change, often focused on the educational institutions which it fosters. Nafīsah, the provincial girl in Ibn Hadūqah's (b. 1929) *Rīḥ al-janūb* ('South wind'), can no longer tolerate or obey the dictates of tradition once she has gone to Algiers to study. Those same educational opportunities, culled from a whole series of cities, lead Muṣṭafā Saᶜīd on his fateful and destructive path in al-Ṭayyib Ṣāliḥ's *Mawsim al-hijrah ilā 'l-shamāl* ('Season of migration to the north'). Throughout the Arab world a generation of young people are shown attending schools and universities in the city and then returning to their homes to face the frustrating prospect of bringing about change in the face of tradition and entrenched interests. One particular city, the capital, is also the seat of government, and it is from there that the city endeavours to impose its societal agenda on the provincial way of life. In those countries with elaborate agricultural networks, the confrontations and crises caused by this situation naturally become a prominent topic for the novel. It is perhaps hardly surprising that many novelists – themselves city-dwellers and advocates of change – tend to portray provincial society as a place of stagnation, stubbornly resisting the forces of change. It is in the desert that the city is at its most distant and alien, and the symbolic potential of this environment as both protector and destroyer is richly explored by both Kanafānī and Munīf.

The fracturing of chronology provides a number of ways in which the reader is drawn into the process of creating the novel's world. Both *Rijāl fī 'l-shams* ('Men in the sun') and *Mā tabaqqā lakum* ('What remains for you') by Ghassān Kanafānī exploit time to the fullest. In the first, three separate narrative strands – the lives of the three Palestinians from different generations – are gradually drawn together towards the final tragedy, while in the second Time itself becomes one of the 'heroes' of the work. The element of synchronicity is seen at its most vivid in Ḥalīm Barakāt's *ᶜAwdat al-ṭāʾir ilā 'l-baḥr* ('Return of the Flying Dutchman to the sea'), in which the scale of the 1967 defeat is demonstrated with a cinematic sweep. Changes in the way in which 'the uninterrupted flow of time' (Lukacs's phrase) is presented also permit creative presentation of the narrative voice, and no more so than in the use of multiple narrators. The Iraqi novelist, Ghāʾib Ṭuᶜmah Farmān, uses no fewer than five narrators in his *Khamsat aṣwāt* ('Five voices') to present a portrait of Baghdadi society immediately before the 1958 Revolution and to show the many tensions felt by the intelligentsia during that period. In Jabrā's *al-Safīnah* ('The ship'), the reader learns via the differing viewpoints of three narrators the events of a Mediterranean cruise which lasts just seven days but, through a whole series of flashbacks and discussions, the temporal, spatial and intellectual scope of the work is expanded into a complex picture of alienation and despair among the intellectual elite. The technique is honed even more in *al-Baḥth ʿan Walīd Masʿūd* ('In search of Walīd Masʿūd') where a tape recording triggers narratives by a number of characters, including the 'lost' hero.

From the earliest period in the development of the Arabic novel, the subject of language has been the focus of much debate. Since independence, there have been fierce debates in the Maghrib over 'arabization' (*taʿrīb*) and the writing of literature in Arabic as opposed to French. Equally keen throughout the Arab world has been the debate over the use of the colloquial dialects in fictional dialogue. The issue is put forcefully by the Tunisian writer al-Bashīr Khurayyif (cited by Abdelkabir Khatibi in *Le roman maghrebin* (1969):

> Parmi les calamités de la langue classique est que d'une part chaque Arabe emploie l'arabe dialectale dans sa vie quotidienne et que d'une autre part quand il désire écrire, il s'engage dans un continent étranger, son écriture perd alors son caractère naturel et simple. (pp. 40–1)

Needless to say, a large number of novelists writing in the Arab world today do not share this view. Indeed the quotation itself lends credence to the 'risky generalisation' which Charles Vial permits himself in his article on the Arabic novel (in the second edition of *The encyclopedia of Islam*):

> The tendency to use the spoken 'popular' language is more widespread in countries where the literary public is greatest and which believe, rightly or wrongly, that they have a better established 'Arab' character – thus, in Egypt, rather than Algeria.

Thus, not only have a large number of novelists throughout the region used the standard written language of Arabic as the vehicle for expressing every aspect of novelistic technique, but a stage seems now to have been reached when novelists have the freedom to choose for themselves the register(s) of language that they will use in their works. The dilemma that they face is that, while the use of the dialect of their own area may lend authenticity to dialogue, it is liable at the same time to give the work a more local readership rather than a broader Arab world one. Here, of course, the receptivity of the dialect itself becomes an issue; one might suggest that the 'central' dialects (Egyptian and 'Levantine') tend to be more readily transportable than the outlying ones (Maghribi and Iraqi).

Turning from problems of the nature of the language itself to matters of style, it is clear that the contemporary Arabic novel can show an almost endless variety. Building on the efforts of pioneers such as al-Manfalūṭī and Zaydān, who provided a prose style which was both concise and adaptable, and of early writers of fiction such as Jibrān, Haykal, Mīkhāʾīl Nuʿaymah, Ṭāhā Ḥusayn and Maḥmūd al-Sayyid, all of whom experimented with the application of language to the requirements of fiction in different ways, the more recent tradition of the Arabic novel has had at its disposal modes of expression of great versatility. To those who preferred a vehicle for description within the bounds of a more traditional realism, ᶜAbd al-Karīm Ghallāb, Ghāʾib Ṭuᶜman Farmān, Dhū 'l-Nūn Ayyūb and the early Ḥannā Mīnah, a prose style of simplicity and directness was available. With an increase in pace and tension, as in the writings of Ḥalīm Barakāt and Ghādah al-Sammān, a shorter, more staccato sentence structure provided the necessary mood. Ḥannā Mīnah's style was to develop into a more symbolic vehicle in later works, as does the writing of al-Ṭāhir Waṭṭār, most particularly in *al-Ḥawwāt wa'l-qaṣr* ('The fisherman and the palace', 1987), although it is also evident in *al-Zilzāl* ('The earthquake') mentioned above. The effective use of imagery and symbol is a particular feature of many, if not most, of the distinguished writers of mature Arabic fiction; whether it is used to underline the particular thematic focus of works such as those of Ghassān Kanafānī and al-Ṭayyib Ṣāliḥ or to lend an atmosphere of disillusionment and obscurity as in the cases of al-ᶜArwī (Laroui) and Ilyās Khūrī, the resulting novels provide a challenge for the reader which greatly enriches the process of discovery. Several authors choose a language which comes close to that of poetry. Jabrā Ibrāhīm Jabrā is, of course, a poet, and thus it comes as no surprise that his novels are replete with passages akin to prose poetry. His friend ᶜAbd al-Raḥmān Munīf is also capable of producing passages of great poetic sensitivity. It is this combination which makes of *ᶜĀlam bi-lā kharāʾiṭ* ('Mapless world') such an interesting exercise in its own right and one which clearly would not work without a meeting of minds on matters of style.

Thus, we would suggest that the very wealth of the Arabic language – with its many structures, modes and registers – far from constituting a problem for the truly creative writer of fiction, provides for the future of the genre a large number of opportunities for creative experiment.

THE NOVEL IN THE ARAB WORLD TODAY: WRITER, READER, TEXT

The writer

Mubārak Rabīᶜ expresses (in Barrādah, *al-Riwāyah al-ᶜArabiyyah*, p. 79) the position of the novelist in the Arab World in the following terms: 'questioning, argument, criticism, review and evaluation of everything which comes within our purview . . .' On a personal and institutional level it has been the fate of novelists to discover with regrettable frequency that, in a period of radical societal transformation which has followed independence, such a posture has often not coincided with the political and societal goals of the regime. To the inherent difficulties of writing such a complex genre and reflecting a changing world have been added other pressures and risks. The many examples of imprisonment, torture and exile to be found in the works of fiction themselves can be duplicated in the real world of the Arab novelist: imprisonment for ᶜAbd al-Karīm Ghallāb, dismissal from university in the case of Ḥalīm Barakāt, and arrest and trial with Laylā Baᶜalbakī. ᶜAbd al-Raḥmān Munīf and Dhū 'l-Nūn Ayyūb are two among many writers living outside their homeland, a fate which has become almost a way of life for the majority of Palestinian authors.

Another factor which has a major impact on the role of the novelist in the Arab world is the entire question of profession. Even the Arab world's most widely acknowledged novelist, Najīb Maḥfūẓ, now in his seventies, was not able to earn a living as a novelist. A writer such as Ḥannā Mīnah has held a bewildering variety of jobs, from barber to stevedore, and a large number of commentators have drawn attention to the distractions which have prevented talented writers from pursuing their real interests during their younger years. Beyond this, however, resides a further, more sinister reality, namely that most of the jobs which will permit writers to pursue their craft are to be found in the area of the state cultural bureaucracy – as editors of newspapers, journals and the like – positions in which they can often be easily controlled and from which they can be dismissed with equal ease. The situation is well described by Abdelkabir Khatibi (*Le roman maghrebin*, Rabat, 1979, p. 35)

> Les régimes autoritaires se fabriquent un code culturel, un autopanégyrique pour masquer leur destin d'oppresseur. L'écrivain qui est payé pour jouer un rôle est un véritable fabricant de l'alienation.

And, when long careers of public service are at an end, novelists sometimes choose to retire simultaneously from both bureaucracy and writing.

The reader

The Arabic novels that we have surveyed in this chapter are, in general, written by an educated élite to be read by the members of that same class. Thus, in spite of the attention that many novelists who are committed to the ideas of social reform pay to the plight of the poor classes, there is the ever-present irony that more often than not, the very classes which are the subject of the novels do not possess the literacy level needed to read them.

Q. D. Leavis points out in her study of publics for fiction that the novel is a demanding genre and that other media are more immediately accessible. From the point of view of the reception of a work of fiction and the 'implied reader', we may wonder about the purpose of references to Rachmaninov in Barakāt's *ʿAwdat al-ṭāʾir ilā 'l-baḥr* and to Neapolitan art and Dostoevsky in Jabrā's *al-Safīnah*. Such detail may, of course, suggest to the reader certain things about the distance between the narrative voice and the author, but many critics have chosen to question the cultural relevance of such references. The use of experimental techniques and their effect on the question of readership is reflected in this comment (also by Muʾayyad al-Ṭalāl) on Walīd Ikhlāṣī's novels:

> The problem with this tendency is that . . . the littérateur is spiritually and mentally isolated, and his literature is turned into a kind of élitist art; it merely widens the gap between the intellect of the symbolist writer with his technical skills on the one hand and the ordinary reader's less sophisticated abilities on the other. (*Al-Thawrah*, Damascus, 15 June 1976)

Turning to the role and practice of criticism, it should be remembered that within the western tradition the development of the field of narratology in all its different aspects is not of great vintage; if the current tradition of fictional criticism in the Arab world is predominantly historical, national and thematic in focus, then it sits firmly within the developmental pattern of its analogue in the western world. The predominance of realistic novels is reflected in critical writing through an emphasis on works written within an individual country or on a particular topic such as war, sexual roles or social trends. Works which adopt a particular critical approach – discussing variations in treatment of point of view, of time and place, or of style – are relatively rare; studies which deal with the Arabic tradition across the Arab world are few and far between. In both these last two regards the situation is certainly in the process of change, as a new generation of critics endeavours to overcome entrenched cultural attitudes and stereotypes and finds or founds publication outlets for their opinions.

The text

One of the major problems facing the Arab novelist is the question of publication and distribution. The daily and periodical press continues to play a crucial role in the dissemination of works of literature throughout the region. However, while this method of distribution and the later process of publication in book form (of one kind or another) ensures that the work reaches a local public, it remains true that both practical and political barriers often prevent works from reaching a wider readership. In this regard, the cultural establishments of some countries in the region are more liberal than others in both the books and the periodicals which they permit to enter the country from other states within the Arab world. Thus, while the Arabic novel has a potentially broad readership 'from the Ocean to the Gulf', a great deal depends on the reception which new works receive from those periodicals which enjoy a wide circulation, such as *al-Ādāb*, *al-Fikr*, *al-Aqlām*, *Fuṣūl*, *al-Mawqif al-Adabī* and *al-Maʿrifah*. This may help to account for a certain regionalism which affects the reception accorded to new novels in the Arab world; most particularly, it suggests that the process whereby writers in such countries as the Sudan, the Yemen and the Emirates, have their works published and disseminated is an extremely difficult one.

Data concerning the number of novels published are extremely difficult to obtain. It is only relatively recently that national libraries and other state-administered organizations have begun to keep records and to require the deposition of books. Curiously enough, it is mostly in countries where the emergence of a novelistic tradition has been fairly recent and where the number of novels can be effectively counted that the most precise information is available: thus in the Maghreb and Syria rather than in Egypt (where the number of published novels is enormous). If the current trend towards maintaining national library collections and producing bibliographical resources of criticism published throughout the Arab world (such as the welcome new initiative *al-Fihrist*, published in Beirut) continues and spreads to other regions, it should become more feasible to conduct comparative studies of the Arabic novel throughout the region in greater detail than has been possible in this chapter.

CHAPTER 7

THE EGYPTIAN NOVEL FROM *ZAYNAB* TO 1980*

Even twenty years ago the Arabic novel was regarded as practically synonymous with the Egyptian novel. Since then the novel has acquired an established place in the literary production of most, if not all, Arab countries, as is described elsewhere in this volume. Yet the Egyptian novel still deserves a place apart in a survey of modern Arabic literature because of the number of works of quality written in Egypt, while the relatively longer history of the genre there enables its different stages of development to be distinguished and studied more easily than is the case in countries where it has had a life of only two or three decades. It is a far cry from Haykal's *Zaynab* to Idwār al-Kharrāṭ's *al-Zaman al-ākhar*, but thanks to the abundance of material it is possible to explain, at least in some measure, the relationship between the restrained and rather conventional grandmother and her adventurous and unbridled grandchild.

PIONEERS

When Muḥammad Ḥusayn Haykal[1] published his novel *Zaynab* in 1913 he had some models to follow. Apart from the translations and adaptations of European fiction other examples from which he could learn included Zaydān's historical novels, Ṣarrūf's novels of social concern, al-Manfalūṭī's sentimental fiction and al-Muwayliḥī's *Ḥadīth ʿĪsā b. Hishām* with its combination of classical form and modern subject matter. Maḥmūd Ṭāhir Ḥaqqī's novella *ʿAdhrāʾ Dinshawāy* (*The Maiden of Dinshway*; 1906) had shown how a book treating a burning issue of the day humanely and imaginatively could achieve such success that it was immediately reprinted;[2] at the same time it marked an advance in technique by its use of

* I would like to thank Dr Ed de Moor and especially Ms Rianne Tamis for their help in obtaining copies of many of the novels discussed here.

1 From an Egyptian landowning family, Muḥammad Ḥusayn Haykal (1888–1956) studied law in Cairo and Paris. After a brief spell as a lawyer he devoted his career to politics, journalism and literature. As well as *Zaynab* he wrote one other novel at the end of his life, *Hākadhā khuliqat* ('Thus she was created'; 1955); he also published a series of biographies of the Prophet Muḥammad and the first caliphs.

2 English translation by Saad El-Gabalawy in *Three pioneering Egyptian novels*; for a discussion of the work see Rotraud Wielandt, *Das bild der Europäer in der modernen arabischen Erzähl- und Theaterliteratur*, Beirut, 1980, pp. 196–200.

colloquial Arabic in dialogues. As he remarks in the preface to the third edition of *Zaynab*, Haykal himself had read English and French as well as Arabic literature. But it is not only because Haykal could profit from the works of other writers and from his own reading that *Zaynab* is a landmark in Egyptian literature; its themes and the literary and intellectual qualities which its author reveals endow it with the necessary complexity and richness to make it the first artistic novel in Arabic.

Zaynab has two plots. The one with which the novel begins and ends centres on the peasant girl Zaynab who, after a slight flirtation with the landowner's son Ḥāmid, falls in love with Ibrāhīm, an overseer on the estate. Ibrāhīm feels unable to ask for her hand, however, because there is talk of her being married off to Ḥasan, a friend of his and the son of a richer peasant. After Zaynab's marriage to Ḥasan she is torn between her love and her loyalty to her husband. When Ibrāhīm is called up as a conscript to serve in the Sudan she goes into a decline and dies of tuberculosis.

The second plot centres on Ḥāmid, who is sixteen when the novel opens; he is studying in Cairo and only returns to his family on the estate for summer holidays and festivals. He has developed an idealized image of his cousin ʿAzīzah, with whom he played as a child but whom he has not seen since she put on the veil. During his summer visit to his family he watches the peasant girls working and his eye is caught by Zaynab, but despite several secret meetings he is not seriously involved with her. During his next summer visit ʿAzīzah comes to stay, but he cannot see her alone, surrounded as she is by relatives; Zaynab meanwhile is taken up with Ibrāhīm. The following year Ḥāmid and ʿAzīzah succeed in exchanging letters and even meet, only to find they are tongue-tied in each other's presence. Shortly after ʿAzīzah's return to her home she writes to tell Ḥāmid her marriage has been arranged. Ḥāmid seeks to renew his acquaintance with Zaynab, but she, reminding him that she is married now, politely rebuffs him. Embittered and disappointed, he leaves for Cairo, having in vain sought counsel from a Sufi shaykh, but the knowledge that all his efforts to meet a girl whom he could love and marry will be frustrated in the present state of Egyptian society bring him to abandon his studies and disappear, leaving a letter to his parents in which he explains all.

These two plots unfold against the background of the Lower Egyptian countryside, loving and careful descriptions of which occur regularly throughout the book. But the author's attention to the book's setting is dictated less by his genuine interest in agricultural life than by his nostalgia for his native land (*Zaynab* was written during the years in which he was studying in Paris) and above all by the romantic tone which dominates the novel and which requires that the protagonists spend long hours communing with nature and reflecting on their emotional states and, in Ḥāmid's case, on general metaphysical issues.

That *Zaynab* owes much to Rousseau's thought is evident,[3] the defence of feeling against the established codes and moral laws is proof of this romantic tendency, while in many respects Ḥāmid's character is modelled on that of the heroes of Rousseau's novels. This romanticism is placed in the service of a central reforming trend in Egyptian society of the time, the campaign for women's emancipation and against arranged marriages, which was led by Qāsim Amīn, one of Haykal's masters. A subsidiary theme, the disapproval of popular religious practice, also reflects the reformers' concerns. A third theme, only intermittently pursued, is that of the harsh conditions of the poor peasants and the injustice they suffer; this borrowing from Rousseau is at variance with Haykal's own appreciation, as the son of a landowner, of the peasants' conditions, and it leads to inconsistency in the presentation of the character of Ḥāmid.

On the whole, though, Ḥāmid, the only extended character study, is coherently drawn: a boy looking for a first love, a philosophical dreamer, happy in the openness of the countryside but otherwise rather bored on the estate and missing his friends and books in Cairo. In the course of the novel he develops somewhat, becoming disillusioned with Egyptian society as a result of his disappointment in love, and reaching physical maturity, as is discreetly suggested through the change in the intensity of his attraction to Zaynab. But although he is the main character, and closer than the others to the author in his concerns and attitude to life, Haykal does not identify with him; thus, for instance, the technique of dramatizing a character's thoughts is used for Ibrāhīm and Zaynab as well as for Ḥāmid.

It is easy to identify awkwardnesses in technique, such as the inconsistent portrayal of characters like ᶜAzīzah or Ḥasan, the heavy-handed introduction of characters whom the author needs only for a few pages, the use of coincidences to help the plot along, and the author's intervention with generalizations. On the credit side, however, the plots are skilfully interwoven and there is a considerable degree of balance in the book, not only in respect of characters and incidents, but also, for instance, in the fact that while Ḥāmid's plot is open-ended and his fate unknown, Zaynab's is rounded off with her death. And the borrowing of western themes and plots is, I believe, to some extent balanced by a recourse to elements of the Arabic literary heritage. Thus, rather than representing an extensively modified derivation from Rousseau's novels, the real parallel *Zaynab*'s plot offers is to the traditional Arabic stories of the ᶜUdhrī lovers, slightly altered in detail

[3] For a detailed discussion of this see Ali B. Jad, *Form and technique in the Egyptian novel 1912–1971*, London, 1983, pp. 58–64.

to fit into Egyptian village life; Zaynab's and Ibrāhīm's unshakeable chastity, otherwise unexplained, then falls into place as a literary convention. There is considerable artistry in the way in which *Zaynab*'s traditional Arabic plot with its closed ending is made to frame the western-derived plot of Ḥāmid, himself the character who has undergone the greatest degree of westernization, with its open ending.

An Egyptian setting, characters who are recognizably Egyptian, competent narrative organization, issues of great contemporary relevance, some dialogues in dialect: *Zaynab* pointed the way to what the Egyptian novel could become and set a standard which was not attained again for a long time.

It was not, however, followed by a spate of imitations; indeed, if *al-Shabāb al-ḍāʾiʿ* ('Lost youth'), the novel which Muḥammad Taymūr left unfinished at his death in 1921, and one or two obscure and abortive attempts are disregarded, more than a decade passed before serious writers tried their hand at the novel form again. The main reason for this is not hard to find. The novel form, which is characterized by dramatic and structural complexity as well as considerable length, requires a degree of command of techniques of fiction which Egyptian writers at the time did not have. Those who worked towards the establishing of fiction as serious literature, such as the ʿUbayd brothers and the members of *al-Madrasah al-ḥadīthah* (the New School), preferred to concentrate on the short story, and then they confined themselves to a very small number of significant characters, a single plot and simple situations. Their concern with the creation of a realistic literature and the expression of the Egyptian personality, their development of a register of themes and the acquiring of experience in the areas of characterization and dialogue were, however, important steps towards the creation of a tradition of modern fiction. At least two of the writers associated with *al-Madrasah al-Ḥadīthah*, Maḥmūd Ṭāhir Lāshīn and Maḥmūd Taymūr, later turned to the novel.

Another direct contribution to the foundation of a tradition of the novel was the publication of autobiographies by leading men of letters. The autobiography, by its nature, possesses the scope which short stories lack and has a single unifying focus throughout. The first work of this genre to reach a wide public was part one of *al-Ayyām* (*The Days*; published serially in 1926–7 and in book form in 1929),[4] the autobiography of Ṭāhā Ḥusayn[5]

[4] English translation by E. H. Paxton: *An Egyptian childhood* (London, 1932).

[5] From a rural middle class family, Ṭāhā Ḥusayn (1889–1973) became blind at the age of three. He overcame this handicap, studying at al-Azhar and the newly established Egyptian University, and later in Paris. He became a professor at Cairo University and was for a short time Minister of Culture. As a literary scholar and thinker he criticized blind obedience to tradition and preached openness to rational scientific methods. His three-part autobiography and four novels are only a small part of an extensive literary oeuvre.

which he wrote ostensibly for his daughter, relating with insight and some irony his childhood before he left his village to study in Cairo. Although the events are those of the author's life, the hero is spoken of in the third person and the presentation is consistent with the perception of a small boy. The style is rhythmic and unaffected, making use of rhetorical questions and appeals to the reader in a manner reminiscent of an oral narrative. In its psychological insight into the world of childhood, its treatment of the formative years of the central figure and its consistent handling of perspective, this book offered a model which novelists could profit from, in particular when embarking on a *Bildungsroman*.

The year 1926 also saw the publication of Muḥammad Farīd Abū Ḥadīd's[6] first historical novel, *Ibnat al-mamlūk* ('The mamluk's daughter'). Unlike Zaydān, Abū Ḥadīd does not subordinate everything to the teaching of history; he endeavours to achieve a realistic presentation of action and characters in a historical setting. His style is clear and betrays his thorough familiarity with and love for the Arabic language. The historical novel did not come into its own until the end of the thirties, however, when the periods preferred were Pharaonic or pre-Islamic and early Islamic Arab history; Egyptian Islamic history and particularly the Mamluk period, the close of which is the setting for *Ibnat al-Mamlūk*, became popular only much later.

From 1931, novels began to appear regularly; their authors were mostly men of letters for whom the novel was one genre among many at which they tried their hand. Some of these works are of merely historical interest today, as for instance *Sārah* (a woman's name; 1938)[7] by ᶜAbbās Mahmūd al-ᶜAqqād, one of the dominating literary figures of the period. *Sārah* portrays a love affair between the woman after whom the novel is named and Hammām, who seems little more than a mouthpiece of the author. Poorly endowed with dialogue and dramatic incident, it is lopsided in its psychological analysis, for while the hero can reflect endlessly on the nature of women he appears devoid of insight into his own motivations. His attitude is thoroughly patriarchal, apparently marked by the idea of *kayd al-nisā'* (women's deviousness), frequent in the Islamic tradition.

It is an indication of the gradual acceptance of fiction as a serious literary form that none of these authors found it necessary to publish their novels under a pseudonym, as Haykal had done for the first edition of *Zaynab*. The

6 Muḥammad Farīd Abū Ḥadīd (1893–1967) received a solid grounding in Arabic at Dār al-ᶜUlūm and studied law at Cairo University. As a civil servant he held influential posts in various educational and cultural institutions. He published a series of works in the 1940s which earned him his reputation as the leading historical novelist of the period.

7 English translation by Mustafa Badawi, Cairo 1978. For further information on al-ᶜAqqād, see Chapter 3.

thirties was a decade of apprenticeship, characterized by efforts to master the techniques needed for the genre and to discover what subjects could be appropriately handled in it.

Ibrāhīm al-kātib (*Ibrahim the writer*; 1931)[8] by Ibrāhīm ʿAbd al-Qādir al-Māzinī,[9] the first of these novels of apprenticeship, illustrates the teething troubles of the genre. It relates the love affairs of the protagonist, the writer Ibrāhīm, with three women: Marie, a young Syrian widow who nurses him after an operation; Shūshū, his cousin, with whom he falls in love while visiting her and her married sister Najiyyah on their country estate; and Laylā, the westernized Egyptian girl whom he meets in a hotel in Luxor. All these affairs come to nothing. Ibrāhīm feels that Marie is somehow beneath him, despite the fact that in many ways their situations are complementary (he is a widower); his proposal to Shūshū is rejected by Najiyyah on the grounds that her older sister must marry first; Laylā decides to relinquish him when she learns of his love for Shūshū and achieves this by representing herself as a girl of easy virtue. Disillusioned, depressed and restless, Ibrāhīm's thoughts turn to death, but a mysterious voice from the grave, presumably that of his late wife, entreats him to remain alive, if only to preserve her memory.

In several respects this novel marks an advance on *Zaynab*. Haykal's measured style, with its conventional imagery, has been replaced by a far more lively one, able to convey different moods and portray a wide range of situations. Although there is still a pronounced Romantic tendency to muse, the dramatic element is much more developed, with some lively dialogues and scenes of action. The setting moves from a country estate to a luxury hotel, with brief visits to a fortune-teller and even an abortion clinic, but it is the typically Egyptian countryside which al-Māzinī is most at pains to describe. The humour for which the author is justly famous inspires some farcical situations and comic minor characters; where Ibrāhīm is the butt of his wit al-Māzinī can be credited with an attack on the Romantic hero.

But over against these achievements stand a number of grave weaknesses: gross inconsistencies in characterization, inadequate motivation, and a tendency, increasingly pronounced as the book progresses and the balance between gravity and humour is abandoned, to present Ibrāhīm as the object of admiration of all those around him. The final impression is of a book in which the author, who in this case is his hero's *alter ego*, is

[8] English translation by Magdi Wahba, Cairo, 1976.

[9] Ibrāhīm ʿAbd al-Qādir al-Māzinī (1890–1949) trained as a teacher but devoted his life to creative writing and journalism. He made his name as a critic of poetry, but was most at home writing short stories and comic sketches. He published two other novels and two novellas; these latter are much more successful than his novels.

seeking to make up for his disappointments in real life by projecting a series of self-gratifying scenes of success with women. *Ibrāhīm al-kātib* is perhaps a unique example of a novel of *fakhr* (self-praise).

Partly concealed behind all the self-glorification, however, another theme can be discerned. Although the book traces three relationships, one, the affair with Marie, is despatched in a few pages; the main focus is on Ibrāhīm's love for Shūshū and for Laylā. Reflecting on these affairs after they have ended, Ibrāhīm characterizes Laylā, with her independence and emancipated approach to love relationships, as essentially western, and contrasts her with the typically Egyptian Shūshū, living in semi-seclusion in the bosom of her family. In other words, the theme of the conflict between west and east, so important in the literature of this period, is reflected, however indistinctly, in this book, too; the equation 'Woman = Life in an abridged form'[10] which Ibrāhīm puts forward, not only allows his love affairs to be read by an outsider as his attempt to enter into relationship with the outside world, but also indicates how he himself perceives these love affairs as having a certain symbolic character.

Ṭāhā Ḥusayn, whose autobiography has been mentioned above, had a greater sense than al-Māzinī of the possibilities offered by the novel. His two main contributions in the genre are *Shajarat al-buʾs* ('The tree of misery'; 1944), the first Egyptian novel dealing with several generations, and especially *Duʿāʾ al-karawān* (*The call of the curlew*; 1934),[11] a study of vengeance. There is indeed something improbable about the subject matter, which concerns the decision of Āminah, a young Bedouin girl, to take revenge for her sister, seduced by her employer and then killed by her uncle to save the family honour. Āminah sets out to be employed by the same man, a young engineer, and to resist his attempts to seduce her, proving that her will-power is stronger than his. But the importance of the book lies in its consistent maintenance of one point of view, that of Āminah, and its careful analysis of her feelings as the nature of her relationship with her employer evolves from hostility to love. The technique of a consistently maintained point of view, which is one of the strengths of the author's autobiography, is equally successfully employed in this novel. The curlew's call, which regularly reminds Āminah of her sister's fate and her duty towards her, is perhaps the first instance in an Egyptian novel of a motif being used to underline important moments in the action; its repetition gives the book a poetic rhythm.

Like al-Māzinī and Ṭāhā Ḥusayn, Tawfīq al-Ḥakīm (1898–1987) was not in the first place a novelist; his invaluable contribution to the establishing of

[10] Ibrāhīm ʿAbd al-Qādir al-Māzinī, *Ibrāhīm al-kātib*, repr. Cairo, 1953, p. 97.

[11] English translation by A. B. al-Safi, Leiden, 1980.

the Arabic drama is dealt with elsewhere in this volume.[12] The three novels which he published in the 1930s, however, demonstrated in different ways the relevance of the form to the discussion of important issues in Egyptian culture, and treated themes and situations which were to become established items in the repertory of the Egyptian novel.

ʿAwdat al-rūḥ ('The return of the soul'; written in Paris in 1927, published 1933) falls into two parts. The first details, with gentle humour, the life of a lower-middle-class Egyptian household consisting of a teenage schoolboy, Muḥsin, his two unmarried uncles and a cousin, his spinster aunt who keeps house and their servant. Two love interests, one focusing on the feelings of the teenager, his cousin and one of his uncles for their neighbour's beautiful daughter, and the other on the aunt's desperate attempts to ensnare a young bachelor who lives in the flat below theirs, provide a narrative foundation for this picture of urban Egyptian life. The second part begins with Muḥsin's visit to his parents in the country and allows al-Ḥakīm to introduce, through two subsidiary characters, certain theories on the eternal existence of the Egyptian soul; then the scene moves back to Cairo, where the members of the household see their hopes of bliss dashed while the love of the neighbour's daughter and the bachelor for each other unfolds. The household is sunk in gloom until suddenly its members are caught up in the nationalist movement of 1919, demonstrating and distributing leaflets. This nationalist movement is the modern 'Return' of the eternal Egyptian soul referred to in the title.

Among the characters it is Muḥsin who is given pride of place. The development of his feelings for the neighbour's daughter is portrayed in great detail and conveys the pain of first love convincingly. The episode of the visit to the countryside serves to emphasize the warmth and humaneness of the boy's Cairo surroundings in contrast to the artificiality and loveless atmosphere of his parents' home, where his Turkish mother is constantly at pains to distance herself from everything Egyptian and thus boorish.

In a sense there is more than one book in the nearly six hundred pages of *ʿAwdat al-rūḥ*, for Muḥsin's growing up and his integration into a

[12] See Chapter 10. Tawfīq al-Ḥakīm was born into a well-to-do family: his father occupied a senior post in the legal profession and his mother was proud of her Turkish origin. Immediately after his graduation in law in 1925, he was sent by his father to France to pursue higher studies in the hope that this would cure him of his passion for the theatre, which he had developed while still a student. In Paris he became deeply immersed in the world of the theatre and its culture, and so he returned home in 1928 without his degree. In Egypt he held several legal posts, including that of Deputy Public Prosecutor, in provincial towns, but in 1943 he resigned from government service to devote his time to writing. He published five novels and more than eighty plays. Al-Ḥakīm received several honours, and in recognition of his service to the cause of Egyptian drama a theatre was named after him in Cairo in 1963.

community (a recurrent theme) could have been an adequate subject for a *Bildungsroman*, while the Cairo love affairs are a novel in themselves. The fundamentally realistic mode which prevails in the main part of the book is at odds with the attempt at a symbolical representation of the household as 'the people', '*al-shaᶜb*', and with the last two chapters, where the revolution is suddenly brought in as a miraculous event, restoring her soul to Egypt although there have been no previous references to the political agitation which followed the end of the First World War. (It is worth noting that the few pages devoted to Egypt's national identity have struck such a deep chord among many readers that this novel is often regarded as the fictional expression of Egyptian patriotism *par excellence*.)

Al-Ḥakīm's real achievement, however, is in presenting a number of clearly drawn characters in lively interaction with each other. Well contrasted, they remain consistent to themselves, and in their limited surroundings they constitute an independent world; they are the first example of the small close-knit community of relatives and neighbours which peoples so many Egyptian novels of urban life. The generous use of dialogues in the colloquial and the unaffected, clear style contribute much to the total effect.

A later novel, *ᶜUṣfūr min al-sharq* (*Bird from the east*; 1938)[13] uses a subsequent period of Muḥsin's life, his student years in Paris, as the occasion for an exploration of the theme of the conflict between the materialist west and the spiritual east. Young students from Egypt and other Arab countries studying in Europe and experiencing in their own lives the clash of cultures were to reappear in later works of fiction of much greater artistic maturity; al-Ḥakīm's merit lies in having identified the theme and stated it for the first time in Egyptian literature.

Al-Ḥakīm's most profound and technically most accomplished novel is *Yawmiyyāt nāʾib fī 'l-aryāf* ('The diary of a deputy public prosecutor in the country').[14] The prosecutor begins his diary as a murder is reported, and the investigation of this crime forms the plot of the work. But the investigation has to be combined with all the prosecutor's other duties, and thus a picture gradually emerges from the diary of the way in which the secular legal code is applied in the countryside. As is pointed out more than once, the law has been drawn up in offices in Cairo without any thought for the conditions of the peasants who are expected to abide by it, and the gap between the assumptions on which the law is based and the actual conditions in which it must be applied generates a series of dramatic situations. Some are simply comic, arising out of misunderstandings between peasants and administra-

[13] English translation by R. Bayly Winder, Beirut, 1966.

[14] Translated under the apt title *The maze of justice* by Aubrey S. Eban, London, 1947.

tors, but when the peasants' utter poverty is involved the humour quickly becomes black. Yet, although these scenes and the ironic observations of the diarist provide for a good deal of amusement, this book is more than a series of sketches of Egyptian peasant life.

The central character in the novel, the diarist, begins his record when he is feeling ill; he appears to have an attack of laryngitis threatening. Otherwise, however, he is in a resigned, quietly ironic mood. At the end of the book the laryngitis is forgotten, but he has so far lost control of himself as to burst out that he has had enough of the country and wants to go back to Cairo. Closing the diary he himself characterizes his mood as bitter and mocking. Although he displays no insight into the real workings of peasant life and no great sympathy for the peasants, his resistance has been worn down by what he has noted of successive instances of injustice, the petty corruption and dishonesty of almost all his fellow-officials and the appalling conditions of health care and hygiene prevailing in the countryside. For al-Ḥakīm's prosecutor, city intellectual that he is, is imbued with a belief in basic human dignity and a natural justice beyond the justice of the courts, and some of what he has seen is a gross violation of these ideals.

There are some contradictions in this novel. One is that although the diary includes twelve entries, the actual number of days it covers is seven; in fact the 'dates' correspond to chapters rather than real days. And while the prosecutor refers more than once to his lengthy experience in the work, the acquiring of insight which has been outlined above and which is at the centre of the book is consistent with a much less experienced character. But these are minor points when set against al-Ḥakīm's signal achievement here: the exploration of a fundamental issue of Egyptian culture, the relationship between the city-based government and the peasantry, within an appropriate narrative framework and a realistic setting, and with economy and humour.

The last work of the pioneering period to be treated here, Maḥmūd Ṭāhir Lāshīn's[15] *Ḥawwāʾ bilā Ādam* ('Eve without Adam'; 1934)[16] passed almost unnoticed when it was published. It is, however, important because it points the way to certain developments in the next period of the novel. It tells the story of an Egyptian middle-class woman teacher, Ḥawwāʾ, who devotes all her time and energy to education and the cause of women's emancipation, allowing her emotions no outlet. Engaged as piano teacher for the young daughter of a Pasha, she falls in love with the Pasha's son Ramzī, nine years her junior. Although she comes to realise, in a moment of

[15] Maḥmūd Ṭāhir Lāshīn (1894–1954) graduated as an engineer and was employed in the Ministry of Public Works. A member of *al-Madrasah al-ḥadīthah*, for which see pp. 282–85, he published three collections of stories as well as this novel, but he abandoned writing at the end of the thirties.

[16] Translation in El-Gabalawy: *Three pioneering Egyptian novels*, pp. 49–94.

lucidity, that background, age and inclinations all separate them, in her imagination she continues to picture Ramzī reciprocating her feelings, until the day when his engagement to the daughter of a landowning family is announced. From then on she disintegrates emotionally and intellectually, finally committing suicide on the day Ramzī's wedding is celebrated.

Lāshīn, in this novel, breaks with the habit of including a character who is a projection of the author; he creates an independent world. The heroine's thoughts and feelings are presented with considerable success, so that her suicide appears as the logical outcome of the novel's actions and not, like Zaynab's decline, as a romantic convention imposed on the material. There are several advances in technique; thus, for instance, the introduction of characters for the first time displays appropriate variations. Whereas Shaykh Muṣṭafā and Ḥājj Imām, Ḥawwāʾ's superstitious grandmother's friends and helpers, are described as soon as they appear, Ḥawwāʾ herself is presented first as the author of a letter to a friend in which she sets out her principles and her aim to revolt against the chaos and corruption of Egyptian life, and it is only later that the reader learns what she looks like.

Like al-Ḥakīm, Lāshīn contributes characters and themes to which later novelists return. Ḥawwāʾ is the first of the urban lower-middle-class intellectuals, hampered by material worries yet driven by their aspirations for themselves and their country to feats of great self-sacrifice. Her grandmother, who brought her up, is the first of the loving, uneducated women who try, through the warmth of their affection, to palliate the hurts suffered by their educated offspring in a changing world but who cannot offer advice derived from their own experience of life. Class conflict, mentioned here but not consistently developed, and the emancipated woman's search for new forms of relationships with men, are both themes taken up by later novelists.

The central issue of the novel, however, is the criticism of two ways of life, in which either the emotions or the intellect hold exclusive sway. In both cases the repressed part of the personality finds an outlet through dreams. Ḥawwāʾ's grandmother devotes her mental energy to their interpretation, while Ḥawwāʾ lives out her emotions in them. Ḥawwāʾ is a very lonely woman, because she has not only rejected the traditional roles of wife and mother but also keeps aloof from her colleagues in the school where she works, thus depriving herself of the emotional satisfactions of friendship. When she realises her feelings for Ramzī she had no-one to turn to for advice, and she must fight her battle alone as she discovers that her pent-up emotions have focused themselves on an unattainable object.

Her suffering leads almost to a crisis of faith. Religious motifs, some of them directly linked to Ḥawwāʾ, occur throughout the book, and her last act is to pray that God will not regard her suicide as an act of rebellion. Her silent protest, towards the end, that there is no-one to explain the meaning of her suffering to her, may echo Moses' words in the Quran, but it has a modern ring.

This extremely interesting novel leaves the impression that it is unfinished. The themes are not always integrated with each other; this is especially true of the theme of class conflict, which is not related in any way to Ḥawwāʾ's relations with the Pashā's family. A promising subplot, the maid Najiyyah's love affair with the butcher's son, is not developed, although it would have formed a nice contrast to Ḥawwāʾ's plot. The author's fondness for the grotesque leads him to include some unnecessary digressions and he is at times facetious. Nonetheless, with its sense of social conflicts and its pin-pointing of moments of crisis in the life of an individual, it is the forerunner of the realistic novels of the 1940s.

A NOTE ON THE NOVELLA

The history of modern Arabic literature has generally paid little attention to the distinction between novel and novella or long short story. As far as terminology is concerned, *riwāyah* and *qiṣṣah* or *qiṣṣah qaṣīrah* are now recognized designations for the novel and short story respectively, but the essential difference between novel and novella has not yet been reflected in the acceptance of a standard term for the latter. Thus a writer as well-versed in literature as ʿAbd al-Ḥakīm Qāsim could recently bring out two novellas in one volume and label them *riwāyatān*.[17]

This is not merely playing with words. The external mark of the novella, which is that it is shorter than the novel, springs from a particular approach to the use of the resources of fiction. What marks a novella off from a novel is a combination of several characteristics, for instance concentration on one character or on a limited action, a preference for the presentation of significant moments rather than detailed frescos, flashes of insight rather than extensive analysis. There are always some borderline cases; the length of *Ḥawwāʾ bilā Ādam*, for instance, might lead one to consider it to be a novella, but according to internal criteria it must be judged as a novel, albeit a little underdone.

There are many instances of novellas in modern Egyptian, and Arabic, literature, some of them very successful: al-Māzinī's *ʿAwd ʿalā badʾ* (*Return to a beginning*; 1943), Yaḥyā Ḥaqqī's *Qindīl Umm Hāshim* (*The saint's lamp*; 1944) and Yūsuf Idrīs's *Qāʿ al-madinah* (*City dregs*; 1957) are but a few well-known examples from Egypt. To devote a study to this genre in modern

[17] *Al-mahdī wa-ṭuraf min khabar al-ākhirah*, Beirut, 1984.

Arabic literature would be well worth while, not only because of the intrinsic interest of the works concerned but also because it could shed light on some aspects of the approach to writing fiction which are characteristic of this literature.

REALISTS

No clear-cut division can be made between periods in literary history; some writers will always continue working within the old conventions and in the old style when their younger colleagues are occupied with innovation. In a country like Egypt, whose literary history in this century is marked by successive attempts to catch up with Europe and thus by many changes in a short space of time, two or more periods often overlap. Pioneering novelists continued to publish in the 1940s, and even after the Revolution, but their later novels still breathe the atmosphere of the 1930s. The end of the 1930s, however, saw the emergence of young writers who in thematic concerns and technique belong to a new period in the Egyptian novel.

All the members of the pioneering generation, with the exception of Haykal, had undergone the influence of the 1919 Revolution, with its affirmation of the Egyptian identity and its optimistic vision of the Egyptian future, when they wrote their novels. Their successors were too young to have appreciated the Revolution's significance at the time; it was the degradation of political life under opportunistic party politicians and harsh dictators and the achievement of a less than complete independence which formed the background to their adolescence and early manhood. They were witness to increased social tensions, the result of a growth in population, falling cotton prices, the drift of peasants to the cities and the concentration of more wealth in fewer hands. The Second World War, in which Egypt became willy-nilly a base for the British war effort, brought greater economic dislocation and the alienating effect of the stationing of large numbers of Allied troops in the country.

The new generation of novelists had at least one great advantage over their elders; they had a natural audience in the new class of technicians, officials and professional men and women, graduates of secondary schools and Cairo University, who sought for a more adequate analysis of the social and political order and the profound changes taking place in Egyptian culture. This new intelligentsia lacked the distrust of its predecessors for the novel as a serious literary form, for not only were the works of the pioneers in existence to show what possibilities the genre offered, but European novels (and plays), accessible either in the original or in translation, also proved the effectiveness of these imported forms in discussing central issues of society and culture.

A clear sign of the rising status of the novel was the institution by the Ministry of Education in 1941 of a competition in novel-writing, judged by a committee nominated by the Arabic Language Academy. Although the difference of opinions between competitors and judges sometimes took the guise of a quarrel between Ancients and Moderns,[18] the existence of the contest undoubtedly fostered the endeavours of young writers.

Another encouraging development was the increase in outlets for publication. Whereas beginners had had to turn to magazines to publish their work (Najīb Maḥfūẓ's first novel, *ᶜAbath al-aqdār*, was accepted by Salāmah Mūsā for a special issue of *al-Majallah al-jadīdah*), in 1943 an enterprising young writer, ᶜAbd al-Ḥamīd Jūdah al-Saḥḥār, set up a publishing body with the revealing name Lajnat al-nashr li-'l-jāmiᶜiyyīn (the University graduates' publishing committee), which brought out nineteen titles in its first year and a half, most of them novels or plays by young writers. The same year a well-known publisher, Dār al-Maᶜārif, began a series of paperbacks, *Iqraʾ* ('Read'), which included some fiction, though generally by established names.

Although realism made its breakthrough in the forties, the decade opened with a marked interest in the historical novel, as is indicated by the results of the first novel-writing competition in which three of the five best novels were historical. Several historical novelists, foremost among them the already mentioned Muḥammad Farīd Abū Ḥadīd, established themselves, while two who later turned to contemporary themes made their first essays in novels set in the past.

The enthusiasm for historical subjects in this period arose in part out of a desire to affirm the country's cultural identity. The choice of a Pharaonic setting reflected a new Egyptian interest in the distant past, on which recent archaeological discoveries had thrown much light; it also affirmed Egyptian nationalism and the specificity of Egyptian culture. Those writers who chose subjects from pre-Islamic or early Islamic history, on the other hand, stressed the Arabic and Islamic component of Egyptian culture; that their interest was basically cultural rather than religious is shown by the relatively high incidence of pre-Islamic settings and heroes who were poets. (It is likely that the greater number of novels in this second category is also connected with the availability of suitable source material; writers on the Pharaonic period had only meagre data at their disposal.) Both periods had a mythical status as founding eras of Egyptian history, and it is perhaps this which explains why they attracted more attention than later ages.

The recourse to historical subjects does not necessarily entail a flight

[18] One side of this is recorded in the preface to ᶜĀdil Kāmil's *Millīm al-akbar*, Cairo, 1944, pp. 3–128.

from the present, as will be clear in the discussion of the first novels of the realist writers ʿĀdil Kāmil and Najīb Maḥfūẓ. ʿĀdil Kāmil's[19] *Malik min shuʿāʿ* ('A king of sunbeams'; submitted for the first novel competition in 1942, published 1945), is a psychological study of the pharaoh and religious reformer Akhnaton, which shows how an introverted and reflective young man goes through a profound crisis of belief, loses his faith in the Egyptian gods but then receives a series of revelations for a new religion. Thereafter he seeks to assert himself as a ruler and to apply the tenets of his new religion, monism and non-violence. He encounters resistance from the priests of Amon and other representatives of the established order, especially when he refuses to put down a revolt in the Asian provinces; finally he is deposed and dies. The emphasis in this novel is on the hero's psychological development and the issues raised by his spiritual conversion, and the historical setting is incidental to them. Moreover the theme of non-violence had a contemporary relevance, and its prophet Mahatma Gandhi was much admired by progressive Egyptian thinkers.

Millīm al-akbar ('Millim the great'; 1944) illustrates its author's concern with the theme of reforming society in a contemporary context. Of its two heroes one, Khālid, is the son of a wealthy and cynical pasha who will stop at nothing to safeguard the interests of his family and class. Khālid has just returned from an English university full of idealistic notions of social justice and convinced of the rottenness of the established order. The second hero, Millīm, is the son of a vagabond and drug-peddlar who tries to earn an honest living when his father is imprisoned. Unjustly accused of theft by Khālid's father, he ends up in prison; Khālid, disgusted by his family, leaves home. In the second part of the novel Millīm, who has served his sentence, is the factotum of Naṣīf, a disciple of Nietzsche who has founded a commune in a Mamluk palace in the old part of Cairo. The members of the commune are artists and writers all more or less in revolt against society; Naṣīf himself is apparently involved in some secret political activity. Khālid, having met Millīm by chance, is introduced to the commune and decides to move in, but whereas for the others revolution is a matter of words he decides to go out and actively preach it, mainly in the hope of winning the admiration of the only woman in the group, Hāniyā. A spy of his father's leads the police to him, and he is thrown into prison. The epilogue shows the two heroes four years later. Millīm has grown rich supplying the British army, but mindful of his origins he is generous to the poor. Khālid, meanwhile, has struck a bargain with his father and bought

[19] ʿĀdil Kāmil (b. 1916), the son of a lawyer, studied law and literature at Cairo University. While practising as a lawyer he pursued his interest in literature, writing three plays and two novels. Lack of response, however, led to his abandoning the pen.

his freedom with political quiescence; he is set on a course of physical and moral degradation.

The raw material of this novel is clearly the social and political reality of Egypt at the outbreak of the Second World War, with its great inequalities in wealth, its corrupt aristocracy and its poor who are at the mercy of all. The political shadow-world of secret societies and conspiracies appears here for the first time, as does the prison, later an all too frequent setting. New, too, is the author's socialist *parti pris*.

Technically *Millīm al-akbar* introduces some important features; for instance it begins with two parallel snatches of dialogue to which it then provides the background. The same technique of parallel development brings Millīm at the end of part one and Khālid at the end of part two into prison, and in this case the superficial similarity underlines profounder differences. The novel moves quickly, and several times there is a cut from one situation to another which heightens the reader's curiosity. The style is precise and economical, and the dialogues, although in literary Arabic, reflect the different characters of the speakers.

Yet, despite his wide reading in European literature and literary criticism, Kāmil was unable to create two consistent psychological portraits in his heroes. The one, Millīm, is insufficiently explored, and in the absence of any other explanation his unshakeable moral sense in the midst of so much corruption must be put down to the author's romantic idealization of the poor. The other, Khālid, suffers from a discrepancy between what the reader is told about him and how he is shown behaving. Whereas he is described as a warm emotional person who leaves none of those who know him indifferent, he appears as a rather weak, dreamy, isolated and self-centred young man who in moments of crisis tends to betray his principles. Given this difficulty with the two main characters it is not easy to determine what the novel is trying to say.

Kāmil's concern with politics, his socialist convictions and his pessimism about the state of Egypt were shared by his friend, a fellow disciple of Salāmah Mūsā, Najīb Maḥfūẓ (Naguib Mahfouz). They differed, however, in their approach to literature. While Kāmil was an innovator in technique and saw a radical break with the Arabic literary tradition as the only way forward,[20] Maḥfūẓ was far less adventurous, carefully constructing his early novels in the manner of the nineteenth-century European realists and avoiding statements of intent. Their literary careers are poles apart; over against Kāmil's one very original historical novel and his equally striking contemporary one must be set Maḥfūẓ's three historical novels of no great

[20] The preface to *Millīm al-akbar* (see note 18) writes off classical Arabic literature *en bloc* in an extreme statement of this position.

distinction and his series of explorations of the contemporary scene, which reveal increasing mastery of the craft of fiction and culminate in his magnificent Trilogy.

His application and his capacity to develop his literary talents are two of the reasons why Najīb Maḥfūẓ[21] has become the most famous Egyptian novelist, dominating the fictional scene for more than two decades. Unlike the pioneers, he felt called to devote himself to the genre of the novel, even to the extent of abandoning an incipient academic career because he felt it was irreconcilable with the claims laid on him by literature. His work as a civil servant left him less time to read but it did not occupy his mind as philosophy would have done.

Maḥfūẓ's first historical novel illustrates the idea of the inescapability of fate, a theme to which he was to return. His other two historical novels relate the tragic fate of a young Pharaoh carried away by his love for a courtisan, and the Egyptian success in driving out a foreign invader; their chief interest lies in their relevance to the contemporary Egyptian situation.

Although he had originally planned a series of historical novels, Maḥfūẓ then turned to the world around him. This realistic period of his work includes four novels of city life, one psychological study in depth and three novels which together relate the destiny of a Cairene middle-class family in the first half of this century – the 'Trilogy'. The first novel's title, *al-Qāhirah al-jadīdah* ('New Cairo'; 1946) suggests the author's concern with contemporary issues. It starts out by introducing three university students, representatives of different trends in Egyptian culture, one open to socialism and scientific thought, another a deeply committed Muslim and the third a penniless opportunist. The opportunist turns out to be the main character, and his attainment of a good position thanks to his willingness to sacrifice his honour and integrity forms the plot. This allows the author to explore the rottenness of the political system, corruption, ambition and the search for values in a changing world; here Maḥfūẓ's outspokenness brought him into conflict with the censors. There is as yet no development of the characters, and their psychology is painstakingly set out, while the interventions of fate play an excessive part.

The world of intellectuals gives place to that of the lower middle classes in the next three novels, which all reveal a greater richness, either because the setting and minor characters are evoked in detail, or because there is

21 Najīb Maḥfūẓ (b. 1911 in Cairo) studied philosophy at Cairo University. Abandoning graduate work he joined the civil service, being employed first in the Ministry of *Waqfs* (religious foundations) and later in the Ministry of Culture. For a time he headed the State Cinema Organisation. He has written at least thirty novels (although some of the later ones, such as *al-Karnak*, are in fact novellas) and ten collections of short stories and plays. He is the first Arab writer to be awarded the Nobel Prize for literature (in 1988).

more than one plot. *Khān al-Khalīlī* (name of a quarter; 1945) and *Zuqāq al-midaqq* (*Midaqq Alley*; 1947)[22] depict quarters of Old Cairo with their mixture of inhabitants: minor civil servants, merchants, café owners, tradesmen, matchmakers, wives and mothers, and destitutes. Whereas the first of these two books ventures rather cautiously into this, for Maḥfūẓ and for the Egyptian novel, unfamiliar world – its hero retreats back into the modern quarters after a year – the second is centred in it and scarcely leaves it. Both books carry further the depiction of a close-knit community already embarked upon in al-Ḥakīm's *ᶜAwdat al-rūḥ* and create their own coherent universe. *Khān al-Khalīlī* stands out, however, because its central figure, the diffident minor civil servant Aḥmad ᶜĀkif, who is on the threshhold of middle age, is poles apart from the young ambitious heroes of Maḥfūẓ's other novels of this period.

As a fairly typical example of these novels *Zuqāq al-midaqq* may be discussed in detail. The scene is set with the description of the alley and its inhabitants, some at their work, others at the café, the hub of the men's social life, and the women in their homes. The action starts as the alley's one emigrant, Ḥusayn Kirshah the café owner's son, returns on leave. The outside world represents opportunities for enrichment, but it is a place of moral anarchy, in which the tone is set by an occupying army. Ḥusayn persuades his friend the barber, ᶜAbbās Ḥilw, to go to work for the British, not out of any ambition, but because he wants to marry Ḥamīdah, the strong-willed tigerish beauty of the alley. Although ᶜAbbās becomes engaged to Ḥamīdah before his departure, the girl does not hesitate to break the engagement when a better match, in the shape of an elderly merchant, presents itself; when he suddenly falls ill the ground has been prepared for her to fall in love with a pimp, who skilfully lures her into his ring of prostitutes. ᶜAbbās, on leave from the army camp where he works, learns of Ḥamīdah's disappearance, and when he sees her in a café surrounded by Allied soldiers he attacks her, only to be beaten to death himself while his friend Ḥusayn looks on helplessly.

Interwoven with this main plot are a sub-plot and several scenes through which the minor characters reveal their habitual preoccupations. As a foil to the ill-starred love of ᶜAbbās and Ḥamidah, the widow Saniyyah ᶜAfīfī's steps to acquire a new husband with the help of Ḥamīdah's foster-mother, the matchmaker, provide a consistent ironic note. The typical scenes include the quarrel between the café owner Kirshah and his wife arising out of his homosexual affairs, Zayṭah's meeting with the beggars he is to maim, and the recourse to Shaykh Riḍwān al-Ḥusaynī as the alley's moral authority; all these are regular events in the life of the alley. Even in the

[22] English translation by Trevor Le Gassick, Beirut, 1966; revised edn, London, 1975.

portrayal of the habitual, however, Maḥfūẓ introduces some dramatic touches, such as the arrest of Zayṭa and Doctor Būshī while they are robbing a grave, and the arrival of Ḥusayn with his wife and brother-in-law. But in contrast to the main plot these incidents do not bring any lasting change in the lives of any of the alley's inhabitants.

The search for moral values in a changing society which is at the heart of Maḥfūẓ's preoccupations in this period is illustrated in the careers of the alley's younger generation, Ḥusayn and ʿAbbās, as well as Ḥamīdah, when they come into contact with the outside world. Ḥamīdah's case is the most dramatic, for society offers her no accepted place except that of wife and mother, a lot to which she is too ambitious to reconcile herself and which, on the evidence of the ménages in the alley, is far from attractive; thus her fate is inevitable. Not that the alley is a haven of moral rectitude. But its inhabitants, for all their quirks, weaknesses and even perversions, share a consensus on certain basic standards and possess a moral arbiter in the person of Shaykh Riḍwān. Their world is a known world; outside is an uncharted jungle, and it is there that Ḥamīdah and ʿAbbās come to grief.

As has been observed, Maḥfūẓ in this period of his work shows a preoccupation with sex which is well illustrated in *Zuqāq al-midaqq*. Granted this, the novel offers a wide range of contrasted characters and some subtle psychological analysis, especially in Ḥamīdah's case. There is a nice sense of the tension between words and the intentions behind them in some of the dialogues of the less aggressive characters, notably Saniyyah ʿAfīfī and Shaykh Riḍwān. The language is moving away from the stiffness of the early novels, becoming more fluent and imaginative, although Maḥfūẓ's faithfulness to the literary language is still sometimes an obstacle to the creation of lifelike dialogue, and prevents the differentiation of one character from another.

A note on Maḥfūẓ's attitude to the dichotomy between literary language (*fuṣḥā*) and colloquial (*ʿāmmiyyah*) is in order here. It has been suggested that because of the nature of Egyptian society, to which 'a nearly fanatical resentment against any inroads on inherited values'[23] has been imputed, any social criticism was a hazardous undertaking, and to couple this with the use of colloquial Arabic might have proved too explosive. As has been noted above, however, in the preceding generation Haykal, al-Māzinī, al-Ḥakīm and Lāshīn used the colloquial and combined it with social criticism, as writers of subsequent generations were to do. The explanation must be sought, rather, in Maḥfūẓ's own attitude to language; for him the *fuṣḥā* is superior to the *ʿāmmiyyah*, both because it is common to the whole of the

23 Mattityahu Peled, *Religion, My Own*, New Brunswick and London, 1983, p. 6. This argument is set out on pp. 5–7.

Arab world and because it has been the vehicle of religion and (élite) culture from ancient times. This view is shared by many, inside and outside Egypt, but it has had relatively little influence on the practice of Egyptian novelists treating contemporary subjects; Maḥfūẓ's achievement in stretching the *fuṣḥā* to convey realistic dialogue is perhaps more important in the context of the Arabic novel outside Egypt than in his own country.

The last of the Cairene realist novels, *Bidāyah wa-nihāyah* (*The beginning and the end*),[24] has a family at its centre. There is far less interest in grotesque human types here, and although ambition and sex are driving forces of two of the main characters, a third represents a more mature approach, the capacity to make sacrifices and to turn to good account the limited possibilities for satisfaction and happiness which are offered him.

Maḥfūẓ's next work, *al-Sarāb* ('The mirage'; although written after *Bidāyah wa-nihāyah* it was published earlier, around 1949) stands out for several reasons. It introduces a first-person narrator and turns its back on sociological concerns to concentrate on the psychology of its protagonist. This is a young man who, due to an excessive mother-fixation and a precocious sexual experience, cannot develop a normal marital relationship. Freud's shadow looms darkly here. But although the novel is longwinded and there is a contradiction between the main character's representation of himself as stupid and his articulateness as a narrator, it is important as a pioneering attempt to treat the theme of sexual frustration without sensationalism.

For his masterpiece, *al-Thulāthiyyah* ('The trilogy'), Maḥfūẓ returns to familiar ground, the old quarters of Cairo and the traditional middle class. Its three volumes, *Bayn al-qaṣrayn*, *Qaṣr al-shawq* and *al-Sukkariyyah* (all street names; 1956–7) trace the destiny of one family over nearly thirty years. The beginning of the work is dominated by the patriarchal figure of Aḥmad ʿAbd al-Jawād, a tyrant to his wife, Amīnah, their children Khadījah, Fahmī, ʿĀʾishah and Kamāl and his son by an earlier marriage, Yāsīn, but outside the home an approachable and sociable man with a marked penchant for wine, women and song. Gradually his children follow their own paths. ʿĀʾishah and Khadījah marry and move to their husbands' house, Fahmī, who has played an active part in the Revolution of 1919, dies, shot during a peaceful demonstration to celebrate Zaghlūl's release from prison, Yāsīn moves to a house his mother left him after a series of marital and extramarital scandals, and only Kamāl continues to live at home, deterred from marrying by the unhappy outcome of his first love affair. In the final volume the third generation is embarking on adult life, Khadījah's two sons ʿAbd al-Munʿim and Aḥmad as members of the Muslim

[24] Translated by Ramses Awad, Cairo, 1985.

Brotherhood and the Communist Party respectively, Yāsīn's son Riḍwān less idealistically in the political establishment. The patriarch himself dies during an air raid in 1941 after a period of ill-health, and the work closes as Amīnah, the archetypal mother-figure, lies in a coma close to death.

In its length and the scale of its conception the 'Trilogy' far surpasses any previous Egyptian novel; indeed, in its own genre it has remained unequalled. Maḥfūẓ's achievement here is many-sided. The writing has attained a new poetic quality, immediately apparent in the first pages of *Bayn al-qaṣrayn* where Amīnah is described as she waits for her husband to come home from his nightly revels. The factual presentation of her surroundings is interwoven with her subjective experiencing of them and with memories drawn from the different periods of her life in her husband's house in such a way as to reveal much of her character, and when al-Sayyid Aḥmad arrives she has already given the reader a first introduction to him too, as befits a wife devoted to her husband's service. Precision of language is combined with the repetition of significant words and phrases and a fresh use of imagery to create a medium fully able to convey the rich, complex and sometimes contradictory world which is brought to life before the reader's eyes.

The description of the characters' material surroundings and their subjective interaction is a major concern, especially in the first part of the 'Trilogy'. In the two later volumes, however, attention to the surroundings decreases, while dialogue and exploration of the characters' thoughts and feelings are correspondingly more prominent. This is to some extent a natural result of the fact that most of the characters continue to live and move in the same surroundings throughout the work, but it is also related to a modification in the focus of interest in the course of the 'Trilogy', a point to which I will come back later.

A constant trait is the painstaking analysis of the characters' experiencing of the different circumstances of life: first love, the death of loved and unloved relatives, marriage, separation from friends, war and the presence of occupying troops, or the more every-day bickering between sisters, the maintenance of friendships, the pursuit of rather undistinguished careers, the discussion of public and private affairs. When a character is at the centre of the stage his or her consciousness is effectively dramatized, and the contrasts thus revealed contribute much to the affirmation of each one's individuality.

Interest in the variety of human characters and in their responses to life's trivialities as well as the fundamental events of birth and death are part of the motivation behind the writing of the 'Trilogy'. On this level the work avoids banality. 'None of the stories embodied in [it] are simple and there are no happy endings. Life is a complicated web where tragedy lies in every corner.'[25] But – and this is its greatness – it can be read on very many other levels too, all of them connected with the passing of time.

The universal theme of the seven ages of man is expressed through al-Sayyid Aḥmad's decline from limitless vigour to infirmity and death, together with Kamāl's passage from boyhood (he is the only detailed child study in Maḥfūẓ's work) to disillusioned maturity; ᶜĀʾishah and Khadījah are the female equivalents of these two characters, although Khadījah, like all the other women characters except Amīnah, is less fully explored than the men and so she is not truly comparable with Kamāl.

As these and the other characters move through time, situations are repeated and patterns appear. Both al-Sayyid Aḥmad and Yāsīn love the lute-girl Zannūbah, Yāsīn's first two marriages follow the same course, Kamāl and his nephew Aḥmad Shawkat are both rejected by girls from wealthier backgrounds. But the repetitive aspect of these situations may point up essential changes; whereas at the beginning of *Bayn al-qaṣrayn* it is Amīnah who, confined by her husband to her house, looks out from the moucharaby, her only window on the world, in *al-Sukkariyyah* Aḥmad ᶜAbd al-Jawād, old and ill, occupies this vantage point while his wife makes her daily round of the shrines of Cairo, praying for all her loved ones.

Maḥfūẓ has placed this one family's destiny firmly in its historical context, and this enables the 'Trilogy' to explore essential themes of Egyptian culture and their development through time. Most obviously the work focuses on the change from a traditional to a modern way of life. In the traditional society, so carefully portrayed in *Bayn al-qaṣrayn*, men and women have separate spheres, the women confined to the house, where they rear the children, the men spending their time either at their work or among friends, free to choose their pleasures. The husband and father is a dictator in his family, and preservation of his power stands between him and spontaneous expression of his affection for his children. As modern patterns of behaviour gain ground, the barriers between the male and female spheres break down; girls continue their education and take professional jobs, fathers cannot, and will not, take decisions affecting their children's lives without consulting them, the distance between the head of the family and its members decreases.

The change from an autocratic to a more democratic system within the family can also be read as an expression, on another level, of the struggle of the Egyptian nation to end autocratic rule, obtain independence and establish democracy. It is no accident that the first great challenge to al-Sayyid Aḥmad's authority comes from Fahmī, whose nationalist convic-

[25] Sasson Somekh, *The changing rhythm*, Leiden, 1973, p. 107.

tions impel him to take part in the 1919 Revolution despite his father's opposition. At the same time the family, which has been kept outside history by its patriarch, is caught up in it and even, in the younger generation, contributes modestly to the making of it.

Together with social changes, the transition to the modern world brings metaphysical doubts and uncertainties. Al-Sayyid Aḥmad and Amīnah have a profound and spontaneous faith in God capable of withstanding all the trials to which it is put. It is this faith which enables Aḥmad to live his double life of the autocrat within the home and the pleasure-seeker outside it harmoniously, reconciling apparently irreconcilable tendencies in his nature. The great drama of Kamāl's life, besides his disappointment in love, is his loss of faith and subsequent search for the meaning of life; perplexity, an ever-critical spirit and world-weariness are his lot. His nephews have discovered their own certainties, but ᶜAbd al-Munᶜim's Islam is just as much an ideology as his brother's Marxism, and the 'Trilogy' ends too soon for the young men's beliefs to be put to the test. In any case, the quest which has led them to their respective positions remains obscure, whereas the stages of Kamāl's spiritual journey are painstakingly documented; it is his predicament, the existential predicament of modern man, which stands out as one of the main themes of the work.

The 'Trilogy' cannot, however, be reduced to straightforward equations and contrasts. For, as has been remarked, the focus of interest is modified in the course of it. In *Bayn al-qaṣrayn* a way of life is evoked in all its aspects, including the details of every-day routine and even the pleasant repetitiveness of chit-chat amongst friends. As time passes the focus of attention becomes increasingly restricted, finally being confined to politics and the quest for meaning. The change in technique observable in the course of the work is directly related to this modification in focus, as is, for instance, the imbalance in the treatment of different characters, notably the female ones. Over against the figures of Amīnah, a signal achievement in Maḥfūẓ's writing, and Khadījah, are set only nonentities in the subsequent generation, while Zannūbah's accession to the ranks of the respectable middle class, the reverse of the path taken by the heroine of *Bidāyah wa-Nihāyah*, is scarcely dwelt upon. The reduction of the role of the women in the 'Trilogy' is symptomatic of the narrowing and concentration of the author's concerns, features to be affirmed in his post-revolutionary novels.

Somekh, in his classic study referred to earlier, has argued that the main concern in the 'Trilogy' is with Time and Change, and that this finds its expression both in themes and in technique. It can be added that the comprehensive portrayal of life in *Bayn al-Qasrayn*, with its extravagancies, its changes of tone and its richness, belongs to a medieval tradition of literature which yields in the later volumes to a modern, concentrated but also fragmented and reductive approach. Whether Maḥfūẓ has overdrawn the contrast, whether the modern world is quite as bleak as he represents it, is open to question, but the fact remains that the 'Trilogy' documents and interprets a turning point in Egyptian life and culture as no other novel has done.

POPULAR ROMANTICS

The end of the 1940s marks the affirmation of a trend in the novel centred on love and at times remote from contemporary reality which is associated especially with the names of Yūsuf al-Sibāʿī, Muḥammad ʿAbd al-Ḥalīm ʿAbdallāh and Iḥsān ʿAbd al-Quddūs. ʿAbdallāh's (1913–70) characters tend to be from the lower middle class, poor, idealistic and self-sacrificing: though given to sentimental outbursts they prove incapable of forging their own destiny. He consistently puts an unalloyed literary language into their mouths, as befits a man who worked for the Arabic Language Academy. His novels, which frequently trace the main character's itinerary from the countryside to the city, appeal especially to those who themselves have left their village to study or work in Cairo.

The novels of Yūsuf al-Sibāʿī (1917–78), a less conservative man, are melodramas generally set in prosperous circles, and they focus on the struggles of lovers to overcome stifling traditions and achieve happiness. His work has been seen as a modern prolongation of the *ʿudhrī* tradition.[26] On occasion he adopts a more realistic vein when writing of the popular quarters of Cairo, and here he employs humour and a capacity for sharp observation to good effect: some of his most notable novels are those set during moments of national crisis, such as the Palestine war of 1948, which express authentic patriotic feeling.

The most provocative of these writers is Iḥsān ʿAbd al-Quddūs (b. 1919), whose novels are generally devoted to delineating the struggles of young girls from good families to liberate themselves, chiefly on the emotional and sexual plane. His declared aim has been to break down the taboos concerning what can be mentioned in literature, but in his manner of pursuing this aim he has failed, or perhaps has not even tried, to avoid sensationalism and titillation.

However the novels of these writers and their disciples are evaluated, they indicate the recognition among wide sections of the literate public that the novel has become an authentic Egyptian literary genre. Within this category of literature there are distinct trends, as the above summary

[26] Charles Vial, *Le personnage de la femme dans le roman et la nouvelle en Egypte de 1914 à 1960*, Damascus, 1979, pp. 121–2.

suggests, and it would repay further study, both for the insight it might provide into the Egyptian novel as a whole and for the information it could give about the preoccupations and aesthetic expectations of the broader reading public.

A PHILOLOGICAL PARENTHESIS

Several of the novels to be studied in subsequent sections of this chapter display textual variants, and so a short discussion of this subject, which has generally been neglected in work on modern Arabic fiction, is in order.

As recent research has shown, the assumption that the text of a given novel or story is identical in all editions is not always warranted. While the most extensive study of textual variants is devoted to Maḥmūd Taymūr's short stories,[27] the issue has also been raised in connection with Muḥammad Farīd Abū Ḥadīd's *Azhār al-shawk*, which was extensively rewritten in response to changing political realities[28] and Yūsuf Idrīs's *al-Ḥarām*, where the addition or modification of a few phrases reflects the author's reaction to the course of Egyptian politics, and a number of other variants are due to a typesetter or copy-editor attempting to correct a misprint.[29] And other instances exist; Ṣunᶜ Allāh Ibrāhīm's *Najmat aghusṭus*, conceived and originally published as a novel in three parts, appears in the Beirut 1980 edition with part two tacked on to part one and part three relabelled as part two, as a paper-saving measure by the publisher.[30] Al-Sharqāwī's *al-Arḍ* has undergone a thorough stylistic revision between the first and the third (1968) edition and one of its chapters has been divided into two; here a comparison with other editions would be necessary to show whether this is the only revision and when it occurred.

The problem is exacerbated because the term '*ṭabᶜah*' denotes 'impression', 'edition' and sometimes 'reprint'. Publishers of fiction have not yet established a convention of mentioning when a given edition includes revisions or alterations of the text of earlier editions of the same work. Ideally the study of any novel should therefore begin with a comparison of the available editions to see whether they yield any variants.

AFTER THE REVOLUTION: AN INTERLUDE OF OPTIMISM

The correspondence between political and literary history is never exact. The influence of political events on literature usually occurs indirectly

27 Rotraud Wielandt, *Das erzählerische Frühwerk Maḥmūd Taymūrs*, Beirut, 1983.

28 Jad, *Form and Technique*, pp. 214–16 and 410–13.

29 Albert-Jan van Hoek, 'al-Ḥarām: Drie Verkenningen', (unpublished M.A. thesis, Nÿmegen, 1988), pp. 1–32.

30 Personal communication by the author.

through a modification of both the social facts which are the writer's starting point and the intellectual climate in which he lives. So it was with the revolution of 1952. The overthrow of the monarchy and the breaking of the great landowners' power marked a step towards the social justice called for by so many writers of the 1940s including Kāmil, Maḥfūẓ and Luwīs ʿAwaḍ. (Luwīs ʿAwaḍ's novel *al-ʿAnqāʾ* ('The phoenix'; 1966) was written in the late 1940s and reveals the same social concerns as Maḥfūẓ's and Kāmil's novels of the period, interwoven with some original metaphysical and ethical themes. Unfortunately the delay in its publication prevented it influencing the development of the genre.) The Free Officers' declared intention to rid Egypt of British bases and end foreign domination reflected profound and wide-spread nationalist feeling. Their populist stance earned them the allegiance of many younger intellectuals who had been influenced by left-wing ideas. On the other hand their tendency to authoritarianism, which emerged rapidly, aroused the misgivings of those who valued intellectual freedom and political pluralism.

One or two authors caught by events in mid-novel had to modify their work, and as already mentioned *Azhār al-shawk* was reissued in a revised edition. Others, among them Maḥmūd Taymūr (1894–1973) and Yaḥyā Ḥaqqī (b. 1905), were moved to respond to the new situation somewhat superficially. Taymūr, whose reputation rests on his short stories and plays, had published three novels before 1952: *Nidāʾ al-majhūl* (1940; tr. as *The Call of the Unknown* by H. Horan, Beirut, 1964), *Kilyūbaṭrā fī Khān al-Khalīlī* (1946) and *Salwā fi mahabb al-riḥ* (1947); a certain mysticism and an interest in psychology are to be found in them, but no sense of social realities. *Ilā 'l-liqāʾ, ayyuhā' l-ḥubb* ('Until we meet again, love'; 1959) attempts to create an upper-class heroine who can come to terms with post-revolutionary conditions, but the author's own profound class-consciousness prevents his portrayal of a committed journalist from being convincing.

Ḥaqqī treated the changes brought about by the Revolution in his *Ṣaḥḥ al-nawm* ('You've slept well!'; 1956), his longest venture into fiction. Conceived as an allegory, it consists chiefly of a series of sketches portraying characters in a Lower Egyptian village before and after 1952. Lacking as it does plot and dramatic incident, it cannot be called a novel and deserves better the designation 'album', which the book's narrator uses once.[31] A comparison with Ḥaqqī's novellas supports the premise that this is a book in a category of its own. Whereas the former reveal the inner depths of named individuals with often exceptional destinies, the sketches

[31] Yaḥyā Ḥaqqī, *Ṣaḥḥ al-nawm*, Cairo, n.d., p. 72. On the preceding page he refers to it as 'memoirs' (*mudhakkirāt*). Tr. by Miriam Cooke as *Good morning and other stories*, Washington, 1987.

present anonymous exemplars from the external narrator's viewpoint. And whereas the novellas and short stories are conveyed in his unique style, in which a supple literary Arabic is enriched with carefully chosen, evocative expressions from Egyptian dialect, *Ṣaḥḥ al-nawm* is written exclusively in *fuṣḥā*, with some uncharacteristically archaic turns of phrase. The reader cannot avoid the impression that Ḥaqqī's great creative powers were here under a form of constraint, perhaps connected with the equivocal response to the Revolution which his narrator voices.

The major change in the novel came about through the emergence into prominence of a number of young leftist writers who had already started publishing before 1952 but who now felt freer to express their commitment to the cause of the poor and oppressed.

The first, and perhaps most typical, product of this new trend is ʿAbd al-Raḥmān al-Sharqāwī's[32] *al-Arḍ*.[33] Unlike *Zaynab*, *al-Arḍ* seeks to portray peasant life as the peasants themselves experience it. Its main plot is simple; against the background of Ismāʿīl Ṣidqī's dictatorship in the early thirties the inhabitants of a village in the Delta try to resist two attempts by the local large landowner to encroach on their rights, first by depriving them of the water they need for irrigation and then by arranging for a road to his estate to be built across their land. The villagers are by no means united, and quarrels over sharing the available water and similar matters as well as rivalry for the hand of the village beauty furnish many subsidiary episodes, as do incursions by the government's representatives.

This plot is framed in the recollections of a boy about to start secondary school, who returns from Cairo for the summer holidays, and the whole action takes place during this period. But while the schoolboy narrates the first and last three chapters in the first person, he disappears from the main part of the book, which is the work of an omniscient third-person narrator.

This is not the only way in which *al-Arḍ* deviates from the conventional novel. There are inconsistencies in plot, notably when the matter of the reduction in water for irrigation is abandoned unresolved and when at the end the focus is shifted from the building of the road, which represents a defeat for the village, to the release of the villagers who had tried to sabotage it and the fostering of mass opposition to the government. Some of the characters, too, are inconsistent, such as the village beauty, Waṣīfah, who changes inexplicably from a tomboy indulging in coarse repartee with passing boatmen to a proud young woman capable of keeping the boldest

32 ʿAbd al-Raḥmān al-Sharqāwī (1920–87) studied law at Cairo University and later worked in journalism. First associated with the Free Verse movement, he later turned to fiction and drama.

33 Published serially in 1953. Tr. Desmond Stewart, *Egyptian earth*, London, 1962.

admirer at a respectful distance.[34] The pace of narration is unusually slow.

Al-Arḍ's success has other reasons. First, despite its somewhat shaky plot it authentically expresses the villagers' grievances against central authority in general and especially the oppressive dictatorships of Ṣidqī and his like. Equally authentic is its representation of village types and forms of behaviour. *ᶜUmdah* (village headman), imam, shopkeeper, schoolteacher, smallholder, landless peasants, all come to vigorous life, even if most of them are stereotypes. Unexpectedly for an author with pronounced Marxist convictions, the vanguard of the struggle against oppression is represented by the smallholders, the most heroic figures in the novel, and this serves to justify some lyrical passages conveying the peasant's profound attachment to his land. Indeed in its expression of the unbreakable bond which exists between the earth and those who work it *al-Arḍ* has affinities with later Palestinian writing. All three themes, the struggle against oppression, the realistic portrayal of village life and the love of the land, were in tune with the mood of the first months after the Revolution.

The concern with the village extends to language and technique. Breaking away from the practice of the previous generation of novelists, *al-Arḍ* makes extensive use of dialogue in the colloquial of the Delta; the feel for the violent, aggressive way of speaking characteristic of the peasants is perhaps the single most important factor contributing to the illusion of realism in the novel. And where it deviates from conventional novelistic technique it appears to reflect the influence of oral tradition, as in its episodic structure, its repetitions, the concentration on external events with a high proportion of conflictual situations, even the fluid state of the text. The links with oral narrative may well have contributed to *al-Arḍ's* immediate and widespread popularity.

None of al-Sharqāwī's three later novels achieve the epic quality of his first, while their flaws are more marked.[35] They belong to the trend of committed literature, common and influential in the late 1950s and the 1960s, which was inspired by the tenets of socialist realism; its lasting importance lies perhaps less in its own achievements than in the reactions it called forth from more thoughtful and less dogmatic writers.

Like *al-Arḍ*, Laṭīfah al-Zayyāt's[36] *al-Bāb al-maftūḥ* ('The open door'; 1960) focuses on an oppressed social group and conveys an optimistic vision of Egypt's future. Here, however, the issue is women's emancipa-

[34] Cf. Jad, *Form and Technique*, pp. 228–9.

[35] Their titles are: *Qulūb khāliyah* (Fancy free; 1957), *al-Shawāriᶜ al khalifiyyah* (The back streets; 1958) and *al-Fallāḥ* (The peasant; 1967). Cf. Fāṭimah Mūsā, *Fī ʾl-riwāyah al-ᶜarabiyyah al-muᶜāṣirah*, Cairo, 1972, pp. 172–86.

[36] Laṭīfah al-Zayyāt (b. 1925) has been Professor of English at Ain Shams University. She has published critical studies and articles on women's rights as well as short stories and one novel.

tion, which is represented as inseparable from national liberation. The heroine, Laylā, grows up surrounded by the usual taboos of middle-class Egyptian society, in which material possessions and status rank higher than authentic feeling and girls are carefully guarded until they can be married off to a suitably prosperous husband. Laylā's first love affair, with her cousin ᶜIṣām, is shipwrecked on the '*uṣūl*', the conventions of how to behave, and, intimidated, she agrees to become engaged to one of her professors, the ideal son-in-law in her parents' eyes; meanwhile a friend of her brother, who is involved in the liberation movement, falls in love with her. Having discovered her fiancé's hypocrisy and infidelity, Laylā plucks up the courage to defy him and applies to teach in Port Said. There she joins her brother and sister-in-law in the resistance to the 1956 invasion and is reunited with her brother's friend, Ḥusayn.

At the end of the novel, and also earlier, Laylā's efforts to emancipate herself are mirrored in Egypt's struggle for national liberation. The intellectual justification for this is that the bourgeoisie, whose values Laylā finds so stifling, is unwilling to make sacrifices for the common good and is incapable of taking its destiny into its own hands. Although not consistently politically motivated, Laylā turns to nationalism and the affirmation of Egypt's independence as an alternative ideology which enables her to see herself not as an isolated individual pitting her strength against a whole class but as a member of a nation learning to shape its own destiny.

The marriage of the two themes of individual and national liberation is not entirely happy; it is one of the weaknesses of the novel that some important political events in the period which it covers, 1946–56, are ignored when they are incompatible with a certain stage in the heroine's development. Another difficulty arises with the portrayal of the positive characters, Ḥusayn and also Laylā's brother Maḥmūd and her friend and later sister-in-law Sanā', none of whom are entirely credible. The revolution and all its works are bathed in a positive light, too, which dates the novel irremediably.

In other respects *al-Bāb al-maftūḥ* is more successful. Its texture is enriched by two subplots tracing alternative responses to the proposed bourgeois model for women of the arranged marriage and a life centred on home-making and motherhood. There is an effective use of motifs and recurrent striking images. But the novel's principal strength lies in its detailed analysis of the emotions of an Egyptian girl growing up. The struggle between Laylā's natural tendency to express her feelings spontaneously and involve herself in public life and her family's efforts to stifle her initiative and confine her mentally to the home are portrayed with finesse and authenticity. This is achieved through the use of dramatized consciousness and especially dialogue. *Al-Bāb al-maftūḥ* is full of verbal exchanges on the most varied subjects, and it seeks to represent the level of colloquial appropriate to different speakers; such nuances in language may have a functional use, such as when Jamīlah's fiancé betrays his uncouthness and the fate of their marriage is foreshadowed. In the end it is the voices of Laylā and her friends, as they move from school to university and seek their path in life, which give the book its tone, a tone as distinctive as that of *al-Arḍ*. In its treatment of its main subject, women's emancipation, it is still unrivalled.

Among representatives of revolutionary optimism Yūsuf Idrīs,[37] who is better known for his short stories and plays, is a borderline case. His novels illustrate the progression of a highly gifted and original writer away from the treatment of conventional topics to the exploration of issues which preoccupy him personally. Whereas his first novel *Qiṣṣat ḥubb* ('Love story'; 1956) depicts characters involved in the resistance to the British in the Canal Zone and reflects a straightforward nationalist commitment and populist attitude, *al-Bayḍāʾ* ('The white woman'; 1959) shows more concern with exploring the psychology of its hero than with the narration of events. It contains the confessions[38] of a young doctor, a member of an underground political group, who falls in love with a married woman of European origin. The hero's soul-searching, on both the political and personal level, reveals him to be self-centred, obstinate and somewhat unstable, but his capacity for subtle psychological analysis and his refusal to abandon his critical faculty make him an interesting character. *Al-Ḥarām*,[39] Idrīs's best novel, depicts the reactions of a rural community to the discovery of a dead new-born baby and the motives of its mother, who accidentally killed it; its concern is with how taboos about sex affect individual and group psychology. The use of free indirect discourse and interior monologue combined with a subtle movement between *fuṣḥā* and colloquial Egyptian give the presentation of the characters' inner world a remarkable intensity and vividness, and this far outweighs the carelessness in construction from which Idrīs's longer fiction suffers. Traces of the revolutionary spirit can still be found in the concern with the *tarāḥīl*, the wretched migrant farm labourers, far poorer than the peasants of *al-Arḍ*, and in the novel's optimistic ending.

37 Yūsuf Idrīs (1927–91) qualified as a doctor but gave up practising medicine early in his career to devote himself to writing and journalism.

38 Cf. V. N. Kirpichenko, *Sovremennaya egipetskaya proza 60–70e gody*, Moscow, 1986, pp. 53 ff.

39 Translation by Kristin Peterson-Ishaq, *The sinners*, Washington DC, 1984.

EXTENDING THE CANVAS

Until the late 1950s the Egyptian novel is virtually synonymous with the Cairene novel; only a handful of works are set in the Delta. The publication in 1957 of Fatḥī Ghānim's *al-Jabal* ('The mountain') marks the beginning of a trend to explore less familiar areas of the country and depict their inhabitants' characteristic ways of life, which are different from, and often threatened by, the customs of the capital. This book relates the course of an investigation into accusations of theft of building material from the site of a proposed model village in Upper Egypt. The investigator discovers that the planned village, while providing salubrious modern housing, would tear the peasants away from the mountain on which they have lived for centuries and which, with its archaeological remains, provides them with a source of livelihood. Essentially Ghānim's novel still represents an outsider's view of the region round Luxor in which later the insider Yaḥyā al-Ṭāhir ʿAbdallāh sets his *al-Ṭawq wa'l-aswirah* ('The ring and the bracelets'; 1975). Further south a village near Aswan is the scene of ʿAbd al-Wahhāb al-Aswānī's *Salmā al-aswāniyyah* ('Salma from Aswan'; 1965), which portrays a young man who has had a modern education in Alexandria being forced to comply with the Bedouin code of honour in operation in his birthplace. Perhaps with a nod to *Zuqāq al-midaqq*, Ṣāliḥ Mursī's *Zuqāq al-sayyid al-bulṭī* ('Mr. Bulti's alley'; 1963) is set in a fishermen's quarter in Alexandria at a time when the fishermen's livelihood is threatened by the introduction of modern fishing methods, and it provides some nice specimens of Alexandrian dialect. Maḥmūd Diyāb's *Aḥzān madīnah* ('A city's sorrows'; 1971) portrays the childhood of a boy in the Arab quarter of one of the Canal cities, Ismailiya. The experience of working abroad, increasingly common for Egyptian graduates, is reflected in Jamīl ʿAṭiyyah Ibrāhīm's *Aṣīla* ('Arzila'; completed in 1966 but not published until 1980), in which the empty and frustrating life of a community of expatriates of different nationalities is juxtaposed with the disillusionment of the inhabitants of this Moroccan coastal town several years after independence, and their continuing material and cultural deprivation. The extension in geographical scope indicates how far the novelists' vision has progressed beyond the days of the New School which aimed to present authentic – but undifferentiated – Egyptian characters.

EXPERIMENTING BEYOND REALISM

Simultaneously with the exploration of new and remoter settings several of the books mentioned above exhibit new techniques and a concern with typically modern times. In this they reflect a development in the Egyptian novel which can be dated to the late 1950s. It arose out of, on the one hand, the recognition that realism, as practised notably by Maḥfūẓ in *Bayn al-qaṣrayn*, had been carried to its furthest possible point and, on the other, the need to express an increasing mood of disillusionment and subjection resulting from the failure of the revolution to fulfil its promises, widespread corruption and the government's reliance on oppression to silence the opposition. Acquaintance with existentialism, especially the concepts of the absurd and alienation, and awareness of modern developments in the western novel, played an important part in determining novelists' responses to this situation.

Maḥfūẓ's *Awlād ḥāratinā* ('The children of our quarter'; 1959)[40] proclaims the onset of this new phase in the novel as well as in its author's career. It uses certain religious stories – the Fall, the lives of Moses, Christ and Muhammad – in such a way as to bring out two aspects of the history of mankind, the search for social justice and the problem of the existence of God. The stories are set in a poor quarter of traditional Cairo, with its cafés, its drug peddlars and prostitutes, its poets and strong men (*futuwwahs*) and on the realistic level they focus on the need for a just political and economic organization; on a deeper level they seek to trace the evolution in man's belief in God up to and including the denial by science of His existence. The book is memorable for several reasons; it introduces the allegory into modern Arabic fiction, it broaches an extremely sensitive subject with courage and it depicts for the first time the Maḥfūẓian *ḥārah*, that pre-modern urban world ridden with violence, exploitation and misery which reappears in several of his later works. As literature it is, however, less than successful because of a disequilibrium between the richness of the metaphysical issues and the rudimentary character of the society in which they are represented and because, despite vivid dialogue and some effective use of motifs, a certain repetitiveness in conception can be observed.

Maḥfūẓ's next five novels, published between 1961 and 1966, share certain characteristics which justify them being considered as a group. In each the hero is involved in a search which, while it may have other aspects, is concerned with essential questions of man's existence: the meaning of life, responsibility, death. In each the plot is single-stranded and the focus of interest is the hero's consciousness, his thoughts and instinctive reactions, the flux of his emotions; external events are important only in so far as they have a bearing on his behaviour and experiencing of the world around him. Techniques of interior monologue, flashback, the abandonment of the traditional concern with description of peoples and places are typical of

[40] Tr. by Philip Stewart, *Children of Gebelawi*, London, 1981.

these novels, in which dialogue, more colourful and varied than before, takes up an important place. Yet despite the evident change in manner they display some continuity with the author's earlier work, notably in the concern for social justice, the interest in politics and in the destiny of Egypt, the search for a resolution to the conflict between religion and science, and the author's weakness for those on the fringes of the underworld.

Perhaps because of his own established position in life, Maḥfūẓ at this stage seems to have needed the underworld to stimulate his poetic imagination to the utmost. For it is the two novels from which the underworld is absent, *al-Summān wa'l-kharīf* ('The quail and the autumn'; 1962)[41] and *al-Shaḥḥādh* (*The beggar*; 1965)[42] which are the most prosaic and artistically unsatisfying. The first of these traces the predicament of a former Wafdist politician who cannot come to terms with the Revolution which has broken his promising career and achieved many of the goals his party had set itself, while in the latter a successful lawyer suddenly perceives the monotonous futility of his life and drops out, searching for ecstasy first through sex and then through mysticism, while haunted by the realization that he has betrayed the socialist ideals of his youth. Although technically proficient, these novels suffer from an overly rational and at times unsympathetic presentation of the hero's consciousness and a certain poverty of imagination.

In the three other novels, *al-Liṣṣ wa'l-kilāb* (*The thief and the dogs*; 1961),[43] *al-Ṭarīq* ('The way'; 1964)[44] and *Thartharah fawq al-nīl* ('Chattering on the Nile'; 1966), by contrast, the subject can be interpreted on at least two levels, while the consciousness of the main character is the prism through which the events are reflected and the author abstains from moral judgements. *Al-Ṭarīq*, the record of a playboy's search for his mysterious and wealthy father and his losing his way between two women, uses a universal motif and endows it with emotional, social and mystical significance; in this last respect the novel treats one of Maḥfūẓ's abiding preoccupations, the problem of belief.

Most original are the first and last novels of the group. *Al-Liṣṣ wa'l-kilāb* starts as Saᶜīd Mahrān, who has just served a sentence for theft, sets out to avenge himself on his former wife and his former assistant, whom he suspects of having had a clandestine affair and having betrayed him to the police and robbed him, and to retrieve his little daughter from them. Unable to achieve his aims, he seeks refuge with his father's Sufi shaykh, and turns for help to Raᵓūf ᶜAlwān, his mentor in days gone by and

[41] Tr. by Roger Allen, *Autumn quail*, Cairo, 1985.
[42] Tr. by Kristin Walker Henry and Nariman al-Warraki, Cairo, 1986.
[43] Tr. by Mustafa Badawi and Trevor Le Gassick, Cairo, 1985.
[44] Tr. under the title *The search* by Mohamed Islam, Cairo, 1987.

proponent of theft as a means to redistribute wealth. Raʾūf has meanwhile abandoned his socialist convictions and become a successful journalist whose only advice to Saʿīd is to start a new life. Saʿīd, betrayed again, tries to take revenge but his efforts end in the death of an innocent man. Hunted by the police and with public opinion whipped up against him by Raʾūf's newspaper, he finds shelter with Nūr, a prostitute who loves him, but when she disappears and he has to go out in search of food the police corner him and gun him down in a graveyard.

To begin with, Saʿīd's is the classic situation of the released prisoner out to get those who informed on him, and his thirst for revenge is all the greater because he had loved his wife; when his little daughter fails to recognize him this is the ultimate example of the general treachery. But with his realization that Raʾūf has abandoned his former socialist principles his betrayal acquires another dimension, and he comes to see himself as the representation of the poor and oppressed who have been tricked and finally abandoned by those who claimed to help them. Saʿīd's animosity is further fuelled by the fact that, having imbibed Raʾūf's materialism, he has lost the ability to understand the Sufi attitude to life exemplified in his father's shaykh, ʿAlī al-Junaydī, with whom he first takes refuge. The shaykh, undoubtedly Maḥfūẓ's most effective portrayal of a Sufi, realises very well the psychological and spiritual predicament of his guest, but the advice he offers is that of the mystic, and Saʿīd is a captive of this world.

Saʿīd's mental state is such that, having left prison, he cannot feel at ease in the shaykh's house with its doors which always stand open, and he moves to the prostitute Nūr's flat, where he dare not make a sound or turn the light on when alone for fear of arousing the neighbour's suspicion. Nūr, with her love and kindness, does succeed in breaking down his mistrust of humanity, but she cannot turn him from the obsession with revenge which in the end destroys him.

The novel is distinguished by great economy. Many motifs can be interpreted on several levels of symbolism and often have an ironic charge too, such as the references to enclosed and open spaces, or to light and darkness. The consciousness of Saʿīd, with its movement between impressions of the present, plans for the future, memories of the past and the incursions of the irrational through dreams, is presented with great skill, enabling his progress into total alienation from his fellow men to emerge in all its tragedy.

Thartharah fawq al-nīl is also a novel of alienation, but here the characters, most of them drug addicts, are already advanced on the path of estrangement from worldly cares. Their meeting-place, a barge on the Nile where most of the novel is set, suggests their tangential relationship to every-day Egyptian reality. The foundation of this book is the regular evening hashish-session (a structural element similar to that of the regular meetings between Aḥmad ᶜAbd al-Jawād and his friends in the 'Trilogy') presided over by Anīs Zakī, a minor civil servant who, in his flight from grief over the death of his wife and baby daughter, loneliness in the city and frustration in his dreary and insignificant job, has almost succeeded in cutting himself adrift from the conventional world; most of his time is spent in fantastic trips through history and reflections on the cosmos, against the background of which man's absurdity becomes only too apparent. The other members of the group, a film star and inveterate skirt chaser, a short story writer, a lawyer, a journalist and critic, and two successful civil servants, one of whom is an example of the emancipated woman, represent different sections of the prosperous new middle class who, on the face of it, would have no reason to escape from reality but all suffer from some feeling of failure or moral corruption. When faced with the need to act responsibly after the film star has run someone over while driving them back from the Pyramids at night, they all except Anīs take the cowardly way out, preferring not to endanger their positions by declaring their part in the accident. Anīs, who admittedly has less to lose than the others, has not managed to kill his sense of solidarity with other suffering human beings and it is he who decides to go to the police.

This novel is clearly a commentary on certain aspects of Egyptian society in the mid sixties, and its exposure of opportunism, cynicism, disillusionment with the government's discourse and a sense of powerlessness to influence events can, with hindsight, be seen as prophesying the defeat of 1967. But escapism, whether hashish-induced or not, is a universal phenomenon and the sense of the absurd is a typical affliction of modern man. Moreover Anīs's hallucinations, which are an important component of the book, reflect his personal sorrows and his sense that injustice has occurred throughout history: they reinforce the universal human dimension.

The consciousness of Anīs is poles apart from that of Saᶜīd Mahrān, the man with a mission, and to have conveyed it with enough incoherence to make it credible and yet to have given it meaning through the use of recurrent motifs is a real achievement. An unusual aspect of this novel is the lightness, sometimes even playfulness of tone and the feeling of bonhomie which the hashish sessions exude; for once Maḥfūẓ is using some humour, desperate though it may be, in treating serious issues.

Mīrāmār (the name of a pension; 1967),[45] the last of Maḥfūẓ's novels of this decade, explores through a handful of characters the predominating

[45] Tr. by Fatma Moussa-Mahmoud, London and Washington DC, 1974.

political trends in contemporary Egypt. It abandons the single hero to describe a series of events through the eyes of four different narrators, a technique introduced in Egypt by Fatḥī Ghānim in his *al-Rajul alladhī faqada ẓillah* (*The man who lost his shadow*; 1962)[46] but used here to greater effect since the narrators have distinctive moods and attitudes to life which they express each in his own characteristic fashion.

Although Maḥfūẓ dominates the Egyptian novel of the sixties, other more adventurous experimenters were at work too, seeking like him to apply techniques developed in the contemporary western novel to the exploration of Egyptian society. The French existentialist novelists, the practitioners of the Nouveau Roman, Kafka, Faulkner and Dos Passos, provided much of their inspiration, as they concentrated on representing the sense of estrangement from society, the profound disillusionment and consciousness of impotence, the oppression and lack of freedom which were the lot of them and their fellow-countrymen and which they as young unknown intellectuals felt keenly. Even if the political situation must bear much of the responsibility for this predicament, other factors such as the modernization of the cities and their increasing anonymity and the ever-growing pressure of population contributed to it too. These experimenters were also protesting against the Egyptian version of socialist realism, which had many supporters in the State cultural apparatus, and the ever-popular romantic escapist fiction.

Many of these innovators belong to the 'missing link' generation,[47] and their work still awaits a thorough study. It is clear, however, that without their challenging of novelistic conventions such as the omniscient or single narrator, the adherence to chronological sequence, the plot with a closed end, clarity of exposition and the concept of the active, not to say positive, hero, subsequent developments would not have been possible. Even if their novels, when judged on their merits, leave much to be desired,[48] it must be recognized that they played an essential role as pioneers.

MATURITY IN DIVERSITY

From the late 1960s a number of younger writers, each with their own specific vision and interests, begin to make a name for themselves as novelists. As they admit, though not always in so many words, they have all come out from under Maḥfūẓ's overcoat, but they are independent of him as well as of each other. The general level of technical competence is higher

[46] Tr. by Desmond Stewart, London, 1980.
[47] Cf. Sayyid Ḥāmid al-Nassāj, *Bānūrāmā al-riwāyah al-ʿarabīyyah al-ḥadīthah*, 2nd edn, Cairo, 1985, p. 100.
[48] Cf. Jad, *Form and Technique*, pp. 325–42, 353–67.

in their work than in that of their predecessors and, although they are aware of the innovations associated with both modernism and post-modernism, they are eclectic in their borrowing from abroad. They have realized more clearly the possibilities that the classical Arabic literary heritage and oral tradition offer and often make extensive use of them. The process of catching up has been completed, for Egyptian novelists now are working within the same general frame of reference as their colleagues all over the world, while their books have an unmistakably Egyptian inspiration.

It is because Egyptians are now collaborating in the worldwide enterprise of the novel on the same terms as, for instance, the Latin Americans, that I believe the Egyptian novel has now entered into its period of maturity. Of course, as time passes and new generations of novelists appear this period of maturity will acquire subdivisions, but the starting-point will remain the same. The awarding of the Nobel Prize for Literature to Najīb Maḥfūẓ in 1988 indicates international recognition of the standing of the Egyptian novel as well as of Maḥfūẓ's achievements as a creative artist in his own right and as the person who has done more than any other to make this maturity a fact. Another indication, albeit somewhat arbitrary, of the changing status of the Egyptian novel abroad is that several recent works have been translated within a few years of their appearance, whereas in the case of earlier works translations, where they exist, usually lag twenty or more years behind publication.

The work of fiction which ushers in the period, Ṣunᶜ Allāh Ibrāhīm's novella *Tilka 'l-rāʾiḥah* (*The smell of it*)[49] came out originally in 1966. Some experimental novels of the 1960s, such as Naᶜīm Aṭiyyah's *al-Mirʾāh wa'l-miṣbāḥ* ('The mirror and the lamp'; written 1966–7) with its evocation of a fear-ridden claustrophobic household ruled by a brutal, arbitrary and authoritarian father, foreshadow typical preoccupations of writers of this period. But it was only after the defeat of 1967 had publicly shown up the failings of the Revolution that the new generation came together round a literary and cultural magazine, *Gallīrī 68* ('Gallery 68') to voice their revolt against the establishment in all its forms and to work out their own values and style. Most of the novelists to be discussed in this final section first attracted attention for the short stories they published there.

It seems to be a recurring phenomenon, when a new phase in the Egyptian novel begins, for some writers to return to the countryside and present their own original interpretation of peasant life. Those who revisited the village in the *Gallīrī 68* generation include Muḥammad Yūsuf al-Quᶜayyid, Yaḥyā al-Ṭāhir ᶜAbdallāh and ᶜAbd al-Ḥakīm Qāsim, all of

[49] Tr. by Denys Johnson-Davies. London, 1971.

them of peasant origin and concerned to explore the essence of peasant culture as they knew it.

One of the most prolific writers of fiction of his generation, Muḥammad Yūsuf al-Quᶜayyid[50] started his career with novels constructed round violent deaths. The first of these, *al-Ḥidād* ('Mourning'; 1969) opens just after the unexplained strangling of al-Ḥājj Manṣūr Abū 'l-layl and consists of four monologues, those of the victim's daughter ᶜAyshah, his unacknowledged illegitimate son Ḥasan, ᶜAyshah's suitor Zahrān and her full brother Ḥāmid. Through these monologues, which include emotions and reflections evoked by the murder interwoven with memories from the past and snatches of dialogue, the character of the dead man and the ambiguous attitudes of the four towards him gradually emerge. A domineering, sometimes cruel personality, he prevented his daughter continuing her education or marrying, and kept Ḥasan in an ambiguous position halfway between a farmhand and a recognized member of the family. He humiliated Zahrān when refusing his request to marry ᶜAyshah on the grounds of his lawless behaviour and rejection by his own father, although it seems that Zahrān and al-Ḥājj Manṣūr have more than a little in common as far as wrong-doing is concerned. Ḥāmid, finally, although he is the most articulate of the four narrators and the only one to have put some distance between himself and al-Ḥājj Manṣūr, cannot escape the spell of his father's authority. He is uncertain of his place in the world, as a distant relative of the Ḥāmid in *Zaynab* might well be, and no longer at ease in the village, but at ᶜAyshah's urging he goes to avenge his father at the sakieh where he was struck down, after Ḥasan and Zahrān have paid with their lives for trying to do so. The novel ends without answering the question of whether Ḥāmid will succeed, or whether he will succumb to the mysterious afreet who is held responsible for the deaths of his father and the other two young men.

Although the afreet is rumoured to be the vengeful spirit of a peasant whose land Manṣūr Abū 'l-layl seized to add to his extensive domains, the book is not about socio-economic issues. It is a powerful study of paternal domination and exploitation and of the structures of ignorance and superstition in the village which support them. The main setting is the murdered man's house in a dark alley, and this contributes to the creating of a morbid, claustrophobic atmosphere, while appropriately the site of the murders, the sakieh, is a place inhabited in peasant belief by spirits who manifest themselves at night. Each monologue has its own tone,

[50] Muḥammad Yūsuf al-Quᶜayyid (also transcribed al-Qaᶜīd) was born in 1944 into a family of landless peasants in the Delta. He has published more than a dozen works of fiction, including novels, novellas and short story collections.

established and reaffirmed through the repetition of motifs and phrases, and often approaching poetry. Together these constitute a terrible indictment of the structures of authority, represented as paternal but capable of wider interpretations, crushing the spontaneity and originality of the young and weak.

Al-Quᶜayyid's next novel, *Akhbār ᶜizbat al-Manīsī* ('What happened on the Manīsī estate'; 1971) deals with another traditional killing, this time of a girl who has violated the code of honour. Ṣābirīn's death opens the book, and it gradually emerges that her brother, al-Zanātī, has poisoned her to erase the shame brought on the family by her seduction by the landowner's son Ṣafwat al-Manīsī. By a tragic irony al-Zanātī only takes this step after al-Ḥājj Hibat Allāh al-Manīsī has paid for Ṣābirīn's father to take her to the nearest town for an abortion; although psychologically Ṣābirīn (and her father, the nightwatchman) have already been damaged irreparably, it is al-Zanātī's action which exposes the family scandal. In this novel there are no real villains, for even Ṣafwat, with his failures at university and in love, cannot fill the bill, but only victims, Ṣābirīn's whole family, her fiancé and her pathetic seducer. The relations between landlord and peasants, but also the time-honoured ethical code conveyed in the folk epics, traditional structures of paternal authority and above all the isolation of the estate and the peasants' harsh, monotonous life contribute to making the tragedy possible.

But in this novel the claustrophobic gloom and oppression of *al-Ḥidād* have been dispelled. The characters' inarticulate sorrow and unvoiced hopes are juxtaposed with a celebration of nature and the never-ceasing fertility of the earth in extensive descriptive passages which distantly recall those of *Zaynab*.[51] Description here has several functions, to express the way in which the peasants experience the land, to emphasize the repetitive aspects of their life, to orchestrate the central events in Ṣābirīn's tragedy, and to create an almost entirely isolated world, a microcosm with multiple symbolic significations. It is an integral part of both the novel and the author's method.

Two subsequent novels by al-Quᶜayyid set in the same area, *Yaḥduth fī Miṣr al-ān* ('It happens in Egypt now'; 1977) and *al-Ḥarb fī barr Miṣr* (*War in the land of Egypt*; 1978[52]) are concerned with the political and economic situation in Sadat's Egypt. The former boldly attacks the impoverishment of the peasants resulting from the Open Door policy and the abolition of land reform measures, while the latter questions the commitment of the wealthier classes to the defence of Egypt, for which the poor pay with their

[51] As noted by Yūsuf al-Shārūnī in an unpublished lecture.

[52] Tr. by Olive Kenny *et al.*, London, 1986 (the author's name is spelt 'al-Qa'id').

lives. Like his earlier novels they manipulate chronology and employ a number of points of view to penetrate beneath the surface of the official version of events. Yet the poetically charged language and suggestive symbolism are absent here, and they have something of the character of good investigative journalism, combined, in the case of *War in the land of Egypt*, with almost too neat a construction.

Set in the same fiercely traditional Upper Egyptian milieu as his short stories, Yaḥyā al-Ṭāhir ᶜAbdallāh's[53] *Al-Ṭawq wa'l-aswirah* ('The hoop and the bracelets'; 1975) depicts a rigidly authoritarian, patriarchal society, merciless to those who challenge its values, in his characteristic poetic style, elliptic and rich in symbolism. In this writer's fiction his novel is distinguished by the fact that it spans the lives of three generations of women, so introducing the dimension of time and allowing change to take place in a generally static world. Thus the grandmother's submissiveness to her husband makes way, in her granddaughter's life, for heroic loyalty to a lover and a suicidal defiance of social customs. Parallel to the destinies of Fahīmah and Nabawiyyah the novel portrays the career of Fahīmah's brother, Muṣṭafā, who leaves the village to work in the Sudan, Palestine and later the Canal Zone. His long separation from family and community leaves him rootless, and his attachment to money cannot compensate for his fundamental alienation; on his return his failure fully to apply the punishment his niece's behaviour requires leads to his public dishonour and virtual suicide.

Al-Ṭawq wa'l-aswirah is constructed as a series of separate scenes, reduced to bare essentials, which represent the main events in the principal characters' lives and elucidate their meaning through symbols and recurring motifs. ᶜAbd al-Ḥakīm Qāsim's[54] method, in his first novel *Ayyām al-insān al-sabᶜah* ('The seven days of man'; 1969), is somewhat more conventional; he evokes, with a wealth of detail, life in a Lower Egyptian village as experienced by the main character, ᶜAbd al-ᶜAzīz. But here too the dimension of time is central, for the seven 'days', the seven stages of preparation and performance of the pilgrimage to Tanta for the *mawlid* (festival) of al-Sayyid al-Badawī, are spaced over ᶜAbd al-ᶜAzīz's early years in such a way that whereas the first stage, the announcement of the date of the pilgrimage, is recorded by a very small ᶜAbd al-ᶜAzīz, he is a young adult when the final stage, the departure after attendance at the *mawlid*, occurs. In

[53] Born in Old Karnak in Upper Egypt in 1942, he died tragically young in 1981. Although he received little formal education, his fiction contains an eloquent and vivid description of life in Upper Egypt.

[54] ᶜAbd al-Hakīm Qāsim (1935–90) was born in Gharbiyyah province. He studied law in Alexandria. Imprisoned under Nasser, he later worked as a civil servant but left the country in 1974 to spend several years in West Berlin. He returned to Egypt in the early 1980s. Three novels, two novellas and three short story collections appeared during his lifetime.

the years between the beginning and end of the book two crucial developments occur. On the one hand the hero's family's economic situation deteriorates, while the group of dervishes to which his father belongs gradually disintegrates through illness and old age, and on the other he himself comes to perceive his family's way of life differently as he pursues his education in the provincial capital and then at university in Alexandria.

ᶜAbd al-ᶜAzīz's changing attitude to his family can be regarded as a result of the normal development in an adolescent of a critical faculty. But the specific reasons for his estrangement are significant. After the boy moves to the city he learns to look at his family and village with the eyes of a city dweller, becoming aware of the dirt, overcrowding and poverty in which they live, and realizing their deep-rooted feeling of inferiority to anything urban or official. At the same time the modern education he receives encourages him to question the spiritual foundations of his father's world. His father is not only a hard-working farmer and authoritarian *pater familias* but also the friendly and hospitable leader in his village of the members of the mystical brotherhood. His eyes are fixed on the hereafter, he models his behaviour on that of the earliest Muslims and his generosity knows no bounds, convinced as he is that God will always provide. ᶜAbd al-ᶜAzīz's mother, a more down-to-earth soul concerned to balance the family budget, is the first to sow seeds of doubt in her son's mind, while his attendance at school outside the village places an insurmountable barrier between him and his father's religious certainties. Yet despite his intellectual refusal of them, in the end he is still bound by ties of love and friendship to the people with whom he has spent his childhood and through whom he has known a more harmonious world than the present one, harsh and full of bitterness.

The perspective, essentially that of ᶜAbd al-ᶜAzīz throughout the novel, is carefully controlled, keeping pace with the boy's understanding of life around him, and it is through the evolution in perception, unfalteringly managed, that the hero's psychological and intellectual development is revealed. Even if the changes which ᶜAbd al-ᶜAzīz notes in the village when he finally returns to it are so profound that the reader may be surprised that they have not struck him before,[55] this is a minor difficulty set against Qāsim's achievement in portraying an intellectual as well as geographical move from the village to the city in this *Bildungsroman*.

Ayyām al-insān al-sabᶜah is memorable also for its evocation of Egyptian village life. Woven unobtrusively into the narrative framework are descriptive passages conveying a scene or atmosphere through a small number of significant details in the manner of brush strokes, and enhanced

[55] Roger Allen, *The Arabic novel*, Manchester, 1982, p. 131.

by the frequent use of vivid images. The style, stripped of connecting particles, conveys a sense of urgency, while the colloquial is not only used for the dialogues but also influences passages of interior monologue, often poetic in their rhythmic repetition of words or phrases, and is well-suited to express the emotional significance of people, animals and objects for the main character which is a constant motif. Rather than a rose-water flavoured evocation of Egyptian folklore and a description of religious rites[56] this novel is a classic study of growing awareness, acceptance of secular urban attitudes and corresponding alienation from a peasant community.

Qāsim was one of the most innovative Egyptian novelists of his generation. His brand of innovation is not spectacular, but consists of taking material or themes already in his personal repertoire or in that of the Egyptian novel and reconsidering them, developing them further through the application of new or more appropriate techniques surely mastered. This is the case with *Ayyām al-insān al-sabʿah* in relation to *Zaynab* or *al-Arḍ*. His second novel, *Muḥāwalah li'l-khurūj* ('An attempt to get away'; 1980) takes the time-honoured theme of the love affair between an Egyptian and a European girl, but sets it in Egypt, which Elsbeth is visiting as a tourist. The novel takes place in the space of two weeks, during which the first-person narrator shows Elsbeth round Cairo and takes her to his village. By means of dialogues between the two main characters and the narrator's memories the state of Egyptian society in the 1970s is examined: its rich history, its age-old traditions still observed by the peasants, the heat and dirt of Cairo and the miserable living conditions of most of its inhabitants, their sexual and emotional deprivation and, in the background, the repressive, authoritarian state. It is not only the tourist who learns from this visit but also the Egyptian narrator, who comes to perceive the reality of his society more sharply and is forced to define his attitude towards it.

A typographical distinction is made between the narrative of Ḥakīm's meetings with Elsbeth and his unspoken comments, memories and associations. This split between interior consciousness and narration mirrors the split in Ḥakīm's personality, his emotional ties with friends, family and the heritage of his country being set against his hatred of the inhuman conditions in which he and so many others are forced to live.

The isolated individual confronting crushingly oppressive structures of authority, whether in the family, the social or economic system, or the apparatus of government, is one of the representative characters of Egyptian fiction in this period. In his first novel, *al-Zaynī Barakāt* (a man's

[56] Nada Tomiche, *Histoire de la Littérature Romanesque de l'Egypte Moderne*, Paris, 1981, pp. 78–9.

name; 1974),[57] Jamāl al-Ghīṭānī[58] examines the mechanisms by which a despotic regime succeeds in eliminating opposition. Although set in Mamluk Cairo it is clearly intended as a commentary on contemporary Egyptian society; the choice of historical period is not accidental, for a parallel is established between the last years of Sultan Qānṣūh al-Ghūrī, on the eve of the Ottoman conquest of Egypt, and the period of Nasser's rule immediately preceding the 1967 defeat. Of the four main characters two, the Azhar student Saᶜīd al-Juhaynī and the destitute ᶜAmr ibn ᶜAdawī, initially take no explicit stand towards the government, while a third, Zakariyyā ibn Rāḍī, head of the secret police, devotes all his energy to protecting the regime in whose shadow he can operate. The fourth character, al-Zaynī Barakāt, occupies an official function, that of *muḥtasib*, (inspector of the markets and supervisor of public morals), but since his point of view is never given his real attitude to the state and the strength of his commitment to reform can only be guessed at.

In the course of the novel ᶜAmr is driven to working for the secret police as an informer, whereas Saᶜīd, who has the support of a Sufi shaykh, publicly protests against the morally unjustifiable rulings of the *muḥtasib*, whom he had initially welcomed as a reformer. Zakariyyā, having at first seen al-Zaynī as a rival, in the end recognizes that they both need each other if the existing political system is to continue to function.

The coming together and divergence of the main characters is worked out against the background of medieval Cairo, powerfully evoked through descriptive passages interspersed with characteristic types of text: the Sultan's formal proclamations, the concise, formulaic announcements of the street criers, the smooth expository prose of technical reports. These, together with the passages in a more abrupt, nervous tempo (again partly achieved by the omission of connecting particles) narrating events and depicting the characters' reflections on them, provide the author with a range of levels of style and diction which he exploits to point up the contrasts between those in authority and the private citizen, the state apparatus and the isolated individual. Perhaps the clearest indication of his essentially contemporary purpose is that although he owes a debt to the Maluk historians Ibn Iyās and al-Maqrīzī, he has modified their style to enable it to reflect the inner world of consciousness, a typical preoccupation of the modern writer.

Waqāᵓiᶜ ḥārat al-Zaᶜfarānī (*Incidents in Zafrani Alley*; 1976)[59] continues al-

[57] Tr. under the title *Zayni Barakat* by Farouk Abdel Wahab, London, 1988.

[58] Jamāl al-Ghīṭānī (b. 1945) grew up in the old part of Cairo. After an apprenticeship in carpet-weaving he turned to journalism. He has published more than a dozen novels and short story collections, as well as historical studies and collections of interviews.

[59] Indifferently translated by Peter O'Daniel, Cairo, 1986.

Ghīṭānī's examination of the mechanisms of coercion in society, but its tone is lightened by liberal doses of phantasy and humour. It is an example of a recurrent type in Egyptian writing, the 'street novel' whose prototype is *Zuqāq al-midaqq*:[60] centred on a street or neighbourhood, such a novel usually has one central character but also includes prominent subsidiary characters who have their own plots. Although the characters' concerns and activities may vary widely, they are bound to interact because they are neighbours and the opportunities for dramatic clashes are almost unlimited. The inhabitants of Zafrani Alley are a varied cross-section of lower-middle- and working-class society, with their aspirations, their failings, and the phantasies they escape into to compensate for their failures. Despite the fact that some of them are grotesque and others rather pathetic, they are sympathetic thanks to the tolerant humour, sometimes tinged with irony, with which their thoughts and feeling are depicted. The same ironic humour inspires the initial situation, the epidemic of impotence, which drives the men of the alley to consult the sinister and mysterious shaykh who has just returned from a long absence. The shaykh, the only character whose thoughts remain opaque, sets out to exploit his neighbours' affliction in order to establish his domination over them. By manipulating their fears he gradually isolates them from one another and reduces them to obedient pawns, and this, the end of the book implies, is a prelude to a more ambitious, worldwide campaign.

The variety of the characters, the inventive conception of the whole, the careful reconstruction of every-day life in a Cairo back street which reaches its dramatic climax in the epic quarrels between the women, the subtle transitions from the real to the magical or other-worldly, make this one of the most remarkable novels of the 1970s. And, incidentally, the fact that the highly symbolic theme of impotence is at the centre of the work and is treated explicitly indicates how far contemporary Egyptian writers have succeeded in liberating themselves from taboos about what can, or cannot, be discussed.

Exposing the mechanisms of coercion and repression is also one of the purposes of Ṣunᶜ Allāh Ibrāhīm[61] in *Najmat aghusṭus* ('August star'; 1974). This novel relates a journalist's visit to the Aswan High Dam and the region beyond it at the moment when the newly completed construction must hold back the full force of the Nile flood for the first time. The first and third parts, written in a matter-of-fact style, record against a background of hotels and construction sites conversations with workers on the dam, other

[60] Cf. Hilary Kilpatrick, 'Egyptian novels and Arabic literary tradition' *Proceedings of the 14th Congress of the Union Européenne des Arabisants et Islamisants, Budapest 1988* (in press).

[61] Ṣunᶜ Allāh Ibrāhīm (b. 1937) studied at Cairo University and spent five years in prison for political activities. He works as a journalist and translator and has published two novels, two novellas, short stories and science fiction for children.

journalists, western tourists, Russian experts and local people; their cumulative effect is to establish a balance-sheet of the building of the dam, the great prestige project of Nasser's regime. The main character does not question the principle of the dam, needed to further Egypt's development, but he notes that while it has provided work and training opportunities for some, it has disrupted the lives of others, such as the Nubians whose villages have been submerged. By interweaving the investigation of the dam project with observation of the social and economic situation of the other characters and memories of his own period in prison, the journalist also portrays the state of Egyptian culture, and here the verdict is clearer and harsher. Under the repressive system established by a government with whose socialist ideology he agrees, class distinctions, materialism and corruption continue to exist, and because of lack of freedom the benefits brought by the dam will be limited to basic material conditions. The reflection on lack of liberty and the personal ambitions of rulers acquires a historical dimension with the visit to the Abu Simbel temples, built by the self-glorifying Ramses II, while by means of quotations from a life of Michelangelo the connection between freedom and creativity is affirmed.

The second part of this meticulously constructed novel contrasts stylistically with the rest. In one long, fluid sentence the different threads of the work, the climax of the dam's construction as it meets and withstands the flood waters, the artist's faith in his material as an element of stability in a chaotic world, and the narrator's moment of physical and emotional fulfilment with a Russian girl he meets in Aswan, are woven together in a profusion of images and allusions ignoring the barriers of time and place.

The concern for the individual facing a repressive state, the urge to denounce lack of freedom and an interest in experimental techniques can be traced in the works of the other significant writers of the period too. Najīb Maḥfūẓ, for instance, has continued to analyse the contemporary problems of Egypt even when using a setting in the more or less distant past, as in *Malḥamat al-ḥarāfīsh* ('The riffraff's epic'; 1977). It must be admitted, however, that his recent novels betray a general decline in poetic force and originality and do not stand comparison with the better writing of younger generations. In the future his reputation will no doubt be founded on the works he published before the age of sixty – which is in the end the destiny of most writers.

Idwār al-Kharrāṭ[62] occupies a place apart in Egyptian fiction. For long a lonely pioneer of modernist techniques and vision, he has found his place in

62 Born in 1926 in Alexandria, he graduated in law. Although he is best known for his short stories, he published a number of experimental novels, including the semi-autobiographical *Turābuhā Zaʿfarān*, translated as *City of saffron* by Frances Liardet, London, 1989.

the generation of writers of the late 1960s and the 1970s, consistently supporting and encouraging them and their younger colleagues. His first novel, *Rāmah wa'l-tinnīn* (Rama and the dragon; 1979),[63] is marked by his experience with the short story, for its fourteen chapters may be read as separate entities. The narrative thread, the main character Mīkhāʾīl's love affair with Rāmah, is subordinated to a more important structuring element, Mīkhāʾīl's consciousness, and the chapters move back and forth through time as he lives, remembers and reconsiders his experiences with this sexually and intellectually stimulating woman who is capable of playing a multitude of roles but in the end rejects any permanent loyalty. It is easy to identify in this novel many typical preoccupations of the modernist school, the difficulty of communicating, the uncertain status of external reality, the concentration on subjective perception, the expression of philosophical preoccupations. But this modernist stance, itself an implicit protest against modern conditions of existence, is combined with references to periods of revolutionary struggle in Egypt's recent history and the contemporary economic and social malaise. In two other respects *Rāmah wa'l-tinnīn* is an important contribution to the Egyptian novel; though not the first attempt to portray a love affair and analyse it in detail without resorting to moral judgements, it is the first in which the protagonists are a Copt and a Muslim woman, thus openly challenging traditional Islamic attitudes which exclude marriages between Muslim women and non-Muslim men. And, thanks to Mīkhāʾīl's and Rāmah's professional interest in Egypt's past, it integrates into a contemporary work of fiction a historical dimension stretching back to Pharaonic and early Christian Egypt; this latter is especially real for Mīkhāʾīl since it forms the basis of his specific cultural heritage.

Although, like many other novels of this type, *Rāmah wa'l-tinnīn* is occasionally wearisome reading, the quality of the style is consistently remarkable. Al-Kharrāṭ has an extraordinary command of the Arabic language and he exploits it to present all aspects of life and human experience. The long, meandering sentences with their qualifications and parentheses are obviously appropriate to the rendering of the main character's psychological processes, but they also serve to describe the external world with great precision and sensitivity, as though affirming the certainty of its existence in the face of the characters' metaphysical perplexity.

Especially in discussing the recent period of the Egyptian novel I am aware that I have given a less than complete or adequate account. This has to do

[63] His second novel, *Al-zaman al-ākhar* (*The other time*; 1985) reworks, alters and adds to the material in *Rāmah wa'l-tinnīn*; it falls, however, outside the period covered in this chapter.

partly with the general difficulty of writing contemporary literary history, but also with the problem of obtaining sources. This is especially evident for the Sadat period, when many intellectuals left the country, or at least published their work abroad, often in very limited editions. But if I have left some serious blanks on the canvas, I have perhaps added a few unexpected details here and there.

The history of the Egyptian novel from 1913 to 1980 traces the process, gradual at first and then gathering momentum, by which a genre of foreign origin has been naturalized and assimilated, and has then taken on specifically Egyptian features. The range of themes has widened, the language has developed new registers, in particular thanks to the breaking down of barriers between colloquial and *fuṣḥā*, the possibilities for enrichment offered by the Arabic oral and written literary tradition have been recognized, the techniques used have become increasingly sophisticated.

Other literatures have witnessed analogous developments. What, then, are the characteristics of the Egyptian novel in its maturity?

First, it has at its disposal the rich arsenal both of a literary language with a long and impressive poetic, intellectual and religious tradition and a colourful, direct dialect, whose dramatic qualities range from the rough and aggressive to the subtly ironic. Second, after a solid grounding in European realism it has increasingly frequently drawn on the mythical, fantastic and otherwise non-realistic heritage of Arabic narrative literature. As far as motifs are concerned, social interaction is an abiding interest, and this is more than simply a reflection of population pressure. The choice of themes reflects the commitment (broadly interpreted) of Egyptian writers to their society; much of their work can be defined as exploring the passage from traditional to modern, in social, cultural and metaphysical terms, and portraying the search for new values to replace the old religious ones, most frequently represented as an ideal through the figure of the Sufi. Another consistent concern is to create a space in which the individual may develop freely, in the face of coercion by the political authorities and a repressive attitude on the part of society at large.

That the Egyptian novel in its period of maturity offers such rich variety as it does should not be a cause for surprise. On the one hand, this is the natural consequence of the developments outlined above; on the other, the political, economic and social near impasse from which the country now suffers seems to have acted to channel much creative energy into literature, and more especially fiction. Whatever the outlook for Egypt, the prospects for the Egyptian novel are very good.

CHAPTER 8

THE MODERN ARABIC SHORT STORY

INTRODUCTION

In modern Arabic literature the close interaction between literature and socio-political issues makes it difficult to isolate one from the other. The importance of the socio-cultural dimension is particularly relevant in dealing with narrative forms, because narrative mediates human experience and derives its significance from probing it. This chapter describes briefly the context necessary for an understanding of the modern Arabic short story throughout the various stages of its development, and also outlines the history of the genre itself and the development of its formal and thematic elements. As is shown in the most comprehensive survey of the genre, published in *The Kenyon Review* (vols 30–32, 1968–70), the short story has been marginalized in most advanced western cultures. In the Arab world, however, as in other developing and semi-developed countries such as India, South Africa and Yugoslavia, for various reasons the short story has emerged as the most popular and arguably the most significant literary medium.

In Arabic literature, while one can trace its descent from other traditional forms of narrative going back to the *Arabian Nights*, the short story in the modern sense of the term is a new literary genre that developed in the last few decades of the nineteenth century and reached maturity only in the early decades of this century. The existence in the culture of a rich tradition of short narrative forms made it inevitable that the question of the genealogy of Arabic fiction should attract the attention of many scholars. Some endeavour to establish a long linear connection between modern Arabic fiction and its medieval narrative ancestors. Although classical and medieval Arabic is relatively rich in archetypal prose fiction, the *maqāmah* has been chosen by most scholars as the ancestor of the novel, the short story and even drama. Others deny any connection with the past and claim simply that the short story is 'borrowed from the west'. But the relationship between modern Arabic narrative and either western narrative forms or classical Arabic archetypal fiction is not one of genealogy alone but of dynamic intertextuality.

The emergence of a new literary genre is part of a lengthy and intricate process that changes people's understanding of their society and their perception of themselves before changing the discourses that process their experience. This started at the beginning of the last century and continued to seep slowly into every aspect of social and cultural life in Egypt and the Levant (Greater Syria, which was later divided into Syria, Palestine and the Lebanon). Since the time of the Crusades this part of the Arab world has borne the brunt of the dialogue with the west and has played a major pioneering role in synthesizing and harmonizing its various elements. The dialogue with western culture entered a new phase during the last century, following Napoleon's campaign in Egypt, through the ambitious programme of reform undertaken by Muhammad ᶜAli and completed later by his grandson Ismāᶜīl, whose reign is described by P. J. Vatikiotis in *The Modern History of Egypt* (London, 1969, pp. 73–4) as the epoch that 'provided the basis for the genesis of an Europeanised Egyptian élite in government, education and letters. The membership of this élite soon expanded and its knowledge increased appreciably until it became the leader of the reform'. The other parts of the Levant witnessed a similar development affecting education, the press, journalism, translation and urbanization, the main factors that accelerated the cultural renaissance.

A NEW READING PUBLIC AND THE CHANGE IN LITERARY SENSIBILITY

Apart from the spread of education, the press is one of the vital factors that participated in the creation of a new reading public, because without printing reading becomes a very specialized activity limited to a small number of manuscripts. The press is linked to journalism and their development went hand in hand throughout the last century. Newspaper publications rose in Egypt during the reign of Ismāᶜīl to twenty-seven Arabic newspapers, and between his deposition in 1879 and the end of the century this number increased to 310 in Egypt alone with many others in the Levant. After the declaration of the Ottoman constitution in 1908, the number and quality of newspapers in Iraq and the Levant rose dramatically. Palestine had more than ninety newspapers, thirty-six of them in Jerusalem; and Iraq had more than seventy. By 1897, according to *al-Hilāl* (October), the readership of newspapers was estimated to have reached 200,000 in Egypt alone, and probably a little more than this number in the rest of the educated Arab world.

In 1861 Lebanon, after its recent tragic civil strife, became autonomous, and both this and its strong historic affinities with Europe enabled it to play a more active role in the cultural revival of the area. Its autonomy provided for relative stability and encouraged missionaries to embark on numerous educational projects, enhancing the interaction with western culture and emphasizing the study of Arabic language and culture in opposition to the domination of Turkish.

Ismāʿīl's era also witnessed the translation of fictional literature, familiarizing the reader with the conventions of narrative and serving as a training-ground for would-be writers. It is not surprising that many of the translators of the early period played a pioneering role in the development of various forms of narrative. The names are numerous, such as Khalīl Baydas, Najātī Ṣidqī, Kulthūm Naṣr ʿAwdah and Anṭūn Ballān (Palestine), Najīb al-Ḥaddād, Sulaymān al-Bustānī, and Nasīb Mashʿalānī (Lebanon), Maḥmūd Aḥmad al-Sayyid, Salīm Baṭṭī and Anwar Shāʿūl (Iraq), Muḥammad Kurd ʿAlī, Najīb Ṭarrād and Ṭanyūs ʿAbduh (Syria) and Ḥāfiẓ Ibrāhīm, ʿAbd al-Qādir Ḥamzah, and Ṣāliḥ Ḥamdī Ḥammād (Egypt). The constant popularity of translated fictional works motivated many of the leading writers of the time to try their hand at fiction. By the last two decades of the nineteenth century the steady growth in the reading public and the popularity of narrative discourse in either its traditional or its modern translated form paved the way for the rise of fiction. More importantly the growing sense of individualism and the development of a clear sense of national identity had altered the very nature of experience and, more significantly, the individual's perception of it. The European colonization of the region and the national resistance that ensued accelerated the forging of a strong sense of national identity, and provided the newly educated class with a clear direction. This gave rise to the early embryonic forms of short narrative, generating a new mode of expression which proved crucial in developing the early works in this genre. The authors of these early works were aware of a need to tell the stories of everyday life. The primacy of this urge to tell a story over any preconception of the form most suitable for expressing it is demonstrated by the fact that the early pioneers did not even canonize the changed nature of their writing by a change in nomenclature; for in Arabic the specific use of the term 'short story' was not fully established until the 1920s.

A NEW FICTIONAL FORM IN EMBRYO

ʿAbdullah Nadīm (1854–96), the most outstanding pioneer of the short fictional form in embryo, led a life which enabled him to move with utmost ease through all strata of society, probe its various social classes, groups and races and absorb its numerous and often contradictory cultural strands from the most traditional to the highly Europeanized. He defined for narrative treatment a number of areas which provided the thematic territories of successive writers. He started his literary career in the early 1870s and worked as a journalist for some years before editing his weekly magazines. Although a number of Levantine writers such as Fransīs al-Marrāsh (1836–73), Salīm al-Bustānī (1848–84) and Nuʿmān al-Qasāṭilī (1854–1920) started publishing rudimentary short fictional pieces in *al-Jinān* (1870–85), a Levantine magazine published in Cairo and then in Beirut, Nadīm's early works in this vein are the most outstanding of their kind. They share with those of Marrāsh certain themes, particularly those dealing with the devastating impact of the adoption of European ideals, but they are characterized by their clarity, distinctively new language and markedly subdued didacticism by the standard of their time. Nadīm deliberately wrote for the new reading public whose language and literary canons were different from those of the traditional reading public, to whom most of the works of his Levantine counterparts were directed. His simple language with its stark, intimate tone and lack of the customary verbal embellishments was well suited to the familiar topics and daily concerns of the common folk. It was his passport to a wide audience and at the same time his contribution to the development of a language of fiction, for the traditional language with its stultified style was inimical to narrative presentation. He even resorted to allegorical narrative in communicating his ideas.

The first, promotional, issue of his first weekly (*al-Tankīt wa'l-tabkīt*), which he distributed free with the daily *al-Maḥrūsah*, contained five of these allegorical narrative pieces. The magazine continued to publish these allegorical pieces until the outbreak of the ʿUrābi revolution when burning patriotic issues became dominant. Nadīm's serious interest in both fictional and patriotic issues established from a very early stage the strong bond between the newly emerging literary form and the national question. Any study of Nadīm's early fictional works, as well as those of al-Bustānī and Marrāsh, reveals the strong connection between these works and the socio-cultural reality in which they emerged, and confirms the link between their themes and the process of sharpening the readers' awareness of their national identity. The narrative pieces dealt with the pitfalls of slavish imitation of western behaviour, the alienation resulting from excessive adoption of European ideals, the danger of seeking refuge in drugs, the social disparity between upper and lower classes and the suffering of the poor, the usurious transactions of foreigners and their exploitation of the natives, the torment and suffering of deserted wives of dissolute husbands, the importance of women's emancipation and education and of an independendent economy, the corruption of the religious establishment and, above all, pride in one's country and its glorious past in an attempt to measure up to it.

At the same time, these fictional works, some of which came very close to a rudimentary form of short story, developed a number of fictional strategies such as the allegorical manipulation of concrete details and factual data, the double meaning of the title and its suggestive interpretative power, the vivid presentation of issues, the power of metaphorical treatment in probing complex or sensitive issues, a sketchy use of the setting and the artistic use of humour and sarcasm harshly to ridicule characters or situations without stripping them of their plausibility.

EXPERIMENTING WITH VARIOUS NARRATIVE WORKS

The development of the Arabic short story from the early fictional seeds sown in *al-Jinān* in 1870 and evolved a few years later in Nadīm's work, to its maturation with the publication of *Ḥadīth al-qaryah* by Maḥmūd Ṭāhir Lāshīn in 1929, took half a century of constant and energetic effort. The process went on throughout the culturally developed part of the Arab world and involved two main groups of writers. One sought to express the new experiences and realities resulting from the socio-cultural transition and outlined in Nadīm's work, by rejuvenating the form of the *maqāmah* and widening its scope and variation; while the other attempted to achieve the same end through a hybrid form which Shukrī ʿAyyād terms 'narrative essay', which is a direct descendant of Nadīm's fictional episodes. In addition there was a third, minor group of writers, confined to Iraq, who experimented with a unique variation on the 'narrative essay' by using *al-ruʾyah* (visionary dream) as a mode of narrative expression.

As far as the first group is concerned, the period saw the publication of many new works in the old form of the *maqāmah* by journalists (Nadīm, Muḥammad al-Muwayliḥī and his father Ibrāhīm al-Muwayliḥī), poets (Aḥmad Shawqī and Ḥāfiẓ Ibrāhīm) and translators (Muḥammad Luṭfī Jumʿah). These new *maqāmāt* are radically different in aim, language and form from the traditional ones and even from those produced a few years earlier by traditionalists such as Abū'l-Thanāʾ al-Alūsī (d. 1854) in Iraq, Nāṣīf al-Yāzijī, Nīqūlā al-Turk (d. 1828), Aḥmad Fāris al-Shidyāq (1805–87) and Ibrāhīm al-Aḥdab (d. 1891) in the Lebanon and ʿAbdullah Fikrī (1834–90) in Egypt. The use of the *maqāmah* to express the new experience of the time in short narrative pieces was also pioneered by Nadīm, but his successors paid more attention to the overall structure of the whole book and to the link between the various *maqāmāt* in it than to the autonomy of each single *maqāmah*, to the extent of considering their work the precursor of the novel rather than the short story. The only *maqāmāt* which pay special attention to the coherence of each episode and therefore come closest to the form of the short story are those of Jumʿah. Unlike the others, who wrote only one work in this form, he demonstrated an earnest desire to continue writing and developing the new form over a considerable period of time and displayed a high degree of awareness of what he was doing. In the introduction to his second book, *Fī Wādī al-humūm*, he conceives of the art of fiction as being divided into two main trends: *al-Ḥaqīqī* (the realistic) and *al-Khayālī* (the fantastic); the former is that of Balzac and Zola, and the latter is that of Scott and Dumas. He declares his intention to pursue the former and write his work *ʿala asās al-ḥaqīqah* (according to the dictates of reality).

Yet when it comes to his creative writing, particularly in its maturest form in his last book *Layālī al-rūḥ al-ḥāʾir* (1912), Jumʿah is a world away from any realistic form of discourse. His work is of a romantic nature, not only because it appeared during the period of what Shukrī ʿAyyād terms 'the romantic explosion', but also because of its sentimental overtones and strong impact upon succeeding romantic works, for which Jumʿah's works set the tone and mapped the thematic ground. His concern for social injustice and the misery of the destitute, which is accompanied by a clamour of loud laments and sentimentality, became a standard motif in many romantic short stories for years to come. His second major theme, that of torment in love, also became a favourite theme; his third theme, which owed a great deal to the work of Qāsim Amīn, that of women's emancipation, also proved popular with successive romantic writers. Yet his romantic characteristics are more evident in his presentation which stresses, if not exaggerates, the emotions and sentiments at the expense of other social factors, and attempts to emphasize the role of imagination both in writing and in life. Another romantic trait, more relevant to the present study, is his attempt to release his writing from the confines of the *maqāmah*, for romanticism is generally associated with the break with and the revolt against old forms.

THE IMPACT OF THE ROMANTIC EXPLOSION

ʿAyyād points out that in the four years 1906–9 Jibrān Khalīl Jibrān published *ʿArāʾis al-murūj* (1906) and *al-Arwāḥ al-mutamarridah* (1908), Muṣṭafā Luṭfī al-Manfalūṭī (1876–1924) started to publish his highly influential and sentimental pieces in *al-Muʾayyad* in 1907 and ʿAbd al-Raḥmān Shukrī published his first collection of romantic poems in 1909. Among these works Jibrān's and al-Manfalūṭī's were the most influential.

Romanticism involves a break with traditional form, and those who were sensitive to such changes and to the needs of the new reading public began to develop certain aspects of the form and to familiarize the reader with some narrative conventions necessary for the reception of the short story. Jibrān, Manfalūṭī and others did not attempt to reproduce the form of the *maqāmah* in a new guise, but were genuinely experimenting with a new form without being completely aware of the nature of this form. They had been exposed to European narrative, either in translation or in the original language, but were responding more to a genuine need to communicate certain ideas, rather than to an experimental urge to pioneer the creation of the Arabic short story.

Although Jibrān was writing his works in the *Mahjar* (North America), their setting was his home in Lebanon and their impact was immediately felt throughout the Arab world and particularly in the Levant. He is considered by many critics as the greatest romantic of the Levant. His early short narrative pieces, which were called *riwāyāt* (narratives) or *ḥikāyāt* (tales) by his friend, the editor of the *al-Mahjar* newspaper, attempt to 'illustrate the sentiments of the various strata of society from the beggar to the prince and from the blasphemous to the saintly'. But they end up by exaggerating these sentiments and creating a highly romanticized view of the suffering of the poor and the torment of love. Jibrān linked these themes to the lack of freedom and the various forms of social and political oppression including those practised by men against women. Like Nadīm, his view of women is generally positive compared with his view of men and his attacks on the Christian religious establishment and its clergy echo those of Nadīm on hypocritical shaikhs. Although his narrative is still rudimentary and lacks vigour and coherence, it is more sophisticated than that of Nadīm and manifests a deeper understanding of the progression of action, functional description and characterization. But his didactic aims, which are just as crude, mar the effectiveness of his narrative.

Like Jibrān's, al-Manfalūṭī's work is distinguished among those of the pioneers by its stylistic and emotive power. This increases the importance of his contribution for it sustained the reading public's need for fiction. He succeeded in this because he aimed his writing not at the elite or the intellectuals, but at the public at large – the intelligent common reader. His short fictional works, which he called in his famous *al-ᶜAbarāt* (1915) *riwāyāt qaṣīrah* (short narratives), pay considerable attention to emotive language and elegant style and are particularly skilful in emotional agitation. But this stylistic gift does not save them from serious shortcomings, it disturbs the balance of the text and hampers the integration of its various components in a harmonious manner. A writer of his school, Muṣṭafā Ṣādiq al-Rāfiʿī (1880–1937), who was strongly influenced by the success of *al-ʿAbarāt*, came very close to creating the first mature short story in his *Miskīnah . . . Miskīnah* in his book *al-Masākīn* (1917). It deals with the theme of social disparity by resorting to skilful characterization, coherent structure, plausible progression of the action which turns full circle in the course of the story and subtle use of the title; this is only marred by the author's rhetorical style and his direct intervention to deliver his unneeded didactic message.

The third group of writers, whom ʿAbd al-Ilāh Aḥmad, the eminent scholar of Iraqi fiction, calls *kuttāb al-ruʾyah*, the writers of visions, also experimented with narrative modes independent of the traditional form of the *maqāmah*. They started publishing their work in the influential magazine *Tanwīr al-afkār* in 1909 and continued until 1921, spreading to other publications. Like Nadīm's narrative sketches, it seems that the new form captured the imagination of young writers at the time who experimented with it with varying degrees of success. Although al-Muwayliḥī used the dream as a literary device in his *Ḥadīth ʿĪsā ibn Hishām*, the Iraqi narrative form seems to be unconnected with this experiment. Like Nadīm's sketches, 'the visionary dreams' were highly didactic with a clear moral message concerned with the nationalistic issues of the time. Despite their name they can be read as a commentary on the present more than a blueprint for the future. In its best examples, in the later work of ʿAṭāʾ Amīn, this form developed a relatively simple narrative language liberated from the heavy verbal decorations which continued to burden most work in this mode.

These three groups contributed, each in its different way, to the development of the conventions of short narrative forms. They helped to popularize the form, stimulate demand for it and encourage a number of new writers to experiment with its potential.

THE EARLY PIONEERS OF THE GENRE

By the second decade of this century most of the writers who were experimenting with the form realised that it was more fruitful to develop the rubrics of narrative outside the realm of the *maqāmah*. The closer one comes to a true reflection of reality the further one gets from the *maqāmah*, as was clearly demonstrated in Jumʿah's work. However, it is no accident that this break with the traditional form of narrative coincided with the disintegration of the tenuous Ottoman hold over the area, and the emergence of a new order and a new phase in the relationship between the Arab world and Europe. By the end of World War I all the countries of this part of the Arab world had come under British colonial domination. This accelerated the development of national identity in the struggle against foreign occupation. The need to use the written word to enhance the readers' awareness of the burning issues of the time, whether political, social or cultural, gave a new impetus to the development of a form of writing capable of expressing these needs.

The pioneers of this form had a clear understanding of both the formal limitations of the short story and the nature of the issues they wanted to tackle. Major revolts against colonial domination in the area (the 1919 revolution in Egypt, the 1920 revolutions in Iraq and Palestine, the 1920 and 1922 uprisings in Syria) were all products and precipitators of a clear awareness of national identity and are closely linked to the rise of the modern Arabic short story. Furthermore, the suppression of these revolutions bred a sense of failure and frustration which, as Frank O'Connor shows in detail in *The Lonely Voice* (London, 1963), is particularly conducive to the form of the short story. Writers representative of this newly emerging genre include Khalīl Baydas (1875–1949) in Palestine, Labībah Hāshim (1880–1947) in Lebanon, ʿAbd al-Masīḥ Ḥaddād (1881–1950) and Mīkhāʾīl Nuʿaymah (1889–1988), who represent the *Mahjar* dimension of Levantine literature, ʿĪsā (189?–1922) and Shiḥātah ʿUbayd (189?–1961), who demonstrate the bond between the Levantine cultural movement and its Egyptian counterpart, Muḥammad Taymūr (1892–1921) from Egypt and Maḥmūd Aḥmad al-Sayyid (1901–37) from Iraq. Those were the most eminent names among many writers who were trying to develop their work simultaneously and without much awareness of each other's work. They were responding to the change in literary sensibility and the demands of the new reading public more than to each other's work.

Baydas was one of the early pioneers of Palestinian literature who started with the conscious intention of producing short stories when he edited his influential magazine *al-Nafāʾis al-ʿaṣriyyah* (1908–14). He started as an active translator from, and even into, Russian, but soon turned to writing his own novels and short stories which were clearly influenced by his translation of and his familiarity with Russian literature. He was aware of the nature of narrative, the vital role of fiction and its popularity with the reading public, as is revealed in his introduction to the first issue of his magazine. Yet when he started writing his own short stories he demonstrated that there was a wide gulf between theoretical awareness of the nature of fiction and its realization. In some of his stories he debates the difference between fact and fiction; in others he uses a mythological, historic, philosophical, pedagogical, symbolic or even social framework. But most of his formal experimentation was marred by authorial intrusion in the narrative, an obtrusive didactic tone, redundant moral messages and the excessive use of chance and surprise.

Like Baydas, Labībah Hāshim was primarily a translator and the editor of a successful magazine, *Fatāt al-sharq* (1906–39). She published a number of short stories in her magazine and later collected them in book form. Although she lacked talent, her journalistic skills, simple language and ability to tell a story and sustain a relatively complicated plot made her the pioneer of a trend of simplistic narrative. Her stories are more like a summary of longer works telling an elaborate and sentimental love story, but she managed to popularize narrative among the female reading public.

Extending the scope of the readership of fiction was also the main contribution of Ḥaddād's collection, *Ḥikāyāt al-Mahjar* ('The stories of expatriation', 1921). Some of these stories appeared in the *Mahjar* while others were published in Levantine periodicals. They mostly deal with the problems which the Arab expatriate faces in his new life away from home. The main theme of these stories is the disparity between expectations and reality, and the hardship of life away from the protective domain of home. His expatriates experience difficult cultural adjustments particularly related to ethical values and the relationship between the sexes, and they nostalgically yearn for the world they left behind. The positive contribution of his work is that it does not idolize or romanticize the past, but treats this nostalgia with humour and sarcasm.

Unlike his compatriots in the *Mahjar*, Nuᶜaymah maintained strong ties with Lebanon and his solid knowledge of its reality is clearly reflected in the early short stories he wrote between 1914–25 particularly in the literary journal *al-Sāʾiḥ*. These stories compare favourably with the most mature works of the early pioneers of the genre and are marked by their understanding of the nature of artistic experience and the techniques of its presentation.

SIGNIFICANT EARLY CONTRIBUTIONS

The two Syrian brothers, ᶜĪsā and Shiḥātah ᶜUbayd, have a curious position which demonstrates the unity of the Arabic short story at the time and the difficulty of drawing a rigid line between the various geographical locations of its origination. They were born in Syria but, like many Syrian intellectuals, migrated to Egypt and played their literary role there. ᶜĪsā ᶜUbayd, the more talented of the two, dedicated his first collection to Saᶜd Zaghlūl, the leader of the Egyptian national revolution of 1919, yet their collections were generally peopled with Syrian, not Egyptian, characters.

ʿĪsā ʿUbayd died prematurely in his twenties, but during his short but fecund literary career he tried his hand at drama, the novel, the short story and literary criticism. His brother, Shiḥātah, chose after ʿĪsā's death to become a recluse and cut himself off from literary life. ʿĪsā published two collections of short stories and Shiḥātah published only one, but both of them began their books with elaborate introductions in which they stated the need for a new form of literature, emphasizing the organic link and interaction between the independence of the country and the shaping of a distinguishable national identity and the creation of indigenous literature. This also showed a strong awareness of the shortcomings of the early attempts to create narrative genres and a sound and mature understanding of the art of fiction, aided no doubt by their solid knowledge of French literature. They called for the literature of the future to be established on a solid 'base of accurate observation, creative imagination and psychological analysis, describing life as it is without exaggeration and diminution: life in its absolute and naked truth, for this is the essence of what is called in the Introduction of *Iḥsān Hānim* '*madhhab al-ḥaqāʾiq*, realism'. Their understanding of both realism and the art of narrative was far superior to that of their predecessors in terms of description, characterization, language, motivation of both the character and action, dialogue and the vitality of verisimilitude. Their stories were unprecedented in their endeavour to illustrate authentic relationships between the two sexes, and to explore the undercurrents of family life, particularly in Christian circles. They were the first to reveal the different dimensions of the life of middle-class women, and to touch upon various aspects of female emancipation.

Their central theme is the incompatibility of partners in a marriage which takes place in a closed social atmosphere, and the grave consequences of such marriages for the coherence of the family. Yet they tackled many other themes such as the tension between the nation's aspirations and the ability of individuals to realize them, the problems arising from polygamy and the conflict between the city and the countryside. Their convincing characterization enabled them to go beyond the two-dimensional characters which their predecessors had created and they developed the technique of using sub-plots or parallel symbolic action. But they burdened their stories with too many issues and used them as vehicles to deliver ideas and information to the extent that many of them became more like synopses of longer works than balanced and well-structured short stories.

Despite his premature death at the age of twenty-nine, Muḥammad Taymūr is generally considered the pioneer of the Arabic short story in Egypt. After three years in Europe, during which he broadened his knowledge of French and European literature, he returned to Egypt in

1914 full of enthusiasm for the creation of a new Egyptian theatre, and an adequate form of expression for the modern short story, the novel and literary criticism. He was convinced that literary independence is inseparable from political independence and he therefore saw the creation of indigenous literature as a patriotic task contributing to the shaping of the national identity and the articulation of its aspirations and goals. At first theatre took the lion's share of his attention, but he started publishing short stories in the *avant-garde* magazine *al-Sufūr* in 1917, and they were collected posthumously in *Mā Tarāh al-ᶜuyūn* ('What the eyes can see', 1922). His stories, which attempt to capture various facets of life's contradictions and depict truly Egyptian characters, played a significant role in providing the newly emerging genre with a clear sense of purpose: a definite nationalistic and spiritual function, to substitute, or at least attenuate, the traditionally pedagogic role.

Although his stories did not venture outside the thematic grounds mapped out by Nadīm, Taymūr managed to some extent to free his work from the prevailing sentimentality of the period. Hence his presentation and treatment of the old themes (the impact of addiction to drugs or alcohol upon the community and the coherence of the family, the wasting of much-needed energy and talent, the injustice of social disparities, the false attraction of western habits and the disunity of the Egyptians in the face of their enemies) is artistically more advanced and effective than that of his predecessors. Yet his works failed to develop their own internal memory, motivation, intrinsic cohesion and integral scale of values. Even his description of the fictional scene, something completely neglected by his predecessors, relies on reference to real places, streets, bars and cafés known to the reader, to convince him of the authenticity of his fictional account. This appears to be a substitute for the lack of what Wayne Booth calls in *The Rhetoric of Fiction* (Chicago, 1961, pp. 3–16) the artificial authority of the author over the reader who is invited to accept unquestioningly all the facts and information the writer gives him. Taymūr succeeded in achieving a complete break with the conventions of traditional prose writing and storytelling, impelled by a desire to find an appropriate means of expressing the new ideas, experiences and vision of the changing literary sensibility and of meeting the readers' demands. In his characterization, he was a pioneer in using similarity and contrast as an effective structural device, in the skilful use of irony and in broadening the scope of narrative discourse by incorporating letters and diaries and other forms of discourse into his fictional text.

The last of the pioneers of the genre, Maḥmūd Aḥmad al-Sayyid, was also a translator, but this time from Turkish. Despite his premature death he published numerous articles, three novels and three collections of short stories – *al-Nakabāt* (1922), *al-Ṭalāʾiʿ* (1929) and *Fī Sāʿ min al-Zaman* (1935). The most interesting feature of these three collections is that they reflect, in their very themes and structure, a strong urge to develop the new literary genre and master it. The last two collections contain attempts to rework some of the stories of the first one to remedy their failures or improve on their theme or narrative presentation.

THE MATURATION OF THE NEW GENRE

After the end of World War I with the victory of the allies, the promised independence was not granted. This resulted in the intensification of the nationalist struggle, the rise of plurality in political thinking and the formation of several political parties, indicative of a growing individualism and an increasing sense of common identity among the urban bourgeoisie. Writers no longer saw themselves as teachers but as individuals caught in social, intellectual, or even political dilemmas. This in turn was reflected in the development of the Arabic short story in three distinct ways: it led to the maturation of the genre in the prevalent atmosphere of frustration and broken hopes of the 1920s; it resulted in a mellowing of the realistic trend; and it enhanced the appeal of the romantic narrative. In countries like Egypt, where the literary movement was very active, the three phenomena were separate and distinct from each other; in other parts of the Arab world they converged and intermingled, often in the work of a single author. It is therefore necessary to distinguish the three phenomena as they took shape in Egypt before dealing with their counterparts in the rest of the Arab world at the time.

The main key contributors to the maturation of the Arabic short story in Egypt are Maḥmūd Taymūr (1894–1973), Maḥmūd Ṭāhir Lāshīn (1894–1954) and other members of *Jamāʿat al-Madrasah al-Ḥadīthah* (the New School of Writers), who brought out the first issue of their weekly *al-Fajr* in 1925. Maḥmūd Taymūr was the younger brother of Muḥammad Taymūr and was strongly influenced by his brother's endeavour to create a modern literary genre. But unlike his elder brother he was also influenced by the solidly classical culture of his father Aḥmad Taymūr (1871–1930), who was one of the pillars of the traditional literary establishment, as well as being influenced by the many orientalists who frequented his father's house. He published his early work under the pseudonym *Mūbāsān al-Miṣrī* (the Egyptian Maupassant) but soon outgrew this practice and used his own name. He wrote with a rigour and frequency that made him, with more than thirty collections of short stories to his name (in addition to his many novels and numerous plays), one of the major short-story writers of his generation. Earlier on in his career he travelled to Europe three times and spent two years in Switzerland during one of these trips. This improved his command of foreign languages and also had a profound impact on his understanding of both art and man. He was particularly influenced by the works of Maupassant, Tolstoy, Turgenev and Chekhov. He started his short-story writing with great enthusiasm for the genre, prophesying in the introduction to his first collection *al-Shaykh Jumʿah* (1925) that the short story would soon be the only heir to all the forms of narrative writing, a statement which he himself regretted and corrected two years later.

He was the most productive among the Arab short-story writers of his time: in the six years from 1925–30 he published five collections of short stories and one novel accompanied by a short story. But his fictional world remained narrow, his themes limited, and there was a lack of variety in his characterization. Nevertheless, the continuous flow of his works played an important role in familiarizing the reading public with the new literary genre and its conventions. In many of the stories of this period, he continued to treat the main themes of his elder brother; namely the neglected and depressed wife, and the frivolous man who wastes his wealth and health in shameless sensual behaviour. In dealing with the latter Taymūr treated his reckless protagonists with a blend of moral harshness and ridicule, explaining the cause of their fall without real understanding of their motives. However, Taymūr was successful in dealing with another of his brother's themes: that of the world of traditional religious shaikhs, against whom he launched a strong attack in numerous short stories. The common stand of the brothers Taymūr as well as many of the preceding short-story writers reflected the deep-rooted struggle between the new generation of Arab intellectuals, with their rationalism and enlightenment, and the older generation with its traditional belief and metaphysical leanings. In their quest for intellectual leadership, the new intelligentsia could no longer tolerate the exaggerated respect which the old intellectual class of the shaikhs enjoyed among the general public. They wanted to unseat them from the hearts of the masses and they embarked on the arduous task of revealing that behind the mask of piety and learning there hid cruel, ignorant, licentious, and even mad men.

Thus the short story became a tool in the battle for public influence and a weapon for the subversion and destruction of the traditional intellectual establishment and its social status. In the work of Taymūr this theme was coupled with that of the predicament of young writers and artists in a society which turns a deaf ear to their activities and ambitions. The stories in which he reached the peak of his literary attainments in this period are those in which he explored the inner life of his characters such as *al-ᶜAwdah* ('The return'). In this mature and well-written story about a grandmother who has made her grandson the centre of her life and waits for his return from the city oblivious to the passage of time, the balance between the individual and the archetypal in the story transforms the simple situation into a profound one that shows the harshness of life in its treatment of those who fail to fathom its complex dynamics. Here, under the influence of the Chekhovian approach, Taymūr achieves a sensitive balance between the various elements of narrative, and creates a convincing human character, a mature fictional situation rich in its texture, structure and conflict.

Taymūr's conscious desire to root the short story in Egyptian literary life led him to use all that he observed of rural life in his summer visits to the country, and all that he had grasped from that world of traditional intellectuals who surrounded his father. He used local settings, but failed to transcend their parochial limits. Nonetheless his works broadened and heightened the artistic and conceptual qualities of the Arabic short story, his concentration on characterization, especially forlorn, injured and defeated figures, was a step forward in the development of the genre. His stories succeeded in decreasing the short story's reliance on what Sean O'Faolain calls in *The Short Story* (London, 1948, p. 137) a 'preamble in which the writer tells us how he came into possession of the facts', and paved the way for dispensing with it altogether. The artistic question around which Taymūr's stories revolved was that concerning the language of fiction, its nature, scope and limits.

The whole question of language was, in fact, the subject of a lengthy controversial discussion among the writers and the critics of the twenties. They dealt with it from the static position of the traditional view of prose language and not from the dynamic position of the aesthetic and structural function of language in a creative work of narrative fiction. Taymūr's treatment of the problem of language as a mere vessel to contain meaning and not as an integral part of the meaning itself, was in harmony with his understanding of the nature and function of narrative. The narrative in his work depended on 'telling' the reader all that he wished him to know about the character and actions. He failed – with few exceptions – to 'show' him the characters evolving in situations which revealed them as three-dimensional people, or to go beneath the surface of the action to obtain a reliable view of a character's mind and heart, so enabling the reader to examine the accuracy of the writer's description. Ironically, Taymūr's sentimentality and other shortcomings concerning language and directness served as a bridge between the new literary form and the traditional reader and were, thus, praised by some of the reviewers of the period. Taymūr's work played an important role in affirming this new literary form and gained considerable support for it from the pillars of the literary establishment.

THE SEMINAL ROLE OF THE 'NEW SCHOOL'

Taymūr's shortcomings were overcome by his gifted contemporary Lāshīn and his group of the New School whose arrival on the literary scene marked a turning-point in the history of the modern Arabic short story. His writings represent the culmination, in both form and content, of the work of previous writers and of his contemporaries. He was also the major figure of the New School, a versatile literary group which played a decisive role in developing the modern Arabic short story, extending its reading public and shaping the characteristics of the new sensibility of that period. The writers of this influential school fell entirely under the spell of Russian literature until it became their main source of inspiration. They identified easily with the world of pre-revolutionary Russian literature and, like their contemporaries in Palestine, read Pushkin, Gogol, Lermontov, Turgenev, Dostoyevsky, Tolstoy, Chekhov, Gorky and Artzybashev, the impact of whose works upon them was enormous.

In addition to being socially and politically oriented, this group of young writers was also aware of what Max Weber calls 'ideal types'. The attempt to mirror these 'ideal types' in their works was the basis of their call to create *adab qaṣaṣī qawmī*, 'national narrative literature'. Their weekly, *al-Fajr*, disseminated their new ideas on a wide scale and prepared the ground for well-established and respected magazines to publish short stories, and to encourage authors to write them. It also established new critical criteria in dealing with literature, not as something incidental to political and ideological writing, but as a significant independent activity, underlining the interrelationship between literary work and other media of artistic expression. This shifted the emphasis from the political relevance of the work to its artistic form without sacrificing its social or edifying role, and helped to create a new concept of indigenous literature which was not confined by the limitations of local situations but was capable of portraying the human aspects of this experience. Lāshīn commenced writing short stories as early as 1921, but he refrained from publishing any of his early attempts and continued to improve on them until late 1924. From then on he wrote and published frequently in *al-Fajr*, and several other magazines after its closure. His first collection, *Sukhriyat al-nāy*, appeared in 1926 and his second, *Yuḥkā ann*, in 1929, bringing most of his work within the context of the New School which went into decline before the end of the twenties. In these two collections he was able to create a coherent artistic vision and to put the new ideas of his group into practice.

Lāshīn, a son of the rather self-centred middle class, naturally focused his work on its characters and values. Although there is a small group drawn from the lower middle classes who remain on the fringe of his world, they are never allowed to occupy the centre. However, lower-class characters are carefully illustrated and sensitively depicted in Lāshīn's world in spite of the obvious overtones of sarcasm and disdain in his representation of them. The main setting of most of his stories is the town, where he concentrates on two main scenes: the first private, inside the houses of the urban middle class, and the second public, cafés, government offices and streets of the poor and crowded areas of Cairo. He was concerned about accomplishing a comprehensive social survey of the life of the city and its inhabitants through the form of the short story as an attempt to root the short story itself in the life of the middle class who formed the major part of the new reading public. His treatment of the various aspects of the social life of the time developed many of the thematic concerns of his predecessors by reflecting their essence in a mature form of narrative. In addition to his treatment of the major contemporary themes of modern Arabic short stories, he excelled in developing the theme of the sensitive conflict between town and country.

Ḥadīth al-qaryah: a turning point

A brief analysis of Lāshīn's masterpiece *Ḥadīth al-qaryah* ('The talk of the village') may serve to demonstrate his masterly sense of structure, and provide the reader with an insight into the story that closed the chapter of trial and experimentation with the rubrics of the new genre, and opened the way for its maturation. It is an important work not only because it marks the real birth of the coherent indigenous realistic Arabic short story but also because it focused its attention on the crossroads at which modern Egypt, and by extension the rest of the Arab world at the time, stood, where the conflict between rural and urban views and values, between modernism and traditional religious thought was greatest. Yet it treats these complicated issues without falling into the trap of presenting foregone conclusions. Though it uses stereotypes it shuns exaggeration and endeavours to resort only to artistic representation of reality.

The story starts with the narrator using the first-person narrative to tell us about a day he spent in the country. He is enchanted by its beauty and freshness, and at the same time amazed by the wretched peasants whose misery is in sharp contrast to the infinite beauty of their surroundings.

When he commiserates with the peasants his friend, who has invited him to the country, holds his view up to ridicule and accuses him of over-sentimentality. From the very beginning, the story presents these two opposing views and sustains a continuous tension between them throughout. This provides it with a form of polyphonic narrative in which various views contend to attain recognition within the text and attract the attention of the reader. In the evening the confrontation between these two urban views about the imaginary country life and the real life of the village takes place when the two urban visitors join in the villagers' nightly chat, the only form of entertainment known to the peasants. Here the story employs a sophisticated narrative structure generated by the interaction between the main story and the story within it which is told during this nightly chat. The two stories come into conflict through another conflict between the urban visitors and the *Imām*, the religious leader of the peasants' community and the representative of the traditional intellectual leadership at the same time. The *Imām* not only presents a completely different view of the life of the village but also seeks to attain recognition and influence within the narrative by becoming the narrator of the story within. The conflict between the urban and rural intellectuals (which on one level represents that waged between the traditional and the newly emerging intelligentsia) is reflected on the structural plane through the successive narration of the two different stories in the narrative.

Lāshīn calls his story 'The talk of the village' to draw the reader's attention to the nightly chat which forms the core of the story's structure, and to emphasize that the story is not that of the tragedy of adultery and revenge which forms the main plot of the story within the story, and which occupies no more than one third of the whole text, but that of the talk which preceded, accompanied, and followed its telling. This is so because Lāshīn is as interested in the conflict of power between the urban and the rural narrators as in the tragedy of the story's main character. It is this talk which penetrates the action and gives shape to the various contradictions within the story. One of the main structural elements in this story is that of identification with the argument. Through a stroke of Lāshīn's genius the hero is a character with whom the peasants can easily identify yet they can be detached from him, look down upon him and mock his ridiculous attempt to climb the social ladder. The narrator seems passionate and sincere in his call for reform, but what is the point of mere talk, however virtuous, when seen in the light of the deeds of the other urban man who deceived their fellow villager and destroyed his life. There is also the way in which the narrator expresses his views, which seem to be difficult even for his urban friend, let alone the peasants, to comprehend, and whose failure to communicate is symptomatic of the inability of the new class of intellectuals to play an effective role in their society.

The story is rich, economic in style, and makes a profound analysis of the clash between two distinct cultures. It maintains a delicate artistic balance and uses words to their full poetic value. It employs some suggestive symbols which draw upon the different shades of light for illuminating both the scene and the characters. Lāshīn uses the description of the setting to enrich his action and characters by means of suggestion and implication and to accomplish the integration of fictional elements. He also introduces, in this story and in many others, elements of irony and parallelism in the structure, especially in the contradictory characters and the complex network of relationships operative within the text. The polarization between two different groups of characters establishes an elaborate network of similarities and contrasts between the major characters of the story which enables the reader to comprehend the various layers of meaning in the text. This story also produces the most convincing attempt to integrate the author's preamble into the story by making it a functional and inseparable part of both its texture and its structure.

THE OSCILLATION BETWEEN ROMANTIC AND REALISTIC NORMS

By the end of the 1920s the works of Taymūr and Lāshīn had brought the stage of the genesis of the indigenous Arabic short story in Egypt to an end. Taymūr laid the foundation for the romantic short story, while Lāshīn established the rigorous tenets of the realistic one. But the maturation of the short story in other parts of the Arab world took place a few years later. The development of the genre in the Levant and Iraq followed the same pattern as Taymūr's work in which elements of realism were mixed with a great deal of sentimentality and romanticism. Throughout the 1930s none of the Arab short-story writers produced anything that equalled, let alone rivalled, Lāshīn's masterpiece, which was published in 1929.

In Iraq in the 1930s, Jaᶜfar al-Khalīlī continued to write the type of stories which were being written in Egypt at the beginning of the century. They were based on traditional themes and concepts of narrative and were deeply rooted in the Arabic folk tradition. But the work of Dhū'l-Nūn Ayyūb (1908–88) and ᶜAbd al-Ḥaqq Fāḍil (b. 1910) in the 1930s owed a great deal to that of Taymūr in both form and content. Fāḍil and Ayyūb started publishing in 1934 and 1935 respectively, but the latter was more prolific and published six collections of short stories in three years (1937–9). Like their Egyptian counterparts they were influenced by Russian literature and felt the need to justify their work by lengthy preambles that made many of

Ayyūb's works, in particular, closer to the literary essay than the short story. He was clearly concerned with political issues, corruption, nepotism and social dissimulation, and launched a vehement attack on bureaucracy. He treated with some understanding the question of the two oppressed groups in his society – women and peasants – both of whom he considered to be main assets of the country, his aim being to advocate a radical change in their situation.

Like Taymūr, these writers used the short story as a means of enhancing the position of the artist in general and the writer in particular in society, and portrayed the newly emerging intellectual in an extremely positive light. In the stories of *Burj Bābil* ('The Tower of Babel', 1939), Ayyūb's best collection of that period, he demonstrated his ability to probe the characters and analyse their motivation, a quality he learnt from his reading of Dostoyevsky. In most of his earlier stories his over-reliance on dialogue and his rudimentary characterization overemphasized the authorial presence in the narrative and marred its effectiveness. The sheer productive capacity of Ayyūb overshadowed the mature work of the less prolific Fāḍil, who was a discerning critic and produced more coherent work than that of his compatriot in the early stage of his writing. Fāḍil's fluid language and the dexterity of his dialogue contributed to the coherent characterization and convincing motivation of the plot in creating more mature stories. His fine sense of humour, in which one can easily detect the influence of the narrative of Ibrāhīm ʿAbd al-Qādir al-Māzinī, spared him the labouring of social-reform messages. He used some mythological elements, possibly under the influence of Tawfīq al-Ḥakīm, which widen the scope of meaning of many of the stories of his first collection, *Mizāḥ wa mā ashbah* ('Humour and the like').

In Syria Ṣubḥī Abū-Ghanīmah's first collection *Aghānī al-layl* ('Nocturnal songs', 1922) was faithful to the romantic overtone in the work of Jibrān and Ḥaddād, and tried to extend its sentiments to the patriotic questions of Syrian independence, but failed to develop the rudimentary narrative of his predecessors. ʿAlī Khalqī (1911–84), in his collection *Rabīʿ wa kharīf* ('Spring and autumn', 1931), and Muḥammad al-Najjār, in *Fī Quṣūr Dimashq* ('In Damascene palaces', 1937), succeeded in taking the Syrian short story beyond the domain of rudimentary sketches and raw sentiments and into a more elaborate narrative form. They brought the Syrians' attempts to create an indigenous short story closer to achieving its aim by exploring various aspects of social reality and rooting the new genre in the daily life of the Damascene middle class.

In Palestine Najātī Ṣidqī (b. 1905) was the most significant short-story writer during the 1930s. Like his predecessor, Baydas, he started his literary career as a translator, critic and a student of Russian literature (graduating from Moscow University) and was fluent in a number of languages. Although his short stories were few and far between he succeeded in bringing the Palestinians' preoccupation with their national question and the danger of the influx of European Zionists into the realm of the short story. Despite his wide culture and extensive knowledge of literary techniques, his stories lack artistic coherence and were far behind their time in characterization and narrative structure.

In the Lebanon Khalīl Taqiyy al-Dīn's work was praised in the 1930s as the most significant contribution to the development of the genre. This was true in comparison with the rudimentary works of his contemporary Mārūn ʿAbbūd (who continued to write a combination of sketches and didactic tales inspired by the folk literature of Lebanese villages), but only until the work of the most gifted Lebanese writer of the period, Tawfīq Yūsuf ʿAwwād (1911–89) appeared. Taqiyy al-Dīn's work is noteworthy for its insightful treatment of the relationship between the migrating Lebanese and their homeland. The interaction between love for the land and love for the sweetheart takes the two themes onto a new plane beyond the naivety of the previous treatment of both issues. Like many of his compatriots he paid a great deal of attention to the lyrical aspects of language and employed the power of imagination to compensate for the bleakness of life in the mountain villages.

NARRATIVE TRENDS AND SOCIO-POLITICAL REALITIES

After the completion of the period of the formation of the genre there was a rapid increase in the number of writers trying to use the newly shaped form as a means of expressing their ideas and visions. This was accompanied by an expansion of the reading public, its subdivision into various reading publics, and the increase in the number of short stories published.

The three decades stretching from 1930 to 1960 witnessed a number of conflicts and contradictions in the Arab world, not only because of the various social and political upheavals which began with the economic crisis of the 1930s and included a number of major wars, but also because of polarization in the national and patriotic movements and the growth of dissent and agitation throughout the area. This period was rich in historical events that raised hopes of independence only to be dashed, leaving behind suffering and frustration. It witnessed rioting and rebellion in Egypt, Iraq and Palestine, an increasing number of political assassinations, widespread corruption, the loss of Palestine with its deep-reaching ramifications, the emergence of new nationalist and leftist ideologies and the anti-climactic realization of political independence. The latter part of this period was marked by the increasing involvement of the army in politics which led to successive military takeovers.

There appears to be a homology between the main socio-political realities of this period and the three major literary trends into which the modern Arabic story was divided. There was the pragmatic political establishment which is represented by the various minority governments which ruled throughout the period. They elected to ignore popular demands for independence and social change, compromised with the colonial forces and satisfied themselves with the status quo under which they attained tremendous privileges even if this required certain repressive measures or false promises. The second political force was the national patriotic one which was represented in the *Wafd* party in Egypt and similar national movements in Syria and Iraq, characterized by their dynamism, reformist ideologies and a commitment to achieving political, economic and cultural independence. The third was that of the rising rebellious popular movement represented by radical students and small and often divided groups of leftist intellectuals rejecting the very fabric of the prevailing establishment and directing their anger against the various occupying forces in an attempt to rally the widest possible support for their political visions. They were unable to unite yet they offered a wide variety of new ideas and ideals and embarked occasionally on radical application of some of them in a manner that generated tremendous vitality and vigour.

These three socio-political forces represent three different perceptions of national identity and correspond with the three major literary trends of the modern Arabic short story. The first was a natural product of the work of the most prolific pioneer of the genre, Maḥmūd Taymūr, but took a significant turn towards the sentimental in the work of the most influential short-story writer of the 1930s, Maḥmūd Kāmil. As Shukrī ʿAyyād explained, Kāmil has discovered that there are many elements of the middle class which have accepted and even gained from the political and social status quo and started to enjoy its new bourgeois life and identify with the European ideal, developing a type of self-centered Franco- or Anglo-Arab mentality. 'From this new class Kāmil drew his inspiration and his fame, and to them, as well as to a large section of the poor who aspire to attain their privileges, he directed his writing and for them he invented what he called the "Arab love story".' The second literary force was a natural continuation of the early development of the modern Arabic short story in its drive to attain maturity and coherence. It continued to adhere to the major principles of this approach and to explore the various facets of national identity and articulate its aspirations and dreams. This trend made its contribution in the framework of realistic presentation, as elaborated and developed by the mature work of the New School of the 1920s, which reached its acme in Lāshīn's eminent contribution. Therefore it is not surprising that this school starts with the work of its youngest and most talented member, Yaḥyā Ḥaqqī (b. 1905), and continued its development with the work of a number of talented writers throughout the Arab world. The third trend, which led to the development of modernistic narrative, was as divided and as fragmentary as the socio-political realities which inspired it. Its insightful pioneers were naturally marginalized throughout the period, despite their continuous impact on a number of talented writers.

THE ROMANTIC SHORT STORY

It is no mere coincidence that the rise and blossoming of romanticism in the Arabic short story took place in the 1930s and 1940s. The gloom of the 1930s and its failure to provide favourable conditions for the achievement of national aspirations was a suitable atmosphere for the development of some of the romantic themes. The early attempts at industrialization were weak and unable either to capture people's imagination or to set the tone for a new era. The awakening of a national identity and the consequent spread of patriotic fervour demanded an artistic expression undiluted by realistic presentation which often contradicts or at least dampens such a movement. On the cultural front neo-classicism, especially in poetry, had already reached its zenith and had started to decline. Realism was unable to catch the attention of the increasing reading public, or to satisfy its thirst for fiction which ends happily and makes no serious demands on the reader.

The glorification of nature and the animation of its beauty is a dominant idea in the romantic short story, not only because this romantic notion struck a genuine chord in the Arab writer with his deep-rooted affection for his homeland, but also because it served to strengthen the reader's patriotic fervour in the struggle for independence. It trained the reader in a new activity and aspired to educate him and strengthen his relationship with his surroundings. A corollary theme, the exaltation of art and the artist, is both a reaction to the state of art and the status of the artist in Arab society, and the product of the strong influence of European romanticism which emphasized the supreme gift of the artist and saw the function of art as that of exploring those areas of the mind and the universe which lie beyond the confines of rational thought and the perceptions of the common man. The hero of romantic writings became none other than the artist himself, who is both the explorer of this unknown realm and the priestly mediator between it and the reader.

The exaggeration of sentiment beyond what is conventionally acceptable within the standard structural framework is what one terms sentimentality. Indeed, in the Arabic short story sentimentality is mainly the product of the inability to assimilate emotional responses and justify them within the internal laws and logic of the creative work. The individual romantic hero is presented as having emotions, ideas and aspirations that cannot be adequately satisfied within the society in which he must operate. There is thus a pervasive air of sorrow and grief at the loss of hope but in the bleakest moments of despair the romantic hero allows us a glimpse of his dream, with a new ethical scale superior to that of the existing morality. Yet the romantic hero is no preacher, he is more a dreamer who prefers his own dreams to reality and whose salvation is often achieved through his love or art, not as two means to a specific end but as ends in themselves. Ironically the romantic Arab short-story writer who is a self-professed seeker of beauty often overlooks design, ordinance and the interrelationship of parts in the structure of his work. But he pays considerable attention to the representation in words of aesthetic qualities and shades of feelings.

In the modern Arabic short story it is possible to discern three categories of romantic texts. The first consists of the more serious romantic works which endeavoured to shape and develop a romantic sensibility, the second encompasses the more commercial ones concerned with the popularization of the short story amongst a wider reading public, and the third includes the works of socialist romanticism which are mistakenly known as works of socialist realism. In the first category the development of a romantic system of ideas is inseparable from the course of the development of the Arabic short story in general and that of the realistic trend in particular. The works of this category participated in the development of both the form and the content of this new literary genre. They also aspired to widen the scope of the form and to root it in the cultural life of the Arab reader. Because the aims of this category of romantic short story were identical to those of the realistic one, it is natural that the two should overlap and that many writers wrote in both indiscriminately.

It is appropriate to begin the discussion of the works in this category with those of the Egyptian writers, and particularly with the stories of Maḥmūd Taymūr, not only because this will provide us with a fine example of the overlapping of romantic and realistic qualities, but also because it demonstrates that romanticism was there from the start of the development of the Arabic short story. Taymūr's work underwent a significant change in the 1930s and 1940s without completely abandoning the old pattern. The didactic tone of the twenties disappeared and his attempt to portray social defects faded away. In their place appeared a concern to indulge the reader with beautiful pastoral scenes and elevated passions. Love is the main pivot around which rotate other subsidiary themes with strong romantic qualities. The chastity of love is a precondition for any emotional involvement in most of his love stories, for he links sex to sin, idiocy, ugliness and vulgarity.

Another theme which is closely associated with the theme of love is Taymūr's treatment of the question of art and the artist, which is clearly influenced by various romantic concepts. The emergence of romantic themes in Taymūr's work corresponds to a shift in his social emphasis in which he replaces the middle and lower classes of his early works with a segment of the aristocracy, a group of artists and intellectuals and a handful of eccentric characters. This was almost necessary to introduce the new romantic themes, one of which is the beauty of nature which can only be appreciated by those who can articulate this appreciation. Nature is a symbol of love, freedom and harmony so that departure from her is unbearable and always leads to the ugly, material town.

One other romantic short-story writer who was keen to introduce a political dimension into the Arabic short story is Muḥammad Amīn Ḥassūnah (1908–58?), who is one of the six signatories of the important 1930 literary manifesto *al-daᶜwah ilā khalq adab qawmī* ('The call for the creation of a national literature'), which was published in *al-Siyasah al-usbūᶜiyyah* on 28 June 1930. Like many of his contemporaries and colleagues his romanticism is distinguished by its patriotic flavour. Unlike Taymūr, who relished the beauty of nature in Europe and adored the mountains of the Lebanon, Ḥassūnah takes delight in describing the bucolic scenes of the Egyptian village and uncovering the charm of its ritualistic life. His stories extol the beauty of rural Egypt and amalgamate it with a strong religious tone so that the combination of the two solace the hero and enable him to endure his tragic misfortune. Like many romantics his dreams are in complete contradiction to reality, and they are naturally dashed to pieces in the first confrontation with it.

Romanticism was to await the arrival of the talented and prolific Saᶜd Makkāwī (1916–85) to reach its acme: in *Shahīrah* one finds a complete and extremely coherent characterization of the romantic hero, not only as an innocent full of dreams and aspirations, but also as a sensitive artist endowed with deep insight and great talent, facing a macabre atmosphere and a corrupt society. Another significant interaction is that between art and love, for *Shahīrah* combines, sometimes movingly, the two favourite themes of romanticism. In addition love is often strongly associated with mysticism or with yet another romantic theme – nostalgia – through which previous love affairs are presented and tenderly cherished. Conflict between the child's view of the world and that of the conformist adult is one of Makkāwī's main themes which involves, at one of its levels, the theme of romantic rebellion. Like his predecessor Ḥassūnah, he is fond of the theme of rebellion against conformity, and especially the rebellion of female characters against unjust social conventions. His stories accentuate the feelings of alienation and discontent and associate them with a Byronic hero constantly oscillating between impossible dreams and an overwhelming longing for destruction, including self-destruction. Like most romantics, Makkāwī is also fond of nature, which he often glorifies, animates and sees as a source of happiness and great hope. But he is the only romantic writer whose work shows a constant, even remarkable, development towards the consolidation of structure and coherence of romantic ideas.

In Syria, the short stories of Muẓaffar Sulṭān (b. 1913), Murād al-Sibāʿī (b. 1914), Badīʿ Ḥaqqī (b. 1922) and Ulfat ʿUmar al-Idlibī (b. 1912) combine the patriotic flair of Ḥassūnah with the romantic sensibility of Taymūr who introduced the first two collections of al-Idlibī. The patriotic element is one of the major components of their narrative to the extent that Badīʿ Ḥaqqī's very influencial and widely read collection, *al-Turāb al-ḥazīn*, revolved around the main theme of the Palestinian question. The stories of these three writers reflect both the desire to mirror social reality and the need to use the short story as a vehicle for didactic, patriotic and moral ends. They deal mostly with themes similar to those of their Egyptian counterparts, with a clear emphasis on national and patriotic issues. Al-Idlibī brought the concerns and preoccupations of women into mainsteam writing and illustrated their barren existence in contrast to their sensitive souls and romantic dreams. She was the founder of a tradition of female narrative rich in texture, mood and emotion, but fragile in structure, which continued to thrive both in Syria and in other parts of the Levant. Like her mentor, Taymūr, she addressed the life of the upper class and her unique concern for the vanishing social norms and rituals provided her stories with a distinct hue of nostalgia and made them valuable records of the past.

But the most significant Syrian short-story writer of the romantic school is ʿAbd al-Salām al-ʿUjaylī (b. 1919), who started writing in the early 1940s and attracted the attention of discerning readers throughout the Arab world. He was a volunteer in the Arab army in the Palestinian war of 1948, an experience that informed a large number of his stories and enhanced the nationalistic element in his writing. Like Ibrāhīm Nājī (1898–1953) and Yūsuf Idrīs (1927–91), his medical training period provided him with the power of sharp observation and an ability to trace the various symptoms to the core of the problem, a quality which enhanced the plausibility of his work and the coherence of its structure. He had the sensitivity and breadth of Makkāwī's experience and shared his concern for the theme of art, the place of the artist in society and the vitality of artistic excellence. Like Makkāwī he saw the artist as a man endowed with the divine power of creativity, but encumbered with the trivialities of life and denied by a dull and unappreciative society. A deep fascination with metaphysical elements and blind inexplicable fate colours his stories with a pensive nature and a touch of the absurd and brings a strong element of melancholy into many of them.

SHADES OF TRAGEDY AND LOSS

A profound melancholy is prevalent in most of romantic Palestinian short stories, particularly in the early part of this period, and is always combined with a strong element of patriotism. The devastating shock of the loss of their homeland, the stagnation of their cause, the sub-human conditions in the refugee camps and the closed horizon before them generated sorrow and despair that naturally penetrated all forms of Palestinian literature. The main Palestinian writers of this vein are Maḥmūd Sayf al-Dīn al-Īrānī (1914–74), ᶜĪsā al-Nāᶜūrī and Samīrah ᶜAzzām (1927–67). Īrānī is indeed the Taymūr of the Palestinian short story, for he wrote prolifically and vigorously in an attempt to consolidate its position and implant its conventions firmly in the life of Palestinian society. The comparison between the works he wrote before the loss of his country and those written afterwards reveals the nature and extent of the transformation in the Palestinians' perception of themselves, their national identity and their future. His last two collections are devoted almost entirely to the problematic existence of the uprooted Palestinians and their tragic conditions: they live on distant memories of their paradise that they were forced to abandon. Al-Nāᶜūrī's stories unite the various political causes of the Palestinian tragedy with concern for the realities of their victims. But the most elaborate and sensitive treatment of the suffering of the Palestinians is found in the work of the most talented Palestinian writer, and one of the most competent female short-story writers of her generation, Samīrah ᶜAzzām, who died prematurely at the peak of her literary maturity and productivity, having published four collections in less than fifteen years.

Samīrah ᶜAzzām is the leading woman writer of this romantic trend; some of her counterparts in Egypt and Syria such as Ṣūfi ᶜAbdullah (b. 1925), Najībah al-ᶜAssāl (b. 1921), Jābhibiyyah Ṣidqī (b. 1927), Widād Sakākīnī, Nawāl al-Saᶜdāwī (b. 1930) and Ulfat ᶜUmar al-Īdlibī may be more productive but only a few of them attain her density and vigour. The excessive idealization of the past in her work enhances the prevalent sense of gloom and pessimism. However, in many of her stories the devastating sense of indignation leads the characters to undertake quixotic acts, born of good intention, which bring about self-destruction and so tighten the grip of the tragic events around the character. Her themes are of a predominantly romantic nature in which the conflict is always between a highly sensitive soul and a morbid, traumatic context which the character fails either to accept or to change. She succeeds in presenting a coherent narrative which is mostly seen from a female point of view, whose confinement in space and by strict social conventions enhances the plausibility of the closed world which takes the situation in some stories beyond both the realistic setting and logical development into a world of dream and fantasy. This is occasionally enhanced by ᶜAzzām's poetic language and by her sensitive description of minute meaningful details. Her female characters are endowed with a strong sense of idealism which sets them apart from the rest of society and particularly from their male counterparts. They are sensitive, but socially naïve and highly vulnerable; armed only with their strong idealism they confront decayed social values and male manipulation.

In the Lebanon the major romantic short-story writers at this time were Nuᶜaymah and Saᶜīd Taqiyy al-Dīn; the former divided his attention between several literary genres but the latter was the most active and prolific Lebanese short-story writer in the 1940s and the early 1950s. His short stories endeavour to encompass what he saw as a major feature of Lebanese society: the divide between those who stayed at home and those who emigrated. Both share the strong love for the homeland and the desire to communicate with its beauty and social environment. The motherland is the main source of emotion and vision in his world and it has the power to hold the Lebanese in its grip however far from its geographical domain. As soon as the link between the Lebanese and their motherland is weakened this opens the gates of deviations and destruction. He portrays the life of the Druze community with nostalgia and a deep appreciation of its stern ethical codes and dignified and simple life. Divorce from the land by migration to foreign countries submerges his characters in an ugly, materialistic world in which money is portrayed as the source of all evil and the means of severing the bond between the person and his roots.

In Iraq the romantic trend enjoyed some popularity in the 1930s and the 1940s despite the declining production of short stories in that period. The main contribution is that of Ayyūb, whose early works have been discussed above. He was the major short-story writer actively publishing throughout the 1940s and 1950s. This period witnessed the peak of his productivity and was also marked by his active involvement in the political scene, a fact that left an evident mark on his narrative works. His main theme in this period continued to be social criticism, but his presentation and philosophical outlook remained predominantly romantic. He emphasized the patriotic element in a manner similar to that of Ḥassūnah, using his stories as a tool in the struggle against British occupation and for elaborating the various aspects of the political question. This brought him into a great deal of trouble with the authorities which in turn led him to use various literary strategies such as symbols, fantasy and foreign locations to mask his presentation.

SENTIMENTALITY: TWO DIFFERENT EXTREMES

The sentimental variety of the romantic Arabic short story took two ostensibly different directions: the escapist and the socialist. Romanticism's strong emphasis on certain aspects of human experience leads, in many romantic works, to a pervasive tone of sentimentality. So also does its conceptual approach to reality implying a tendency to beautify, perfect and glorify and an inclination towards exaggeration, a rich source of sentimentality. The success, even prevalence, of sentimental works hindered the process of the artistic development of the Arabic short story and encouraged the dilettante and the careless. Yet it played a significant role in popularizing the genre and familiarizing the wider reading public with its conventions, especially in the 1930s when good works of fiction were few and far between.

In Egypt Maḥmūd Kāmil (b. 1906) is an important figure in the history of the Arabic short story because it is largely to him that the new literary genre owes not only its success and popularity throughout the 1930s and the early 1940s, but also a great deal of the respectability which it earned amongst both readers and writers. He was a successful lawyer who in 1932 launched *al-Jāmiʿah*, the first successful popular magazine devoted to and deriving its success, indeed its *raison d'être*, from fiction. The success of his magazine in general and his works in particular led to the foundation of a publishing house in 1937 and the publication of a new bi-weekly to cope with the thriving narrative business. Ironically he is now little remembered and when his works are mentioned serious critics and highbrow intellectuals treat them with disdain for he is the father of the sentimental short story. He peopled his world with middle- and upper-class characters eschewing their social problems to concentrate on their emotional and moral ones. Hence love is the major theme in his world, many of the stories presenting it as an unattainable dream associated with sweet music, refined thoughts and poetry. Kāmil combines his attack on decaying social norms with a call for the emancipation of women. In many stories he presents women as helpless victims of the closed social environment, and particularly of man's inability to appreciate their situation or realise the extent of the cultural changes they have undergone. Another corollary theme is the conflict between European and Egyptian life and ideals which is presented in almost the same terms as the urban–rural conflict. European, and particularly Parisian, life is painted with a great deal of nostalgia and reverence as a paradise of civility, culture and art.

Although Kāmil was the most popular figure among the writers of sentimental short stories throughout the 1930s and much of the 1940s, there are other writers who deserve mention, such as Ḥabīb Tawfīq (1909–74), Ībrāhīm Ḥusayn al-ᶜAqqād (1910–83), Amīn Yūsuf Ghurāb (1911–70) and later Tharwat Abāẓah (b. 1926), amongst others. Some of them continued to produce Kāmil-like works in which sentimentality is blended with romantic and didactic elements, and on rare occasions with a faint realistic flavour. Others, such as Yūsuf al-Sibāᶜī (1917–78), Muḥammad ᶜAbd al-Ḥalīm ᶜAbdullah (1913–71), Iḥsān ᶜAbd al-Quddūs (1919–90), Ībrāhīm al-Wirdānī (1919–91) and Jādhibiyyah Ṣidqī (b. 1927), tried to keep Kāmil's sentimentality alive, not by the mere reproduction of his themes, techniques and characters but by developing the escapist elements in his work and amalgamating them with either social or idyllic details.

The Palestinian followers of Kāmil are numerous (ᶜAbd al-Ḥamīd Yāsīn (1908–75), Nabīl al-Khūrī, Muḥammad Adīb al-ᶜĀmirī (b. 1907) and Īsā al-Nāᶜūrī) as are the Syrians (Murād al-Sibāᶜī (b. 1914), Waṣfī al-Bunnī (1915–83), Muḥammad ᶜAlī Shalaq (b. 1915), Widād Sakākīnī (1918–86), Salmā al-Ḥaffār al-Kuzbarī (b. 1922), Iskandar Lūqā (b. 1929) and ᶜAbd al-ᶜAzīz Hilāl (b. 1933)), the Lebanese (Khalīl Hindāwī (1905–76) and Nasīb Nimr (b. 1925)) and the Iraqis (Jaᶜfar al-Khalīlī (b. 1908), Mīr Baṣrī (b. 1911), Shālūm Darwīsh (b. 1913) and Idmūn Ṣabrī (1921–75)). The work of all these writers attained significant popularity and diverted the attention of the reading public from more serious writings being produced at the time. The spread and apparent popularity of these works made the task of the more serious writers more difficult, for they had to deal with the twofold problem of uprooting sloppy and false concepts about the short story, then establishing new adequate ones.

SOCIALIST ROMANTICISM: THE DREAMS OF THE POOR

The second variety of sentimental short story is the socialistic strand which appeared as a reaction to the prevalence of middle-class ideals and the escapist sentimental short stories of the 1940s. This strand is known in modern Arabic literature as 'socialist realism'. It appeared within the context of the unique amalgam of revolutionary fervour and overt optimism of the late 1940s and the early 1950s with the attainment of the long-sought independence and the change of political regimes. Indeed, the emergence of the conception of socialist realism is a corollary to the dissemination of revolutionary ideas and is strongly associated with Marxist ideology, which had its heyday in the Arab world in the 1950s. Both the theory and the practice of this literary doctrine are advocated by Marxist writers, who were obviously under the influence of Soviet thought and literature. The exponents of this type of writing conceived of the development of society in terms of a battle for the future through a revolutionary class struggle, in which the writer, under the guidance of the party, becomes the artist in uniform. So he is obliged to portray what is positive and reveal and condemn the imperfections that hinder the forward march of society.

The term 'socialist realism' was coined by Gorky, who had in mind a vague combination of realism and socialist romanticism. When the term came into use in Arabic in the early 1950s, the battle for commitment was in full swing. For those who made full use of the favourable atmosphere, socialist realism was synonymous with commitment, for others it was an expression of the steadfastness of *la littérature engagée*. Yet when it came to praxis socialist realism was a lax discipline which appealed to many writers in many ways and influenced numerous works. The influence varied considerably from one writer to another, for while some, such as Zakariyyā al-Ḥijjāwī (1914–76), Ībrāhīm ᶜAbd al-Ḥalīm (1919–81), ᶜAbd al-Raḥmān al-Sharqāwī (1920–87) and Muḥammad Ṣidqī (b. 1927) in Egypt, Ḥasīb al-Kayyālī (b. 1921), Ṣalāḥ Duhnī (b. 1925), Shawqī Baghdādī (b. 1928) and ᶜĀdil Abū-Shanab (b. 1931) in Syria, Muḥammad Dakrūb (b. 1929) in the Lebanon and Ghā'ib Ṭiᶜmah Firmān, Mahdī ᶜĪsā al-Ṣaqr and ᶜAbd al-Razzāq al-Shaykh ᶜAlī in Iraq fell heavily under its spell, others, such as ᶜAbd al-Raḥmān al-Khamīsī (1919–87), Aḥmad Rushdī Ṣāliḥ (1920–82) and Maḥmūd al-Saᶜdanī (b. 1925) in Egypt, Ṣidqī Ismāᶜīl (1924–72), Ḥannā Mīnah (b. 1924), Adīb Naḥawī (b. 1924) and Saᶜīd Ḥūrāniyyah (b. 1929) in Syria and Shākir Khiṣbāk, ᶜAbd al-Razzāq al-Shaykh ᶜAlī, Dhū'l-Nūn Ayyūb and Nizār Salīm in Iraq were only partially influenced by it. In addition many tenets of socialist realism, especially those with romantic connotations, can be easily detected in the work of other writers. Yet this influence, whether total or partial, was short lived. For after sweeping through Arabic literature in the 1950s it waned and by the middle of the 1960s had almost died out, but not before leaving a lasting impact on the development of some literary genres.

Since the product of this romantic strand is relatively homogeneous in its vision and form, it suffices to deal with only a few of the founders of this large literary battalion. One of the major writers of this socialist strand is al-Sharqāwī, who started his literary career as a Marxist writer and ended closer to Islam. His first collection, *Arḍ al-maᶜrakah* ('The battlefield'), appeared in 1953 and was shortly followed by his second in 1956. In these two collections, he laid the foundation for Arabic socialist romanticism in prose fiction, and although he stopped writing short stories after the publication of his second collection, the socialist romantic vein remains noticeable in his subsequent writings. This vein strikes a genuine chord in al-Sharqāwī's temperament, and he succeeds in interweaving socialist romanticism with a strong sense of history, a sense which he cherished and developed throughout his literary career. In his first collection, as the title accurately states, the prevalent theme is the people's resistance to all forms of social and political oppression, while that of the second collection, *Aḥlām ṣaghīrah* ('Small dreams'), is the hope of the oppressed and the underdogs for a better future, the means of transforming their dreams into reality.

Another major writer of this strand is Muḥammad Ṣidqī, who was the first self-taught Egyptian worker to write literature to any significant extent. He had a Gorky-like upbringing, hence he was qualified to develop the early socialist romantic qualities which al-Sharqāwī's works had presented. Indeed it is not mere coincidence that his first collection appeared hard on the heels of al-Sharqāwī's second and last collection. Nor is it coincidence that his first collection was enthusiastically introduced by the ardent exponent of socialist romantic doctrine in Egypt at the time, Maḥmūd Amīn al-ᶜĀlim. Ṣidqī's work takes the pioneering achievement of al-Sharqāwī as its departure point, elaborates on its views and discoveries, and widens their applications and implications. He carried socialist romantic writing almost to its pinnacle, for he developed both the positive and the negative aspects of this literary vein to their limits. He emphasized, through his presentation of conceptually controlled reality, the suffering of the underprivileged and the agony of poverty, and described them in extended scenes.

In Syria, the brothers Mawāhib (b. 1919) and Ḥasīb Kayyālī (b. 1921) are two more of this battalion who brought the narrative of everyday life into the realm of the short story. Their stories were filled with extremely poor people suffering from the evils of social disparity and exploitation, yet full of optimism and a strong desire to change their situation. Unrealistically, the poor illiterate characters are armed with highly elaborate and well-articulated views which are evidently those of the authors. Ḥasib's work was distinguished by its strong sense of humour and by its resort to the structural irony that illuminates the situation from inside rather than from outside, while his brother's work was extremely parochial and tinged with sentimentality. The language of narrative in most of the works of this vein tends towards the simple and uses a great number of spoken idioms. In some of these works the use of the vernacular was confused with the viewpoint of the simple folk, and one of its exponents in Egypt, Badr Nashʾat (b. 1927), wrote his short stories solely in the colloquial using it in both dialogue and narrative presentation.

Socialist romanticism began to disappear in the early 1960s. This was not the result of a calculated decision, nor the failure of its social project which was more a dream than a carefully planned programme, but ironically as a consequence of a political blow. For by 1960 most of its writers were imprisoned throughout the Arab world, and when they were released, a few years later, everything was changing. Socialist romanticism was falling out of favour, even in Russia itself, and a new artistic sensibility was developing, more faithful both to the spirit of the early founders of the genre and to the complex and changing realities of the Arab world. Yet a few writers continued to tread the old path, while others, including their leading critic, al-ʿĀlim, tried to comprehend the new sensibility and adapt to its modern features and requirements. But none of the leading writers of socialist romanticism succeeded in surviving the radical changes of the modern sensibility, for artistically it was a very demanding one.

THE REALISTIC SHORT STORY

This study does not use the term realism as a period concept, not only because of the coexistence of realism and romanticism throughout the period under discussion, but also because realism in the Arabic short story is not a school or movement. It knows no theoretical programme or manifesto. Its range is wide, encompassing all the main forms of the short story, from the social and regional to the idyllic, humorous, lyrical and psychological, and there are no common links, philosophical, cultural or even personal, amongst those who produced what this study terms the realistic short story, apart from their artistic approach. The dynamic nature of reality demands an equally dynamic literary form to express its diversities. Realism, with its comprehension of this complexity and dynamism, provided this, for it dispenses with conceptual knowledge in its attempt to fathom reality.

In Arabic literature realism is also attributed to the rise of a literate middle class, the ever-increasing expansion of the reading public, the rise of rationalism, interest in the daily, the humdrum, and the contemporary in literature, the spread of the urban norms of life and the attempt of the new groups who were educated outside the old traditional system to dictate their own visions and tastes. It is also associated with the middle-class attempt to express itself in literature, and to speak for the lower classes – the peasants and the workers – from a moralistic and humanistic viewpoint at the beginning and from an ideological standpoint later on. The emergence of realism coincides with the rise of indigenous literary works which were at pains to distinguish themselves from the translated works or the sketchy adaptations of the earlier period. The novelty of the literary form, which was used as an excuse or a licence for artistic mediocrity, was no longer a valid pretext by the early 1930s. Not only had some of the pioneers in a few of their works succeeded in attaining literary heights, but also the rising popularity of the genre and the accumulation of original and translated short stories acquainted the reading public with most of the conventions and devices of this genre. The artistic sensibility of the second third of this century became less simple than that of the first, and tended, towards the late 1950s and throughout the 1960s, to be highly complex. These changes were in keeping with the Arab world's burning desire for progress in every field; the period was full of hope for a new future. The Arab realist, like his European counterpart, expresses his growing awareness of the contradictions of the age, not in radical representations of external reality, but in a poetic inward synthesis of the real and the ideal. He does not show the social and historical world as it exists objectively, rather this world is revealed as it is experienced and understood by the individual.

The contribution of realism to the development of the Arabic short story will be delineated through a critical investigation of the works of some of its leading writers, and any list of those writers, whether long or short, must start with the towering figure, the master of the genre, Yaḥyā Ḥaqqī. While the works of Taymūr and Kāmil received a great deal of attention and popularity, Yaḥyā Ḥaqqī's works, which are few and far between, were quietly making a major contribution to the development of the genre. He started writing and publishing short stories as early as 1926 and continued to do so until 1968, yet he did not publish more than seven collections of short stories. But the contribution of these seven collections to the development of the Arabic short story is by any standards an important one, not only because of their remarkable artistic quality, but also because of their highly acknowledged role of evolving the genre and influencing many short-story writers. Although Ḥaqqī was among the youngest of his contemporary writers, he was more aware of the importance of artistic criteria in creative works than many of them. This is evident both in his early critical writing and in his experimentation in form and style. He used a wide variety of techniques and attempted to explore new ground both in theme and in form, experimenting with form more than any of his contemporaries. The sparseness of his output does not imply any narrowness of his fictional work. Unlike most of his contemporaries, Ḥaqqī does not confine himself to the urban middle class or see the world through this class's perspective. In addition to middle-class characters his world is peopled with the poor from throughout urban and rural Egypt. Through these two realms Ḥaqqī touches the very spirit of Egypt and explores the undercurrents of Egyptian social life.

From the beginning of his literary career Ḥaqqī was aware of the fact that a good short-story writer needs to understand not only the subject, and the limits and the nature, of his characters, but also all the social rituals, details of life, sets of values and beliefs, traditional legends, tales, songs and proverbs, and pseudo-scientific lore about the weather, plants and animals that the character portrayed ought to possess, or the ramifications the situation ought to suggest. In Ḥaqqī's work, fondness for clarity is closely connected with contemplative elements throughout the narrative to demonstrate the perceptive insight and the quality of creative imagination which this writer possesses to such a supreme degree. His work is distinguished by its richness and uniqueness and unlike Taymūr, who imitates Maupassant, or Lāshīn, who was clearly influenced by Chekhov, Ḥaqqī does not fall under the shadow of any specific European writer despite his wide knowledge of European literature. Although he was fascinated by the racy descriptive technique of Thomas Mann and by Dostoyevsky's aptitude for the analysis of inner feeling, his greatest debt is to Egyptian folktales and oral literature with their simplicity, depth, vivid imagery and far-reaching effects. Ḥaqqī's stories focus on character and treat it in the context of the appropriate social milieu. Conflict in his story has two main strands: an inner conflict as well as a struggle between the protagonist and the outside world. In most of his stories the two conflicts are thoroughly interrelated, and each participates in the development of the other. This is particularly so in his stories about Upper Egypt where the tragic elements were interwoven with the rituals of everyday life and with the character's attitude towards both self and society.

One of the major attainments of Ḥaqqī's work is its ability to herald the change in artistic sensibility and to be always in the forefront of its development. This makes him unique among his contemporaries. Some of the stories of Ibrāhīm al-Miṣrī (1909–81?) exhibit certain of Ḥaqqī's characteristics, and the later works of Najīb Maḥfūẓ (b. 1911) in the genre of the short story benefit from his awareness of the necessity of endowing the short story with multiple layers of meaning which can assume symbolic value. In the early period of Maḥfūẓ's career, when he divided his attention between the essay, the short story and the novel, he produced very chequered short stories which oscillate between the romanticism of Taymūr or even the sentimentality of Kāmil and the realistic works of Ḥaqqī, without ever succeeding in attaining the artistic heights that Ḥaqqī achieved in the same period (the 1930s). Yet when Maḥfuẓ returned to the genre in the early 1960s, after dedicating the intervening period entirely to the novel, he brought to the genre the dexterity and coherence of narrative structure which he had mastered in the novel. But he failed to detect, let alone assimilate, the elements of the modern sensibility that had germinated in the short story since he stopped writing it. Only after the devastating shock of the 1967 Arab defeat did he become aware of these changes and assimilate some of these strategies into his traditional narrative edifice. He elaborated a set of imploding symbols which he skilfully interwove with his ostensibly innocent description. Elsewhere in the Arab world, the standard of the short story among his contemporaries was still far behind what Ḥaqqī had achieved, as in the work of Fuʾād al-Shāyib (1910–70), Michel ʿAflaq (19?–1989), Liyān Dīranī (b. 1909) in Syria and Shālūm Darwīsh (b. 1913) and the few works of ʿAbd al-Ḥaqq Fāḍil in this period in Iraq.

Capturing the essence of reality

But the major Arab writer of Ḥaqqī's generation who made a significant contribution to the development of the genre is the Lebanese Tawfīq Yūsuf ʿAwwād. The publication of his first two collections in 1936 and 1937 was a milestone in the development of the modern Arabic short story in the Levant. In these early collections one finds a mature literary rendering of the questions of daily Levantine life and the vision of the various strata of Lebanese society presented in economic language using a coherent narrative structure. His perception of the genre, expressed in the Introduction to *al-Ṣabiyy al-aʿraj* as the literary form most capable of capturing the flow of life with its multiple facets and conflicting concerns, enabled him to use it as a means of exploring the undercurrents of reality and expressing its complexity in a sophisticated artistic manner. Although some of his early stories are mere narrative sketches and are still marked by simple journalistic qualities, his more mature works are characterized by profound insight into the human psyche and the ability to present vivid and convincing narrative situations and delicate poetic touches. His sensitivity to detail and economy of style combined with his skill in sustaining the reader's interest and engaging him in the narrative stratagem through a carefully structured progression of the action and a convincing motivation of the characters provided his stories with a high degree of maturity without alienating them from the wider reading public.

ʿAwwād's stories integrated the genre into the major questions of his society which was torn between the harsh life of the countryside and the tragic problems associated with both migration to the city and emigration to other countries. The adherence to the land, its values and way of life is seen in his work as a question of honour and the only viable alternative despite the heavy price which it exacts; for abandoning the homeland opens the gates to disaster. Although the homeland is often seen in his work through a highly romantic concept of patriotism blended with idealization of its natural beauty and good-hearted people, the presentation of the rough life of its cities is profoundly realistic in its portrayal of the prevalent double standards of morality. Both the administrative and religious symbols of authority are exposed in his work for their hypocrisy, ignobility and meanness. His harsh criticism of vicars is reminiscent of that of the early pioneers of the short story in their portrayal of the hypocritical sheikhs. The association of both administrative and religious leaders with the old feudal lords in his work demonstrates a strong social awareness and a deep antipathy to the cruelty of the rich, whom he holds responsible for the suffering of the poor. He calls for radical social reform and strongly criticizes those who call for reform only to further their own aims.

ʿAwwād's stories are peopled with simple folk from the lower and middle strata of Lebanese society, but their simplicity is depicted with love and empathy for their condition in a manner that reveals the human essence beyond the specific traits of the individuals. He pays great attention to characterization; the majority of his characters endure difficult social or psychological conditions and are presented in a tense, complex and plausible situation which enables the author, despite his occasional authorial intrusion, to develop them and provide his action with strong motivation. His most effective works are those which attempt to illuminate deep human emotion, particularly love, to illustrate passion, innocence or compassion, and to record the rituals of simple life and strong human bonds. His interest in death as the culmination of the human tragedy, the ultimate truth and supreme arbiter, endows some of his stories with a metaphysical hue which imparts to them a philosophical significance.

Another major realistic short-story writer is the Egyptian Maḥmūd al-Badawī (1908–85) who started his literary career in 1933 by translating Chekhov's short stories, and in 1935 published his first book, *al-Raḥīl.* Apart from a descriptive travel book about a journey to the Far East, he wrote nothing but short stories, of which he published eighteen collections spanning forty years. This makes him the only Arab writer to devote his life entirely to this literary genre and to become one of the major Arab writers through the short story alone. His works break the limited circle of location and character type which, up to the middle 1930s, were conceived to be the main realm of the Arabic short story. His stories take place in both town and village settings. Apart from Cairo, he is particularly fond of Alexandria and the coastal towns, for the complex relationship between man and the sea fascinated him. The small provincial towns of Upper Egypt provide the arena for the confrontation between the villagers and the wonders of urban life, and for the villagers' sense of loss and bewilderment in the city. In his world the social barrier is impenetrable even if there is a blood bond between those who live on opposite sides of the class divide. Naturally the destitute who endure the inhumanity of poverty attract more of his attention than the wealthy. The gypsies of Egypt, who seldom appear in literature, are depicted in several stories with their special and fascinating values and way of life, as are the outlaws, tramps and footpads of Upper Egypt with their masculine, rough and somewhat heroically mysterious world, as well as the various foreign communities with their exotic life and eccentricities who lived in Egypt's major towns. One major theme in al-Badawī's fictional world is human suffering and endurance. Another is sex, which is closely associated with death and violence and is also an integral part of his investigation of the attractive–repulsive nature of the relationship between the two sexes. Since his first collection, he has tried to express the multidimensional relationship between sex and human destiny through a carefully interwoven set of imploding symbols. In many of his stories sex is a vital urge for life, is almost its essence, not only because it is a life-giving power, but also because it is a means of unfolding the human personality and the beginning of the build-up of tension at the same time. Through these associations and moods of presentation, al-Badawī succeeds in overcoming the taboo that is attached to the treatment of this vital subject in modern Arabic literature at such an early stage of its development. A third major theme is the interrelationship between man's action and what seems to be universal reason, the mystery of the unknown. Fate or destiny interferes in the development of the action not merely as a moral power which restores order, but often as an irrational power which strikes the most lively and leaves them in despair. In some stories the social nature of fate is more in view than its metaphysical one, especially when it is associated with external conditions and crucial events such as war; for al-Badawī's world shows the impact of the various major national events and wars since the 1919 revolution. Another recurring theme is failure and its social and psychological ramifications, particularly in the somewhat indolent and morally loose urban life of the city-dwellers. Through this wide range of themes and characters, al-Badawī widened the scope of the Arabic short story and illustrated its ability to tackle, in a subtle and artistic manner, the major issues of society.

The pinnacle of realistic narrative

By the early 1940s, the euphoria which followed the 1936 Treaty of Independence of Egypt and the Palestinian uprising of the same year turned to frustration and despair, particularly after the failure of the 1941 uprising in Iraq and of the attempt to expel the French from Syria and the Lebanon and the entanglement with the economic and political ramifications of World War II, the full impact of which was not felt in the Arab world until the late 1940s. Hopes of independence were dashed by the war and there arose a wave of popular anger. An atmosphere similar to that of the early 1920s, in which the maturation of the Arabic short story was accomplished, prevailed and was conducive to the development of the realistic trend. A seminal role was played by *al-Muʿadhdhabūn fī'l-arḍ*, ('The wretched of the earth', 1948) whose author, Ṭāhā Ḥusayn, was at pains to assert that it is not a book of short stories. The literary stature of Ḥusayn, the elegance of his style, the justice of his cause and the powerful emotions that he invoked compensated for the rudimentary structure of some of his short narrative pieces, and enabled this book to change the course of the short story by positing a new way of writing about the poor and vindicating such writings. The compelling tableaux of the life, sufferings and tribulations of the underdogs provided many Egyptian writers of the younger generation, at the time, with a strong sense of purpose and a literary direction to express their social and political anger.

This anger seemed to have found in the profound and highly productive talent of Yūsuf Idrīs its supreme expression. Idrīs's towering talent eclipsed that of his contemporaries, because his work is not only rich in form as well as in subject matter, but also abundant and constantly developing. He wrote and published his first five collections before reaching the age of thirty, at a time of great social and political aspiration. The publication of his early collections coincided with the dismantling of the old regime in Egypt, the evacuation of British troops, the declaration of the republic and the foundation of a new political order. Their main aim appears to be to put a set of priorities before the new regime and to shape the aspirations of the poor and exploited so that the new regime can act on them. The issues appeared crystal clear in this period and equally clear were the goals and identities of friends and enemies. This left its mark on both the nature of the narrative world and its structure. In this fervent atmosphere, Idrīs's stories became a significant part of the prevalent radical atmosphere. They aspired to be the voice of the underprivileged, the protest of the desolate poor against the literature of entertainment. They countered those tales which take place in luxurious settings, lofty villas, elegant cars and stylish surroundings. They also spoke against the fantasies of those who seek salvation through dreams of winning first prize in the lottery.

In his first five collections Idrīs did not confine himself to a limited number of themes or ideas. Nor did he restrict himself to a forlorn, marginalized or depressed group of people; he moved freely through the whole social spectrum and across a wide range of locations. The diversity of human characters is as rich as, or even richer than, that of his locations. However, one character type is dominant, the frustrated man, full of dreams and projects, often larger than life, yet unable for all sorts of reasons to fulfil them. His craving for life with its sensual pleasures is as great as the insurmountable obstacles which stand between him and his aspirations. He lives in a world which seems to be enveloped in a miasma of oppression, manipulated by failure, and suffused in insecurity and lack of fulfilment. To present this oppressive atmosphere of frustration, in which the character's dreams never come to fruition, without descending to crude melodrama, Idrīs treats his material as if it were part of a nightmare. The second major theme in this period is the conflict between the group and the individual, which reaches in some stories a high degree of sophistication and richness.

The second group of Idrīs's collections of short stories – that is to say, his seven collections which were published after *Ākhir al-dunyā* in 1961 – are marked by a substantial change in theme and form, despite a certain element of continuity. Just as his early works managed to infuse a breath of fresh air into the realistic short story and bring it back into vogue, so his later works play an important role in shaping and sustaining the modern sensibility. Most of the stories of this period deal with two main themes, the first being the central character's discovery of the futility and absurdity of the life he has been leading. This discovery, coming too late, places the character at the mercy of self-reproach and exposes him to censure, and consequently fills him with bitterness and despair. The second theme is the perpetual feeling of loneliness, a lack of fulfilment and security, of being the quarry in a mysterious pursuit. Another important change is the elimination or reduction of the element of claustrophobic nightmare. What survives of this early feature is only a tendency to preserve a pessimistic strand of gloom, for he now tends to water down the nightmarish elements and prefers to lean towards abstract structures and the use of a dream-like progression of the action which involves unrealistic images or details and a fondness for maxims. The third change affects his dominant character, who leaves his state of oppression or heroic failure for its complete opposite. He becomes an enigmatic and often miraculous creature, and those two qualities are neither rare nor confined to a certain class or group.

In terms of location and action, Idrīs accentuates the enigmatic, miraculous aspect through the confrontation between the individual and the group. Unlike the previous stage, the group is no longer sacred and infallible, rather it is stupid, hostile, immoral and submissive. It is an accomplice of the status quo and suppresses any individual who defies it in a world in which the dreams of the past have turned sour. The individual's reaction frequently takes the form of withdrawal from an outside reality that is oppressive, hostile, and increasingly incomprehensible. Although this tendency to withdraw seems to be in apparent contradiction to the new rebellious character of the individual, it underlines the pervasiveness of the corruption from which the individual seeks to escape, and imbues his rebellion with tragedy. Other changes linked to this are the disappearance of interest in the rituals of life, and the absence of the positive aspects of the patriarchal pattern of society. The stories of this stage are more concerned with structure and experimentation than the previous ones. Irony, both structural and cosmic, still constitutes the core of Idrīs's work. His previously intrusive authorial presence almost disappears, and he succeeds in omitting all undesirable preambles and in concentrating on the basic situation. There is the emergence of a particularly significant technique: a narrative time with its own autonomous logic, time with a unique duration, almost stagnant and unreal but possessing supreme authority over its dream-like world. Within this particular time Idrīs presents his fictional situation as if seen in slow-motion, a method which allows him to account for the minutest detail and to ponder over the slightest movement. He employs these new techniques and others to suspend the narrative situation in the limbo between illusion and reality, where dreams and facts interpenetrate and become complementary.

The proliferation of the realistic short story

Coinciding with the emergence of Idrīs and his generation of short-story writers such as Muṣṭafā Maḥmūd, Salāḥ Ḥāfiẓ, Lutfī al-Khūlī, Aḥmad ʿAbbās Ṣāliḥ and Maḥmūd Ṣubḥī, and in response to similar socio-political conditions and more importantly to similar literary needs, the realistic trend flourished in other parts of the Arab world. Particularly notable is the work of ʿAbd al-Malik Nūrī (b. 1921), Firmān, Nazār Salīm, Shākir Khiṣbāk, Muḥammad Ruznāmjī and Nazār ʿAbbās in Iraq, Ḥannā Mīnah (b. 1924),

Saʿīd Ḥūrāniyyah (b. 1929), Fāris Zarzūr (b. 1930) and Fāḍil al-Sibāʿī (b. 1929) in Syria, Shuhayl Idrīs (b. 1924) in Lebanon, and the Palestinian writers Amīn Fāris Milḥis, Jabrā Ibrāhīm Jabrā and Ghassān Kanafānī. In their work, the real pulse, spirit and particularities of life in Arab society are elevated to a common experience capable of illuminating the various aspects of the human condition. Apart from the many students of Idrīs's narrative approach in Egypt, such as ʿAbd al-Raḥmān Fahmī, Saʿd-l-Dīn Wahbah, Ḥilmī Murād, and Fārūq Munīb whose work replicated most of the achievements of Idrīs, these writers are the most talented among a large number of authors who participated in the development of the realistic short story at the time. We shall deal very briefly with one writer from each country.

Nūrī is the major Iraqi writer who contributed to the development of the realistic short story in the 1950s and brought it to a high level of coherence and maturity virtually unknown previously in its Iraqi output. By 1946 he had published his first collection, and in 1948 he was awarded the prestigious short story award of *Al-Adīb* monthly in Beirut which brought him, as well as the Iraqi short story, national recognition. His two collections, and the numerous short stories that appeared in periodicals and were not collected in book form, show a great deal of sensitivity and a constant striving to experiment and to develop the rubrics of the genre. Like Ḥaqqī, he manifested in his early critical articles a profound perception of the nature and function of narrative and treated his own work with a great deal of rigour and insight, for he was one of the few Iraqi short-story writers who read widely, in both Arabic and English, and brought his extensive reading to bear on his own creative output. His artistic use of language, which reveals the influence of major Egyptian writers, combines with a mature understanding of narrative structure which varies according to the needs of the situation and characterization. In his use of time he is clearly one of the early pioneers of Iraq, whose work certainly influenced that of his outstanding contemporary and friend, Fuʾād al-Takarlī (b. 1927). His racy description, which he occasionally succeeds in integrating in both the process of characterization and the progression of the action, is coupled with a skilful use of the cinematic technique of the montage which enriches the theme through dialectics of juxtaposition and the controlled rhythm of successive scenes, as well as the rudimentary use of the interior monologue or stream of consciousness. Yet the irony is that Nūrī used such sophisticated narrative to deal with the stock in trade of the realistic short story at the time, the issues of social disparity and marital incompatibility. His characters are alienated from their social surroundings by either oppressive poverty or excessive sensitivity. Yet in the most successful stories of his second collection he developed the use of the internal monologue in a manner capable of illuminating the inner life of his characters, and created convincing characterization and plausible action despite his use of feeble plots. He was strongly aware of the dramatic tension that permeates the narrative in successful short stories and managed to provide some of his successful works with a polyphony of language capable of providing each character with his/her distinct voice. The Iraqi literary movement's neglect of his significant achievement and his own strong sense of discontent led him to stop writing altogether by the end of the 1950s, a fact that deprived Arabic literature in general, and the Iraqi short story in particular, of one of its most talented writers.

Ḥūrāniyyah is the most talented writer of the large number of realistic short-story writers in Syria in the 1950s. He started writing in 1947 but attained recognition with the ascent of the progressive literary movement which culminated in the establishment of *Rābiṭat al-Kuttāb al-Sūriyyīn* (Syrian Writers Association) which later became *Rābiṭat al-Kuttāb al-ᶜArab* (Arab Writers Association) whose secretary general was no other than Ḥūrāniyyah himself. He was also one of the authors of the seminal anthology, *Darb ilā al-qimmah* (1951), whose introduction served as the literary manifesto of the new realistic short story in the Levant. Like Idrīs and his generation, Ḥūrāniyyah and his associates were riding on the crest of the euphoria surrounding Syria's independence and were eager to articulate the dreams and aspirations of the oppressed and the poor. His first collection, which appeared a few months after the publication of this seminal anthology, opened a new era in the Syrian short story and announced the birth of a new breed of writers whose patriotic love for the country is free from the romantic overtones of the previous generation. The conflict between the two generations is one of the major themes in Ḥūrāniyyah's work, in which the action is seen through the eyes of the younger generation whose views are associated with progress, freedom, rebellion and patriotism. He amalgamated the struggle for the freedom of his country with the wider pan-Arab dimension of the Palestinian tragedy. The nationalistic issue in his stories is clearly linked with the struggle for social justice and the importance of maintaining the dignity of the individual. He developed new descriptive strategy using nature as a tool that reflects the internal mood of the situation. His poetic use of language turns the short descriptive passages that present the locus of the action into a suggestive force which enables the surroundings to radiate with meaning and illuminate the reality of the interaction between the character and nature. Yet his poetic description was void of any sentimental or romantic connotation, for it succeeded in relating both nature and the locus of the action to the individual character as well as to class perception of man and nature. Ḥūrāniyyah's other contribution to the development of the realistic short story is his use of what may be called the dialectics of parallel structures in the development of the action. This is achieved through the presentation of two concurrent plots whose dialectical interaction during the course of their development enriches both and widens the scope of meaning in the story. Through his sophisticated technique many of the realistic details serve the double function of developing the action and enhancing its plausibility yet transforming it into imploding symbols rich in their meaning and connotations.

Ghassān Kanafānī (1936–72) was the most gifted Palestinian short-story writer whose prolific narrative changed both the nature and the character of Palestinian literature. He started writing short stories in the late 1950s, a fact indicative of the late development of realistic narrative among Palestinian writers whose perception of their tragic condition remained within the boundaries of romanticism until Kanafānī's arrival on the literary scene. From the outset of his literary career his main concern was the creation of a literature capable of expressing the complexity and intricacy of the Palestinian predicament. The search for what one may call the essence of Palestinianness is behind every narrative work that Kanafānī wrote, for it is clear that the project of his life was to change the Palestinians' awareness of themselves, their recent history, their tragic predicament and their perception of their own identity. Kanafānī depicted the plight of the various generations of Palestinians who were uprooted from their country, from the older generation who lived all their life in Palestine but were denied the right to die in peace in the land of their forefathers, to the younger generations whose main memories of childhood are those of the flight from brutality and persecution, or who were born in refugee camps and endured a sub-human existence. But the generation that took up the major part of his attention was his own generation whose happy childhood among their extended families in Palestine is presented as a paradise lost and who experienced in their teens or early youth the devastating shock of the loss of their country. Their education was interrupted and their national and cultural consciousness suffered unique and unprecedented scars that cannot heal and have no remedy. The quandary of their being is as much in their inability to digest the tragic logic of their abrupt transformation from citizens to refugees, as in their inability to accept their unjust present. Their suffering at the hands of those who displaced them is seen as only the beginning of a chain of endless anguish and tribulation.

In his attempt to illustrate their various endeavours at improving their condition, Kanafānī was keen to mirror the stages of development of the

Palestinian national consciousness from the passive resentment of their situation to the active quest to control their fate and struggle to regain their lost country. He sketched throughout his numerous collections and long short stories the diverse solutions open to the Palestinians and demonstrated that all lead to loss and destruction, bar one – going back to their homeland. Unlike romantic Palestinian writers who wanted to put the clock back and shrug off the nightmarish present, Kanafānī acknowledges the complexity of the situation and the need to recognize differences. This is achieved as much in the theme as in the nature of his narrative and its polyphonic language. He was aware of the importance of attenuating his language to assimilate the complex realities of the Palestinians, and of subjecting the form to the moods of what was being expressed and the demands of the theme. He experimented with diverse narrative strategies and attempted a new form of collection of short stories in which the book is not a mere collection of different and often discordant works in the genre accumulated over a period of time, but a unified work with an organic structure. In his collection, *ᶜĀlam lays lanā* ('A world not for us', 1965), the whole book investigates the various facets of the theme embodied in the title: the basic elements of life that constitute the normal and simple 'world' and are denied to the Palestinian, and the impact of such denial on the human psyche. Although this new form of collection exhibits certain weaknesses resulting from the supremacy of an idea over narrative technique, the harmony between the autonomous short stories compensates for such shortcomings and extends the horizons of the genre.

In Egypt, the work of Idrīs was both so powerful and so popular that it overshadowed that of many writers of his own generation, as well as some slightly older or younger writers. Shukrī ᶜAyyād (b. 1921) stands as the most gifted amongst the older, and Abū'l-Maᶜāṭī Abū'l-Nagā (b. 1931) as the most eminent amongst the younger group, which was particularly numerous and contained a large number of competent writers such as ᶜAbdullah al-Ṭūkhī (b. 1928), Fārūq Munīb (1929–8?), Ṣāliḥ Mursī (b. 1930), Ṣabrī Mūsā (b. 1930?) and Maḥfūẓ ᶜAbd al-Raḥmān (b. 1933). ᶜAyyād published five collections of short stories, in which he combines the sensitivity and spontaneity of the artist with the intellect of the literary critic. He endeavours to maintain the delicate balance necessary to save creative writing from academic dryness without sacrificing intellectual depth. He succeeds partly because he selects a number of his characters from the educated, even intellectual, class in a manner which justifies the introduction of intellectual and contemplative elements. He is ceaselessly fascinated by the effect of temporal human encounters on the life, views or feelings of man, and tries to explore and understand the mechanism of such encounters. The corollary to this fascination with unique relationships is his concern about distinctive and unforgettable memories in the life of the individual.

The appearance of Abū'l-Nagā and his contemporary Sulaymān Fayyāḍ (b. 1929) on the literary scene marked the success of the new literary forms which started as a break with tradition. These two writers were the first to emerge from a totally traditional (Azharite) educational background and this gives their contribution to the development of the Arabic short story a distinctive significance. The interaction in the former's work is between the individual and the group as a collective. The group in Abū'l-Nagā's works is not an ambiguous societal entity, but a collective hero, a distinguishable entity with specific social and psychological characteristics and with a collective reason which operates as if it has a single mind. Abū'l-Nagā had to develop a set of technical devices to enable him to illustrate the singular will of the group without obliterating its collectiveness or cancelling out its social or political implications.

THE CONTRADICTIONS OF CHANGING REALITY

The decades from 1960 until the end of the 1980s were radically different from the preceding period. They were marked by great contradictions and rapidly shifting realities, particularly on the political and cultural planes. They started with the euphoria of independence from colonial rule and the ecstasy of the collective pan-Arab dream, and ended with a number of civil wars and inter-Arab hostilities. The dreams of independence, industrialization and economic development soon turned into bitter defeat and the destruction of the spirit of opposition. The period started with the inter-Arab war in the Yemen and ended with the long and bloody Iran–Iraq war in the Gulf. In between it witnessed two major Arab–Israeli wars, the invasion of the Lebanon, two long civil wars in Lebanon and the Sudan, and a number of flaring regional conflicts from the Gulf to the Moroccan desert. It began with a sense of purpose and national self-confidence that gave rise to a significant literary output articulating these dreams and drawing attention to their inherent contradictions. One major result of this was the rise of narrative genres in parts of the Arab world that had until then made no significant contribution. From Bahrain and the Gulf to the Sudan and Morocco a new wave of short-story writing started to emerge and to enrich and complement the continuing production of the genre in the rest of the Arab world. The 1950s and 1960s witnessed the formation of an educated class for the first time in many parts of the Arab world. This provided the socio-cultural basis for the production of intellectual and literary works which began to appear in the 1950s and 1960s.

This coincided with the weakening of the old cultural centres in the Arab world and emergence of new relationships between the old centres and the peripheries. It also coincided with the change in literary sensibility in the old centres in Egypt and the Levant and with the emergence of modernistic narrative there. The embryo of the second change in literary sensibility was conceived in the heat of World War II and the loss of the Palestinian war that followed, and matured in the heat of another war – that of June 1967. Nothing alters human relations as rapidly and intensely as wars, for they shake the ensconced order and breed social upheavals, discontent and a sense of loss and estrangement. War can be recognized as the apocalyptic moment of transition into the new, not only because it brings about a new reality, but also because it poses crucial questions that often entail a complete reappraisal of values and culture. Apart from these wars, the Arab world witnessed during this period two major factors which played a significant role in developing this change in literary sensibility: the spread of political coercion and intimidation which had started in the 1940s and reigned supreme by the 1960s, and the introduction of new European ideas and modern modes of discourse. The former created a new reality in which the world becomes transferable and arbitrary, the latter deepened the writers' perception of this new reality and provided them with both a theoretical background that suited the modifications in the human experience, and the techniques capable of assimilating and expressing them.

The new literary sensibility, which was heralded by Nadīm at the turn of the century and was responsible for the emergence of the early forms of narrative in Arabic during the following decade, reached its apogee by the middle of the century and started to experience substantial changes in the old centres, at the same time that it was being picked up by the emerging cultural movement in the peripheries. Its early strengths and vigour, which attracted many talents in the Arab peripheries to the new narrative genre, had dwindled under the influence of sentimentality and socialist romanticism in the old centres, for neither was responsive to the many cultural shifts and social displacements which were taking place and which gave rise to a new and complex reality. Although the shift was gradual, it took place with great vigour strongly aided by the process of rapid urbanization in the Arab world. The ramifications and contradictions of this penetrated every aspect of social life, and the cumulative effects of wars and growing cities changed the writers' perceptions of both themselves and the reality that surrounded them. The vast and varied output of the Arabic short story in Egypt, Iraq and the Levant played a vital role in accelerating the development of the local product and justifying its relevance. The early works of narrative in these countries emerged during the heyday of pan-Arab nationalism during which the influence of the old centres was not only acceptable, but desirable. As a result, the pioneers of the genre in these countries had a much easier task in justifying their work, developing their language and educating the reader in the conventions of narrative. A study of the work of the pioneers of the genre in these countries demonstrates elements of similarity in their work and a homology between their pioneering efforts and those of the early period of the rise of the genre in Arabic literature. Their work oscillates between romantic and realistic narrative and attempts to root the genre in the concerns of the newly emerging semi-urban middle class. The major theme of their work is that of the impact of rapid change in social values and the radical alteration of the perspective of reality on the common man. The conflict between the country and the city in the stories of the old centres appears in their work in the guise of the impact of oil on traditional ways of life, or the clash between tribal and modern life.

EXPERIMENTATION AND MODERN SENSIBILITY

The works of modern sensibility in the traditional centres – Egypt, Iraq and the Levant – are complementary to the main strand of the realistic short story, not only because they adopt an artistic approach to reality (though their means of realising this approach are different and have their alternative set of emphases) but also because many of the realistic works are the forerunners of the modern sensibility, as we have seen in the work of Ḥaqqī. Realism is, indeed, a transmutable concept that can often include many features of the modern. Yet the radical change in outlook and in the artist's perception of the world was associated in the Arabic short story with the development of new technical devices. The search for a style and a typology becomes a self-conscious element in the modernist's literary production, for he is engaged in a profound and ceaseless journey through the means and integrity of art. The modernist search for technique is in its very essence a search for new meaning, content and experience. The techniques and devices associated with the modern sensibility drew attention to the autonomy of the fictive structure itself and not to that of the narrator, as was the case in previous works. The process of change towards modernistic narrative was gradual and was entangled with many other social, intellectual and political transformations.

The early pioneers of modernist narrative in the Arabic short story were a group of French-educated writers, whose works appeared in experimental magazines, some of whom wrote in French like Albert Quṣayrī and others, like Bishr Fāris, in Arabic. In 1942, Fāris published a collection of short stories, *Sūʾ tafāhum* ('Misunderstandings'), in which he includes works of a symbolic nature. Although Fāris developed variable new techniques of lyrical presentation of action, characterization and other narrative elements, the transformation of action to a fine pattern of rich and suggestive imagery reached its apogee in the work of ᶜĀdil Kāmil (b. 1916). Kāmil had stopped writing by the mid 1940s and is better known for his novels, but he wrote and published a few short stories, some of which are very significant for the study of the schism in artistic sensibility in the modern Arabic short story. His story, '*Ḍabāb wa ramād*', published in *al-Muqṭaṭaf* (January 1943), is particularly significant for its coherent structure and mature symbolism. It is a story of a symbolic search for an impossible dream of an unreal character whose world is made up of fog and ashes. The progression of narrative is not determined by the causality of external reality, but by the inner logic of symbolic association in which place and time are shifting, constantly modified and reinterpreted in the light of subjective exigencies.

Unlike Fāris and Kāmil, who were relatively isolated from the literary movement, Fatḥī Ghānim (b. 1927) was an active member of the literary coterie that established the experimental magazine *al-Bashīr* in 1948. He was also the most talented amongst the members of the group who experimented with the short story at the time. Ghānim's works are more experimental and less symmetric, with a host of novel techniques and devices, through which he develops alongside his main theme of the relativity of life and events the important theme of the lack of communication with its undertone of absurdity. Time and location lose their conventional nature, so action is deliberately situated in a world where time runs in neutral and space is stripped of its geographical or realistic nature.

PIONEERS OF MODERNISM AND THE RETREAT TO THE INNER SELF

The modernist works of the 1940s are, in a sense, no more than a prelude to the works of Yūsuf al-Shārūnī (b. 1924) and Idwār al-Kharrāṭ (b. 1926) in Egypt, Fuʾād al-Takarlī (b. 1927) in Iraq and Zakariyyā Tāmir (b. 1931) in Syria, which constitute the core of modernist writing in the 1950s and 1960s. The shaping of modern sensibility through their work took place side by side with the triumph of the older sensibility and at the same time was opposed to it. They were breaking new ground and developing a radically different type of short story that was largely ahead of its time. Shārūnī started publishing his short stories in a Lebanese monthly review while living in Egypt. However, he benefited from the upsurge of cultural activities at the beginning of the 1950s in Cairo and his first collection, *al-*

ʿUshshāq al-khamsah, ('Five lovers') was published on a wide scale in 1954, in the same year and in the same series as that of Idrīs. Yet he failed to attract the enthusiastic reception which Idrīs attained and his collection failed to affect the cultural scene in a way comparable to that of Idrīs's *The cheapest nights*. Shārūnī is not a prolific writer; he is a writer of limited but significant means. His work neither depends on the richness of feeling and texture nor draws upon a wide variety of profound experience; it rather relies on a carefully balanced and coolly structured edifice. His study of philosophy has left a clear mark on his thematic scheme and on the type of modern sensibility discernible in his work.

The craving for communication and the cherishing of solitude are two of Shārūnī's main themes which are both contradictory and complementary, for the conflict between them is an expression of wider and deeper conflicts between society and individual, the objective and the subjective, the outer and inner realities. His favourite hero, or more appropriately anti-hero, is a man tormented by his vision, whose knowledge and sensitivity put him at a disadvantage for he fails either to unbind or to protect himself from hostile reality. He is aware that he is ordained to live in a world that has closed around and before him, for he is forced to come to terms with realities that he neither understands nor controls. His nightmare, and the weak point through which fear tightens its grip on him, is his uncertainty which in turn is a symptom of submission to fear. The biblical phraseology of the opening of one of his well known stories, 'In the Beginning was the fear. All things were made by fear and without fear was not anything made that was made', is followed by an inverted Cartesian *cogito*, 'I fear, therefore I am'. He uses a technique that may be called duality of perspective, a technique associated with the treatment of the favourite theme of the modernists, the relativity of truth. Shārūnī created the first, most coherent world of modern sensibility with its distinct views, visions, techniques, characteristics, archetypes and modes of discourse. He succeeded in articulating many of the ambiguous fears and anxieties that had characterized the atmosphere of Arab society since the late 1940s and became almost palpable towards the 1960s.

Like Shārūnī, Kharrāṭ, who conducted a successful campaign of self-promotion and was able to attain more fame and influence than Shārūnī, is a Copt with a strong sense of being a member of a minority that suited him to certain aspects of the modernist experience. He claims that he started writing short stories in the 1940s, but he did not publish any until his first collection came out in 1958. He is generally a more complex writer than Shārūnī, for he explored in the 1950s many of the realms and visions which remained largely untouched by others until the 1960s. Unlike Shārūnī, whose modernist works are tainted by conventional graces, Kharrāṭ removes any form of conventionalism from his work and gives all themes and visions a clearly modernist and apocalyptic touch. In addition, his modernist beginnings, which benefited from the earlier accomplishments of Kāmil and Ghānim, did not stop him from developing his discoveries and maturing his visions particularly in some of his later works. In the world of Kharrāṭ, a man, although influenced by social factors and phenomena, is not perceived as a social entity but as a complex individual who aspires to assert his will and his existential being over nothingness and meaninglessness. His protagonist is an anti-hero, a hypersensitive creature whose constant surprise vis-à-vis everyday events strips the ordinary of its familiarity and renders external reality crude and illogical.

In Kharrāṭ's early works man is presented as being bored with his own life above everything else, so he naturally looks down upon those who live in harmony with life and submerge themselves in its trivialities. He prefers his solitude to communicating with, or submitting to, the banality of life. To articulate this complex stand, Kharrāṭ endeavours to provide his protagonist with exceptionally, and often implausibly, sharp insights and a comprehensive awareness of his surroundings. He is a seeker after meaning, who is forced to live in an unjustifiable way, the incomprehensible presence of which is conveyed through the dexterous use of language. The use of the passive mode in the narrative implies that many things are taking place despite man and beyond his control or comprehension. Hence absurdity, meaninglessness and fear creep in, and man loses his centrality and starts to doubt himself. In his later work, and after attaining some recognition through the triumph of modern sensibilitity in the works of the generation of the sixties, he turned his attention to the world of dreams and old memories in which the innocent world of childhood is mixed with hedonistic elements. Although many of his works are marred by his excessive linguistic or mere lexical investigations and overwriting, he succeeds in some of them in invoking old memories and restoring time past. Kharrāṭ's is a world of senses and feelings, perceived through smells, tastes and touches rather than through any rationalized precepts. As a result, the narrative becomes charged with an overflowing presence in a manner that tries to convey the power of the momentary existence of perceptible data by avoiding the frequent use of the perfect tense of verbs and concentrating on the imperfect and present tenses despite the fact that many of his works are told in the third person which is usually associated, at least in the Arabic short story, with the use of past tenses. The linguistic shift from the present to the past tense in his recent work is associated with a strong sense of nostalgia for time past and a certain recourse to some rubrics of traditional narrative. Instead of placing man in a universe of gloom and the characters in a nocturnal world, a world in which the interests in daily activities are minimal, the recent works are marked by their clarity, simplicity, stark feelings, mundane dealings and daily activities, and their action takes place mostly in the light of day. However, even in his earlier works, which show man leading a sheltered existence controlled by an inherent and unconscious yearning to return to the darkness, to the protective existence of the womb, from his solitude, his characters continue to view life with a great deal of affection and reverence.

Takarlī, who started writing in the 1950s and whose first collection appeared in 1960, became a landmark in the development of the Arabic short story in general and the Iraqi in particular. From the outset of his literary career he demonstrated a profound understanding of the nature of modernistic narrative and a unique ability to avoid excessive experimentation. He is one of the rare masters of narrative structure in the modern Arabic short story, preceded only by Ḥaqqī and succeeded by Ṭāhir and Aṣlān. His sensitivity to the dialectical interaction between texture and structure can be seen in his awareness of the motivations of every textual device that he uses. This gives his narrative a coherence of vision that penetrates every detail and remains undisturbed by the turbulent changes in the socio-political milieu that he tries to express. He encodes the details of his narrative into a chain of actions that constitute a well-wrought plot which is usually organized as a crescendo culminating in an effective dénouement that keeps the reader in its grip long after reaching the end of the story. This is so because most of his dénouements have an explosive nature which ignites fertile possibilities in the mind of the reader and leads him to explore the multiple layers of meaning in the text.

Unlike the alienated hero of his Egyptian counterparts, Takarlī's hero is completely integrated in the social setting and the temporal experience in which he participates, but like him, he is deeply enveloped in his existential concerns. His main theme, the investigation of the dark side of sexuality, would have provided another writer with an easy path to fame and excitement, but his dexterous treatment of the theme, and his concern for the exploration of its social undercurrent, turns it into a serious and complex issue. His bold and insightful exploration of the many facets of this theme takes the Arabic short story to new grounds, and initiates new methods of dealing with such complex and forbidden issues. The repressive values that control the nature of sexuality in Arab society are called into question, for they are seen as a senseless imposition that impoverishes the quality of life of the individual, while the various forms of lascivious and incestuous relationships are presented only as symptoms of more radical deformities. In addition to his treatment of sexuality, Takarlī has a full range of modernistic themes, such as the various forms of political repression and their impact on society and the individual, the brutalities of life and man's ability to act against himself, and the ability of simple people to cherish rich and complex feelings or to manifest heroic qualities which gives their failure a tragic dimension. In Takarlī's work the real pulse, spirit and particularities of life in Iraqi society are portrayed with love and compassion and are elevated to a universal experience capable of illuminating the various aspects of the human condition. His mastery of narrative structure led him to vary the form, technique and textual devices from one story to another, with a complete suppression of the authorial presence and the adoption of the character's vision, perspective and voice in each story, and the use of stream of consciousness with its two different manifestations as interior monologue or narrated monologue, a characteristic that he shares with the Syrian writer Zakariyyā Tāmir.

With Tāmir the stream of consciousness assumes a new life in its investigation of the area of expression which blurs the boundaries between rational and irrational, logical and illogical, intuitive and mechanical. For it not only aims at the displacement of the outer or external space by inner ones, but also attempts to draw a new map of reality in which fantasy and the labyrinth are not the opposite of reality, but its more accurate manifestation. Tāmir is the poet of the Arabic short story par excellence, both because of his use of lyrical language, dense and sustained imagery, allegory, irony and metaphor, and because of his ability to exempt his narrative from the common fate of prose as a simple transaction by perpetually withholding some indefinable remainder of its meaning, forcing us to come back to the language itself again and again. The poetry penetrates every aspect of the narrative, inspires its structure, liberates the action from the shackles of realistic plausibility, and suggests a new logic and a different order. The flight into fantasy in his work is a unique approach to reality in which the author suspends, even abrogates, resemblance in order to enhance the text's affinity with reality and its relevance to its essence. For what one encounters in this flight is a kind of compensatory imagination which sheds light on the nature of reality and its inhuman pressures.

With his unique background as a self-taught worker rising from poverty, Tāmir saw the shifting Arab realities of the 1950s and 1960s with fresh eyes, free of hypocrisy and, more importantly, free of the stale narrative conventions that stultify human experience and corrupt the readers' perception of reality. This fresh approach combined with the dexterous use of structural irony gives Tāmir's narrative a unique place in the development of modern sensibility far greater than that of the self-professed pioneers of modernism, for it was executed with innocence and simplicity that were multi-levelled in their seductive power to create new sensations, move dream and reality onto another plane of existence, and breathe new life into old forms and themes. It has affected both the temporal and the spatial dimensions of narrative and shaped an apocalyptic vision of a peculiar metamorphosis of reality. The five collections of short stories which Tāmir published between 1960 and 1978 constitute five different aspects of this metamorphosis, for each collection presents a homogeneous experiment.

The first collection creates both the narrative perspective of Tāmir's fictional world, that of the poor and downtrodden strata of society, and the domain of their experience: their dreams of an alternative existence and their quest for life, passion and pleasure amidst the harsh conditions of their present. The stories create a perpetual tension between dream and reality in order to shape a utopian world which is the counter-image of present conditions. The man who dwells in this tension does not suffer from the intellectual malaise of alienation, but from more serious and real neuroses which often lead him to explosions of rage and impulsive destruction. His yearning for material or spiritual comfort, communication and acceptance, or physical and carnal pleasures, is seen as an impossible dream; thus the shock of recognition often leads the protagonist to murder, which is viewed as the other side of the denied creativity. This 'creative' killing in which fantasy blends with reality is our entry to Tāmir's second collection, where it pervades the collection and assumes a multiplicity of meanings. It becomes a positive act of rebellion in which the extermination of a person is less significant than the concurrent removal of obstacles, limits, oppression and misery with the ensuing fulfilment and pleasure. It is an inverted act of creation conducted in an elaborately ritualistic manner with cold brutality and cherished violence, and like many violent actions it contains an element of absurdity and fate. The reasons for this killing pale into insignificance before the pleasures of the act, which is often carried out with a kind of consecration, emphasized by the use of folkloric and mythological elements necessitating the use of knives, swords and daggers which enhances the sexual connotations of the act. The third collection portrays a world of brutality and absurdity in which man suffers more from spiritual than from material poverty and is driven by his hunger for justice and freedom to the brink of destruction; irony, sarcasm and abstract presentation turn the story into a nightmare or a mythical narrative. In the last two collections, which have political connotations, man is seen as both corrupt and guilty, having lost his innocence since childhood, hence it is necessary to rewrite history and purge from it any trace of humanism or glory. The contemporary Arab man does not deserve his own history, particularly after 1967. In a world without history man returns to his animal self, loses his innocence, abandons reason and becomes involved in a crescendo of violence. The tidal wave of violence sweeps through Tāmir's narrative as an act of ritualistic ablution in blood, shocking the reader to the core.

Besides those four pioneers of the modern sensibility there are others whose short stories played a significant role in exploring some facets of this new type of discourse, consolidating or even popularizing certain aspects of the modern experience, such as Muṭāᶜ Ṣafadī (b. 1930?) and Ṣidqī Ismāᶜīl (1924–72) in Syria, Yūsuf Ḥabashī al-Ashqar and Ḥalīm Barakāt (b. 1936) in Lebanon, Jabrā Ibrāhīm Jabrā and Imīl Ḥabībī (b. 1921) in Palestine and al-Ṭayyib Ṣāliḥ in the Sudan. The importance of the role of the established masters of the genre such as Ḥaqqī, Idrīs and the later works of Maḥfūẓ, whose short stories are worthy forerunners of this discourse, in exploring new grounds with their innovative writing, cannot be exaggerated.

THE PROPHETS OF DOOM AND CONTRADICTION

The 1960s is an important decade in the history of the modern Arabic short story, for it is the decade which dealt a substantial blow to the romantic, sentimental and photographic approach to reality and rooted the modern sensibility in the literary scene. It witnessed the emergence of a new generation of writers and the formation of a new mode of discourse and a new understanding of the complex relationship between art and reality. This was also the decade in which the short story started to appear in those areas of the Arab world that had not had any significant narrative output. Despite the severe contradictions of this decade and the apparent lack of political freedom, men of letters enjoyed a relatively substantial freedom of expression even if their works contained a constant flow of overt or latent social and political criticisms, as did those of Maḥfūẓ. It was indeed a decade of paradox, for despite its heavy paternalistic atmosphere many opponents of the prevalent establishment became the pillars of its literary movement and enjoyed substantial influence and freedom. Some of them were even honoured by the very regime they continued to oppose. Maḥfūẓ is a strong case in point.

The young writers who started their careers in the 1960s and who are now known as the sixties generation encountered a difficult situation, for they shared with the 'established' authors their opposition to aspects of the social and political phenomena, but they did not necessarily have identical convictions. The conflict between the young writers and the older ones, especially those who controlled the literary establishment, is clearly associated with a significant development in the mode of literary presentation and the code of reference to external reality. Censorship led the young writers to develop certain methods of narrative codification to express effectively their critical views and escape the damaging effect of censorship. The new generation was destined to impose upon itself an extra censor, indeed the censor moved from outside to inside the creative process and became one of its components, for without this self-imposed censorship it was almost impossible to publish. Nevertheless the development of a new code and new techniques was both a curse and a blessing, for it alienated the work of the new writers from the wider reading public, unaccustomed to such codes and techniques and subsequently impaired its effectiveness but, at the same time, it eliminated didacticism and sentimentality.

As a reaction to the prevalence of sentimental notions and ideals and as an attempt to portray the disintegration of the individual self which is only matched by the disintegration of external reality, these writers gave substantial attention to sense-data and momentary sensory impressions through which persons or events emerge fleetingly from the stream and vanish again. The emphasis on sense-data and momentary impressions is closely associated with the feeling of an existence without essence which runs deep in the art and gives it a sense of internal strain – a certain terminal quality which reveals that it is attempting to reach towards the limits of language. It is also associated with yet another modernist phenomenon, the perception of the world as a prison. A large number of the young writers of the 1960s suffered as a result of their defiance of the established order: they lived through the experience of political intimidation or endured detention. Even those who did not experience such trauma realised that the contemporary self has discovered the strange secrets of all eternal prisons: that though doors are never locked, no prisoner wishes to escape; that all avenues of escape lead to the same cell; that nothing may really exist beyond the prison walls. The withdrawal from the world, which is the most momentous characteristic of the new anti-hero, is a recoil both into and against the self. It is a withdrawal into the self in as much as it explores the human psyche or, more accurately, the impact of grotesque reality upon man. It is a recoil into the self, because outer reality is absurdly cruel and any movement to alter it is futile and condemned to impotence, so the hero has no choice but to become an anti-hero. The idea of victimization is combined with a feeling of alienation and an implicit rebellion that involves a sense of revulsion as an attitude towards history. The plight of the displaced person and his isolation becomes a form of rebellion which aims to verify the existence of the anti-hero and his compatriots.

The sixties generation paid great attention to techniques and explored the limits and potential of the genre in an unprecedented manner, so that they could create, through their narrative, a new reality which was neither identical to external reality nor completely alien to it. At the same time, they use techniques that shed substantial doubts on the realistic data and make them appear absurd and unreal. The two complementary processes are sustained by maintaining interactions between explicit statements and implicit imagery, and by preferring subjective to chronometric time. The writers of the sixties were more conscious than their predecessors of the precarious nature of time. They were interested in exploring time and understanding the distortion of its logical sequence in a manner that was linked to the technique of the cluster of images which are deployed in a certain succession, in a stream of association which is a carefully plotted sequence, gradually piercing to the core of the situation without any detailed illustration of its composition. The internal logic of a modernist work of narrative does not necessarily comply with the strict order of outer reality nor with its chronometric time. Fictional time has its unique duration, which permits the fusion of times, of things remembered and hoped for, desired, or even feared, and allows the constant modification and reinterpretation of the whole fusion in the light of present exigencies, past frustrations and future fantasies.

The advent of the sixties generation is marked by tension and trauma. They appeared at first to be the prophets of doom in the highly optimistic world of the early 1960s and when their prophecy came true they were the first to suffer. The 1970s, which would normally have been the years of their flowering and wide recognition, witnessed their dispersal and displacement. Yet they continued to write, even if some of them had difficulties in publishing their work, and many of them reached remarkable maturity after three decades of continuous writing. By the end of the 1980s it has become clear that some of the most interesting and stimulating work of the last two decades has been written by writers belonging in one way or another to this generation. Although the odds were often against them, the powerful impact of their writing can be felt from Bahrain to Morocco and this made it impossible for the new writers emerging in the peripheries of the Arab world to avoid their influence. The most interesting phenomenon in this regard is that, unlike the previous generations, of which one can easily identify one or two major names in each country, there are numerous distinguished writers in every Arab country in this generation. This can be easily explained by the sheer population growth in the Arab world which more than doubled, and in the old centres more than tripled, since the 1920s, and by the wide spread of education and the entry of lower classes into the realm of literacy.

In Egypt alone there are at least ten prominent names of the sixties generation, such as Sulaymān Fayyāḍ (b. 1929), Muḥammad Ḥāfiẓ Rajab (b. 1933), ʿAbd al-Ḥakīm Qāsim (1935–90), Bahāʾ Ṭāhir (b. 1935), Ibrāhīm Aṣlān (b. 1935), Muḥammad Rūmaysh (b. 1937), Muḥammad al-Bisāṭī (b. 1938), Muḥammad Mustajāb (b. 1939), Majīd Ṭūbyā (b. 1939), Yaḥyā al-Ṭāhir ʿAbdullah (1940–81), Muḥammad Ibrāhīm Mabrūk (b. 1940) and Jamāl al-Ghīṭānī (b. 1945), each of whom merits as detailed a treatment as that granted to any of the major writers already discussed. This is also the case in Iraq and the Levantine countries. There the following names come to mind: Jūrj Sālim (1933–76), Walīd Ikhlāṣī (b. 1935), Nādyā Khust (b. 1935), Kūlīt al-Khūrī (b. 1936), Hānī al-Rāhib (b. 1939), Ḥaydar Ḥaydar (b. 1940?) and Ghādah al-Sammān (b. 1942) in Syria, Ghālib Halasā (1932–89) and Fakhrī Qiʿwār (b. 1945) in Jordan, Laylā Baʿalbakī, Ḥanān al-Shaykh (b. 1945) and Ilyās al-Khūrī (b. 194?) in Lebanon, Ghāzī al-ʿIbādī (b. 1935), Dīzī al-ʿAmīr (b. 1935), Maḥmūd Jindārī (b. 1939), ʿAbd al-Raḥmān al-Rubayʿī (b. 1939), Muḥammad Khuḍayyir (b. 1940), Mūsā Kirīdī (b. 1940), ʿĀʾid Khiṣbāk (b. 1945) and Aḥmad Khalaf in Iraq and ʿAḥmad ʿInānī, Nawwāf Abū-l-Hayjā' (b. 1938), Tawfīq Fayyāḍ (b. 1939), Yūsuf Shurūrū (b. 1940), Rashād Abū-Shāwir (b. 1942), Yaḥyā Yakhluf (b. 1944) and Maḥmūd al-Rīmāwī (b. 1946) in Palestine.

It will be noticed that the list includes several women writers to whom could be added others, such as Saḥar Khalīfah, Iqbāl Barakah, Alīfah Rifʿat, Nawāl Saʿdāwī and Samar al-ʿAṭṭār. In fact, one of the major contributions of the sixties generation is the large number of its talented female writers who participated in the development of the genre and widened the scope of its experience. They differ from earlier women writers in their strong awareness of their feminine perspective and their feminist view of the world.

Unfortunately, for lack of space it will not be possible to discuss individually, however briefly, the work of these important writers of the sixties generation in the old centres. Nor will it be possible to treat in any detail the ever-increasing importance of the peripheries whose literary output was, until recently, artistically and conceptually far behind that of the old centres of Arab culture in Egypt and the Levant. It is only in the past few years that the literary product of the Gulf, Yemen, Saudi Arabia, Sudan, Tunisia, Morocco and Algeria has gained wider recognition and has been thought not only to be worthy of consideration, but to contribute to the exploration of new horizons and techniques in Arabic literature. We shall have to content ourselves with mentioning the names of those writers from the peripheries, who are imposing themselves on the centres and challenging them for attention, such as al-Ṭayyib Ṣāliḥ, al-Ṭayyib Zarrūq (b. 1935) and Malak Jaʿfar in the Sudan, Muḥammad Barrādah (b. 1938),

Khunāthah Binnūnah (b. 1943), Aḥmad Būzfūr, Idrīs al-Khūrī (b. 1939), Aḥmad al-Middīnī (b. 1948), Muṣṭafā al-Misnāwī (b. 1953), Mubārak Rabīᶜ (b. 1935), Mīlūdī Shaghmūm (b. 1947), Muḥammad Shukrī (b. 1935), ᶜAbd al-Jabbār al-Suḥaymī (b. 1939), Muḥammad ᶜIzz al-Dīn al-Tāzī (b. 1948), Muḥammad Zifzāf (b. 1945) and Rafīqat al-Ṭabīᶜah (b. 1940) in Morocco, al-Ṭāhir Waṭṭār, ᶜAbd al-Ḥamīd bin Haddūqah, ᶜAbdullah al-Rikībī and Zuhūr Wanīsī in Algeria, Maḥmūd al-Masᶜadī, ᶜIzz-l-Dīn al-Madanī, Samīr al-ᶜAyyādī (b. 1947) and Ḥasan Naṣr (b. 1937) in Tunisia, Aḥmad Ibrāhīm al-Faqīh (b. 1942), Khalīfah Ḥusayn (b. 1947?), Kāmil Ḥasan al-Maqhūr and Muḥammad al-Suwayhidīn in Libya, Muḥammad ᶜAbd al-Walī, Aḥmad Maḥfūẓ ᶜUmar, ᶜAlī Bādhīb and ᶜAbdullah Sālim Bāwazīr in Yemen, ᶜAbdullah Jamᶜān (b. 1938), Khalīl al-Fazīᶜ (b. 1943), Muḥammad ᶜUlwān (b. 1948), ᶜAbdullah al-Jafrī (b. 1948), ᶜAbdullah Bākhishwayn (b. 1953), ᶜAbduh Khāl, ᶜAbdullah Mannāᶜ (b. 1938), ᶜAbd al-ᶜAzīz Mishrī (b. 1955), Ruqayyah Maḥmūd al-Shabīb (b. 1957), Muḥammad Manṣūr al-Shaqḥā' (b. 1947), ᶜAlī Muḥammad Ḥassūn (b. 1951), Fāṭimah Ḥinnāwī (b. 1949) and Ḥusayn ᶜAlī Ḥusayn (b. 1950) in Saudi Arabia, ᶜAbd al-Qādir ᶜAqīl (b. 1949), ᶜAlī ᶜAbdullah Khalīfah and Amīn Ṣāliḥ (b. 1950) in Bahrain, Ẓabyah Khamīs, Salmā Maṭar Sayf, Muḥammad Ḥasan al-Ḥarbī, ᶜAbd al-Ḥamīd Aḥmad and Muḥammad al-Murr in UAE, and Ismāᶜīl Fahd Ismāᶜīl (b. 194?), Walīd al-Rujayb, Sulaymān al-Shaykh, Sulaymān al-Shaṭṭī and Laylā al-ᶜUthmān in Kuwait. What they have published so far carries the tidings of a rich future full of promise that will take the Arabic short story to new horizons.

CHAPTER 9

ARABIC DRAMA: EARLY DEVELOPMENTS

TRADITIONAL FORMS OF DRAMATIC ENTERTAINMENT

In spite of several well-intentioned attempts to prove the contrary, classical Arab literature did not know drama as it was conceived in the west from the times of the ancient Greeks to the present, namely as an art form in which an action is 'imitated' through dialogue spoken by human actors on a stage. True enough, a specifically Arabic literary form, the *maqāmah*, developed in the tenth century, generally assumed to be the invention of al-Hamadhānī (969–1008): a tale in elaborate euphuistic rhyming prose intermixed with verse, often relating the adventures of an eloquent vagabond who ekes out a living by impersonating other characters and fooling people. It is a unique form, incorporating both narrative and dramatic elements without being either a short story or a drama proper. Clearly, out of the *maqāmah* grew the Arabic shadow play (*khayāl al-ẓill*), probably under Far Eastern influence, in which human characters are represented by shadows cast upon a screen by flat, coloured leather puppets held in front of a torch and manipulated by a hidden puppet master (*khayāliyy* or *rayyis*), who also introduced the characters and delivered dialogue and songs with the help of associates.

The shadow play, particularly in its earliest (and, as it happens, most sophisticated) surviving examples, namely the work of Ibn Dāniyāl (1248–1311), is the closest thing in classical Arabic literature to western drama, even though the actors are only puppets. Ibn Dāniyāl's three plays are obviously the work of a conscious craftsman working within the Fool literary tradition. In spirit and in some of their dramatic techniques they are not far removed from medieval western drama, from the Mysteries and Moralities as well as the *Sotties*. Although they have many features in common such as singing, music and dancing, and their interest in conmen, tricksters and the lower strata of society, they differ from one another in form and structure, ranging from the fairly well-organized plot to the loosely connected pageant of human types, but their characterization can attain a surprisingly high degree of sophistication and subtlety as, for instance, in the character of the unforgettable matchmaker Umm Rashīd in *Ṭayf al-khayāl*, who is a cross between Juliet's Nurse and Celestina.

The later developments of the shadow theatre, judging by the examples that have come down to us from the seventeenth century, show a marked change in spirit, form and language. Written in *zajal* (verse in the colloquial) and meant to be almost wholly sung, they seem to be the work of several hands. They are therefore closer to other popular folk entertainments that possess a dramatic element. These include the dramatic recitation from memory of popular medieval romances such as the Hilālī cycles by highly skilled 'rhapsodes' in public places like coffee shops, together with the *faṣl muḍḥik* (a comic act), a primitive kind of *commedia dell'arte*, which despite its crudity sometimes contained an element of social satire, as well as the rough-and-tumble Punch and Judy type of show, known as *qaraqōz*. Less of an entertainment is the religious passion play of *ta*ᶜ*ziyah*, in which Shiᶜite Muslims commemorated the massacre by the ruling house of Umayyads of Ḥusyan, the son of the fourth Caliph, in scenes or tableaux which combined crude symbolic props and all too realistic representations of physical suffering and grief. The *ta*ᶜ*ziyah*, however, should be regarded more as an extension of religious ritual than as drama, and it is more relevant to Persian than to Arabic literature.

Although traditional forms of dramatic entertainment never ceased to exercise some influence on the writings of many modern Arabic playwrights, they never developed into drama in the western sense defined above. The latter was imported to Arabic literature only around the middle of the nineteenth century. It is true that during the brief French occupation of Egypt (1798–1801) the French troops were entertained by French dramatic spectacles presented in a make-shift sort of theatre which attracted the bemused attention of the Egyptian historian al-Jabartī. As the European community in Egypt increased under the modernizing rule of Muḥammad ᶜAlī and his successors, the interest in European opera and drama grew and performances were given both by visiting foreign companies as well as local amateurs. Gradually theatres began to be opened in Cairo and Alexandria, culminating in the Cairo Opera House built in 1869 as part of the celebrations planned by Khedive Ismail on the occasion of the opening of the Suez Canal, with a view to having the first performance of Verdi's *Aida* given in it (in the event *Rigoletto* was performed instead as the former opera was not finished in time). It is clear that in such theatres the audience consisted of Europeans or the westernized local aristocratic elite who probably did not know much Arabic. However, it was not long before Arabic plays were performed even in the imposing Cairo Opera House.

THE PIONEERS (I) MĀRŪN AL-NAQQĀSH

The birth of Arabic drama

But it was in Beirut, not Cairo, that the very first play in Arabic appeared. This was the work of Mārūn al-Naqqāsh (1817–55), a widely travelled, prosperous and cultured businessman from Lebanon, who knew French and Italian. During a visit to Italy in 1846 he fell under the spell of the Italian theatre and opera, and in the following year he wrote and produced, in his own house with the help of his family and friends before an invited audience which included local notables and foreign dignitaries, *al-Bakhīl* ('The miser'), a play inspired by, but not (as was thought for a long time) adapted from, Molière's *L'Avare*. Al-Naqqāsh, who can be regarded as the father of modern Arabic drama, thought it wise to introduce his novel work to those unacquainted with the theatre by a speech explaining briefly what drama is and what his intentions are. In this speech, which reveals his awareness of the civilizing influence of the theatre, al-Naqqāsh said that he had deliberately chosen a dramatic form which relied upon singing not only because of his own preference for opera, but also because he was convinced that his Arab audience with their passion for singing would find the musical theatre more congenial to their taste. Encouraged by the favourable response to his endeavour, he went on to write and produce (also in his house) *Abū'l-Ḥasan al-mughaffal* ('Abu'l Ḥasan the fool') in 1849–50, then his third and last play *al-Salīṭ al-ḥasūd* ('The sharp-tongued envious man') which he performed in 1853 in a theatre which he had built close to his house after obtaining the necessary Ottoman decree.

Given that it was the very first attempt at writing drama in Arabic, *al-Bakhīl* is for the most part a remarkably competent work. Despite much padding the plot is fairly straightforward. Al-Thaᶜālibī is intent on marrying his young and beautiful daughter Hind to the ugly and elderly miser Qarrād because of his wealth. Horrified at the prospect, al-Thaᶜālibī's son tries to dissuade his father and to obtain his consent to marry her instead to his friend ᶜĪsā, the young man she distinctly prefers. The action consists of the successful attempt by the young people to get rid of old Qarrād and marry Hind to ᶜĪsā, in the course of which they resort to a variety of tricks and disguises which enable them to punish the old miser and to divest him of all his money. Surprisingly enough he eventually forgives them and the drama ends with all the characters singing 'Let this be a lesson to all misers', thus explicitly stating the moral of the play. *Al-Bakhīl* is a lively play, packed with action, intrigue and horseplay humour. The dialogue, written mostly in classical Arabic of sorts and in somewhat irregular verse, is meant to be sung to the tunes of well-known Arabic songs (as well as two arabized French songs), all carefully indicated by the author. Some attempt is made to reproduce local dialect by making the Lebanese maidservant and those who impersonate Egyptian and Turkish characters use appropriate modes of expression. Beside the main characters there are a host of minor ones, together with a chorus. Some are given names denoting their dominant attributes, but not all of them remain lifeless: Qarrād with his comical antics is a lively caricature and Hind comes to life when in her attempt to scare Qarrād away she acts the part of the spoiled woman of the world. For obvious reasons the female parts were all played by young men in disguise.

In introducing much singing in his play al-Naqqāsh set his seal on the form much Arabic drama was to take, for singing was to become an indispensable part of Arabic plays for many decades to come. Al-Naqqāsh also influenced the development of modern Arabic drama in another respect. In his second play *Abū'l-Ḥasan al-mughaffal* he derived his theme from the tales of the *Arabian Nights*, thus setting an example which many Arab dramatists have been following to this day.

The plot of *Abū'l-Ḥasan* may be summarized as follows: the Caliph Hārūn al-Rashīd and his vizier Jaʿfar, disguised as dervishes, make frequent visits to the once rich merchant Abū'l-Ḥasan who partly through his own folly, partly through the dishonesty and cheating of his trustees, loses all his fortune and is deserted by the horde of flatterers and sycophants who used to live off him. The Caliph is attracted by Abū'l-Ḥasan's singing and amused by his gullibility. When he hears Abū'l-Ḥasan express the wish to be Caliph for one day to put the world to rights, he has him drugged and transported to the court, and with the help of his servant made to believe that he is Caliph in reality, hoping thereby to be entertained by the misadventures this foolish man is likely to be embroiled in in his attempt to avenge himself on his enemies. Into this tale al-Naqqāsh brings a love interest: Abū'l-Ḥusan is in love with the young woman whom his younger and more handsome and presentable brother wishes to marry and who reciprocates the brother's feeling. Likewise, the young woman's brother is in love with Abū'l-Ḥasan's daughter, and in the hope of obtaining his consent to their marriage he falsely assures Abū'l-Ḥasan, that he is trying to persuade his sister to accept him. After a series of complicated and amusing adventures in the court while ruling as Caliph, Abū'l-Ḥasan is transported back to his more humble dwelling, his mind slightly unhinged, unable to distinguish between reality and dream. However, the play ends happily with the two pairs of young lovers married and the Caliph making amends for the trick he has played on Abū'l-Ḥasan by giving him the slave girl he has fallen in love with at the court.

Abū'l-Ḥasan is easily Mārūn al-Naqqāsh's most accomplished play. Although written in a mixture of rhyming prose and verse in imperfect classical Arabic, the dialogue is not wholly sung, and the language is at times powerfully expressive, as in the colourful abuse exchanged by Abū'l-Ḥasan and his rival brother, which still sounds comical today. The two themes, Abū'l-Ḥasan's caliphate of a day and the love interest, are skilfully interwoven, even though the resolution of the complicated plot, which takes up the whole of the third and final Act, is exceedingly long. But it is in characterization that this play impresses us most, in the two memorable portraits, those of the simpleton Abū'l-Ḥasan, and more especially his servant ʿUrqūb, by far the liveliest and most consistent and amusing character, who, despite his age, is full of zest and vitality, a plausible rogue, prepared to plot against even his own master for material gain. His resourcefulness, vitality and charm are such that he has been compared with Scapin and the valet in the classical French comedy. Echoes of Molière's *L'Avare* can be heard in *Abū'l-Ḥasan* as in *al-Bakhīl*.

Molière's influence can also be seen in al-Naqqāsh' last play *al-Salīṭ al-Ḥasūd*, the protagonist of which is clearly modelled on Alceste of *Le Misanthrope*, but in which some traces of *Le Bourgeois Gentilhomme* and *Precieuses Ridicules* can also be detected. The plot is extremely complicated, involving intrigues and disguises, elopement in the dark, duels, a foiled attempt at poisoning, stealing and hair-breadth escape. In its essentials the story relates how, because of his unbearable jealousy and his sharp tongue and mean view of human nature, Samʿān, a handsome young man, gradually loses the affection of Rāḥīl, the young woman whom he loves, and who ends up by rejecting him in favour of a charming and generous rival. Despite Samʿān's attempt to poison Rāḥīl and her bridegroom with his gift box of poisoned sweets he is forgiven in the end as 'forgiveness is the best policy'. The play is symmetrically structured: for example Rāḥīl's marriage, which is the subject of the main plot, is paralleled in the subplot, which deals with the marriage of her maidservant, Barbara. Like her mistress, Barbara, too, has two rival suitors. Although it creates an effect of artificiality, this parallelism can at times be a source of humour, as, for example, in the scene in which Rāḥīl's singing about her love for Samʿān is echoed by her maid's singing of her passion for Samʿān's servant, or when the mutual recriminations of the lovers is parodied by the recriminations of their servants, in which language is used to suit the character and status of each speaker. Here, too, the author evinces his power of characterization in the portrait of the servant Jabbūr, who shares some of the liveliness and charm of ʿUrqūb in the earlier play, but more particularly in the character of the misanthropist Samʿān, a compelling figure with his striking mixture of cruelty and cowardice, pathological jealousy, unreasonable behaviour, self-pity and insensitivity to the feelings of others. Like *Abū'l-Ḥasan, al-Salīṭ* is written in a mixture of verse and rhyming prose and it is not meant to be entirely sung. It too suffers from much padding, with far too many moral precepts and wise sayings in its lengthy speeches, and irrelevant material inserted in the dialogue with no obvious dramatic function, such as the discussion on the theatre and al-Naqqāsh's own three plays.

After his premature death, Mārūn al-Naqqāsh's theatre was turned into a church in accordance with the terms of his will. His brother Nīqūlā published his works in 1869 and is recorded as having once produced *al-Salīṭ* for purposes of charity. But it was his nephew Salīm al-Naqqāsh (d. 1884) who continued his activities in Beirut and formed a troupe, which included actresses, and in a newly built theatre performed his uncle's plays as well as his own. In 1876 he took his troupe to Egypt, thereby setting an example to several gifted Lebanese and Syrians who were attracted by what they had heard about the Khedive's munificence and encouragement of the theatre arts.

(2) YAᶜQŪB ṢANNŪᶜ

The first Egyptian experiment

Before the arrival of Salīm al-Naqqāsh and his troupe in Egypt, an Arabic theatre had already been started quite independently in Cairo (in 1870) by Yaᶜqūb Ṣannūᶜ (1839–1912), a Jewish-born Egyptian who, like Mārūn al-Naqqāsh, derived his inspiration from the Italian opera. A precocious child, Ṣannūᶜ was sent in his youth to Italy to study at the expense of a member of the ruling house of Muhammad Ali. In Italy, besides mastering the Italian language, he developed a passion for the theatre arts and on his return to Cairo where he earned his living as a schoolteacher he took part in the productions of French and Italian works given by local European troupes. Because of his passionate belief in the civilizing influence of drama he was resolved to create an Arabic theatre. He formed a troupe of players out of some of his old pupils whom he trained to perform an Arabic play which he claimed he had written specially for them after having studied works by Molière, Goldoni and Sheridan in their original languages. He managed to arouse the interest of Khedive Ismail, who granted him permission to perform before him in a show attended by the court, several diplomats and local dignitaries. The play, the text of which is now lost, aimed at correcting European prejudices concerning women in the Egyptian harem and it involved intrigues and disguises and contained much singing. The favourable reception with which he met encouraged Ṣannūᶜ to reconstitute his troupe, including actresses in it, and to write more plays, which earned him from the Khedive the honorific title of the Egyptian Molière.

Ṣannūᶜ continued to write and perform plays (his own probably exaggerated claim was that he produced thirty-two) until 1872, when for reasons which still remain unclear Ismail abruptly withdrew his patronage and ordered him to close his theatre. Later on Ṣannūᶜ launched upon a career of satirical journalism and political activity connected with the nascent Egyptian nationalist movement, and as a result of his attacks on Ismail he was exiled in 1878, but from his exile in France he pursued his political journalism, publishing a series of dramatic dialogues full of biting political satire directed against Ismail and his successor Tawfiq. Although of considerable interest to the student of modern Egyptian journalism and politics, these sketches, which he called *Muḥāwarāt* (dialogues) or *Luᶜbāt* (scenes or playlets) do not contain much merit as drama: they are too brief to possess any dramatic structure, with caricatures instead of characters. However, interestingly enough, in them he developed a crude kind of symbolism in which recurrent characters stood for certain political figures of the day.

It is in his longer plays that Ṣannūᶜ made his contribution to Arabic drama. Apart from his last play, which was published in 1912, these were either lost or remained in unknown manuscript form until 1963, when Professor Yūsuf Najm published a collection of them, making them available to the student of Arabic drama for the first time. The collection contains eight works of unequal length: *al-Sawwāḥ wa'l ḥammār* ('The tourist and the muleteer') is only a two-page dialogue, poking fun at an English tourist's determined attempt to speak (very faulty) classical Arabic, and *al-Ḍurratayn* ('The two rival co-wives') in a short play, no more than a farce, which despite its serious aim of ridiculing bigamy relies upon cheap horseplay humour. Each of the remaining six plays, however, averages about half the size of a normal full-length play. They are all written in the Egyptian colloquial and contain much less singing than Mārūn al-Naqqāsh's plays.

The first in the collection, *Būrṣat Miṣr* ('The Cairo stock exchange'), a comedy of manners and intrigue betraying the influence of Ṣannūᶜ's European mentors, revolves around the rivalry between two suitors for the hand of the daughter of a rich banker, which results in the success of the good suitor, thanks to the intrigue of his agent/servant, and the failure of the wicked one, who is only after the girl's fortune. A comic subplot depicts the hopeless passion the humble Egyptian servant of the family develops for the higher-class European housekeeper. The play is in two acts, each of which ends with a song. To facilitate social intercourse between the sexes, the main characters are chosen from the westernized Levantine middle class. Although the characters are to some extent distinguished from one another, understandably the characterization is on the whole somewhat crude, the possible exception being the lively character of the Egyptian servant. By using spoken (that is, colloquial) Arabic in the dialogue, Ṣannūᶜ succeeds in making his characters sound life-like and distinct from one another. The money-dealers at the stock exchange are portrayed fairly realistically and their language is studded with Italian phrases. The Arabic of the Nubian servant is recognizably Nubian in accent. The author's satirical intent is clear: he points out the dangers of money speculation, makes fun of the foolish imitation of western manners by Arabs, attacks the practice of prearranged marriages, and condemns the prevalent contemptuous attitude towards the Egyptian lower classes. But despite its satiric content and its somewhat primitive technique, its inordinately large number of scenes and its excessive use of soliloquy, the play is a lively and amusing dramatic spectacle, relying for good measure upon some of the devices used in traditional popular dramatic entertainment, particularly the use of defective or quaint Arabic for humorous effects.

Al-ᶜAlīl ('The invalid') is also a comedy of manners, turning round the successful attempt of a young couple to overcome the obstacle in the way of their marriage, this being the mysterious illness of the girl's father. The events take place against the background of medical practice in Egypt, in particular the newly opened Ḥulwān Sanatorium. The play satirizes quack medicine and ridicules the foolish practice of parents who force their daughters to marry against their wishes. Much less satiric in intent is *al-Ṣadāqah* ('Fidelity'), a light-weight one-act play beginning and ending with a song, which is marked by Ṣannūᶜ's usual humour and lively dialogue. It is a variation on the Griselda theme, in which the protagonist resorts to a bizarre course of action in an attempt to test his fiancée's constancy.

Ṣannūᶜ's most accomplished plays in this collection are undoubtedly *Abū Rīdah wa Kaᶜb al-Khayr* and *al-Amīrah al-Iskandaraniyyah* ('The Alexandrian princess'). The former, a comedy of manners set in Alexandria, opens with a song by the black manservant Abū Rīdah, who complains in an amusingly colourful language of his desperate passion for the Nubian maid Kaᶜb al-Khayr. He confides in the mistress of the house, the young rich widow Banbah, who promptly promises to use her influence to further his cause. Parallel to this theme of the servant's love for the maid is that of the eligible merchant Nakhlah for Banbah, an interesting inversion of the more common dramatic practice of making the servants' love a subplot echoing the main theme of love between their masters and mistresses. Nakhlah's case is successfully pleaded by the resourceful matchmaker-cum-saleswoman Mabrūkah, but Banbah vows not to allow her own wedding to take place until she has succeeded in her efforts to bring about the marriage of her servants, thus providing a rather tenuous link between the two main strands of the action. Banbah's undertaking proves more difficult than she imagined because of the intransigence of the maid who is shown to suffer from the mulish obstinacy commonly attributed to Nubians: she agrees to marry Abū Rīdah only at the end when she sees him in despair, about to commit suicide in her presence.

Abū Rīdah is not at all the kind of work one expects from a nascent theatre: it is a skilful piece of dramatic writing which is well constructed and moves smoothly, with enough action to sustain the audience's interest throughout. We are given the necessary information indirectly, through a dialogue which is lively and exploits to the full the potentialities of the highly expressive colloquial medium. Characters are given the type of language appropriate to their temperament, sex, origin and station in life. Although Ṣannūᶜ still makes use of the popular traditional sources of humour such as dialect, mispronunciation and malapropism, he does not set out merely to raise a laugh by resorting to a facile device. The humour arises from the comedy of situation and character. In *Abū Rīdah* he has created at least two memorable characters: the Nubian servant Abū Rīdah and, more particularly, the matchmaker Mabrūkah, who is strongly reminiscent of the other matchmaker Umm Rashīd in the medieval shadow play *Ṭayf al-khayāl* by Ibn Dāniyāl. She is sly and materialistic, yet not without some concern for the welfare of her clients; because of her persuasive eloquence and her mature understanding of human nature she easily manipulates her clients to her advantage while giving them the impression that she is only trying to please them.

Unlike *Abū Rīdah, al-Amīrah al-Iskandaraniyyah* does not merely depict amusing aspects of the human comedy. Although basically a comedy of intrigue and impersonation, it sets out to satirize the blind imitation of the outward forms of western life in Egyptian society. It is perhaps the first Arabic play to launch a frontal attack on the negative aspects of superficial westernization, while at the same time benefiting from the dramatic technique of Molière in *Le Bourgeois Gentilhomme* and *Georges Dandin*. The action also takes place in Alexandria: Maryam, the wife of a prosperous Alexandrian merchant of humble origins, is a social climber and a snob, who forces her henpecked husband to agree reluctantly to her adopting the outward form of the French way of life at home, up to the minutest and most ridiculous details. She is totally opposed to the idea of her daughter marrying Yūsuf, a decent young man who is in love with her, because he is an Egyptian and a commoner, having made up her mind to try to marry her off to Victor, whom she takes to be a titled Frenchman on a visit to Alexandria, the son of a nobleman she had met when she and her husband were holidaying in Paris the previous summer. The action of the play consists of the attempt of the young couple to fool the mother and secure their marriage. Yūsuf pretends to be Victor, forges a letter of introduction to the family, pays his attentions to the daughter and asks for her hand in marriage, to the delight of the mother. Only after their marriage takes place does the mother discover the deception when the real French nobleman unexpectedly arrives in Alexandria, but despite her initial shock she gradually learns to accept the *fait accompli*.

The two pivots of action, namely the battle of the sexes (which the husband seems to lose until the final twist in the events proves the opposite) and the blind imitation of western manners, provide rich sources of humour. Moreover, the author shows considerable skill in the construction of his play: the opening scene which shows us the Egyptian male servant's ridiculous infatuation with the beauty of the high-class European maid adumbrates, in a more comic vein, the juxtaposition between the Egyptian and the European which is the main theme of the play. To maintain interest and suspense, the audience is not told until very late in the play of the young couple's plot. Furthermore, to add to the credibility of the events, Ṣannūᶜ makes the husband equally ignorant of it and allows him to pass comments on the strange course of action, comments which forestall any feeling of incredulity on the audience's part. Far from being primitive drama, *al-Amīrah al-Iskandaraniyyah* is therefore an intelligent work, which makes its point concisely and tellingly without ceasing to be entertaining. The fact that there are no songs in it indicates that Ṣannūᶜ has freed himself from the influence of Italian opera.

Ṣannūᶜ's last play, the only one to appear in print in his lifetime, *Molière Miṣr wa mā yuqāsīh* ('The Egyptian Molière and what he suffers') was obviously revised by him when he came to publish it some forty years after he was forced to cease his theatrical activity. In its published form it is a disappointing play, in spite of the light it may shed on its author's career in the theatre and the early history of modern Egyptian drama. Inspired by Molière's *L'Impromptu de Versailles*, the play deals with the difficulties faced by Ṣannūᶜ vis-à-vis his company of actors and actresses in rehearsing for a performance, depicting the efforts he made to establish Arabic drama in Egypt, the envy and hostility he aroused and the problems he encountered in paying his troupe. The play ends with the members of the troupe patching up their quarrel and getting ready to perform. As an account of the beginning of the Egyptian theatre it must be treated with some circumspection, because of Ṣannūʿ's notorious habit of exaggeration and possible failure of memory so many years later. However, it may shed some light on many points, such as the practice of putting on two plays in the same evening (which accounts for the shortness of the plays), the employment of actresses (Jewish or Levantine) on the Egyptian stage from the beginning, or the tendency to build up stock characters around members of the troupe, each of whom specialized in certain recognizable roles or types. As a play, however, *Molière Miṣr* represents a sharp decline in Ṣannūʿ's dramatic art. Apart from its loose structure, one possible reason is Ṣannūʿ's unexpected use of *sajʿ* (rhyming prose) for dialogue, which is probably due to the influence of Lebanese and Syrian drama (although he did use rhyming prose in some of his later short pieces published in his satirical periodical), or may even be a mark of atavism, since rhyming prose was used on a large scale in medieval shadow drama. By resorting to rhyming prose Ṣannūʿ denied himself the free use of his extraordinary gift of producing realistic dialogue which expresses the speakers' characters, a gift amply illustrated in his earlier plays. As a result *Molière Miṣr* is also weak in characterization and on the whole constitutes a retrogressive step in Ṣannūʿ's dramatic art.

Despite the gap of twenty-three years that separates their first plays, the two pioneers of modern Arabic drama, Ṣannūʿ and Mārūn al-Naqqāsh, have a number of features in common. Because both were influenced by Italian opera, they emphasized the role of singing in drama (albeit to different degrees and, as we have seen, Ṣannūʿ managed to write at least one play devoid of all singing). The work of both betrays the strong influence of Molière, whose comedies played a crucial role in shaping the early attempts at writing Arabic drama. The plays of these two pioneers are clearly indebted to the artificial comedy of intrigue: in their complicated plots servants and masters alike engage in stratagems involving disguises and mistaken identity, which provide a source of humour as rich and as popular as malapropisms, dialect and misuse of language. Love and marriage, money and greed, provide the themes of many of their plays. Where the plot requires the mixing of the sexes, non-Muslim characters are understandably introduced. In Ṣannūʿ's plays the main characters are usually Levantine Christians, while the minor ones such as servants and doorkeepers are Egyptian Muslims, be they Alexandrian, Cairene or Nubian. Another common feature is that both dramatists wrote only comedies or farces: however dark and threatening the events may look, their outcome is always a happy one. In establishing comedy in this fashion these pioneers determined the course of future Arabic drama for several generations to come. Few attempts at writing tragedies were to be made and these tended to be more akin to melodrama. While comedy developed sufficiently to cater for the needs of Arab society, tragedy lagged behind, the theatre relying in this field more on Arabic translations of European dramatists such as Shakespeare or Corneille. Despite their similarities, however, Ṣannūʿ differed greatly from al-Naqqāsh in both the content and the language of his plays. Ṣannūʿ's drama is more intimately related to contemporary social reality than al-Naqqāsh's, the action in the latter occurring either in a social vacuum or in the fantasy world of the *Arabian Nights*. Ṣannūʿ viewed his drama seriously as a means of social change. Partly because of this, unlike Naqqāsh he did not hesitate to use spoken (that is, colloquial) Arabic in his dialogue and, except in *Molière Miṣr*, he avoided the use of traditional rhyming prose. As far as the art of drama is concerned, no significant advance was made on the work of these pioneers in the voluminous production of their immediate successors, most of whom seem to rely heavily upon free adaptations of western drama.

MĀRŪN AL-NAQQĀSH'S FOLLOWERS IN SYRIA AND LEBANON

Translators, adaptors and actor/managers

Salīm al-Naqqāsh brought with him to Egypt, together with his uncle's plays, five works which he himself had adapted or loosely translated: *ʿĀʾida*, adapted from Ghislanzoni's libretto of Verdi's opera, *Mayy aw Horace* and *al-Kadhūb* based on Corneille's *Horace* and *Le Menteur* respectively, as well as *Gharāʾib al-ṣudaf* ('Strange coincidences') and *al-Ẓalūm* ('The tyrant') obviously inspired by European plays which have not been identified. In these works the dialogue, which was meant to be mainly, but not wholly, sung to popular Arab tunes of the time, consists of a mixture of verse and rhyming prose, much of which is irregular and unmetrical, all in classical Arabic. The speeches are more declamatory than dramatic: they tend to follow the conventions of traditional Arabic poetic genres of love poetry and martial boastfulness (*fakhr*). The characterization is poor: the lovers no less than the warriors express their emotions in the purely traditional idiom. The love interest is dominant in these plays, although the lovers are not always happily united in the end but, as in the first two plays, may die in tragic circumstances. Love is never portrayed in a realistic setting but, as the title of one of the plays suggests, it is often intermixed with a tale of adventure, improbabilities and coincidence.

The same combination of the dominance of love themes, the romance-like quality of events, the passion for singing and the desire to point out overtly the moral significance of the action is to be found in the work of the more popular Syrian actor/dramatist Aḥmad Abū Khalīl al-Qabbānī (1833–1902), generally regarded as the father of Syrian drama. Inspired by the Lebanese example, a product of traditional Arab education with no knowledge of a European language, al-Qabbānī began in the late 1870s to produce plays of his own in Damascus, but after an initial period of success and encouragement he met with ridicule and strong opposition from the extremist 'puritans' who brought pressure to bear upon the Ottoman authorities to force him to close his theatre. In 1884 he moved his troupe to Egypt, where he had an active career until 1900 when he returned to Damascus. Together with his own work, he performed plays by other Arab writers, ranging from Mārūn and Salīm al-Naqqāsh to Najīb al-Ḥaddād, as well as free translations of works by Corneille, Racine, Victor Hugo and Alexandre Dumas. He enjoyed considerable success, largely because his performances contained much singing, music and dancing at which he was eminently skilful. His own plays, which number fifteen, are either adaptations and free translations of European works, or original efforts based upon Arab and Islamic history and folktales, notably the *Arabian Nights*. They are all episodic in structure, with hardly any characterization, and their dialogue consists of a series of long speeches in verse. Among the most popular of the first category were *Nākir al-jamīl* ('The ungrateful man'), a play of deception and intrigues, murder and attempted murder, improbable events and the final triumph of virtue and *Lūsiyā aw ḥiyal al-nisāʾ* ('Lucia, or the trickeries of women'), which again celebrates, against the background of miraculous events, the victory of good over evil exemplified in the unprincipled lust of a woman and her male accomplice. *ʿAfīfah* ('The chaste woman') is a variation on the theme of *Geneviève* where the wronged chaste heroine is improbably saved and rewarded. In *Lubāb al-gharām aw al-Malik Mitridāt*, al-Qabbānī's version of Racine's *Mithridate*, the love interest is predictably emphasized and the tragedy is turned into a melodrama of love, treachery and war.

No less popular in their day were al-Qabbānī's plays derived from traditional Arab sources. *Hārūn al-Rashīd maʿ Uns al-Jalīs* revolves round envy and scheming, but it provides a happy ending for the innocent lovers, after a number of typical jail scenes which serve as an excuse for tear-jerking, self-pitying verse and much singing. The same folktale combination of love, adventures and improbabilities, with virtue rewarded in the end, can be seen again in other plays: *Hārūn al-Rashīd maʿa al-Amīr Ghānim wa Qūt al-Qulūb, al-Amīr Maḥmūd Najl Shāh al-ʿAjam* and especially in *ʿAntar ibn Shaddād*, where there is plenty of ranting and complaining about the pangs of love, but no characterization or dramatic structure: we are offered the world of the popular tale where wars are waged, fought and won in the space of a few lines and the whole play is no more than an excuse for a number of songs about love and war.

FURTHER DEVELOPMENTS IN EGYPT

Although as far as dramatic technique is concerned, neither Salīm al-Naqqāsh nor al-Qabbānī improved upon the art of the pioneers Mārūn al-Naqqāsh and Ṣannūʿ, they did contribute towards the strengthening of certain strands in the nascent Arabic dramatic tradition, namely singing and music, and the predominance of the theme of love as well as emotionalism. Of the two, al-Qabbānī exercised the greater influence. Because of his great musical talent he helped to popularize musical drama enormously and because of his more traditional cultural background, which enabled him to attain a greater command of classical Arabic, he played no small part in the establishment of the tradition, started by Mārūn al-Naqqāsh, of using the Arabic cultural and literary heritage, particularly the *Arabian Nights*, as a rich source of inspiration for Arab dramatists. Moreover, these Lebanese and Syrian dramatists/actors/managers and their successors and Egyptian imitators, together with their various splinter troupes, created a healthy sort of competition which led to the prosperity of the theatre in Egypt, thus making possible the rise of talented actors and singers such as al-Shaykh Salāmah Ḥijāzī, Jūrj Abyaḍ and later Najīb al-Rīḥānī, who contributed greatly to the popularity of the Arabic theatre. To satisfy the demands of the public, an abundance of musical plays were producced, adapted or freely translated from western works. Indeed it is to this popular theatre that the more important Arab dramatists first turned their attention before attempting, with varying degrees of success, to reconcile their more serious dramatic intentions and ideas with the needs of their unsophisticated public, dramatists such as Faraḥ Anṭūn, Ibrāhīm Ramzī, Muḥammad Taymūr and Anṭūn Yazbak. Even Tawfīq al-Ḥakīm began his dramatic career by trying to cater for the needs of this public. At the same time, because the theatre was becoming a familiar feature of urban life, it came to be used for political ends. In fact by 1900 Egyptian drama had become a political force of sufficient importance to warrant the banning of the performance of certain works by the British authorities for fear of inflaming nationalist feeling.

It is understandable, then, that it was in Egypt that the real developments in Arabic drama took place. This is not only because of the concentration of so much theatrical activity there following the arrival of Lebanese and Syrian troupes. In Egypt the birth of modern drama coincided with the rise and growth of Egyptian nationalism, with the consequent desire to create a specifically Egyptian literature in general and drama in particular to express the Egyptian ethos and character. Not surprisingly the first notable attempt to Egyptianize drama occurred in the field of translation and adaptation: ʿUthmān Jalāl's (1829–94) bold rendering of French drama into the Egyptian colloquial (verse). This was not just another example of the universal practice of adapting foreign drama to make it more palatable to local tastes, a practice known to students of comparative literature and easily illustrated, for instance, in studies of the fortunes of Shakespeare in France, Russia, Poland or India. The Arabic *Romeo and Juliet* in Najīb al-Ḥaddād's free translation entitled *Shuhadāʾ al-gharām* ('Martyrs of love', staged in 1890 but published in 1901) opens with an interpolation: Romeo, looking lovelorn and addressing the moon in a love poem, which answered all the requirements of traditional Arabic love poetry and which was sung in the mellifluous voice of the celebrated actor/singer Salāmah Ḥijāzī. ʿUthmān Jalāl's version of Molière's *Tartuffe* (*al-Shaykh Matlūf*, 1873), on the other hand, goes beyond the mere attempt to substitute Arab names for the French ones of the dramatis personae or to clothe events in a local garb. It is nothing short of a *tour de force*: while remaining faithful to the original French to a surprising degree, Jalāl's translation embodies so much of the Egyptian spirit that in it the reader is hardly aware, except in a very few almost unavoidable details, that he is reading a non-Egyptian work.

THE SEARCH FOR TRULY EGYPTIAN DRAMA

Faraḥ Anṭūn

The search for Egyptian identity became the guiding principle for the serious dramatists, who both in their critical utterances and in their practice emphasized the need for Egyptian drama to be related to local concerns and to be genuinely expressive of the Egyptian spirit if it was to be not only good drama, but also capable of performing successfully its civilizing function in modern Egyptian society. Faraḥ Anṭūn (1874–1922), one of the most highly educated and well-read journalists and men of letters of his generation, advocated plays with serious social messages, what he called *al-riwāyāt al-ijtimāʿiyyah* (social plays), that is plays which dealt with the problems and issues of present-day society, instead of historical drama or works translated from western theatre, or works written merely for entertainment, although later in life he himself was driven by financial considerations to produce musical comedies and historical drama as well as translations of western plays, ancient and modern. Anṭūn's main contribution is *Miṣr al-jadīdah wa Miṣr al-qadīmah* ('Egypt new and old', 1913) which,

which, although inspired by Emile Zola, deals didactically and in a somewhat transparently symbolical manner with several problems of Egyptian society, arising largely from negative aspects of westernization. It points out the need to maintain virtue and traditional values through the development of the strength of willpower, work, self-discipline and serious application, and to combat excessive and misguided women's liberation, as well as the temptations of gambling, drinking and sex provided by self-interested European owners of nightclubs. Despite several lively scenes in which details of Egyptian life are faithfully reproduced, the play is too didactic in tone and its characters, which are crudely symbolical, lack warmth and individuality. Because of the importance he attached to writing about contemporary social reality, Anṭūn had to face squarely one of the main problems posed by modern Arabic drama, namely the question of the language of dialogue, caused by the large gap that separates the language of speech (*ᶜāmmiyyah*) from the literary language of writing (*al-fuṣḥā*). Anṭūn's analysis of the problem is acutely perceptive; it is based on the commonsense assumption that drama is meant to be an imitation of life. He felt that whereas it is permissible to use the literary language in translated plays which are set in foreign countries and in which characters are not meant to be Arabic speakers anyway, the case is different in plays set in modern Egypt. Yet, in his reluctance to abandon altogether literary or classical Arabic, which he believed to be the sole medium fit to express noble ideas, he decided in his *Miṣr al-jadīdah* to employ three levels of language: the spoken for the lower-class characters, the literary for the higher strata of society who, however, use the spoken when conversing with the lower classes, and a reduced *fuṣḥā* or heightened *ᶜāmmiyyah* for the ladies of society to use among themselves. Anṭūn's cumbersome solution cannot be described as successful and may have contributed to the lifelessness of the characters. Fortunately it has not been followed by many dramatists.

Ibrāhīm Ramzī

Unlike Anṭūn, Ibrāhīm Ramzī (1884–1949) did not flinch from using spoken (that is, colloquial) Arabic throughout in his social comedies and satires, although he wrote the entire dialogue for his historical drama in the classical. Like Anṭūn, Ramzī was a well-educated man who obtained first-hand experience of the western theatre while studying in London. Ramzī was a prolific writer and translator, not only of plays but also of works in history, sociology and even science. Besides his translations, which included works by Shakespeare, Sheridan, Shaw and Ibsen, he wrote six historical plays, four social comedies and two serious *drames*. It is interesting to note that all of Ramzī's plays, whether historical drama or social comedy, are set in Egypt and they treat subjects connected with Egypt's past or present – a fact which clearly expresses his desire to create Egyptian drama. Of these only two will be discussed here because in them Ramzī managed to make a historical contribution to the development of Arabic drama, a contribution which is still not fully appreciated by historians of Arabic literature. They are the long one-act comedy *Dukhūl al-ḥammām mish zayy khurūguh* ('Admission to the baths is a lot less difficult than coming out of them') and the historical play *Abṭāl al-Manṣūrah* ('The heroes of Mansura'), both of which seem to have been written around 1915.

There is no doubt that *Dukhūl al-ḥammām* is the first fully fledged truly Egyptian social comedy. Set in a Cairo public baths in the poor quarter of Bulaq, ostensibly in the late nineteenth century, the play really depicts contemporary Egypt, and particularly the impact of the First World War on the economy and the hardships suffered by the poor as a result of the high cost of living. Lack of custom drives the despairing manager of the baths, Abū Ḥasan, to think of giving up his job and working as a hired 'official false witness in the court of law', which he sees as a more lucrative trade. To be able to do that he has to smarten up his appearance, so he thinks of disposing of some of the baths' equipment to raise enough money to purchase some new clothes. However, his wife, Zaynab, will not let him close down the baths or remove the equipment without his agreeing that first she should be allowed to try her luck in running the baths in his absence, with the assistance of the bath attendant, Nashāshqī, who is anxious not to lose his job. Soon after Abū Ḥasan's departure chance brings them a village chief (*ᶜUmdah*) laden with money after having sold his cotton crop, accompanied by his bailiff: they are on a brief visit to Cairo to pay homage to a high official. Attracted by the wife's singing, in their innocence they assume it is the voice of the most famous woman singer of the day. The main action of the play consists of the elaborate trick successfully played by the wife and the attendant to rob the village chief of his money, with the help of the husband, who has come back, wearing his new garments and looking impressively like a judge, in time to take an active and plausible part in the plot. Noting instinctively his weakness for women, Zaynab uses her female powers of seduction to get the ᶜUmdah to propose to her. When she falsely informs him that she must first get a divorce from her husband, who abandoned her seven years ago, they agree to go to the judge, pretending that he is her husband, suddenly returned and now prepared to give her a divorce. The judge (Abū Ḥasan in disguise) grants her a divorce, but orders the ᶜUmdah to pay her huge sums of money in the form of a delayed portion of dowry, alimony and maintenance for the whole of the seven years. The play ends with the horrified ʿUmdah, fleeced of all his possessions, only too grateful to be allowed to escape alive, and the tricksters singing that in such hard times the poor have to live off fools.

In *Dukhūl al-ḥammām* we suddenly meet with a surprisingly high level of sophistication in dramatic writing: for the first time we find an author providing full stage directions, including a description of the scenery which meticulously covers the minutest details. In this matter of full stage directions, which this play shares with his other works, Ramzī was influenced by Shaw, whom he had translated into Arabic. *Dukhūl al-ḥammām* is such a well-written, close-knit play that not a word in it seems redundant or out of place. Although it is supposed to take an hour and a quarter to perform, it is not divided into acts or scenes. Yet the attention of the audience is not allowed to flag because of the swift movement of the action. The events are so carefully organized that we are prepared for every turn they take. We are given the necessary information indirectly in the course of a dialogue which sounds spontaneous and natural. For instance, we are not completely surprised at the behaviour of Abū Ḥasan and Zaynab, because we are given early on a hint of their unscrupulous past. When he sees his master in his new clothes, Nashāshqī exclaims that he looks like the judge, so it is not unreasonable for the ʿUmdah to think he is the judge when the plot requires that Abū Ḥasan should pose as one. Trying to entice the reluctant ʿUmdah to use the baths, Zaynab skilfully drops the false remark that the judge is one of their regular patrons, with the result that the ʿUmdah is prepared to believe the lie that the judge has just arrived. Even the songs in the play, of which there are no more than three, are strictly functional: so far have we moved from the world of musical comedy in which dramatic action provides an excuse for singing.

Dukhūl al-ḥammām is rich in humour which arises from several sources ranging from word play and malapropism to character and situation, from traditional popular devices and horseplay to subtle overall irony. The ʿUmdah, who is almost pathologically and obsessively anxious to avoid the fate of simple country folk who are duped by the notorious conmen of Cairo, ends up an easy prey to the tricks of a Cairene woman. In the beginning, and as a result of his misunderstanding an expression used by Nashāshqī, he thinks she is one of the evil spirits that are reputed to haunt public baths. In fear, and to the delight of the audience, he tries to hide from her, but she reassures him that she is only a human being who means no harm. Yet in the end she does him more harm than any evil spirit is likely to inflict upon him. One of the most remarkable features of this excellent comedy is the memorable character of Zaynab: undaunted by her husband's harsh words, she proves an invaluable help to him. She is, as I have described her elsewhere, 'earthy and coquetish, shrewd and resourceful and by an unerring instinct she knows how to get what she wants; while remaining every whit an Egyptian and Muslim female, she is easily the strongest and most dominant character in the whole play' (M. M. Badawi, *Early Arabic drama*, Cambridge, 1988, pp. 84–5).

Despite its hilariously comic effect, the play never ceases to be seriously satirical, attacking various aspects of contemporary society: the war inflation, which drives the poor to resort to crime and deception, the miscarriage of justice and the malpractices of the courts of law in town and country, where an army of 'official false witnesses' are available to testify to anything for a fee, the absurdly mechanical application of the Sharīᶜah law, and the widespread phenomenon of the village chief who after selling his cotton crop would go to Cairo in search of a good time but would end up losing his money to the conmen of the wicked city – a theme vividly treated by Muḥammad al-Muwayliḥī in his articles, later published in book form in *Ḥadīth ᶜĪsā ibn Hishām* (1907).

Just as Ramzī can be described as the author of the first mature Arabic comedy, in *Abṭāl al-Manṣūrah* ('The heroes of Mansura', 1915) it can be claimed that he produced the first historical drama of literary merit in modern Arabic literature. Because the play deals with events of the ill-fated Sixth Crusade of 1248 by Louis IX of France, Ramzī, in accordance with his explicitly stated views on the proper language of dialogue in drama, chose literary/classical Arabic (*fuṣḥā*) for his medium. Since the characters came from either Islamic or European medieval history, the problem of producing the illusion of contemporary Egyptian reality by means of spoken Egyptian Arabic did not arise. The play is in four acts. Act I takes place in the royal palace in Mansura, shortly after the Crusaders had treacherously captured Damietta: the courtiers have been summoned by Queen Shajarat al-Durr, who breaks the news of the death of the ailing Sultan and asks their advice about their next move. She declines the offer of the throne and it is decided that, because of the war, it would be wiser to suppress the news of the Sultan's death until his son returns from abroad to succeed his father. In Act II the scene shifts to a farm in Faraskur, owned by Shaykh Bernard, an aged Frenchman, who has been taken as a prisoner of war in an earlier crusade, but who managed to escape and has been living for many years as a local farmer, outwardly adopting Egyptian ways while remaining loyal to his mother country. He has been acting as a spy in conjunction with Hibat Allah, the court physician, whose real name is Philippe and who, under the pretext of treating the Sultan, has in fact been administering to him the poison prepared by Bernard. The French nobility come to his farm before they proceed to attack Mansura. Act III takes us back to Mansura and the last-minute preparations for the war, which is fought and the act ends with the victory of the Muslims and the capture of King Louis. The events of the fourth and final act deal with the aftermath of the war, and take place in the palace of the new Sultan Ṭūrānshāh, whose autocratic and selfish behaviour has confirmed the fears of the nobility on account of his bad reputation. He falls under the evil influence of Hibat Allah, divests the Queen of all authority and attempts to destroy the power of the nobility, to whom he declares he is the sole ruler of Egypt. However, he is forced by the generals, under the leadership of Baybars, to make his apologies to the Queen, and to accept the fact that Egypt has changed, that the age of absolute monarchy has gone and that he must keep to the principle that he cannot rule without consultation.

The two main themes of the play are therefore the heroic struggle of the Egyptians/Muslims to drive out the western invaders and the successful attempt to curb the autocratic rule of the Sultan. *Abṭāl al-Manṣūrah* is, then, not a purely historical play without much relevance to contemporary Egypt. On the contrary, and as the author himself admits in the introduction to the printed text, it was inspired by deep nationalist feeling in the wake of the British Government imposing Husayn Kamil as Sultan of Egypt. That is why its stage performance was not allowed by the British authorities until 1918. The play is in fact pervaded by an intensely nationalistic sentiment: the treachery is committed not by Egyptians but by people of French origin, and the Muslim champions are often referred to not as Muslims but as Egyptians. Yet the author does not allow his patriotism to drive him to paint his characters in black and white. Not all the French are portrayed as vile, neither are all the Egyptian Muslim leaders shown as heroic or good. They are drawn primarily as complex human beings, acting from mixed motives. Ramzī's characters are credible and sufficiently distinguished from one another; this is particularly true of the three major figures: Baybars, Queen Shajarat al-Durr and the physician Hibat Allah. Baybars is the nearest dramatic creation to the ideal knight; no less idealized is Queen Shajarat al-Durr: in both characters the author deviated from history for his own dramatic ends. A more complex creation is Hibat Allah, a character invented by Ramzī: his evil may be somewhat exaggerated, but he certainly does not suffer from motiveless malignity: we are given sufficient facts about his person and his history to make his behaviour totally credible.

Abṭāl al-Manṣūrah is packed with action: fighting, spying, plotting and intrigue, romance-like elements, such as a daughter kidnapped in early childhood and restored to her parents as a young woman. The author even adds a love interest to make his historical facts more exciting. Yet the play does not strike us as confused or overcrowded; it is a well-constructed work in which the line of progression is clear, with few melodramatic surprises, since later developments are cunningly prepared for earlier in the play. Suspense is skilfully aroused and intelligently gratified.

No less remarkable is the dramatist's style. The classical Arabic of the dialogue is totally free from the artificialities, bombast and rhyming prose which characterized most of the plays hitherto written in the classical language. The poetic atmosphere is enforced by ceremonial and almost ritualistic action, such as the oath-taking scene in which all the noblemen together with Queen Shajarat al-Durr take a ceremonial oath by placing their hands on the open Koran with Baybars' sword drawn swearing to keep the departed Sultan's death a secret until his son's return to Egypt, or the colourful procession of the Queen, carried in a litter preceded by torchmen, flanked by the princes in the splendour of full armour. Ramzī even resorts to symbolism, as in the game of chess with which the play opens, in which a pawn checkmates a king, pointing not only to the impending death of the Sultan, but presaging the conclusion of the play in which the new Sultan is mastered by his people. Significant phrases, running like leitmotifs, are reiterated at certain crucial moments in the play, marking the political message the author wished to convey. Such complexity of dramatic structure as we find in *Abṭāl al-Manṣūrah* shows beyond any doubt that in Egypt modern Arabic drama has come of age.

Muḥammad Taymūr

Like Ramzī, Muḥammad Taymūr (1891–1921) set out to write specifically Egyptian drama. Taymūr, who came from a wealthy family of distinguished men of letters – his younger brother Maḥmūd became a leading Arab novelist and dramatist – was perhaps the most articulate advocate of the movement of the Egyptianization (*Tamṣīr*) of the theatre of his generation. He had developed a passion for the theatre while he was still a schoolboy in Cairo, but his views on drama became more sharply defined after a three-year stay in France, which came to an abrupt end because of the war and during which, besides studying law, he was a frequent visitor to the theatre. He was convinced that the primary reason for the low standard of the theatre in Egypt was that the serious troupes were anxious to put on translated European plays which could not be digested by an Egyptian and in which no Egyptian was able to identify his national manners and customs, believing that the public should be given instead plays which discussed popular current issues in order to derive useful lessons from them.

Taymūr's first full-length play *al-ʿUṣfūr fi'l-qafaṣ* (The bird in the cage') was performed in 1918: it is a domestic drama, treating life in the upper classes of Egyptian society. Written originally in classical Arabic, it was later expanded and recast in the Egyptian colloquial, which Taymūr became convinced was the proper medium for modern Egyptian drama and in which he wrote the rest of his plays. It had a limited commercial success, because it could not compete with the popular dramatic entertainments of the day: the cheap revue, what was known as *Franco-Arabe* farce, operetta and melodrama. Anxious about the fate of serious drama, Taymūr published a number of critical articles on the state of the Egyptian theatre and on the leading actors and singers. Hoping to appeal to a wider audience, he wrote *ᶜAbd al-Sattār Afandī* (performed in 1918), a comedy depicting the life and problems of a middle-class Egyptian family. This proved to be no greater commercial success than its predecessor, as it contained neither singing nor sexual titillation. Bitterly disappointed by his failure, he turned away from playwriting altogether, concentrating on editing his periodical *al-Sufūr*, where he published a series of critical articles on contemporary Egyptian dramatists in the form of mock trials which take place within the framework of a dream: despite their lighthearted tone they provide the best account of Egyptian drama of the day. Taymūr, however, did return to serious drama in his last work, which he apparently wrote only to please himself, with no thought of an audience in mind: *al-Hāwiyah* ('The precipice', 1921). Ironically enough, it met with greater success on the stage than that achieved by his other work, but unfortunately the author did not live long enough to see it performed.

In *al-ᶜUṣfūr* Ziftāwī Pasha, a rich but miserly landlord with sophisticated pretensions, who has lost his seat on a provincial council, spends his time in Cairo, where he has an expensive villa with all the trappings of western civilization, trying to ingratiate himself with the influential Raḍwān Pacha, in the hope that the latter may help him regain his seat. He rules his family like a tyrant, and his son Ḥasan, starved of affection, turns for sympathy to the westernized Levantine maid, Marguerite. The affair is discovered and stopped by Ziftāwī, who dismisses the maid instantly. Marguerite, who finds she is pregnant, returns to ask for help, but the irate father brutally orders her out of the house. At this point Ḥasan decides to go with her: he marries her and gives up his education, and they live on his meagre income as a minor clerk which is barely sufficient to support them and their child. Chance has it that he saves from being run over by a tram-car a man who turns out to be Raḍwān Pacha. In gratitude the latter, when he hears Ḥasan's story, puts pressure upon his father and manages to bring about a reconciliation between father and son, a reconciliation which is strengthened by the father seeing his grandson for the first time.

Considering it is Taymūr's first play, *ᶜUṣfūr* is a remarkably competent work, with a reasonably compact and fast-moving plot and lively dialogue. The atmosphere and the characters are genuinely Egyptian. Most of the characters are convincing because they are not painted in black and white. The father, who has been described, with some exaggeration, as an Egyptian mixture of Molière's Harpagon and Monsieur Jordain, is an amusing but not incredible bundle of contradictions, and the son is not a mere innocent victim of circumstances. The main theme is not simply the conflict between generations, but also the disastrous results of the excessively conservative and restrictive way of bringing up children. The plot may be about a small section of the upper classes, but the author manages to raise several wider issues of Egyptian society at large, such as relations between town and country and the state of flux of the social values at the time. Despite its serious subject, the play is not devoid of humour, such as we find in the ludicrous imitation of outward western manners by the Egyptian higher classes, or in the language and behaviour of the Nubian servant, both, as we have seen, favourite targets of fun in Ṣannūᶜ's plays.

Unlike *ᶜUṣfūr*, *ᶜAbd al-Sattār Afandī* is about a middle-class Egyptian family, yet it has some features in common with the earlier play: it also deals with the conflict of generations, and tyranny within the family (although the tyranny here is practised by the son against the father), and the threat posed to traditional norms by a veneer of westernization which allows parental authority to be eroded. ᶜAbd al-Sattār Afandī, a minor civil servant, is henpecked by his shrewish wife Nafūsah, who in her turn is completely under the thumb of her spoilt, unemployed, good-for-nothing son, ᶜAfīfī. With his mother on his side, and aided by the young maid, Hānim, ᶜAfīfī schemes to marry off his older sister, Jamīlah, against her wishes to his friend Faraḥāt, a plausible crook who in return has promised to obtain for him as a wife the daughter of a rich aristocratic acquaintance of his. ᶜAbd al-Sattār, however, who has no illusions about Faraḥāt, manages, after many trials and much humiliation, with the help of the manservant, Khalīfah, but more importantly through the interference of chance, to foil the scheme and marry Jamīlah to Balīgh, the upright young man, who loves her and whom she wishes to marry. Like *ᶜUṣfūr*, *ᶜAbd al-Sattār Afandī* is a well-constructed play, with a fast-moving plot and considerable humour arising from language, situation and character, although traces of *Tartuffe* can be detected not only in a comic eavesdropping scene, but also in its *deus ex machina* ending. But it is Taymūr's power of characterization that impresses us most in this play, which contains a rich gallery of interesting characters: ᶜAbd al-Sattār, weak and ineffectual, easily cowed, but capable of occasional bursts of courage and self-assertiveness, susceptible to female charms, and suffering from a false self-image as a womanizer and a Don Juan to compensate for his wife's scornful attitude; his wife Nafūsah, of whom everybody except her son is scared and who justifies her bad temper by claiming that she is possessed by evil spirits. The worthless, unemployed and totally unprincipled son ᶜAfīfī behaves as if he was a gentleman of leisure and regards his membership of an amateur dramatic society and of a society against cruelty to animals as his passport to social respectability, bullies the entire household because one of his dogs has been allowed to fall ill, treats his father vilely, accusing him of being boorish and old-fashioned and incapable of appreciating his son's sophistication, and is prepared to sacrifice his sister's happiness for his own material gain. Not the least interesting is the maidservant Hānim, one of the liveliest and most memorable characters in Taymūr's work: aware of her physical charms, she flirts her way through life, a sexual tease, behaving seductively not only towards ᶜAbd al-Sattār, whom she blackmails, but also toward the old servant Khalīfah, making a fool of him, constantly tormenting and mocking him. She allows ᶜAfīfī to take money from her because he has led her to believe he will marry her, but as soon as she learns of his plans to marry someone else she becomes such a formidable rival that not even her mistress Nafūsah is a match for her.

In his last play Taymūr returned to the upper-class world he knew so well. *Al-Hāwiyah* is a bourgeois tragedy in which the author tackles the problem of drug addiction in Egyptian high society, and its destructive effect particularly on marriage. Amīn, a wealthy dissolute young man, lives with his superficially westernized wife Ratībah and his more conventional mother in an opulent villa in Cairo. Far from reforming his character, as his mother had hoped, his marriage had led him to add cocaine addiction to the list of his vices, which already included drinking, gambling and whoring. His desire to be regarded as 'modern' drives him to introduce his wife to his two companions, Magdī and Shafīq – a daring step to take at the time, since no Muslim was supposed to show his womenfolk to any man not closely related to the family. Shafīq has designs on his friend's wife, and his land. Taking advantage of his friendship, he induces him to sell him the land at a ruinously low price, despite the advice given to Amīn by his caring uncle, and would have succeeded in seducing his wife, had they not been interrupted during her visit to his house. Both Amīn and Magdī, who are aware that Amīn had been entertaining a married ladyfriend in his house, assume that they know who she is: the former thinking that she is Magdī's sister, while the latter knows that it is Amīn's wife. Under the influence of cocaine, Magdī reveals the truth to Amīn, who promptly throws him out of the house. Amīn then forces the truth out of his wife, and is about to assault her, calling her an unfaithful whore, but she roundly accuses him of being himself partly to blame for nearly driving her to the brink of unfaithfulness because of his shameless neglect of his duties as a husband. Under the impact of the shock, and being full of cocaine, Amīn falls into a fit of impotent rage which proves fatal to him.

Al-Hāwiyah is another well-made play, in which every word serves a dramatic purpose, whether it be to advance the plot or further to delineate the characters. The result is that all the characters are vividly portrayed and distinguished from one another. This applies even to Amīn's two friends: Magdī, the tiresome playboy, who lives for the moment and who is always short of money, is different from Shafīq, who is strong and unscrupulous, scheming to steal his friend's fortune and his wife. As for Amīn and his wife, they are utterly convincing characters, who in the course of the play undergo considerable development. Amīn, like ᶜAfīfī, has been spoilt by his mother, who had made up her mind to deny him nothing as he had lost his father as a young child, with the result that he has grown into a weak and self-indulgent man. He deteriorates rapidly, driven to self-destruction by his rebellion against the traditional family values and his mistrust of his uncle, together with his increasing dependence upon cocaine. His wife, on the other hand, grows under the impact of events from a spoilt, superficial middle-class girl, interested in social life, going to the opera and women's fashions, to a more healthily liberated Egyptian woman, who saves her honour in time and stands up against her neglectful husband without any feeling of inferiority. Although the play deals mostly with cocaine addiction, there is no doubt that in his portrayal of Ratībah Taymūr struck a blow for the emancipation of the Egyptian woman, and *al-Hāwiyah* may be rightly described as a plea for responsible relations between partners in marriage. Although neglected for many decades, *al-Hāwiyah* has been generally regarded alike by those who witnessed it on the stage when it first appeared and the critics who rediscovered it nearly forty years later as the best play Muḥammad Taymūr ever wrote. In any case it constitutes ample evidence that his untimely death robbed the world of Egyptian drama of a figure that held great promise.

Anṭūn Yazbak

Marriage also provides the theme of what is arguably the most accomplished tragic work written in the Egyptian colloquial during the first half of this century, namely Anṭūn Yazbak's *al-Dhabāʾiḥ* ('The sacrifices'), which met with tremendous success when it was first produced on the stage in 1925, but was soon inexplicably to be ignored by critics until

Muḥammad Mandūr rescued it from oblivion in 1959 in his book *al-Masraḥ al-nathrī*. Mandūr describes the play as dealing with problems that arise from Egyptians marrying European women, but this is only one of its many themes.

Hammām Pacha, a retired army general, after a brief marriage to Amīnah, meets and falls in love with a European woman, Noreska, whom he marries after divorcing his first wife. His second marriage proves a disaster, although it has lasted twenty years and has resulted in a son, ᶜUthmān, now a hypersensitive youth, who is in his final year at school. They also have living with them his niece, Laylā, who lost both her parents several years ago, and for whom ᶜUthmān entertains a passion which is requited by the girl. Because of his unhappy marriage, Hammām is now a sick man, in need of nursing, which is provided by Ḥafīẓah, the nurse, with whose arrival on the scene the action of the play begins. Ḥafīẓah turns out to be none other than Amīnah, his ex-wife, who, having fallen upon hard times, has taken up nursing to support herself. Moved by her kindness and conscience-stricken for his past cruelty to her, Ḥammām decides to make amends and marries her again, setting up home with her, while still being married to Noreska whom he deserts, taking Laylā with him to save her from the corrupting influence of his liberated European wife. ᶜUthmān is naturally distressed not only by the rupture between his parents but also by the separation from Laylā. Noreska calls to discuss the new situation with Amīnah, and to confront her husband, who in his fury declares her divorced, and removes ᶜUthmān from her custody. ᶜUthmān witnesses the closing moments of the angry scene between his parents, and this has a shattering effect upon him. When his father decides to send Laylā away to live with an aunt, safe from the tempting company of her cousin, in a fit of despair the young man puts an end to his life and the shock of his suicide unhinges Laylā's mind. The contrite Hammām, unable to face the consequences of his actions, plans to commit suicide too, but the sight of the pathetically helpless Laylā makes him change his mind. Just at the moment when the much humbled Hammām decides to remain alive to face up to his responsibilities, Noreska, who has just received the news of her son's suicide, arrives, beside herself with rage, and shoots him dead as a punishment for the harm he has caused to so many people.

Such in brief is the outline of the main plot (for there is a subplot, relating to a failed army conspiracy in which Hammām's junior ex-colleagues are involved), an outline which may emphasize the melodramatic character of *al-Dhabāʾiḥ* and therefore may not do justice to a sensitively and carefully written play, free from the sensational surprises and the flat stereotypes characteristic of melodrama. Here, using subtle devices, the dramatist prepares us for what is to come, and he has created characters who are complex, credible and capable of enlisting our genuine sympathy. *Al-Dhabāʾiḥ* is so well constructed, so highly organized, that more than any previous Arabic play it is permeated by tragic irony. For the first time in drama the Egyptian colloquial rises to truly poetic heights and a powerful atmosphere is created in which certain objects become potent symbols expressing the characters' state of mind and feeling.

The characterization is truly admirable. In Hammām, if we confine our brief remarks to one character, we have a convincing tragic hero. His character is drawn on a grand scale. He is a tyrannical *pater familias*, domineering, used to command and incapable of brooking being crossed, and his explosive anger has terrifying proportions. The confrontation with Noreska is one of the most memorable scenes of the war of the sexes in Egyptian drama, the intensity of the conflict reminiscent of the work of Strindberg. His fatal flaw, his *hamartia*, is his lack of self-knowledge: assuming as he does, with his typical tidy military mind, his clear, but limited vision, that all his troubles are the result of his marriage to a European woman and of his having foolishly divorced his first wife. Yet what he is really seeking is not an Egyptian wife, but a wife prepared to be his doormat. As Noreska (obviously a descendant of Ibsen's Nora) points out to him, he wants to control his wife's mind as well as her body, and he is genuinely incapable of understanding her need to have her mind free. He attributes this need to her being European, ignoring Noreska's remark that it is a universal need which even Egyptian women are bound to feel soon if they do not already do so. He is totally unaware of the complexities of life that make human beings unique individuals and impel them to take what seem to be irrational actions. It is easier for him to think of Noreska as a European woman than as the individual Noreska. Nor can he understand how young people can commit suicide because of failure in love or school examinations. Yet he undoubtedly wins our sympathy for his concern about his family and his colleagues, and the intensity of his suffering and penance. In the course of the play his initial dogmatic position is thoroughly destroyed, causing his mental anguish when he sees his world collapse around him; his overbearing pride and cocksureness give place to humility, doubt and uncertainty, which drive him to contemplate suicide. It is truly tragic that when in utter humility he has painfully learnt to accept responsibility in continuing to live, he is cut down by Noreska's bullet.

One of the merits of this remarkable play is that, while it is firmly set in a specific social context with references to several problems of Egyptian society such as the position of women in Egypt and the tyranny of fathers, it is primarily a play about human relations. It shows the extent to which in their ruthless pursuit of their own quarrels the self-absorbed older generation can thoughtlessly destroy the lives of the impressionable and sensitive young.

ACHIEVEMENTS IN EGYPT: A COMPARISON WITH THE REST OF THE ARAB WORLD

It can safely be said that with the work of Ibrāhīm Ramzī, Muḥammad Taymūr, and Anṭūn Yazbak Arabic drama reached its maturity. Just how far ahead of the rest of Arabic drama Egyptian plays were at the time can be gauged if any of these works is compared with the best known non-Egyptian play of the period, one of the few works listed by Jacob Landau in *Studies in the Arab theater and cinema*, Philadelphia, 1958, pp. 117–18, as good drama, *al-Ābāᵓ wa'l-banūn* ('Parents and children', 1917) by the Lebanese poet and man of letters Mīkhāᵓīl Nuᶜaymah (1889–1988), a play meant to dramatize the conflict between the generations and to show the need of the young to rebel against the cruel and outworn traditions of the old. *Al-Ābāᵓ wa 'l-banūn* is really no more than a melodramatic story with an unsatisfactory plot, shallow and unconvincing characterization, excessive abstract discussions and a seriously flawed dialogue in which, instead of opting for either the colloquial or the classical, Nuᶜaymah resorts (albeit inconsistently) to the method advocated by Faraḥ Anṭūn, that of making the educated speak in the literary idiom while putting the colloquial in the mouths of the rest, with artificial and at times downright ridiculous results, as when two brothers engaged in a conversation are not made to speak the same language.

Like Nuᶜaymah, Saᶜīd Taqiyy al-Dīn, the best known Lebanese dramatist in the first half of the twentieth century, chose the classical for the higher classes and the colloquial for the peasants and the underworld characters in his well-known play *Lawla'l-muḥāmī* ('But for the lawyer', 1924), although surprisingly enough the leader of the gang of brigands is made to speak in the classical. Compared with the Egyptian plays we have been discussing, *Lawla 'l-muḥāmī*, too, is no more than a melodrama with a happy ending in which virtue is vindicated and vice punished: its events are improbable, its characterization is primitive and its dialogue is unsure.

By the third decade of this century certain norms had become more or less established in Egyptian drama. Regarding the language of dialogue, an issue which cannot be said to have been completely resolved even today, on the whole plays set in modern Egypt and designed to be performed on the stage were written in the colloquial, while the classical or a simplified form of it was used in those with historical themes. In the second and third decades Egyptian dramatists were able to write plays of considerable merit in both classical and colloquial Arabic which deserve to be taken seriously by the literary critics. Alike in social satirical comedy, *drame*, tragedy and historical drama, any imperfections that can be detected are no longer those resulting from teething troubles. As I have pointed out in my *Early Arabic Drama* (p. 134), convincing characters reveal their nature in crisp, natural dialogue and they develop, when they do, within the framework of reasonably well-constructed plots. The world they inhabit, their preoccupations and problems, are all recognizably Egyptian. In them controversial issues of the time figure prominently, ranging from such questions as the emancipation of women, the relation between the sexes and the conflict between generations, aggravated by the transition of society from tradition to modernity when certain values are in a state of flux, to economic and political problems such as the war inflation and the nationalist struggle for independence, on to the perennial tension between town and country.

From the late twenties the Egyptian government began to take steps to encourage serious Egyptian theatre, which was threatened by the popular commercial theatre, offering prizes for playwriting and scholarships to study drama and acting in Europe and even setting up a school of dramatic arts in 1930. By the thirties drama and acting had acquired a modicum of respectability in Egypt, at least officially, for various reasons. These include the increasing number of well-educated or highly born individuals such as Muḥammad Taymūr and Yūsuf Wahbī who became involved in the theatre, and the growth of theatre criticism, published first in national newspapers, then in many magazines devoted almost exclusively to the theatre which began to flood the market in the twenties. Another relevant factor is the interest taken in drama, ancient and modern, by the influential and highly esteemed author and critic Ṭāhā Ḥusayn. Furthermore, the fact that a great poet with an enormous reputation in the Arab world, Aḥmad Shawqī, who wrote within the classical Arabic tradition, turned to writing verse drama during the last four years of his life (1928–32), helped considerably to render drama an acceptable form of literature. We must remember that Tawfīq al-Ḥakīm (1898–1987), easily the best known and most important figure in the history of Arabic drama, although his career as a dramatist really belongs to a later and more sophisticated stage in the development of this genre, had his first experience of the Egyptian theatre during this period.

CHAPTER 10

ARABIC DRAMA SINCE THE THIRTIES

By the 1930s the theatre had become firmly rooted in the Egyptian soil: seeds sown in the previous decades now began to shoot up and bear some fruit. Egyptian theatregoers were getting used to the presence of good actors and actresses, particularly the talented Jūrj Abyaḍ who had received a proper training in Paris. They were also introduced to the concepts of a director (ᶜAzīz ᶜĪd), a theatre-manager and producer (Yūsuf Wahbī), and a highly disciplined company (Ramsīs, founded in 1923). A national company was formed under government auspices (1935), was given financial support and placed under the joint management of a poet with wide and varied cultural interests, Khalīl Muṭrān, and some of the most prominent men of letters of the day, including Ṭāhā Ḥusayn. No less important was the emergence of a gifted playwright who dedicated his best abilities to dramatic writing and who was soon to become, by dint of hard work and continuous presence on the scene, Egypt's national dramatist, Tawfīq al-Ḥakīm. The forties brought with them further consolidation. The High Institute of Drama, which had been forced to close down after a brief appearance in 1931, was reopened in 1944, headed by the properly trained Zakī Ṭulaymāt. At long last the theatre arts were beginning to receive serious attention from the state. The clamours of the pioneers that the theatre was not the abode of immorality, but a house for the education and re-education of men, no less important than schools, were being heeded.

THE ADVENT OF POETIC DRAMA

The Arabic theatre acquired more respectability when its ranks were joined by the leading poet Aḥmad Shawqī (1868–1932). He had been sent to France for higher studies in law, but in Paris he experienced, at first hand, the glories of the French classic theatre, mainly Racine and Corneille, as well as Shakespeare. His secret passion, the theatre, was thus given a powerful impetus. He had written his first play in Paris in 1893, under the title of *ᶜAlī Bey al-Kabīr* ('Ali Bey the Great'), but received little encouragement from his patron, and it was many years after his return to Egypt that he revised it, and felt that he could start on the task of introducing Arabic poetic drama. Shawqī wrote seven plays, all but one in verse. He took his themes from Ancient Egyptian history: *Qambīz* ('Cambyses', 1931); Egypt under the Ptolemies: *Maṣra*ᶜ *Kilyubaṭra* ('The death of Cleopatra', 1929); the Arab poetic heritage: *Majnūn Laylā* ('The mad lover of Layla', 1931); Mameluke Egypt: *ᶜAlī Bey al-Kabīr*; Spain under the Arabs: *Amīrat al-Andalus* ('The princess of Andalusia', 1932), the only play in prose and *Al-Sit Hudā*, (published posthumously), from Egyptian life in his day. He left uncompleted an eighth play: *Al-Bakhīlah* ('The miser').

It is commonly accepted that Shawqī was under the influence of Racine, Corneille and Shakespeare's tragedies when he wrote his verse plays. From Corneille, in particular, he took the theme of Love versus Duty and made the action of his plays turn round this axis. Especially is this the case in *Maṣra*ᶜ *Kilyubaṭra*, where the beautiful Queen of Egypt and her doting warrior-lover are virtually reduced to the size of puppets, tossed back and forth by conflicting allegiancies, at one time to Love and at another to Duty. Shawqī also tried to defend Cleopatra against the Roman charge that she was a strong-willed temptress seeking to bring about the downfall of Rome through seducing one after another of her Caesars. Instead of this degrading picture Shawqī presented Cleopatra as an astute leader and dedicated lover of her country, whose suicide is the final sacrifice she makes for her country. Rather than accepting the shame of surrendering her country and herself to Roman tutelage, she prefers to die. Anthony, likewise, dies to save himself from the consequences of his defeat at Actium. As he is breathing his last, he announces proudly that he is a fighter whom war has failed to subjugate, one who has chosen to die under the banner of love.

Despite its good intentions the work fails to convince us dramatically. The poetry is sonorous at times, sweet and tender at others. But the poet has not come anywhere near forging the proper dramatic tool with which alone he could have carved his characters, manipulated his events and created the conflict necessary for good tragedies. The poetry in the play is frankly lyrical, so much so that it was suggested more than once that Shawqī's plays be turned into operas where they stand a better chance of success.

The same could be said of the other verse plays. What is lacking is a dramatic point of view, a feeling of the true exigencies of the dramatic art. It is of course unfair to expect this of a poet who was writing in classical Arabic verse which is rhymed, meticulously measured and proud of being able to express a whole idea, or picture an event within the confines of one single line. Although Shawqī tried to modernize Arabic poetry, it was quite beyond his intention to do away with rhyme, or with the concept of the one line as the basis of poetic composition. What happened sometimes when he wanted to produce a dialogue was that he wrote a full passage and then divided it up between two or more characters. This, of course, hardly makes for drama, good or bad.

Curiously enough, when Shawqī decided to turn his back on historic themes and write on the contemporary scene in *al-Sitt Hudā*, he showed unmistakable signs of good dramaturgy. *Al-Sitt Hudā* clearly belongs to the comedy of social criticism, not very far removed from the comedy of Congreve or the easier, much less restricted, comedy of Goldsmith. The explanation of his unexpected success here lies in the fact that Shawqī took his characters from a section of Egyptian life he knew very well. The classical poetry form, instead of being an impediment, provided the play, a comedy, with effective irony, emanating from the contrast between commonplace characters and the lofty poetic language they were using.

Lesser poets followed in the wake of Shawqī, using the same classical Arabic poetry form, with all the limitations alluded to above. But they came up with much less gain. One such was ᶜĀzīz Abāẓah (1898–1969) who drew his themes mainly from Arabic history. He lacked the knowledge of theatre Shawqī had gained in Paris. His bent was lyrical through and through. His choice of language was unhappy, since he was particularly fond of big outlandish words hardly fit for dramatic expression, mistaking them for eloquence. The fact that in the printed editions of his works he explained in footnotes the meanings of little-known words betrays the dramatist's conception of dramatic works as being primarily books to be read, works of literature to be valued as such, irrespective of dramatic merit. Abāẓah wrote several plays, almost all suffering from the same limitations.

It was left to a younger generation to come up with verse plays appreciably nearer to dramatic art. In Egypt, ᶜAbd al-Raḥmān al-Sharqāwī (1920–87), one of a group of poets who, in the forties, were agitating for and producing the 'new' poetry, turned his hand in the fifties to verse drama. He had written a poem which had attracted much attention, 'From an Egyptian father to President Truman', which clearly revealed a dramatic bent, aided by the freedom afforded by the new poetry's doing away with rhyme and the concept of the one-line unit. In place of this the new poets insisted on the organic unity emanating from the poem as a whole as a result of interaction between theme, form and point of view. From this it was not very difficult to step into the domain of verse drama. The poetry, made more pliant, was easier to forge into some sort of dramatic tool which al-Sharqāwī could use to delineate character and create atmosphere. This was made easier still by the dramatist's choice of themes. For his first play *Maʾsāt Jamīlah* ('The tragedy of Jamilah', 1962) he used the story of the Algerian young woman who turned to guerilla fighting to help liberate her country from the French. Having been subjected to most inhuman torture, she stood out as a present-day Joan of Arc. In her story Sharqāwī could give vent to his talent for rhetoric and lyricism as well as expressing his political views. A gain had undoubtedly been made in the direction of proper verse drama. But the goal was still far away: Sharqāwī got nearer to it in his subsequent plays, notably in *al-Ḥusayn, Thāʾiran* ('Al-Husayn, a Revolutionary') and its sequel *al-Ḥusayn, Shahīdan* ('Al-Husayn, a martyr', 1969).

Once more, the dramatist chooses a character from real life who can be easily turned into a tragic hero. Al-Ḥusayn, grandson of the Prophet, is presented as an engaging young man, pure of heart and soul, determined to serve God and the Prophet by always righting wrongs. His adversary, Caliph Muʿāwiyah, has perpetrated an act of political aggression almost tantamount to a sin by forcing his people to choose his son, Yazīd, as his successor, thus annulling the orthodox Muslim principle of *al-shūrā*, a democratic discussion among Muslims, resorted to when a serious decision, political or religious, has to be made. Al-Ḥusayn has no other course but to take up arms, knowing full well that victory will not be his lot against such a vastly superior enemy. It is his fate that he should be chosen to fight God's battle, irrespective of the result. The battle, not the consequence, is what confers greatness upon a man. Though defeated, the soul of man emerges victorious.

Al-Ḥusayn is convincingly portrayed as a tragic hero. Though little or no self-conflict rages in his soul, the fact that he feels sorrow for what is going on around him gives him the tragic dimension one finds in a Cordelia or a Hamlet. Part of the success al-Sharqāwī achieves here has been made possible by his choice of the historical figure of al-Ḥusayn, whom generations of devout Muslims have turned into a legend. The martyrdom of al-Ḥusayn has for many centuries been reenacted every year in the streets by devout Shiʿites in what must be considered Islam's only tragic spectacle (*taʿziyah*). Sharqāwī's play undoubtedly draws on the treasured-up sympathy for al-Ḥusayn. He is also aided by what progress his poetry has made on the way to becoming dramatic. This progress is somewhat limited, though, for the poetry does not do away with lyricism altogether. Though writing for the stage, Sharqāwī never forgets that he is primarily a poet. He does not create proper dramatic verse.

A younger poet, Ṣalāḥ ʿAbd al-Ṣabūr (1931–81), was destined to write what can be fairly considered poetic drama. He was more sensitive and had a more refined taste than Sharqāwī and had the advantage of a better knowledge of Arabic literature, old and new, as well as a considerable reading in western literature, particularly the poetry and drama of T. S. Eliot, with whom, like many other writers, scholars and critics in the forties and fifties in Egypt, he had fallen in love. Shakespeare and the Greek dramatists were also among his tutors. Like Sharqāwī, ᶜAbd al-Ṣabūr had begun with poetry which betrayed an unmistakable dramatic talent, such as we find in his striking poem *Shanq Zahrān* ('The hanging of Zahran'). This treats the tragic fate of some Egyptian fellaheen who tried to defend their precious pigeons against the bullets of a company of British soldiers who had gone out shooting. One of the soldiers died of sunstroke and the whole village of Dinshway was held responsible. Zahrān, together with other young fellaheen, was summarily tried and subsequently hanged on the spot. The event (which took place in 1906) soon became a national cause and thenceforth became a landmark and a symbol in the movement for national liberation.

When he began to write his poetic dramas, ᶜAbd al-Ṣabūr had widened his scope to include all forms of protest against oppression. His *Maᵓsāt al-Ḥallāj* ('The tragic fate of al-Hallaj', 1965) pictures this eminent ninth-century mystic trying in vain to defend his right of conscience against despotic rule. Like Christ, he is defeated by both enemies and potential friends. *Laylā wa 'l-Majnūn* ('Laylā and the mad lover', 1970), another interesting play, uses Shawqī's verse play on the unhappy love of Laylā and Qays as background to tell the contemporary story of a group of young men and women journalists working together to put an end to the political and social injustice prior to the 1952 revolution. One of the editors of their revolutionary magazine is Saᶜīd, ᶜĀbd al-Ṣabūr's Qays, whose love for Laylā is weighed down with many a heavy burden. He had seen his (widowed) mother in bed with her second husband, whom she hated and had married merely to secure support for herself and her child.

Saᶜīd, Hamlet-like, chooses to look upon his mother's husband as the 'murderer' of his father. The act of lying with him is a sin his mother, Gertrude-like, commits. Hence Saᶜīd's abhorrence of sexual love. When Laylā offers him her full love, body and soul, he turns away in disgust: 'Love is our eternal curse, our downfall'. Laylā, undesirous of wasting her life and her dream of creating a new life, heeds the call of one of Saᶜīd's friends, the revolutionary-turned-spy Ḥusām. When Saᶜīd discovers her just rising from Ḥusām's bed after lovemaking, his mother's sin is enacted again before his eyes and he attempts to kill the spy Ḥusām. Seeing the complete disintegration of Saᶜīd, Laylā discovers that her true love is for him and not Ḥusām. In Shawqī's play the two lovers are separated by prohibitive conventions. In ᶜAbd al-Ṣabūr's the cause of the lovers' misfortune is both personal and political. Poverty, social injustice and lack of decision are national maladies which sow dissension and treason in the ranks of the revolutionaries. In some ways Laylā is seen as a symbol of Egypt. Both Laylā and Egypt are victims of indecision, lack of purpose and selfishness on the part of their lovers and supporters. A whole generation of revolutionaries has failed to defend the revolution. But this is not the end. If Saʿīd, the man of words and not of deeds, has failed, a time will come when a new prophet will arise, sword in hand, to replace the defeated prophet, Saʿīd, who only has a pen in his hand.

The play ends with Cairo set on fire and the group dispersing in different directions in a scene clearly reminiscent of Eliot's *The Cocktail Party*, Ziyād, feeling disgraced for having spent an evening in a brothel, vows not to write another word; Salwā, a Copt, renounces her plans to marry Ḥusām and decides to 'marry Christ', in a convent; Ziyād and Ḥanān go to a small village to supervise a kindergarten; Saʿīd goes to prison to serve a sentence for attempting to kill Ḥusām; while the chief editor of the group's magazine, and their leader, seeing Cairo in flames and his magazine closed down, declares, 'This is a time unfit to write in, to contemplate, sing, or even exist'. A picture on the wall in his office representing Don Quixote underlines his ineffectual leadership of the group.

ʿAbd al-Ṣabūr has another point of contact with Eliot: the desire to popularize poetic drama by using a kind of verse which can sound like prose, but which rises to poetic heights and gains more intensity if a given situation demands it. In *Laylā wa'l-Majnūn*, ʿAbd al-Ṣabūr does not choose historical, mythical or folktale characters as he does in *Baʿd an Yamūt al-Malik* ('After the king is dead', 1973) and *al-Amīrah tantaẓir* ('The princess is waiting', 1971), respectively, but picks a contemporary theme, again profiting by the experience of Eliot in *The Cocktail Party* and *The Confidential Clerk*. The result is clearly rewarding. In *Laylā wa'l-Majnūn*, poetry serves well the purpose of the play: theme, exposition, dialogue and character delineation in their entirety. It proves that contemporary themes can be better treated in poetic drama, for the tragedy in the play is made more, not less, effective by the poetic mould. Taking ʿAbd al-Ṣabūr's other plays into consideration, it is fair to say that this painstaking dramatist has succeeded in producing good poetic drama. *Al-Amīrah tantaẓir*, for instance, is a folktale in which the techniques of popular Egyptian theatre as well as ancient Greek and Renaissance drama and Ṣabūr's luxuriant poetry unite to give a richly poetic play.

To poetic drama also belong the plays of a younger poet, Najīb Surūr (1932–78). Unlike the two previous writers, Surūr had been trained in the theatre arts both in Cairo's High Institute for Drama and in Moscow, where he was sent on a scholarship. Surūr thus brought to drama his talent as a poet and his training as a director and would-be actor. In 1964 the Cairo Experimental Theatre, known as the Pocket Theatre, presented his poignant popular verse play *Yāsīn wa Bahiyyah* ('Yasin and Bahiyya') directed by the gifted Karam Muṭāwiᶜ.

The play takes the form of a folkloric tale: the unhappy love of the young man Yāsīn and his cousin, the beautiful Bahiyyah, who since their childhood have been promised to each other. Now fully grown young man and woman, they impatiently await the fixing of the date for their wedding, which is put off year after year because of their parents' poverty. Yāsīn's father is the victim of the feudal lord to whom Bahut, the village where the lovers live, belongs. Year after year the feudal lord has been whittling away pieces of the little land which Yāsīn's father owns and this year the Pasha has come for what is left, half an acre. Rather than face utter ruin, the father puts up a fierce resistance which takes him to prison from which he never comes back alive.

Now the Pasha is after Bahiyyah, her 'services' at the Pasha's palace are required. Full well does Yāsīn know what these services are, for many an innocent maid has gone there light as a sparrow, and come back with a big belly. Rather than accept this shame, Yāsīn is determined to die if need be. When the Pasha's men come to requisition the crop, Yāsīn leads an armed revolt by the desperate fellaheen. In the ensuing battle a victory is gained over the Pasha's men, his granaries are forced open and burnt out and his livestock taken away. But the victory is too serious a threat for the authorities to accept with complacency. The camel corps, men notorious for their savage dealings with such situations, descend upon the village and ransack it, torture the insurgents and kill Yāsīn. The play ends with Bahiyyah left alone, sitting under the twin palm tree where she had enjoyed the love of her deceased would-be husband. The play is cast in the folkloric mould of the *Shāᶜir* of old, a story-teller who recited the epic exploits of popular heroes, playing his *rabābah*, a primitive violin, and seeking to impress his listeners by acting the events of epics, impersonating their many characters. Because of what looked like an undramatic tale, the play was deemed stagnant, static and unfit for the stage, but because of the deep insight and expert knowledge of stagecraft of Muṭāwiᶜ, the director, it proved a resounding success. The old form of the *rabābah-shāᶜir* was demonstrated to be capable of dealing with contemporary themes; one more proof that the Arabic dramatic or potentially dramatic heritage could be used to bridge the gap between theatre and the simple people.

Surūr wrote other plays in the form of popular theatre. Noteworthy among these is his *Min ayn ajīb nās* ('O, would that I had listeners', 1976), which abandons the western formula of drama-writing in favour of a popular form which combines acting, narration, song, folkloric chanting, direct political commentary, a lively chorus taking part in and directing, the action, and a very plastic decor, all used to engage the attention of the audience and inculcate a sense of belonging in them, turning them from placid, passive spectators into participants in the show, highly and joyfully involved in its events.

* * *

Poetic drama in other Arab countries does not seem to have progressed as far as it has in Egypt, with the possible exceptions of Syrian and Palestinian drama.

In Syria, as in other Arab countries, attracted by the shining example set by Shawqī in Egypt, gifted poets were tempted to try their hand at this fascinating genre which promised a wider area of attention and more latitude for their poetry. But the approach was mainly literary, not dramatic. One of Syria's talented poets, ʿUmar Abū Rīshah (1910–) produced, in 1936, a verse drama called *Rāyāt Dhī Qār* ('The banners of Dhī-Qār')[1] which soon attracted great attention in literary circles and was deemed a piece of fine literature. ʿAdnān Mardam, another literary verse dramatist, has written some seven plays, all in the classical form of rhymed verse. But judging by two of these plays, *al-Ḥallāj* (1971) and *Filasṭīn al-thāʾirah* ('Palestine in revolution', 1974), his contribution to verse drama is weak indeed: the poetry is rather poor, the drama poorer still.

Khālid Muḥyildīn al-Barādiʿī is a better poet and dramatist. He wrote two plays, of which *al-Salām yuḥāṣir Qarṭājannah* ('Peace besieges Carthage', 1979) is noteworthy. It is a quasi-historical play, using the theme of war between Carthage and Rome to pass judgement on present-day events. Carthage stands for Egypt under Sadat, and Rome Israel. The dramatist manages to produce a reasonably convincing verse drama in which his rhyme-free poetry is turned into a pliant tool, which makes possible good character delineation and a plot that secures our attention. Some of his characters stand out, particularly ʿAbd al-Shams, a strolling poet who sings the woes of his country in the streets of Carthage, unafraid of being heard by the weak despotic king who has capitulated to Rome in return for an illusory peace. He joins the ranks of those who have denounced the peace and defied both the king and his Roman allies. When, at the end of the play, Carthage is razed to the ground by Roman soldiers and utter defeat is the lot of those who have taken up arms in defence of their people, their homes and their land, the poet ends his tale of woe on a hopeful note: the defeated warriors vow to build Carthage anew.

[1] An Iraqi governorate.

Samīḥ al-Qāsim, a prominent Palestinian poet living under Israeli rule, has written an impressive poetic drama called *Qaraqāsh* (1970). Qaraqāsh is a despotic ruler whose name calls to mind Qaraqosh, who lived in Egypt under Saladin and who, though an efficient warrior and statesman, was turned by popular imagination into a symbol of arbitrariness and dictatorial behaviour. In Qāsim's play Qaraqāsh is made to represent despotism throughout the centuries. He is the slave-driver of Ancient Greece and Ancient Egypt, as well as the modern dictator and mass murderer, Hitler. He is out for war and conquest, preaches the philosophy of aggression as a way out of economic difficulties, regards human beings as cannon-fodder and lubrication for the war machine. Since he is one-eyed and shows interest in archaeology, he also stands for Dayan.

As this is meant to be a popular entertainment, the events of the play are cast in the mould of a fable. Qaraqāsh's son, a noble spirit, falls in love with a beautiful peasant girl and insists on marrying her, despite the girl's attempt to remind him of the huge social barrier that separates them. The Vizir is sent by the lover as mediator between the prince and his father. When the question is put to the despot, 'What would be his judgement if a prince in his land should fall in love with a commoner?', he unhesitatingly pronounces the death of the lovers and asks that their bodies be carried to him. Discovering that he has unwittingly put his own son to death, he is driven by shock and grief to declare a new war in which his people should be compelled to take part. However, his people are unable to stand any more of the dictator's crimes and an open revolt ensues in which both Qaraqāsh and his minister are killed. A popular rule is soon set up amid universal jubilation, with the soldiers throwing away their helmets and joining in. Despite its serious content, *Qaraqāsh* is never allowed to be a song of hatred and vengeance. Indeed, acts of murder, mutilation and treason abound; victims fall in the despot's wars. But the emphasis is put on the people's power to overcome all misery, all insanity of judgement, and emerge victorious. In fulfilment of the traditions of the fables of old, a prince loves a peasant girl. Although the result is not at all happy, the young prince's desire that the castle should lower itself a little and the cottage rise a little is achieved, even though the union may be in death. Qāsim's simple, free-running poetry, his purity of heart and mind, his eye for the comic and the amusing, as well as his concern for good human beings no matter what station they are in, help him a great deal to create a truly entertaining poetic drama.

Another Palestinian poet and dramatist, who lived outside Israel, is Muᶜīn Basīsū. He wrote three full-length plays: *Maʾsāt Guevara* ('The tragedy of Guevara', 1969), *Thawrat al-Zanj* ('The revolution of the Zanj',

1970) and *Shamshūn wa Dalīlah* ('Samson and Delilah', 1971), as well as three other short plays and playlets. Of these *Shamshūn wa Dalīlah* is particularly worthy of consideration. In it, the dramatist, who has taken the tragedy of his people and his homeland very much to heart, succeeds in translating his emotions of anger and sorrow into convincing dramatic terms, thus producing an impressive poetic drama on a very thorny problem. His view of Palestine is the simple one of a land unlawfully seized by an alien force, and a people that has been either expelled into the wilderness or subjugated inside Israel, and rendered subservient to the foreign master.

The play gives an impressive picture of the subjugation. A Palestinian family of five has to deal with the situation created by the successive wars, all lost, culminating in the 1967 major defeat. The family – parents, two sons and a daughter – have different views as to what must be done. One of the sons, Māzin, can no longer tolerate life under the Israelis, and he also brands as futile his father's action in keeping a key and documents proving that he owns a well in Jaffa, since Jaffa and other towns have fallen to the enemy, and an Arab return to Palestine as promised in the fiery press articles and radio and television programmes is no more than a dream: the North Pole is nearer to the Palestinians than Jaffa. He therefore decides to run away from such an impossible situation. The other son, ᶜĀṣim, holds a different view. To his father's protest that leaving the land to the Israelis was a fatal mistake, ᶜĀṣim points out that henceforth it is the duty of every Palestinian to shape his own destiny with his own hands. Life in exile is just another prison. Of no avail is the crying and wailing of his sister Rīm, who is driven mad by her own personal as well as by the general tragedy. Besides her country she has lost her baby in an Israeli raid, mistaking a bundle she was carrying for the baby, and throwing away the latter. Armed revolution, maintains ᶜĀṣim, is the only way out. Part One of the play ends with the rise of the revolution.

Part Two deals with the 1967 defeat: Israel has won more Arab lands and is now stronger than ever. But the resistance movement has also gained momentum. As the play is drawing to an end, the Israelis try to win to their side Rīm, who is now in their hands. If she denounces her friends, she will be allowed to leave and then she can become a heroine overnight by pretending she has escaped. Her interlocutor is a present-day Samson, whose long hair is made of bullet tapes. The failure of this new Samson to win Rīm over is taken by Samson's lover, a young woman called Rachel, to mean that the new Delilah has robbed Samson of his strength, by once again cutting his hair.

Shamshūn wa Dalīlah is a phantasy in some of its parts, a prophecy in others. But throughout it never abandons its strong stand for the people of

Palestine and their revolution. In fact Basīsū supports all revolutions seeking to liberate people from the yoke of foreign rule, internal exploitation and the loss of freedom of speech. His two other long plays draw a comparison between the Palestinian revolution and the revolution of the Zanj (negroes) who lived under the Abbasid empire in untold misery. The fate of the Red Indians of North America is presented in the Zanj play as a grave warning to the Palestinians who stand in danger of utter extermination, which was the lot of the 'red-skins'. As for Basīsū's poetry, it is simple enough to accommodate the events on the two levels of phantasy and realism which *Shamshūn wa Dalīlah* embraces. It is a marked step towards creating a truly dramatic poetry.

TAWFĪQ AL-ḤAKĪM: BIRTH OF A NATIONAL PLAYWRIGHT IN EGYPT

To al-Ḥakīm (1898–1987) goes the credit of making prose drama an accepted form of Arabic literature. Previous to his works, dramatic writing had never gained the recognition, let alone the respect, of Arabic critics and writers, old or new. Dramatic art was looked down upon as being the occupation of, at best, bizarre people; at worst, of people of doubtful morals, who lived a life of licence, very low on the social scale. This was so much so that, when al-Ḥakīm wrote his first two plays, *al-ᶜArīs* (The bridegroom', 1924) and *Khātim Sulaymān* ('Solomon's ring', 1924), he had to omit his surname to avoid both family censure and social disgrace. The problem was made even more difficult by the kind of plays al-Ḥakīm chose to begin with. Two of these, *al-Marᵓah al-jadīdah* ('The new woman', 1923) and *Ali Baba* (1926), were not calculated to gain a good name for the art al-Ḥakīm was championing. The events of the first, in part an adaptation from French theatre, revolve around a womanizer who expects his mistress at his love-nest, only to find his plans thwarted by the arrival of one wrong person after another. The kill-joys include friends who refuse to hide away in a room unless they are bribed, as well as Laylā, his daughter, who also arrives. She is a good example of the new woman who has gained her freedom and exercises her will to live exactly as she pleases. Al-Ḥakīm wrote his play to attack precisely this type of woman. In the early twenties he was very much against the liberation of women and he used the play to point out that freedom for women meant moral laxity. Laylā is a powerfully created character, full of life, intelligence and credibility. But al-Ḥakīm, to gain his point against liberated woman, shows her, against all probability, as being the mistress of one of her father's friends. This is the first instance of al-Ḥakīm's tendency to make character subservient to idea. Henceforth, his drama will follow this line, thus bringing upon itself the accusation that his is no living theatre, but a drama in the mind, better read than acted. Al-Ḥakīm himself contributed to this inaccurate description when, in the forties, he called his works intellectual drama.

Ali Baba, by sharp contrast, is unashamed entertainment. The *Arabian Nights* is very much depended upon to produce a first-class popular show, including love, adventure, a hidden treasure, dance, song and intrigue. Nowhere in his writings does al-Ḥakīm account for this change from the thesis play to light-hearted operetta. But in a recent interview (February 1987), he told the present writer that *al-Marʾah al-jadīdah* was accorded a fairly good reception. It could not have been, therefore, that al-Ḥakīm turned from *drame à thèse* to light-hearted entertainment because of lack of appreciation of his more serious work. The reason must be looked for elsewhere. A reasonably good explanation lies in the fact that a careful study of al-Ḥakīm's dramatic career shows clearly that inside the dramatist there were two artists, one a thinker, the other a clown, with neither leaving the other alone. When they were not working harmoniously with each other, as indeed they did at a certain phase in al-Ḥakīm's career, one or the other gained the ascendancy. This will be discussed later in more detail.

In 1925 al-Ḥakīm went to Paris to read for a higher degree in law. But his secret desire was to acquaint himself with the cultural, artistic and dramatic life of the French capital. Of these facets of art he seems to have drunk his fill, but it was drama that was his passion. Having seen the plays of the top dramatists of the day – Ibsen, Shaw, Maeterlink and Pirandello – the word 'drama' had come to mean to the young aspiring dramatist something palpably different from its connotation in Cairo. Gone were the days of farce, vaudeville, operetta and popular theatrical entertainment. These specimens of theatrical arts were now regarded as beneath the consideration of one who had come to know the high and mighty in drama.

The works of those masters were to become al-Ḥakīm's ideal, his guide in fulfilling the self-imposed task of saving Arabic drama from contempt. By writing dramas which could be considered literary works of value, good in their own right, that is apart from their meeting the exigencies of the stage, al-Ḥakīm hoped to gain a sufficiently good name for his favourite art to allow it to take its place alongside poetry, long considered by the Arabs as their major achievement.

When al-Ḥakīm came back to Cairo in 1928 without his law degree, he started to write his 'lofty' plays, replete with sublime ideas, philosophic contemplation and a good intellectual dialogue: the latter being one of al-Ḥakīm's special assets. He wrote his *Shahrazād* in 1934, but this was not acted until much later, in the early sixties; the explanation is not hard to find, for the play provides fascinating reading, but is difficult to perform. The theme is knowledge – what constitutes it; how to seek it; where to find it. Shahrazād embodies knowledge and indeed is made to represent life itself. After the thousand and one nights are over Shahrayār is transformed. He turns away, in disgust, from both body and heart, and would be content to live the life of the mind. Unfortunately, he gets nowhere. Shahrazād rightly describes him as a man suspended in the air, somewhere between heaven and earth. The journey he suddenly embarks upon shows his bewilderment: he claims it is a search for knowledge, but in fact it is an attempt to escape from the Shahrazād dilemma. Qamar, his minister, is equally unable to resist the lure of Shahrazād: he loves her dearly and would very much have her return his love. But this vital woman does not feel she belongs to any particular man – neither to the king who now sees her as a great mind, nor to Qamar, to whom she is a big heart. The black slave whom Shahrazād encourages to acquaint himself with the treasures of her body, sees her erotically, as a luscious body. Shahrazād agrees she is all these things put together, but she is much more, since she is life itself. An attempt is made to link Shahrazād to Isis, the Queen of Ancient Egypt and symbol of dedication to recurrent life. Both the king and his minister cry out in astonishment when they see the image of Isis in Egypt: the likeness is striking, they both agree.

Shahrazād, then, is Life Eternal, life that seeks to grow, produce plant and bear fruit. This explains why it is that the black slave, full of the lust for life, is the only one of the three lovers who is allowed to enjoy Shahrazād. Not for her the squabbles of the King and his Minister over her real meaning. In the third scene, which is oddly reminiscent of the auction scene in Shaw's *Candida*, Shahrazād dicusses herself with her two lovers. Qamar the Minister, is Ḥakīm's Marchbanks, Shahrayār is Morell. One can hear the echo of Marchbanks's final words in *Candida*: 'Out with me then into the impatient night'. The poet, renouncing romantic love, goes out to seek knowledge in the wide world.

The search for knowledge is one of the main themes in al-Ḥakīm's drama. In *Shahrazād* he makes the King adopt various means of gaining knowledge, renunciation of heart and feeling, the deification of the human mind and magic, are all tested for possible sources of knowledge. He is to come back to the same theme in *Yā Ṭāliᶜ al-shajarah* ('The tree climber', 1962), where direct questioning, mystical revelations, magic and ritual are successively used to gain knowledge.

But prior to *Shahrazād*, al-Ḥakīm had written, in 1931, a significant play: *Raṣāṣah fi'l-qalb* ('A bullet in the heart'), a comedy of character and situation in which the playwright sought to integrate thought and entertainment into an attractive play which could appeal to all sections of theatregoers.

The theme is the conflict between idealistic and practical behaviour. Naguīb, a high-grade civil servant and a spendthrift, is always in debt, ever afraid of creditors pursuing and persecuting him. He lives alone in a Cairo apartment, using up his monthly salary a few hours after receiving it to pay some of his debts and borrowing his way through the rest of the month. A nerve-racking life, but he likes it, and would not trade it for the secure, well-financed life of his doctor friend Sāmī, who lives in an apartment upstairs in the same building. The doctor is Naguīb's exact opposite: money, not beauty, is his first goal. He is about to be engaged to Fīfī, a well-to-do modern young woman, who drives her own car, a roomy Packard. Now, as fate would have it, Naguīb falls for this same beautiful young lady, whom he has seen eating ice-cream at a fashionable shop. It is a case of love at first sight, a bullet in the heart, as Naguīb puts it. He immediately runs to his friend to tell him of the incident, little knowing that he has fallen in love with his friend's fiancée. Fīfī comes to see her fiancé and, not finding him at home, gets into a deliciously comic banter with Naguīb. Being an intelligent woman, she notices at once the difference between the two men. She finds herself more attracted to the beauty-worshipping eternal bankrupt, and audaciously offers him her heart. Though he could ask for no happier end to his celibacy, Naguīb, with a broken heart, declines the offer. Fīfī thinks he does this because he would not take away his friend's future wife. But Naguīb comments to himself: 'I am not the marrying sort. My lot will always be financial troubles.'

Raṣāṣah fi'l-qalb is an early specimen of al-Ḥakīm's plays dealing with the theme of realist versus idealist. In a measure the playwright projects here his own dilemma: whether to address his art to the masses and compromise his own ideals or stick to his goal of producing only 'fine' plays, irrespective of their reception at the box office. The first alternative would mean fame and fortune, two privileges which al-Ḥakīm was not at all against. The second would bring with it respect, the recognition of the powerful intellectual elite, and a place for drama among the recognized literary genres.

The play could have solved the dilemma for al-Ḥakīm. It is many-faceted, comprising farce and high comedy. The dialogue, written in spoken (that is, colloquial) Arabic, is easy-flowing, rising from down-to-earth words and phrases to moments of feeling and pathos. The story of the play is one that is readily appreciated by a multiple audience. Unfortunately it was not immediately acted, although some distinguished actors of the day were prepared to take it. There was a quarrel over the principal part of Naguīb between two eminent actors, Muḥammad ʿAbd al-Quddūs and Sulaymān Naguīb, the latter claiming that the part was especially written for him, while al-Rīḥānī, a prominent comedian, would produce the play if al-Ḥakīm gave him permission to pepper it up. Al-Ḥakīm would not agree.

Thus it was that Egyptian comedy was denied the opportunity to rise above the poor-quality slapstick that was the bill of fare for many playhouses. The play had to wait for several years before being turned into a film in the forties, proving an immediate success. Part of the success must be attributed to the songs of Muḥammad ᶜAbd al-Wahhāb, who played Naguīb, and the words of Ḥusayn al-Sayyid, a songwriter with a palpable gift for comedy, who entered into the spirit of the main situation.

Finding himself unable to reach his coveted wide audience, al-Ḥakīm had to content himself with his intellectual drama project. If wide popular acclaim was not to be had, then the recognition of distinguished literary critics such as Ṭāhā Ḥusayn or Muḥammad Ḥusayn Haykal must be considered compensation enough. Hence the series of plays which al-Ḥakīm himself helped to dub 'intellectual drama': *Shahrazād* (1934), *Ahl al-kahf* ('The men of the cave', 1933), *Praxa* (1939, enlarged in 1954), *Pygmalion* (1942), *Sulaymān al-Ḥakīm* ('Solomon the wise', 1943) and *al-Malik Ūdīb* (King Oedipus, 1949). In each of these plays al-Ḥakīm tries hard to write a play of ideas which could please both thinker and seeker of entertainment. The attempt at an amalgam of entertainment and thought is particularly evident in two of these plays: *Praxa* and *Sulaymān*.

The full title of the first play is 'Praxa or: How to govern'. Al-Ḥakim is here inspired by the first part of Aristophanes' *Lysistrata*. In the introduction to the first version, which comprised three acts, he advises readers and critics to read the Greek play first. Actually, the two plays are different in both approach and incidents. The main theme is the same: the revolt of women against war-loving men. But Aristophanes contents himself with poking fun at men and women alike, not forgetting to dart a shaft of criticism at the dignitaries of Greek cities. Al-Ḥakīm is more ambitious: he tackles, in the comic vein, the problem of government in Cairo, thinly veiled as Athens. The year the play was written (1939) witnessed a chaotic state of affairs in Egypt: a weak government, bickering short-sighted parties and a playboy king – enough to support a call for a strong-man government which is answered in al-Ḥakīm's play by an army officer, Hironimus. Praxa, the leader of women, has successfully rallied her folk against men, and by a ruse, has planted those women, in men's guise, into the ranks of citizens attending a national assembly session where a motion is being presented to give government over to women. The motion is carried and Praxa installed in office. She takes the liberal approach to ever-growing problems. Things prove too much for her and she soon falls into the clutches of the army officer, after having first fallen into his arms as her lover. The officer takes over and the three-act first version ends with Praxa chained and put in prison.

In 1954, using the occasion of *Praxa* having been translated in Paris, al-Ḥakīm adds three more acts. He intimates, in a short introductory note, that in 1939 he had to stop at the limit of three acts for reasons of prudence, though he had much more to say. The 1952 revolution gave him the opportunity to express himself in full. In this second part, Praxa's husband, a weak plaything of a man, is asked to ascend the throne, to help save the nation from chaos and prevent Hironimus, the army officer and leader of the nation, from having to commit suicide. The man easily allows himself to be talked into acceptance, but once king, he takes himself seriously, and with the help of a bad retinue, actually becomes a dictator. He plans to put his wife Praxa, her philosopher/counsellor and the ex-dictator on trial for misgovernment, embezzlement of public funds and encouraging corruption in high places. When the three so-called culprits appear before the people, they soon turn the tables against their accusers, and Praxa and her philosopher emerge triumphant. The philosopher now firmly believes that it is the duty of thinkers to be in the swim of things. To think and not to act is untenable and harmful.

It is quite obvious that al-Ḥakīm was thinking mainly of Egypt, her King, her revolution and finally himself as he wrote this second part. We have only his word that he had stored up all this until a convenient moment presented itself. The point, however, is not of any major importance. Al-Ḥakīm has always been quick to respond to circumstances, both politically and intellectually as well as dramatically, as we will have occasion to see later. What is important is that the playwright has here successfully used the two components of thought and entertainment to produce an interesting play. The thought is not as austere or puzzling as in *Shahrazād*, or *Ahl al-kahf*: there is nothing difficult to grasp in what the philosopher says. In the first three acts he maintains an attitude of neutrality between Praxa, representing liberalism, and Hironimus, who stands for naked power. Neither is fit for government, in the philosopher's view. Towards the end of Act Three the philosopher dares to express his conviction that liberalism, in weak hands, becomes chaos, and naked power is despotism. A third party has to join to see that a balance is maintained between freedom and power; that is, the rule of wisdom, emanating from the enlightened human mind. His proposal is turned down by Hironimus, and Praxa is chained and imprisoned with her counsellor. In the following three acts the philosopher's proposal is accepted, a triumvirate is set up, and Praxa's husband becomes king. Only when there is a public commotion against the king and his regime does the philosopher join the ranks of revolution. Without much ado he becomes a man of action.

Throughout, the philosopher plays the double part of thinker and clown.

He openly flirts with Praxa, makes fun of her sensual love for Hironimus, accuses her at a convenient moment of being a weak ruler and joins in her game of installing her unintelligent husband as king, thus providing comedy in the play. But Praxa's husband is the real fool: the scene where the members of the triumvirate try to convince him that he is a born king is delicious first-rate farce. Another element of entertainment is the two-faced secretary who acts as a spy against her mistress, and goes over to the King's side to aid and abet him in his projects for bringing about the downfall of Praxa's government. Besides, there is the melodramatic trial at the end and the sheepish manner in which the people turn many different ways, moving from one extreme to another.

Al-Ḥakīm does not seem to be much aware that throughout his dramatic career he has been attempting to bring together the two elements of thought and entertainment in his plays. Although he mentions outright that in *al-Marʾah al-jadīdah* he has poured his thesis-play into the mould of farce and ribald comedy in order to make it more palatable to the less sensitive part of his audience, he soon forgets that he has done so. Thus we find him putting such plays of ideas as *Ahl al-kahf* and *Shahrazād* together with *Praxa* and *Pygmalion* as being of the same nature, although the last two are clearly different in that an attempt is made in each of them to tip the balance in favour of entertainment. When he came to write *al-Malik Ūdīb*, he stated clearly that one of his main concerns was to hide ideas behind action, and preserve the full dramatic and theatrical force of the myth. To do this, he says, he had to summarize what had happened to Oedipus before his tragedy had begun. He also had to strip the Greek play of all that the Arab and Islamic mind would not accept. This meant he had to do away with the fable of the Sphinx altogether, with the idea of man defying the gods and with the insurmountable Greek fate.

In this play Oedipus's tragedy lies in Oedipus himself: his search for the truth, which unchains the series of events leading to his downfall. He is not a mythical figure at all and the beast he overcomes is a mere lion he courageously kills. But unlike the Greek Oedipus, the damning truth does not make him want to atone for his deeds by deserting his queen/mother or breaking up a family life based on an unclean bed. Al-Ḥakīm chooses to make Oedipus a family man, too fond of his mother/wife and his brothers and sisters/children to want to leave them. After the appalling revelation he is quite content to be allowed to leave Thebes with his family for some other place. Only when Jocasta commits suicide does he tear out his own eyes and show readiness to go into exile, leaving his precious family to the care of a loving uncle. Al-Ḥakīm turns Tiresias into a strong-willed conspirator who does not believe in the voices coming from on high any more than Oedipus does. It is he who convinces Laius that he will be killed by his own son. It is also he who teaches Oedipus to solve the riddle and pretend that the lion was the terrible beast. In this way Tiresias is changed from a seer into an ambitious politician. He becomes the originator of the tragedy and takes the place of fate. Al-Ḥakīm would not have the gods work against man, and has to put the blame for the downfall of Oedipus on Tiresias, in the first place, and on Oedipus's insistent search for the truth. As an Oriental, he says, he cannot see man as the only power in the universe, as his own god. The gods are just: they give us what we deserve.

In *al-Malik Ūdīb,* al-Ḥakīm produced a play which reads well, one that has gained for the author and for Arabic drama enough prestige to make traditionalists and purists more willing to look upon drama as a genre of Arabic literature. This dearly acquired prestige had been steadily building up ever since al-Ḥakīm wrote his series of dramas of ideas starting with *Shahrazād*, and moving on to *Ahl al-kahf, Pygmalion, Sulaymān al-Ḥakīm, al-Malik Ūdīb* and *Īsīs.* In each of these plays the dramatist displays keen interest in mythology, religious tales and folklore as sources of the type of drama that should have both quality and wide appeal. None of them ever gave him anything other than the respect of the enlightened audience, by nature few in number and of little effect as far as wide audiences are concerned. Hence al-Ḥakīm's deep regret that he never could reach the masses, and his continuous efforts to work out ways and means that would enable him to reach that goal.

In this continuous effort al-Ḥakīm was well served by an eclectic nature and a quick response to what new things were in the air. Thus in 1945, when he was offered the chance to write a one-act play for an Egyptian weekly, *Akhbār al-Yawm*, he seized eagerly upon the chance and wrote week after week one-act plays with themes taken from everyday life. Al-Ḥakīm describes this phase of his career as 'the theatre on paper period'. Obviously not very happy that his drama should be metamorphosed into cold words on colder paper, illustrated instead of being performed on the stage, he tried to look at the brighter side of this development. At least, he argued, he had full freedom to choose what subjects he liked, not perturbed by the exigencies of mounting a production, the ups and downs of acting companies and the size of audiences.

His freedom, however, was not absolute. He had been not a little dismayed by the poor attendance accorded to previous plays and had to bear in mind that in order to reach a wider audience he had to water down his intellectual content, and put more entertainment into the plays. Moreover, the consideration of the tastes of the readers of those plays impressed itself on him since he was writing for a wide-circulation, popular weekly, given to sensationalism in reporting and news selection. The obvious solution was to look around for daily events of dramatic interest. An opportunity soon presented itself: a butcher who owned a three-storey apartment building wanted to marry off his three daughters who could not boast of good looks. He hit on the ingenious idea of promising suitors to his daughters a flat each, should they agree to take the young women as wives. Enough suitors presented themselves. But those actually chosen soon found out that a wife and not a flat was all that fell to their lot. The story had been reported by the press. Al-Ḥakīm fashioned it to his own taste in his *ᶜImārat al-Muᶜallim Kandūz* ('Mr Kanduz's property', 1950), pouring his events into the mould of comedy, and at times of farce. The centuries-old theme of the trickster tricked is ingeniously pumped for carefree laughter, and a moral is unobtrusively pointed out: if you agree to play the game of tricking, then you must not complain if events turn against you. To the angry suitors who incriminate him the butcher retorts: 'I may be a trickster. But at least I have worked hard to own this building. What about you? What have you offered to own the flats? Only your greed and the desire to possess that which you have not sweated for.'

There are other works in this light satirical vein. One such is *Aᶜmāl ḥurrah* ('Private enterprise'), which unmasks corruption in government departments and private companies. A cynical team of civil servants work for a government department in the mornings and serve a private company in the afternoons. They receive in the morning, on behalf of the government department, goods and other equipment which they themselves have bought for the company, receiving some kind of commission from both sides. The head of the government department has a mistress, a singer of very lax morals. When he visits the company to find out whether his subordinates actually have double jobs he is soon surprised by his wife who turns up to satisfy herself as to rumours about love affairs her husband is reported to be indulging in. She finds him with the singer. A crisis is avoided when the head of the company offers the wife a gold bracelet as part of the payment her husband will soon be receiving, since the latter will shortly be appointed adviser to the company. Everybody is satisfied. Here again corruption is universal; al-Ḥakīm sees no one as being innocent.

In other plays of this period al-Ḥakīm tackles again in a lighter vein some of the themes he has previously treated in the plays of ideas. Time is absolute: you cannot go round it, bypass or ignore it. Thus it is expressed in *Ahl al-kahf* ('The men of the cave', 1933), al-Ḥakīm's serious and philosophic treatment of the Koranic version of the Christian legend of the Seven Sleepers of Ephesus. Three men seek shelter in a cave to save their lives from the Roman persecution of early Christians. They soon fall asleep, but when they wake up, over three hundred years have elapsed. Of this terrifying fact they are at first unaware, thinking their slumber lasted only for one night, but gradually as the truth is revealed to them, they find their situation unbearable. With every contact with reality they are made to feel alien, antiquated and unwanted. They finally realise that the past they represent has no place in the present, and are forced to go back to die in their cave. Al-Ḥakīm treats this theme with a mixture of humour and tragic pathos, and he returns to it in a later play, *Law ᶜaraf al-shabāb* ('If youth only knew', 1950), in which an old man regains his youth after having been given a rejuvenating elixir. The man soon finds out that a youthful skin is no guarantee for happiness. To look young and feel old is a daily torment which the man cannot endure for long. He asks to be given back his old age. The analogy with *Ahl al-kahf* is obvious. But the treatment is markedly different. The later play reports what goes on currently in modern Egyptian high society. It is full of characters who live in the here and now and makes no attempt at philosophizing.

Although al-Ḥakīm in this phase is clearly marking time, busying himself with drama of a sort, trying hard not to lose touch with his art or his audience, the results are not of small consequence. One obvious benefit that has accrued to al-Ḥakīm here is that he was learning, practising and developing the technique of integrating thought with entertainment. He does achieve a balance which gives lustre and vitality to the plays he is to write henceforth.

One such play is *al-Aydī al-nāᶜimah*, ('Soft hands', 1954), written two years after the 1952 revolution. The soft hands are those of a prince of the Royal Family, who loses, together with his title, the right to dispose of his luxurious palace by rent or sale; he can only benefit by it for his own use. The play shows how the soft hands of the former prince become gradually rough through housework. He has agreed to let a family of two, an aged father and his adult daughter, live with him on condition they look after him and secure food for him and his friend, a grammarian who wrote a doctoral thesis on the Arabic preposition *ḥattā*. The prince falls in love with the daughter of the tenant, who lets him help her with the housework. The idea that work is important for one's integrity and peace of mind is inculcated into the prince. This is further emphasized by subsequent events. One of the prince's two daughters has married an engineer who has worked so hard that he has come to own a car factory. This engineer preaches the advantages of work to the prince and his friend, and sees that each gets a job to suit his hidden talent. The grammarian marries the other daughter of the prince. The latter marries the mature woman who won him for a productive life. Al-Ḥakīm is of course paying homage here to the slogan raised by the revolution: 'Work is a right, an honour and a duty'. But the way he does it is both convincing and deliciously comic. The prince and his grammarian doctor are a couple of good-for-nothings; both penniless, they soon become little more than two vagabonds, living outside the pale of respect and enjoying the immense freedom this life gives. Their childish bickerings, their continuous attempts to offload responsibilities onto each other's shoulders soon turns them into a comic duet. Al-Ḥakīm is once more the same master of the comic whom we have met in some of his non-dramatic works such as *ᶜAwdat al-rūḥ* ('Return of the spirit') and *Yawmiyyāt nāʾib fil'-aryāf* ('Diary of a County District Attorney'), as well as in some of the earlier plays, notably *Raṣāṣah fi'l-qalb*. But here he shows his astuteness in turning an essentially serious theme into matter for real comedy, without allowing the message of the play to be in any way belittled or made fun of. It is the balance between thought and entertainment for which the dramatist has been working which has led to this happy result. *Al-Aydī al-nāᶜimah* was a box-office success and, like *Raṣāṣah*, was subsequently turned into a film.

In 1956 al-Ḥakīm wrote *al-Ṣafqah* ('The deal'), a significant play because in it the dramatist uses the form and technique of total theatre to write a popular play aimed at all sections of theatregoers. In a postscript to the play which he calls 'A Manifesto', al-Ḥakīm discusses the various problems that face the Arabic theatre. One of these is that plays have ceased to have a general appeal: they address themselves to certain sections of the audiences, either the intellectuals or the broad masses. The need exists for a play that should please all parts of a united audience because this kind of play has always been the bulwark of all thriving theatre. Hence the present attempt by the writer: a play cast into the mould of what we call today 'the poor theatre'. It can be played in the open air – a barn or a marketplace; it needs no sets or props, and the dialogue is written in such a way that it can be readily understood by everybody, in the town as well as in the countryside, in Egypt and in all other parts of the Arab fatherland. Al-Ḥakīm chooses words common to all Arabs and hopes thereby to solve the thorny problem of colloquial versus classical Arabic, for the dialogue lends itself easily to either: al-Ḥakīm calls this the 'third' language. He succeeds markedly in suiting the dramatic diction of Arabic drama to the needs of an easily flowing dialogue.

For the theme of the play al-Ḥakīm chooses a story taken from real life. A small village is trying with great difficulty to secure the ownership of two feddans which a foreign land company is offering for sale. They have finally collected the money needed when a big landowner is seen on the outskirts of the village. He has had a car accident and is waiting with his assistant to catch a train to Cairo. The villagers immediately believe he has come to outbid them at the land sale. They decide to bribe him off and hand him one hundred pounds. Neither he nor his assistant understands why the money is offered. When they do, the landowner will not allow the villagers to have the two feddans unless they let him take a pretty young peasant woman for whom he has developed a liking, to work as a nurse to his son in his Cairo palace. Everybody is appalled: they know what this would in effect mean. But Mabrūkah, the young woman in question, agrees to go. She uses a ruse to thwart the plans of Ḥāmīd Bey, the landowner: in his luxurious palace she pretends to have caught cholera. The palace is immediately cordoned off and its residents, including Ḥāmīd Bey, become internees. Mabrūkah is taken to hospital but is released two days later – enough time to give the peasants the chance to finalize the sale with the company. Mabrūkah returns home, her honour fully preserved. Al-Ḥakīm does not say how much of this has actually taken place, but it is easy to see that he was building on the basic situation of the coincidence and the misunderstanding. The rest belongs to the writer's imagination, aided by folktales in which enterprising men and women face difficult situations by means of courage and ruse and emerge victorious. The play offers a fascinating picture of a typical Egyptian village; the characters, who are vivid and true to life, are keenly observed and sympathetically portrayed, even though one can detect an undertone of criticism directed against the peasants' credulousness and their petty quarrels. Some of them are rash; others are timid and yielding. One is a trickster and a double-dealer; another, though a drunkard, is honest and helpful.

Al-Ṣafqah reaches the goal set by al-Ḥakīm: it pleases everybody. When presented on the stage in 1958, it was an immediate success. It is a precursor of a group of plays which were termed 'Operettas without music', that is, plays which have the basic requirements for an operetta: a phantasy, a situation turned upside down, or a delicious illogical premise which, once accepted, entails perfectly logical sequences. These plays lend themselves easily to the operetta form. Al-Ḥakīm's stage directions to *al-Ṣafqah* mention music, dance, song and other festive happenings. But it is the main situation in the play which draws it very close to being an operetta.

Al-Sulṭān al-ḥāʾir ('The Sultan's dilemma', 1960), is even more obviously an operetta in essence, based as it is on a delightfully fantastic situation. A Sultan in Mameluke times suddenly finds himself in a very awkward situation. The previous Sultan, for whom as a child of six he had been bought, has died without ever emancipating his slave, the present Sultan. This means that the courageous ruler, loved and respected by everybody for the many battles he has won for his country, has either to abdicate or to suffer himself to be publicly sold by auction. This second alternative is the only way by which the Sultan can keep his throne; being a slave, he is not entitled to enjoy the rights of free men. He is merely a thing that belongs to the public coffers and only by auction can he hope to be freed. The bidder to whose lot he will fall would be asked to forfeit his right to own him as a manifestation of his love for Sultan and country alike. Then and then only can the Sultan resume his rule. When this is put to the Sultan by the Chief Judge he is astounded, infuriated and scandalized by turns. He is sorely tempted to use force to end this ridiculous situation. Who would gainsay him if, sword in hand, he would asseverate that he has actually been emancipated by his predecessor? No one, answers the Chief Judge, except himself for he would make it known that the Sultan is a slave. The Sultan can indeed do what he likes, but the Chief Judge points out to him that swords do cut knots and necks, but they never offer a good way out of a tremendous difficulty such as the present one.

The Sultan's dilemma is a choice between naked power and the rule of law. He hesitates for a while before deciding to abide by the law. When offered for sale the highest bidder proves to be a woman whom everybody takes for a prostitute. Actually she is a very cultured, many-talented young widow, who was formerly the slave and then the wife of a rich merchant. In her husband's lifetime she and her husband kept a salon where poetry, song and dance were permanent fare and when her husband died she kept the salon going. Hence the ill repute she has brought upon herself, for only men attended her salon. The lady, who cares for the souls of men, not for their bodies, is a latter-day Shahrazād. Because of this interest in improving men's souls she decides to buy the Sultan. She has heard of his insolence and his ferociousness and so she decides to have him fully in her power. Once he is in her grip, she discovers what a truly gentle and good-natured man he is. She is fascinated by his quiet decision to shun force and resort to the civilized position of bowing to the law. She is also elated by the power which she suddenly has over the first and greatest man in the country. One word said by her would decide his ultimate end: to be either a permanent slave to her or a free man fully entitled to become again the good, courageous Sultan he was. The lady, too, has to make a difficult choice: to keep the man she likes, even though he be a slave, or to set him free and lose him for ever. She decides to obey the dictates of honour. The Sultan is given his freedom.

In this fairy-tale atmosphere where everything is topsy-turvey – a Sultan is discovered to be a slave and has to be sold by public auction to gain his freedom; a prostitute turns out to be a truly virtuous and noble soul – al-Ḥakīm discusses the serious question of how a country should be governed.

The question was becoming increasingly important for those liberals who were daily dismayed by the sight of power being concentrated in the hands of a few men around Nasser. Some of those liberals, while supporting Nasser's main lines in the international field, felt the need for more freedom at home. Now that the revolution was firmly in the driving seat they argued, the country should go back to the rule of law, instead of the revolutionary measures previously used. *Al-Sulṭān al-ḥāʾir* is an urge in this direction. It is a fully dramatic plea for freedom, pleasant as well as instructive. Despite the light, easy-going manner in which events develop, the message is easily put across; no ruler is himself free, who uses force to support freedom. This is the last of al-Ḥakīm's political plays to end on a cheerful note. When he came to write such political plays as *Maṣīr ṣarṣār* ('Fate of a cockroach', 1966), *Kull shayʾ fī maḥallih* ('Not a thing out of place', 1966) and *Bank al-qalaq* ('The bank of worry', 1967), the tone was bitterly critical.

But before saying goodbye to cheerfulness, al-Hakīm wrote two truly fascinating plays: *Yā Ṭāliʿ al-shajarah* ('The tree climber', 1962) and *Shams al-Nahār* (1965). In the former play he goes back to the eternal situation of Adam and Eve and the Tree. Al-Ḥakīm's Adam is called Bahādir, a former low-grade civil servant, who lives on his small pension with his wife Bahānah. Bahādir is not at all what he seems: a former employee who, without work, is only fit for the scrap heap. Deep down within he is in fact a philosopher in search of Full Knowledge. He believes he will attain this knowledge when he has succeeded in growing an evergreen tree with a miraculous attribute: it bears fruit all four seasons of the year. Bahādir is convinced that the tree will not grow until it has been fertilized with his wife's blood. He keeps this intention a dark secret until the proper time comes to put it into effect. Meanwhile he lives a life of disharmony with his wife: the two are at opposite poles. Bahānah, for her part, also seeks to 'kill' her husband, that is she tries to pull him away from his philosophic project and turn him into a woman-fertilizer, a bread-winner and a father to their daughter. In this way she, too, is a creative person. The discord between her and her husband is not the usual petty quarrels experienced by some married people. It is a clash of opposites in which one party only can win. The situation is very near what we see in some of Shaw's plays, notably *Man and Superman*, where an artist and a vital woman are involved in a tug-of-war, which decides what type of creation will result: art and philosophy or a race of supermen. The play ends by Bahādir actually killing his wife. When he gets ready to bury the body under his tree, he is horrified to find that the symbol of his achievement, a small green lizard which he calls *Sheikha Khaḍrah*, has been killed and thrown into the pit he has prepared for his dead wife. The body of Bahānah disappears. By killing his wife he has killed creativity. The Tree, Bahānah and the lizard are essential parts of his dream of creation.

When *Yā Ṭāliᶜ al-shajarah* was published, al-Ḥakīm agreed with those critics who classified it as belonging to the Theatre of the Absurd. Those critics believed that the parallel dialogue between husband and wife which discloses their inability to meet and communicate was enough to term the play absurd. Actually the play has nothing of the absurd in it. It is a philosophic work very cleverly using the detective technique to secure the attention of its audiences and readers and to probe the problem of knowledge, which has always interested al-Ḥakīm. Various methods of trying to acquire knowledge are presented in the play: the police officer uses the cross-examination method to try to come to know why and where the wife has disappeared to previous to her subsequent murder. The Sufi mystic taps his inner sources for knowledge. Bahādir tries to achieve knowledge by something like black magic rituals. The title which al-Ḥakīm uses for his play is taken from a folkloric song with symbolic undertones. The relation between the song and the content of the play is not easy to decide: it can only be guessed at. The tree of the song is as magical as that of the play. In song and play alike a project is destroyed, a dream does not come true.

Shams al-Nahār is a frankly didactic play. Thus states al-Ḥakīm in his short introductory word in which he says he wants his play to teach a lesson as directly as did *Kalīlah wa Dimnah*, La Fontaine's *Fables* and some of Brecht's plays. For the lesson he goes to the *Arabian Nights* and picks out a tale about a princess, Shams al-Nahār, who, unlike her sisters, would not marry a rich prince or a wealthy vizir's son, but a man who would deserve her in his own right. She has it announced in the town that whosoever wants to marry the Princess can present himself and, if fit, he will win the great prize, otherwise he will receive three lashes. Many rich young men come to present their suits to her, and they all are found wanting. The Sultan, her father, and his Minister are about to give up in despair, when an interesting man comes forward. He is a nobody, obviously poor and untutored in the good manners of royal life, but he has a strong personality. The princess is interested, but the suitor has his own terms: Shams al-Nahār should step down and live the life of an ordinary woman of her age. She should go out with him into the open fields and the mountains, there to learn how to earn the food and pleasure she is now getting out of life undeservingly. She should work in order to become a fully developed human being. Most reluctantly, the Sultan lets the princess and her suitor have their way. The two go off on a trip during which the princess learns a great deal. Work makes her independent of her position and her wealth. She also becomes independent of her tutor, her would-be fiancé. Towards the end of the play she surprises him by saying that if she marries him she will all the time be thinking of a certain prince, Ḥamdān, whom the two travellers had come to know. Ḥamdān has fallen in love with Shams and has agreed to go on foot to her father's palace, to ask for her hand in marriage. Shams believes he has the makings of a good ruler and so is tempted to marry him. With a broken heart the would-be fiancé, Badr is his assumed name, points out to Shams that she should marry Ḥamdān. She has created him in her own image, and is bound to love him, since we all love those whom we fashion. Equally sadly, Shams concurs and the farewell scene is very much reminiscent of Higgins and Eliza's separation. Al-Ḥakīm's Higgins, Badr, has created the princess anew, has given her a soul and a will of her own. She is fit to go on her way and marry a man who belongs to her own class; Badr, like Higgins, has a greater goal than matrimonial happiness. He will appear in other places, in different guises and professions, to help fashion interesting people anew. Such is his lot in life.

Thus ends a fascinating play where thought and entertainment have been welded together to make a beautiful whole. Like *al-Ṣafqah*, *al-Sulṭān al-ḥāʾir* and *Yā Ṭāliʿ al-shajarah*, this is an operetta in essence ready to lend itself easily to any enterprising composer. Although the obvious kinship of al-Ḥakīm's plays to music has been laughed away by more than one Arab critic, al-Ḥakīm himself is conscious of music permeating many of his plays. In an article published in the Egyptian weekly *Ākhir Sāʿah*, he describes how he went to see a production of *Ahl al-kahf* ('The men of the cave') given at Palermo, in Italy, in 1954, where the acting took place in the courtyard of a monastery. Al-Ḥakīm was pleasantly surprised to find that a corps of ballet dancers was used to give expression to the thoughts and dreams of the sleepers. The second and third acts used the columns of the monastery as a natural and very fitting decor. When the actress who played Presca started to bewail her dead lover, al-Ḥakīm could hear music, but coming seemingly from nowhere. The words, he could feel, were not merely articulated but sung. Next to al-Ḥakīm sat a high-ranking Italian official, who, when the acting was over, turned to the playwright and said: 'How fit this play is to become an opera.' The same remark had been made by an Austrian composer commenting on a production of al-Ḥakīm's *Pygmalion* at Salzburg.

THE NEW EGYPTIAN DRAMATISTS

When the 1952 revolution broke out al-Ḥakīm had succeeded in keeping alive the idea and practice of drama and theatre in Egypt. He had managed to bestow respect on a profession and a form of writing which had enjoyed little consideration both socially and in literary circles. A printed play was now securely accepted as good literature read for its own merits irrespective of actability. And al-Ḥakīm could boast that to him went most of the credit.

But, as shown above, the playwright was far from satisfied by this result. Do what he would, his plays never could reach the broad audiences he was eager to address. Something other than social respect and the continued presence of a prominent writer was needed: a great national event. This was supplied by the 1952 army revolution. New vistas were opened before the nation, enormous problems were encountered, different solutions contemplated and tried. Everybody felt invited to take part in the national awakening, to shape his and the nation's destiny. This is the precious moment which makes a truly alive theatre possible.

The group of young writers, who began to make their appearance after the revolution, had talents, big dreams and a direct contact with reality. Quite a number of them had known prisons and concentration camps before and after the revolution. One of them, at least, Alfred Farag (1929–), had been recently released from a concentration camp when his first successful play *Ḥāllaq Baghdād* ('The barber of Baghdad') was accepted and produced by the National Theatre.

The group was headed by Nuᶜmān ᶜĀshūr (1918–87), a many-talented young man who, before the revolution, had written articles and short stories for magazines agitating for radical change. Endowed with a marked histrionic talent he now found it possible to give vent to his secret desire of becoming a dramatist. ᶜĀshūr wrote many good plays, the most mature of these being *ᶜĀʾilat al-Dughrī* ('The Dughri family', 1962), which depicts a lower-middle-class Egyptian family. The dramatist captures the family at a very low ebb of its fortunes – approaching disintegration. Sayyid, the eldest member, is a tailor who was once fashionable but has been driven out of business by new techniques in tailoring he is unable to take in; he becomes almost a bankrupt. His younger brother, Muṣṭafā, is a history teacher who has recently obtained his M.A. He thinks that by virtue of the degree he has mounted many steps above the rest of the family, and so looks despisingly at all around him. He divorces his downtrodden wife and plans to marry a former faculty colleague, Azhār, who looks upon marriage as a mere business deal, so devoid is she of any finer feeling. There is also Zaynab, the older of two sisters; she is a sharp-tongued woman who holds perfect sway over Aḥmad, her hen-pecked husband, a low-grade civil servant, but despite her biting words she has a good heart. ᶜĀʾishah, the younger sister, is a teacher of gymnastics who, having reached her twenty-seventh year, has to look urgently for a husband. The youngest member of the Dughri family is Ḥasan, a promising football player who, having completed his secondary school studies, has allowed football to entice him away from further education.

This is mainly a play of characters. ʿĀshūr paints a mural of an Egyptian family, and contemplates it, meting out criticism here and there, expressing compassion, showing up social deficiencies and passing a final judgement. Very little happens in the play. There is a dispute about the family house: Muṣṭafā, the history master, convinces his sister Zaynab that it would be to their advantage if the two of them sold their shares in the house. When they try to do so they discover that Sayyid had mortgaged the premises. They accuse him of double-dealing and Muṣṭafā threatens to inform the police. The crisis is soon averted when Sayyid proves by documents he has laid aside and forgotten that he had regained ownership of the house while still solvent. But though peace is made a big crack now mars the family edifice. Disintegration presents itself. The members of the family all go their separate ways, leaving behind an aged servant who has served each one of them young and old and whose life-long dream has been to own a pair of shoes. When he is offered a pair in the end by Ḥasan, he discovers that having gone barefoot for so long, his feet have become too flattened for any shoes. As he sees everybody going away he bitterly comments: 'May God forgive you. May God forgive you all.'

In subject-matter, in character portrayal and in the attitude the dramatist takes towards his characters, *ʿĀʾilat al-Dughrī* is unprecedented in Arabic drama. The main characters, Sayyid, Muṣṭafā and Zaynab, are carefully portrayed with an objectivity that looks deep into them, irrespective of the dramatist's own feelings which, nevertheless, transpire unobtrusively throughout. Sayyid is a drunkard, a spendthrift and a benighted manager of his own affairs. But he is shown to possess a heart of gold. Zaynab is delineated sympathetically despite her biting tongue and foolish behaviour. Though she teams up with Muṣṭafā, she does not share his hatred and contempt for everybody. The old servant, al-Ṭawwāf, though he appears for only a few minutes in the play, is allowed to unmask the utter selfishness of the family. That the dramatist should give this opportunity to the old servant, is a good proof of maturity, since ʿĀshūr belongs to the same social stratum as the Dughri family.

Comparable to ʿĀshūr's works are those of Alfred Farag (Faraj), a dramatist who embraced many styles of dramatic writing, ranging from plays based on the Arab heritage, such as *Ḥallāq Baghdād* (1963), *al-Zīr Sālim* ('Prince Salim', 1967) and *ʿAlī Janāḥ al-Tabrīzī* (1968) to political plays, such as *Sulaymān al-Ḥalabī* (1964), *al-Nār wa'l-zaytūn* ('Fire and olives', 1970) and social critical plays like *ʿAskar wa ḥaramiyyah* ('Cops and robbers',

1966) and *Zawāj ᶜalā waraqat ṭalāq* ('Marriage on a divorce licence', 1973). Of these, *ᶜAlī Janaḥ al-Tabrīzī* deserves special mention, since it represents one of the mature attempts to draw on the sources of the *Arabian Nights* for dramatic material likely to appeal to wide audiences. Out of two tales from the *Arabian Nights*, Farag weaves the text of a fascinating play. The theme is the interlocking of myth and reality, how easy it is to pass from the one into the other, how powerful myth is when embraced by a firm believer in its all-pervading potency, how miraculous it becomes when taken up by the masses.

ᶜAlī Janāh al-Tabrīzī is a spendthrift lord who has wasted away his wealth on drink and entertainment. When the play opens he is about to leave his castle for ever, having sold it. He expects the new owner every minute and meanwhile lives in imagination the life, and maintains the ways and airs of the wealthy lord he once was. When a cobbler knocks at the door asking for alms, he is well received by ᶜAlī, who invites him to a banquet. This turns out to be an imaginary meal, full of the names of the most delicious dishes which the cobbler, under threat of bodily punishment, has to pretend he is actually enjoying. The cobbler is soon talked into agreeing to serve the wayward master. Though he strikes him as being not a little bizarre, he finds himself unable to resist the charm of his eloquence, his fiery imagination and his contagious play-acting. The poor cobbler gives away what little he has saved to his bankrupt master and agrees to go with him on a voyage to the Far East. The two will pretend that the master is a very wealthy merchant who is ahead of a richly endowed caravan extending all the way from Baghdad to China.

When they arrive at their destination, ᶜAlī immediately starts his play-acting. He instructs his follower to introduce him to the town in the grand manner that befits an emir. The cobbler enters into the spirit of the little play and soon convinces a merchant that his master is the dignitary he pretends to be. When the King's daughter comes to buy a piece of very rich cloth, ᶜAlī pretends that all that the shop contains is far beneath the princess's dignity, and commands his follower to give away to the poor all the stock. When the princess asks who ᶜAlī is, the latter's answer is: 'a stranger who would fain serve the princess with his heart, his sword and his wealth'. The royal personage is much impressed.

ᶜAlī Janāḥ soon becomes a myth. The wealthy lend him money on the strength of the very rich caravan he expects. The King himself comes to believe in the caravan, and agrees to let ᶜAlī marry the Princess. But when months pass by and no caravan appears, all, including the King, lose patience. Even ᶜAlī's follower, piqued by his master's squandering of money on the poor and never giving him any, becomes a turncoat and informs the King against his master with the result that ʿAlī is sentenced to death. However, appalled by the awful deed he has done, the cobbler puts on a mantle and a huge turban, pretending he is Ḥasan, one of ʿAlī's attendants who has just arrived to announce the good news of the arrival of the caravan. ʿAlī is immediately released and has barely time to flee on horseback, taking away with him, besides his follower, the princess, his wife. She has always believed in the essential goodness of a man who created a myth and made it serve a very good end.

A good myth or an atrocious lie? The play intimates that the answer depends on how one see things. To the poor the imaginary caravan has worked miracles: it effected a more just distribution of wealth since it gave to the have-nots the surplus of those who have. Thus, in their eyes, ʿAlī stands out as a reformer, a visionary, a dreamer of dreams. If enormous good has come through a myth in one place, it could do the same in many other places. In this sense, the caravan ceases to be pure imagination, it becomes a possibility capable of materialization elsewhere. The borderline between myth and reality is seen to be gross by gross people only. For those who have dreams the border does not exist. This is what the princess has come to realise. Hence she joins the ranks of the dreamers.

Another significant playwright of the period is Mīkhāʾīl Rūmān (1927–73), who wrote many social-critical and political plays, prominent among which is his first, *al-Dukhkhān* ('Smoke', 1962). The play introduces the character of an intelligent young man called Ḥamdī, who is to appear in many of the plays by Rūmān under the same name, presenting almost the same features. He is an oppressed youth, suffering from social and political persecution and condemned to dire poverty. In *al-Dukhkhān* he is a downtrodden typist, who cannot make both ends meet. He has to resort to hashish to forget his troubles, but hashish only increases them and emphasizes his utter loss. Ḥamdī represents many Egyptian young men belonging to the lower middle class who managed, under most trying conditions, to obtain higher education. Their university degrees, however, never could raise them above the very low level of government or private-company employees, grossly overworked and meagrely paid. Ḥamdī has the additional misery of having discovered the truth about himself and his society – indeed, about the human condition itself. He very much hates what he has discovered, and would be happy, were it possible for him, to do battle with all injustices to right the wrong, as did Don Quixote with whom Ḥamdī identifies.

We meet the character again, but initially without the name, in a fascinating one-act play called *al-Wāfid* ('The newcomer', 1965). The young man arrives at an hotel after a long trying journey, and he is famished. He sits at a table, his mouth watering at the very thought that soon he will help himself to a sumptuous meal. Immediately a person called the Deputy appears, embraces the Newcomer warmly and talks to him cordially as he would to an old friend. The Newcomer is at once put on his guard as he does not remember ever having met the Deputy, but the latter does not mind the cold reception of his old friend. When the Deputy suggests that the Newcomer work with him at the hotel, the latter hesitates. The Deputy construes this as turning down the offer, expresses his sorrow and leaves his friend, saying he has a journey to make, but since this is the opportunity of a life-time, he hopes his friend will contact him some other time.

A waiter comes, and before the Newcomer has had time to order his meal of choice food, he is asked whether he is on the list of the hotel's guests. Unable to return a satisfactory answer to this and to very many other questions concerning the time and manner of his arrival, the guest is left to the good care of the Commissioner. The Newcomer learns that the Commissioner was once a comrade in the nationalist struggle. The two of them soon take part in an imaginary political demonstration in which they denounce past traitors. When the Newcomer, suddenly feeling the pangs of hunger, calls for food the Commissioner asks the excruciating question: 'Are you on the list?' Utterly dejected, the Newcomer decides to do without food altogether, but he discovers that food is obligatory. He discovers more: he is in fact under arrest and his case has to be examined by the Expert. The Expert turns out to be a dear old friend, but he too asks the painful question. When no positive answer is given the Expert informs his friend that not until he has gained full information about him, can he be of any service to him. This information will have to be fed into a computer and it alone will decide whether food can be given. Short of this the Newcomer would become a nobody – a person without identity, without a past, without a future. His patience utterly exhausted, the Newcomer is driven to extreme rage. He denounces everybody and everything, accusing people at the hotel of having been reduced to ciphers. What good has the hotel brought them? Each of them is ridiculously proud of the button he is assigned to press and deems this glorious work. He, the Newcomer, is the only truly free man among the lot of them, having done away with identity card, luggage and all other social manacles. But before he has exhausted his rage, the long arm of the mechanized contemporary age seizes him. He is liquidated without much ado. The play is an effective unmasking of all political regimes where the individual is ruthlessly squeezed by the huge wheels of an inhumanly efficient state. It is an outcry for the freedom of the individual and a denunciation of all efforts to make man subservient to the machine. Despite its romanticism it grips us with its sincerity and acute pathos.

Maḥmūd Diyāb (1932–83), despite his short life, managed to contribute to Arabic drama some of its more mature plays. He varied his style – beginning with the realism of *al-Zawbaʿah* ('The storm', 1967), a drama about village life, moving to experiment with popular forms of drama such as *al-Sāmir*, a village form of entertainment which he coupled with the quasi-improvised form to give us a fascinating play, *Layālī al-ḥiṣād* ('Harvest nights', 1967). Its theme is illusion and reality in the lives of simple villagers whom a beautiful temptress drives to mortal disputes and crime. But it is *Bāb al-Futūḥ* (1971) which has earned Diyāb the esteem of critics and playgoers alike – an esteem which has been growing steadily even after his death. The play captures a preeminently dramatic moment in the life of the Arab nation – the excruciating pains of the 1967 major defeat. The air sits heavy on every chest; silence is heavier and to have to wait is heaviest. A group of young men are conversing. What is to be done? To keep silent? To shout out? To laugh? To become furious? Some of this is without avail and fury is not allowed. The young men, therefore, decide to play the game of history – to refashion its events and bring them nearer to truth and their hearts. History says that it is kings, sultans and great warriors who make major events. It gives as a shining example the august warrior and leader hero, Ṣalāḥ al-Dīn (Saladin). It says that it was the courage and genius of this great leader which enabled the Muslims to liberate Jerusalem after the battle of Hittin. The young men think otherwise. They believe that it is the people who make history, that when a war of liberation is taking place, it is they who join its ranks to defend themselves, their families, their homes and their country. They are the material of which victory is made. And yet hypocritical historians insist on looking upon them as mere tools by which great leaders march to their glories. The discontented, disillusioned group, after reviewing different periods of Arab history, choose to play the age of Saladin. But why think that the age gave birth to one great man only? Could it not have produced an equally great person, some revolutionary or other who had the interests of his Arab nation at heart? This they imagine to be Usāmah Ibn Yaʿqūb, a young man who has come all the way from Andalusia, with Seville soldiers hot at his heels. He has decided to turn his back on the disintegrating Arab sway in Spain where Arab factions fight each other with the help of their mutual enemies, and come to the east with an abundant hope in his heart and a great book in his hand. He wants to meet Saladin and explain his book to him. But the revolutionary ideas it contains terrify ʿImād al-Dīn, the personal historian of Saladin, who informs against Usāmah and his book and a series of persecutions ensue. The book, however, attracts many followers and believers, but its copies are burnt one after another. Usāmah's supporters all fall into the hands of their enemies and the end comes when

Usāmah himself is taken. Before he meets his death he addresses his persecutors:

> I know you all, I have met you in Andalusia, Morocco, Egypt and Syria and all the other countries I set foot in. I wish my comrades could see you now, in this devilish meeting you are holding. They would then discover the truth which your eyes reveal. We are right: never will this nation achieve victory until it has felled down your bodies – all, and ruthlessly.

Usāmah had wanted to warn Saladin against his retinue, who constitute a barrier between him and the simple folk in whose interests he is waging his wars. We meet some of these simple people among the throngs of Muslims who are on their way to Jerusalem, of whom the most interesting is the resolute, aged Abu'l-Fāḍil, who unfortunately fails to get back his house in Jerusalem; it has been turned into a *Khān*, a small wayside hotel, managed by a wily Jewess and her daughter. The victory of Saladin is only beneficial to the rich and their protegés, while the have-nots will be back where they were. This is a war by the people, but not for the people.

From the point of view of dramatic technique, *Bāb al-futūḥ* is a remarkable example of the mastery over dramatic writing the new generation of writers have been steadily gaining. The smooth way in which events run from reality into illusion and back is one aspect of this mastery. Thus the discontented are at one time young men living in the present and at another participants in the historic events. At a third time they represent Usāmah, whose words they declaim in a loud tone. They also assume the part of commentators on events, as well as representing the common folk in the play, those who embrace Usāmah's words and turn them into a dream that has to be fulfilled. These many parts are played with a grace that makes *Bāb al-Futūḥ* the first Arab play fully to integrate the chorus and turn it into an essential part of the play.

Limited space has not made it possible to give other dramatists the consideration they deserve. Among them is Yūsuf Idrīs (1927–91), whose *al-Farāfīr* ('The stooges', 1964) caused a big stir among theatregoers and critics alike. Idrīs claimed that his play is a good example of the truly national theatre form he was aiming at. *Al-Farāfīr* was a success, but it did not prove the dramatist's claim. ᶜAlī Sālim (1936–) gained wide acclaim with his play *Inta illi qatalt al-waḥsh* ('You killed the monster', 1970), in which he uses the Oedipus myth to discuss the state of affairs that led to the 1967 Arab defeat. In a vein of ironic humour it levels some biting criticism at both people and leader in an imaginary country where hero-worship has led to catastrophe. Saᶜd al-Dīn Wahbah (1925–) has many interesting plays to his credit, of which *Bīr al-sillim* ('The stairwell', 1966) is a good example. The head of the family suffers from paralysis, and lies helpless under the staircase. None except his loving daughter, ʿAzīzah, believe that he will ever recover. Thus they go their own selfish ways. Disintegration wins the day. But the family reunites towards the end, when its head begins to move again. The work offers many opportunities for different interpretations. It also harks back to Nuʿmān ʿĀshūr's *ʿĀʾilat al-Dughrī*, and utilizes some of the technique of Beckett's *Waiting for Godot*.

Because the section on Egypt has been designed to deal with the main dramatic current, that emanating from al-Ḥakīm, it was not possible to consider the plays of Maḥmūd Taymūr (1894–1973) and ʿAli Aḥmad Bākathīr (1910–69). Had more space been allotted, a different design would surely have included their works.

DRAMA OUTSIDE EGYPT

Lebanon and Syria

Although Syria and Lebanon helped the Egyptian theatre to flourish, giving it whole companies as well as some dramatic fare, at home, however, theatre lights were all put out. In both countries, especially in Syria, the attitude which prevailed regarded the theatre as a despicable art and relegated drama to books, providing reading material only, printed plays which are unactable.

Lebanese writers are very much aware that in their country, until very recently, drama existed only as a literary genre. Thus confessed ʿAbd al-Laṭīf Sharārah in an article entitled 'Contemporary Lebanese theatre', (*al-Ādāb* magazine, January 1967). Sharārah, after having divided Lebanese dramatic effort into three phases – translation from the west; the attempt to resurrect Arab national glories; and the realist period – ended his article by asking whether there existed the possibility for a thriving Arab dramatic literature. The question was answered by another Lebanese writer, Ghassān Salāmah (Salamé), who, in a book written in French, maintained that Lebanese theatre only began in 1960. All efforts to introduce theatre into Lebanon prior to this date he unceremoniously dismissed as either attempts to entertain neighbours by Arabizing Molière (al-Naqqāsh) or end-of-the-academic-year school plays written for edification. The author then described in some detail theatrical activities in Lebanon during the years 1960–74. Five drama companies were busy giving performances in Beirut, one of them directed by two theatre artists who had had dramatic training in London and Strasbourg. Some dramatists and actors were also trained in France and Moscow. Most of the plays given were designed to cater for the tastes of the intellectuals. Quite a number were chosen from world drama. The director of one drama company, The Beirut School for Contemporary Drama, Munīr al-Dibs, presented plays by Sophocles, Shakespeare, Sartre, Ionesco, Goethe, Büchner and Brecht against a background of historical sites. He was later (1970) to alienate himself from the limited audiences of these masterpieces and embrace a kind of mysticism akin to Grotowski's, preferring to derive his inspiration from non-dramatic works such as Jibrān's *The Prophet*.

But there were others who sought to give expression to burning social questions, such as the artists who gathered round Roger ^c^Assāf and his enterprising actress and partner Niḍāl al-Ashqar, who together ran the Beirut Studio. They presented an interesting play called *Iḍrāb al-ḥaramiyyah* ('The thieves on strike', 1971) which has some kinship with Brecht's *The Threepenny Opera*. Both works deal with the relationship that exists between crime and the police: one of mutal aid and benefit. The thieves in the play are not the common ones, but are the industrialist who underpays his workers, the doctor who shares with the pharmacist the price of expensive medicine he unnecessarily prescribes for his patients, and so on. When the people rise in protest against this exploitation and succeed in pushing the robbers out they soon discover that a new set of robbers have come to replace the old. The evil lies much deeper. A whole regime has to be done away with and not particular persons only. The play was given the framework of a festival: audiences were met at the entrances by actors and the author; folkloric music greeted them and Arab coffee and Turkish delight were circulated. Theatregoers either sat on chairs or on the carpeted floor and the events of the play were presented on three stages in different parts of the auditorium. The play itself was treated as a social as well as a dramatic event, the aim being to plant theatre in the daily activities of the people and do away with the assumption that it concerned intellectuals only. People from every walk of life flocked to see it.

Using the same method of directly addressing the people, the Raḥabānī brothers, aided by a superstar, the celebrated singer Fayrūz, gave one operetta after another, in which they extolled the simple life of the Lebanese peasants, their solidarity in the face of danger and their continuous efforts to combat evil – in persons as well as in systems. These operettas must be considered Lebanon's main contribution to the art of theatre. But for drama proper, that is fixed texts of literary merit which are actable, Lebanon had to wait until the poet ^c^Iṣām Maḥfūẓ (b. 1939) produced his *avant garde* plays such as *al-Zanzalakht* ('The china tree', 1968), an absurdist play attacking political tyranny.

Syria, without al-Qabbānī, went on for many decades enjoying popular theatre shows such as *qaraqoz* theatre, comic fragments and al-Samāḥ dance.

This fare was successfully given at coffee houses by a popular artist called Muḥammad Ḥabīb. Besides this, as ᶜAdnān Ibn Dhurayl shows in his study of the Syrian Theatre from Khalīl al-Qabbānī to the present (Damascus, 1971), there were coffee-house presentations of *ḥakawātī* (story-teller) and the comic numbers of the famous clown Jūrj Dakhūl, which had some influence on Arabic comedy, popular and literary alike, especially when Jurj Dakhūl also migrated from Syria into Egypt. Alongside this popular fare were the usual literary dramatic pieces, some written by noted poets such as ᶜUmar Abū Rīshah, but these were hopelessly weak and unactable. This situation continued until 1959, when the state decided to intervene. A little earlier two noted theatre artists, Rafīq al-Ṣabbān and Sharīf Khazandar, had come back to Damascus from France where both had been trained by two of the foremost French men of the theatre, Jean Louis Barraut and Jean Vilar. The young Syrian pair began to give plays from world theatre calculated to attract wide attention. Al-Ṣabbān formed a drama nucleus, which he called '*Nadwat al-Fann wa'l-Fikr*', which gave good support to the new Syrian drama. When the state decided it was time to help, it formed a National Theatre Company in 1959, making use of al-Ṣabbān's group and of some directors who had graduated in America and Egypt. Thus the Syrian Theatre began to build up its team of artists and technicians. As it did so, a young dramatist, Saᶜdallah Wannūs (1940–) was busy equipping himself for the part he was to play in Syrian theatre life: that of a national dramatist.

Wannūs wrote five one-act plays and a long play in two parts in which he was clearly looking for a direction and a mode of expression before writing the play that marked him as an initiator: *Ḥaflat samar min ajl khamsa Ḥuzayrān* ('A party to celebrate the Fifth of June', 1968) a courageous dramatic search into the minds and souls of Arabs and an attempt to discover the circumstances that led to the major defeat of 1967. In it Wannūs used the seemingly improvised dramatic form to extract bitter laughter and unmask serious shortcomings in the Arab situation. This was followed by two other plays: *Mughāmarat raʾs al-mamlūk Jābir* ('The adventures of the head of Mamluk Jabir', 1969) and *Sahrah maᶜa Abī Khalīl al-Qabbānī* ('An evening with Abu Khalil al-Qabbani', 1972). In them Wannūs used the traditions of popular presentations: direct address to the audience, the brushing aside of illusion and a seemingly improvised text (*Sahrah*) and the adventures, intrigues, warring princes and impassioned love between their dependants, all reminiscent of the *Arabian Nights* (*Mughāmarat*).

But it was in his *al-Malik huwa'l-malik* ('The king is the king', 1977), that Wannūs revealed his dramatic genius. Making use of two tales from the

Arabian Nights, he wrote a fascinating play in which the major theme of how to govern was tackled profoundly, intelligently and very entertainingly. A bored king, to pass time agreeably, picks on one of his subjects to make him king for a day. The counterfeit king, once the sceptre is in his grip actually becomes king in word and deed. He is recognized as such even by the true king's own queen and his closest attendants. The post, the retinue, the costume and the other regalia all make a king what he is and not the person who is blessed with these. What is more, the fake king, a downtrodden bankrupt merchant, impoverished by the machinations of the Shabandar of merchants, defends, in his new capacity, this same Shabandar, and endorses all the wrongs that the previous regime has perpetrated against the people, as being in the nature of things. The moral of the play, namely that to achieve universal justice, regimes, not persons, must go, is sung by the chorus. As well as being a chorus its members are characters in the play who represent a group of young men and a woman looking for revolutionary change. The play uses the techniques of various popular presentations to tell a story and act a play as well as drive home a lesson.

Iraq

In Iraq dramatic art was introduced through visiting companies, largely Egyptian. In 1926 an Egyptian company headed by Jūrj Abyaḍ gave performances in Baghdad and Basra and the visit proved to be pivotal to nascent Iraqi drama, boosting the morale of Iraqi amateurs. *Oedipus Rex* was given and a certain Iraqi amateur, Haqqī al-Shiblī, was so taken with the performance in which he acted the part of Oedipus's son that he went out and formed a drama company in the following year, for which both Iraqi and Egyptian actors played. In 1935 Shiblī was given a scholarship to study theatre arts in France. He came back four years later, and started a department attached to the Arts Academy, for training would-be theatre artists as actors and directors. The department also took on the responsibility of arranging and presenting dramatic seasons. Everything was ready for the birth of a theatre. One thing only was lacking: a dramatist who would be able to achieve both presence and continuity on the dramatic scene. Such a dramatist did not take long to appear. He was Yūsūf al-ᶜĀnī (1927–) whose rich output earned him the stature of a national dramatist.

Al-ᶜĀnī wrote several plays. *Anā ummuk yā Shākir* ('I am your mother, Shakir', 1955) treats of affairs of an Iraqi lower-middle-class family whose members take an active part in the events of the national movement raging around them. Shākir, the eldest, has been put to death by the despots of Iraq and his younger brother, Saᶜūdī, will meet with the same fate by the end of the play. Kawthar, their sister, is arrested as she comes out of hiding to inform her mother of Saᶜūdī's death. Thus the mother, Umm Shākir, is left alone, but she does not weaken or hesitate in her belief that all must work for the national cause. Despite some overwriting, the characters are powerfully created. The mould is decidedly melodramatic, but this happens to suit the patriotic theme of the play.

Al-ᶜĀnī was to learn the important lesson of welding successfully the two elements of entertainment and message in his *al-Miftaḥ* ('The key'), written some twelve years later (1967–68). For the form of his play, the dramatist chooses the fable, making use of a popular song about a magic chest which has variants in other Arab countries (thus making it possible for his play also to be appreciated outside Iraq). A newly married young couple go on a journey to look for guarantees for a child they intend to have. The husband has insisted on not having a child before a good life is secured for it. The couple put a dress and a cake in a chest, but in order to safeguard the contents they have to have a key for the chest. The key can only be made by a blacksmith, but the blacksmith demands money and money is kept by a bride. When the couple get to meet her she is having a bath and she tells them that she needs a lamp, which is at the bottom of a well. To reach the lamp, a rope is needed, but the rope is tied to a bull's horn and the bull needs grass. Grass will be in the garden, but the garden needs rain and rain is with God.

At every phase of their journey, the couple, called Ḥayrān and Ḥayrānah (Mr and Mrs At-a-loss) meet disappointments. However, in the end the blacksmith gives them the key free of charge, but when they open the chest it is empty. Thus the couple come to learn a good lesson. Exertion alone is not sufficient; far more important is to define one's goal and the means of reaching it. Nothing given to us free of charge is worth having, and we must look for concrete things that will make our lives fuller and more secure. At the end of the play Ḥayrānah reveals a secret that she has been keeping dark: she is actually pregnant and will soon have a baby. She had decided not to tell her husband until the chest has been opened. Now that the child is a certainty the husband has to accept the unexpected situation. He and his wife, and a third person who has been accompanying them, have to find a new approach to life – have to run and rush to meet the new demands made by the arrival of the child. The play fascinates by a delightful reinterpretation of folklore which is both sympathetic and clear-sighted.

Al-ᶜĀnī wrote other equally significant plays, one of which is *al-Kharābah* ('The waste land', 1970), which is a phantasy making use of many dramatic styles such as the documentary and the popular and puppet theatres to produce a dramatic investigation into the problem of good and evil in its many aspects and under contemporary conditions. *Al-Khān* ('The Khan', 1976) is an impressive dramatic mural of national events that took place during the tempestuous years of the struggle for national liberation since the forties. It contains some powerfully created popular characters such as Najmah, an experienced woman of the people who, robbed of her much-loved husband, has dedicated her life to look after his handicapped friend who had once stood by her husband when in dire need. Najmah is reminiscent of comparable characters in Gorky.

Kuwait and Bahrain

Though Egyptian theatre artists have been instrumental in shaping and developing the theatre in Kuwait ever since the early sixties, the roots of the truly national Kuwaiti theatre strike deeper. Since the early forties, Kuwait has shown considerable interest in the dramatic arts. This manifested itself mainly in the improvised plays of Muḥammad al-Nashmī, a talented man of the theatre who perceived clearly that to reach the hearts of his audiences he had to give them what they liked best: comic themes taken directly from real life and charged with criticism of social and personal shortcomings, in the framework of improvisation. Al-Nashmī produced some twenty plays between 1956 and 1962, which left a deep impression on subsequent writers (who, unlike him, opted for the written text) and helped to determine the form and content of popular comedies and farces. One of them was Ṣaqr al-Rashūd, who was later to distinguish himself both as dramatist and as director.

Al-Rashūd wrote a series of plays in which he tackled the problem of the relationship between fathers and children in a changing Kuwait. The father stands apart, aloof and domineering, totally unprepared to yield one inch of the seemingly firm ground on which he stands: absolute domination over his family. The wife is either downtrodden and completely negligible when it comes to decision-taking, or she fully supports the father's despotism. The struggle that goes on ends invariably in the break-up of the family. Women suffer most. Prominent among Rashūd's plays is *al-Ṭīn* ('The mud', 1965), where an old father insists on marrying a young woman, not much older than his daughter. The latter is a plain Jane, who has to buy herself a husband. This man soon attracts the attention of the old man's beautiful wife. The two indulge in illicit love. The daughter knows this and has to accept it, as she loves her unfaithful husband. Then comes the break-up. The old man dies; his wife leaves both the house and her lover, for she has others to go to. The lover turns his back on his wife. Before the final curtain falls the corpse of the old man is treated to a severe lecture by Marzūq, the old servant who had also waited on the dead man's father. The theme is the undeserved wealth of the rich and the dire lot of the poor, who actually produce the wealth.

ᶜAbd al-ᶜAzīz al-Surayyiᶜ is another noteworthy dramatist. His plays are preoccupied with the twin themes of patriarchal despotism and the social earthquake which oil has brought to Kuwait. His play *Fulūs wa nufūs* ('Money and souls', 1969–70) deals effectively with this theme. A whole family breaks up. The father, who used to be honest and content with his lot, obtains a large sum of money from the sale of his house to the government. Immediately he becomes another man: he dons sumptuous clothes, gets himself a new wife from abroad, and stands in defiance against the whole family, accusing them of attempting to rob him of the lawful fruits of his newly acquired wealth.

Theatre in Bahrain presents a picture very similar to that of Kuwait. The themes are very much the same: patriarchal despotism, social injustice, sons and daughters in revolt against family coercion which soon produces frustration, madness or desertion of family and country.

Al-ᶜAnīd ('Steadfast', 197?), by Sulṭān Sālim, is different: it deals with the wider theme of revolt against the despotism of Salmān, a high-ranking civil servant. Aḥmad, a junior employee under Salmān, comes to inform him that he and the whole body of employees in the department have decided to go on strike unless their demands are met. Salmān tries to intimidate Aḥmad, but the young man stands firm. We are then shown the private life of Salmān when his mistress comes to see him. He is her virtual slave. A necklace of pearls he gives her she contemptuously rejects, but deigns to accept it when Salmān promises to give her the diamond one she very much desires. This scene of frivolity and looseness is contrasted with another of shameless oppression. Mahdī, a very poor old tenant, comes to seek clemency from Salmān. He cannot pay his landlord the three hundred dinars he had promised: this has been a very poor year for dates and Mahdī can only pay two hundred. But Salmān's decree is: either pay the sum in full or give up the palm trees. The callousness moves the mistress to compassion. From her handbag she takes one hundred dinars and gives them to poor old Mahdī. Aḥmad comes to see Salmān again, this time he is heartbroken: his colleagues have decided to abandon the strike, they are too poor to be able to afford dismissal. However, Aḥmad, clearly shaken, sticks to his own decision. In vain does Salmān try to bribe him with money, a house and a farm. The young man rejects it all, saying: 'This was only one battle. To try and lose is far better than not to try at all.' The play ends with a scene of dire warning against injustice: an earthquake breaks an island in two; a young woman in Bahreini national dress severely castigates those who squander wealth and deny the lawful rights of others: the workers and the needy. These will awaken one day.

Sudan

Sudan was introduced to the theatre by some Egyptian amateurs on the teaching staff of Gordon College, Khartum. In 1912 these amateurs worked together to write and produce a play called *al-Tawbah al-ṣādiqah* ('True penitence'), which was entirely Egyptian in subject, principal characters and players. This sparked off a continued effort by Sudanese intellectuals and amateur theatre artists who were very much impressed by the play as idea and practice. In 1932 Khālid Abū'l-Rūs wrote the first play by a Sudanese: *Tājūj wa'l-Muḥalliq* ('Tagug and al-Muhalliq'), which describes a tragic love between a beautiful wife and her husband. Though immature, the play presented Sudanese drama with a Sudanese theme, and took theatre to the wider audience of a sports club, where it was performed. Other clubs followed suit.

In 1946 the first Sudanese actress appeared on stage and in 1964 the first truly popular company was formed, which sought to go deep into Sudanese society and present its burning questions on the stage, touring provinces and giving performances at every suitable site. This was the Abad Amak drama company which attracted many to the theatre arts by dint of enthusiasm, dedication and the adoption of the people's causes, in and outside Sudan. In 1967 al-Fakkī ᶜAbd al-Ḥamīd, back from theatre and drama training in Britain, headed the National Theatre. He sought to give continuous theatre seasons, comprising Sudanese, Arab and world plays. He formed all the necessary crews of technicians and skilled workers, inculcated the teamwork spirit into them and paid playwrights more for their works. A department for theatre and other performing arts soon came into existence. But despite all these efforts, a national playwright has never yet been born.

Libya

In Libya the case is not at all different from many other Arab countries: the usual visits by Egyptian companies awaken the latent interest of local intellectuals and lovers of the theatre in the dramatic arts. They soon perceive that as well as an art, the theatre is a political and social means of effecting radical change. Hence the great enthusiasm of amateurs to plant the seed of the theatre in the national soil, and the many sacrifices they are prepared to make to this effect.

Some interesting plays have been written in Libya, such as *Zarīʿat al-shayaṭīn* ('The devil's farm', 1973) by al-Mahdī Abū Qurayn, depicting the malpractices of al-Haddār, a contractor and rich landowner, who oppresses his womenfolk (a wife and a helpless daughter) and pampers his good-for-nothing semi-illiterate son. But al-Haddār is soon unmasked. On his estate he grows narcotics and gains enormous sums of money, but the long arm of the law reaches him. The play is carefully written, the characters are clearly delineated and the fight between good and evil is well defined and convincing.

ʿAbd al-Karīm al-Dannāʿ is another significant playwright. He wrote some five plays, among which *Saʿdūn* (1974) stands out because of the careful balance he strikes between protagonists and antagonists, Libyan nationalists and Italian conquerors. Though heroic deeds of Saʿdūn are extolled, neither the good that lies in the other camp nor the shortcomings in the Libyan one are neglected. The writer shows deftness and keen political awareness when he differentiates between the leaders of the conquest and their victims in the Italian camp: simple folk who are led to their deaths in a war that is not theirs.

Al-Aqniʿah ('Masks'), by Muḥammad ʿAbd al-Jalīl Qunaydī, is a different play. Cast in the form of a fable, it attacks the injustices of a whole regime: Sultan, Vizir, Head of the Royal Guard and Queen. The Vizir and the Queen seek to kill the Sultan, the better to enjoy their illicit love. When the attempt fails, a frame-up is prepared for a simple citizen who is summarily put into prison to await trial. However, the citizen turns the tables on everybody, Sultan, Vizir and Queen alike: all are wrongdoers. When this is made clear to the people they rise in revolt, the Sultan is deposed and killed and the citizen is asked to succeed him. Unwillingly he agrees, but he makes no promises, except one: he will be the last to eat if there is a shortage of food. Universal justice is hard to achieve, but he will try. The play is very effective, avoiding, as it does, preaching and hyperbole. Like others it shows that the Libyan dramatists can write well-constructed plays. However, they have failed to produce a national dramatist who is one of the mainstays of every dramatic movement.

Tunisia

Tunisia is another clear case of indebtedness to the Egyptian theatre. Starting from 1908 a series of Egyptian troupes visited the country. Towards the end of the same year, a company headed by Sulaymān al-Qurdāḥī gave several plays which created considerable interest among Tunisian intellectuals, who regarded the Arabic theatre as a much-needed force to confront continuous efforts made by the French to obliterate all

Tunisians' feelings of belonging to the Arab nation. One direct result of Qurdāḥī's visit was the formation of a Tunisian–Egyptian company which began its career by performing an Egyptian play *Ṣidq al-Ikhāʾ* ('True friendship') in 1909. This was followed by two Tunisian drama groups: *al-Ādāb al-ᶜArabiyyah* (1911) and *al-Shahāmah al-ᶜArabiyyah*. The two companies competed with each other to the benefit of the nascent Tunisian drama. In the course of this competition a Tunisian play *al-Intiqām* ('Revenge') was performed.

Later events proved that there was no shortage of plays or of companies. In 1932 Tunisia had four companies. In 1959 *al-Masraḥ al-Ḥadīth* (The Modern Theatre) was formed, which gathered together men and women who were all relatives, as a means of getting round the difficulty of public censure of female performers. Al-Munṣif Sharaf al-Dīn, head of the company, let his wife take a part in one of the two plays given by the troupe. Muṣṭafā al-Fārisī, a playwright, computed the number of plays given on the Tunisian stage between the years 1966–71 as over five hundred. In 1965 another Tunisian writer, Ḥasan al-Zamūlī, complained that the various plays performed did not reflect the national sentiment and did not satisfy Tunisian aspirations and outlook on life in the fields of writing, acting and directing. What al-Zamūlī was missing was a truly national Tunisian theatre. Five years after al-Zamūlī had expressed himself thus frankly on the subject, there appeared a dramatist, ᶜIzz al-Dīn al-Madanī, who was to gain for himself the stature and prestige of a national dramatist. This he achieved through indefatigable effort to look into the heritage of Arab literature, in search of the form and content which should prove nearest to Arab hearts.

Ever since the early sixties many Arab writers were showing increasing dissatisfaction with the western dramatic formula. They were eagerly looking for a dramatic form inspired by dramatic and quasi-dramatic presentations inherent in folk entertainment such as shadow plays, street and marketplace performances given by strolling players on national, religious and private occasions. These were taken by some writers as offering opportunities for producing a specific Arab dramatic form. They were duly put to the test, and some significant plays were written, using folk entertainment as form for contemporary content. Yūsuf Idrīs (Egypt), Saᶜdalla Wannūs (Syria), Qāsim Muḥammad (Iraq) and al-Ṭayyib al-Ṣiddīqī (Morocco) are good examples of these. None of these dramatists actually claimed that they would ultimately produce an Arab dramatic form by using folk entertainment. They were quite content to use the folk material for its worth and appeal, and when the result was more people coming to see their plays, they believed they were on the right track.

ᶜIzz al-Dīn al-Madanī alone expressed a different opinion. In an introductory word to his play *Dīwān al-Zanj* ('The Diwan of the Zang Revolution', 1972) he points out that folk material would not, of itself, lead to an Arab dramatic form. The theme, the approach, the writer's sensibility, his ability to come as near as possible to his people, his determination not to look upon heritage as sacred, are all needed to put a dramatist on the right road. A thorough knowledge of past achievements should go hand in hand with a critical attitude towards these achievements. Only living values from the past should be allowed to live on in the present. Al-Madanī wrote six plays, in all of which he tried to conform to the above requirements. Four of these: *Thawrat Ṣāḥib al-Ḥimār* ('The revolution of the donkey rider', 1970), *Dīwān al-Zanj* (1972), *Riḥlat al-Ḥallāj* ('Al-Hallaj's progress', 1973) and *Mawlāy al-Sulṭān Ḥasan al-Ḥafṣī* (1977), are looked upon by the dramatist as a quartet, since they have the same theme: people's revolutions. Al-Madanī looks critically at these people's revolutions against despotic rulers and compares past events with present ones. Like revolutions in the Third World nations of today, these liberation movements achieve initial success. The revolutionaries gain power, only to engage in internal strife, which destroys from the inside the revolutions they have so successfully led. The counter-revolutionary powers march in and destroy them all. To give dramatic expression to this main line of thought, that people's revolutions defeat themselves even before their enemies have marched to bring about their downfall, the dramatist has recourse to some interesting devices. In his wide reading of classical Arabic literature, he has noticed that one salient characteristic of this literature is digression. An event is told in a general way, then is tapped later for details. The treatment is easy-going, impulsive, piecemeal, surface-deep and never all-embracing. The aim is to entertain a reader or an audience and give them pleasure.

This digression al-Madanī translates in *Dīwān al-Zanj* into three separate stages on which the play is acted out: the first stage is devoted to dramatic events; in the second the author of the play addresses his audience and informs them that he wrote his play inspired by the revolutions of the Third World. He then poses different questions as to the sources of dramatic writing and asks whether there are good themes to be used and bad ones to be avoided. Serious as well as trivial suggestions are then made by the dramatist. In the third stage a medley of non-dramatic material is given: poems of complaint bearing advice and threats to the Abbasid Caliph, preceded by passages from history chronicles such as al-Ṭabarī's. There is nothing essentially new in all this. In popular plays drama comprises commentary, narration and direct appeal to the audience. Illusion is done away with and performers act their parts and present their real identities at one and the same time. What al-Madanī has done here is to relegate all drama to the first stage, and devote the other two to the digressional non-dramatic material. When a character in the second and third stages experiences dramatic development, as has happened to al-Ṭabarī, he is moved to stage one to explain what has happened to make him move, say, from antagonism to the revolution to palpable sympathy with it.

Algeria and Morocco

The development of the theatre in Algeria followed a different course from that in other Arab countries. The usual visit of an Egyptian company – Jūrj Abyaḍ's in 1921 – was not accorded the enthusiastic welcome it received in Libya and Tunisia. Algerian intellectuals were too much taken up by French culture to give any serious attention to the plays presented by the company: Jūrj Ḥaddād's *Saladin*, and *Thārārt al-ᶜArab* ('Arab epic wars'). The general public was not particularly enamoured of plays given in classical Arabic. They did not much like literary drama, and preferred the Algerian national dramatic entertainment, which was a mixture of song, laughter and improvised scenes provided by the company members, and simple direct talk that goes straight to the heart. Such was the power of this preference to see shows rather than literary, well-constructed plays, that Kātib Yāsīn, Algeria's celebrated novelist and dramatist, who had written his major works in French, had to bow to popular demand. Pushing aside his works in drama, his impressive intellectual plays translated into Arabic, such as *al-Juththah al-Muḥāṣarah* ('The encircled corpse', tr. 1968) and *al-Aṣlāf* ('The ancestors'), he wrote a popular play called *Muḥammad, khudh ḥaqībatak* ('Take your suitcase', Muhammad). The work is replete with Algerian popular laughter, using improvization. Right from the start, Yāsīn looked upon his work as something of a scenario for which he provided the broad outlines. The theatre artists had to give it a shape – not a final one, since the play was never given a fixed text. This kept changing from time to time, and from place to place. Thus the audience got what they wanted: a very plastic presentation which reflected their tastes and allowed them to take part in shaping and reshaping events. The same method is used by the other Algerian man of the theatre, Kākī Wild ᶜAbd al-Raḥmān, who filled his work with folktales cast in popular forms, even though he made use of skeletons of plays borrowed from the west. The younger generation of theatre artists stand firmly by collective authorship as being the only means of freeing actors from parrot-fashion delivery of other people's words. They even welcome the participation of theatregoers, not only in acting, but also in filling in blanks in a given play. For instance in a play called *Qīmat al-Ittifāq* ('The value of agreement'), given by the al-Baḥr Company, a whole scene was contributed by a member of the audience.

Morocco was introduced to theatre through a visit to the country by a Tunisian company headed by Muḥammad ᶜIzz al-Dīn in 1923. As happened elsewhere in the Arab world, the visit had a tremendous impact on theatre lovers. It was enthusiastically welcomed even by religious leaders as well as by intellectuals and men of letters. Other visits were to ensue. The first Moroccan company was formed in 1924 by students of Fez Secondary school, aided by some artists from the eastern part of the Arab world. Other companies were to follow. But despite the undeniable services rendered by amateurs, the theatre in Morocco attained maturity only through the efforts of two leading men: Aḥmad al-Ṭayyib al-ᶜIlg (1928–) and al-Ṭayyib al-Ṣiddīqī (1938–). The two men worked together for some time, before each went his separate way. Al-ᶜIlg is the author of some forty dramas, as well as of a greater number of Moroccanized plays. His *Waliy Allāh* is an impressive Moroccanization of Molière's *Tartuffe*, so cleverly done that it looks perfectly Moroccan when shown on stage. An eminent Moroccan student of drama, Dr Ḥasan al-Minayᶜī, describes him as the only dramatist with sufficient mastery of the dramatic art to enable him to produce truly Moroccan plays.

Al-Ṣiddīqī used his remarkable talent for the theatre to become a true theatre man: actor, director, writer and producer, all in one. He used popular forms of Moroccan drama to give to his many audiences dramatic fare that kept them on their seats for many an hour. *Dīwān Sīdī ᶜAbd al-Raḥmān al-Majdhūb* (1966) is a good case in point. In it he uses the actor-narrator form to dramatize the life and sayings of the strolling popular poet whose name the play bears. An equally important work is *Maqāmāt Badīᶜ al-Zamān al-Hamadhānī* (1971), which is a brilliant exploration of the dramatic content of the *maqāmah* and a no less brilliant use of it to produce a satiric comedy very much akin to that of Ben Jonson.

CHAPTER 11

THE PROSE STYLISTS

The Arab literary establishment of the period immediately preceding the nineteenth century had reached such stability in social status, such homogeneity in education and such unanimity in cultural values that it was no longer searching for innovative ideas, and of its men of letters – poets and prose writers alike – it expected not originality but consummate skill in the use of words. The prose that it favoured was not only rhymed, but laden with tropes, especially those developed in the branch of rhetoric known as *badīᶜ*, which concerns itself not so much with imagery as with verbal artifices[1] (such as the paronomasia, the double entendre, and the palindrome) of which by then over 150 varieties had been devised.

INHERITED PRIORITIES

An indication of the priorities of the period is that one of the most celebrated prose writers whose activities extended into the modern period, Ḥasan al-ᶜAṭṭār (c. 1766–1834 or 1838), devoted some of his energies to a book of *inshāʾ*[2] which he described as 'divided into two sections: the drafting of contracts and title-deeds, and the composition of letters and communications exchanged between common people and kings. With these two arts is the ordering of the world effected, for they form one of the wings of kingship, the other being its sword.' One of its gems (pp. 19–20) is a model of how a letter addressed to a grammarian should start. Taken in their everyday sense, the words may be read as:

My initial greeting conveys a love strongly based and loftily erected, and the stimuli of my yearnings give tongue to deeds of praise and eulogy; the affirmations of affection describe what is hidden in the inner core of conscousness: true love, the wholeness of which is immune from fragmentation . . . Having thus lifted up an invocation based upon insight and an encomium set upon praise, and having communicated a yearning the inspirer of which is exalted, and an unceasing desire the stimulation of which is never nullified, I say . . .

[1] Technically known as 'schemes'. See P. Cachia, 'From sound to echo: the values underlying late *badīᶜ* literature', in *Journal of the American Oriental Society*, 108, 2 (Apr.–Jun. 1988), pp. 219–25.
[2] Published in AH 1275/AD 1858–9.

But the point of the piece is that it is studded with words that double as technical terms of grammar, so that – with little more tortuousness than in the original – it may be rendered:

My *inchoative* greeting *enunciates* a love strongly *backed* and loftily *indeclinable*, and the *operatives* of yearning *inflect* the *verbs of praise* and eulogy; *emphatic* expressions of affection *qualify* what is *covert* within the *pronoun*: manifestations of true love the *plurality* of which is *sound* and *immune to irregularity* . . . After a *subjective* invocation *invariably* open-*vowelled* and a eulogy made *accusative* upon reception of the praise, and having communicated a yearning whose *verb* is *indicative* and a desire never *restrained* and whose *operative* is *unsuppressed*, I say . . .

Largely as a result of the irruption of western European powers, the Arab world was soon to undergo far-reaching political, economic and social changes that were sure to transform cultural values as well – but not at the same pace. At least through the first three-quarters of the nineteenth century, the aesthetic priorities of the preceding age continued to be proclaimed, and to a somewhat lesser extent applied.[3]

Literary reputations continued to be made by displays of linguistic dexterity and familiarity with an antiquated lexicon. One may open Nāṣīf al-Yāzijī's (1800–71) *Majmaᶜ al-baḥrayn*[4] at any page and find a *maqāmah* as full of finely chiselled rhyming phrases and learned allusions as any by al-Ḥarīrī, whom al-Yāzijī greatly admired and consciously imitated. Even translators and authors who aimed mainly at being informative had to make obeisance to prevailing standards by giving their works ornate titles and prefaces. When, for example, Rifāᶜah Rāfiᶜ al-Ṭahṭāwī (1801–73) recorded his observations on French life and thought in purposeful prose, he still drew upon an art close to a Cellini's in calling his book *Takhlīṣ al-ibrīz ilā talkhīṣ Bārīz*, literally 'The extraction of gold in the summing up of Paris'.

The wonders of western science were readily accepted, but their recognition in literature was first enshrined in time-hallowed formulae. In the 1870s, for example, a mathematician introduced a series of articles on the atmosphere[5] with a traditional, but unusually worded, pious invocation:

I bear witness that there is no god but Thou, o Lord of Lords, Who hast reduced air and stars and clouds to obedience; and that Muḥammad is the Apostle of God, the magnet of pious hearts and the electric impulse among the prophets, the elect, and the believers.

A more genuinely literary treatment of some of the marvels of the new technology comes from the pen of ᶜAbd Allāh al-Nadīm (1854–96). On the

3 Here and at several other points, the chapter on 'The critics' is relevant. 4 Beirut, 1872.

5 By ᶜAlī al-Darandah-lī, 'al-Hawāʾ al-Jawwī', as quoted in Muḥammad ᶜAbd al-Ghanī Ḥasan and ᶜAbd al-ᶜAzīz al-Disūqī, *Rawḍat al-Madāris: nashʾatuhā wa 'ttijāhātuhā 'l-adabiyyah wa 'l-ᶜilmiyyah*, Cairo, 1975, p. 234.

model of traditional pieces of fine writing in which comparisons of, say, spring and summer flowers were cast in the form of a debate, he has a train and a steamboat outboasting each other.[6] In the finely balanced versicles of rhymed prose and with an apt allusion to the arch-enemy of the Prophet nicknamed 'Father of the Flames' in the Qurʾān, the boat's apostrophe runs, in part:

Soft, o Father of the Flames, you have exceeded the bounds of courtesy! I must dock into your territory and burn you with the blaze of your own coals. You are limited in movement by wheel and rail, and have fallen into boiling water and flames. You feed upon wood and coal, and have oil and grease for dessert . . . Rage is so firmly established and so confined in you that it has become a head of steam . . . If you collide with anything you are finished: you halt and find no means of going forward. If your piston-arm breaks you collapse, and seldom move on again. When your nose emits smoke, the entire sight of you is blotted, and if some day you go thirsty, your boiler bursts. You race through open spaces and deserts, shouting: 'The fire rather than disgrace!' How filthy your attendants are, and how limited is your scope, o you who part lovers and terrify passengers! More desirable is my drowning than your burning, and safer is my river than your track.

A CHANGE IN PRACTICE

And yet, almost unheralded, a new style of writing was coming into being.

Much credit for the popularization of simpler forms of self-expression has been given to Syrian Christian journalists who, as Muṣṭafā Luṭfī 'l-Manfalūṭī (1876–1924) put it, preferred 'that the ignorant should learn from them than that the pedants should approve of them'.[7]

Some attention to the career of Fāris (known, after his conversion to Islam, as Aḥmad Fāris) al-Shidyāq (1804–87) shows that there was more to it than that. Al-Shidyāq was indeed born a Lebanese Christian and he did eventually found, in 1861, the very popular and influential journal *al-Jawāʾib*; but even before Arab journalism had taken wing, he had made his mark as a highly individualistic writer of insatiable curiosity and of irrepressible verve, even if sometimes erratic and inconsistent.

Al-Shidyāq lived and worked in European countries for many years; but although remarkably open-minded about many practices and institutions at variance with those he had known in his formative years, he was not overawed by European literary norms, and specifically crowed over the fact that none could vie with the Arabs in the 'miracle' of rhymed prose.[8]

A look at his discursive, lively, often Rabelaisian fictionalized autobiography *al-Sāq ʿalā 'l-sāq fī mā huwa 'l-Fāriyāq*, first published in Paris in

[6] *Sulāfat al-Nadīm*, vol. 1, Cairo, 1914, pp. 24 ff.

[7] H. A. R. Gibb, *Studies on the civilization of Islam*, London, 1962, p. 251.

[8] Hāshim Yāghī, *al-Naqd al-adabī al-ḥadīth fī Lubnān*, vol. 1, Cairo, 1968, p. 102.

1955[9] shows that al-Shidyāq could indeed hold his own against any contemporary in ornate writing, and since his greatest expertise was in lexicography, he particularly delighted in stringing together long lists of synonyms or near synonyms, as when he reeled off 164 words that denote or connote coquettishness (pp. 215–16, in Pt. 2, Ch. 2).

But al-Shidyāq also warned his readers in the very first chapter (p. 82) not to expect the whole of his discourse to be 'spiced with paronomasias, allusions, metaphors and metonymies', and he followed his lights in writing now with all the resources of rhetoric and of antiquarian philology, now with a simplicity and directness that a writer a century later would be pleased to claim for himself, as in this passage (p. 437, in Pt. 3, Ch. 6), which conveys in a flippant way information that was novel and intriguing to the public of the time, and which may be set out as a dialogue initiated by the narrator's wife:

- I have seen strange things in this country!
- What things?
- I see that hair does not grow on men's faces over here, and they know no shame.
- How so?
- I have not seen any with a beard or a moustache. Are they all callow?
- Don't you know that they shave their faces with a razor every day?
- What for?
- To please their women, for they like clean, smooth cheeks.
- Oh, no! What delights a woman in a man is anything that marks out his masculinity, so that the abundance of hair on a man's face is equivalent to its absence in a woman's.
- And what did you mean when you said that they know no shame? Has any of them made an indecent demand of you?
- That has not happened yet, but I notice that they have their trousers made so tight that their private parts show behind them.
- By the logic of what you said, that ought to delight the women!

He does not abandon rhymed prose thereafter, nor does he specify to what contexts either style is better fitted, but he comes closest to pinpointing his motivation at the outset of the tenth chapter of Part I (p. 123):

Rhymed prose is to a writer what a wooden leg is to a walker: I must not lean upon it in all manner of discourse lest it prove too limiting or lead me into a tight corner from which there is no escape. I have found that commitment to rhymed prose is more burdensome than commitment to verse, for the lines of a poem do not require as close a linkage and affinity between them as do the versicles of rhymed prose. One often finds that the writer of rhymed prose is forced to stray from the road in which he is engaged and is led to a different position from the one that would have satisfied him if he had not been bound to the rhyme. Our purpose here is to weave

[9] The references that follow are from the edition of Nasīb Wahībah al-Khāzin, Beirut, n.d.

our narrative in a form acceptable to any reader. Let him who wishes to hear discourse that is rhymed throughout, interspersed with metaphors and decorated with metonymies, betake himself to the *maqāmāt* of al-Ḥarīrī or the *Nawābigh* of al-Zamakhsharī.

What we have here is neither a condemnation of ornate writing, nor an imitation of western practice. Least of all is it a concession to half-educated readers. It is rather that, unlike his immediate predecessors, the writer now had something novel to say, and the very nature of the exercise imposed upon him a functional style.

It is not surprising either to find that the great Islamic reformist Muḥammad ʿAbduh (d. 1905) who, although not primarily a man of letters, did much to infuse a purposeful spirit in his contemporaries, was among the first to abandon rhymed prose – at the suggestion, it is reported, of Jamāl al-Dīn al-Afghānī.[10]

The new direction was inevitable, for a new reading public had appeared: no longer a coterie of people who shared the same formation and the same devotion to inherited values, but men operating in a variety of occupations where new techniques originating in the west were being tried out, who were eager to learn more about the sources of the new wisdom, and who believed that the greatest good lay in its propagation. And printing presses were available to fulfil just such a purpose.

Although they did not initiate the trend, the Syrian Christian journalists mentioned by al-Manfalūṭī were soon to accelerate and accentuate it. From the 1870s onwards, journals and even newspapers were to provide the main outlet for writers, and their need to reach a wide readership and to meet deadlines were added incentives for the adoption of a simple style.

Even the thorny question of whether the long-despised colloquial might have a place in literature was first raised at that time,[11] but its most determined exponent, Muḥammad ʿUthmān Jalāl (1829–94) was active mainly in verse translations of European plays.

The change of direction is nowhere more strikingly illustrated than in the career of ʿAbd Allāh al-Nadīm. Although long established and much admired as a master of ornate prose, he largely abandoned it when, with increasing involvement in politics, he turned to journalism. This is said to have been in 1879, when articles of his appeared in the publications of Adīb Isḥāq (1856–85) and Salīm al-Naqqāsh (d. 1884), under their signature,[12] and he proclaimed his new standard in the inaugural number of his own short-lived *al-Tankīt wa 'l-tabkīt* (it ran only from 6 June to 22 October

[10] Muḥammad ʿAbd al-Ghanī Ḥasan and ʿAbd al-ʿAzīz al-Disūqī, *Rawḍat al-Madāris*, p. 63.

[11] See P. Cachia, 'The Use of the Colloquial in Modern Arabic Literature', *J.A.O.S.*, 87, 1 (Jan.–Mar. 1967), pp. 12–22.

[12] Aḥmad Samīr's introduction to *Sulāfat al-Nadīm*.

1881) when he undertook to write 'in a style which the learned will not despise, and the ignorant will not need to have interpreted'.

Later still, after he had been pardoned for his part in the ʿUrābī rebellion, al-Nadīm founded *al-Ustādh* in 1892. Here, despite his commitment to the purity of the Arabic language, he tried his hand at some dialogues in the colloquial, explicitly for the edification of the unlearned, arguing[13] that this was not as objectionable as the introduction of foreign terms as it amounts only to 'the representation of the condition of someone speaking in his everyday language'. Although these were apparently well received, they soon became less and less frequent, and tailed off entirely within two years. As early as in the tenth number of his journal (25 October 1892), he had expressed his uneasiness about their effect, much preferring to address even the humblest of his readers 'in simple words, as flowing as the colloquial, but in correct Arabic'.

This al-Nadīm could do in a manner that has scarcely been topped since, as in this piece in which some simple women are discussing how to deal with a drunken husband. When one of them suggests beating him, another objects:[14]

> The good lady Najiyyah said, 'First of all, for men to be beaten by women is something abominable, which only a shameless, ill-bred woman would do, and which would be tolerated only by a vile man with no sense of honour and of no standing among men. Secondly, matrimonial authority is in the men's hands, and if a woman beats her husband he may well repudiate her if there is any spirit in him, and after having been the mistress of her own house she would become a mere nothing. The worst calamity is that if she has children and is poor, she will be at a loss what to do with them. And if she returns to her father's house, she will merely sit there like a stranger . . .'

Except for two negated phrases (*lā tafʿaluhu* and *laysa lahu*) and one declined noun (*abūhā*) on which classical grammar imposes distinctive but not unrecognizable forms, the entire passage could be read as colloquial.

Yet there are few indications that at the time clear and direct prose was recognized as good literature, rather than merely a necessity of mass communication. All through the nineteenth century, the great majority of works of criticism went on detailing the linguistic and rhetorical skills deemed essential to the man of letters.

All the same, the very dynamics observable in Shidyāq's writing was bound to prove decisive. The acceptance of Europe's values, initially of its technology and science, was reinforced in the 1880s by all too palpable manifestations of its power. With or without logic, its achievements gave it

[13] In 'al-Lughah wa 'l-inshāʾ', *al-Ustādh*, Yr. 1, No. 9 (11 Oct. 1892), pp. 169–84.

[14] *Sulāfat al-Nadīm*, vol. 2, p. 86.

authority in other fields as well: one of Qāsim Amīn's (1865–1908) arguments for the emancipation of women[15] was that people who had discovered the power of steam and electricity could not be wrong in their sexual mores. Besides, the appeal of European plays, novels and short stories – all new genres to the Arabs – was genuine. By the 1890s, countless articles began not by contending but by conceding the overall superiority of the west in everything except religion and morality: 'No two people disagree on the fact that Westerners remain active and earnest in raising the status of knowledge and pulling down the ramparts of ignorance...'[16] or 'It is well known that the makings of our recent scientific renaissance are derived, wholly or in part, from the Europeans'.[17] By the same token, inherited values were being explicitly or implicitly invalidated.

THE ROMANTIC VIEW

At the turn of the century, the new élite was ripe for an aesthetic reorientation. The pendulum was swinging away from the formalism of the previous age, and the handiest alternative models came from France and England. It is no wonder that the chord that was most insistently struck in Arab hearts was therefore a romantic one.

Initially, the feature of romanticism that most impressed the Arabs is indicated by an observation made by Muḥammad Ḥusayn Haykal (1888–1956) in the early 1920s, in the course of a study on Rousseau:[18]

> For ladies and young persons, and even for the old, the need to cry is one of the most urgent needs of life... French literature had become arid after Racine,... and it was necessary for a writer of throbbing sensibility ... to shed his tears on souls that had become barren of emotion ... in order to restore them to life and to fertility.

The demands of style were not forgotten, but the effects now sought were not ornamental but emotional. A telling judgement was made by Mayy Ziyādah (1886–1941):[19]

> Prose is nothing but poetry that escapes from the strict rules of metre. Even so, it is not satisfying unless it subjects itself to the rules of composition which include balance of sentences, musicality of diction, and expression of thought systematically and simply. Therefore prose is free verse.

[15] *Taḥrīr al-marʾah*, Cairo, 1970, p. 114.

[16] ʿAbd Allāh Salīm Yāzijī in *al-Hilāl*, Yr. 3, No. 17 (1 May 1895), p. 659.

[17] Jurjī Zaydān, 'Kuttāb al-ʿArabiyyah wa qurrāʾuhā', *al-Hilāl*, Yr. 6, No. 4 (15 Oct. 1897), p. 126.

[18] *Jān Jāk Rūsū*, Cairo, 1965, p. 210.

[19] *Al-Muʾallafāt al-kāmilah*, vol. 2, ed. Salmā 'l-Ḥaffār al-Kuzbarī, Beirut, 1982, p. 389.

Mayy herself could write both effusively and with considerable vigour, as in this remarkably early plea for a right approach to women writers:[20]

The public asserts that its desire to sample women's writings does not bespeak admiration for these writings or acknowledgement of the truth of their perceptions, but arises from the fact that in their writings is some manifestation of the feminine essence in general. This is a worthy step towards the honouring of feminine literature, but it is not without some injustice and some denial of rights . . . Some thinkers – especially some who have convinced themselves that they are thinkers – have gone beyond the score in isolating women from the human species, which they have all but restricted to the man. The fact is that every passion that moves a woman derives from the all-inclusive human spirit, and every product of her acumen is an aspect of general human thought.

The writer who best articulated the taste of the first quarter of the twentieth century, however, was Muṣṭafā Luṭfī 'l-Manfalūṭī. Apart from 'arabizing' – without any knowledge of a European language – four French romantic novels, he delighted the public of the day with short prose pieces which were always emotional, high-minded and elegantly worded, and which have been published and republished in two collections appropriately titled *Views* (*al-Naẓarāt*) and *Tears* (*al-ᶜAbarāt*), for they often depicted harrowing scenes from which some lofty moral was to be derived. One of them[21] depicts a rich man lying on his death-bed, his sufferings compounded by the knowledge that, instead of attending to him, his wife is out enjoying herself; but then:

The servant approached him and said, '. . . Do you not recall those long nights which you used to spend away from home, pursuing some appetite, draining a cup, dragging your coattails in some place of entertainment, wasting your money in dance halls – and leaving your wife in this very room, on this very bed, sighing in her loneliness, weeping in her solitude, writhing on what was hotter than live embers in her yearning for you and her sorrow over you? Yet you would not return to her until the raven of the night had turned white with age and the eagle of morn was on the wing. You robbed her of those past nights, and thus did you become her debtor. Now she is claiming these nights back from you, one after another, down to the very last one.'

An issue that generated a great deal of heat then was the extent to which Arabic needed to evolve in order to meet the needs of modern life.[22] Conservatives maintained that the language had reached perfection and needed no tampering; but by the middle of the 1920s these had been not so much silenced as by-passed by the modernists, who by precept or practice

[20] Jamīl Jabr (comp.), *Mayy Ziyādah fī mudhakkarātihā*, Dār al-Rīḥānī, 6–7, n.d., pp. 105–6.

[21] *Al-Naẓarāt*, Vol. 1, Cairo, n.d., p. 85.

[22] See Jaroslav Stetkevych, *The modern Arabic literary language*, Chicago, 1970.

had recognized the necessity and established the right to coin new words.

However, most of the writers who had risen to prominence by then and were to dominate the next generation were wary of disrupting the structure of the language, and in fact perpetuated al-Nadīm's formula of combining simple diction with strict respect for classical grammar. This concern for correctness was shared by a conservative like Muṣṭafā Ṣādiq al-Rāfiʿī (1880–1937), mainstream modernists like ʿAbbās Maḥmūd al-ʿAqqād (1889–1964) or Muḥammad Ḥusayn Haykal (1888–1956), and a socialist like Salāmah Mūsā (1887–1958), who in his zeal to reach the people decried all past Arabic literature as 'regal'.[23] Prodigiously productive and versatile, these writers demonstrated how impeccably and with what suppleness Arabic could be made to deal with the most modern and elaborate of subjects.

Of these, the most celebrated as a stylist, Ṭāhā Ḥusayn (1889–1973), was also one of the most puristic. His ideal was to combine the beauty of classical Arabic as it was used by writers of the first four centuries of Islam, especially al-Jāḥiẓ, with the charm and imaginativeness he encountered in French and English literatures.[24] Foreign words for which no equivalent could be coined from an Arabic root are rare in his writings, and the colloquial he could tolerate only in small doses,[25] at times arguing that true democracy consisted of raising the common people to the level at which they could appreciate fine literature,[26] at others boasting that he was as aristocratic in matters of language as he was democratic in his political philosophy.[27]

Even when, in a novel, he reported a conversation between the narrator, a casually educated woman and a countryside character encountered in a village guesthouse, Ṭāhā Ḥusayn allowed himself only one colloquialism which he placed between quotation marks (as is done in the translation below), and for the rest had to use his considerable ingenuity to suggest the tanginess of their expressions:[28]

The woman turned to me and burst out, 'You mother is silent and has nothing to say; your sister is so downcast that there seems to be no hope that she will take in or answer anything – so let's hear *you* speak! I can see some brazenness in your eye, something not unlike cheekiness in your features. I daresay there's no salt in your eye . . . Speak! Who are you and where have you come from? What's your story? Why are you off your food? Why do you keep your mouth shut?' Before this strange and sudden onslaught . . . I could not help laughing as I retorted, 'And you – who

[23] *Al-Adab li 'l-shaʿb*, Cairo, 1956, especially p. 41.

[24] *Falsafat Ibn Khaldūn al-ijtimāʿiyyah* (Muḥammad ʿAbd Allāh ʿInān's translation of 'Étude analytique et critique de la philosophie sociale d'Ibn Khaldoun', doctoral dissertation, University of Paris), Cairo, *al-Iʿtimād*, 1925, pp. 28–9.

[25] Interview in *al-Ṭalabah al-ʿArab*, Yr. 5, No. 182 (5 Mar. 1966).

[26] *Fuṣūl fī 'l-adab wa 'l-naqd*, Cairo, 1945, pp. 20–1.

[27] Discussion at Fu'ād Academy of the Arabic Language. 26 Dec. 1949, reported in *al-Risālah*, Yr. 18, No. 863 (16 Jan. 1950), pp. 122–4.

[28] *Duʿāʾ al-karawān*, Cairo, 1946, p. 40.

are you and where do you come from? What business have you to question us and press us?' Addressing her friends she said quickly, 'Didn't I tell you that she was "crouse" and had no salt in her eye – that she'd be the one to listen to me and answer me?' Then she turned to me: 'An investigation – do you hear? It's an investigation . . .'

Even in the same generation, not all were so inhibited. Yaḥyā Ḥaqqī (b. 1905), although no less concerned with the demands of art, resorts freely to loan-words and to colloquialisms when he deems them most appropriate, and this not in dialogue alone but also in descriptive passages, as in this pen-portrait of a fellow-passenger on public transport[29] which is not only studded with non-classical words and usages (italicized in the translation) but also in which the foreign word *kilo* is not given the Arabic plural form required by the syntax:

. . . A lady like a sack of cotton! Her lipstick is *smudged*, her eye-paint is *running*. On her breast is a *brooch* the size of which is a measure only of its cheapness. Lord! How can a woman's face suggest such grossness and insensitivity? . . . This lady, who if she were to lean against a wall would bring it down, has a son weighing some ten *kilos* – restless mercury – who wades through our bodies with his shoes in order to get to the window. The *lady* does not carry him – that would be an offence against her *chic* and elegance. Do you know to whom she leaves him? To a little maid who herself weighs no more than ten *kilos*, who *ought to be* dandled on somebody's knees, to be hugged, to sleep in somebody's arms, to have a doll to play with . . .

The use of the colloquial has implications that extend far beyond the concerns of literature, and there are still those who fulminate against it as a corruption, divisive of the Arabs, its advocacy ascribed to a strange alliance between imperialists, Zionists and communists.[30]

Nevertheless, the colloquial has established itself as a virtual necessity of comic dialogue from the time that Mārūn al-Naqqāsh (1818–55) put on his first play in 1847, and its use in the dialogue of novels and short stories, although far from universal, has long ceased to raise eyebrows. That the practice is due to genuinely artistic considerations is shown by the fact that the stage directions of plays – even, I am assured, in unpublished scripts intended only for the performers – are invariably in the literary language.

In the last twenty-five years or so, the colloquial has made some inroads into poetry, but these are not under consideration here. In prose, the boldest experiment was made by Luwīs ʿAwaḍ (1915–90) who, specifically to test its suitability to serious purposes, wrote – in 1942, although it was not published until much later – an account of his student days at

29 *Fikrah fa 'btisāmah*, Cairo, n.d., pp. 14–15.

30 See for example, Anwar al-Jindī, *al-Shuʿūbiyyah fī 'l-adab al-ʿArabī al-ḥadīth*, Cairo, n.d. (but not earlier than 1970), especially pp. 216, 221, and 229.

Cambridge entirely in the colloquial; but he states in his preface to the 1965 edition[31] that, although undaunted by the furious attacks to which he was subjected, he has not followed it up because in his subsequent career as an academic and a critic he found that the literary idiom presented him with no problem.

One may also note that in 1956 Tawfīq al-Ḥakīm (born between 1899 and 1903, d. 1987) wrote a play which, partly by taking advantage of the ambiguities of the Arabic script, may be read as being either in the classical or in the colloquial;[32] that another established playwright, Rashād Rushdī, turned to the colloquial in writing his melodrama, *al-Farāshah*,[33] and that the novelist Fatḥī Ghānim (b. 1924) achieved much the same purpose by greatly extending the dialogue in his *al-Muṭallaqah*[34] so that it reads rather like a film script. But there is here no harbinger of a significant breach of the walls of the literary establishment.

VARIETY AND MATURITY

If there has been a shift of emphasis in the present generation, it has been towards a measure of acceptance that fidelity to the strictest rules of classical morphology and syntax is not necessarily the supreme criterion of literary writing. So it is that some highly-regarded writers like ʿAbd al-Raḥmān Majīd al-Rubayʿī (b. 1939), whose prose is generally taut and purposeful, may without rousing the ire of critics sprinkle his writing with redundant particles, unparadigmatic formations and somewhat idiosyncratic idioms.[35]

The liberties taken are not merely a result of growing laxity. Rather, there is a realization that the immensity of literature embraces contexts in which correctness and polish must give way to special needs. It is obvious, for example, that there are situations in which the fragmentary and the inexplicit may do better service than the finely rounded sentence, as when Jamāl al-Ghīṭānī (b. 1945) writes:[36]

> ... I was at a loss – what was he thinking? I swear to you that his head was ablaze ... No, not sorrows. Rather . . . what would you call them? Sensations here get jumbled. They are of special kinds. Perhaps he remembered some distant situations – some close. Snatches of a tune precipitated in one's depth. Perhaps a child's cry, Muṣṭafā's laughter, a word dropped by some unknown passer-by, a look from a soldier on his way to eternity . . .

Other considerations, too, have militated against a uniformly puristic and exalted style. For the sake of truer characterization, fiction writers readily

[31] *Mudhakkirāt ṭālib biʿthah*, Cairo, Nov. 1965, p. 9. [32] *al-Ṣafqah*, Cairo, [1965].

[33] Cairo, 1960. [34] Cairo, Feb. 1963.

[35] See my review of Hans Wehr, *A Dictionary of Modern Written Arabic*, in *J.A.O.S.* 105, 4 (1985), pp. 742–4. [36] *Arḍ – Arḍ*, Beirut, 1980, p. 62.

sacrifice such orotund speeches as al-Manfalūṭī placed on a servant's lips, not least when what they reproduce is 'the stream of consciousness', as is expertly done by Najīb Maḥfūẓ (b. 1911) in several novels. Others, like Jamāl al-Ghīṭānī, may want to project themselves into a different century and adopt its linguistic peculiarities,[37] or heighten the hero's predicament by expounding it in the form of police reports.[38] Yūsuf Idrīs (1927–91) has long striven to develop a distinctively Egyptian style,[39] and he has experimented boldly with unconventional word order, as in this opening of a short story:[40]

From the car she alighted. Fātinah alighted. The pass made by a hurrying passer-by revived her spirit. She entered the park. Slowly she crossed it. The steps – she climbed them: a step; a pause; a step. At the top step, she flustered. Fearful, she flustered.

Of course there is much else that, without jarring convention, makes its point by dint of precise wording and carefully chosen imagery, as in the same Yūsuf Idrīs's masterly description of a journey from one of Cairo's most fashionable quarters to one of its most sordid,[41] or as when Adūnīs (ʿAlī Aḥmad Saʿīd, b. 1930) attempts to define key concepts of poetry:[42]

Every innovation is the innovation of a world, for the true poet presents his poetry as a special, personal world, not a collection of impressions and adornments . . . And innovation and novelty are often intermingled, for the apparel always comes along with newness; but novelty is a passing stream, whereas innovation is a deep, permanent river . . . Novelty is a garb, but innovation is prophecy, and garbs reflect the ripples of life, whereas prophecy reflects its depths.

The Arab public of today is well served by prose writers who recognize no limit to their art and are constantly trying out new modes of expression. Nor is the public restricted to the writings of the avant-garde: from al-Manfalūṭī's onward, the major works of this century are constantly being printed and reprinted.

Only rhymed prose is entirely out of favour, being used solely for comic effect, as in the piquant work of ʿAbbās al-Aswānī, the flavour of whose writing may be conveyed in this loose translation:[43]

European letters present me with no mystery, and in Groppi's tea-rooms I have a history. I take mayonnaise, and read the Lettres Françaises. I have studied Corneille

37 *Awrāq shābb ʿāsha mundh alf ʿāmm*, Cairo, 1969. Also *al-Zaynī Barakāt*, Cairo, 1980, translated into French by Jean-François Fourcade, Paris, 1985.

38 A favourite device of al-Ghīṭānī's, as in 'Mudhakkirah īḍāḥiyyah ḥawl wāqiʿah raqm 106, Qism al-Jamāliyyah, al-Qāhirah', in *al-Ḥiṣār min thalāth jihāt*, Damascus, 1975, pp. 119–35.

39 See Sasson Somekh, *Lughat al-Qiṣṣah fī adab Yūsuf Idrīs*, Acre, Tel-Aviv, 1984.

40 'ʿAlā Waraq Silūfān', in his *Bayt min laḥm*, Cairo, 1971, p. 37.

41 Chapter 7 of *Qāʿ al-madīnah*, translated in *In the eye of the beholder*, ed. Roger Allen, Minneapolis, 1978.

42 *Muqaddimah li 'l-shiʿr al-ʿArabī*, Beirut, 1971, p. 100.

43 *Al-Maqāmāt al-Aswāniyyah*, Cairo, 1970, p. 2.

and Racine, and the poetry of Lamartine. I have led guests to the treasure-trove of the articles of Sainte-Beuve . . .

In mocking alike the artificiality of predecessors and the senseless aping of the west al-Aswānī points in a backhanded way to the long road travelled by Arab prose writers from formalism to functionalism and to experimentation and virtuosity.

CHAPTER 12

THE CRITICS

By the eighteenth century, Arab literary criticism had been reduced to blanket judgements, usually unsupported, on the literary qualities of men of learning who earned a place in biographical dictionaries, and to ever more elaborate treatises on rhetoric, especially on that branch of it known as *badīʿ*, which concerned itself mostly with tropes that exploit not imagery but the forms of words. In prose and poetry alike, it was the ability to juggle with words that was most highly prized.

The challenge set by European powers, first to the Ottomans in the Balkans then more directly through the Bonaparte expedition to Egypt in 1798, was soon to lead to changes that were initially designed to strengthen the armed forces, but that inevitably went on to affect administrative, educational and economic practices in one Arab country after another. Not surprisingly, it was the material benefits of western technology that were most readily accepted – Egypt had a railway line as early as 1854 – whereas an appreciation of its intellectual underpinnings came later, and of European aesthetic perceptions later still.

INITIAL CONSERVATISM

Of the first Arabs to be directly exposed to European life, Rifāʿah Rāfiʿ al-Ṭahṭāwī (1801–73) readily opened his gigantic intellect to new ideas without surrendering his independence of judgement. In his *Takhlīṣ al-ibrīz ilā talkhīṣ Bārīz*, first published in 1834–5,[1] he conscientiously noted that Europeans also had a science called *rītūrīqī* although not so elaborate as its Arabic counterpart especially with regard to *badīʿ*, and he conceded that different peoples may share some modes of expression, as in comparing a brave man to a lion, but differ in others, as when Europeans object to amatory verses which refer to the beloved's saliva (p. 288); but this did not alter his view (p. 129) that 'there is no doubt that Arabic is of all languages the greatest and most splendid – indeed can gold be approximated by tinsel?' And the examples he gives of Arabic verses he admired (pp. 280–5),

[1] Page references are to the edition by Mahdī ʿAllām *et al.*, Cairo 1958.

although not particularly heavy with verbal ornamentation, are broadly consistent with the taste of the preceding century.

Although more mercurial and less consistent, Fāris (later, Aḥmad Fāris) al-Shidyāq (1804–87) exhibits much the same balance. He too was bold enough to proclaim his admiration for many of the ways of Europeans even in the sensitive area of relations between the sexes,[2] and at one time went as far as to say that 'all sciences had come into their hands and all arts were theirs alone'. He was also well aware that excessive concern with *badīʿ* could, and often did, lead to the subordination of substance to form.[3] Nevertheless, he cited monorhyme poetry and rhymed prose – which he deemed superior even to poetry in that it alone requires the concatenation of ideas – as marks of the superiority of Arabic literature. He also observed that Europeans were repelled by sexually explicit descriptions of women in an encomium, and even more by the ascription of female characteristics to ephebes; but in his usual salty manner he drew from this the conclusion that 'the whole of their poetry is castrated'.[4] He did, all the same, refrain from adding an erotic prelude to the ode he presented to Queen Victoria.[5]

It is, alas, in a far from edifying context that one encounters the first expression of admiration for European literature. In 1840, Buṭrus Karāmah (1774–1851) composed a poem with a pun on the word *khāl* used as the rhyme in each of its 23 lines. The one-time governor of Iraq, Dāwūd Pasha, issued a challenge to the poets of Baghdad to do better, but one of them, Ṣāliḥ Tamīmī, was stung into retorting to the would-be patron:

> We know you to spare the repentant,
> So spare us responding to Nazarene verse;
> In eloquent poetry that has mellowed and blossomed,
> Is there a Christian to be reckoned as eloquent?

To this Buṭrus Karāmah responded adequately by citing great Christian Arab poets of the past. But forty years later Rushayd al-Daḥdāḥ (1813–89) picked up the cudgels again, this time adding to the rebuttal:

> If the argument refers to eloquence in general, in all languages and under all climes, then by no stretch of the imagination is there anyone who deserves mention alongside the eloquent Christians writing in European languages, for their lands are resplendent with their intellects, their pulpits are crowded with their orators, and their learned men have filled the earth with books on every art. This is a fact, well known to all who are knowledgeable.[6]

2 *Al-Wāsiṭah fī maʿrifat aḥwāl Māliṭah*, printed in one vol. with *Kashf al-mukhabbā fī funūn Urubbā*, 2nd edn, Constantinople, AH 1299/AD 1881, p. 37. The next quotation is from p. 53 of the same.

3 *Al-Sāq ʿalā 'l-sāq fī mā huwa 'l-Fāriyāq*, ed. Nasīb Wahībah al-Khāzin, Beirut, n.d., pp. 82, 357.

4 See Hāshim Yāghī, *al-Naqd al-adabī al-ḥadīth fī Lubnān*, vol. 1, Cairo, 1965, pp. 102, 117, which brings together quotations from several of al-Shidyāq's works.

5 See A. J. Arberry, *Arabic poetry: a primer for students*, Cambridge, 1965, pp. 136–49.

6 Hāshim Yāghī, *al-Naqd al-adabī al-ḥadīth fī Lubnān*, pp. 26–31.

At a time when other writers, such as the Christian Ḥunayn al-Khūrī[7] and the Muslims al-Ṭahṭāwī[8] and – somewhat later – ʿAbd Allāh al-Nadīm (1845–96)[9] were groping towards the formulation of a regionally-based loyalty that would unite men of different ethnic and religious backgrounds, such a blanket assertion as al-Daḥdāḥ's bespeaks a deep turmoil in the society, but not its penetration by European literary norms.

In fact, although by 1870 some voices were being raised against young men who affected to speak French and expressed a preference for European books,[10] and although western literary works were being translated into Arabic, it seems that few even among the educated had more than extremely patchy notions of the literatures produced by other cultures than their own.

This is evidenced in the work of someone so well placed to gather authoritative information as ʿAlī Fahmī Rifāʿah (1848–1903), the great al-Ṭahṭāwī's son and editor of the prestigious *Rawḍat al-madāris*, founded in April 1870. In an article entitled 'Nubdhah fī 'l-shiʿr wa 'l-mūsīqā',[11] he blatantly plagiarized an earlier one by Nawfal Niʿmat Allāh Nawfal[12] (1812–87) but extended its range to cover, in about five pages, the poetry and the music of any country under the sun that either author had heard of. Like its model, it is a farrago of totally unsubstantiated assertions which starts from the premiss that 'the excellence of Arabic verses is well-known' but concedes that talent is to be found in other climes 'even in cold regions', dismisses the production of some other nations – such as Afghanistan – with a few uncomplimentary adjectives, and takes no note of development over the centuries, as when it bundles together the output of the Romans and of the modern Italians. Its tenor and quality may be judged from this extract:

In Spain, odes are composed in Spanish and have been popular for generations. Spaniards have put into verse accounts of battle, especially the story of the Arabs, as well as the wonders of magic, the condition of mankind, the history of the Ancients, the Old Testament and the New. Having composed these, they have set them to the music of their guitar. When one of them falls in love and is rejected by his lady love, he takes his guitar, stations himself under her window, and describes his condition in verse sung to the accompaniment of his guitar so that she may take pity on him; but it may happen that he is driven away from under her window, or she may be in love with another who will come and fight him. Spanish verses are devoid of brilliance or fine expression, and are therefore not favoured.

7 'Al-Dīn wa 'l-Waṭan', *al-Jinān*, Yr. 1 (1870), pp. 435–6.

8 *Manāhij al-albāb al-miṣriyyah fī mabāhij al-ādāb al-ʿaṣriyyah*, Cairo, 1912, especially p. 99.

9 In numerous articles in *al-Ustādh*, notably 'al-Hayāh al-waṭaniyyah', Yr. 1, No. 2 (30 Aug. 1892), and 'al-Jāmiʿah al-waṭaniyyah wa 'l-ikhtilāṭ al-ʿimrānī', Yr. 1, No. 4 (13 Sep. 1892).

10 'Al-Lughah al-ʿArabiyyah', unsigned article presumably by Yūsuf al-Shalfūn, the editor of *al-Zahra*, Yr. 1, No. 18 (30 Apr. 1870), quoted in Hāshim Yāghī, *al-Naqd al-adabī al-ḥadīth fī Lubnān*, vol. 1, p. 59.

11 *Rawḍat al-madāris*, Yr. 5, No. 15, as quoted in Muḥammad Abd al-Ghanī Ḥasan and ʿAbd al-ʿAzīz al-Disūqī, *Rawḍat al-madāris*, Beirut, n.d., pp. 104–9, where it is highly praised.

12 'Al-Shiʿr wa 'l-Shuʿarāʾ', *al-Jinān*, Yr. 2, No. 7 (Apr. 1871), pp. 230–40.

It is not altogether surprising, therefore, that through the first three-quarters of the nineteenth century, hardly any consciously and significantly new literary criteria were formulated. The most substantial works of criticism published continued to be handbooks of rhetoric. Other, apparently innovative, productions are in much the same spirit. Characteristic of the time is Shākir Shuqayr's (1850–96) *Misbāḥ al-afkār fī naẓm al-ashʿār*,[13] published in 1871, which gives precise step-by-step instructions on how to teach oneself to write poetry. One may also note the composition by a Maronite priest of two *badīʿiyyahs* in which the conventional theme of praise of the Prophet is changed to praise of Jesus.[14] Pressing a new art form into the service of traditional values are two three-act verse plays by Ibrāhīm al-Aḥdab (1824–91), one on grammar and one on rhetoric[15] – both end-of-term productions which had their premiere in the Rushdiyyah school run by the author. These may be mere curiosities, but they are indicative of the priorities of the time.

More solid evidence is that as late as 1885, Shākir al-Batlūnī published *Dalīl al-hāʾim fī sināʿat al-nāthir wa 'l-nāẓim*[16] which draws its material entirely from such classics as Ibn al-Athīr's *al-Mathal al-sāʾir*, Ibn ʿAbd Rabbih's *al-ʿIqd al-farīd*, Ibn Khaldūn's *Muqaddimah*, Abū Isḥāq Ibrāhīm al-Ḥuṣrī's *Zahr al-ādāb* and al-Māwardī's *Adab al-dunyā wa 'l-dīn*.

The anthologies and biographical dictionaries published at that time bear witness, implicitly or explicitly, to broadly the same conservative taste.

No less indicative of the pulse of the intellectuals were the many periodicals which appeared from the middle of the century onward. It is here that one encounters examples of applied criticism. These consist largely of extremely one-sided comments on individual works, either praising them fulsomely or carping on minute points of linguistic usage, the word *takhṭiʾah*, 'fault-finding', actually appearing in the titles of some articles. Personal animosities were not absent from these nit-picking exercises. Clear evidence has been adduced that al-Shidyāq actually paid Yūsuf al-Asīr (1817–89) to attack his rivals Salīm al-Shartūnī and Nāṣīf al-Yāzijī[17] (d. 1870). They are nevertheless indicative of the basis on which judgements were made.

That this concern with minutiae persisted throughout the century is shown by the admiration with which the editor of *Miṣbāḥ al-sharq* reported

13 See Muḥammad Yūsuf Najm, *Naẓariyyat al-naqd wa 'l-funūn wa 'l-madhāhib al-adabiyyah fī 'l-adab al-ʿarabī al-ḥadīth*, Muqaddimah wa Dalīl, Beirut, 1985, pp. 24–8.

14 Al-Khūrī Arsānyūs al-Fākhūrī, *Zahr al-rabīʿ fī fann al-badīʿ*, Beirut, 1868, in which is mentioned an earlier one entitled *al-Rawḍah al-Lubnāniyyah fī sharḥ al-badīʿiyyah*.

15 *Tuḥfat al-rushdiyyah fī ʿulūm al-ʿarabiyyah*, and *Washy al-yarāʿah fī ʿulūm al-balāghah wa 'l-barāʿah*, both published in Beirut, the first in AH 1285 (AD 1868–9), the second in AH 1286/AD 1870.

16 Beirut, al-Maṭbaʿah al-Adabiyyah; see Hāshim Yāghī, *al-Naqd al-adabī al-ḥadīth fī Lubnān*, pp. 48–9.

17 ʿImād al-Ṣulḥ, *Aḥmad Fāris al-Shidyāq – āthāruh wa ʿaṣruh*, Beirut, 1980, p. 125.

that Shaykh al-Shinqīṭī[18] had spotted no fewer than fifteen errors in the transmission of a single line of poetry, which al-Ashmūnī had misattributed to Ruʾbah.[19]

All in all, the perceptions of most of the learned may be summed up in the words of ʿAbd al-Hādī Najā ʾl-Ibyārī who in a brief article[20] reviewed the various definitions of *ʿilm al-adab*, the 'science of literature', in classical Arabic sources, and ended with the observation that

> Nowadays *ʿilm al-adab* is generally used for philology, the making of verse – by which I mean the ability to compose it in accordance with the rules of Rhetoric, and of distinguishing the good from the bad in it – the science of *badīʿ*, and colloquies (*muḥāḍarāt*), i.e. matching one's companion in the retailing of witticisms, delicate verses, and anecdotes.

HARBINGERS OF CHANGE

An intriguing and potentially far-reaching new departure, however, was the appearance in 1876 of a rendering into *rajaz* of selected passages from Boileau's *Art Poétique* by Muḥammad ʿUthmān, almost certainly the enterprising translator better known as Muḥammad ʿUthmān Jalāl[21] (1829–1908). An editorial preface starts with the assertion that 'Europeans do have an interest in "literary poetic sciences", these not being confined to the Arabic language as a minority of the educated imagine', and expresses the hope that the translator will complete his project. The piece itself consists of 100 distiches corresponding to 138 of the first 218 lines of Boileau's poem. It is largely confined to general advice to the budding poet to acquaint himself with the work of predecessors and to seek the opinion of honest, critically minded friends rather than flatterers. It does not, therefore, touch upon the essence of poetry.

The editor's expression of a pious hope and the fact that the order of Boileau's lines is not jumbled imply that more was to follow. But the initial effort does not seem to have made much of an impression at the time, and no sequel of any kind has been traced. The piece is significant, nevertheless, if not as a harbinger of receptivity to totally foreign influences, at least as an indicator of changing tastes; for the models commended by Muḥammad ʿUthmān Jalāl to the attention of his contemporaries are neither those named by Boileau in lines 13–26 of his composition nor those of the Arabs of the immediate past. They are (in lines 9–11 of the translation) the works

18 Presumably Aḥmad ibn al-Amīn al-Shinqīṭī, 1872–1913.

19 'Bayt ʿāmir bi 'l-ghalaṭ maskūn bi 'l-khiṭāʾ' *Miṣbāḥ al-sharq*, Yr. 1, No. 21 (8 Sep. 1898).

20 In *Rawḍat al-madāris*, No. 13 (15 Rajab 1287/Sep. 1870), as quoted in ʿAbd al-ʿAzīz al-Disūqī, *Tatawwur al-naqd al-ḥadīth fī Miṣr*, Cairo, 1977 (hereafter referred to as *Disūqī*), p. 28.

21 'Qawāʿid fī fann al-shiʿr', *Rawḍat al-madāris*, Yr. 6, No. 7, pp. 11–15.

of al-Mutanabbī, Abū Tammām, Abū 'l-ʿAtāhiyah, Abū Nuwās, al-Buḥturī, Abū Firās al-Ḥamdānī, Ṣafiyy al-Dīn al-Ḥillī, al-Sariyy al-Raffāʾ and al-Ṣūlī – mostly the great poets of the early Abbasid age, precisely those who were to be admired and imitated during the next two generations.

For a new spirit was stirring among the creative writers and their public. The political, social and technological results of European penetration had undermined the order which for centuries had found satisfaction in unchanging values. The most energetic minds of the day perceived the potential benefits of Europe's civilization, but also its challenge. A growing readership of men not steeped in traditional learning but exposed to some branch of western knowledge was avid for more, and the importation of printing presses made catering for this possible. The movement led by Jamāl al-Dīn al-Afghānī (1839–97) and Muḥammad ʿAbduh (1849–1905) sensed the need to emulate Europeans, but sought to preserve the Islamic character of the culture by citing the example of predecessors in a livelier age, and this not in religious matters alone. ʿAbduh once summed up his priorities as follows:[22]

> I raised my voice in the service of two great causes. The first was the liberation of thought from the bonds of tradition and the understanding of religion as it had been understood by the forefathers of the *ummah*, and the second the reform of the style of Arabic writing . . . Arabic writing in Egypt was limited to two kinds, both abhorrent to good taste and incompatible with the language of early Arabs. One was the kind in use in government offices and the like, and that amounted to stringing words together in an outworn, vile manner beyond the reach of understanding . . . The other was that of the men of letters and the graduates of the Azhar in which rhyming was maintained even if inane, and balanced periods and varieties of paronomasias were sought even at the expense of taste, clarity, euphony, and effective communication of one's purpose.

Accordingly, Muḥammad ʿAbduh gave a fillip to the revival of Arabic classics, himself edited *Nahj al-Balāghah* and the *maqāmāt* of al-Hamadhānī, and gave support and guidance to Ḥusayn al-Marṣafī (c. 1815–90) in his efforts to reform the teaching of literature.

Among the critics of that period, al-Marṣafī was indeed to prove the most open to new perceptions in the lectures which he delivered at Dār al-ʿUlūm, and which were summarized in *Rawḍat al-madāris* and then made into a two-volume work, *al-Wasīlah al-adabiyyah* (1872, 1875). Estimates of his influence have differed widely. Some, basing themselves on passing observations in his book, would make him the forerunner of psychological and historico-social literary studies.[23] Others, noting that the comparisons

[22] As quoted by Aḥmad Amīn in *Zuʿamāʾ al-iṣlāḥ* and reproduced in *Disūqī*, pp. 46–7.
[23] *Disūqī*, pp. 61–91.

he drew were mainly with writers of the past, see his modernity as 'only a thin veneer'.[24]

If by modernity is meant the explicit abandonment of past standards and the proclamation of new ones derived from Europe, there is not even a veneer of this in al-Marṣafī's work. Indeed the bulk of his book is a review of grammar and rhetoric, together with substantial discussion of authors and texts, ancient and recent, so that the difference with other laborious compilations is not immediately apparent. What is significant, however, is that he reserved his admiration for Jāhilī and early Islamic poets as having set the Arab literary tradition and for the Abbasid 'modernists' as having maintained it, but treated the later taste for excessive verbal ornamentation virtually as an aberration.[25] His was the literary counterpart of the '*salafiyyah*' that was to inform Islamic reformism.

Al-Marṣafī defined literature as 'knowledge of the conditions which make the man of letters acceptable to the percipient, who are God's trustees over the inhabitants of His earth, by placing each discourse in the place that befits it'.[26] Quaint though it is, this definition does have the virtue of subjecting literature to informed taste rather than to the automatic application of the rules of rhetoric, and he likened the mere retention of 'rules' and 'the treatment of instruments as if they were ends' to 'the storing of cereals in places that may or may not be suitable for the purpose'.[27] Indeed the very title of his book implies that the cherished 'sciences' he expounded were the *means* by which the man of letters normally attained proficiency, but did not embody the essence of literature. He displayed his own firm taste and independence of judgement in dealing with particular issues, such as al-Bāqillānī's treatment of Imruʾ al-Qays, and above all in his recognition of the talent of Maḥmūd Sāmī al-Bārūdī (1838–1904) who had *not* been through the mill painstakingly described in the *Wasīlah*.

The achievement of al-Bārūdī, now recognized as the founder of the neo-classical school of modern Arabic poetry, is itself significant. Heirs to an immense and immensely powerful tradition but cast into a challenging situation, the most gifted poets of the period turned away from decorative versifying to the models provided by the poets of a more purposeful age. Their early efforts may well be labelled imitative, but their imitativeness was spontaneous, creative and formative.

They had not waited for the guidance of the critics, the majority of whom – as has already been indicated – continued to pay lip service to the values of the immediate past.

24 J. Brugman, *An introduction to the history of modern Arabic literature in Egypt*, Leiden, 1984, p. 325.
25 *Disūqī*, pp. 79–81.
26 *Al-Wasīlah al-adabiyyah*, vol. 1, Maṭbaʿat al-Madāris al-Malakiyyah, AH 1292, p. 4.
27 *Al-Wasīlah al-adabiyyah*, p. 211.

It may be worth adding that the general readership, too, was slow in sensing the change of direction which, with the benefit of hindsight, we now see as the most significant. Even in the 1890s *al-Hilāl*, a journal widely regarded as a signal organ of modernization, invited readers to nominate the best contemporary poets, and published the submissions of thirteen individuals between 15 November 1893 and 15 April 1894. In those lists Aḥmad Shawqī (1868–1932) was named only once, whereas the conservative ʿAlī al-Laythī (d. 1897) earned four mentions. These are of course not expert opinions and the sampling is too limited to carry much weight, but it is also worth noting that when another reader submitted two highly ornate lines for editorial comment, the unsigned response praised them highly as being 'delicate in diction, valid in sense, and decorated with *badīʿ*'[28] but criticized them for some redundancy, apparently occasioned only by the desire to include a paronomasia.

Moved by somewhat different considerations, some prose writers also had taken, even earlier in the century, to a simple, functional style,[29] but this appears to have been accepted as a necessity in some circumstances rather than as a desirable literary feature. A rare positive argument in its favour was made at a comparatively early stage by the extremely talented but short-lived Adīb Isḥāq (1856–85), one of the few who made occasional references to European sources in his scant essays in literary criticism. His point was that correct and chaste but unfettered prose was more *natural* than *sajʿ*, as is evidenced by the fact that the latter is virtually unknown in other literary traditions. But even he, although suspicious of verbal artifice as tempting the writer to substitute fancies for 'the beauties of the truth', admitted that it had a more immediate effect on hearts and minds, and allowed it a place in introductory and transitional passages.[30]

How far these perceptions were from being widely accepted even by the end of the century is shown, paradoxically, by the views expressed by one of the giants of modern writing, Jurjī Zaydān (1861–1914).

Zaydān was always impatient of writers who made a display of a recondite vocabulary and obscure construction, but if the unsigned comment mentioned earlier on two lines of poetry submitted to his journal is his, it shows him to have been at least moderately conservative in his taste. And in a long study published by instalments in the same *al-Hilāl* between February 1897 and April 1899,[31] also unsigned but undoubtedly from his pen for he referred in it to his authorship of historical romances (1 Mar. 1897, p. 495), he wrote (1 Jun. 1897, p. 735):

[28] *al-Hilāl* (1 Oct. 1895), p. 101. [29] See the chapter on 'Prose stylists'.
[30] Hāshim Yāghī, *al-Naqd al-adabī al-ḥadīth fī Lubnān*, vol. 1, pp. 118–22.
[31] 'Kuttāb al-ʿArabiyyah wa qurrāʾuhā'. Specific references will be indicated within the text of this paragraph and the next two by date and page.

Another basis on which the style of writing may vary is the subject dealt with . . . for the language of science differs in style from the language of literature, and the language of writing is other than the language of oratory. Ornate expressions are as undesirable in the natural and mathematical sciences as simple ones are in literary subjects, where the aim is to stir the emotions and rouse men's zeal.

Zaydān seems in fact to embody, in attenuated fashion, the dilemma of a generation leaning away from the standards of the immediate past yet unwilling to jettison them altogether. His own historical romances, which have earned him a place of note among pioneers of the novel in Arabic, are in a very simple, bare style; but – as if at pains to exempt them somehow from the full demands of literature – he classes them sometimes as popularized history (1 Mar. 1897, p. 495), sometimes as 'entertainment' (*fukāhah*; 1 Apr. 1899, p. 397); at yet another point (15 Feb. 1897, pp. 457–8) he spoke of there being many kinds of novels, such as the historical, the scientific, the literary, the entertaining and the edifying, all approached by readers 'in their hours of leisure, to relieve their minds of the pressure of work, not to resort to dictionaries in order to solve riddles set by their diction'.

He also acknowledged that it was precisely this kind of writing that was most in demand (1 Apr. 1899, p. 395). Whatever their literary pretensions, those who had first resorted to a direct and functional style had set an irreversible trend. Their prose lacked purple, but their books were read.

The indications, therefore, are that throughout most of the nineteenth century, despite the forces stirring in society and in many areas of intellectual endeavour, the majority of the critics remained conservative and stood like a dam across a mighty river, with only a few sluice-gates open. Among the most responsive creative writers and poets, new trends were taking shape that owed much indirectly to European stimulation, but little to the direct example of its literature. At the same time, a growing admiration for the achievements of Europe was building up a massive head of water. And when – mainly in the 1890s – the dam gave way, change came in a tremendous flood, and was deep-stained with awareness of Europe.

THE EXAMPLE OF EUROPE

Even in its most formalistic stages, Arab literary criticism had never claimed that proficiency in language and rhetoric was the essence of the literary experience. If only in a perfunctory manner, the critics allowed for the fact that poets are born, not made.[32] Some went a little further: Aḥmad

32 On the controversy in classical times about natural and artificial poetry, see Mansour Agami, *The neckveins of winter*, Leiden, 1984. A reaffirmation early in the nineteenth century may be found in Ṭahṭāwī's *Takhlīṣ al-ibrīz*, p. 281.

al-Barbīr (1745?–1811) argued – echoing and perhaps also widening the view of Ibn Rashīq – that the derivation at an early stage of the word *shāʿir* (poet) from *shaʿara* (to be aware) implies more than that he was the repository of tribal lore, for the root denotes something wider than knowledge; rather, the poet is so called 'because he perceives what others do not'.[33]

Yet it is not from such cracks in the dam that modernistic notions of literature flowed. Rather, it became commonplace to claim a European antecedent for any new initiative. Even in urging a more even-handed evaluation of literary works, both *al-Hilāl*[34] and *al-Muqtaṭaf*[35] appealed not merely to a sense of justice or common sense, but to the example of Europeans.

The all too obvious successes of European powers – mainly Great Britain and France – were all the more impressive as they were achieved at the expense of the Arabs. They created the illusion that western civilization was uniform, uniformly excellent and universally valid, so there seemed no way forward except by emulating it. Already in 1870 in an unsigned article in *al-Jinān*[36] presumably by the editor Buṭrus al-Bustānī (1819–93) we read:

> The East, which of old had been the centre of good taste and brilliance, which has bestowed religion and law and civilization upon the rest of the world, has sunk – thanks to the prevalence of fanaticism, of selfishly motivated revolutions, and of divisions – to a condition of ignorance and stupidity . . . What can possibly result from railways and other means of locomotion, from the telegraph, the printing presses, the newspapers, the schools, the cutting of the Suez Canal and the extension of means of contact with the peoples of Europe . . . except the good tidings of the spread of civilization and the gradual widening of its reach?

Noticeable in this passage is not only the indiscriminate admiration of the achievements of Europe – an acceptance of what may be called 'excellence by association' – but also a tendency to paint the local scene in extremely drab colours. This was soon to gather strength, as in an unsigned article in *Miṣbāḥ al-sharq*,[37] which may be assumed to have been written by Ibrāhīm al-Muwayliḥī (1846–1906), which contrasted the low standard of language used in government offices with the fact that the British paid bonuses to their own men if they learned Arabic, then went on to say what scarcely corresponds with the observable reality:

> Is it not strange, is it not to be wondered at, to find an English soldier addressing you, in speech or in writing, in correct Arabic, whereas a member of the Egyptian

[33] Hāshim Yāghī, *al-Naqd al-adabī al-ḥadīth fī Lubnān*, p. 17.

[34] Yr. 1, No. 7 (1 Mar. 1893), p. 245.

[35] Yaʿqūb Ṣarrūf, 'al-Intiqād', (Dec. 1887), as quoted in *Disūqī*, pp. 114–17.

[36] 'Al-Sharq', Yr. 1, No. 2, (January 1870), pp. 15, 17.

[37] 'Lughat al-ḥukūmah', Yr. 1, No. 3 (28 Apr. 1898).

élite, an Arab, is incapable of expressing himself in his own tongue and must resort to a foreign one?

It became commonplace to bewail the lack of stimulation in contemporary intellectual life.[38] In addition some went on to wholesale condemnation of the heritage of the past. Khalīl Mutrān (1872–1949) stated baldly that[39] 'the Arabs did not follow any known method in their criticism, nor did they make of it an art with principles of its own; there were only casual notions that they scattered piecemeal in their discourses'. This view was echoed later by Tāhā Ḥusayn (1889–1973).[40]

Mayy Ziyādah (1886–1941) characterized the whole of the Arab poetic tradition in these terms:[41]

Out of admiration for Beduin purity of style came a fondness for copying and imitation, and out of it resulted the poverty of Arab imagination, attachment to diction rather than content, the formulation of ideas in single verses, defects in the correlation of ideas, and shortcomings in the marshalling of parts of a discourse, so that one often finds that the end of an ode ought to be placed at the beginning, and the middle at the end. Imitativeness also resulted in the confinement of Arabic poetry to the motifs of praise, satire, elegy, heroism, self-glorification, and some gnomic verse.

Similarly Abū 'l-Qāsim al-Shābbī's (1909–34) book on poetic imagination,[42] sensitive and perceptive though it was, all but denied the existence of this quality in past Arabic poetry.

The derogation could even acquire a racialist tone, as when Ibrāhīm ʿAbd al-Qādir al-Māzinī (1890–1949), after again asserting that *all* Arab poets were confined to one path by dint of imitation, added[43] that of all the poets writing in Arabic, writers and great men, the ones most deserving of being designated as geniuses were of non-Arab extraction.

It needs to be said that such exaggerations are due at least in part to a desire to shame one's contemporaries into self-improvement. Unflattering comparisons with the zeal of Europeans are found even in the writings of ʿAbd Allāh al-Nadīm, whose fierce loyalty to his nation is not in doubt. A glimpse at the true motivation may be had in Ṭāhā Ḥusayn's review of a book entitled *Harem*, written in French, in which Qūt al-Qulūb al-Dimirdāshiyyah exposed disturbing aspects of family life.[44] He wished that

38 For example, Mayy Ziyādah, *ʿĀʾishah Taymūr*, Beirut, Muʾassasat Nawfal, 1975, p. 104.

39 'Al-Intiqād', in inaugural number of *al-Majallah al-Jadīdah* (June 1900), as quoted in *Disūqī*, p. 99.

40 *Ḥadīth al-arbiʿāʾ*, vol. 2, Cairo, 1937, p. 63.

41 Introduction to the *Dīwān* of ʿĀʾishah Taymūr, as quoted in Hāshim Yāghī, *al-Naqd al-adabī al-ḥadīth fī Lubnān*, vol. 2, p. 22.

42 *Al-Khayāl al-shiʿrī ʿind al-ʿArab*, (the text of a lecture given in Tunis in 1929, and since often reprinted), Tunis, n.d.

43 In an article on Ibn al-Rūmī in *al-Bayān*, Yr. 2 (1912), as quoted in *Disūqī*, p. 366.

44 *Fuṣūl fī 'l-adab wa l-naqd*, Cairo, 1945, p. 69.

it had been written in Arabic to point at weaknesses to be remedied, and would not have minded if it had then been translated into foreign languages, as proof of Arab capacity for self-criticism.

As late as 1949, Muḥammad Mandūr (1907–65) was writing:[45]

> We cannot – without being guilty of fatuous bigotry and dense ignorance – pretend that we need not be the pupils of Europe, need not import Western culture, then digest and assimilate it, that we may then be able to contribute in earnest to the advancement of human civilization.

Even this statement is open to argument, but it is an accurate formulation of Arabs' hopes and expectations as they embarked on a radical re-orientation of their literature.

MODERNISM

What the critics who were to make their mark early in the twentieth century had inherited from the previous generation was – together with a gathering momentum for change – a concern for the purity of the Arabic language, a taste for a direct, functional style now enshrined as a principle of modernism, and an interest in the literature which their forefathers had produced in a more vigorous period of their history. But those who remained within the limits of these notions, believing that neither their language nor their literature had any need of foreign importations, now appeared in the guise of conservatives. They had their eloquent representatives – such as Muṣṭafā Ṣādiq al-Rāfiʿī (1880–1937) – and they engaged in bitter polemics in defence of their stand; but since the late 1920s their voice has been not so much silenced as swamped by a breed of writers who had exciting new perspectives to offer the reading public. These are broadly referred to as 'modernists'.

Of these, a few, like the early socialist Salāmah Mūsā (c. 1887–1958), considered all past writing to be upper class, and therefore irrelevant. The majority, however, looked for a blending, in a variety of formulae, of their Arab–Islamic heritage with such western ideas as seemed to offer the best hope of self-assertion in the modern world. Secularism, liberalism and nationalism were part of the same package. And the new élite was most willing to give a hearing to those who, like Ṭāhā Ḥusayn,[46] claimed to be true to the spirit of the Arab past even in their openness to foreign influences. What was radically new was that they treated their heritage not

[45] 'Rusul al-thaqāfah al-gharbiyyah', *al-Ahrām*, 10 May 1949.

[46] See P. Cachia, *Ṭāhā Ḥusayn: his place in the Egyptian literary renaissance*, London, 1956, especially Ch. 7, pp. 86–103.

as a directive force, but as raw material to be studied in the light of principles derived from the west.

With a keen sense of urgency and a multitude of ready models to follow, these authors quickly formed a corpus of critical writing so immense that only its broadest trends can be delineated here.

A factor affecting not criticism alone but all modern writing is that, initially at least, the readership was too small to enable an author to live by his pen. To those with a literary bent, the main avenues of employment were in education or in journalism. Virtually all theoretical expositions and many broad attempts at literary history were born within the far-from-cloistered walls of the new universities, and many major works were first published serially in the pages of journals or even in the literary columns of newspapers.

A remarkable early example of the way foreign criteria were grafted onto native stock is Jabr Ḍūmiṭ's (1859–1930) *Falsafat al-balāghah*, first published in 1898.[47]

Jabr Ḍūmiṭ, who taught at the American University of Beirut and remained active until the late 1920s, had already published in Cairo, two years earlier, *al-Khawāṭir al-ḥisān fī 'l-mā*ᶜ*anī wa 'l-bayān* which despite its rhyming title was an innnovative book. It explored the relationship between grammar, rhetoric and logic and insisted on the unity and clarity of conception of a literary work.[48]

Falsafat al-balāghah, however, was basically a translation of Herbert Spencer's *Philosophy of style*, at times so replete with collocations unfamiliar in Arabic[49] that the public of the time must have had some difficulty in following the argument; but it did more than make up for this by conjoining Spencer's arguments with dicta from the classical Arab critics and illustrating them with passages from Arabic literature. It identified, for example, classical preferences for pithiness and directness with the principle of economy of the hearer's attention. Where Spencer praised Emerson's use of the compound metaphor in the first of his 'Lectures on the times',[50] Jabr Ḍūmiṭ referred to the effectiveness of the similes in al-Ghazālī's *Iḥyā*ᵓ ᶜ*ulūm al-dīn*; and he paralleled Spencer's remarks on 'the error committed both by Pope in his poems and by Bacon in his essays . . . of constantly employing forcible forms of expression' by observing that rhymed prose, which he conceded was pleasing, becomes tiresome if maintained without a break.

47 Baᶜabdā, al-Maṭbaᶜah al-ᶜUthmāniyyah, usefully summarized in Hāshim Yāghī, *al-Naqd al-adabī al-ḥadīth fī Lubnān*, vol. 1, pp. 212–29.

48 Extract entitled 'Shurūṭ al-balāghah' in *al-Hilāl* (15 Dec. 1896).

49 Such as *al-iqtiṣād* ᶜ*alā mutaᵓaththiriyyāt al-sāmi*ᶜ for 'the economy of the mental sensibilities'.

50 H. Spencer, *The philosophy of style*, ed. Fred. N. Scott, Boston, 1892, p. 26.

His was to prove the most direct and concentrated method by which western criteria were integrated into Arab literary perception. Not all his successors followed exactly his scheme: some have been content with a straightforward translation which then affected other works; others leaned heavily on a foreign source while elaborating their own views; but the road followed by Arab criticism is studded with importations felt to be as relevant to Arabic as they are to the culture that produced them. Qusṭākī al-Ḥimṣī (1858–1941) published a long series of summaries of the works of classical Arab and modern French critics.[51] Even before the middle of the century, Naẓmī Khalīl had translated Shelley's *Defence of poetry* in 1935; Aḥmad al-Shāyib had closely followed Winchester's *Principles of literary criticism* in his *Uṣūl al-naqd al-adabī* in 1940; Muḥammad ʿAwaḍ Muḥammad had translated Abercrombie's work of the same title in 1942; Luwīs ʿAwaḍ (1914–90) had done the same with Horace's *Ars poetica* in 1947; and Muḥammad Mandūr's translation of Lanson's *Méthode de l'historie littéraire* informed much of his own early work.

Increasingly since then, Arab authors have tended to form their own synthesis rather than concentrate on a single foreign source, but interest in the thinking of western critics remains intense, as witness the translations of selections from René Wellek's *Concepts of criticism* and *Discriminations* by Muḥammad ʿAṣfūr in 1987.

So it is that all the tools and auxiliary techniques of literary criticism have passed into the hands of the Arabs. One may instance the application of psychology to the understanding of literary works. Some literary figures had, from an early date, invited a psychological approach – notably Ibn al-Rūmī and Abū Nuwās in studies by Ibrāhīm ʿAbd al-Qādir al-Māzinī as early as in 1913[52] and particularly by ʿAbbās Maḥmūd al-ʿAqqād (1889–1964). But a significant landmark was reached when Cairo University instituted, in 1938, a course on the connection between psychology and literature, entrusting it to Aḥmad Amīn (1879–1954) and Muḥammad Khalaf Allāh. The latter went on to publish a number of studies,[53] of which the theoretical ones were based mainly on Cyril Burt's *How the mind works* and Spearman's *The creative mind*. Among his students were Muḥammad al-Nuwayhī and ʿIzz al-Dīn Ismāʿīl, who actively followed his lead.

More recently, the interest in semiology, form criticism and other modern literary approaches was attested in the bi-lingual journal *Alif*, published by the American University in Cairo, of which the second number (Spring 1982) is devoted to 'Criticism and the avant-garde'. And

[51] *Manhal al-wurrād fī ʿilm al-intiqād*, vols 1 and 2 published Cairo 1907, vol. 3 in Aleppo, 1925.
[52] 'Kalimah ʿan Ibn al-Rūmī', in al-Barqūqī's *al-Bayān*; see *Disūqī*, pp. 410–12.
[53] Collected in *Min al-wujhah al-nafsiyyah fī dirāsat al-adab wa naqdih*, Cairo, 1947.

Kamāl Abū Dīb's enthusiasms may be gauged from the fact that in a volume explicitly intended to revolutionize not only Arab literary perceptions but the whole of Arab thought, he declared that the three modern movements which have 'made it impossible to view the universe as it was previously viewed' are Marxism, Picasso's vision, and structuralism,[54] and he has followed this up with a structuralist study of pre-Islamic poetry.[55]

For the theories have not remained theories. Apart from the constant give-and-take between modern creative writers and their critics, there has been a pervasive reevaluation of the entire heritage of the past.

Once again, it is a western example that initiated Arab literary history. On 1 August 1893, *al-Hilāl* carried an unsigned review of a book by Edward van Dyck and Constantine Philippides entitled *History of the Arabs and their literature*. One of the reviewer's comments was that 'Europeans have a science called the science of *lītiratūr* which examines the nation's men of letters, the history of their compositions and their writings, the ranks of the authors in different periods and similar topics, the like of which we have not encountered in Arab books'. Exactly five months later, Jurjī Zaydān began publishing in the same journal a long series of articles entitled 'Tārīkh ādāb al-lughah al-ʿarabiyyah', later (1911–14) collected in four volumes under the same title.[56]

The approach was more historical than literary, but if only because of the need of textbooks for secondary schools, the genre was soon established although it was only after the 1930s that mature literary histories began to be produced, as well as solid studies on particular periods or particular features or genres, classical and modern.

A negative hangover from the past is that initially the critics gave little attention to prose genres.[57] Style was very much a matter of debate, and illustrations of rhetorical features were drawn from prose as well as poetry, but there seemed to be an assumption that poetry held the quintessence of literary values, and that prose was literary only inasmuch as it shared in these. Even the immense popularity of short stories and novels drew only brief and almost casual comments from the early critics.[58] But a turning point was reached when Zakī Mubārak wrote his doctoral thesis in Paris, *La prose arabe au 4e siècle de l'hégire*, published in 1931.[59]

54 *Jadaliyyat al-khafāʾ wa 'l-tajallī*, Beirut, 1979, pp. 7–8.
55 *al-Ruʾā 'l-Muqannaʿah*, Cairo, 1986.
56 Cf. Brugman, *History of Modern Arabic literature*, p. 328, who takes note only of the date of publication in book form, and reports a surmise that it was inspired by Brockelmann.
57 Muḥammad Yūsuf Najm, *Naẓariyyat al-Naqd*, p. 6.
58 For example, Ḥabīb Bannūt in 1890, Yaʿqūb Ṣarrūf and especially Jabr Ḍūmiṭ in 1906, all as recorded in Hāshim Yāghī, *al-Naqd al-adabī al-ḥadīth fī Lubnān*, pp. 139–41, 127–35, and 229–35.
59 Paris.

Of particular interest in the present context is the attention belatedly given to the positive achievements of classical Arab critics. An impressive sweeping view of these was taken by Muhammad Mandūr in his *al-Naqd al-manhajī ᶜind al-ᶜarab*, first published in 1948,[60] and the magisterial *Tārīkh al-naqd al-adabī* by Iḥsān ᶜAbbās (b. 1920) in 1971.[61]

Not surprisingly, the great majority of theoretical presentations and broad literary histories have been academic in provenance and character. No less effective, however, in the formation of trends and perceptions has been a multitude of articles and books, many consisting of collected articles, by men and a very few women who, whether or not they also had a place in the educational establishment, found their readiest outlet in journalism. Especially in the first half of the twentieth century, they were prodigiously productive and versatile. Ṭāhā Ḥusayn, for example, is credited with sixty-seven books and 1325 articles in addition to twenty-three poems composed in his early youth, joint authorship of another twenty books, introductions to thirty-six books by other authors, the editing of eight texts, ten volumes of translations, twenty-nine shorter translations that appeared in journals and contributions to 110 published interviews and discussions.[62]

Because Ṭāhā Ḥusayn and many of his most eminent contemporaries such as ᶜAbbās Maḥmūd al-ᶜAqqād, Muḥammad Ḥusayn Haykal (1888–1956)[63] and Mārūn ᶜAbbūd (1886–1962) were polymaths active in a variety of fields, it is sometimes difficult to determine by what channels they influenced their public most. It is noticeable that none of these set out his guiding principles in one explicit, systematic book; and yet by a careful perusal of their many individual studies, one can detect either a clear progression in their literary perceptions, as in the case of Ṭāhā Ḥusayn, or an impressive degree of self-consistency, as is true of al-ᶜAqqād.[64]

It has become common to speak of various literary 'schools' functioning then, such as the Dīwān school named after a single book that two of three temporarily allied poet-critics produced together,[65] or the Apollo Group who did have an organized nucleus and contributed to a journal so named,[66] or the Syro-Americans who were mostly Christian émigrés to the Americas and as such shared a common experience. These 'schools', however, were

[60] Cairo. [61] Beirut.

[62] Ḥamdī al-Sakkūt and Marsden Jones, *Aᶜlām al-adab al-muᶜāṣir fī Misr – 1. Ṭāhā Ḥusayn*, Cairo, 1975.

[63] On these and on Ṭāhā Ḥusayn and Muḥammad Mandūr, see David Semah, *Four Egyptian literary critics*, Leiden, 1974.

[64] ᶜAbd al-Munᶜim Khiḍir az-Zubaidī, 'Al-ᶜAḳḳād's critical theories', PhD dissertation, Edinburgh University, 1965–6.

[65] The two were ᶜAbbās Maḥmūd al-ᶜAqqād and ᶜAbd al-Qādir al-Māzinī, who soon fell out with the third member of the group, ᶜAbd al-Raḥmān Shukrī.

[66] Founded by Aḥmad Zakī Abū Shādī.

seldom extensive, markedly cohesive or long-lived. It may be truer to speak of variations in a common movement.

What gave the movement a common direction is not in doubt. Although individuals differed in their choice of a particular guru, it is to western authorities and western examples that they appealed, and by western criteria that they judged, either by explicit comparisons or implicitly by characterizing, say, al-Jāḥiẓ as 'the Voltaire of the Arabic language'[67] or al-Maᶜarrī as 'the Lucretius of Islam', 'the Diogenes of the Arabs', or 'the Voltaire of the Levant'.[68] Whether it was Ṭāhā Ḥusayn writing the first doctoral thesis accepted by the new Egyptian University, or the self-educated al-ᶜAqqād freelancing in *Shuᶜarāʾ Miṣr wa bīʾātuhum*, they gave the attention to their subject's cultural and social background that western scholarship expected. Even if their documentation was not always very rigorous, their sampling of the material was so immense as to give weight to their opinions, and the perceptiveness of such as Ṭāhā Ḥusayn and Mārūn ᶜAbbūd has been recognized by a later critic even when he deplored the lack of method in their approach.[69]

THE ROMANTIC PHASE

It is arguable that, whereas throughout most of the nineteenth century the critics proved more conservative than the creative writers, they were during the first three or four decades of the twentieth century very much in the vanguard, in that by drawing on prestigious ready-made formulae more easily advocated than applied, they were accustoming the reading public to expectations which the poets and prose-writers then had to fulfil. The members of the Dīwān group, for example, were undoubtedly more influential as critics than as poets.[70] And whereas at the beginning of the century it was the neo-classicists Aḥmad Shawqī and Ḥāfiẓ Ibrāhīm (1872–1932) who dominated the poetic scene, they were badgered by critics who constantly represented them as inferior to the great poets of the west; and in time it was a western-inspired romanticism that triumphed in poetry as it had already triumphed in prose.

Of course criticism was not the only factor at work. Romanticism in its most popular conception as an outpouring of personal emotion benefited from the swing of the pendulum away from the excessive formalism of the

67 Khalīl Shaybūb, 'Fī 'l-Ṭarīq', *al-Ahrām*, 3 Aug. 1949.

68 Amīn al-Rayḥānī, as quoted in Hāshim Yāghī, *al-Naqd al-adabī al-ḥidāth fī Lubnān*, vol. 1, p. 321.

69 Muḥammad Yūsuf Najm, *Naẓariyyat al-naqd*, p. 37.

70 M. M. Badawi, *A critical introduction to modern Arabic poetry*, Cambridge, 1975, p. 115. Also ᶜAbd al-Muḥsin Ṭāhā Badr, *Taṭawwur al-riwāyah al-ᶜarabiyyah al-ḥadīthah*, Cairo, 1963, p. 285.

immediate past. At a time when the great powers of Europe were overwhelming one Arab country after another politically and militarily, an emotional response was one of the very few that remained open. And romanticism does reflect one perennial aspect of the human reality with which Arabs, like others, could genuinely identify. So it was that romanticism was to colour virtually all of the first half of the twentieth century in Arabic writing.

The strictest understanding of romanticism came through the Dīwān 'school', two of whose members, al-Māzinī and ʿAbd al-Raḥmān Shukrī (1886–1958), attended the Teachers' Training College in Cairo where they were exposed to English literature; the third, al-ʿAqqād, although his only formal schooling was at the primary level, proved the most constant and energetic and perhaps also the most scholarly. Influenced by Hazlitt, Coleridge and other leading English critics of the preceding century, he perceived that the mark of the true poet is not merely to give vent to his emotions, but to capture a vision of reality, and fit his creative activity to it.[71] To this key understanding he attached a number of related concepts, such as the organic unity of the poem and the distinction between wit and imagination, which have earned a permanent place in the vocabulary of Arab critics.

The great majority of al-ʿAqqād's contemporaries, however, were content to give emotion free rein. One of the distinctive features of the Dīwān group was that their foreign culture was English, whereas even in the Arab countries controlled by Britain it was the French who were more active in the educational field and made the deeper mark on literature. Some of the critics therefore perceived the difference between the rival notions in terms of their provenance and were impatient with what seemed to be unnecessary complications. The mutual antipathies of the two camps are well illustrated in these two contrasting passages.[72] The first is by Khalīl Shaybūb (1891–1951):

> The young generation is bent on emulating Saxon civilization in straining after recondite, far-fetched imaginings and notions. The previous one drew its inspiration from Latin civilization and tried to draw near to the ways of its people and its poets. And there is no doubt that Orientals are – by nature, by instinct, by their tendency to flights of imagination which wisdom weighs in the scales of life – closer to duplicating Latin civilization.

No less pungent was al-ʿAqqād's judgement:

[71] Zubaidī, *Critical theories*, p. 292.

[72] Khalīl Shaybūb's occurs in the introduction of his volume of poetry, *al-Fajr al-awwal*, published in 1921; al-ʿAqqād's is in *Sāʿāt bayn al-kutub*, first published in book form in 1929. I traced them from information given in Shmuel Moreh, *Modern Arabic poetry 1800–1970*, Leiden, 1976, p. 66, notes 55 and 56.

We learned French and read its literature before we learned English and other tongues, so what is diffused amongst us is the popular criteria of French literature – namely a superficial brilliance and frivolous subtlety. We went along with its defects and its qualities, which are similar to ours, with the result that we have not come to perceive the difference between the true and the counterfeit, between sincerity and speciousness. We never in fact got out of our rut and into a different way. Still hidden from us are the criteria of earnestness, straightforwardness, and simplicity which are the mark of English and German poetry.

It was Ṭāhā Ḥusayn who was to encapsulate the preference of the many when, echoing Lamartine's 'Je chantais, mes amis, comme chante l'oiseau', he defined literature as 'such writings as issue from the writer as a song is emitted from a warbling bird, as a perfume is diffused from a fragrant flower, as light emanates from the brilliant sun'.[73] He refused to limit the spontaneity of the creative writer by any considerations of self-discipline, of craftsmanship or of the character of the emotion to be expressed. Correspondingly, although at one time he sought some objective basis for criticism, the position to which he ultimately came was that the critic's judgement was essentially a subjective response to a subjective outflow.

In virtually all the varieties of criticism practised then, from the academic to the impressionistic, one finds a marked concentration on the emotional power of the individual poet or writer.[74] And ᶜAbd al-Raḥmān Shukrī was giving voice to a widespread assumption, close to that of the late Victorians, when he wrote that

the great poet is not someone who concerns himself with little matters, but one who soars above the day in which he happens to be living, then looks into the depths of Time and reaches out to the utmost of what has been and what is to be, so that his poetry comes forth as eternal as is his vision.[75]

There was, as a result, an element of escapism in Arab romanticism, and certainly a great deal of pathos. A few voices, such as Amīn al-Rayḥānī's[76] (1876–1940), were raised against excessively lachrymose outpourings, but had not Alfred de Musset once said:

Les plus désespérés sont les chants les plus beaux,
Et j'en sais d'éternels qui sont des purs sanglots?

Yet all the time, the appreciation of the true nature of artistic perception and expression was growing and being refined. The entire trend found its summation in the first part of the career of Muḥammad Mandūr. A disciple of Ṭāhā Ḥusayn, he commended to his contemporaries the subtler power of

73 See P. Cachia, *Ṭāhā Ḥusayn*, especially p. 132.

74 See quotations from ᶜAbd al-Raḥmān Shukrī, Aḥmad Amīn, and Sayyid Quṭb in *Disūqī*, pp. 336, 419, 406 and 437.

75 Also quoted in *Disūqī*, pp. 341–2.

76 Quoted in Hāshim Yāghī, *al-Naqd al-adabī al-ḥadīth fī Lubnān*, p. 30.

a literature that was 'whispered' rather than one that trumpeted its effects, and although still holding on to the essential subjectiveness of criticism, he put his faith in honing its instruments by insisting on the critic's acquisition of a wide culture.

Arab romanticism was never without challenges either from remnants of conservatism or from voguish importations from the west. Ilyās Abū Shabakah (1903–47), who owed not a little to French romanticism but consistently resisted any kind of curb on creative impulses and roundly declared that 'in literature, theories are diseases',[77] dismissed its rivals with considerable irritation as pretentious foreign importations; bandying the French words, he wrote:[78]

> The market-place of criticism has got busy, and a brand of dewy-eyed critics has popped up, proclaiming it necessary to follow the lead of the West in so-called living literature, advocating modern theories (as if literature were expendable goods, to be changed as one changes shoes). So some sing the praises of 'cubisme' – and that was the start of 'snobisme' in Egypt and especially in the Lebanon; others call for 'réalisme' or 'impressionisme' or 'futurisme' or 'symbolisme'. So have all theses 'ismes' become the badge of erudition.

Yet some, notably symbolism, were to create a sizable enclave for themselves. Its high priest in the Arab world, both as practitioner and as early exponent, was Saʿīd ʿAql (b. 1913). He characterized it in rather extreme terms as being born solely of the subconscious. By not only denying that emotion had any part in the process of creation but also insisting that the stronger the emotion, the greater was the damage done to poetry,[79] he did little to endear it to the romantics. And yet ironically, perhaps because it still focuses on the vision of the individual, some critics look upon symbolism as no more than a sub-species of romanticism.

But by the late 1940s a more radical change of emphasis was in the air.

REALISM AND COMMITMENT

In 1947 there appeared the first experiments with free verse, in which both regularity in rhyming and uniformity in the length of the lines were abandoned, and one of its first exponents, Nāzik al-Malāʾikah (b. 1923), went on to attempt to codify the new poetry.[80]

The break with practices so long established that they seemed to be of the very essence of the language, let alone the literary tradition, roused fierce

[77] Muḥammad Yūsuf Najm, *Naẓariyyat al-Naqd*, p. 39.

[78] *Rawābiṭ al-fikr wa 'l-rūḥ bayn al-ʿArab wa 'l-firinjah*, Beirut, 1943, as quoted in Hāshim Yāghī, *al-Naqd al-adabī al-ḥadīth fī Lubnān*, vol. 2, p. 132.

[79] In the lecture 'Kayfa afham al-shiʿr', delivered in Beirut in 1937, as quoted in Yāghī, *al-Naqd al-adabī al-ḥadīth fī Lubnān*, vol. 2, p. 176.

[80] In *Qaḍāyā 'l-shiʿr almuʿāṣir*, Beirut, 1962.

polemics among the critics; and yet it was only one symptom of a sea change in Arab consciousness. Limited as they were, the advances made by Arabs in running their own affairs generated more dynamism. At the same time, renewed impositions made by the colonial powers during the Second World War showed how precarious those advances had been. The wounds inflicted on Palestine, soon to be widened, added rage and bitterness. The course of the war also demonstrated that there were other viable ideologies than those of Great Britain or France. Even without these goads, the broadening of education and advances in maturity were making a new generation impatient with the escapism that had been a feature of Arab romanticism. Commitment was now the keyword.

Once again, there were to be many moods, varying from activism to discomposure, many labels, ranging from existentialism to rejectionism, and many variations in the formulae to which individual critics and men of letters swore loyalty, to say nothing of idiosyncratic '-isms' and the persistence of outdated ones. For most, however, the focus was no longer on the richness of the experience of the individual creative writer, but on his social relevance. Commitment is as dominant a note in the second half of the twentieth century as romanticism had been in the first. And Marxism has become a substantial component of the creed of the most dynamic and most widely read critics today.

The new thinking had long been in the making. There had been, from quite early days, socialists like Shiblī Shumayyil (1860–1917), Faraḥ Anṭūn (1874–1922) and Salāmah Mūsā. A concern for the poor and resentment of colonial rule had been staples of all the literary genres,[81] but these had not been central to the writers' self-view. Now the pace of change was quickening, and not always by direct statement. The paradigmatic image of Shelley as an ethereal poet unconcerned with social realities was corrected by Luwīs ʿAwaḍ in the preface to his translation of *Prometheus unbound*.[82] Issues from the Arab past and from the present were tackled from a new, provocative angle by the likes of Raʾīf Khūrī (1911–67). Muḥammad Mandūr, who had once decried all doctrinal approaches to literature, now turned to ideological criticism. A long-established writer noted for his aloofness, Tawfīq al-Ḥakīm (1899 or 1903–1987), was soon to find it necessary to argue that he had been a committed writer all along.[83]

If a turning-point in the prevailing mood needs to be specified, one may pick on the launching in January 1953 of the influential journal *al-Ādāb*, the

[81] See Mustafa Badawi's excellently documented 'Commitment in contemporary Arabic literature', UNESCO's *Cahiers d'histoire mondiale*, XIV, 4 (1972), pp. 859–79.

[82] M. Abdel-Hai, 'Shelley and the Arabs', *Journal of Arabic Literature*, III (1972), pp. 72–89.

[83] P. Cachia, 'Idealism and ideology: the case of Tawfīq al-Ḥakīm', *Journal of the American Oriental Society*, 100, 3 (Jul.–Oct. 1980), pp. 225–35.

proprietor of which, Suhayl Idrīs (b. 1923), proclaimed in the inaugural issue that it would be devoted to the service of committed literature.

A claim to realism, usually with some much disputed qualifier, is the *sine qua non* of contemporary Arab criticism in any of its variations. Yet its main theoretical underpinning, Marxism, is – like its predecessors in popular favour – an importation from Europe, and the glibness with which its vocabulary is used disguises the fact that it does not always sit comfortably on the Middle Eastern set-up.

An example of the strains involved may be seen in Luwīs ʿAwaḍ's analysis of the class structure of Egypt.[84] What he calls the aristocracy bears some resemblance to its European counterpart in that its beginnings involve titles and land grants (not linked to the titles) earned by services to a monarch, although it might more appropriately have been called a meritocracy since there was no hereditary principle involved, and no private ownership of land until Muḥammad ʿAlī, well into the nineteenth century, found it useful to entrust mostly tracts that needed developing to men who had earned his favour. The parallelism breaks down even further when what is called the bourgeoisie is found to consist mainly of the educated who became government functionaries, so that the dividing line between classes is ultimately determined by the rank attained and the wealth accumulated.

The one broad departure from European Marxism acknowledged by the Arabs is over its international character. One of the main reasons may have been the setback to some communist cells when they attempted to represent the struggle against Zionists as irrelevant, and preached instead that it was the enmity to Zionism that was irrelevant, that Arab and Jewish proletarians ought to make common cause against the capitalists of either ilk.[85] At any rate, it is common for writers to commend a Marxism modified by Arab national experience. The mere fact that the modifier is identified as national, not Islamic or communal, is a witness to the hold that nationalism has acquired and retains.

As may be expected of adherents to so self-assertive and cohesive a theory, their application of it to literary criticism has not proved immune to doctrinaire excesses. In the earlier stages especially, there were all too facile attempts to link the positions taken by some littérateurs of the preceding generation with their social origins, without accounting for the fact that men of very different backgrounds, such as the modest villager Ṭāhā Ḥusayn, the son of a city judge like Tawfīq al-Ḥakīm and the son of a Pasha

[84] *Tārīkh al-fikr al-miṣrī al-ḥadīth min ʿaṣr Ismāʿīl ilā thawrat 1919 – al-mabḥath al-awwal: al-khalfiyyah al-tārīkhiyyah*, vol. 1, Cairo; Beirut, 1966.

[85] See Luwīs ʿAwaḍ, introduction to *al-ʿAnqāʾ*, Beirut, 1966.

Maḥmūd Taymūr (1894–1973) had embraced substantially the same liberal, secular, nationalistic values.

The bias may indeed be very pronounced, as in a recent study on the short story in Egypt by Sayyid Ḥāmid al-Nassāj[86] which characterizes the bourgeoisie as self-indulgent and pleasure-seeking and romanticism as pandering to it (pp. 39–40, 51–65), then goes on to illustrate this over more than thirty pages with the effusions of a pornographer who had never been recognized as a literary figure of any standing.

The commoner temptation for a Marxist critic is to be somewhat prescriptive on the subject-matter of literature. This may be innocuous, if somewhat naive, as when Raʾīf Khūrī argued that we need to develop a new kind of 'nature literature':[87]

> Why should we not see in the current of a river a wasted electric power to lighten our darkness and energize factories? Of if the river is unsuitable to the generation of electricity, why do we not visualize in it fertile orchards, prosperous festivals, and happy peasants if only we could devise some irrigation project to water the thirsty land?

At other times, the critic is likely to distort values by restricting the writer to themes consciously perceived as socially relevant, or even insisting on an explicit message. It is, however, a sign of maturity that it was for giving much more space in their criticism to such considerations than to literary features that ʿAbd al-ʿAẓīm Anīs and Maḥmūd Amīn al-ʿĀlim (b. 1922) drew measured rebukes from a fellow Marxist, Ghālī Shukrī,[88] who pointed out that such a practice amounted to political comment but ceased to be literary criticism.

There is in fact no lack of Marxist critics of considerable maturity and originality, such as Jūrj Ṭarābīshī who combines psychology and Marxism in his work,[89] or who display admirable intellectual power and integrity, such as Ḥusayn Muruwwah (1909–87) who has made a major contribution to modern thought in his re-examination of Islamic philosophy.[90] One of the most acute and puristic is Ghālī Shukrī, who distinguishes sharply between propagandist writing designed to serve a cause, which he looks upon as a Leninist aberration, and a truly artistic approach to literature, exemplified by Marx and Engels who admired Shakespeare and Balzac for truthfully portraying the dissolution of their own class.[91]

The ideal Ghālī Shukrī puts forward is that of the writer who is imbued

86 *Ittijāhāt al-qiṣṣah al-Miṣriyyah al-qaṣīrah*, Cairo, 1978.

87 Samāḥ Idrīs, *Raʾīf Khūrī wa turāth al-ʿArab*, Beirut, 1986, p. 78.

88 *Thawrat al-fikr fī adabina 'l-ḥadīth*, Cairo, 1965, pp. 139–62.

89 As in *Sharq wa gharb, rujūlah wa unūthah*, Beirut, 1970.

90 *Al-Nazaʿāt al-māddiyyah fī 'l-falsafah al-ʿarabiyyah*, 2 vols, Beirut, 1978.

91 *Thawrat al-fikr fī adabinā 'l-ḥadīth*, especially pp. 134–8.

with true socialist principles and then truthfully conveys his vision of whatever has moved him. The similarity with St Augustine's 'Love and do what you will'[92] is striking, and underlines the faith-like quality of Marxism.

LINGUISTIC CRITICISM

Although the dominant concern of most of the present-day Arab critics is manifestly ideological, a number of them have been attracted by the basically linguistic techniques developed in the west for dealing with literary texts.

Most of these – but by no means all – have been North Africans who keep closely in touch with intellectual developments in France.[93] Amongst them, the dominant influences have been those of Todorov, Barthes, Propp and Goldman.

From its inaugural issue in November 1968, the review *Mawāqif* provided the main outlet for brief and sometimes partial expositions of the contents of single books by French innovators, sometimes for translations of some chapters or of articles, and for first attempts at testing their applicability to Arabic literary productions. Its example was eventually followed by other journals, such as *al-Ḥayāh al-Thaqāfiyyah* and *al-Aqlām*. Significant advances continue to be made in periodical publications that are not always easily accessible.

One of the pioneers who has also emerged as an active and dedicated contributor to this branch of criticism is the Tunisian ᶜAbd al-Salām al-Musiddī, who has not only produced substantial studies of his own,[94] but has also directed the research of several graduates of the Tunisian University. No less prominent in the Arab heartlands are Ṣalāh Faḍl, who has produced the most substantial exposition of structuralism in Arabic,[95] Khaldūn al-Shamᶜah,[96] Mūrīs Abū Nāṣir[97] and Kamāl Abū Dīb.[98]

Not surprisingly, one of the major problems encountered by the theorists has been the coining of a technical vocabulary that would command wide acceptance. The word 'structuralism' itself has been

[92] 'Homily on the first Epistle of St John', para. 8, in Augustine of Hippo, *Selected writings*, New York, (Classics of western spirituality), 1984, p. 305.

[93] A useful survey is to be found in Tawfīq al-Zaydī, *Athar al-lisāniyyāt fī 'l-naqd al-ᶜArabī al-ḥadīth*, Tripoli and Tunis, 1984.

[94] Notably, in book form, *al-Uslūbiyyah wa 'l-uslūb: Naḥw badīl alsunī fī naqd al-adab*, Tripoli and Tunis, al-Dār al-ᶜArabiyyah li 'l-Kitāb, 1977. He is also the main contributor to *al-Shiᶜr wa mutaghayyirāt al-marḥalah*, Baghdad, 1985.

[95] *Naẓariyyat al-bināʾiyyah fī 'l-naqd al-adabī*, Cairo, 1978.

[96] In an inclusive study of critical theories entitled *al-Shams wa 'l-ᶜanqāʾ*, Damascus, 1974, and in *al-Naqd wa 'l-ḥurriyyah*, by the same publisher, 1977.

[97] *Al-Alsuniyyah wa 'l-naqd al-adabī fī 'l-naẓariyyah wa 'l-mumārasah*, Beirut, 1979.

[98] *Jadaliyyat al-khafāʾ wa 'l-tajallī*, Beirut, 1979.

variously rendered as *bināʾiyyah*, *binyawiyyah*, *binawiyyah*, *bunyāniyyah* and *haykaliyyah*.[99]

The techniques thus propagated are already being applied in book-length studies of literary works both classical[100] and modern.[101] This is yet another instance of the process by which most aspects of western thought have been integrated into Arab consciousness.

THE PRICE OF PROGRESS

The immensity of the strides taken by Arab critics in the last three or four generations may conceal how rocky the road has been. At every step, they have had not only to liberate themselves from the hold of the past, but also to fight a rearguard action against the diehards. There are still those who, by a simplistic identification of anything new with the changes that occurred in early Abbasid times, argue that Arabs need never look beyond the limits of their own tradition. Ibrāhīm ʿAlī Abū 'l-Khashab,[102] for example, makes out that the 'psychological' school (by which he evidently means the 'classical') stands merely for 'those who hallow the old', as did al-Aṣmaʿī, he sees the romantic school as a revolt against anything old and against all limitations placed on the individual, as is exemplified by Abū Nuwās, and all other schools as modifications of these. He also quotes with approval Wadīʿ Filisṭīn (b. c. 1920) – who incidentally is not the product of a traditional education, but a graduate of the American University in Cairo – when he ridicules the symbolists as merely wrapping simple metaphors in layers of obscurity, and declares that all these so-called schools are the inventions of critics, no poet ever having been known to 'put in an application to join this school or that'.

The effort and the cost of progress have not been intellectual only. The first modernists were kicking against a tradition that had been invested with a religious character, and they have therefore had to wage a long struggle against popular prejudice and a well-entrenched establishment. The later committed writers are by definition political activists who incur the ire of the authorities. For citing Islamic 'myths' as one factor that may have led to literary forgeries, Ṭāhā Ḥusayn was at one time accused of heresy and at another dismissed from his job and denied the right to lecture in public.

99 See glossary, Tawfīq al-Zaydī, *Athar al-lisāniyyāt*, pp. 163–75, and Ḥammādī Ṣamūd, 'Muʿjam li muṣṭalaḥāt al-naqd al-ḥadīth', *Ḥawliyyāt al-Jāmiʿah al-Tūnisiyyah*, 15 (1977) pp. 125–59.

100 For example, Ḥusayn al-Wād, *al-Binyah al-qaṣaṣiyyah fī Risālat al-ghufrān*, Tripoli and Tunis, 1972.

101 For example, Muḥammad Rashīd Thābit, *al-Binyah al-haykaliyyah wa 'l-ijtimāʿiyyah li Ḥadīth ʿĪsā 'bn Hishām*, Tripoli and Tunis, 1976; Tarshūnah Maḥmūd, *al-Adab al-murīd fī muʾallafāt al-Masʿadī*, Tunis, 1978; Maḥmūd Ghanāyim *Fī Mabnā 'l-naṣṣ* (on Imīl Ḥabībī's novel *al-Mutashāʾil*), Haifa, 1987.

102 In *Fī Muḥīṭ al-naqd al-adabī*, Cairo, 1985, pp. 83–7.

Others, from al-ᶜAqqād to Luwīs ᶜAwaḍ, have seen the inside of monarchic and republican prisons. Ḥusayn Muruwwah has died a violent death in the factionalism that is tearing the Lebanon apart. There is a heroic dimension to modern Arabic writing.

Sustaining it is an exalted notion of the function of literature. It is most richly condensed in the ascription of a prophetic function to the poet. One need only recall al-Mutanabbī's sobriquet to realise that the comparison would have been unthinkable before modern times. Yet it has been a recurring note in modern Arab writing.

It must have suggested itself from the time – perhaps as early as 1876[103] – that poetry began to be seen as a matter of inspiration rather than craftsmanship, although one must note that it is the word *ilhām* rather than the Qurʾanic *waḥy* that is most commonly used to describe the process. It was taken up by Asᶜad Dāghir (d. 1935) in his review of the *Dīwān* of Ḥāfiẓ Ibrāhīm in 1901,[104] where the word *ilhām* seems to be equated with *shuᶜūr* (sentiment, feeling). It was widely adopted by the Syro-Americans, as the title of Jibrān Khalīl Jibrān's best-known book attests.

It is re-echoed even now, but with a difference: The emphasis is no longer on the poet's visionary capacity, but on the social – and indeed the universal – significance of his vision. Adūnīs (ᶜAlī Aḥmad Saᶜīd, b. 1930) who has much to say on the subject,[105] has a self-consistent view of poetry in which every innovation is tantamount to the creation of a new world. For by concerning itself with the ultimate of Man's potential, it acquires what – in a characteristically striking and suggestive phrase – he calls 'the lyricism of becoming'. It is this lyricism that gives it the vital impetus of prophecy. Far from being fanciful or ineffectual, it is prophetic in that it leads us to a universe beyond our limitations.

[103] See the views ascribed to one Muḥammad Saᶜīd, but rather loosely reproduced, in *Disūqī*, p. 34.
[104] Quoted in Hāshim Yāghī, *al-Naqd al-adabī al-ḥadīth fī Lubnān*, vol. 1, p. 250.
[105] *Muqaddimah li 'l-shiᶜr al-ᶜArabī*, Beirut, 1943, pp. 100, 102, 106, 122–3.

CHAPTER 13

ARAB WOMEN WRITERS

WRITING IN THE WILDERNESS

To assess Arab women's writings in the twentieth century, we must go back to the latter half of the nineteenth. The late 1880s were a time of turmoil in Egypt, the contemporary cultural heartland of the Arab world. There was a climate of openness and acceptance of the new. Egypt was attracting Arab intellectuals – including women like the Lebanese Zaynab Fawwāz (1850–1914) in 1870, Wardah al-Yāzijī (1838–1924) in 1899 and the Palestinian-Lebanese Mayy Ziyādah (1886–1941) in 1908 – who could not find such intellectual freedom at home. Many of these immigrants became journalists, thus overcoming their outsider status and becoming intellectually integrated into their new society. Persistent contact with Europe throughout the nineteenth century was beginning to have a profound effect in Egypt. The values and philosophies of this alien culture were being absorbed and slowly transformed into indigenous commodities. The novel and the short story became for the Egyptians, as for their European counterparts, forays into reality. Writers, using these genres, could begin to create themselves as subjects within their transforming social context.

Women, too, were beginning to write. Contrary to what is generally believed, there were some women in the nineteenth century who were educated and could write. They were, for the most part, from the urban upper and middle classes and they were coming into contact, however indirectly, with Europeans. They were able to compare themselves with their European counterparts and could see in the comparison the contrast: European society welcomed women in the public sphere. Hence, despite their economic privilege, these women knew that they were not socially or emotionally privileged. Their exclusion and oppression as women cut across class lines, so that their expression mirrored the experience of others and in that reflection raised a consciousness of injustice suffered because of gender.

It is now common knowledge that liberal nationalists like Qāsim Amīn and Luṭfī al-Sayyid, and Islamic reformers like Muḥammad ʿAbduh and Rashīd Riḍā, rallied around the issue of women's education and its importance to the family and to society as a whole. What is less commonly known is that women also took up the banner. Understandably their contribution to modern Arabic literature was often inextricably bound up with the question of women's emancipation.

Between 1886 and 1925, women like the Lebanese Wardah al-Yāzijī and Zaynab Fawwāz, and the Egyptians ᶜĀʾishah al-Taymūriyyah (1840–1902) and Malak Ḥifnī Nāṣif, better known as Bāḥithat al-Bādiyah (1886–1918), began to speak, even if only within restricted circles, that is, in private homes or meetings of women's charitable organizations, the 'legitimate' gathering places for women in restricted societies. They also began to write in newspapers like *al-Jarīdah*, Aḥmad Luṭfī al-Sayyid's liberal nationalist paper, and *al-Maḥrūsah*, the paper that Mayy Ziyādah's father edited.

ᶜĀʾishah al-Taymūriyyah is the earliest of these writers, and is regarded by some as the best. She was born in Cairo into an aristocratic Turkish/Kurdish family with a long literary tradition. In addition to her almost feminist treatise entitled *Mirʾāt al-taʾammul fī 'l-umūr* ('The mirror of contemplation', 1892?), al-Taymūriyyah published *Natāʾij al-aḥwāl fī 'l-aqwāl wa'l-afᶜāl* ('The results of circumstances in words and deeds') in 1888. In her introduction to this work of fiction, she states quite plainly that as a child she had no interest in learning the graceful skills of embroidery and weaving. Her real interest, she boldly asserts, was to learn and, above all, to write. Mayy Ziyādah in her biography of al-Taymūriyyah claims that she was the first to call for gender equality.[1] She was lucky to have a father who found such recalcitrant unconventionality intriguing. Despite his wife's remonstrances, he engaged a Farsi and an Arabic tutor for ᶜĀʾishah. She studied eagerly, while remaining aware that to be a woman involved certain limitations. She writes, 'Whoever may censure me for lapses in that which I write must see that this seclusion is the greatest of excuses'. Her prose fiction is designed to distract women from 'the grief they feel in the exile of solitude, which is harder to bear than exile from one's homeland'.[2] However, al-Taymūriyyah's main output was not in prose but in poetry. She began to write when she was thirteen. Her lyrical poetry focuses on love and death and some of her best poetry consists of elegies written for her daughter. Since she spent much time in the khedivial harem, often translating for European women visitors, she also composed occasional poetry, including eulogies to the khedive, not only in Arabic but also in Turkish and Persian. Much of this poetry was anthologized in her *Ḥilyat al-*

1 Mayy Ziyādah, *ᶜĀʾishah Taymūr: shāᶜirat al-ṭalīᶜah*, Cairo, 1926, p. 219.

2 ᶜĀʾishah al-Taymūriyyah, *Natāʾij al-aḥwāl fī 'l-aqwāl wa 'l-afᶜal*, 1888, section introduced and translated by Marilyn Booth in Margot Badran and Miriam Cooke, *Opening the gates. A century of Arab feminist writing*, London/Bloomington, 1990.

ṭirāz ('Embroidered ornaments'), which was first published in Cairo c. 1885. She signed her Turkish and Persian poetry with the name ᶜIṣmat and the Arabic poetry with ᶜĀʾishah.

Like al-Taymūriyyah, with whom she had some correspondence, Wardah al-Yāzijī was born into a highly cultured family that was deeply involved in the late-nineteenth-century attempts to renew the Arabic language. Like al-Taymūriyyah, she had an exceptional father – Nāṣīf al-Yāzijī – who recognized his daughter's talent. She began to write poetry at the age of thirteen, and all her correspondence with her father when he was away from home was in verse.[3] Like al-Taymūriyyah, also, she wrote much occasional poetry, especially elegies for her six brothers, her sister, her father, her husband and then, most painful of all, for her two sons and her daughter. But it is in her elegy for her famous brother Ibrāhīm that she has been compared with her illustrious pre-Islamic foremother, al-Khansāʾ. Her sad anthology *Ḥadīqat al-ward* ('Rose garden') was the first book written by an Arab woman to appear in print. It was published four times: 1867, 1887, 1894 and 1914, each time with some additions. Al-Yāzijī was very conservative in her lifestyle as in her poetry, and she admonished women who rejected tradition in favour of a slavish imitation of western fashions, particularly when this involved the rejection of Arabic. However, this warning did not preclude a certain admiration of western women's accomplishments. When Wardah al-Yāzijī died, a group of Lebanese women wrote an obituary for her. It was the first time that women had publicly recognized another woman's literary achievements.

Zaynab Fawwāz's background was quite different and disproves the notion that it was only upper-class women who had access to education. She was born into a poor family in South Lebanon. As a young girl she went to Alexandria with the Egyptian family for whom she worked. Her mistress was intrigued by her maid's native intelligence and arranged for her to be taught the 'three Rs'. Zaynab quickly learnt what her teachers had to offer and in time went on to study with Egyptian scholars. Eventually, she became very active in women's issues and she wrote some pioneering poetry and essays focused on women's rights. The most famous of her essays were *al-Rasāʾil al-Zaynabiyyah* ('The Zaynab letters') which have been considered to be forerunners to Qāsim Amīn's *Taḥrīr al-marʾah* ('Liberation of woman', 1899). When Jurjī Nīqūla Bāz founded *al-Ḥasnāʾ*, a woman's magazine that is still published today, Zaynab was the first to be published. She also wrote two novels entitled *al-Malik Qurūsh* ('King Qurush'), a historical romance criticizing slavery during the Persians' conquest of the Medes, and *Ḥusn al-ᶜawāqib aw al-ghādah al-ẓāhirah* ('Good outcomes or the

[3] Emily Naṣrallāh, *Nisāʾ rāʾidāt* ('Pioneering women'), Beirut, 1986, p. 128.

shining maiden', 1899); and an unpublished four-act play, *al-Hawā wa 'l-wafā'* ('Passion and loyalty').

The last of these four nineteenth-century women writers, Bāḥithat al-Bādiyah, was a devout Muslim and the partially secluded second wife of a homosexual Bedouin chief. She was the first Egyptian woman to obtain a primary school certificate in 1893 and then a teacher's diploma in 1900. For four years she taught the princesses in the khedivial palace. Her famous collection of articles *Nisā'iyyāt* (*Concerning women*) build on Qāsim Amīn's call for the emancipation of women in his *Taḥrīr al-mar'ah*. Bāḥithat al-Bādiyah serialized her *Nisā'iyyāt* in *al-Jarīdah*, and then published them in 1910 in two volumes.

In literary discourse, these writers were echoing the questions that social reformers were asking. Why were women debarred from education and professional opportunities? Was gender a sufficient reason? What effect did their invisibility have on society? These debates entered the mainstream through women's participation in journalism. By writing to be published – that is, to be made public – these women were refusing the privateness of the world to which they had been condemned from birth. They were rejecting the belief that women's voices are *ʿawrah*, a shame and dishonour. Yet their 'construction from within a masculine world of that women's world' allowed them to touch on both.[4] Writing provided an escape from a gender-determined role while seeming to affirm it. Al-Taymūriyyah, Fawwāz and Bāḥithat al-Bādiyah might challenge the patriarchy and advocate reform within the until-then untouchable space of the home. But they could only do this by placing themselves on the margins of both worlds. They were building bridges, but at first only a few chose to cross.

WOMEN'S JOURNALISM

In the Egypt of the late nineteenth century, women were not only writing columns and supplements devoted to women's issues, they were also establishing newspapers. *Al-Fatāh*, which was founded in Alexandria in 1892 by the Lebanese Ḥind Nawfal, was the first Arabic monthly for women. Although it was only in existence for two years, it launched women's journalism. During the following twenty-one years, fourteen more women's magazines came into existence. *Al-Fatāh* included news, book reviews, poems, fashion articles and, above all, biographies of famous women.

Such biographies became a regular feature in many newspapers and

[4] Mary Eagleton (ed.), *Feminist literary theory. A reader*, Oxford/NY, 1986, p. 101.

periodicals.[5] By affirming the importance of women in the past, they served as a model for contemporary women. Zaynab Fawwāz also worked within the biographical tradition and in 1895 anthologized her encyclopaedic *al-Durr al-manthūr fī ṭabaqāt rabbāt al-khudūr* ('Scattered pearls on the classes of women'). It was a huge volume. In it she brought together the lives of about 450 eastern and western women famous for their literary and social accomplishments. Like her compatriots al-Yāzijī and Ziyādah, Fawwāz did not feel as threatened as Egyptian women by the west. Not having had Egypt's experience of intense western colonial rule, these Syro-Lebanese seem to have felt free to acknowledge western women.

Mayy Ziyādah, who was the first woman to be accepted into the mainstream of early-twentieth-century Arabic literature and who had a well-attended weekly literary salon, also wrote biographies. Her biographies were literary bio-histories of women writers she had known personally or by reputation: Bāḥithat al-Bādiyah (1920); ʿĀʾishah al-Taymūriyyah (1924); and a lecture that was published in *al-Muqtaṭaf* on Wardah al-Yāzijī (1924). By choosing to write of contemporary women writers, and not historical or legendary figures, she was already helping to create a female canon, a tradition on which others could build. Although these women were hardly activists, Ziyādah presents them 'not as isolated individuals merely aware of their own subjugation as women, but rather as actual participants in the history of women's struggle for equality'.[6] Besides recovering the lives of women relegated to the attic of history, women's biographies served another purpose: they provided a screen, allowing their writers to make otherwise censurable political statements.

Women and advocates of women's rights recognized the revolutionary potential of the press. They published articles and stories and ultimately serialized novels calculated to educate and persuade segments of the population they had never before dreamt they might reach. Journalism became the platform for social protest as well as for literary expression. It is a role which continues even today. In the Arabian Peninsula, the press has played a vital role in the emergence of a class of professional women who have been fully accepted into the ranks of journalism. The first Saudi newspaper to be founded was the Meccan *Umm al-Qurā* in 1924. Only

5 Biographical novels pertaining to famous women, particularly those who had fought alongside men, were also published later, for example Bint al-Shāṭiʾ, *Baṭalat Karbalāʾ. Zaynab Bint al-Zahrāʾ* ('The heroine of Karbala. Zaynab Bint al-Zahrāʾ', Beirut, n.d.), *Banāt al-nabiy* ('The daughters of the Prophet', Cairo, 1956) and *Al-Khansāʾ*, 1957; Ṣūfī ʿAbdallāh wrote *Nisāʾ muḥāribāt* ('Fighting women', 1951) and *Nifirtītī*, 1952; Saniyyah Qurrāʿah, *Umm al-mulūk. Hind Bint ʿUṭba* ('The mother of kings', 1959) and *ʿArūs al-zuhd Rabīʿah al-ʿAdawiyyah* ('The bride of Austerity', 1960).

6 Marilyn Booth, 'Mayy Ziyadah and the feminist perspective in Egypt 1908–1931', unpublished BA Hons. Thesis, Harvard University, p. 100.

twenty-eight years later, *Majallat al-Yamāmah* began publication, and its editors frequently championed women's education. And in 1961, Dr Fātinah Shākir became the first woman in Saudi Arabia to edit a woman's page: it was introduced by *ʿUkāẓ*. Later she founded the women's magazine *Sayyidātī*, which is regarded as the most feminist journal to come out of the Arabian Gulf region. Women's literary involvement in the press has increased over the years. It has been said that in the 1980s the newspaper *al-Riyāḍ* has almost unwittingly fostered a novel feminist expression.[7] The women journalists self-consciously call themselves *muḥarrirāt*, with its 'double entendre' of female editor and liberator. Under the dynamic leadership of women such as the short-story writer Khayriyyah al-Saqqāf (b. 1951), these *muḥarrirāt* have made their presence known not only in Saudi Arabia but also outside the country.

In Qatar, journalism emerged simultaneously with the winning of independence in the early 1970s. Unlike most other women writers, however, Qatari women did not lag behind the men in publishing. In what appeared to be one of the most traditional societies in the world they assumed a responsibility to their society: they had to maintain the tension between a desire to modernize and a fear of radical change. Fāṭimah Turkī (b. 1953), who sometimes takes the pseudonym of Umm Aktham, might attack her society because it disadvantages women, but she is quick to point out that the libertine western model is not one she admires. She strikes the balance between self-criticism and nationalist apologetics.[8] Persistently, these journalists use the press to disseminate models, to validate difference, and also to raise consciousness. Journalism, then, became a vehicle for new ideas and models relayed as articles but often also as literature, since most newspapers in the Arab world have literary pages and supplements in which much of the fiction published first appears in serial form. For women who did not know how their newly found voice was going to be appreciated, the cellophane of fiction was a safe release.

ISOLATED VOICES

While men like Yaḥyā Ḥaqqī, Maḥmūd Ṭāhir Lāshīn and the Taymūr brothers were writing their first realistic short stories, women were also writing. The men's stories were usually reflective of a reality that demanded

[7] Laylā Ṣāliḥ has discovered that there are now more women writers in *al-Riyāḍ* than there are men (*Adab al-marʾah fī 'l-jazīrah al-ʿarabīyah wa 'l-khalīj*, Kuwait, 1982), p. 31. These women reject a feminine press claiming that this further marginalizes women. In 1980, Juhayr Musāʿid (b. 1956) wrote a fierce indictment of the Saudi Ministry of Information which had not responded to her angry criticism of the publication of the women's magazine, *Balqīs* (*al-Riyāḍ*, No. 14194, 1980).

[8] Ṣāliḥ, *Adab al-marʾah fī 'l-jazīrah*, p. 266.

reform. The women's writings were less graphic, less violent and perhaps for that reason less known. Among the first women fiction writers are the Syrian ʿUlfah al-Idlibī (b. 1912) who describes traditional middle-class Damascene society, and the Egyptian Suhayr Qalamāwī (b. 1911). Qalamāwī's *Aḥādīth jaddatī* ('My grandmother's tales', 1935), which was introduced by Ṭāhā Ḥusayn, contains wistful vignettes of Cairo at the end of the nineteenth century. They conjure up a traditional world on the brink of the new. The grandmother is at once the beloved story teller and the repository of a cultural heritage. In 1943, Qalamāwī published her study *Alf laylah wa laylah* ('One thousand and one nights') for which she was awarded the first prize of the Cairo Language Academy. Most of her work, however, has been in literary criticism. Another important and prolific writer is ʿĀʾishah ʿAbd al-Raḥmān, who used the nom de plume Bint al-Shāṭiʾ (1912–74). She is best known for her feminist religious and linguistic studies, but she, too, produced some fiction about the position of women in rural Egyptian life. In 1944, she published *Sayyid al-ʿizbah* ('The landlord'); and then in the fifties she published three collections of short stories: *Sirr al-shāṭiʾ* ('The secret of the coast', 1952); *Imraʾah khāṭiʾah* ('A fallen woman', 1958) and *Ṣuwar min ḥayātihinna* ('Images from women's lives', 1959). In 1967, she wrote her autobiography entitled *ʿAlā 'l-jisr* ('On the bridge').

In the thirties, forties and early fifties, women were writing in isolation from the mainstream literary tradition and from each other. As women writers, they did not form a unit that might be retrospectively called a feminine voice. But in the late fifties there was a change as experimentation in form and content within all genres became the norm, and romantic escapism and gentle questioning gave way to a literature of angry protest.

Although women joined the ranks of novelists and short story writers quite late, in poetry they were in the forefront. Iraq might be the last of the countries of the Fertile Crescent to be fully integrated into the *Nahḍah*, but, on the other hand, it was the first to produce revolutionary experimentation in poetry, the most resilient of all the classical genres to change. There is controversy as to who was the first poet successfully to implement free verse, al-Sayyāb or Nāzik al-Malāʾikah (b. 1923). Al-Malāʾikah was from a family of poets, and her mother was the first Iraqi poet to call for women's rights. In 1945, al-Malāʾikah wrote her romantic *Maʾsāt al-ḥayāh* ('Life's tragedy') in traditional forms, but in 1949 she published *Shaẓāyā wa ramād* ('Splinters and ashes'), which included some poems in free verse. The experiment was hailed a success and others finally felt free to introduce new poetic forms. The Palestinian poet and critic Salmā al-Khaḍrāʾ al-Jayyūsī (b. 1924) has argued that al-Malāʾikah was able to achieve what men could not because she did not adhere to the received literary canon, and had nothing to lose if she were to violate sacred rules.[9] Free verse soon gained currency throughout the Arab world as men and women rallied to this newly liberated form. In Saudi Arabia volumes of verse by women such as Thurayyā Qābil's diwan *Awzān bākīyah* ('Weeping metres', 1972) and ᶜAzzah Fuʾād Shākir's *Ashriᶜat al-layl* ('The sails of night', 1978) contain immediate and intense free-verse evocations of a painful reality. However, their poetry has not met with general critical acclaim.[10]

In prose fiction women's contribution continued to grow in size and importance. In the mid fifties their novels and short stories were appearing not only in Egypt, Lebanon, Syria and Iraq, but also in the Gulf countries. In 1955, the Bahraini newspaper *al-Waṭan* published Mūzah al-Zayd's 'Ṭawāhā 'l-nisyān' ('Oblivion swallowed her'). This was the first piece of fiction by a woman to be published in Bahrain. In 1957 in Egypt, the short-story writer Jādhibiyyah Ṣidqī (b. 1927) published *Wa bakā qalbī* ('My heart wept'), and the prolific journalist, novelist and translator Ṣūfī ᶜAbdallāh (b. 1925) published her powerful novel *Laᶜnat al-jasad* ('The curse of the body'). ᶜAbdallāh had begun to publish in 1948. Her entire oeuvre comprises over fifty books which have elicited criticism from men like ᶜAbbās Maḥmūd al-ᶜAqqād and Ghālī Shukrī.

REJECTION

But the novel that aroused the greatest critical response was *Ana aḥyā* ('I live', 1958). This unprecedented novel of revolt was written by the Lebanese Laylā Baᶜalbakī (b. 1936). In somewhat violent terms, it exposes the hollowness of a Middle Eastern woman's life, the superficiality of social values, the prison of the home. The protagonist is involved in herself to the exclusion of all else, proudly proclaiming that she needs no one, particularly not her family. This novel and the by now infamous short story 'Safīnat ḥanān ilā 'l-qamar' ('Spaceship of tenderness to the moon', 1964) sound the bugle to a new stage in women's writings: not only to challenge society but also to assert their own needs and strengths as women.

Laylā Baᶜalbakī's battlecry was taken up enthusiastically by others, including the Egyptians Laṭīfah al-Zayyāt (b. 1925) and Najībah al-ᶜAssāl (b. 1921). In her novel *al-Bāb al-Maftūḥ* ('The open door', 1960), al-Zayyāt

9 Jayyūsī, 'Al-marʾah wa ṣūrat al-marʾah ᶜinda Nāzik al-Malāʾikah' ('Woman and her image in the writings of Nazik al-Malaʾikah'), in *Nāzik al-Malāʾikah. Dirāsāt fī al-shiᶜr wa al-shāᶜirah*, Kuwait, 1986, pp. 235, 248.

10 Abū ᶜAbd al-Raḥmān b. ᶜUqayl al-Ẓāhirī, for example, has commented: 'The paucity of women's poetry and of women with anthologies is not a matter of pride. Women's poetry whether it be in the colloquial or in the classical language is very weak when compared with male poets' outpourings'. He considers the only exception to be the Saudi popular poet Rīm al-Ṣaḥrāʾ, whose first anthology *Zahrat ḥanan* ('The flower of tenderness') came out in 1979; see Ṣāliḥ, *Adab al-marʾah fī 'l-jazīrah*, p. 134.

describes the protagonist's struggle to gain control over her life during the decade surrounding Egypt's fight for independence. For her, the liberation of the woman and of the nation had to go hand in hand. In her collection of short stories entitled *Bayt al-ṭāʿah* ('House of obedience', 1962), al-ʿAssāl attacked this invidious institution that sanctions a man's imprisoning his wife. Already in the 1920s male writers had decried social sanction of the 'house of obedience', but now a woman writer was adding her voice, declaring that divorce with all the hardship and ignominy entailed was preferable to this conjugal jail.

But the writer who has continued to attract the most consistent attention in the Arab world is the Syrian Ghādah al-Sammān (b. 1942). Her first collection of short stories, *ʿAynāk qadarī* ('Your eyes are my destiny') was published in 1962. Fourteen of the sixteen stories focus on women and the problems they face as they try to relate to men in a traditional Middle Eastern society. This collection has been widely circulated throughout the Arab world and has had a great influence on Saudi women writers in particular.[11] Among the most prolific Arab women writers, al-Sammān in her later works, and particularly in *Layl al-ghurabāʾ* ('Night of the strangers', 1966), articulates an angry, frustrated rebellion against sexual oppression and discrimination, the 'honour' system and political corruption.[12]

In 1962 also, the Lebanese Emily Naṣrallāh (b. 1938) wrote her *Ṭuyūr Aylūl* ('September birds'). It is the romantic tale of a girl's departure from her village to the big city. This familiar theme of the journey is given a special resonance when referring to a woman. Men were expected to make this journey, and then not only to the city but beyond to the lands of emigration. Women were expected to stay at home. Yet Munā – whose life story parallels that of her creator – refuses the passivity of the female condition and destiny: she persuades an uncle who had emigrated to the USA to pay for her education. She leaves the village, only to discover ultimately that women who do not play the game by the usual rules are debarred: she is ostracized.

Naṣrallāh's concern with the question of emigration coincides with a time when many Arabs were leaving their native countries in search of fortune and freedom of expression in exile. Many, particularly the North Africans who had experienced French colonial rule, went to Paris. Some followed in the footsteps of the *Mahjar* writers like Jibrān Khalīl Jibrān,

11 Before I left Riyadh in May 1983, Dahlia Hawwir (a *muḥarrirah*) gave me her copy of *ʿAynāk qadarī* even though I had assured her that I already had one.

12 In the wake of the burning of her private library during the Lebanese Civil War and the loss of much unpublished material, she has begun to republish and publish anew everything she has written. Her series of *al-Aʿmāl ghayr al-kāmilah* is not complete, as the title suggests, and already comprises fourteen volumes.

Mikhaʾīl Nuʿaymah and Amīn Rīḥānī who had left their native lands to make their homes in the Americas. Some chose their exile status, others did not.

PALESTINIAN ECHOES

The most numerous of these writers in exile in the latter half of the twentieth century have been the Palestinians. The literature that they produced inspired a whole generation of Arab writers. Palestinian poetry and fiction wept for a lost past, called for protest against a cruel occupier and promised renewal through the blood of the sacrifice. This literature became emblematic for Arab literary production as a whole. Two women poets have been central to this movement: Salmā al-Khaḍrāʾ al-Jayyūsī and Fadwā Ṭūqān (b. 1923). However, mention should also be made of Samīrah ʿAzzām (1927–67) who has been described as a bridge between the older generation of Palestinian writers and the diaspora generally, and whose short stories focus on economic and social oppression suffered by all members of Palestinian society. Al-Jayyūsī wrote from outside, Tūqān from inside. Al-Jayyūsī published her romantic *al-ʿAwdah min al-nabʿ al-ḥālim* ('Return from the dreaming source') in 1960. It called for love of the motherland and resistance. However, in the wake of the 1967 disaster she seems to have stopped writing poetry altogether. Most of her later writings have focused on literary criticism and translation of Arabic literature into English. From within the West Bank, Fadwā Ṭūqān has written poems of resistance that have galvanized the Palestinian youth and not allowed them to forget their roots. Before 1967, she wrote three volumes of poetry: *Waḥdī maʿa 'l-ayyām* ('Alone with the days', 1955), *Wajadtuhā* ('I found her', 1957) and *Aʿṭinā ḥubban* ('Give us love', 1960). Like many of the pre-1967 poets, Ṭūqān emphasized the importance of love as she shied away from overt political statement. However, her *Amām al-bāb al-mughlaq* ('Before the locked gate', 1967) heralds a new stage in which she talks defiantly about freedom fighters and the endless nightmare that the Palestinians live – compare also *al-Fidāʾī wa 'l-arḍ* ('The guerilla and the land', 1968) and *Kābūs al-layl wa 'l-nahār* ('The nightmare of night and day', 1974). More recently, another Palestinian woman has been publishing novels on the plight of the Palestinians, and particularly of women, in the occupied territories. In *al-Subār* ('Wild thorns', 1976) and *ʿAbbād al-shams* ('Sunflower', 1980), Saḥar Khalīfah (b. 1941) has asked questions none have known how to answer: How is Palestine best defended? Is it by staying on the land, even if that staying involves collusion with the enemy to the extent that work must be sought in Israel for survival? Or, is it by leaving and plotting and then returning to carry out grandiose missions that do not count the sacrifices? What role can women play? Does the nationalist agenda have any space for feminist activism? In all her novels Khalīfah has tried to resolve the conflict between nationalist and feminist goals. In her Künstlerroman, *Mudhakkirāt imraʾah ghayr wāqiʿiyyah* ('Memoirs of an unrealistic woman', 1986), Khalīfah has presented a protagonist who is trying to construct herself outside the prison of socialization. ʿAfāf is a woman who uses art to escape her body and to carve out a different destiny for herself and by extension her society. Prophetically, all of Khalīfah's works seem to anticipate the *Intifāḍah* with its transformed role for women.

It was not only the Palestinians who expressed the agony that arose out of the 1967 disaster and its aftermath. Throughout the Arab world echoes were heard. Indeed, it became for many writers a political agenda that guided their writing. Works that were not obviously committed, *engagés*, were considered self-indulgent. Even at the furthest extremes of the Arab world, writers, including women, were responding. Although most North African littérateurs have been francophone until very recently, there were a few in the late sixties who were already writing in Arabic. In Morocco, Khannātah Bannūnah wove allusions to the Palestinian cause into her angry stories that derive their abstract rhetorical style from North African francophone literature. The year 1967 – elliptically referred to as 'June' – for her also is a radical turning point: 'We have to remain completely separate from all that precedes June when we were sure, insistent, insightful and independent, so that we might truly be launched on the path to the future.'[13] Bannūnah is not so much concerned with gender rights and relations as she is about politics, particularly about global Arab politics. There is certainly some exploration of mood and character, but the personal delving is subordinated to the political declaiming. It is the prioritization of the political over the social that makes her writing unusual for a woman.

ACTIVISM

Most Arab women writers, to the contrary, eschew political specificity to deal with its effect on personal life. The controversial Egyptian feminist physician Nawāl al-Saʿdāwī (b. 1930) affirms that fiction writing is one of the most effective ways to advance the cause of Arab women. She has not only been censured for her beliefs, she has also been imprisoned. And yet,

[13] Khannātah Bannūnah, *al-Ṣūrah wa 'l-ṣawt* ('The image and the voice'), Casablanca, 1975, p. 12.

she continues to write and to find publishing outlets outside Egypt. Her *Mudhakkirātī fī sijn al-nisāʾ* ('My memoirs out of the women's prison') was published by the Beiruti Dār al-Mustaqbal in 1983 and was translated into English four years later as *Prison memoirs.* In the mid-1970s she published three feminist novels: *Mawt al-rajul al-waḥīd ʿalā 'l-arḍ* ('The death of the only man on earth', 1974); *Imraʾatān fī imraʾah* ('Two women in one', 1975) and *Imraʾah ʿind nuqṭat al-ṣifr* ('Woman at point zero', 1975).[14] The latter is the ballad of a woman's inevitable passage from incest to prostitution to murder as she struggles for autonomy and love. In al-Saʿdāwī's work, prostitution is seen to be an inevitable part of patriarchy, women cannot escape physical exploitation. Firdaws refuses the game of submission, commits murder and is therefore executed. Al-Saʿdāwī's novel has had a considerable impact on Arab women, and particularly on women writers as can be seen in the introduction written by the Algerian francophone writer Assia Djebar (b. 1943) to the French translation that was entitled *Ferdaous: Une voix à l'enfer* (1981).[15] Djebar's encomium places this novel within its literary historical context and bears witness to a significant development – women are beginning to recognize the development of a women's literary tradition not in retrospect but at the time of its formation.

SURVIVAL IN BEIRUT

The mid-1970s have been considered to be an important period in the history of international feminist criticism and literature. Feminist literary theory is no longer an alternative optic, it is becoming as necessary to literary inquiry as a materialist approach. Feminist fiction at the same time is becoming more radical in its demand for a restructuring of society. To some extent this is also true for Arabic literature. The arena for this radical break was Lebanon. The occasion was the Lebanese Civil War which broke out in 1975.

Writers in Lebanon had to assert life in the face of destruction. In Lebanon, and particularly in Beirut, a group of women gradually came to recognize the power of the word.[16] The Beirut decentrists are a group of Arab women writers of about the same generation who are arabophone, francophone and anglophone. The arabophone writers include among their numbers the Lebanese Nūr Salmān (b. 1932), Ḥanān al-Shaykh (b. 1945), Emily Naṣrallāh and Layla ʿUsayrān (b. 1934), the Palestinian Nuhā

[14] Translated into English as *God dies by the Nile*, London, 1985; *Two women in one*, London, 1985; *Woman at point zero*, London, 1983.

[15] al-Saʿadāwī, *Ferdaous: Une voix à l'enfer*, Paris, 1981, pp. 7–10.

[16] Cf. Miriam Cooke, *War's other voices: Women writers on the Lebanese Civil War 1975–82*, Cambridge, 1988.

Samārah (b. 1943), the Syrian Ghādah al-Sammān and the Iraqi Daisy al-Amīr (b. 1935), to mention only a few. They centred their concern on Beirut but they were decentred culturally and often physically. They wrote searchingly about the war and about their own roles in it. Ghādah al-Sammān's *Kawābīs Bayrūt* ('Beirut nightmares', 1980) chronicles a few days and hundreds of nightmares that she had to endure as her house came under sniper fire during the infamous hotels battle in October and November of 1975. In the madness and absurdity of this violence the protagonist still tries to weigh the pros and cons of the pen over the gun. Ḥanān al-Shaykh's *Ḥikāyat Zahrah* ('Zahra's story', 1980)[17] is the haunting tale of a young woman driven crazy by sexual abuse who finds in the war a solace and a temporary normalization of her madness.

Unlike the men, the Beirut decentrists did not describe the war as a revolution; it was patently unjust. They did not locate enemies whom they could conveniently blame. They described the dailiness of a violence that grows dull through habit. Daisy al-Amīr's *Fī dawwāmat al-ḥubb wa 'l-karāhiyah* ('In the vortex of love and hate', 1979) and *Wuᶜūd li 'l-bayᶜ* ('Promises for sale', 1981) are collections of leaden little stories that try to wrest some normality out of anarchy. The Beirut decentrists traced through the dizzying alternations of alliance and hatred, as in Nuhā Samārah's *al-Ṭāwilāt ᶜāshat akthar min Amīn* ('The tables lived longer than Amin', 1981), where the narrator is involuntarily drawn into the fighting of which he had so heartily disapproved.

And finally, these writers began to describe the new society that war-torn Lebanon was becoming. It was a society that was made up of militia boys, old men, women and children. The fit adult men had left. Although at first the Beirut decentrists did not censure this departure, by the end of the 1970s the tone began to change. Naṣrallāh's *Tilka 'l-dhikrayāt* ('Those memories', 1980) and *al-Iqlāᶜ ᶜaks al-zaman* ('Flight against time', 1981)[18] and Samārah's 'Wajhān li imraʾah' ('Two faces one woman' in *al-Ṭāwilāt*) register this change of mood on the part of those who stayed. It was writing that allowed the Beirut decentrists to articulate a reality they might not have otherwise perceived: the weak and helpless had been left to struggle alone. Consciousness of this fact brought into focus another: the weak and helpless had survived and had through survival become strong and independent. An explicit portrayal of this growing strength can be seen in ᶜUsayrān's *Qalᶜat al-usṭa* ('Usta's citadel', 1979), where the female protagonist is expected to galvanize all energies. Any moments of weakness and fear must be hidden, converted into a new strength.

[17] Translated into French as *Histoire de Zahra*, Paris, 1985; into English as *The story of Zahra*, London 1986. [18] Translated into English as *Flight against time*, Montreal, 1987.

In this transforming society, only those who stayed could call themselves citizens. The Beirut decentrists vividly depict a society which has acquired the space to look back on its past. Their writings question the patriarchal principles of the Lebanese, and by extension of Arab society, show them to be corrupt and suicidal, undermine them and construct a new national ethos that is feminine as defined in pre-war terminology. The Beirut decentrists have collectively described in their literature the unprecedented feminization of society, and not the masculinization of society that feminist historians have ascribed to other societies at war.[19]

The Beirut decentrists have created the model of an activist literature. Reality is not to be copied romantically, realistically or impressionistically. It must be changed. This call for fundamental change and renewal is finding adherents in the first generation of young women writers of the Arabian Peninsula to be educated in their own countries.

These young women are revolting against the oppression that has been their condition, and they are for the first time dealing discursively with their feelings of alienation. Since 1973 and the publication of her anthology *Ilā matā yakhtaṭifūnak laylat al-ᶜurs* ('How long will they keep raping you on your wedding night?'), the Saudi poet Fawziyyah Abū Khālid (b. 1955) has been shouting for awareness. She has worked on creating a new language that, she says, must explode out of the present. Even her symbolism describing her own work seems to derive from the violence of the Lebanese Civil War that so many have come to consider a microcosm for the rest of the Arab world. Khayriyyah al-Saqqāf writes in 'Qiṣṣat al-wāqiᶜ' ('A true story', 1979) and in her collection of very short stories *An tubḥir naḥwa al-abᶜad* ('Let her take off into the blue', 1982) of the need for women's education so that they may participate fully in a transforming society. In her poignant vignettes that are each informed by a deeply Islamic spirit, she reiterates the weakness of man in the face of the majesty of nature. The association of nature and woman is only lightly, if at all, disguised. Ruqayyah Shabīb (b. 1952) calls for a society reordered to accommodate women, but she has used a double distancing device: a historical context and an obscure language filled with opaque symbolism. She would agree with her colleague Fawziyyah al-Bikr (b. 1958) who has said: 'Writing is like walking along a firing range. It is the confrontation with social problems in their entirety so as to change culture.'[20] In Bahrain, Fawziyyah Muḥammad al-Sanadī (b. 1956) is rebelling against tradition but indicates

[19] Sandra M. Gilbert, 'Soldier's heart: literary men, literary women, and the Great War', In *Signs: journal of women in culture and society*, Spring, 1983, pp. 422–50.

[20] Ṣāliḥ, *Adab al-marʾah fī 'l-jazīrah*, p. 92.

that it is the women alone who are free enough to achieve a separation from tradition; men remain attached and therefore cannot reject it nor truly progress. In Qatar, Kulthūm Jabar (b. 1960) has been writing since the age of fourteen for the media. In 1978, she published her first collection of short stories *Anta wa ghābat al-ṣamt wa 'l-taraddud* ('You and the jungle of silence and hesitation'). She demands nothing less than a restructuring of the norms of sexual behaviour.

COMING OF AGE

The 1980s have seen the emergence of many new women's voices throughout the Arab world. Few concern themselves any longer with belonging to the dominant tradition. They have found a new readership in the growing numbers of educated women. And it is to them that they are increasingly addressing themselves. In 1983, the Moroccan Laylā Abū Zayd published *ᶜĀm al-fīl* ('The year of the elephant'). In this evocative novel, Abū Zayd journeys through a divorce and in the process examines Arab attitudes to women. A sign of the growing interest in women's writings is that the novel almost immediately sold out and had to be reprinted. In 1982, Ḥanān al-Shaykh published *Wardat al-ṣaḥrāʾ* ('Desert rose'). It is a collection of short stories each one of which features a woman who is trying to deal with a situation into which she has been forced. Although women are often portrayed as victims, they are no longer passive. These protagonists are, in some cases almost unconsciously forging a future for themselves that does not accord with social expectations. In 1988, she published *Misk al-ghazāl* which was immediately translated into English with the title *Women of sand and myrrh*. This long novel in four women's voices criticizes female seclusion prevalent in an unnamed desert society. As with her earlier novel on the Lebanese Civil War, *Ḥikāyat Zahrah*, al-Shaykh has defied convention and propriety. She has written with passion and violence of Arab women's sexuality, daring even to use the hitherto unheard voice of a lesbian. This erstwhile maverick has become a literary presence none can ignore.

In any study that deals with the Arab world of the 1980s, mention must be made of the emergence of fundamentalist Islam. Within two decades, this movement has established itself in many parts of the Arab world. Most of the writings produced by fundamentalists are not in fiction, but there are some isolated cases of writers who have been inspired by the new emphasis on literalism and the valorization of Islam in the face of modernity. Some women have turned to the Quran and to the Sunnah and have searched there for an interpretation of their rights that they do not find in reality. The

Egyptian Alīfah Rifᶜat (b. 1930) is a case in point. Rifᶜat has been writing since the 1940s, and she published her first short stories in 1947. They were 'Ḥadīth imraᵓatayn' ('A story of two women'), 'Ḥawwāᵓ tuᶜīd Ādam īlā 'l-jannah' ('Eve takes Adam back to Paradise') and 'ᶜĀlamī al-majhūl' ('My secret world'). The last of these stories is a sophisticated chronicling of a woman's growing madness as her obsession with a female snake becomes overwhelming. This story has the same tense quality as Charlotte Perkins Gilman's recently revived 'The yellow wallpaper' (1892). When these stories appeared in *al-Taḥrīr*, *al-Thaqāfah al-Usbūᶜiyyah* and *al-Zuhūr* respectively, Rifᶜat's husband was incensed. How could his wife dare to flaunt herself in public? He forbade her to write another word. He could forbid her to publish, he could not stop her from writing. Between 1955 and 1974, the date of his death, Alīfah Rifᶜat published nothing. However, throughout those years whenever she felt the urge to write she would lock herself up in her bathroom, run the bath and, stretching herself out on the floor, she would write and write.[21] In 1974 with the ban on publication lifted after the demise of her spouse, Rifᶜat published eighteen short stories, most of them in *al-Thaqāfah al-Usbūᶜiyyah*. The following year these stories were anthologized in *Ḥawwāᵓ taᶜūd bi Ādam* ('Eve brings Adam back'). She has continued to write and to publish. In 1981, she published another collection of short stories entitled, *Man yakūn al-rajul* ('Who'll be the man'). And in 1984, a collection of short stories, many of which had not yet been published in Arabic, was brought out in London with the title *Distant view of a minaret*. She writes of the promise that a newly revitalized Islam holds out. Islam gave women their rights in the seventh century. These rights must be restored so that men may no longer be free to contravene Quranic dictates in the realms of personal behaviour. She writes of frustrated love, of loneliness, of dreams, and against women's cruelty to each other (for example, clitoridectomy).

Nawāl al-Saᶜdāwī's reaction to the growth of fundamentalist rhetoric and activism in her native Egypt has been outspoken and uncompromising. In 1988, at risk to her personal safety, she brought out *Suqūṭ al-imām* (translated immediately into English as *Fall of the Imam*, 1989). This angry, liturgical novel eloquently attacks zealotry whether it be that of the Party of God or the Party of Satan. As long as men arrogate to themselves the right to control and abuse women's bodies in the name of some god, the society in which they live will be corrupt. This novel is not an attack on Islam, but on patriarchy and its exploitation of Islam. As expected, the novel elicited threats from religious activists and al-Saᶜdāwī has had to be kept under 24-hour guard.

[21] Interview with Alīfah Rifᶜat, London, 10 August 1984.

TEXTUAL STRATEGIES

These pioneering women were orphans who had no parents and who belonged to no one. They were writing, as Elaine Showalter has put it for American women writers and critics, in the wilderness. But by the early 1970s these scattered writings were beginning to gel even though this process was not noticed at the time and could only be comprehended in hindsight. Women were creating a tradition. They were looking to models – foremothers – who were not exceptional women of history, like Shajarat al-Durr and Zubaydah, but modern creative women. A vivid example is the Lebanese intellectual Nūr Salmān. As a very young woman she had been told of her resemblance, both physical and spiritual, to Mayy Ziyādah. She now believes herself to be the latter's literary legatee.[22]

Others have used intertextuality to draw attention to the new canon in the making. This was particularly evident in the use of almost identical titles. In 1963, the Saudi writer Sulṭānah al-Sudīrī published *ᶜAynāya fidāk* ('My eyes are your ransom'). This novelist has established a double connection with al-Sammān: her title obviously refers to the latter's *ᶜAynāk qadarī* (1962), and the novel was published by the Ghādah al-Sammān Publishing House. In 1982, the Saudi Rajāʾ Muḥammad ᶜAwdah published *Innahu qadarī* ('He is my destiny'). Another Saudi, Fawziyyah al-Bikr, published in 1979 a short story entitled 'al-Sibāḥah fī buḥayrat al-ᶜadam' ('Swimming in the lake of nothingness') which mimics al-Sammān's *al-Sibāḥa fī buḥayrat al-shayṭān* ('Swimming in the lake of the devil'), first published in 1974. Al-Sammān in turn used this device, but, ironically, with a male writer. Her *Kawābīs Bayrūt* was derived from and in turn subverts Tawfīq ᶜAwwād's *Ṭawāḥīn Bayrūt* ('Beirut mills', 1975).[23] Whereas ᶜAwwād presents an unbelievable whirlwind of commitments, love and death, al-Sammān enters one person's head to show that the chaos was not only outside but particularly inside people's war-torn minds.

Other women also were subverting male discourse through ironic use of intertextuality. In 1950, Tawfīq al-Ḥakīm wrote his *Ughniyyat al-mawt* ('Song of death'). The theme is a blood feud, and the mother's insistence that her Cairo-educated son avenge his father's death. The son finds this practice abhorrent and refuses to comply. The mother is horrified at her son's cowardice and orders him to be killed. In this play, the mother stands for tradition and honour in its preservation. In 1975, Ṣūfī ᶜAbdallāh wrote *Thamānī ᶜuyūn* ('Eight eyes'). The theme is the same, except that the mother

22 Interview with Nūr Salmān, Durham, North Carolina, 3 October 1987.

23 Tawfīq ᶜAwwād expressed annoyance at what he referred to as plagiarism (interview, Beirut, 27 May 1982).

applauds what her son had perceived to be cowardice. She assures him that she had brought him up for this very refusal. This refusal, she assures him, is the sign of true virility: the ability to uphold convictions in the face of patently contradictory social expectations. In this case, the mother stands for progress and rupture with destructive values. Sasson Somekh, when discussing these two stories, refers to the plot relationship as indirect intertextuality.[24] Saḥar Khalīfah's *al-Ṣubār* subverts Ghassān Kanafānī's *Rijāl fī 'l-shams* ('Men in the sun', 1961). Both write of Palestinians: those who stay on their land and those who leave. In each case, the land of exile is Kuwait. In *Rijāl fī 'l-shams*, Kanafānī censures those who seek individual solutions and are not actively committed to the collective national problem. In *al-Ṣubār*, Khalīfah takes the commitment Kanafānī advocates to its logical extreme, thereby questioning its validity as a political desideratum. Had the three men who died in the inferno of the empty water tank drawn attention to their plight and then made it to Kuwait, they might have returned to the West Bank years later as guerrillas to kill their cousins who had stayed. On the other hand, had they stayed out of commitment to the land, they might have been killed by their cousins coming from Kuwait. It is not enough to write blithely of commitment. Such an attitude must be examined to reveal its consequences. Is there a programme beyond commitment?

CONCLUSION

In twentieth-century Arabic literature, men and women have written from different perspectives.[25] The men have in general remained in closer touch with political reality, to the point that their work can almost be dated by its contents. Many have represented and belonged to certain political persuasions. They were often expected by their groups to write in a particular way. The message was paramount. Nothing, however, has been expected of women writers. They have been free to dream radically, and not

[24] Sasson Somekh, 'Al-ʿilāqāt al-naṣṣiyyah fī 'l-niẓām al-adabī al-wāḥid', in *Al-Karmil studies in Arabic language and literature* (Haifa), vol. 7, 1986, pp. 123–8.

[25] It is undesirable to try to find essentialist differences as Mahmoud Bikheet el Rabie did in his 1965 thesis. He writes of nineteenth-century women's writings as being 'in keeping with the feminine nature which admits of no violence or rebellion. Words chosen tend to be gentle and pleasant sounding, and no special message is given'. Later he lists vocabulary that reappears frequently in women's works, for example *ya's* (despair), *ẓulm* (injustice), *khaybat al-amal* (disappointment), *tashā'um* (pessimism), *qalaq* (anguish) and *ḥayrah* (confusion). Men, he writes, chose the *qaṣīdah* (ode) form, women the *maqṭūʿah* (snippet). Also, women used the colloquial, simple diction, short metres and a great variety of rhyme. 'Women Writers and Critics in Modern Egypt 1888–1963', unpublished PhD Thesis, SOAS, London University, 1965, pp. 85, 107, 110.

in opposition to a political given, for example colonialism, westernization, neo-colonialism. This freedom has allowed for a growing autonomy in literature. Women rarely relay specific political messages; they write of human relationships and of the turbulence of emotions, and not of raw political facts lightly swathed in fiction. In her bemused question to Ilyās Khūrī, Ḥanān al-Shaykh mirrors many women writers' reaction to male writing: 'Before you start to write do you put on a special pair of gloves?'[26] In an interview, Nawāl al-Saᶜdāwī commented on men's political commitment: 'Arabic literature,' she said, 'is becoming more conservative. Especially the men writers, of course. You know, even some of the Marxists have become Islamic writers. Of course, from pragmatic political considerations.'[27]

In *A literature of their own: British women novelists from Brontë to Lessing* (1979), Elaine Showalter outlines the three major stages that minority literatures, and particularly women's literature, must go through before they come into their own:

> First, there is a prolonged phase of *imitation* of the prevailing modes of the dominant tradition, *internalization* of its standards of art and its views on social roles. Second, there is a phase of *protest* against these standards and values, and *advocacy* of minority rights and values, including a demand for autonomy. Finally, there is a phase of *self-discovery*, a turning inward freed from some of the dependency of opposition, a search for identity.[28]

Each of these stages seems as relevant for an analysis of Arab women writers as it is for those in the west.

These three stages also connote in the Arab world a different readership. In the first stage, which was didactic and which lasted until the mid-1950s, the women were writing primarily for women. Much was wrong with society and they were determined that the 'woman' question should not be overlooked in the drive to reform. In the second stage, which began in the late 1950s and went on for about twenty years, the audience was both men and women. Awareness of women's rights and of their oppression was no longer enough. Men had to learn that women were beginning to reject what had previously been, at best, only questioned. The final stage, heralded by the Beirut decentrists and their discursive restructuring of Lebanese society during the Lebanese Civil War galvanized the construction of autonomous women's worlds. Arab women's writings are now being published and

[26] Interview with Ḥanān al-Shaykh, Durham, NC, 28 February 1987.

[27] Interview by Fedwa Malti-Douglas and Allen Douglas with Nawāl al-Saᶜdāwī, Cairo, 15 August 1986, in Badran and Cooke, *Opening the gates*.

[28] Elaine Showalter, *A literature of their own: British women novelists from Brontë to Lessing*, Princeton, 1977, p. 15.

translated by mainstream presses, and while the target readership is often female, men also are reading. Women have had the courage to write and to create 'a literary movement apart from but hardly subordinate to the mainstream: an undercurrent, rapid and powerful'.[29]

[29] Ellen Moers, *Literary women: the great writers*, New York, 1963, p. 8.

CHAPTER 14

POETRY IN THE VERNACULAR

The lively presence of Arabic dialect poetry in the eighth to the fourteenth centuries is remarked upon by Ibn Khaldūn. Criticizing the grammarians' rejection of colloquial poetry, he notes that it has its own rules and eloquence, rooted in each dialect's milieu. Eloquence, he states, has nothing to do with grammatical rules, but is 'the suitability of the utterance to the meaning desired and the demands of the situation.'[1]

DEFINITIONS

Today, vernacular Arabic is chosen by poets who feel that what they want to express, and the milieu in which they practise their art, demand an idiom based on everyday speech. Drawing upon a heritage of local oral folk traditions and an elite colloquial poetry originating in medieval Andalusia, this poetry is often labelled *al-shiʿr al-shaʿbī* (folk or popular poetry), or *zajal*, as colloquial Andalusian strophic verse was called, attesting to these links. Other terms define it by what it 'lacks', echoing attitudes that Ibn Khaldūn attacked: in the Maghrib, it is known as *al-shiʿr al-malḥūn* (from *laḥn*, that is, not adhering to *fuṣḥā* grammar) and, in the Arabian peninsula, as *al-shiʿr al-nabaṭī* (Nabatean, thus 'non-Arab'). While contemporary poets refer to it as *shiʿr al-ʿāmmiyyah* (poetry of the colloquial), negative connotations remain: *ʿāmmī* means not only 'colloquial' but also 'common' or 'vulgar'. Yet this term also bears positive ideological overtones, for one virtue of a colloquial poetic idiom is its potential audience, extending beyond the educated. Another is its indigenous capacity: in the Sudan and Lebanon, this poetry has been called *al-shiʿr al-qawmī* ('poetry of the populace', by extension, 'national poetry'). 'Commonness' and 'localness' are statements in themselves: colloquial poetry is an art of *iltizām* (commitment) par excellence, although the degree, direction and expression of *iltizām* vary along the entire spectrum of personal, political and poetic outlooks.

Colloquial poetry's vitality has not been matched by scholarly attention.

[1] Ibn Khaldūn, ʿAbd al-Raḥmān, *Muqaddimat al-ʿAllāmah ibn Khaldūn*, Beirut, 1982, p. 583.

It falls neither into the folklorists' realm nor into Arabic literary study as constituted at present, and receives relatively little attention in literary journals, critical studies and anthologies. Traditionally negative attitudes plus notions that the vernacular undermines Arab unity have inhibited its study. Morpho-phonological and lexical differences among dialects hamper literary cross-fertilization and critical appreciation. Lacking a standard orthography, poets vary in preferring phono-morphological or etymological transcription. Few studies or collections exist to offer poets access to their premodern colloquial heritage. Finally, this poetry's topicality reduces accessibility but lends force: one of its strengths as art and political voice is its intimate link to the here and now of its environment.

Signs of change are appearing. In Egypt, an infant critical literature has been nourished by posthumous interest in the major poets Fuʾād Ḥaddād (1927–85) and Ṣalāḥ Jāhīn (1930–86) and by acceptance of folk art as a field of academic study. Elsewhere, the example of major poets has led to what can almost be called schools of colloquial poetry. Some poets attempt to cross dialect boundaries by means of glossaries in their *dīwāns*; others search for an idiom which both expresses and transcends a particular linguistic situation. Meanwhile, traditional forms exist alongside experimentation. Not isolated from but influenced by developments in *fuṣḥā* poetry, the performing arts and of course songwriting, colloquial poetry also shows the imprint of other literatures – European, Russian, South American. Most important, colloquial poets are disproving the notion that vernacular Arabic suits only the functional communications of mundane life.

TRADITIONAL FORMS AND THE NINETEENTH CENTURY

As two broad traditions – the oral poetry of the Beduin and the strophic *zajal* first attested for sixth- to twelfth-century Spain – were grafted onto local folk arts, Ṣūfī poetry and other elements, a range of colloquial art emerged from Andalusia to Persia. Beduin poetry, the continuation of what was long ago codified as the classical Arabic ode, is the ancestor of *nabaṭī* poetry and that known as *al-shurūqī* in the Fertile Crescent. Andalusian *zajal*'s identity remains controversial;[2] what is important here is its transmission by merchants and pilgrims across the Maghrib, into Egypt and the Fertile Crescent. The result is an array of traditional forms and terms, defined regionally and by combinations of formal, thematic and performance characteristics – while poets have not conformed to their own or scholars' classifications. Forms noted by medieval scholars remain in use,

[2] See Stern, Samuel, *Hispano-Arabic strophic poetry*, Oxford, 1974; al-Ahwānī, ʿAbd al-ʿAzīz, *al-Zajal fīʾl-Andalus*, Cairo, 1957 and the debate in *Journal of Arabic Literature*, vols VI, IX, XIII, XVII.

but with expanded or modified traits, often moving from *fuṣḥā* to *ᶜāmmiyyah*. The medieval stanzaic *muwashshaḥ* (composed in *fuṣḥā*) became, in the Yemen, *colloquial* poetry echoing, often distantly, patterns typical of the medieval model.[3] The *dūbayt* (Persian *dū* + Arabic *bayt*, 'two lines'), once a four-hemistich *fuṣḥā* poem, refers in the Sudan to a range of couplet-based forms (as does the similarly derived Yemeni *mūbayt*).[4] The medieval *mawāliyā* is probably the ancestor of the *mawwāl*, which branched into several forms, became a basis for multi-stanzaic poems and has been adopted (and often radically adapted) by today's poets.[5]

The term *zajal* is especially problematic. Linked initially to the *muwashshaḥ* in form but composed in colloquial and sub-categorized by theme, its compositional boundaries, and the term's very meaning, expanded as *zajal* spread eastward. In some regions, it came to signify all colloquial poetry. While many contemporary poets prefer to avoid this term, as it connotes a traditionalism of form and to a lesser extent of subject, it still refers in Egypt and Lebanon to poetry with a repeating stanzaic rhyme scheme and single metre based on traditional *buḥūr* (metres). In Lebanon, numerous sub-types of *zajal* exist;[6] in Egypt, to confuse matters further, the *mawwāl* is often considered a kind of *zajal*.

Pre-nineteenth-century sources are sparse, but suggest the presence of a colloquial poetic art for which there existed a consciousness of fixed texts by individual, often highly educated, composers, and to this day each dialect group claims its famous early poets.[7] Thus, this poetry cannot be considered initially 'anonymous' or 'collective' in composition, although it may aim to create or reassert collective sentiments. While an 'oral-written' distinction may be useful in examining specific texts, it is not germane to the problematic relationship between colloquial poetry and folk tradition.

3 al-Maqāliḥ, ᶜAbd al-ᶜAzīz, *Shiᶜr al-ᶜāmmiyyah fi'l-Yaman*, Beirut, 1983, pp. 111, 246–50.

4 al-Maqāliḥ, *Shiᶜr al-ᶜāmmiyyah*, pp. 242–5; Ismāᶜīl, ᶜIzz al-Dīn, *al-Shiᶜr al-qawmī fi'l-Sūdān*, Beirut, 1968, pp. 9–32.

5 Sub-types are: the *mawwāl miṣrī* (AABA), the *aᶜraj* (AAABA) and the *mawwāl baghdādī*, also known as *nuᶜmānī* or *zuhayrī* (AAABBBA). For origins and examples see Cachia, Pierre, 'The Egyptian *Mawwāl*: its ancestry, its development and its present forms', *JAL* VIII (1977), pp. 77–103; al-ᶜAllāf, ᶜAbd al-Karīm, ed., *al-Mawwāl al-Baghdādī*, Baghdad, 1963; al-Khāqānī, ᶜAlī, *Funūn al-adab al-shaᶜbī*, Pt. 1, Baghdad, 1962; al-Sammarrā'ī, Rabīᶜ, *al-ᶜArūḍ fi'l-shiᶜr al-shaᶜbī al-ᶜIrāqī*, Baghdad, 1987; al-Dawīsh, ᶜAbdallāh ᶜAbd al-ᶜAzīz, ed., *Dīwān al-Zuhayrī, majmūᶜah min al-mawāwīl al-mashhūrah*, Kuwait, n.d. Examples of modern use (see in Bibliography): ᶜUways (Jordan), Khalīfah (Bahrain) and in Egypt: Jāhīn, Qāᶜūd and, as a kind of consciousness informing structure, the works of Fu'ād Ḥaddād.

6 On Lebanese forms see Haydar, Adnan, 'The development of Lebanese zajal: genre, meter and verbal duel', MS. courtesy of the author; Lecerf, Jean, 'Littérature dialectale et renaissance Arabe moderne', *Bulletin d'études orientales* II (1932), pp. 179–258, and III (1933), pp. 44–171; Wuhaybah, Munīr Ilyās (al-Khāzinī al-Ghassānī), *al-Zajal: tārīkhuh, adabuh, aᶜlāmuh qadīman wa ḥadīthan*, Ḥarīṣā, 1952.

7 E.g., Jibrā'īl al-Qulāᶜī al-Laḥfadī (844–922/1440–1516, Lebanon); Khalaf al-Ghibārī (eighth/fourteenth c., Egypt); Rāshid al-Kahlāwī (eleventh/seventeenth c.?, Najd); ᶜAbd al-Raḥmān al-Anisī (1168–1250/1754–1824) and ᶜAlī b. al-Ḥasan al-Qāsim 'al-Khafanjī' (d. 1188/1766, Yemen); al-Akhḍar b. Khulūf (tenth/sixteenth c.) and Muḥammad b. Masāyib (d. 1190/1768, Maghrib).

Nineteenth-century social, political and cultural developments broadened colloquial poetry's sphere; new contexts led to thematic, and then formal, shifts. Thus, while Najdī poets continued to be important public voices in a tribal society, an embryonic urban outlook and political struggles in a larger context than inter-tribal relations were articulated in poetry. Muḥammad b. Liᶜbūn al-Wāyilī (1790–1831), who moved from Najd to al-Zubayr and on to Kuwait for political reasons, incorporated the dialects, customs and concerns of both interior and coast into his verse. Poems by Rākān b. Ḥithlayn (d. 1893) and Muḥammad al-ᶜAwnī (c. 1870–1923) express a changing political scene. The nostalgic vision of tribal society expressed by ᶜAbdallāh b. Subayyil (c. 1855–1938) suggests the passing of the old.[8] But these poets preserved the monorhyme form, language and imagery of Beduin poetry.

Elite literature's isolation from society and the desire to convey political messages to a broad audience gave colloquial poetry unique force. In the Yemen, while traditional poetic vehicles remained intact, new themes and a changing language were shaped by the appearance of the British in Aden (1839) and the Turks in North Yemen (1870), and by urbanization. Borrowed vocabulary, acceptable in colloquial but not in *fuṣḥā* poetry, infused an embryonic nationalist poetry.[9] The satirical poet Aḥmad Sharaf al-Dīn al-Qārah (d. 1863), for example, expressed local sentiment towards the Ottomans in a diction sprinkled with Turkish loanwords, and linked the chaos in Sanaa to corruption.[10]

The Maghrib also witnessed an expansion in theme, diction and imagery, while the architecture of the poem remained traditional. Dialect poetry from Morocco, Tunisia, Algeria and Libya remains an important document of socio-political conditions in the nineteenth and early twentieth centuries.[11] With the French occupation of Algeria (1830) and Tunisia

[8] For Ibn Liᶜbūn, see al-Rabīᶜān, Yaḥyā, ed., *Ibn Liᶜbūn: ḥayātuh wa shiᶜruh*, Kuwait, 1982; on Ḥithlayn, see Sowayan, Saad Abdullah, *Nabati Poetry: the oral poetry of Arabia*, Berkeley, 1985, p. 29 and al-Ḥātam, ᶜAbdallāh b. Khālid, ed., *Khiyār mā yultaqaṭ min shiᶜr al-nabaṭ*, Kuwait, 1981, vol. II, pp. 225–33; on al-ᶜAwnī, see Sowayan, *Nabati Poetry*, p. 89 and Abdallāh b. Khālid al-Ḥātam, ed., *Min al-shiᶜr al-Najdī: Dīwān al-shāᶜir Muḥammad ᶜAbdallāh al-ᶜAwnī*, Kuwait, 1984; on Ibn Subayyil, see Sowayan, *Nabati Poetry*, pp. 24–7 and al-Ḥātam ᶜAbdallāh b. Khālid, ed., *Min al-shiᶜr al-Najdī: Dīwān al-shāᶜir ᶜAbdallāh b. Ḥamūd b. Subayyil*, Kuwait, 1984.

[9] al-Maqāliḥ, *Shiᶜr al-ᶜāmmiyyah*, pp. 71, 74–8.

[10] al-Maqāliḥ, *Shiᶜr al-ᶜāmmiyyah*, pp. 176–8, and see Sharaf al-Dīn, Aḥmad Ḥusayn, ed., *al-Ṭarāʾif al-mukhtārah min shiᶜr al-Khafanjī wa'l-Qārah*, n.p. 1970. pt. 2. On other poets, see Serjeant, R.B., *South Arabian Poetry I: poetry and prose from Hadramawt*, London, 1951; al-Maqāliḥ, *Shiᶜr al-ᶜāmmiyyah*; al-Bardūnī, ᶜAbdallāh, *Riḥlah fi'l-shiᶜr al-Yamanī qadīman wa ḥadīthan*, Beirut, 3rd pr., 1978.

[11] See al-Marzūqī, Muḥammad, *al-Shiᶜr al-shaᶜbī wa'l-intifāḍāt al-taḥarruriyyah*, Tunis, 1971; Ibn al-Shaykh, al-Tallī, *Dawr al-shiᶜr al-shaᶜbī al-Jazāʾirī fi'l-thawrah 1830–1945*, Algiers, 1983; al-Ghunayy, ᶜAbd Rabbih, *Dirāsāt fī'l-adab al-shaᶜbī*, pts 1–3, Benghazi, Beirut, 1968; *Āmāl/Promesses*, Special Issue on al-Shiᶜr al-malḥūn, Algiers, 1970.

(1881), colloquial poets encouraged and chronicled popular resistance and expressed pride in a local identity.[12]

As the Sudanese *dūbayt* spread from desert to town, it embraced a growing range of poetic form.[13] Particularly renowned was Muḥammad Aḥmad Abū Sinn 'al-Ḥārdallū' (c. 1830–1917). Of the Shukriyyah tribe, al-Ḥārdallū spent time in Khartoum; his poetry blends desert and city. *Ghazal*, nature description, and hunting narrative gave way to political themes from the 1880s on, and al-Ḥārdallū became so famous that in parts of the Sudan the *dūbayt* is called the *ḥardallū*.[14]

In Iraq, the popular art of *zuhayrī* and other traditional forms proliferated, with experimentation, and served to provoke.[15] Iraq's rich folk heritage produced two famous poets. 'Ḥājj Zāyir' (Zāyir b. ᶜAlī al-Duwayjī, d. 1920) composed in every known form of Iraqi colloquial poetry and invented his own forms; his poems are still sung. ᶜAbbūd al-Karkhī (1861–1946) is remembered for his political satires.

In Transjordan, Syria and Palestine, Beduin poetry dominated, although few texts have survived. As late as the 1930s, Beduin poetry was the liveliest form of literary expression in Jordan.[16] Oral colloquial poetry permeated the culture of Mount Lebanon via competing improvisational troupes. A proliferation of forms, some linked to Syriac liturgy,[17] became the basis of a written colloquial poetry. Poets such as Ilyās al-Farrān (1858–1921) and Manṣūr Shāhīn al-Ghurrayib (1848–1920) gained renown beyond their own areas and published *dīwāns*. *Zajal* travelled into the *mahjar*: Farīd Jabbūr (1872–?) published his *dīwān* in Brazil. Noted *fuṣḥā* poets also composed *zajal*, among them Wardah al-Turk, Nāṣīf al-Yāzijī and Jibrān Khalīl Jibrān – just as, in Egypt, Aḥmad Shawqī composed colloquial songs and the *zajals* of Ismāᶜīl Ṣabrī and Ḥifnī Nāṣif were known to their contemporaries.[18]

In Egypt, an urban tradition of *zajal* is known for the Mamlūk and

12 E.g., the Algerian poets Ṭāhir b. Ḥawwāʾ (see Ibn al-Shaykh, *Dawr al-Shiᶜr*, pp. 136–9, 142–61) and Muḥammad Bilkhayr (ibid., pp. 211–15). *Revue africaine* (Algiers) is an important source for this poetry; see articles by J. Desparmet and A. Cour in the Bibliography.

13 Ismāᶜīl, *al-Shiᶜr al-qawmī*, pp. 33–8.

14 Ismāᶜīl, *al-Shiᶜr al-qawmī*, p. 28. On al-Ḥārdallū, see ᶜAbidīn, ᶜAbd al-Majīd, ᶜal-Ḥārdallū: Amīr al-shiᶜr al-shaᶜbī fī'l-Sūdān', *al-Majallah*, 70 (Cairo, Nov. 1962), pp. 40–5.

15 E.g., in the 1920 revolution (see al-ᶜAllāf, *al-Mawwāl al-Baghdādī*, e.g. p. 90, n. 1.). On traditional forms, see al-ᶜAllāf, *al-Mawwāl al-Baghdādī*, al-Shamarī, Rabīᶜ, *al-ᶜArūḍ fī'l-shiᶜr al-shaᶜbī al-ᶜIrāqī*, Baghdad, 1987 and al-Khāqānī, *Funūn al-adab*.

16 al-Quṣūṣ, Jiryis, ᶜal-Ḥayāh al-adabiyyah fī sharq al-Urdun', *al-Risālah*, (Cairo), 151 (25 May 1936), pp. 866–7.

17 See ᶜAbbūd, Mārūn, *al-Shiᶜr al-ᶜāmmī*, Beirut, 1968, pp. 70–3, 103–10.

18 Wuhaybah, *al-Zajal*, pp. 126–7, 91–3, 107–9; *al-Shawqiyyāt al-majhūlah*, ed. M. Ṣabrī, 2nd edn, Beirut, 1979, II, pp. 299–300, 304–18; Riyāḍ, Ḥusayn Maẓlūm and al-Ṣabāḥī, Muṣṭafā Muḥammad, *Tārīkh adab al-shaᶜb: nashʾatuh, taṭawwuruh, aᶜlāmuh*, Cairo, 1936, pp. 140–8, 328–32.

Ottoman periods,[19] but it was Shaykh ʿAbdallāh al-Faḥḥām who reinvigorated *zajal* composition among the early nineteenth-century *ʿulamāʾ* with his *madāʾ iḥ nabawiyyah* (praises of the Prophet) and *waʿẓ* (sermonic poems), heavily classical in diction and laden with *badīʿ*.[20] Decades later, in conjunction with the rise of a popular press, *zajal*'s public role broadened. ʿAbdallāh Nadīm (1854–96) and Yaʿqūb Ṣannūʿ (1839–1912) recognized colloquial poetry's political potential, using it to shape public awareness from the podium and in their newpapers, Nadīm's *al-Tankīt waʾl-tabkīt* (1881–2) and *al-Ustādh* (1892–3), and Ṣannūʿ's *Abū Naẓẓārah Zarqāʾ* (1877) and its successors. Nadīm and Ṣannūʿ gave *zajal* critical force, extracting it from the domain of *ghazal* and competitive repartee while building on familiar themes. Ṣannūʿ, for example, used *ghazal* satirically: a standoff between an English soldier's wife and an Egyptian 'man on the street' sketches the people's determination to eject England.[21] As in Yemeni poetry, foreign loanwords in the dialogue give a concrete dimension to the colonialist's image.

The *zajjāl* (*zajal*-poet) and publisher Muḥammad Tawfīq (*Ḥimārat munyatī*, founded 1898) experimented to achieve provocative satirical effects. In 'Zajal ḥalafāwī, ʿarabī ʿalā faransāwī',[22] the insertion of French into the Arabic text destroys the harmony of rhyme and rhythm – expressing through form the upheaval in identities which is the poem's theme. Colloquial poetry's flexibility relative to *fuṣḥā* poetry made such outrageous experimentation possible. Tawfīq differed from other prominent *zajjāl*-journalists in avoiding classical diction in favour of what is sometimes contemptuously labelled 'the language of the marketplace'. Other poems in *Ḥimārat munyatī* challenge formal distinctions between *fuṣḥā* and *ʿāmmiyyah* poetry, adhering to *fuṣḥā* syntax and *iʿrāb* which govern utterly colloquial diction.

The *ʿālim* Muḥammad al-Najjār followed al-Faḥḥām's orientation, showing professorial dedication as he moved between al-Azhar and a café where he held training sessions for the next generation, among them the important poets Muḥammad Imām al-ʿAbd, ʿIzzat Ṣaqr and Khalīl Naẓīr. Al-Najjār's *al-Arghūl* (founded 1894) was a vehicle for his own and others' didactic *zajals*. A cautious reformism marks his thematic choices, pithy descriptions of contemporary behaviour and penchant for *waʿẓ* and *ḥikmah*, in poems such as 'Zajal on the fast life' and 'Mawāwīl from which the illiterate will learn his faith's precepts of jurisprudence and the principle of

19 See al-Jammāl, Aḥmad Ṣādiq. *al-Adab al-ʿāmmī fī Miṣr fīʾl-ʿaṣr al-Mamlūkī*, Cairo, 1966.

20 See Riyāḍ and al-Ṣabāḥī, *Tārīkh*, pp. 60–1, 92–7.

21 Text reprinted in ʿAbduh, Ibrāhīm, *Abū Naẓẓārah: imām al-ṣaḥāfah al-fukāhiyyah al-muṣāwwarah wa zaʿīm al-masraḥ fī Miṣr 1839–1912*, Cairo, 1953, pp. 159–60.

22 *Ḥimārat munyatī* II no. 35 (n.d. [1317/1899]), pp. 554–7.

the oneness of God'.[23] Heavily classical and moulded into intricate rhetorical patterns, in harmony with his conservative vision, al-Najjār's diction is the opposite of Tawfīq's

Al-Arghūl and *al-Ustādh* published reader's *zajals*; this was an art in which some of the public participated. The poets identify themselves as students, civil servants and professionals; frequent *fuṣḥā* usages and classical rhetorical figures manifest an elite education. This may say more about editors than potential contributors. Al-Najjār, for example, tried to control the boundaries of colloquial poetry production as he defended *zajal*'s respectability among the arts. An article in *al-Arghūl* entitled 'Fann al-zajal'[24] instructs the reader in 'proper' *zajal* composition, asserting that it requires educated choice and distinguishing the *zajjāl* from the *udabātī*, or extemporaneous composer-entertainer who, it is claimed, does not know the 'science of metre'.

DEVELOPMENTS IN THE TWENTIETH CENTURY

Zajal continued to voice social criticism and political comment. By 1922, over one hundred satirical periodicals had appeared; many employed *zajal* to treat public issues. During the 1919 revolution, *zajal* articulated nationalist rhetoric, berated the government for passivity and called on the populace to act. *Zajjāls* continued to found newspapers, among them *al-Misallah* (Bayram al-Tūnisī, 1919), *al-Nās* (Ḥusayn Shafīq al-Miṣrī, 1924), *Abū Qirdān* (Maḥmūd Ramzī Naẓīm, 1924) and *Alf Ṣinf* (Badīᶜ Khayrī, 1925). Also important were *al-Kashkūl*, and the newspaper of Rābiṭat al-Zajjālīn (the Colloquial Poets' League, founded 1932), *al-Miṭraqah*. Other newspapers had 'resident *zajjāls*' who played the role of columnist.[25]

Zajal-journalism had emerged elsewhere. As in Egypt, poets started their own outlets. In Baghdad, where satirical journals had appeared as early as 1911, ᶜAbbūd al-Karkhī founded *al-Karkh* (1927), in which his own biting verse appeared.[26] Tunisian satirical periodicals appeared from 1906 and were quickly associated with colloquial poetry, which often took up half the newspapers and concretely re-emphasized editorial points.[27] In Tunis in

23 al-Najjār, Muḥammad, *Majmūᶜat al-azjāl*, Cairo, 1318 A.H., pp. 4–8, 68–70.

24 *al-Arghūl* I no. 2 (15 Sept. 1894), pp. 32–3; I no. 3 (1 Oct. 1894), pp. 58–60. Cf. Nadīm in *al-Ustādh*, I no. 41 (6 June 1893), pp. 985–95.

25 See Booth, Marilyn, 'Writing to be heard: colloquial Arabic verse and the press in Egypt (1877–1930)', *ARCE Newsletter* 140 (Winter 1987/1988) and 'Colloquial Arabic Poetry, Politics, and the Press in modern Egypt', *International Journal of Middle East Studies* (August 1992).

26 For examples of his poetry in *al-Karkh* see al-Jabbūrī, Jamil, *Ḥabaz Būz fī tārīkh ṣaḥāfat al-hazl wa'l-Kārīkātūr fī'l-ᶜIrāq*, Baghdad, 1986, pp. 104–5.

27 Gliouiz, Azaiez, 'La Presse humoristique tunisienne de ses origines jusqu'en 1923', diss, 3rd cycle, University of Paris III, 1978, pp. 38, 251–2, 256–8.

the 1930s, newspapers such as *al-Shabāb* (Maḥmūd Bayram al-Tūnisī, 1936) featured political colloquial poetry. In Beirut and Damascus, 'semi-periodicals' published anonymous political *zajal*, while the humorous press welcomed less political verse.[28] Unlike in Egypt, periodicals devoted almost wholly to *zajal* appeared, a trend begun by *al-Zajal al-Lubnānī* (Yūsuf al-Bāḥūṭ, 1933).[29] These published *zajal* for its own sake rather than for political purposes: some bear the words 'collection of non-political *zajals*' on their mastheads. Other periodicals, such as *al-Dabbūr* (Yūsuf Mukarzal, 1923), also published *zajal*, as did periodicals in the *mahjar* like Shukrī al-Khūrī's *Abū'l-Hawl* (founded 1906 in Sao Paolo).

Major figures in *zajal*'s successful invasion of the press were influential in colloquial poetry's development. ʿAbbūd al-Karkhī and Maḥmūd Bayram al-Tūnisī (1893–1961) are still widely read and recited. Both were close observers and trenchant critics of society, their poetry comprising a satirical tapestry of the times. Al-Tūnisī's best poetry combines fine portraiture of human types with ironic vision:

> Thief, you steal a loaf and you're locked up for two months
> Were I the city's judge, I'd imprison you two years
> For your sin, criminal, is two sins indeed.
> You cheapened the profession when you stole a loaf
> And thieved before becoming an honorable dignitary.[30]

A similarly prominent Lebanese poet, ʿUmar al-Zaʿannī (1895–1961), published in the press but composed poetry primarily for oral performance. Popular in his native Beirut, al-Zaʿannī became known beyond Lebanon. His *zajal* is urban in diction, satirical in tone, topically political and punchy in its song-based staccato rhythms.[31] Less famous but perhaps as important to his own milieu in blending political criticism, social satire and public performance was the Damascene poet Salāmah al-Arjawānī (1909–?), who – unlike al-Zaʿannī – was influenced by rural folk poetry.[32]

It is Rashīd Nakhlah (1873–1939), though, who is recognized as having moved Lebanese colloquial poetry into a new stage. His *zajal* derives from the Mount Lebanon tradition in architecture, subject and imagery; although Nakhlah spent much of his adult life in the city, his poetry retained rural images and diction. Most prolific in the traditional sphere of *ghazal*, Nakhlah in his love poetry escapes the trite imagery and repetitive diction

[28] Lecerf, 'Littérature dialectale', pp. 215–16. On the humorous press: e.g. *al-Dabbūs* (1921), *Maʿlaysh* (1926, Beirut); *al-Ḥimārah* (1919), *al-Muḍḥik al-mubkī* (1929, Damascus).

[29] E.g., *Bulbul al-Arz* (Wilyam Ṣaʿb, 1943), *Marqad al-ʿanzah* (Asʿad Sābā, 1947), *al-Shiʿr al-Qawmī* (Khalīl al-Ḥittī, 1950).

[30] 'Ḥarāmī al-raghīf', al-Tūnisi, *al-Aʿmāl al-kāmilah*, IV, Cairo, 1976, pp. 24–5. On the poet, see Booth, Marilyn, *Bayram al-Tunisi's Egypt: Social and Narrative Strategies*, Exeter, 1990.

[31] See his *dīwān*: al-Zaʿannī, ʿUmar, *ʿUmar al-Zaʿannī: Mūliyīr al-sharq*, ed. al-Zaʿannī al-Ṣaghīr, Beirut, 1980.

[32] Lecerf, 'Littérature dialectale', p. 93.

of many contemporaries. As another Lebanese poet has noted, Nakhlah 'represents the intellectual revolution in [Lebanese] popular literature', and helped to make Lebanese *zajal* 'beloved and respected' among the literary elite.[33] The same can be said of Bayram al-Tūnisī in Egypt; both poets gave *zajal* new respectability and broader horizons. While remaining loyal to traditional vernacular poetic forms, Nakhlah, al-Tūnisī, and al-Karkhī and Ḥājj Zāyir in Iraq brought new vitality to this art by rejecting outworn images, exercising lexical precision, experimenting with metre, expanding the thematic sphere and exploiting familiar forms in new ways. The next generations built upon their accomplishments, combining the richness of the colloquial heritage with the achievements of avant-garde *fuṣḥā* poetry.

A NEW COLLOQUIAL POETRY: EGYPT AND LEBANON

The new colloquial poetry movement has been strongest in Egypt and Lebanon, the 1950s witnessing important contextual developments. Having infused popular-satirical newspapers and then the labour press, Egyptian colloquial poetry moved into mainstream news and arts periodicals. In the daily *al-Masāʾ*, Luṭfī al-Khūlī and ʿAlī al-Rāʿī welcomed it in the Worker's Column and on the Literary Page respectively. *Al-Jumhūriyyah* featured Bayram al-Tūnisī in his final decade; *Rūz al-Yūsuf* and *Sabāḥ al-Khayr* published new poets regularly. In Beirut, *al-Ṣayyād*, *al-Dabbūr* and *al-ʿĀsifah* featured poets renowned for their skill at oral poetic duelling. Important poets published in *Al-Dabbūr* between 1946 and 1951 include Rāmiz al-Bustānī, Imīl Mubārak, Asʿad al-Sabʿilī, Wilyam Ṣaʿb and Zaghlūl al-Dāmūr (Jūzīf al-Hāshim).

Colloquial poetry's appearance in the mainstream press did not mean its wholehearted acceptance into the literary fold. *Fuṣḥā* poets and literary critics remained ambivalent. They admitted in theory that its vitality offered an important breath of fresh air, but in practice their acceptance was hesitant and extremely limited. For those associated with highbrow literature to try their hand at colloquial poetry (for example Lūwīs Awaḍ in *Plutoland*, 1947) was still seen by many as an aberration or dismissed as nonliterary play. Al-Khūlī's attempt to recognize it as serious art by inviting prominent writers to comment on poems published in *al-Masāʾ* was tempered by the paternalistic tone of some of the resulting essays. In Lebanon, equivocal attitudes marked the group around the journal *Shiʿr*. Yūsuf al-Khāl and some colleagues supported the admission of colloquial elements into poetic composition in their call for a radical reformation of

[33] Ṣaʿb, Wilyam, 'al-Adab fī'l-zajal', *al-Adīb* II, no. 1 (Beirut, Jan. 1943), pp. 42, 43. See Nakhlah, Rashīd, *Dīwān Rashīd Nakhlah fī'l-zajal*, ed. Amīn Nakhlah, Beirut, 1964.

Arabic poetry, and *Shiʿr* twice published colloquial poems. But the journal's inner circle did not themselves compose colloquial poetry, and *Shiʿr* focused its efforts on publishing avant-garde *fuṣḥā* poetry.[34]

Conflicts of the period sharpened the politics of language, affecting colloquial poetry's status among the literati. In Egypt, the post-1952 regime emphasized 'the production of the people' in literature. Folklore study was the major beneficiary, but colloquial poetry was also recognized as a valuable 'populist' medium. This meant, however, encouragement with tight control. In Lebanon, supporters of a separatist Lebanese nationalism called for the use of colloquial Lebanese as the language of culture, a campaign that reached its height during the 1958 civil war, as Lebanon faced the issue of joining the United Arab Republic. A standard-bearer of this campaign was the symbolist poet Saʿīd ʿAql (b. 1912). Publishing a volume of colloquial poetry (*Yāra*) in 1961, ʿAql took the further step of substituting Latin for Arabic characters. Soon after, he founded Dār Yāra to publish colloquial works, including poetry. He encouraged new colloquial poets by introducing their *dīwāns* in colloquial prose.[35] Orthographically awkward, *Yāra* is an unexceptional colloquial echo of ʿAql's *fuṣḥā* love poetry, centred on the descriptive celebration of idealized womanhood mirrored in nature's rhythms. While ʿAql's French symbolist orientation shows in the evocation of figure and emotion through an interrelated succession of sensual images, his *ʿāmmiyyah* poetry manifests a greater degree of static external description than does his *fuṣḥā* poetry. Yet the vernacular tongue called ʿAql to simpler images and the diction of everyday life lent warmth to his 'cold craftsmanship'.[36] But ʿAql's importance to Lebanese colloquial poetry lies more in his symbolist experiments and linguistic nationalism than in his own colloquial verse.

One of those on whom ʿAql left his symbolist mark (and also one of the two colloquial poets published in *Shiʿr*) has become Lebanon's best-known colloquial poet. When Mīshāl Ṭrād (b. 1912) began writing, he was one of several poets seeking to retain and exploit the elegant simplicity of Lebanese *zajal* at its finest whilst breaking through its formal constraints. These poets included Asʿad Sābā, Ṭalāl Ḥaydar, ʿAbdallāh Ghānim, Mūrīs

[34] See Kheir Beik, Kamal, *Le Mouvement moderniste de la poésie arabe contemporaine*, Paris, 1978, pp. 44–5, 73–81, 126–7, who says al-Khāl, Unsī al-Ḥājj and ʿIṣām Maḥfūz later composed in the vernacular (127n, 174n); these compositions have proved unlocatable.

[35] E.g. Mīshāl Ṭrād's *Julnār* (Beirut, 1951) and Manṣūr al-Riyāshī's *Nafaḥāt min Lubnān*, (Beirut, 1973). On Dār Yāra, which also published J. Ghuṣayn's colloquial *dīwān Nawwār* in Latinate characters, see Grotzfeld, Heinz, 'L'Expérience de Saʿīd ʿAql: l'Arabe Libanais employé comme langue littéraire', *Orientalia Suecana* (Uppsala) 22 (1973).

[36] Badawi, M. M., *A critical introduction to modern Arabic poetry*, Cambridge, 1975, p. 242. ʿAql was writing colloquial poetry long before *Yāra*. 'Mishwār' appears in *al-Dabbūr* 1197 (30 May 1948); Wuhaybah, *al-Zajal*, (pp. 124–5) gives three poems not in *Yāra*. ʿAql's colloquial *Khumāsiyyāt* (1978) has proved unlocatable.

ʿAwwād and Kābī Ḥaddād. Thematically, their romantic celebration of Lebanon's beauty and idyllic picture of rural society seem not far removed from the art of the *zajal*-poets, but a more complicated vision emerges in the attempt at a poetic organization and imagery structured on contradictions between the ideal and the real.

Shiʿr also recognized Ṭrād by publishing al-Khāl's review of the poet's second collection, *Dūlāb*. Supporting Ṭrād's freedom to choose a colloquial medium, al-Khāl criticized him for a traditionalism of form and vision in his optimism based on ahistoricity, reliance on external description and abstract symbolism, preference for ideas over images and linear rather than organic unity. He concluded that Ṭrād had not exploited the vernacular's liberating potential.[37] There is truth in al-Khāl's words, but Ṭrād cannot be entirely circumscribed by them.

Each of Ṭrād's first three collections (*Julnār*, 1951; *Dūlāb*, 1957; *Laysh*, 1964) has a distinct thematic focus. But the poems show formal similarities: they are rhythmically quick and regular, constructed stanzaically and punctuated by regular, simple rhymes. *Julnār* presents Ṭrād's early love poetry, in which an aesthetically controlled treatment of female beauty surfaces in the descriptive passages. A lyrical, subjective tone is overlain by a carefree simplicity invoked through images of rural Lebanon in which Nature and Woman are interwoven. In *Dūlāb*, the countryside emerges in its own right, sounding a pastoral note as the poet celebrates rural Lebanon. The lengthier poems of *Laysh* transform this evocation into a longing for a simpler past, communicated in a detailed cataloguing of village life. Anger at the transformations worked by time, greed and war emerges; nationalist fervour is interspersed with bitter reflections on society's changes for the worse.[38] Diction and imagery drawn from daily life contrast starkly with overarching images of darkness and destruction.

With *Kās ʿa shafāf al-dinī* (composed 1957–72), Ṭrad returned to the shorter forms and lyrical lightness of *Julnār* and *Dūlāb*, treating philosophical questions by juxtaposing simple images and painting portraits of love, human contact and the wandering poet with flute:

Where be you, O vendor
Of dreams? You'll get lost
On the road amidst the fog
When the sun has begun to set!
Tell me: What are you selling?
He said: I am the roving poet.
I circle on the night of the feast
I sell these poems,

37 Shukrī, Ghālī, *Shiʿrunā al-ḥadīth ilā ayn*, Cairo, 1968, pp. 68–9. The review appeared in *Shiʿr* (Beirut), I, no. 4.

38 E.g., in the long catalogue poem 'Ayyām sōdā', *Laysh*, Beirut, 1964, pp. 43–79.

Roses, and jugs of
Red wine, and I sell love,
And with the flute of spring I blow tunes to these lovers![39]

Shadows are protective rather than ominous; carefree childhood still engenders wistful yearning but this is not the bitter longing of *Laysh.* Despite an awareness of time's passage, emphasis on today's pleasures re-emerges. In *ᶜArabiyyī mukhallaᶜā* (1965–74) and *al-Ghurāb al-aᶜwar* (poems undated), a darker note sounds: the broken-down cart bears embalmed mankind, pulled in 'this storm' by 'a rabid dog/ and a one-eyed crow . . .'[40] Humankind wanders lost and lights candles to the devil. The past is erased. Nature echoes the dark chaos of human society where it once mirrored pastoral peace: the butterfly shivers with cold rather than fluttering in the sun. The poet still wanders, but has neither flute nor a sense of destination. Yet images of winter darkness are still invaded by light and colour, the idyllic tones of rural life.

These recent collections show movement towards more concentrated imagery and experimental form, but Ṭrād's lexicon, fund of images and basic themes have not changed markedly. Ṭrād's strength lies in his colourful, sonorous and precise treatment of images and themes rooted in rural Lebanon. A static, superficial quality emerges particularly when he attempts to treat the human condition writ large. Yet he has been important in moving Lebanese colloquial poetry beyond Nakhlah's *zajal* into the realm of contemporary Arabic poetry, whilst retaining echoes of Lebanon's *zajal* tradition.

FURTHER DEVELOPMENTS: NEW COLLOQUIAL POETRY IN EGYPT

Fuʾad Ḥaddād and Ṣalāḥ Jāhīn were influenced by the free verse movement, revolutionary literatures and the ideological ferment of the 1940s. Together, they launched Egypt's new colloquial poetry.

Ḥaddād's French education, romantic Marxism and immersion in Arab-Muslim culture are richly evident in his poetry: steeped in Egyptian popular tradition, it also echoes al-Mutanabbī, Ibn al-ᶜArabī, Aragon and Paul Eluard. Ḥaddād's idiom, particularly in later works, is unique in its harmonious blend of Qurʾān and *mawwāl.* If Bayram al-Tūnisī wrote of daily experience, Ḥaddād struggled with life's contradictions, moving beyond al-Tūnisī's linear poetic logic to a dialectical association of antithetical and metonymic images. Correspondingly metre and rhyme, once chiefly external unifying features, became semantic elements in the

39 'Nāy a-rabīᶜ', *Kās ᶜā shafāf al-dinī*, Beirut, 1972, p. 14.
40 'Jināzat al-insān', *ᶜArabiyyī mikhallaᶜā*, Beirut, 1986, pp. 5–10.

poem's movement. These features are now common in *ʿāmmiyyah* poetry, but Ḥaddād played a major role in introducing them. Yet he preserves the semantic and musical unity of the poetic line: 'an ancient Arab poet in contemporary garb . . . [his] poetry is a defense against all who accuse us of severing our links with the Arabic heritage'.[41] Ḥaddād's more than thirty *dīwāns* (not yet all published) are not so much collections of discrete poems as polyphonic unities. A unifying thread may be, for example, political (*Aḥrār*, *Bi-quwwah*), religious (the Sufi *al-Ḥaḍrah al-zakiyyah*) or historical (*Min nūr al-khayāl*); from each a complex vision emerges.

While Ḥaddād bridged old and new, Jāhīn constructed the directional signals. He began by writing nationalistic *fuṣḥā* poetry but turned to the vernacular, influenced first by al-Tūnisī and then by Ḥaddād. A cartoonist, Jāhīn filled his space in *Rūz al-Yūsuf* one week with the poem 'al-Shāy bi'l-laban' (Aug. 1953):

> Four hands upon the breakfast [table]
> Four lips drink tea with milk
> And kiss, embracing the light of day
> Between her chest and his, between the two smiles,
> And embrace the love which gathered them together
> At breakfast.[42]

The morning sun's warmth upon the couple's faces and the light cast upon their simple home express the hopes of the revolution. Jāhīn's first *dīwān*, *Kalimat salām* (1955), where this poem appears, speaks in simple imagery which links daily experience to global politics in a tone far removed from both romanticism and overt rhetoric: 'Wheat is not like gold/ Wheat is like the peasants/ Lean stalks whose roots feed on mud'.[43]

Beneath these poems' beautiful simplicity lies intricate imagery; a striking visual quality reflects Jāhīn's skill as cartoonist. While these traits continued to mark his poetry, Jāhīn turned to an explicit articulation of Nasserist ideology with the long 'Mawwāl ʿashān al-qanāl' (1956), drawing on such slogans as 'alliance of the popular forces' and 'national construction'. Believing deeply in the aims and promises of the revolution, Jāhīn transcended the role of ideologue with his ironic and sensitive view of the human condition (most fully expressed in *Rubāʿiyyāt*). Through much of his corpus runs an underlying tension, evoking the gap between Nasserism as ideal and as reality.

Jāhīn shared the general intellectual malaise which followed the June 1967 war, with the revolution's evident failure to fulfil its ideals. As a voice

[41] ʿAbd al-Raḥmān al-Abnūdī, quoted in al-Baghdādī, Muḥammad, 'Lā uḥibbu', *Ṣabāḥ al-Khayr*, 1581 (Cairo, 24 April 1986), p. 43. [42] *Kalimat salām*, Cairo, 1955, p. 27.

[43] 'Zayy al-fallāḥīn', *Kalimat salām*, p. 35.

for these ideals, he felt the impact of the defeat violently and responded with silence rather than self-criticism. With the publication of his collected works (1977) and a further *dīwān* (*Anghām Siptimbiriyyah*, 1985), Jāhīn's voice re-emerged to affirm for a new generation the continuing meaning of the revolution.[44]

Jahīn more than Ḥaddād was influenced by *fuṣḥā* poetry's turn to free verse and metrical patterns based on the *tafʿīlah* (foot) rather than the *baḥr* (metre). It is interesting that Jāhīn regarded some of his poetry as *zajal* and some as *shiʿr*. *Zajals* were shorter and lighter, expressing simple meanings, while *shiʿr* arose from contradictory elements in the poet's relationship with his world.[45]

The break with the past had been formally articulated in 1959 by the formation of the Ibn ʿArūs League (named for an eighteenth-century predecessor), which included Jāhīn, ʿAbd al-Raḥmān al-Abnūdī, Sayyid Ḥijāb, Fuʾād Qāʿūd and Farīdah Ilhāmī (Ḥaddād was in prison). Distancing themselves from the label 'folk poet',[46] they held that the vernacular set no *a priori* limits upon creativity or vision. Colloquial as well as *fuṣḥā* poetry could transcend the boundaries and concerns of its own milieu to explore universal issues.

Dār Ibn ʿArūs published al-Abnūdī's first works, *al-Arḍ wa'l-ʿiyāl* (1964) and *al-Zaḥmah* (1967). The first, written while al-Abnūdī still lived in his native Qena province, is Upper Egyptian in rhythm, diction and imagery, echoing the Ṣaʿīd's songs and epics. Surrealistic scenes constructed from realistic elements express alienation from village society: the felucca's sail unfurls, attaches to the body and dissolves into a burial shroud. External logic is absent; a series of moments defines an internal life mingling dream and reality, both made concrete in images of village life. The rhythm of the Ṣaʿīdī *nadb* (lament) sounds a tone of grieving loss, but the ability to dream holds a promise of renewal. Composed after the poet had moved to Cairo, *Al-Zaḥmah's* urban imagery and starker diction add sharpness to the theme of *ghurbah* (life far from home). Scene, form and persona are externally described, shorn of explicit emotional mediation. Subsequent works include experiments in the epistolary form (*Jawābāt Ḥurājī*, *Baʿd al-taḥiyyah*) and extended narrative (*Aḥmad Ismāʿīn*). The gentleness of *Fuṣūl*, the yoking of Egyptian – Saʿīdī identity and experience abroad in *Ṣamt al-jaras*

44 E.g. in 'Anghām Siptimbiriyyah', *Anghām Siptimbiriyyah*, Cairo, 1984, pp. 5–7.

45 *Qaṣāqīṣ waraq*, 2nd edn, Cairo, 1967, p. 7; *Anghām Siptimbiriyyah*, pp. 3–4; author's interviews with Ṣ. Jāhīn, Cairo, March and April 1982.

46 As articulated in the changing subtitles of Jāhīn's first two collections: *Kalimat salām: shiʿr shaʿbī* and *ʿAn al-qamar wa'l-ṭīn: shiʿr bi'l-ʿāmmiyyah al-miṣriyyah*. See also Jāhīn, *Dawāwīn Ṣalāḥ Jāhīn*, Cairo, 1977, p. 6.

and the declamatory tone of recent political poems[47] manifest a poetic talent of many facets.

Poets of the same generation, each carrying on in a distinct way the accomplishments of Ḥaddād and Jāhīn, include those of the Ibn ᶜArūs group plus Maḥmūd ᶜAfīfī, Samīr ᶜAbd al-Bāqī, Ḥajjāj al-Bāy, Muḥsin al-Khayyāṭ, ᶜAbd al-Raḥīm Manṣūr and Majdī Najīb. They have been joined by a stream of new poets – including a growing number of women – who are erasing boundaries between *fuṣḥā* and *ᶜāmmiyyah* poetry in technique, imagery and subject. Syntax and diction move between linguistic levels, a poetic answer to the 'third language' which is the speech of the educated and which *fuṣḥā* poets have also approached.[48] Erasing boundaries is linked to an idea of what choice of language means. Rather than a question of audience or milieu, the choice is posed by the text itself and the need for an idiom whose precision comes from its link to daily experience. The choice of linguistic level in itself is seen as meaningless; how the language is used determines poetic strength and communicative power. National and social issues are expressed less directly and topically, and the folk *turāth* (heritage) is present less as an overt adaptation of form and motif than as a subtle element of style and musicality – as seen first in al-Abnūdī, Ḥijāb and Ḥaddād.

THE HERITAGE AND THE NEW IN THE SUDAN AND IRAQ

While contemporary Sudanese *shiᶜr qawmī* echoes the traditional colloquial *dūbayt*, *shiᶜr al-buṭūlah* (poetry of heroism) and Ṣūfī poetry, and while the grieving tenor of the traditional forms *nāyil* and *abūdhiyyah* run through today's *shiᶜr shaᶜbī ᶜirāqī*, radical changes in vision and poetic organization have emerged. Tradition-bound images become contemporary symbols: for Iraqi poets the *mashḥūf*, a skiff used in Iraq's southern marches, is a mount of war, a vessel for life's journey and a coffin, and Shīᶜī heroes become contemporary martyrs.

While the urban Sudanese *qaṣīdah dūbaytiyyah* signalled a new attempt at internal narrative unity within old forms, some of today's poets have abandoned those forms, selectively retaining their imagery and language. The early *dīwāns* of Sayyid Aḥmad al-Ḥārdallū (b. 1938) – in *fuṣḥā* – are dominated by *ghazal*, but concrete village images, nationalist consciousness

[47] E.g. 'al-Aḥzān al-ᶜādiyyah', *Adab wa-naqd* (Cairo), 4, (May–June 1984), pp. 111–20; 'al-Muttaham', *Adab wa-naqd*, 24 (August 1986), pp. 100–11; 'Zayy mā iḥnā', *al-Ahālī*, (Cairo), X, no. 285 (25 March 1987), p. 10.

[48] See Jayyusi, Salma Khadra, *Trends and movements in modern Arabic poetry*, 2 vols, Leiden, 1977.

and an inclination to folk art appear in the first, *Ghadan naltaqī* (1960). Alienation, a rejection of painful reality and a desire to escape the city for 'simpler' village values emerged more clearly in *Muqaddimāt* (1970). Al-Ḥārdallū's *fuṣḥā* poetry – direct and simple in diction, drawing on colloquialisms and based on single extended images – seems to merge naturally into his turn to the colloquial in the early 1970s. *Misdār . . . ᶜashān baladī*, *Niḥnā* and *Sindabād fī bilād al-sajam wa'l-rumād* vocalize a further escape – linguistically underlined – from urban life's 'artificiality'. *Sindabād*, the most complex, juxtaposes images of exile with Sudanese local colour to express a longing for the homeland and to suggest the absence of human contact outside. An interesting experiment is 'Bābā Jamāl', a hymn to Nasser in which third-world struggles resonate, religious images give the hero legitimacy and Egyptian diction invades Sudanese speech. 'Al-Baḥr' echoes the sailing chanty, posing an extended political metaphor in a monologue addressed by a sailor to his *rayyis* (captain). Hāshim Ṣiddīq also expresses alienation, distance and yearning for the homeland, especially in *al-Zaman wa'l-riḥlah*. English winters described in Sudanese diction convey the gap between surroundings and identity, cold dislocation and the warmth of the beloved/the Sudan, and the blockage of space and silence versus the acts of writing and performing music. Al-Ḥārdallū's imagery stays close to Sudanese experience, using precise portraiture, whereas Ṣiddīq offers polar and universal opposites – light and darkness, silence and music, the static railway station and the moving train. Al-Ḥārdallū's diction is more colloquial, with Nubian elements, and both his orthography and rhythm evoke the spoken tongue, while Ṣiddīq draws on *fuṣḥā* elements.

In Iraq, Muẓaffar al-Nawwāb (b. 1934) led the break from traditional forms, while echoing the images and rhythms of the Shīᶜī *ᶜĀshūrah* pageantry which surrounded him from birth. He began early to write traditional *fuṣḥā* poetry and satirical colloquial verse in the style of ᶜAbbūd al-Karkhī, but he followed the Iraqi free-verse movement closely. The 1958 revolution and a sojourn in the Iraqi marches with Saᶜdī Yūsuf yielded the famous 'Lil-rāyil wa-Ḥamid' ('To the train and Hamid') and other poems[49] in a style and rural diction far removed from al-Karkhī's verse. Elegizing the martyrs of the nationalist struggle, these poems mark an abrupt transition from traditional colloquial poetry. Images of rural society are vivid and spare; first-person narration constructs the hero-figure indirectly through an accumulation of incomplete details, and the poet's voice mingles with the weeping of a mourning woman. The poems also manifest a formal breakthrough in their use of free verse, reliance on internal more than endline rhymes and the interplay of narrative voices, dialogue and

[49] See his collection *Lil-rāyil wa-Ḥamid*, Beirut, n.d. [1969].

dramatic invocation. Yet the hero-figure of al-Nawwāb's narrative elegies is an externally drawn figure, with emotion provided by the narrator's evocation of memory. Poets influenced by al-Nawwāb have carried his achievements further. In the poetry of the brothers ᶜAzīz and Shākir al-Samāwī, the hero-figure is internally presented, beset by contradictions and moulded by struggle in an interplay of personal and collective emotion. Shākir al-Samāwī's varying type and spatial organization suggest an attempt at concrete poetry. Riyāḍ al-Nuᶜmānī's poetry is a direct outcry – the explicit hero-martyr is Iraq – while Jumᶜah al-Ḥilfī creates an ironic and circular lyricism to express loss, boredom and alienation.[50]

AL-NABAṬI AND THE NEW IN THE ARABIAN PENINSULA

Though traditional oral poetry remains popular throughout the Peninsula, social change and the mass media have transformed colloquial poetry 'from a socio-political institution to pure literature'.[51] Regularly broadcast and published in periodicals, *nabaṭī* poetry has inspired numerous and often repetitive anthologies. Young poets have adapted traditional forms and motifs to shorter poems often composed to be sung. Mostly love poems and simple *waṭaniyyāt* (patriotic poems), they employ a simplified urban diction invaded by *fuṣḥā* usages, the shorter, lighter metres and sometimes quatrain-based rhymes.[52] Some poets, influenced by new *fuṣḥā* and *ᶜāmmiyyah* poetry, have attempted to break away from old forms but their poetry remains dominated by traditional themes.[53] In Bahrain, experiments with the *mawwāl* and free verse incorporate familiar images of life drawn from the sea.[54]

Yemen's centuries-old tradition of poets writing in both *fuṣḥā* and *ᶜāmmiyyah*[55] continues: today's major colloquial poets either began by writing in *fuṣḥā* and, influenced largely by political change, turned to the colloquial (Muṭahhar al-ᶜIryānī, ᶜAlī Ṣabrah), or have simultaneously composed *fuṣḥā* verse and *ᶜāmmiyyah* songs (ᶜAbdallāh Hādī Ṣbayt), or have carried experiments with *fuṣḥā* new poetry into the vernacular (ᶜAbdallāh Salām Nājī). One result is that most – including those known *only* as

50 See in Bibliography ᶜA. al-Samāwī and Sh. al-Samāwī; al-Nuᶜmānī and al Ḥilfī, untitled mss. courtesy of the authors.

51 Personal communication to the author from S. Sowayan, 2 June 1987.

52 S. Sowayan, pers. commun.; see in Bibliography al-Lumayyiᶜ, Sālim; al-Ḥarshānī, Shanūf Jāsim; al-Saᶜīd, Ṭalāl ᶜUthmān; al-Ḥamūd, Nawwār ᶜAbd al-Qādir; al-Ghāmidī, ᶜAbd al-Raḥmān; Ibn Sulṭān, al-Sharīf Manṣūr.

53 E.g., al-Dawsirī, Musaffir; ᶜAbd al-Jalīl, Fāyiq.

54 E.g., al-Khalīfah, ᶜAlī; ᶜAbdallāh, ᶜAllām; Rabīᶜ, ᶜAbd al-Raḥmān.

55 'Rarely do we find a poet in Yemen who has not composed colloquial as well as *faṣīḥ* poetry . . .' al-Ḥibshī, ᶜAbdallāh Muḥammad, *al-Adab al-Yamanī ᶜaṣr khurūj al-atrāk al-awwal min al-Yaman*, Beirut, 1986, p. 403.

colloquial poets (Muḥammad al-Dhahbānī, Ṣāliḥ Saḥlūl) – compose in what one critic has called *fuṣʿāmmiyyah*,[56] evident in grammatical structures as well as lexicon.

POETRY, PERFORMANCE, NARRATIVE

Contemporary colloquial poets have crossed traditional genre boundaries, sometimes overtly echoing the narrative patterns and performance contexts of folk epic and balladry. Experiments with colloquial verse theatre, exploiting Arabic theatre's long-established receptivity to the vernacular, have proved especially effective. In Egypt, when Muḥammad ʿUthmān Jalāl (1829–98) 'Egyptianized' Molière's comedies, he did so by freely translating them into *zajal*.[57] The comedic-operatic theatre of the early twentieth century drew upon *zajal*, sung or declaimed, as best seen in the collaborative efforts of Najīb al-Riḥānī and Badīʿ Khayrī, Bayram al-Tūnisī and Sayyid Darwīsh. More recently, in Egypt, Najīb Surūr's verse dramas have received wide acclaim on stage; in the Sudan, H. Ṣiddīq and S. A. al-Ḥārdallū have written plays in colloquial verse. The well-known Yemeni singer and songwriter Ḥusayn Abū Bakr al-Miḥḍār has experimented with vernacular verse musi-drama. Colloquial poetry's potential for sustained dramatic/narrative expression is also demonstrated by the 'drama-poetry' of the Egyptians Samīr ʿAbd al-Bāqī and Yusrī al-ʿAzab, the Sudanese poet al-Jīlī Muḥammad Ṣāliḥ and the Yemenis ʿA. S. Nājī and ʿA. H. Ṣbayt, as well as by the Egyptian colloquial poetry '*riwāyahs*' of al-Abnūdī and Fuʾād Ḥajjāj. Colloquial poetry's ties to the folk epic tradition have inspired, in Egypt, dramatic narratives combining colloquial poetry with prose and turning upon the narrating figure of the *rāwī*; this combination has been exploited by, among others, al-Tūnisī, Ḥaddād and, more recently, Muḥsin al-Khayyāṭ.[58]

[56] al-Bardūnī, *Riḥlah*, p. 353. On the poets, see al-Maqāliḥ, *Shiʿr al-ʿāmmiyyah*, pp. 410–66, and *Shuʿarāʾ min al-Yaman*, Beirut, 1983, pp. 193–212; al-Bardūnī, *Funūn al-adab al-shaʿbī fī'l-Yaman*, Beirut, 1988, pp. 353–83, and *Riḥlah*, pp. 335–51; al-Iryānī; ʿAwlaqī; ʿA. S. Nājī, 'Salām lil-fahm', *al-Ḥikmah* (Sanaa), VI, no. 57 (Feb. 1977), pp. 66–71.

[57] Jalāl, Muḥammad ʿUthmān, *al-Arbaʿ riwāyāt mi nakhb al-tiyatrāt*, Cairo, 1307 A. H. [1889/90].

[58] See works by Surūr, Najīb; Ṣiddīq, Hāshim, *Nabtā habībatī*, Beirut, 1986; al-Ḥārdallū, Sayyid Aḥmad, *ʿArḍaḥāl*, Khartoum, 1980; on al-Miḥḍār see Bilfaqīh, ʿAbdallāh ʿUmar, *al-Hikmah*, VI, no. 50 (May 1976), pp. 77–81; ʿAbd al-Bāqī, Samīr, *al-Nashīd al-faqīr*, Cairo, 1976; al-ʿAzab, Yusrī, *Taghrībah ʿAbrazāq al-Hilālī*, Cairo, 1984; Ṣāliḥ, al-Jīlī Muḥammad, *Aḥājī al-Khirtīt*, Khartoum, n.d.; on Nājī's *Nashwān wa'l-rāʿiyah* (1966) and Ṣbayt's *Qiṣṣat al-fallāḥ wa'l-arḍ*, (1965), see al-Maqāliḥ, *Shiʿr al-ʿāmmiyyah*, pp. 312–23; al-Abnūdī, ʿAbd al-Raḥmān, *Aḥmad Ismāʿīn*, Cairo, 1972; Ḥajjāj, Fu'ād, *Yawmiyyāt ʿAbd al-ʿĀl*, Cairo, 1984; al-Tūnisī, Maḥmūd Bayram, *Muntakhabāt al-shabāb*, Cairo, 1923, pp. 23–30, 32–7; Ḥaddād, Fuʾād, *al-Shāṭir Ḥasan*, Cairo, 1984; al-Khayyāṭ, Muḥsin, *Ḥikayāt Bahiyyah*, Cairo, 1986.

PLATFORM POETRY AND THE ISSUE OF AUDIENCE

Past and present, much colloquial poetry can be described as 'platform poetry' in its declamatory structure and overtly political message. Circulating on tape and from the stage, poetry becomes political action and an awareness of audience is paramount. The Palestinian poet Abū'l-Ṣādiq notes, 'When the illiterate camp resident says '*Ah, dā ṣaḥḥ*' ('Oh, how true'), I know I have attained my goal.' Abū'l-Ṣādiq's *thawriyyāt* (revolutionary poems) seek to organize artistically the experiences and words of the fedayeen, whom he calls 'the real poets' behind his work.[59] Simplicity and a straightforward integration of elements drawn from his audience's lives are important.

Aḥmad Fuʾād Najm (b. 1929) may be the best-known colloquial poet who aims explicitly to provoke political action. Sung by Shaykh Imām ʿĪsā (b. 1918) from 1962 until the late 1980s, Najm's poems are known to Arab communities everywhere. Like Nadīm and al-Tūnisī, Najm has translated a life of hardship among society's poorest elements into poetry which combines provocation with education. His first term in prison on a trumped-up charge produced *Ṣuwar min al-ḥayāh wa'l-sijn* (1964); al-Tūnisī's direct influence shows in the construction of narrative portraits ('Aḥmad Gharīb') and in the form and content of 'Fallāḥ yukhāṭib iqṭāʿiyyan', which echoes al-Tūnisī's 'al-Fallāḥ' and 'al-ʿĀmil al-Maṣrī'. The partnership with Shaykh Imām brought Najm closer to the folk *turāth* and gave prominence to verbal caricature and the joke as structural elements.[60] Najm's brilliance lies in using the vernacular of Cairo's medieval heart to construct a voice speaking from that heart to the society around, distanced through the language itself. Najm's poems of the 1960s exposed the contradictions between the regime's ideology and the continued existence of class division, elite privilege and corruption.[61] A more direct tone conveyed blanket rejection of the post-Nasser era. Najm's poetry moved fully onto the regional stage in tandem with political events and his own broadening sphere of movement, celebrating the Iranian revolution (*Ṭaharān*) and bringing the Palestinian struggle, present in his earlier poetry, into sharp focus as the core of the Arab people's struggle (*ʿĪshī yā Miṣr*). This was accompanied by a shift from poetic complexity to outright sloganeering, but recent experiments suggest the search for a new voice.

59 Author's interview with Abū'l-Ṣādiq, Cairo, Oct. 1987. See Abūʾl-Sādiq in Bibliography.

60 A. F. Najm, quoted in al-Naqqāsh, Farīdah, 'Ẓāhirat al-shāʿir wa'l-shaykh' in Najm', Aḥmad Fuʾād, *Baladī wa habībatī*, Beirut, 3rd pr., 1981, p. 11.

61 See for example the poems in Najm, *Baladī* and *Yaʿīsh ahl baladī*, Beirut, 5th pr., 1981.

For some poets, choosing the vernacular is a question of worldview which certainly includes political commitment, but indirectly. Their diction tends toward a mixture of *fuṣḥā* and *ʿāmmiyyah* elements, while use of the folk *turāth* is less direct. They are concerned more with the communication of personal experience than with the creation of a collective consciousness. For others, whose impulse comes first and foremost from politics and the communicative function, poetic diction tends to be fully associated with colloquial speech. Their finest poetry is far from prosaic propaganda, but the vernacular's potential for mass communication can be overexploited. At its worst, such poetry is repetitive and heavy-handed. But its existence bespeaks an issue hotly debated among colloquial poets, that of audience and function, for some assert that colloquial poetry must be accessible to all but that it has become isolated and thus has lost its legitimacy. This issue has become more urgent because the audience sought is no longer a purely local one. Colloquial poets today address themselves to the Arabic-speaking world as a whole. For some, like Palestinians and Iraqis in exile, this is a necessity, both practical and ideological. For others, it bespeaks a belief that their poetry transcends national boundaries. Greater communication has led to mutual influence; through popular singers' voices colloquial poetry crosses boundaries, while some poets have experimented with writing in more than one dialect.

But political factors and cultural biases still militate against colloquial poetry. In Lebanon, it is feared that colloquial poetry can too easily become an expression of sectarianism. For Palestinians and Syrians, the need to address a regional audience and the ideological emphasis on Arab unity respectively discourage vernacular composition. In the Maghrib, concern to replace French with Arabic as the language of culture de-emphasizes *al-ʿāmmiyyah*, while in the Peninsula battles over its 'legitimacy' rage. When colloquial poetry becomes closely associated with either support for or opposition to a specific regime, as in Iraq and Libya, it often suffers artistically. Constraints on freedom of expression affecting all the arts have a particular impact on colloquial poetry with its potential mass audience. Yet *shiʿr al-ʿāmmiyyah* flourishes throughout the Arab world, and has its own special power to unite *turāth* and *muʿāṣarah* (heritage and contemporaneity), *aṣālah* and *tajdīd* (authenticity and renovation).*

* Portions of this chapter are based on research funded by the National Endowment for the Humanities and the American Research Center in Egypt, to whom I am grateful. I also want to thank the following individuals for help in locating material: Mahmud al-Alim, Ferial Ghazoul, Nadia Gifour, Nadia Harb, Ibrahim al-Hariri, Adnan Haydar, Ibrahim al-Hindi, Sayyid Khamis, Raouf Musʿid and Saʿd Sowayan.

BIBLIOGRAPHY

GENERAL BIBLIOGRAPHY

A. In Arabic

ʿAbidīn, ʿAbd al-Majīd *Tārikh al-thaqāfah al-ʿarabiyyah fī'l sūdān, min nashʾatihā ilā 'l-ʿaṣr al-ḥadīth*, Cairo, 1953.

Al-ʿAlī, Ṣāliḥ *et al. al-Adab al-ʿArabī fī āthār al-dārisīn*, Beirut, 1961.

Amīn, Bakrī Shaykh *al-Ḥarakah al-adabiyyah al-suʿūdiyyah*, Beirut, 1972.

Al-Asad, Nāṣir al-Dīn *al-Ittijāhāt al-adabiyyah al-ḥadīthah fi Filasṭīn wa 'l-Urdun*, Cairo. 1957.

ʿAwwād, G. Ḥannā *Muʿjam al-muʾallifīn al-ʿirāqiyyīn fī'l-qarnayn al-tāsiʿ ʿashar wa'l-ʿishrīn (1800–1969)*, 3 vols, Baghdad, 1969.

Cheikho, Louis *al-Ādāb al-ʿarabiyyah fī'l-qarn al-tāsiʿ ʿashar*, 2 vols, Beirut, 1924–26.

Tārīkh al-ādāb al-ʿarabiyyah fī'l-rubʿ al-awwal min al-qarn al-ʿishrīn, Beirut, 1926.

Dāghir, Yūsuf Asʿad *Maṣādir al-dirāsah al-adabiyyah, vol. 2: al-fikr al-ʿarabī al-ḥadīth fī siyar aʿlāmihi*, Sidon, 1956.

Muʿjam al-masraḥiyyāt al-ʿarabiyyah wa'l-muʿarrabah, Baghdad, 1978.

Al-Daqqāq, 'Umar *Funūn al-adab al-muʿāṣir fī Sūriyyah*, Damascus, 1971.

Dusūqī, ʿUmar *Fī'l-adab al-ḥadīth*, 2 vols, Cairo, 1948–55.

Ḥāfiẓ, Sabrī *'Bibliografiyā al-riwāyah al-miṣriyyah 1876–1969', Majallat al-Kitāb al-ʿArabī*, Cairo, July 1970

Ḥajirī, Ṭāhā *al-Ḥayāh al-adabiyyah fī Lībiya*, Cairo, n.d.

Haykal, Aḥmad *Taṭawwur al-adab al-ḥadīth fī Miṣr*, Cairo, 1967.

al-Ḥusaynī, Isḥāq Mūsā *al-Madkhal ilā 'l-adab al-ʿarabī al-muʿāṣir*, Cairo, 1963.

Ibn ʿĀshūr, Muḥammad al-Fāḍil *al-Ḥarakah al-adabiyyah wa'l-fikriyyah fī Tūnis*, 2 vols, Cairo, 1956.

Kayyālī, Sāmī *al-Adab al-ʿarabī al muʿāṣir fī Sūriya 1850–1950*, Cairo, 1959

Maqdisī, Anīs Khūrī *al-Ittijāhāt al-adabiyyah fī'l-ʿālam al-ʿarabī al-ḥadīth*, Beirut, 1960.

Mubārak, ʿAbd Allāh *al-Adab al-ʿArabī al-muʿāṣir fī'l Jazīrah al-ʿArabiyyah*, Cairo, 1973.

Najm, Muḥammad Yūsuf *Fahāris al-adab al-ʿarabī al-ḥadīth; 1: Al-Qiṣṣah (up to 1962); 2: Al-Uqṣūṣah (up to 1962), Al-Abḥāth* 16 (1963), pp. 53–153, 346–411.

Nassāj, Sayyid Ḥāmid *Dalīl al-qiṣṣah al-miṣriyyah, ṣuḥuf wa majmūʿāt, 1910–61*, Cairo, 1972.

al-Masraḥiyyah fī'l-adab al-ᶜarabī al-ḥadīth, Beirut, 1956.
al-Qiṣṣah fī'l-adab al-ᶜarabī al-ḥadīth, Beirut, 1961.
Saᶜīd, Jamīl *Naẓarāt fī'l-tayyārāt al-adabiyyah al-ḥadīthah fī'l ᶜIrāq*, Cairo, 1954.
Sakkūt, Ḥamdī and Jones, Marsden *Aᶜlām al-adab al-muᶜaṣir fī Miṣr; silsilah biyugrāfiyyah naqdiyyah bibliyugrāfiyyah*, Cairo, 1975.
Sanūsī, Zayn al-ᶜĀbidīn *al-Adab al-muᶜāṣir fī'l-ᶜIrāq (1938–1960)*, Baghdad, 1962.
al-Adab al-tūnisī fī'l-qarn al-rābiᶜ ᶜashar, 2 vols, Tunis, 1346/1927.
Ṣaydaḥ, Jūrj *Adabunā wa udabāʾunā fī'l-mahājir al-amrīkiyyah*, Beirut, 1964.
Sarkīs, Yūsuf *Muᶜjam al-maṭbūᶜāt al-ᶜarabiyyah wa'l-muᶜarrabah*, 2 vols, Cairo, 1928–31.
Yāghī, ᶜAbd al-Raḥmān *al-Adab al-filasṭīnī al-ḥadīth*, Cairo, 1970.
Yāghī, Ḥāshim *al-Naqd al-adabī al-ḥadīth fī Lubnān*, 2 vols, Cairo, 1968.
Yāzijī, Kamāl *Ruwwād al-nahḍah al-adabiyyah fī Lubnān al-ḥadīth 1800–1900*, Beirut, 1962.
Zaydān, Jurjī *Tārīkh ādāb al-lughah al-ᶜarabiyyah*, vol. 4, Cairo, 1914.
Tarājim mashāhīr al-sharq fī'l-qarn al-tāsiᶜ ᶜashar, Cairo, 1910.

B. *In European languages*

Abdul-Hai, Muhammad 'A bibliography of Arabic translations of English and American poetry (1830–1970)', *Journal of Arabic Literature*, VII (1976), pp. 120–50.
Allen, Roger, ed. *Modern Arabic literature. A library of literary criticism*, New York, 1987.
Altoma, Salih, J. *Modern Arabic literature; a bibliography of articles, books, dissertations and translations in English*, Bloomington, Indiana, 1975.
Alwan, Mohamad Bakir 'A bibliography of modern Arabic fiction in English translation', *Middle East Journal*, 26 (1972), pp. 195–200.
'A bibliography of modern Arabic poetry in English translation', *Middle East Journal*, 27 (1973), pp, 373–81.
Ashrawi, Hanan Mikhail *Contemporary Palestinian literature under occupation*, Bir Zeit, 1976.
Badawi, M.M. 'Modern Arabic literature' in Derek Hopwood and D. Grimwood-Jones, eds, *Middle East and Islam: a bibliographical introduction*, Zug, Switzerland, 1972; 2nd edn, 1986.
Berque, J. *et al. Bibliographie de la culture arabe contemporaine*, Paris, 1981.
Brocklemann, C. *Geschichte der arabischen Litteratur, Supplementband III*, Leiden, 1949.
Brugman, J. *An introduction to the history of modern Arabic literature in Egypt*, Leiden, 1984.
Cachia, Pierre *An overview of modern Arabic literature*, Edinburgh, 1990.
Fontaine, Jean '*Bibliographie littéraire tunisienne 1972–79*', *Journal of Arabic Literature*, VI (1975); VII (1977); X (1979); XIII (1982).
Aspects de la littérature tunisienne (1975–83), Tunis, 1985.
Gibb, H. A . R. *Studies on the civilization of Islam*, eds. Stanford J. Shaw and William

R. Polk, London, 1962.
Hafez, Sabry 'A complete bibliography of collections of Egyptian short stories (1921–1970)', *Journal of Arabic Literature*, XI (1980), pp. 123–9.
Hazo, Samuel, ed, *Mundius Artium, Special Arabic Issue*, X (1), Texas, 1977.
Index Islamicus 1906–55, Cambridge, Supplements: 1956–60; 1961–65; 1966–70; 1971–75; 1975–80.
Index Islamicus: the Quarterly vols 1–9 (1977–85).
Khemiri, Taher and Kampffmayer, B. *Leaders in contemporary Arabic literature*, Berlin, 1930.
Moreh, S. ed. *Arabic works by Jewish writers, 1863–1973*, Jerusalem, 1973.
Studies in modern Arabic prose and poetry, Leiden, 1988.
Ostle, R. C., ed. *Studies in modern Arabic literature*, Warminster, Aris & Phillips, 1973.
Pérès, Henri '*Le roman, le conte et la nouvelle dans la littérature arabe moderne*', *Annales de l'Institut d'Etudes Orientales*, III (1937), pp. 266–337.
Somekh, Sasson *Genre and Language in modern Arabic literature*, Wiesbaden, 1991.
de Voogd, I. K. 'Bibliography of modern Moroccan Arabic literature (novels and short stories), published 1956–80', *Journal of Arabic Literature*, XII (1982), pp. 149–51.

ANTHOLOGIES AND SELECTIONS IN ENGLISH TRANSLATION (EXCLUDING POETRY)

(For Poetry see bibliographies to chapters 3 and 4)

Abdel Wahab, Farouk, ed. *Modern Egyptian drama*, Minneapolis and Chicago, 1974.
Abdullah, Yahya Taher *The mountain of green tea*, tr. by Denys Johnson-Davies, London, 1984.
Allen, Roger, ed. *A library of literary criticism: modern Arabic literature*, New York, 1987.
Awad, Louis *The literature of ideas in Egypt*, Atlanta, Georgia, 1986.
Azrak, M., tr. and Young, M. J. L., rev. *Modern Syrian short stories*, Washington, 1989.
Bagader, Abu Bakr and Heinrichsdorff, A. M. *Assassination of Light: Modern Saudi short stories*, Washington, 1990.
Brinner, W. M. and Khuri, Mounah *Readings in modern Arabic literature*, Leiden, 1971.
Ebeid, R. Y. and Young, M. J. L. *Arab stories – east and west*, Leeds, 1977.
El-Gabalawi, Saad *Modern Egyptian short stories*, Fredricton, New Brunswick, 1977.
Three pioneering Egyptian novels, Fredericton, New Brunswick, 1986.
Hafez, Sabry and Cobham, Catherine, eds *A reader in modern Arabic short stories*, London, 1988.
Hafidh, Y. T. and Al-Dilaimi, eds *Iraqi short stories: an anthology*, Baghdad, 1988.
Al-Hakim, Tawfiq *Plays, prefaces and postscripts of Tawfiq al-Hakim*, tr. by W. M. Hutchins, Vol. 1: *Theater of the Mind*, Washington, 1981; Vol. 2: *Theater of society*, Washington, 1984.

The fate of a cockroach and other plays, tr. by D. Johnson-Davies, London, 1973.
Haqqi, Yahya *Good morning and other stories*, tr. by Miriam Cooke, Washington, 1987.
The Saint's Lamp and other stories, tr. by M. M. Badawi, Leiden, 1973.
Hutchins, W. M., ed. *Egyptian short stories*, Cairo, 1986.
Tales and short stories of the 1970s and 1980s, Cairo, 1986.
Ibrahim, Sunᶜallah *The smell of it and other stories*, tr. Denys Johnson-Davies, London, 1971.
Idris, Yusuf *The cheapest nights and other stories*, tr. by Wadida Wassef, London, 1978.
In the eye of the beholder, ed. Roger Allen, Minneapolis and Chicago, 1978.
Rings of burnished brass, tr. by Catherine Cobham, London, 1984.
Jayyusi, Salma Khadra, ed. *The literature of modern Arabia*, London, 1987.
Johnson-Davies, Denys *Arabic short stories*, London, 1983.
Egyptian one-act plays, London, 1981.
Egyptian short stories, 1978.
Modern Arabic short stories, Oxford, 1967.
Kanafani, Ghassan *All that's left to you and other stories*, tr. May Jayyusi and Jeremy Reed, Austin, 1990.
Men in the sun and other Palestinian stories, tr. Hilary Kilpatrick, London, 1978.
Palestine's children, tr. Barbara Harlow, London, 1984.
Kassem, Ceza and Hashem, Malek, eds *Flights of fantasy* (Arabic short stories), Cairo, 1985.
Mahfuz, Najib *God's World*, tr. Akef Abadir and Roger Allen, Minneapolis, 1973.
The time and the place, tr. Denys Johnson-Davies, New York, 1991.
Manzalaoui, Mahmoud, ed. *Arabic writing today – the short story*, Cairo, 1968.
Arabic writing today – drama, Cairo, 1977.
Al-Mazini, Ibrahim ᶜAbd al-Qadir *Al-Mazini's Egypt* (two novels and one short story), tr. by W. M. Hutchins, Washington, 1983.
Nuᶜayma, Mikhaᵓil *A New Year*, tr. by J. R. Perry, Leiden, 1974.
Rifaat, Alifa *Distant view of a minaret and other stories*, tr. by D. Johnson-Davies, London, 1983.
Salih, al-Tayyib (Tayeb) *The wedding of Zein and other stories*, tr. by Denys Johnson-Davies, London, 1968.
Sharuni, Yusuf *Blood feud*, tr. by D. Johnson-Davies, London, 1984.
Tamir, Zakariya *Tigers on the tenth day and other stories*, tr. by Denys Johnson-Davies, London, 1985.
Taymur, Mahmud *Tales from Egyptian life*, tr. by Denys Johnson-Davies, Cairo, 1949.
Woodman, David *Egyptian one-act plays*, Cairo, 1974.

1: INTRODUCTION: THE BACKGROUND; TRANSLATIONS AND ADAPTATIONS

A. Arabic sources

ᶜAbd al-Rāziq, ᶜAlī *al-Islām wa uṣūl al-ḥukm*, Cairo, 1925.
ᶜAbduh, Ibrāhīm *Taṭawwur al-ṣaḥāfah al-miṣriyyah*, Cairo, 1925.

ʿAbduh, Muḥammad *al-Islām wa'l-radd ʿalā muntaqidīhi*, Cairo, 1327 (1909–10).
Risālat al-tawḥīd, Cairo, 1361 (1942–43) (tr. *The theology of unity*, by I. Musaʾad and K. Cragg, London, 1966).
al-ʿĀlim, Mahmūd Amīn and Anīs, ʿA. *Fī'l-thaqāfah al-miṣriyyah*, Beirut, 1955.
Amīn, Aḥmad *Ḥayātī*, Cairo, 1950 (tr. *My life*, by I. J. Boullata, Leiden, 1978).
Zuʿamāʾ al-iṣlāḥ, Cairo, 1948.
Amīn, Qāsim *al-Marʾah al-jadīdah*, Cairo, 1901.
Taḥrīr al-marʾah, Cairo, 1899.
Anīs, M. *Dirāsāt fī thawrat sanat 1919*, Cairo, 1963.
Anṭūn, Faraḥ *Mukhtārāt min Faraḥ Anṭūn, Silsilat manāhil al-adab al-ʿarabī*, No. 29, Beirut, 1950.
al-ʿAqqād, ʿAbbās Maḥmūd *Saʿd Zaghlūl*, Cairo, 1936.
Arslān, Shakīb *Limādhā taʾakhkhar al-Muslimūn*, Cairo, 1358 (1939–40).
ʿAwaḍ, Louis *al-Muʾaththirāt al-ajnabiyyah fī'l-adab alʿarabī al-ḥadīth*, 2 vols, Cairo, 1962–63.
Tārīkh al-fikr al-miṣrī al-ḥadīth, 2 vols, Cairo, 1967–69.
al-Bustānī, Buṭrus *et al.*, eds *Dāʾirat al-maʿārif*, 11 vols,. Beirut, 1876–1900.
al-Fāsī, ʿAllāl *al-Ḥarakāt al-istiqlāliyyah fī'l-Maghrib al-ʿarabī*, Cairo, 1948 (tr. *The independence movements in Arab North Africa*, by H. Z. Nuseibeh, Washington, 1954).
Fayṣal, Shukrī *al-Ṣaḥāfah al-adabiyyah*, Cairo, 1959.
al-Ḥakīm, Tawfīq *Sijn al-ʿumr*, Cairo, 1988.
Ḥamzah, ʿAbd al-Laṭīf *Adab al-maqālah al-ṣuḥufiyyah fī Miṣr*, 5 vols, Cairo, n.d.
Ḥanafī, Ḥasan *Dirāsāt islāmiyyah*, Beirut, 1982.
Qaḍāyā muʿāṣirah, 1, Fī fikrinā al-muʿāṣir, Beirut, 1981.
Qaḍāyā muʿāṣirah, 2, Fī'l-fikr al-gharbī al-muʿāṣir, Beirut, 1982.
Ḥusayn, Ṭāhā *al-Ayyām*, Cairo, 1926–27 (tr. Taha Hussein, *An Egyptian childhood*, by E. H. Paxton, London, 1932).
Mustaqbal al-thaqāfah fī Miṣr, Cairo, 1938 (tr. *The future of culture in Egypt*, by S. Glazer, Washington, 1954).
Isḥāq, Adīb *al-Durar*, Beirut, 1909.
al-Jabartī, ʿAbd al-Raḥmān *ʿAjāʾib al-āthār fī 'l-tarājim wa 'l-akhbār*, 4 vols, Cairo 1322 (1904–5) (tr. *Al-Jabarti's chronicle of the first seven months of the French occupation of Egypt*, by S. Moreh, Leiden, 1975).
al-Jābirī, Muḥammad ʿĀbid *Naḥnu wa'l-turāth*, Casablanca, 1980; 3rd edn, 1983.
al-Kawākibī, ʿAbd al-Raḥmān *Ṭabāʾiʿ al-istibdād*, Cairo, n.d.
Khālid, Khālid Muḥammad *Min hunā nabdaʾ*, Cairo, 1950 (tr. *From here we start*, by I. al-Faruqi, Washington, 1953).
Khayr al-Dīn Pasha *Aqwam al-masālik fī maʿrifat aḥwāl al-mamālik*, Tunis, 1284–85 (1867–68) (tr. *The surest path*, by L. C. Brown, Cambridge, Mass., 1967).
Kurd ʿAlī, Muḥammad *Mudhakkirāt*, 4 vols, Damascus, 1948–51.
Luṭfī al-Sayyid, Aḥmad *al-Muntakhabāt*, 2 vols, Cairo, 1937–45.
Maḥmūd, Zakī Najīb *Tajdīd al-fikr al-ʿarabī*, Beirut, 1971.
Marrāsh, Faransīs *Riḥlah ilā Ūrubbah*, Beirut, 1867.
Mubārak, ʿAlī *ʿAlam al-Dīn*, 4 vols, Alexandria, 1882.
al-Khiṭaṭ al-Tawfīqiyyah, 15 vols, Cairo, 1886–88.

Muruwwah, Ḥusayn *Qaḍāya adabiyyah*, Beirut, 1956.

Mūsā, Salāmah *Tarbiyat Salāmah Mūsā*, Cairo, 1947 (tr. *The Education of Salama Musa*, by L. O. Schuman, Leiden, 1961).

al-Nadīm, ʿAbd Allāh *Sulāfat al-Nadīm*, 2 vols, Cairo, 1897–1901.

Quṭb, Sayyid *al-ʿAdālah al-ijtimāʿiyyah fī'l-Islām*, Cairo, 1954, (tr. Sayed Kotb, *Social justice in Islam*, by J. B. Hardie, Washington, 1953).

al-Rāfiʿī, ʿAbd al-Raḥmān *Tārīkh al-ḥarakah al-qawmiyyah*, 2 vols, Cairo, 1938.

Riḍā, Muḥammad Rashīd *Tārīkh al-ustādh al-imām al-shaykh Muḥammad ʿAbduh*, 3 vols, Cairo, 1931.

Rifāʿī, Shams al-Dīn *Tārīkh al-ṣaḥāfah al-Sūriyyah*, 2 vols, Cairo, 1969.

Saʿādah, Anṭūn *al-Niẓām al-jadīd*, n.p., 1950.

Saʿīd, Rifʿat *Tārīkh al-ḥarakah al-ishtirākiyyah fī Miṣr 1900–1925*, Beirut, 1972.

al-Ṣaʿīdī, ʿAbd al-Mutaʿāl *Tārīkh al-iṣlaḥ fī'l-Azhar*, Cairo, 1943.

al-Shayyāl, Jamāl al-Dīn *Tārīkh al-tarjamah wa ḥarakat al-thaqāfah fī ʿasr Muḥammad ʿAlī*, Cairo, 1951.

Shidyāq, Aḥmad Fāris *Kanz al-raghāʾib fī muntakhabāt al-Jawāʾib*, Constantinople, A. H. 1288–9 (1871–1881).

Kashf al-mukhabbā ʿan funūn Urubbā, (1st edn, Tunis, 1866), Constantinople, 1299 (1881–82).

al-Sāq ʿalā'l-sāq fī mā huwa 'l-Fāriyāq, (1st edn, Paris, 1855), 2 vols, Cairo, n.d.

al-Ṭahṭāwī, Rifāʿah Rāfiʿ *Manāhij al-albāb al-miṣriyyah fī mabāhij al-ādāb al-ʿaṣriyyah*, Cairo, 1912.

al-Murshid al-amīn li 'l-banāt wa 'l-banīn, Cairo, 1912.

Takhlīṣ al-ibrīz ilā talkhīṣ Bārīz, (1st edn, Cairo, 1834), Cairo, 1905.

Tājir, Jāk *Ḥarakat al-tarjamah fī Miṣr khilāl al-qarn al-tāsiʿ ʿashar*, Cairo, 1945.

Ṭarrāzī, Philippe de *Tārīkh al-ṣaḥāfah al-ʿarabiyyah*, 4 vols, Beirut, 1913–33.

al-Zayyāt, Laṭīfah '*Ḥarakat al-tarjamah al-adabiyyah min al-inglīziyyah ilā 'l-ʿarabiyyah fī Miṣr fī'l fatrah mā bayn 1882–1925*', Cairo University unpublished dissertation, 1957.

Zurayq, Qusṭanṭin *Maʿnā al-Nakbah*, Beirut, 1948 (tr. *The meaning of the disaster*, Beirut, 1956).

B. Sources in European languages

Abdallah, Ahmad *The student movement and national politics in Egypt 1923–1973*, London, 1985.

Abdel-Malek, A. *Anthologie de la littérature arabe contemporaine: II les essais*, Paris, 1965.

Idéologie et renaissance nationale: l'Égypte moderne, Paris, 1969.

La pensée politique arabe contemporaine, Paris, 1970.

Abu Jabir, K. S. *The Arab Baʿth Socialist Party: history, ideology and organization*, Syracuse, N.Y., 1966.

Abu-Lughod, Ibrahim *Arab Rediscovery of Europe*, Princeton, 1963.

Abu-Lughod, J. *Cairo: 1001 years of the city victorious*, Princeton, 1971.

Adams, C. C. *Islam and modernism in Egypt*, London, 1933.

Ahmed, J. M. *The intellectual origins of Egyptian nationalism*, London, 1960.
Antonius, G. *The Arab awakening*, London, 1938.
Awad, Louis *The literature of ideas in Egypt. Selection, translation and introductions*, Atlanta, Georgia, 1986.
Baer, Gabriel *A History of landownership in modern Egypt 1800–1950*, Oxford, 1962.
Berque, J. *Les Arabes d'hier à demain*, Paris, 1960.
L'Égypte, impérialisme et révolution, Paris, 1967.
Cultural expression in Arab Society today, Austin, 1978.
Buheiry, M. *et al. Intellectual life in the Arab East, 1890–1939*, Beirut, 1981.
Cachia, P. *Ṭāhā Ḥusayn; his place in the modern Arab literary renaissance*, London, 1956.
Cromer, Lord *Modern Egypt*, 2 vols, London, 1908.
Deeb, Marius *Party politics in Egypt: the Wafd and its rivals, 1919–1939*, London, 1979.
Enayat, H. *Modern Islamic political thought*, London, 1982.
Gershoni, Israel and Jankowski, James R. *Egypt, Islam and the Arabs: The search for Egyptian nationhood, 1900–1930*, Oxford, 1986.
Gibb, H. A. R. *Modern trends in Islam*, Chicago, 1947.
Studies on the civilization of Islam, London, 1962.
Gibb, H. A. R. and Bowen, Harold *Islamic society and the west*, Oxford, vol. I, 1950, vol. II, 1957.
Grünebaum, G. E. von *Islam: essays on the nature and growth of a cultural tradition*. London, 1955.
ed. *Modern Islam: the search for cultural identity*, University of California Press, 1962.
Haim, Sylvia G. *Arab nationalism, an anthology*, London, 1962.
Heyworth-Dunne, J. *Introduction to the history of education in modern Egypt*, London, 1938.
Holt, P. M., ed. *Political and social change in modern Egypt*, London, 1963.
Hopwood, D. *The Russian presence in Syria and Palestine, 1843–1914*, Oxford, 1969.
Egypt 1945–1984: politics and society, London, 1985.
Syria 1945–1986: politics and society, London, 1988.
Hourani, A. H. *Arabic thought in the liberal age, 1798–1939*, London, 1962.
The Emergence of the modern Middle East, London, 1981.
ed. *Saint Antony's Papers*, 17, Middle Eastern Affairs, 4 (1965).
al-Husry, Khaldun S. *Three reformers, a study in modern Arab thought*, Beirut, 1966.
Issawi, Charles *An Economic history of the Middle East and North Africa*, London, 1982.
Keddie, N. R. *Sayyid Jamal al-Din 'al-Afghani': a political biography*, Berkeley, 1972.
Kedourie, E. *The Chatham House version and other Middle Eastern studies*, N.Y., 1970.
Arabic political memoirs and other studies, London, 1974.
Kerr, M. *Islamic reform: the political and legal theories of Muhammad Abduh and Rashid Rida*, Berkeley, 1966.
Khuri, Raʾif. *Modern Arab thought: channels of the French Revolution to the Arab East*, Princeton, 1983.
Lane, Edward William *An account of the manners and customs of the modern Egyptians*, Everyman's Library, n.d.

Laqueur, Walter *Communism and nationalism in the Middle East*, London, 1957.
Laroui, A. *L'idéologie arabe contemporaine*, Paris, 1967.
La Crise des intellectuels arabes, Paris, 1974.
Les origines sociales et culturelles du nationalisme morocain 1830–1912, Paris, 1980.
Lewis, B. *The Muslim discovery of Europe*, London, 1981.
Longrigg, S. H. *Syria and Lebanon under French Mandate*, London, 1958.
Louca, Anouar *Voyageurs et écrivains égyptiens en France au XIX siècle*, Paris, 1970.
Lufti al-Sayyid Marsot, A. *Egypt and Cromer*, London, 1968.
Egypt's liberal experiment, 1922–1936, Berkeley, 1977.
Mabro, Robert *The Egyptian economy 1952–1972*, Oxford, 1974.
Mansfield, Peter *Nasser's Egypt*, London, 1965.
The Arabs, London, 1976; reprinted with a Postscript, 1980.
Máoz, M. *Ottoman reform in Syria and Palestine 1940–1861*, Oxford, 1968.
Mardin, S. *The genesis of young Ottoman thought*, Princeton, 1962.
Mazyad, A. M. H. *Ahmad Amin 1886–1954; advocate of social and literary reform in Egypt*, Leiden, 1963.
Mitchell, R. P. *The Society of the Muslim Brothers*, Oxford, 1969.
Moosa, Matti *The origins of modern Arabic fiction*, Washington, 1983.
Owen, Roger *The Middle East in the world, 1800–1914*, London, 1981.
Philipp, T. *Gurgi Zaidan: his life and thought*, Beirut, 1979.
Polk, W. R. and Chambers, R. L., eds, *Beginnings of modernization in the Middle East: the nineteenth century*, Chicago, 1968.
Reid, D. M. *The odyssey of Farah Antun: a Syrian Christian's quest for secularism*, Minneapolis, 1975.
Renan, E. *L'Islamisme et la science*, Paris, 1883.
Rodinson, M. *Marxisme et monde musulman*, Paris, 1967.
Safran, N. *Egypt in search of political community*, Cambridge, Mass., 1961.
Salibi, K. *The modern history of Lebanon*, London, 1965.
Sayegh, F. A. *Arab unity*, N.Y., 1958.
Schölch, A. *Ägypten den Ägyptern!* Zürich, 1972 (tr. *Egypt for the Egyptians*, London, 1981).
Sharabi, Hisham B. *Nationalism and revolution in the Arab world*, N.Y., 1966.
Arab intellectuals and the west: the formative years 1875–1914, Baltimore, 1970.
Smith, Wilfred Cantwell *Islam in modern history*, Princeton, 1957.
Stetkevych, J. *Modern Arabic literary language; lexical and stylistic development*, Chicago, 1970.
Thompson, J. H., and Reischauer, eds *Modernization of the Arab world*, N.Y., 1966.
Tibawi, A. L. *Islamic education*, London, 1972.
Vatikiotis, P. J. *The modern history of Egypt*, London, 1969.
Vatin, J. C. *L'Algérie politique; histoire et société*, Paris, 1974.
Waterbury, J. *The Egypt of Nasser and Sadat*, Princeton, 1983.
Welch, Alfred, T. and Cachia, P., eds *Islam: Past influence and present challenge*, Edinburgh, 1979.
Wendell, C. *The evolution of the Egyptian national image: from its origins to Ahmad Lutfi al-Sayyid*, Berkeley, 1972.

Wessels, Antonie *A Modern biography of Muhammad*, Leiden, 1972.
Zeine, Z. N. *The struggle for Arab independence*, Beirut, 1960.

2: THE NEO-CLASSICAL ARABIC POETS

A. Dīwāns

As a rule, the poetry of most of the neo-classical poets is included in their respective *dīwān*s. A *Dīwān* (meaning 'the collected poetry of...') is normally put together by the poet at some stage in his life, then reprinted with additions, deletions or alterations within his lifetime. The poems are customarily arranged alphabetically by their rhymes, often divided into *abwāb* encompassing the different *aghrāḍ*. In the case of many eminent poets, comprehensive editions of their *dīwān*s are published after their deaths under the editorship of one or more scholars. Until very recently these editors would not usually indicate the dates of composition and publication of the poems unless the poet in question had done so in the editions he published in his lifetime. Furthermore, the editors would sometimes omit certain poems or sections for extra-literary considerations (political, moral, personal) without acknowledging or explaining their alterations.

Many of the poems of these poets, especially in the early stages of modern Arabic literature, did not have individual titles when they were first published in the press or in the *dīwān*s. However, recent editions of these *dīwan*s sometimes assign individual titles to the poems, but the editors often fail to indicate whether these titles were added by them or by the poets.

Another ambiguity is presented by the explanatory glosses that are appended to the poems. Sometimes the glosses are provided by the poets, but in many cases they are added by the editors or by language experts who are entrusted with the task of explicating difficult words and phrases. The reader is often left in the dark regarding the identities of the authors of these annotations.

The following list specifies the main editions of the *dīwān*s of some of the poets discussed in this chapter. In each case the edition used is indicated.

Al-Bārūdī: Although al-Bārūdī prepared his *dīwān* for publication during the last years of his life, he never saw it in print and it was only a decade after his death that the first two volumes of *Dīwān al-Bārūdī* were published (in 1914 and 1915). It was edited by Maḥmūd al-Imām al-Manṣūrī, who provided it with bulky annotations. The third and final volume of this edition never appeared in print. A fuller edition (though not sufficiently comprehensive) was published in four volumes in 1940, 1942, 1972 and 1974 respectively, with an introduction by Dr Muḥammad Ḥusayn Haykal and glosses and indices by ᶜAlī al-Jārim and Muḥammad Shafīq Maᶜrūf. This edition was reprinted several times. Also noteworthy are the 450 lines which were not included in the earlier editions of the *dīwān* but were unearthed by ᶜAlī Muḥammad al-Ḥadīdī and appended to his book *Maḥmūd Sāmī al-Bārūdī Shāᶜir al-Nahḍah*, second edition, Cairo, 1969. *Edition used*: *Dīwān al-Bārūdī*, ed. al-Jārim and Maᶜrūf, Cairo, 1971–74.

Ḥāfiẓ Ibrāhīm: Several editions of *Dīwān Ḥāfiẓ Ibrāhīm* were published in his lifetime. The first of those appeared with glosses by Muḥammad Ibrāhīm Hilāl (Cairo, 1901), and the second in 1922. After his death an edition appeared entitled *Dīwān Ḥāfiẓ min ṣibāhu ilā wafātihi*, with an introduction by Khalīl Muṭrān (Cairo, 1935). In 1937, a new edition in two volumes was published by Aḥmad Amīn, Aḥmad al-Zayn and Ibrāhīm al-Ibyārī. This edition was reprinted in recent years in Cairo with certain omissions (for example, volume I, seventh edition, 1955; volume II, sixth edition, 1956). *Edition used*: *Dīwān Ḥafiẓ Ibrāhīm*, ed. Aḥmad Amīn *et al.*, vol. I (fourth edition), Cairo, 1948; vol. II (third edition), Cairo, 1939.

Al-Jawāhirī: The early collections of al-Jawāhirī's poetry, published in his youth, did not carry the title *dīwān*. The first edition of *Dīwān al-Jawāhirī* came out in Baghdad in 1949–53. It includes glosses written by the poet himself. In 1961 a new two-volume edition, with several omissions and additions, was also published in Baghdad (it was described in the title page as the fifth edition). Other editions were published outside Iraq (for example Damascus, 1957; Sidon, 1967; and Beirut, 1968, the latter bearing the title *Al-Majmūᶜah al-shiᶜriyyah al-kāmilah*). Finally, a committee of Iraqi scholars, headed by Dr Ibrāhīm al-Sāmarrāʾī and aided by the poet, published in Baghdad between 1973 and 1977 a new version of *Dīwān al-Jawāhirī* in six volumes. Unlike the editions edited by the poet, the poems in this edition are arranged chronologically. *Edition used*: *Dīwān al-Jawāhirī*, Baghdad, 1961.

Al-Ruṣāfī: The first edition of *Dīwān al-Ruṣāfī* was printed in Beirut in 1910, with an introduction by Muḥyī al-Dīn al-Khayyāṭ and annotations by Muṣṭafā al-Ghalāyīnī. Subsequent editions published in the poet's lifetime were the 1925 Cairo edition, and the 1931 Beirut edition introduced by ᶜAbd al-Qādir al-Maghribī. In 1956 an enlarged edition was published in Cairo, and between 1972 and 1975 a new three-volume edition was produced in Baghdad by Muṣṭafā ᶜAlī who later published a five-volume edition (Baghdad, 1986). At least two other editions have been published in Lebanon in recent decades: Beirut, 1969 and Beirut, 1972; the latter is titled *Dīwān Maᶜrūf al-Ruṣāfī*, *Edition used*: *Dīwān al-Ruṣāfī*, Beirut, 1931.

Shawqī: The first edition of *al-Shawqiyyāt* was published by the young Shawqī, with his own autobiographical introduction, in 1898 and reprinted in 1911. In 1925 the first volume of the new *al-Shawqiyyāt* came out in Cairo with an introduction by Dr Haykal. Volume II was published in 1930, and volumes III and IV posthumously in 1936 and 1941 respectively (the last volume was edited by Muḥammad Saᶜīd al-ᶜIryān). This four-volume set became the 'standard edition' of Shawqī's poems, and was repeatedly reprinted. In 1961–62, Dr Muḥammad Ṣabrī published in Cairo two volumes of *al-Shawqiyyāt al-Majhūlah*, in which he included hundreds of poems that were excluded from *al-Shawqiyyāt*. Dr Ṣabrī indicated the original publication dates of the poems and provided useful background information. In recent years, two attempts have been made to republish the entire poetic output of Shawqī in a new form: by Aḥmad Muḥammad al-Ḥūfī (*Dīwān Shawqī*, volume 1, Cairo, 1980), and by

Muḥammad Saʿīd al-ʿIryān (*al-Mawsūʿah al-Shawqiyyah*, four volumes to date, Cairo, 1982). *Editions used*: *al-Shawqiyyāt* I–IV, Cairo, 1964; *al-Shawqiyyāt al-Majhūlah* I–II, Cairo, 1961–62.

B. Secondary works in Arabic

Adūnīs (ʿAlī Aḥmad Saʿīd) *Al-thābit wa 'l-mutaḥawwil*, vol. 3, Beirut, 1978.

Anīs, Ibrāhīm *Mūsīqā 'l-shiʿr*, 3rd edn, Cairo, 1965.

ʿAqqād (al-), ʿAbbās Maḥmūd *Shuʿarāʾ Miṣr wa-biʾātuhum fi ʾl-jīl al-māḍī*, Cairo, 1937.

ʿAwaḍayn, Ibrāhim *Al-muʿāraḍah fī shiʿr Shawqī*, Cairo, 1982.

Ḍayf, Shawqī *Al-Bārūdī rāʾid al-shiʿr al-ḥadīth*, Cairo, 1964.

Shawqī shāʿir al-ʿaṣr al-ḥadīth, Cairo, 1963.

Dusūqī, ʿUmar *Fī 'l-adab al-ḥadīth*, Cairo, 1964.

Ḥadīdī (al-), ʿAlī Muḥammad *Maḥmūd Sāmī al-Bārūdī shāʿir al-nahḍah*, 2nd edn, Cairo, 1969.

Ḥusayn, Ṭāhā *Shawqī wa Ḥāfiẓ*, Cairo, 1933.

Ismāʿīl, ʿIzz al-Din *Al-shiʿr al-ʿArabī al-muʿāṣir: qaḍāyāhu wa-ẓawāhiruhu al-fanniyyah wa 'l-maʿnawiyyah*, Cairo, 1967.

Kayyālī (al-), Sāmī *Al-adab al-ʿArabī al-muʿāṣir fī Sūryā 1850–1950*, Cairo, 1968.

Khayyāṭ (al-), Jalāl *Al-shiʿr al-ʿIrāqi al-ḥadīth: marāḥiluhu wa taṭawwuruhu*, Beirut, 1970.

Mandūr, Muḥammad *Al-shiʿr al-Miṣrī baʿda Shawqī*, vol. 1, Cairo, 1963.

Muḥāḍarāt ʿan shiʿr Ismāʿil Ṣabrī, Cairo, 1955.

Fī 'l-mīzān al-jadīd, Cairo, 1944.

Manfalūṭī (al-), Muṣṭafā Luṭfī *Mukhtārāt al-Manfalūṭī*, Cairo, n.d.

Marṣafī (al-), Ḥusayn *Al-wasīlah al-adabiyyah*, Cairo, 1974.

Nuwayhī (al-), Muḥammad *Qaḍiyyat al-shiʿr al-jadīd*, Cairo, 1964.

Saʿāfīn (al-), Ibrāhim *Madrasat al-iḥyāʾ wa'l-turāth*, Beirut, 1981.

Saḥartī (al-), Muṣṭafā ʿAbd al-Laṭīf *Al-shiʿr al-muʿāṣir ʿalā ḍawʾ al-naqd al-ḥadīth*, Cairo, 1948.

Sāmarrāʾī (al-), Ibrāhīm *Lughat al-shiʿr bayna jīlayn*, Beirut, n.d.

Shahīd, ʿIrfān *Al-ʿawdah ilā Shawqī aw baʿda khamsīna ʿāman*, Beirut, 1986.

Ṭabānah, Badawī *Maʿrūf al-Ruṣāfī*, Cairo, 1957.

C. Secondary works in European languages

Arberry, Arthur J, *Modern Arabic poetry: an anthology with English verse translation*, London, 1950.

Badawi, M. M. *A critical introduction to modern Arabic poetry*, Cambridge, 1975.

'Al-Bārūdī: Precursor of the modern Arabic poetic revival', *Die Welt des Islams*, n.s., XII (1969), 228–45.

Boudot-Lamotte, Antoine *Aḥmad Šawqi: L'homme et l'oeuvre*, Damascus, 1977.

Jayyusi, Salma Khadra *Trends and movements in modern Arabic poetry*, Leiden, 1977.

Khouri, Munah *Poetry and the making of modern Egypt*, Leiden, 1971.

Moreh, S. *Modern Arabic poetry 1800–1970*, Leiden, 1976.

'The neo-classical *qaṣīda*: modern poets and critics', in von Grunebaum, G. E., ed., *Arabic poetry: theory and development*, Wiesbaden, 1973, pp. 155–79.
Somekh, Sasson *Genre and Language in modern Arabic literature*, Wiesbaden, 1991.
von Grunebaum, G. 'The response to nature in Arabic poetry', *Journal of Near Eastern Studies* IV (1945), pp. 137–51.

3: THE ROMANTIC POETS

A. Principal collections of poetry

Abū Māḍī, Īlyā *Tadhkār al-māḍī*, Alexandria, 1911.
Dīwān Īlyā Abū Māḍī, New York, 1919.
al-Jadāwil, New York, 1927.
al-Khamāʾil, Beirut, 1961.
Tibr wa turāb, Beirut, 1960.
Abū Shabakah, Ilyās *al-Qīthārah*, Beirut, 1926.
al-Marīḍ al-ṣāmit, Beirut, 1928.
Afāʿī 'l-firdaws, Beirut, 1938.
al-Alḥān, Beirut, 1941.
Nidāʾ al-qalb, Beirut, 1944.
Ilā 'l-abad, Beirut, 1944.
Ghalwāʾ, Beirut, 1945.
Min ṣaʿīd al-ālihah, Beirut, 1959.
Abū Shādī, Aḥmad Zakī *Andāʾ al-fajr*, 2nd edn, Cairo, 1934.
Zaynab, Cairo, 1924.
Miṣriyyāt,Cairo, 1924.
Anīn wa ranīn, Cairo, 1925.
al-Shafaq al-bākī, Cairo, 1926–27.
Ashiʿʿah wa ẓilāl, Cairo, 1931.
Aṭyāf al-rabīʿ, Cairo, 1933.
al-Shuʿlah, Cairo, 1933.
al-Yanbūʿ, Cairo, 1934.
Fawqa 'l-ʿubāb, Cairo, 1935.
ʿAwdat al-rāʿī, Alexandria, 1942.
Min al-samāʾ, New York, 1949.
al-ʿAqqād, ʿAbbās Maḥmūd *Dīwān al-ʿAqqād*, Cairo, 1928.
ʿĀbir sabīl, Cairo, 1937.
ʿArīḍah, Nasīb *al-Arwāḥ al-ḥāʾirah*, New York, 1946.
Ayyūb, Rashīd *al-Ayyūbiyyāt*, Beirut, 1959.
Aghānī 'l-darwīsh, Beirut, 1959.
Hiya 'l-dunyā, Beirut, 1959.
Farḥāt, Ilyās Ḥabīb *Aḥlām al-rāʿī*, 2nd edn, Beirut, 1962.
Ḥaddād. Nadrah *Awrāq al-kharīf*, New York, 1941.
Jibrān, Jibrān Khalīl *al-Majmūʿah al-kāmilah li muʾallafāt Jibrān Khalīl Jibrān*, (Introduction by M. Nuʿaymah), Beirut, 1959.

al-Khūrī, Rashīd Salīm *Dīwān al-Rashīdiyyāt*, Sao Paulo, 1916.
Dīwān al-qarawiyyāt, Sao Paulo, 1922.
al-Aʿāṣīr, Sao Paulo, 1933.
al-Maʿlūf, Fawzī *ʿAlā bisāṭ al-rīḥ*, Rio de Janeiro, 1929.
al-Māzinī, Ibrāhīm ʿAbd al-Qādir *Dīwān al-Māzinī*, vols I and II, Cairo, 1913, 1917.
Muṭrān, Khalīl *Dīwān al-Khalīl*, Cairo, 1908.
Dīwān al-Khalīl, vols I–IV, Cairo, 1949.
Nāgī (Nājī), Ibrāhīm *Dīwān Nāgī*, eds A. Rāmī, Ṣ. Jawdat, A. A. M. Haykal, and M. Nāgī, Cairo, 1961.
Nuʿaymah, Mīkhāʾīl *Hams al-jufūn*, 5th edn, Beirut, 1966.
al-Shābbī, Abū'l-Qāsim *Aghanī 'l-ḥayah*, Tunis, 1955.
Shukrī, ʿAbd al-Raḥmān *Dīwān ʿAbd al-Raḥmān Shukrī*, ed. Niqūlā Yūsuf, Alexandria, 1960.
Ṭāhā, ʿAlī Mahmūd *al-Mallāḥ al-tāʾih*, Cairo, 1934.
Layālī 'l-mallāḥ al-tāʾih, Cairo, 1940.
Arwāḥ wa ashbāḥ, Cairo, 1942.
Ughniyat al-riyāḥ al-arbaʿ, Cairo, 1943.
Zahr wa khamr, Cairo, 1943.
al-Shawq al-ʿāʾid, Cairo, 1945.

B. *Arabic sources*

ʿAbbās, Iḥsān with Muḥammad Yūsuf Najm *al-Shiʿr al-ʿArabī fī'l-mahjar: Amrīkā al-shamāliyyah*, Beirut, 1967.
ʿAbbūd Mārūn *Ruwwād al-nahḍah al-ḥadīthah*, Beirut, 1968.
Abū Shādī, Aḥmad Zakī *Qaḍāyā al-shiʿr al-muʿāṣir*, Cairo, 1959.
al-ʿAqqād, ʿAbbās Maḥmūd, with Ibrāhīm ʿAbd al-Qādir al-Māzinī *al-Dīwān: Kitāb fī'l naqd wa'l-adab*, Cairo, 1921.
al-ʿAqqād, ʿAbbās Maḥmūd *Shuʿarāʾ miṣr wa bīʾātuhum fī 'l-jīl al-māḍī*, Cairo, 1950.
Ayyūb, Suhayl *ʿAlī Maḥmūd Ṭāhā shiʿr wa dirāsah*, Damascus, 1962.
ʿAwaḍ, Lūwīs *Dirāsāt fī adabinā al-ḥadīth*, Cairo, 1961.
Badawī, Muḥammad Muṣṭafā *Dirāsāt fī'l-shiʿr wa'l-masraḥ*, Alexandria, 1979.
Bullāṭah, ʿĪsā Yūsif *al-Rūmanṭīqiyyah wa maʿālimuhā fī'l-shiʿr al-ʿarabī al-ḥadīth*, Beirut, 1960.
al-Dusūqī, ʿAbd al-ʿAzīz *Jamāʿat Apollo wa atharuhā fī'l-shiʿr al-ʿarabī al-ḥadīth*, Cairo, 1960.
Ḍayf, Shawqī *Dirāsāt fī'l-shiʿr al-ʿarabī al-ḥadīth*, Cairo, 1961.
Fuʾād, Niʿmāt Aḥmad *Adab al-Māzinī*, Cairo, 1961.
Haddārah, Muḥammad Muṣṭafā *al-Tajdīd fī shiʿr al-mahjar*, Cairo, 1957.
Ḥusayn, Ṭāhā *Ḥadīth al-arbaʿāʾ*, vols I–III, Cairo, n.d.
Jawdat, Ṣāliḥ *Nāgī, ḥayātuh wa shiʿruh*, Cairo, 1960.
Karam, Anṭūn Ghaṭṭās *Muḥāḍarāt fī Jibrān Khalīl Jibrān*, Cairo, 1964.
Karrū, Abū'l-Qāsim *al-Shābbī, ḥayātuh wa shiʿruh*, Beirut, 1954.
Āthār al-Shābbī wa ṣadāh fī'l-sharq, Beirut, 1961.

Mandūr, Muḥammad *al-Shiʿr al-miṣrī baʿda Shawqī*, vols I–III, Cairo, 1955–58.
Muḥāḍarāt ʿan Khalīl Muṭrān, Cairo, 1954.
Fī'l-mīzān al-jadīd, Cairo, n.d.
Mīrzā, Zuhayr, ed. *Īlyā Abū Māḍī, shāʿir al-mahjar al-akbar*, Damascus, 1963.
Nāgī, Ibrāhīm *Baudelaire wa qaṣāʾid min azhār al-sharr*, Cairo, 1954.
Nashʾat, Kamāl *Abū Shādī wa ḥarakat al-tajdīd fī'l-shiʿr al-ʿarabī'l-ḥadīth*, Cairo, 1967.
al-Nāʿūrī, ʿĪsā *Adab al-mahjar*, Cairo, 1958.
Nuʿaymah, Mīkhāʾīl *al-Ghirbāl*, Cairo, 1923.
Jibrān Khalīl Jibrān, Beirut, 1960.
Sabʿūn, vols I–III, Beirut, 1959–60.
al-Nuwayhī, Muḥammad *Qaḍiyyat al-shiʿr al-jadīd*, Cairo, 1964.
al-Ramādī, Jamāl al-Dīn *Khalīl Muṭrān, shāʿir al-aqṭār al-ʿarabiyyah*, Cairo, n.d.
Razzūq, Razzūq Faraj *Ilyās Abū Shabakah wa shiʿruh*, Beirut, 1956.
Ṣabrī, Muḥammad *Khalīl Muṭrān, arwaʿ mā katab*, Cairo, 1960.
Sarrāj, Nādira Jamīl *Nasīb ʿArīḍah, al-shāʿir al-kātib al-ṣuḥufī*, Cairo, 1970.
Shuʿarʾa al-rābiṭah al-qalamiyyah, Cairo, 1957.
Ṣaydaḥ, Jūrj *Adabunā wa udabāʾunā fī'l-mahājir al-amrīkiyyah*, Beirut, 1957.
al-Sayyid, Taqī al-Dīn *ʿAlī Maḥmūd Ṭāhā, ḥayātuh wa shiʿruh*, Cairo, 1963.
al-Shābbī, Abū'l-Qāsim *al-Khayāl al-shiʿrī ʿinda 'l-ʿArab*, Tunis, 1961.
Sharārah, ʿAbd al-Laṭīf *Īlyā Abū Māḍī*, Beirut, 1961.
Khalīl Muṭrān, Beirut, 1964.
Shukrī, ʿAbd al-Raḥmān *Kitāb al-iʿtirāf*, Alexandria, 1916.
Kitāb al-thamarāt, Alexandria, 1916.
Ṭāhā, ʿAlī Maḥmūd *Arwāḥ shāridah*, Cairo, 1941.

C. Sources in English

Abdul-Hai, Muhammad *Tradition and English and American influence in Arabic romantic poetry*, London, 1982.
Arberry, A. J. *Modern Arabic poetry* (Anthology with translations), Cambridge, 1967.
Badawi, M. M. *An Anthology of modern Arabic verse*, Oxford, 1970.
A critical introduction to modern Arabic poetry, Cambridge, 1975.
Bellamy, J. A., E. N. McCarus and Adil Yacoub *Contemporary Arabic readers, V, modern Arabic poetry*, Part 2, Ann Arbor, 1966.
Bushrui, Suheil *Gibran of Lebanon*, Gerrards Cross, 1987.
Coleridge, S. T. *Biographia Literaria*, London, 1906.
Edham, I. A. *Abushady the poet*, Leipzig, 1936.
Grunebaum, G. E. von, ed. *Arabic poetry, theory and development*, Wiesbaden, 1973.
Hawi, K. *Khalil Jibran: his background, character, and works*, Beirut, 1963.
Hazlitt, W. *Lectures on the English poets*, London, 1884.
Jayyusi, S. K. *Trends and movements in modern Arabic poetry*, Vols I and II, Leiden, 1977.
Khouri, M. A. *An anthology of modern Arabic poetry, selected, edited, and translated by Mounah A. Khouri and Hamid Algar*, Berkeley, 1975.

Poetry and the making of modern Egypt 1882–1922, Leiden, 1971.
Moreh, S. *Modern Arabic poetry 1800–1970*, Leiden, 1976.
Naimy, N. *Mikhail Naimy: an introduction*, Beirut, 1967.
Nijland, C. *Mikhāʾil Nuʿaymah: promoter of Arabic literary revival*, Istanbul, 1975.
Palgrave, F. T. *The golden treasury*, Oxford, 1935.
Wordsworth, W. *Preface to the lyrical ballads*, London, 1920.
Wordsworth, W. and S. T. Coleridge *The lyrical ballads*, London, 1952.

4: MODERNIST POETRY IN ARABIC

A. Arabic

ʿAbd al-Ṣabūr, Ṣalāḥ *Aqūlu lakum*, 2nd edn, Beirut, 1965.
Al-Majmūʿah al-kāmilah, Beirut, 1972.
Al-Nās fī bilādī, 2nd edn, Cairo, 1962.
Shajar al-layl, 2nd edn, Beirut, 1977.
ʿAbdallah, Ḥasan *Adhkuru annī aḥbabt*, Beirut, 1972.
Abī Shaqrā, Shawqī *Ḥayratī jālisah tuffāḥah ʿalā ʾl-ṭāwilah*, Beirut, 1983.
Khuṭuwāt al-malik, Beirut, 1960.
Yatbaʿ al-sāḥir wa yaksir al-sanābil rākiḍan, Beirut, 1979.
Adūnīs (ʿAlī Aḥmad Saʿīd) *Al-Aʿmāl al-shiʿriyyah al-kāmilah*, Beirut, 1971: a collection of his poetry to date including:
Aghānī Mihyār al-Dimashqī, 1st edn Beirut, 1961.
Kitāb al-taḥawwulāt wa ʾl-hijrah fī aqālīm al-nahār wa ʾl-layl, 1st edn Beirut, 1965.
Al-Masraḥ wa ʾl-marāyā, 1st edn Beirut, 1968.
Waqt bayn al-ramād wa ʾl-ward, Beirut, 1971.
Fī ʾl-shiʿriyyah al-ʿarabiyyah (A Study), Beirut, 1984.
Fātiḥah li nihāyāt al-qarn (Studies), Beirut, 1980.
Kitāb al-ḥiṣār, June 1981–June 1985, Beirut, 1985.
Kitāb al-qaṣāʾid al-khams, Beirut, 1979.
Mufrad bi ṣīghat al-jamʿ, Beirut, 1977.
Muqaddimah li ʾl-shiʿr al-ʿArabī (A Study), Beirut, 1971.
Shahwah tataqaddam fī kharāʾiṭ al-māddah, Casablanca, 1987.
Siyāsat al-shiʿr (Essays), Beirut, 1985.
Al-Thābit wa ʾl-mutaḥawwil: III ṣadmat al-ḥadāthah (A Study), Beirut, 1978.
Zaman al-shiʿr, Beirut, 1972.
Al-Asʿad, Muḥammad *Baḥthan ʿan al-ḥadāthah*, Beirut, 1986.
Al-Ghināʾ fī aqbiyah ʿamīqah, Baghdad, 1974.
Ḥāwaltu rasmaki fī jasad al-baḥr, n.p., n.d. (1976 or later).
Li sāḥiliki al-āna taʾtī ʾl-ṭuyūr, Beirut, n.d. (1979 or after).
Mamlakat al-amthāl, Beirut, 1986.
ʿAql, Saʿīd *Ajmalu minki? Lā!*, Beirut, 1960.
Kaʾsun li khamr, Beirut, 1961.
Al-Majdaliyyah, 2nd edn, Beirut, 1960, (first published 1937).
Al-ʿAẓm, Ṣādiq *Al-Istishrāq wa ʾl-istishrāq maʿkūsan*, Beirut, 1971.
Badawī, Muḥammad Muṣṭafā *Rasāʾil min London*, Alexandria, (1956?).

Bākathīr, ʿAlī Aḥmad *Akhnātūn wa Nefertītī*, Cairo, n.d.
Romeo wa Juliet, Cairo, 1943.
Barakāt, Salīm *Al-Majmūʿāt al-khams* (including *al-Karākī*, 1981), Beirut, 1981.
Bi 'l-shibāk dhātihā, bi 'l-thaʿālib al-latī taqūdu al-rīḥ, Beirut, 1987.
Al-Barghūthī, Murīd *Al-Ayyām al-ṣaʿbah*, Beirut, 1976.
Ṭāla 'l-shatāt, Beirut, 1987.
Bayḍūn, ʿAbbās *Al-Waqt bi jarʿāt kabīrah*, Beirut, 1982.
Zuwwār al-shatwati 'l-ūlā, Beirut, 1985.
Al-Bayyātī, ʿAbd al-Wahhāb *Al-Majmūʿah al-Kāmilah*, Beirut, 1971.
Ashʿār fī 'l-manfā, Cairo, 1957.
Kalimāt lā tamūt, Beirut, 1960.
Al-Majd li 'l-atfāl wa 'l-zaytūn, 2nd edn, Beirut, 1958.
Mamlakat al-sanābil, Beirut, 1979.
Al-Nār wa 'l-kalimāt, Beirut, n.d.
Sifr al-faqr wa 'l-thawrah, Beirut, 1965.
Bennīs, Muḥammad *Fī ittijāh ṣawtaki 'l-ʿamūdiyy*, Casablanca, 1980.
Hadāthat al-suʾāl (Essays on modernity), Casablanca, 1985.
Mawāsim al-sharq, Casablanca, 1985.
Shayʾ ʿan al-iṭṭihaḍ wa 'l-faraḥ, Fez, 1972.
Wajh mutawahhij ʿabra imtidād al-zaman, Fez, 1974.
Waraqat al-bahāʾ, Casablanca, 1988.
Būlus, Sargūn *Al-Ḥayāt qurb al-akrōpōl*, Casablanca, 1985.
Al-Wuṣūl ilā madīnat ayn, Attiki, 1985.
Al-Faytūri, Muḥammad *Sharq al-Shams, gharb al-qamar*, Rabat, 1987.
Gharīb, Samīr *Al-Suryāliyyah fī Misr*, Cairo, 1986.
Al-Ghuzzī, Muḥammad *Kitāb al-māʾ, kitāb al-jamr*, Tunis, 1982.
Gibrān, Gibrān Khalīl (Jibrān) *Al-ʿAwaṣif*, Cairo, 1920.
Dam ah wa ibtisāmah (a new edn), Beirut, 1962.
Ḥaddād, Qāsim *Al-Dam al-thāni*, Bahrain, 1976.
Al-Bishārah, 2nd edn, Kuwait, 1984 (1st edn 1970).
Al-Nahrawān, Bahrain, 1988.
Qalb al-ḥubb, Beirut, 1980.
Al-Qiyāmah, Beirut, 1980.
Shazāyā, Beirut, 1981.
Hāfiẓ, Yāsīn Ṭāhā *Al-Burj*, Baghdad, 1976.
Qaṣāʾid al-aʿrāf, Baghdad, 1974.
Qaṣāʾid al-sayyidah 'l-jamīlah, Baghdad, 1988.
Tamūt al-zuhūr tastayqiz al-afkār, Baghdad, 1986.
Al-Ḥāj, Unsī *Lan*, Beirut, 1960.
Mādhā ṣanaʿta bi 'l-dhahab, mādhā faʿalta bi 'l-wardah, Beirut, 1970.
Māḍī 'l-ayyām al-ʾātiyah, Beirut, 1965.
Al-Raʾs al-maqṭūʿ, Beirut, 1963.
Al-Rasūlah bi shaʿriha 'l-dhahabiyy, Beirut, 1975.
Ḥajjār, Bassām *Li arwī kaman yakhāfu an yarā*, Beirut, 1985.
Ḥāwī, Khalīl *Bayādir al-jūʿ*, Beirut, 1965.
Nahr al-ramād, 3rd edn, Beirut, 1963 (1st edn 1957).

Al-Nāy wa 'l-rīḥ, Beirut, 1961.

Ḥijāzī, Aḥmad ʿAbd al-Muʿṭī *Kāʾināt mamlakat al-layl*, Beirut, 1978.

Lam yabqa illa 'l-iʿtirāf, Beirut, 1965.

Madīnah bilā qalb, Beirut, 1959.

Jabrā, Jabrā Ibrāhīm (tr.) *Adonis, dirārsah fī 'l-asāṭīr wa 'l-adyān al-sharqiyyah al-qadīmah* , Beirut, 1957.

Al-Madār al-mughlaq, Beirut, 1964.

Tammūz fī 'l-madīnah, Beirut, 1959.

Al-Khāl, Yūsuf *Al-Biʾr al-mahjūrah*, Beirut, 1958.

Dafātir al-ayyām, London, 1987.

Al-Ḥadāthah fī 'l shiʿr (Essays), Beirut, 1987.

Qaṣāʾid fī 'l-arbaʿīn, Beirut, 1960.

Khāzindār, Walīd *Afʿāl muḍāriʿah*, Beirut, 1987.

Al-Māghūṭ, Muḥammad *Al-Āthar al-kāmilah*, Beirut, 1973 (including his first, *Ḥuzn fī ḍawʾ al-qamar*, 1959, *Ghurfah bi malāyīn al-judrān* and *Al-faraḥ laysa mihnatī*).

Mahdī, Sāmī *Al-Aʿmāl al-shiʿriyyah, 1965–1985*, Baghdad, 1986, including: *Al-Asʾilah* (1979); *Al-Zawāl* (1981).

Maḥfūẓ, ʿIṣām *Al-Suryāliyyah wa tafāʿulātuha 'l-ʿarabiyyah* (A Study), Beirut, 1987.

Al-Sayf wa burj al-ʿadhrāʾ, Beirut, 1963.

Al-Malāʾikah, Nāzik *Qaḍāyā 'l-shiʿr al-muʿāṣir* (Essays), Beirut, 1962.

Qarārat al-mawjah, Beirut, 1960.

Shajarat al-qamar, Beirut, 1968.

Shaẓāyā wa ramād, 2nd edn, Beirut, 1959.

Yughayyiru alwānahu 'l-baḥr, Baghdad, 1977.

Manṣūr, Khayrī *Ẓilāl*, Baghdad, 1986.

Maṭar, Muḥammad ʿAfīfī *Anta wāḥiduhā wa hiya aʿḍāʾuka intatharat*, Baghdad, 1986.

Shahādat al-bukāʾ fī zaman al-ḍaḥik, Beirut, 1973.

Muyassar, Urkhān and ʿAlī al-Nāṣir *Siryāl*, Aleppo, 1947.

Nāṣir, Amjad *Madīḥ li maqhā ākhar*, Beirut, 1979.

Ruʿāt al-ʿuzlah, Amman, 1986.

Qāṣid, ʿAbd al-Karīm *Al-Ḥaqāʾib*, Beirut, 1975.

Al-Shāhidah, Beirut, 1987.

Raḥabī, Sayf *Ajrās al-qaṭīʿah*, Paris, 1984.

Nawrasat al-junūn, Damascus, n.d.

Riyādh, Ṭāhir *Al-ʿAṣā 'l-ʿarjāʾ*, Amman, 1988.

Saʿīd, Ḥamīd *Ḥarāʾiq al-ḥuḍūr*, Beirut, 1978.

Qirāʾah thāminah Beirut, 1972.

Ṭufūlat al-māʾ, Baghdad, 1985.

Al-Ṣāʾigh, Yūsuf *Sayyidat al-tuffāḥāt al-arbaʿ*, Baghdad, 1976.

Ṣāyigh, Tawfīq *Muʿallaqat Tawfīq Ṣāyigh*, Beirut, 1963.

Al-Qaṣīdah kāf, Beirut, 1960.

Thalathūn qaṣīdah, Beirut, 1954.

Al-Sayyāb, Badr Shākir *Al-Majmūʿah al-kāmilah*, Beirut, 1971 (includes his *Unshūdat al-maṭar*, first published in Beirut, 1960).

Al-Shaykh Jaʿfar, Ḥasab *ʿAbra 'l-ḥāʾiṭ fī 'l-mirʾāh*, Baghdad, 1977.

Ziyārat al-sayyidah 'l-Sūmariyyah, Baghdad, 1974.
Al-Wahāybi, Munṣif *Alwāḥ*, Tunis, 1982.
Yūsuf, Saʿdī *Al-Aʿmāl al-shiʿriyyah, 1952–1977*, Beirut, 1979, including:
Al-Akhḍar Ben Yūsuf wa mashāghiluhu, (1972);
Al-Layālī kulluhā, (1976);
Al-Sāʿah 'l-akhīrah, (1977).
Afkār bi ṣawt hādiʾ, Beirut, 1987.
Kaifa kataba 'l-Akhḍar Ben Yūsuf qaṣīdatahu 'l-jadīdah, Beirut, 1978.
Qaṣāʾid aqall ṣamtan, Beirut, 1979.
Al-Yūsufī, Muḥammad ʿAlī *Ḥāffat al-arḍ*, Beirut, 1988.
Zaqṭān, Ghassān *Buṭūlat al-ashyāʾ*, Beirut, 1988.

B. *English critical studies and anthologies*

Abd al-Sabur, Salah *A journey at night*, tr. Samar Attar, Cairo, 1970.
Murder in Baghdad, tr. Khalil Samaan, Leiden, 1972.
Abdul-Hai, Muhammad *Tradition and English and American Influence in Arabic romantic poetry*, London, 1982.
Adunis *The Blood of Adonis*, tr. Samuel Hazo, Pittsburgh, 1971.
The transformation of the lover, tr. S. Hazo, Ohio, 1983.
Aruri, Naseer and Ghareeb, Edmund, eds *Enemy of the Sun, poetry of Palestinian resistance*, Washington, 1970.
Asfour, John Mikhail *When the words burn, an anthology of modern Arabic poetry 1945–1987*, Ontario, 1988.
al-Asmar, Fauzi *Poems from an Israeli prison*, tr. and ed. Jawad Buraq *et al.* New York, 1973.
Badawi, M. M. *A critical introduction to modern Arabic poetry*, Cambridge, 1975.
al-Bayati, Abd al-Wahhab *Lilies and death*, tr. Mohamed Alwan, Baghdad, 1972.
Eye of the Sun, tr. Desmond Stewart *et al.*, Copenhagen, 1978.
Love under the rain, tr. Desmond Stewart and George Masri, Madrid, 1985.
Bennani, B., ed. and tr. *Bread, hashish and moon: four modern Arab poets*, Greensboro, 1982.
Boullata, Issa, ed. and tr. *Modern Arab poets 1950–1975*, Washington, 1976.
ed. *Critical perspectives on modern Arabic literature 1945–1980*, Washington, 1980.
Boullata, Kamal, ed. *Women of the Fertile Crescent: Modern poetry by Arab women*, Washington, 1978.
Boullata, Kamal and Ghossein, Mirene, eds *The World of Rashid Hussein*, Detroit, 1979.
Darwish, Mahmud *A lover from Palestine and other poems*, ed. and tr. A. W. Elmessiri, Washington, 1970.
Selected poems, tr. Ian Wedde & Fawwaz Tuqan, Cheshire, 1973.
Splinters of bone, tr. B. M. Bennani, New York, 1974.
The music of human flesh, tr. Denis Johnson-Davies, London, 1980.
Sand and other poems, tr. Rana Kabbani, London, 1986.
Elmessiri, A. W., ed. and tr. *The Palestinian wedding*, Washington, 1982.
Enani, M. M. *An anthology of new Arabic poetry*, Cairo, 1986.

Hawi, Khalil *Naked in exile, the threshing floors of hunger*, tr. Adnan Haydar and Michael Beard, Washington, 1984.
al-Haydari, Buland *Songs of the tired guard*, tr. Abdullah al-Udhari, London, 1977.
Hazo, Samuel, ed. *Mundus artium*, special Arabic issue, Vol. X, No. 1 (1977).
Jayyusi, Salma Khadra *Trends and movements in modern Arabic poetry*. Vol. II, Leiden, 1977.
ed. *Modern Arabic poetry, an anthology*, New York, 1987.
ed. *Literature of modern Arabia, an anthology*, London, 1988.
Khouri, Mounah A. and Algar, Hamid, tr. *An anthology of modern Arabic poetry*, Berkeley, 1974.
Lu'lu'a, Abdul Wahid, tr. *Modern Iraqi poetry*, Baghdad, 1989.
Megally, Shafik, tr. *Arabic poetry of resistance: an anthology*, Cairo, 1970.
Moreh, S. *Modern Arabic poetry, 1800–1970*, Leiden, 1976.
Ostle, R. C., ed. *Studies in modern Arabic literature*, Middlesex, 1976.
Stewart, Desmond *Poet of Iraq: Abdul Wahab al-Bayati: an introductory essay with translations*, London, 1976.
Sulaiman, Khalid A. *Palestine and modern Arab poetry*, London, 1984.
al-Udhari, Abdullah, tr. *A mirror for autumn: modern Arab poetry*, London, 1974.
tr. *Victims of a map*, London, 1984.
ed. and tr. *Modern poetry of the Arab world*, London, 1986.

5: THE BEGINNINGS OF THE ARABIC NOVEL

6: THE MATURE ARABIC NOVEL OUTSIDE EGYPT

A. Authors and works discussed (with translations where available)

Abū Shāwir, Rashād [Pal.] *Al-ʿUshshāq* (The lovers), 1977.
Anṭūn, Faraḥ [Leb.] *Al-Ḥubb ḥattā al-mawt* (Love till death), 1898.
Al-ʿIlm wa'l-dīn wa'l-māl (Science, religion and money), 1905.
Ūrishalīm al-jadīdah aw fatḥ al-ʿArab bayt al-maqdis (New Jerusalem or the conquest of the Holy City), 1904.
Al-Waḥsh, al-waḥsh, al-waḥsh, 1903.
al-ʿArwī, ʿAbdallāh [Mor.] *Al-Ghurbah* (Exile), 1971.
al-Ashqar, Yūsuf Ḥabashī [Leb.] *La tanbut judhūr fī 'l-samāʾ* (Roots do not grow in heaven), 1971.
ʿAwwād, Tawfīq Yūsuf [Leb.] *Al-Raghīf* (The loaf), 1939.
Ṭawāḥīn Bayrūt (The mills of Bayrut), 1972; tr. into English by Leslie McLoughlin as *Death in Beirut*, 1976.
Ayyūb, Dhū 'l-Nūn [Irq.] *Al-Duktūr Ibrāhīm* (Dr Ibrahim), 1939.
Al-Yad wa'l-arḍ wa'l-māʾ (Hand, earth and water), 1948.
Baʿalbakī, Laylā [Leb.] *Anā aḥyā* (I am alive), 1964.
Al-Ālihah al-mamsūkhah (Deformed deities), 1965.
Barakāt, Ḥalīm [Syr./Leb.] *ʿAwdat al-ṭāʾir ilā 'l-baḥr* (The flying Dutchman's return to the sea), 1969; tr. Trevor Le Gassick as *Days of Dust*, 1974).
Sittat ayyām (Six days), 1961.
al-Bustānī, Saʿīd [Leb.] *Dhāt al-khidr* (Lady of the boudoir), 1884.

al-Bustānī, Salīm [Leb] *Al-Huyām fī jinān al-Shām* (Passion in Syrian gardens), 1870.
Dabbāgh, Ghānim [Irq.] *Ḍajjah fī 'l-zuqāq* (Din in the alley), 1972.
al-Dūᶜājī, ᶜAlī [Tun.] *Jawlah ḥawla ḥānāt al-baḥr al-abyaḍ al-mutawassiṭ* (A tour of Mediterranean taverns), 1935.
Faḍl, Al-Sirr Ḥasan [Sud.] *Min ajl Laylā* (For Layla's sake), 1960.
Farmān, Ghāʾib Ṭuᶜmah [Irq.] *Khamsat aṣwāt* (Five voices), 1967.
al-Nakhlah wa'l-jīrān (The palm tree and the neighbours), 1966.
Fayḍī, Sulaymān (al-Mawṣilī) [Irq.] *Al-Riwāyah al-Īqāẓiyyah* (The story of *al-Īqāẓ* awakening?), 1919.
Fayyāḍ, Tawfīq [Pal.] *Majmūᶜat 778* (778 Group), 1974.
Ghallāb, ᶜAbd al-Karīm [Mor.] *Dafannā 'l-māḍī* (We have buried the past), 1966.
Sabᶜat abwāb (Seven gates), 1965.
Ḥabībī, Emīl [Pal.] *Sudāsiyyat al-ayyām al-sittah* (Sextet on the six days), 1968.
Al-Waqāʾiᶜ al-gharībah fī-ikhtifāʾ Saᶜīd Abī 'l-naḥs al-mutashāʾil, 1972/74; tr. into English by Trevor Le Gassick and Salma Khadra al-Jayyusi as *The secret life of Saeed, the ill-fated pessoptimist*, 1982).
Ḥaddād, Niqūlā [Leb.] *Asīrat al-ḥubb* (Prisoner of love), n.d.
Fātinat al-imperator (Enchantress of the emperor), 1922.
Ḥawwāʾ al-jadīdah (Modern Eve), 1906.
Ḥaqqī, Maḥmūd Ṭāhir [Eg.] *ᶜAdhrāʾ Dinshawāy* (The virgin of Dinshaway), 1907; tr. Saad El-Gabalawy in *Three pioneering Egyptian novels*, 1986.
Haykal, Muḥammad Ḥusayn [Eg.] *Zaynab*, 1913.
Ḥijāzī, ᶜAbd al-Nabī [Syr.] *Qārib al-zamān* (The boat of time), 1970.
Al-Sindīyānah (The oak tree), 1971.
Ḥūḥū, Aḥmad Riḍā [Alg.] *Ghādat Umm al-Qurā* (The maid of the city), 1947.
ibn Hadūqah, ᶜAbd al-Ḥamīd [Alg.] *Rīḥ al-janūb* (South wind), 1971.
ibn Jallūn, ᶜAbd al-Majīd [Mor.] *Fī 'l-ṭufūlah* (In childhood), 1957.
Ibrāhīm, Ḥāfiz [Eg.] *Layālī Saṭīḥ* (Nights of Saṭīḥ), 1906.
Idrīs, Suhayl [Leb.] *Al-Ḥayy al-Lātīnī* (The Latin quarter), 1953.
Al-Khandaq al-ghamīq (The deep trench), 1958.
Ikhlāṣī, Walīd [Syr.] *Shitāʾ al-baḥr al-yābis* (Winter of the dry sea), 1965.
Aḥzān al-ramād (Sorrows of ashes), 1979.
Ismāᶜīl, Ismāᶜīl Fahd [Kuw.] *Al-Mustanqaᶜāt al-ḍawʾiyyah* (Light swamps), 1972.
Ismāᶜīl, Ṣidqī [Syr.] *Al-ᶜUsāt* (The rebels), 1964.
al-Jābirī, Shakīb [Syr.] *Naham* (Greed), 1937.
Qadar yalhū (Fate at play), 1939.
Qaws quzaḥ (Rainbow), 1946.
Jabrā, Jabrā Ibrāhīm [Pal.] *Al-Baḥth ᶜan Walīd Masᶜūd* (In search of Walīd Masᶜūd), 1978.
Al-Ghuraf al-ukhrā (The other rooms) 1986.
Al-Safīnah (*The ship*), 1969; tr. into English by Adnan Haydar and Roger Allen, 1985.
and ᶜAbd al-Raḥmān Munīf [Sau.] *ᶜĀlam bi-lā kharāʾiṭ* (Mapless world), 1983.
Jibrān, Jibrān Khalīl [Leb.] *Al-Ajniḥah al-mutakassirah* (Broken wings), 1912.

Al-Arwāḥ al-mutamarridah (Spirits rebellious), 1908.

Jumʿah, Muḥammad Luṭfī [Eg.] *Layālī 'l-rūḥ al-ḥāʾir* (Nights of the perplexed spirit), 1912.

Kanafānī, Ghassān [Pal.] *Mā tabaqqā lakum* (What remains for you), 1966, tr. into English by May Jayyusi and Jeremy Reed, 1990.

Rijāl fī 'l-shams (Men in the sun), 1963; tr. into English by Hilary Kilpatrick, 1978.

Kayyālī, Ḥasīb [Syr.] *Makātīb al-gharām* (Love letters), 1957.

Khālid, Abū Bakr [Sud.] *Bidāyat al-rabīʿ* (The beginning of spring), 1958.

Khalīfa, Saḥar [Pal.] *Al-Ṣubār* (Wild thorns), 1976; tr. into English by Trevor Le Gassick and Elizabeth Fernea, 1985.

Khalīl, Badawī ʿAbd al-Qādir [Sud.] *Hāʾim ʿalā 'l-arḍ aw rasāʾil al-ḥirmān* (Roaming the earth or letters of deprivation), 1954.

Khurayyif, Al-Bashīr [Tun.] *Barq al-layl* (Night lightning), 1961.

Khūrī, Colette [Syr.] *Ayyām maʿahu* (Days with him), 1959.

Khūrī, Ilyās [Leb.] *Al-Jabal al-ṣaghīr* (The small mountain), 1977, tr. into English by Maia Tabet, 1989.

Abwāb al-madīnah (City gates), 1981.

Khūrī, Nabīl [Pal.] *Ḥārat al-Naṣārā* (The Christian quarter), 1969.

Al-Raḥīl (The departure), 1969.

al-Manfalūṭī, Muṣṭafā Luṭfī [Eg.] *Al-Naẓarāt*, 1910; selections tr. Nevill Barbour in *Islamic Culture* between 1933 and 1936.

Marrāsh, Faransīs [Leb.] *Durr al-ṣadaf fī gharāʾib al-ṣudaf* (Quirks of fate), 1872.

Ghābat al-ḥaqq (The forest of truth), 1865.

al-Masʿadī, Maḥmūd (Tun.] *Al-Sudd* (The dam), 1955.

al-Middīnī, Aḥmad [Mor.] *Zaman bayna 'l-wilādah wa'l-ḥulm* (Time between birth and dream), 1976.

Midfaʿī, Walīd [Syr.] *Ghurabāʾ fī awṭāninā* (Strangers in our own country), 1974.

Mīnah, Ḥannā [Syr.] *Al-Maṣābīḥ al-zurq* (Blue lamps), 1954.

Al-Shams fī yawm ghāʾim (Sun on a cloudy day), 1973.

Al-Shirāʿ wa'l-ʿāṣifah (The sail and the storm), 1966.

Al-Thalj yaʾtī min al-nāfidhah (The snow comes through the window), 1969.

al-Muʾaqqit, Muḥammad ibn ʿAbdallāh [Mor.] *Al-Riḥlah al-Marākushiyyah aw mirʾāt al-masāʾil al-waqtiyyah* (Marrakesh journey, or, Mirror of problems of the time), 1920s.

Mubārak, ʿAlī [Eg.] *ʿAlam al-dīn*, 1881–82.

Munīf, ʿAbd al-Raḥmān [Sau.] *Al-Ashjār wa'ghtiyāl Marzūq* (The trees and Marzuq's assassination), 1973.

Ḥīna taraknā 'l-jisr (When we abandoned the bridge), 1976.

Al-Nihāyāt (*Endings*), 1978; tr. into English by Roger Allen, 1988.

Sharq al-Mutawassiṭ (East of the Mediterranean), 1977; tr. into French by Kadhem Jihad as *A l'Est du méditerranée*, 1985).

Muṣṭafā, Shākir [Sud.] *Ḥattā taʿūd* (Till she returns), 1959.

al-Muwayliḥī, Ibrāhīm [Eg.] *Mirʾāt al-ʿālam aw Ḥadīth Mūsā ibn ʿIṣām* (Mirror of the world, or, The story of Mūsā ibn ʿIṣām), 1902; tr. into German by G. Widmer

in *Die Welt des Islams*, N.S., 3 (1954), pp. 57 ff.
al-Muwayliḥī, Muḥammad [Eg.] *Ḥadīth ᶜĪsā ibn Hishām* (The story of ᶜĪsā ibn Hishām), 1907; tr. by Roger Allen in *Ḥadīth ᶜĪsā ibn Hishām, Al-Muwayliḥī's study of Egypt During the British Occupation*, Albany, 1974.
Naḥawī, Adīb [Syr.] *Matā yaᶜūd al-maṭar* (When the rain returns), 1960.
Naṣrallāh, Emily [Leb.] *Ṭuyūr Aylūl* (September birds), 1962.
Tilka al-dhikrayāt (Those memories), 1978.
Naṣrallāh, Ibrāhīm [Pal.] *Barārī al-ḥummā* (Fever prairies), 1985.
Nuᶜaymah, Mīkhāʾīl [Leb.] *Mudhakkirāt al-arqash*, 1949; tr. as *The memoirs of a vagrant soul or the pitted face*, 1952.
Rabīᶜ, Mubārak [Mor.] *Al-Ṭayyibūn* (The good folk), 1972.
al-Rāhib, Hānī [Syr.] *Al-Mahzūmūn* (The defeated), 1961.
Sharkh fī tārīkh ṭawīl (Crack in a long history), 1969.
al-Rubayᶜī, ᶜAbd al-Raḥmān [Irq.] *Al-Washm* (The tattoo), 1972.
Ṣafadī, Muṭāᶜ [Syr.] *Jīl al-qadar* (Generation of fate), 1960.
Thāʾir muḥtarif (Professional revolutionary), 1961.
Ṣāliḥ, Al-Ṭayyib [Sud.] *Mawsim al-hijrah ilā 'l-shamāl* (*Season of migration to the north*), 1966; tr. Denys Johnson-Davies, 1969.
Sālim, Jūrj [Syr.] *Fī 'l-manfā* (In exile), 1962.
al-Sammān, Ghādah [Syr.] *Kawābīs Bayrūt* (Beirut nightmares), 1976.
Ṣarrūf, Yaᶜqūb [Leb.] *Amīr Lubnān* (Prince of Lebanon), 1907.
Fatāt al-Fayyūm (Maid of Fayyum), 1908.
Fatāt Miṣr (Maid of Egypt), 1905.
al-Sayyid, Maḥmūd Aḥmad [Irq.] *Jalāl Khālid*, 1928.
al-Shaykh, Ḥanān [Leb.], *Ḥikāyat Zahrah*, 1980; *The Story of Zahra*, tr. into English by the author and Peter Ford, 1986.
al-Shidyāq, Aḥmad Fāris [Leb.] *Al-Sāq ᶜalā 'l-sāq fīmā huwa 'l-Fāriyāq*, 1855.
Shinār, Amīn [Pal.] *Al-Kābūs* (The nightmare), 1968.
al-Sibāᶜī, Al-Bakrī Aḥmad [Mor.] *Bawtaqat al-ḥayāh* (Life's crucible), 1966.
al-Sibāᶜī, Fāḍil [Syr.] *Thumma azhara 'l-ḥuzn* (Then sadness bloomed), 1963.
Sulaymān, Nabīl [Syr.] *Al-Sijn* (Prison), 1972.
al-Ṭahṭāwī, Rifāᶜah Rāfiᶜ [Eg.] *Takhlīṣ al-ibrīz ilā talkhīṣ Bārīz*, 1834–35.
al-Tāzī, Muḥammad ᶜIzz al-Dīn [Mor.] *Abrāj al-madīnah* (City towers), 1978.
ᶜUdwān, Mamdūḥ [Syr.] *Al-Abtar* (Flawed), 1970.
ᶜUsayrān, Laylā [Leb/Eg] *ᶜAṣāfīr al-fajr* (Dawn birds), 1968.
Waṭṭār, Al-Ṭāhir (Alg.] *Al-Ḥawwāt wa'l-qaṣr* (The fisherman and the palace), 1978.
Al-Lāz (the name of the hero), 1974.
Al-Lāz, al-ᶜishq wa'l-mawt fī 'l-zaman al-ḥarāshī (Al-Lāz: Love and death in rough times), 1982.
Al-Zilzāl (The earthquake), 1974.
Yakhlaf, Yaḥyā [Pal.] *Tuffāḥ al-majānīn* (Apples of the insane), n.d.
al-Yāzijī, Nāṣīf [Leb.Eg.] *Majmaᶜ al-baḥrayn*, 1856.
Zarzūr, Fāris [Syr.] *Ḥasan Jabal*, 1969.
Al-Ḥufāt (Without shoes), 1971.
Lan tasquṭ al-madīnah (The city will not fall), 1969.

Al-Mudhnibūn (Sinners), 1974.
Zaydān, Jurjī [Leb./Eg.] *Armanūsah al-Miṣriyyah*, 1889.
Al-Ḥajjāj ibn Yūsuf, 1909.
Istibdād al-Mamālīk (Mamlūk tyranny), 1893.
Shajarat al-Durr, 1914.
Zayn, Amīn Muḥammad [Sud.] *Liqāʾ ʿinda al-ghurūb* (Meeting at sunset), 1963.
Zifzāf, Muḥammad [Mor.] *Al-Marʾah wa'l-wardah* (The Woman and the rose), 1972.

B. Major secondary sources

The combination of limited space and breadth of topic has required the elimination of footnotes in chapters 5 and 6. The following represents a listing of the *principal* sources consulted:

General

(i) In Arabic

ʿAbdallāh, Muḥammad Ḥasan *Al-Wāqiʿiyyah fī 'l-riwāyah al-ʿArabiyyah*, Cairo, 1971.
Abū Nāḍir, Maurice *Al-Alsuniyyah wa'l-naqd al-adabī fī 'l-naẓariyyah wa'l-mumārasah*, Beirut, 1979.
Al-ʿAdwān, Amīnah *Maqālāt fī 'l-riwāyah al-ʿArabiyyah al-muʿāṣirah*, 1976.
Al-ʿĀnī, Shujāʾ Muslim *Al-Riwāyah al-ʿArabiyyah wa'l-ḥaḍārah 'l-Ūrubbiyyah*, Baghdād, 1979.
Al-Ashtar, ʿAbd al-Karīm *Dirāsāt fī adab al-nakbah*, Damascus, 1975.
ʿAṭiyyah, Aḥmad Muḥammad *Al-Baṭal al-thawrī fī 'l-riwāyah al-ʿArabiyyah*, Damascus, 1977.
Al-ʿAwf, Najīb *Darajat al-waʿy fī 'l-kitābah*, Dār al-Bayḍā, 1980.
ʿAyyād, Shukrī 'Al-Riwāyah al-ʿArabiyyah al-muʿāṣirah wa-azmat al-ḍamīr al-ʿArabī', *ʿĀlam al-fikr* Vol. 3 no. 3 (Oct–Dec. 1972), pp. 619–48.
Barrādah, Muḥammad *Al-Riwāyah al-ʿArabiyyah*, Beirut, 1981.
Al-Fayyūmī, Ibrāhīm Ḥusayn ʿAbd al-Hādī *Al-Wāqiʿiyyah fī 'l-riwāyah al-ʿArabiyyah al-ḥadīthah fī bilād al-Shām*, ʿAmmān, 1983.
Ḥāfiẓ, Ṣabrī 'Maʾsāt Filasṭīn fī 'l-riwāyah al-ʿArabiyyah al-muʿāṣirah', *Al-Ādāb* 4 (1964).
Hilāl, Muḥammad Ghunaymī 'Al-muʾaththirāt al-gharbiyyah fī ʾl-riwāyah al-ʿArabiyyah', *Al-Ādāb* (Mar. 1963).
Al-Khaṭīb, Muḥammad Kāmil *Al-Mughāmarah al-muʿaqqadah*, Damascus, 1976.
Khūrī, Ilyās *Tajribat baḥth ʿan ufq*, Beirut, 1974.
Māḍī, Shukrī ʿAzīz *Inʿikās haẓīmat Ḥuẓayrān ʿalā 'l-riwāyah al-ʿArabiyyah*, Beirut, 1978.
Maḥfūẓ, ʿIṣām *Al-Riwāyah al-ʿArabiyyah al-ṭalīʿiyyah*, Beirut, 1982.
Muraydan, ʿAzīzah *Al-Qiṣṣah wa'l-riwāyah*, Damascus, 1980.
Al-Mūsawī, Muḥsin Jāsim *Al-Mawqif al-thawrī fī 'l-riwāyah al-ʿArabiyyah al-muʿāṣirah*, Baghdad, 1975.

Al-Nassāj, Sayyid Ḥāmid *Panorama al-riwāyah al-ᶜArabiyyah al-ḥadītha*, Beirut, 1982.

Qāsim, Qāsim ᶜAbduh and Ḥamīd Ibrāhīm al-Hawārī *Al-Riwāyah al-tārīkhiyyah fī 'l-adab al-ᶜArabī 'l-ḥadīth*, Cairo, 1977.

Al-Riwāyah al-ᶜArabiyyah: Wāqiᶜ wa-āfāq, n.p., 1981.

Al-Rubayᶜī, ᶜAbd al-Raḥmān Majīd *Al-Shāṭiʾ al-jadīd: qirāʾah fī kuttāb al-qiṣṣah al-ᶜArabiyyah*, Tunis, 1983.

Al-Saᶜāfīn, Ibrāhīm ᶜAbd al-Raḥmān Saᶜd *Taṭawwur al-riwāyah al-ᶜArabiyyah al-ḥadīthah fī 'l-Shām*, Baghdad, 1980.

Sālim, Jūrj *Al-Mughāmarah al-riwāʾiyyah*, Damascus, 1973.

Shukrī, Ghālī *Al-Riwāyah al-ᶜArabiyyah fī riḥlat ᶜadhāb*, Cairo, 1971.

Azmat al-jins fī 'l-qiṣṣah al-ᶜArabiyyah, Cairo, 1971.

Ṭarābīshī, Jūrj *Ramziyyat al-marʾah fī 'l-riwāyah al-ᶜArabiyyah*, Beirut, 1981.

Sharq wa-gharb: Rujūlah wa-unūthah, Beirut, 1977.

Ṭarrāzī, Philip de *Tārīkh al-ṣaḥāfah al-ᶜArabiyyah*, Vols 1–3, Beirut, 1913; Vol. 4, Beirut, 1933.

(ii) In European languages

Allen, Roger *The Arabic novel: an historical and critical introduction*, Syracuse, 1982.

ed. *Modern Arabic literature* Library of Literary Criticism Series, New York, 1987.

Badawi, M. M. *Modern Arabic literature and the west*, London, 1985.

Barakat, Halim *Visions of social reality in the contemporary Arab novel*, Georgetown, 1977.

Gibb H. A. R. *Studies on the civilization of Islam*, London, 1962.

Hafez, Sabry 'The state of the contemporary Arabic novel: some reflections', *The Literary Review*, Supplement on the Arabic Cultural Scene (June 1982), pp. 17–24.

Hartmann, M. P. W. *The Arabic press in Egypt*, London, 1899.

Hourani, Albert *Arabic thought in the Liberal Age*, London, 1962.

Monroe, James T. *The art of Badīᶜ az-Zamān al-Hamadhānī as picaresque narrative*, Beirut, 1983.

Moosa, Matti *The origins of modern Arabic fiction*, Washington, 1983, pp. 147–53.

Pérès, Henri 'Le roman, le conte et la nouvelle dans la littérature arabe moderne', *Annales de l'Institut des Études Orientales* 3 (1937), pp. 266 ff.; 5 (1939–41), pp. 137 ff.

'Le roman historique dans la littérature arabe', *Annales de l'Institut des Études Orientales* 15 (1957), pp. 5 ff.

Philipp, Thomas *Gurgi Zaidan, his life and thought*, Beirut and Wiesbaden, 1979.

Siddiq, Muhammad 'The contemporary Arabic novel in perspective', *World Literature Today* (Spring 1986), pp. 206–11.

Wieland, Rotraud *Das Bild der Europaer in der modernen arabischen Erzahl- und Theaterliteratur*, Beirut, 1980.

Algeria

Maṣāyif, Muḥammad *Al-Riwāyah al-ᶜArabiyyah al-Jazāʾiriyyah al-ḥadīthah bayna al-wāqiᶜiyyah wa'l-iltizām*, Algiers, 1983.

Rakībī, ᶜAbdallāh *Al-Nathr al-Jazā'irī al-ḥadīth*, Cairo, 1976.

Egypt: (i) In Arabic

Badr, ᶜAbd al-Muḥsin Ṭāhā *Taṭawwur al-riwāyah al-ᶜArabiyyah al-ḥadīthah fī Miṣr 1870–1938*, Cairo, 1963.

Wādī, Ṭāha *Sūrat al-mar'ah fī 'l-riwāyah al-muᶜāṣirah*, Cairo, 1980.

Egypt: (ii) In European languages

Allen, Roger *Ḥadīh ᶜĪsā ibn Hishām, Al-Muwayliḥī's study of Egypt during the British occupation*, Albany, 1974.

Brugman, J. *An introduction to the history of modern Arabic literature in Egypt*, Leiden, 1984.

Elkhadem, Saad *History of the Egyptian novel: its rise and early beginnings*, Fredericton, New Brunswick, 1985.

Fontaine, Jean 'Le nouveau roman égyptien 1975–1985', *IBLA* Vol. 49 no. 158 (1986), pp. 215–61.

Jad, Ali B, *Form and technique in the Egyptian novel 1912–71*, London, 1983.

Kilpatrick, Hilary *The modern Egyptian novel*, London, 1974.

Sakkut, Hamdi *The Egyptian novel and its main trends 1913–1952*, Cairo, 1971.

Tomiche, Nada *Histoire de la littérature romanesque de l'Egypte moderne*, Paris, 1981.

Iraq

Aḥmad, ᶜAbd al-Ilāh *Nash'at al-qiṣṣah wa taṭawwuruhā fī 'l-ᶜIrāq*, Baghdad, 1979.

Amīn, ᶜAbd al-Qādir Ḥasan *Al-Qaṣaṣ fī 'l-adab al-ᶜIrāqī al-ḥadīth*, Baghdad, 1956.

ᶜIzz al-dīn, Yūsuf *Al-Riwāyah fī 'l-ᶜIrāq: taṭawwuruhā wa-athar al-fikr fīhā*, Cairo, 1973.

Al-Qiṣṣah fī 'l-ᶜIrāq: judhūruhā wa taṭawwuruhā, Cairo, 1974.

Al-Khalīlī, Jaᶜfar *Al-Qiṣṣah al-ᶜIrāqiyyah qadīman wa-ḥadīthan*, Beirut, 1962.

Saᶜīd, Jamīl *Naẓārāt fī 'l-tayyārāt al-adabiyyah al-ḥadīthah fī 'l-ᶜIrāq*, Cairo, 1954.

Al-Ṭāhir, ᶜAlī Jawād *Fī 'l-qaṣaṣ al-ᶜIrāqī al-muᶜāṣir*, Beirut, 1967.

Maḥmūd Aḥmad al-Sayyid, rā'id al-qiṣṣah al-ḥadīthah fī 'l-ᶜIrāq, Beirut, 1969.

Al-Ṭālib, ᶜUmar *Al-Ittijāh al-wāqiᶜī fī 'l-riwāyah al-ᶜIrāqiyyah*, Beirut, 1971.

Al-Fann al-qaṣaṣī fī 'l-adab al-ᶜIrāqī al-ḥadīth, Najaf, 1971.

Al-Zajjājī, Bāqir Jawwād *Al-Riwāyah al-ᶜirāqiyyah wa qaḍiyyat al-rīf*, Baghdād, 1980.

Lebanon (i) In Arabic

ᶜAṭwī, ᶜAlī Najīb *Taṭawwur fann al-qiṣṣah al-Lubnāniyyah al-ᶜArabiyyah baᶜda 'l-ḥarb al-ᶜālamiyyah al-thāniyah*, Beirut, 1982.

Idrīs, Suhayl *Muḥāḍarāt ᶜan al-qiṣṣah fī Lubnān*, Cairo, 1957.

'Al-qiṣṣah al-tārīkhiyyah ᶜinda Zaydān', *Al-Ādāb* (Mar. 1954).

Najm, Muḥammad Yūsuf *Al-qiṣṣah fī 'l-adab al-ᶜArabī 'l-ḥadīth fī Lubnān*, Beirut, 1966.

Lebanon: (ii) In European lanaguages

Accad, Evelyne *Sexuality and War: literary masks of the Middle East*, New York, 1990.

Cooke, Miriam *War's other voices*, Cambridge, 1988.
Ḥāwī, Khalīl *Khalil Gibran: His background, character and works*, Beirut, 1963.
Naimy, Nadim 'The mind and thought of Khalil Gibran', *Journal of Arabic Literature* V (1974), pp. 55–71.
Nijland, C. *Mikhaʾil Nuʿaymah, promotor of the Arabic literary revival*, Istanbul, 1975.
Siddiq, Muhammad 'Mikhail Nʿaimy as Novelist', *Al-ʿArabiyya* Vol. 15 nos 1 and 2 (Spr. & Aut. 1982), pp. 16–33.
Reid, Donald *The odyssey of Farah Antun*, Minneapolis, 1975.

Morocco: (i) In Arabic

Ḥamīd, Laḥmidānī *Fī'l- tanẓīr wa'l-mumārasah: dirāsāt fī 'l-riwāyah al-Maghribiyyah*, Al-Dār al-Bayḍāʾ, 1986.
Al-Riwāyah al-Maghribiyyah waruʾyā 'l-wāqiʿ al-ijtimāʿī, Al-Dār al-Bayḍāʾ, 1985.
al-Nassāj, Sayyid Ḥāmid *Al-Adab al-ʿArabī al-muʿāṣir fī 'l-Maghrib al-aqṣā*, Cairo, 1977.

Morocco (ii) In European languages

Europe: revue littéraire mensuelle, 'Littérature morocaine' (June–July, 1979).
Al-Khaṭībī, ʿAbd al-Kabīr *Le roman maghrebin*, 2nd edn., Rabat, 1979.

Palestine: (i) In Arabic

Abū Maṭar, Aḥmad *Al-Riwāyah fī 'l-adab al-Filasṭīnī: 1950–75*, Beirut, 1980.
ʿĀshūr, Raḍwā *Al-Ṭarīq ilā 'l-khaymah al-ukhrā: dirāsah fī aʿmāl Ghassān Kanafānī*, Beirut, 1977.
Ṣāliḥ, Fakhrī *Fī 'l-riwāyah al-Filasṭīniyyah*, Beirut, 1985.
Wādī, Fārūq *Thalāth ʿalāmāt fī 'l-riwāyah al-Filasṭīniyyah: Ghassān Kanafānī, Emīle Ḥabībī, Jabrā Ibrāhīm Jabrā*, ʿAkkā, 1981.
Yāghī, ʿAbd al-Raḥmān *Fī 'l-adab al-Filasṭīnī qabla 'l-nakbah wa-baʿdahā*, Kuwait, 1983.
Ḥayāt al-adab al-Filasṭīnī al-ḥadīth awwal al-nahḍah ḥattā 'l-nakbah, Beirut, 1968.
Al-Yūsuf, Yūsuf 'Ghassān Kanafānī riwāʾiyyan', *Al-Maʿrifah* 173 (1976).

Palestine: (ii) In European languages

Camera d'Afflitto, Isabella 'Simbolo e realta in Ghassan Kanafani', *Studi in memoria di Maria Nallino*, Rome, 1984, pp. 33–40.
Siddiq, Muhammad *Man is a cause: political consciousness and the fiction of Ghassan Kanafani*, Seattle, 1984.

Sudan: (i) In Arabic

Sallām, Muḥammad Zaghlūl *Al-Qiṣṣah fī 'l-adab al-Sūdānī al-ḥadīth*, Cairo, 1970.

Sudan: (ii) In English

Amyuni, Mona Takieddine, ed. *Tayeb Salih's Season of migration to the north: a casebook*, Beirut, 1985.

Syria: (i) In Arabic
Al-Fayṣal, Samar Rūḥī *Malāmiḥ fī 'l-riwāyah al-Sūriyyah*, Damascus, 1979.
Ibn Dhurayl, ᶜAdnān *Adab al-qiṣṣah fī Sūriyyah*, Damascus, n.d.
Al-Riwāyah al-ᶜArabiyyah al-Sūriyyah, Damascus, 1973.
Al-Kayyālī, Sāmī *Al-Adab al-ᶜArabī al-muᶜāṣir fi Sūriyyā 1850–1950*, Cairo, 1968.
Al-Khaṭīb, Ḥusām *Al-Riwāyah al-Sūriyyah fī marḥalat al-nuhūḍ*, Cairo, 1975.
Riwāyāt taḥt al-mijhar: dirāsāt nuhūḍ al-riwāyah fī Sūriyyā, Damascus, 1983.
Subul al-muʾaththirāt al-ajnabiyyah wa-ashkāluhā fī 'l-qissah al-Sūriyyah, Cairo, 1972.
Lūqā, Iskandar *Al-Ḥarakah al-adabiyyah fī Dimashq 1800-1917*, Damascus, 1976.
Muṣṭafā, Shākir *Al-qiṣṣah fī Sūriyyā ḥattā al-ḥarb al-ᶜālamiyyah al-thāniyah*, Cairo, 1957,

Syria: (In English)
Gouryh, Admer 'The fictional world of Walīd Ikhlāṣī', *World Literature Today* Vol. 58 (1964), pp. 23–7.

Tunis: (i) In Arabic
ᶜĀshūr, Muḥammad al-Fāḍil *Al-Ḥarakah al-fikriyyah wa'l-adabiyyah fī Tūnis*, Tunis, 1972.
Ibrāhīm, Raḍwān *Al-Taᶜrīf bi-'l-adab al-Tūnisī*, Tunis, 1977.
Al-Jābirī, Muḥammad Ṣāliḥ *Al-Qiṣṣah al-Tūnisiyyah; nashʾatuhā waruwwāduhā*, Tunis, 1975.

Tunis: (ii) In European languages
Fontaine, Jean *20 ans de littérature tunisienne 1956–1975*, Tunis, 1977.
Aspects de la littérature tunisienne 1975–1983, Tunis, n.d.
Ghāzī, Ferid *Le roman et la nouvelle en Tunisie*, Tunis, 1970.
Ostle, Robin 'Maḥmūd al-Masᶜadī and Tunisia's "Lost Generation"', *Journal of Arabic Literature*, Vol. 8 (1977), pp. 153–66.

7: THE EGYPTIAN NOVEL FROM ZAYNAB TO THE EARLY 1980S

A. Novels and other fiction*

ᶜAbdallāh, Yaḥyā al-Ṭāhir *Al-Ṭawq wa'l-aswirah*, Cairo, 1975.
ᶜAbd al-Ḥakīm, Shawqī *Aḥzān Nūh*, Cairo, 1964.
Dam Ibn Yaᶜqūb, Cairo, 1967.
Abū Ḥadīd, Muḥammad Farīd *Ibnat al-mamlūk*, Cairo, 1926.
Azhār al-shawk, Cairo, 1948; revised edns 1953 and 1961.
Abū 'l-Najā, Abū 'l-Maᶜāṭī *Al-ᶜAwdah ilā'l-manfā*, Cairo, 1969.
Al-ᶜAqqād, ᶜAbbās Maḥmūd *Sārah*, Cairo, 1938.
Al-Aswānī, ᶜAbd al-Wahhāb *Salmā al-aswāniyyah*, Cairo, 1968.

* This section includes novels mentioned in the text, other works by novelists discussed and novels which, for reasons of space or availability, I was unable to consider but which belong to the significant examples of the genre in Egypt. It does not pretend to be exhaustive.

ᶜAṭiyyah, Naᶜīm *Al-Mirʾāh wa'l-miṣbāḥ*, Cairo, 1968.
ᶜAwad, Luwīs *Al-ᶜAnqāʾ aw taʾrīkh Ḥasan Miftāḥ*, Beirut, 1966.
Diyāb, Maḥmūd *Al-Ẓilāl fī 'l-jānib al-ākhar*, Cairo, 1964.
Aḥzān madīnah. Ṭifl fī 'l-ḥayy al-ᶜarabī, Cairo, 1971.
Ghānim, Fatḥī *Al-Jabal*, Cairo, 1959.
Al-Rajul alladhī faqada ẓillah, Cairo, 1961.
Zaynab wa'l-ᶜarsh, Cairo, 1976.
Al-Ghīṭānī, Jamāl *Al-Zaynī Barakāt*, Damascus, 1974.
Waqāʾiᶜ ḥārat al-Zaᶜfarānī, Cairo, 1976.
Al-Rifāᶜī, Cairo, 1978.
Al-Ḥakīm, Tawfīq *ᶜAwdaṭ al-rūḥ*, Cairo, 1933.
Yawmiyyāt nāʾib fī 'l-aryāf, Cairo, 1937.
ᶜUṣfūr min al-sharq, Cairo, 1938.
Al-Ribāṭ al-muqaddas, Cairo, 1945.
Ḥaqqī, Yaḥyā *Qindīl Umm Hāshim*, Cairo, 1944.
Ṣaḥḥ al-nawm, Cairo, 1956.
Haykal, Muḥammad Ḥusayn *Zaynab*, Cairo, 1913.
Hākadhā khuliqat, Cairo, 1955.
Ḥusayn, Ṭāhā *Al-Ayyām*, part 1, Cairo, 1929.
Duᶜāʾ al-karawān, Cairo, 1934.
Adīb, Cairo, 1935.
Shajarat al-buʾs, Cairo, 1944.
Ibrāhīm, Jamīl ᶜAṭiyyah *Aṣīlā*, Damascus, 1980.
Ibrāhīm, ṢunᶜAllah *Tilka 'l-rāʾiḥah*, Cairo, 1966; censored version, Cairo 1969; original version reprinted 1986.
Najmat aghusṭus, Damascus, 1974.
Idrīs, Yūsuf *Qiṣṣat ḥubb*, Cairo, 1956.
Qāᶜ al-madīnah, Cairo, 1957.
Al-Ḥarām, Cairo, 1959; revised editions 1965, 1970.
Al-ᶜAyb, Cairo, 1962.
Al-Bayḍāʾ, Beirut, 1970.
Kāmil, ᶜĀdil *Malik min shuᶜāᶜ*, Cairo, 1945.
Millīm al-akbar, Cairo, 1944.
Kharrāṭ, Idwār *Rāmah wa'l-tinnīn*, Cairo, 1979.
Lāshīn, Maḥmūd Tāhir *Ḥawwāʾ bilā Ādam*, Cairo, 1934.
Maḥfūẓ, Najīb *ᶜAbath al-aqdār*, Cairo, 1939.
Rādūbīs, Cairo, 1943.
Kifāḥ Ṭībah, Cairo, 1944.
Khān al-Khalīlī, Cairo, 1945.
Al-Qāhirah al-jadīdah, Cairo, 1946.
Zuqāq al-midaqq, Cairo, 1947.
Al-Sarāb, Cairo, 1949.
Bidāyah wa nihāyah, Cairo, 1951.
Bayn al-qaṣrayn, Cairo, 1956.
Qaṣr al-shawq, Cairo, 1957.

Al-Sukkariyyah, Cairo, 1957.
Awlād ḥāratinā, Beirut, 1967.
Al-Liṣṣ wal'l-kilāb, Cairo, 1961.
Al-Summān wa'l-kharīf, Cairo, 1962.
Al-Ṭarīq, Cairo, 1964.
Al-Shaḥḥādh, Cairo, 1965.
Thartharah fawq al-Nīl, Cairo, 1966.
Mīrāmār, Cairo, 1967
Al-Marāyā, Cairo, 1972.
Al-Karnak, Cairo, 1974.
Ḥikāyāt ḥāratinā, Cairo, 1975.
Qalb al-layl, Cairo, 1975.
Ḥaḍrat al-muḥtaram, Cairo, 1975.
Malḥamat al-ḥarāfīsh, Cairo, 1977.
Makkāwī, Saᶜd *Al-Sāʾirūn niyāman*, Cairo, 1965.
Al-Māzinī, Ibrāhīm ᶜAbd al-Qādir *Ibrāhīm al-kātib*, Cairo, 1931.
Ibrāhīm al-thānī, Cairo, 1943.
ᶜAwd ᶜalā badʾ, Cairo, 1943.
Thalāthat rijāl wa-imraʾah, Cairo, 1944.
Mursī, Ṣāliḥ *Zuqāq al-Sayyid al-Bulṭī*, Cairo, 1963.
Mūsā, Sabrī *Fasād al-amkinah*, Cairo, 1973.
Qāsim, ᶜAbd al-Ḥakīm *Ayyām al-insān al-sabᶜah*, Cairo, 1969.
Muḥāwala li'l-khurūj, Beirut, 1980.
Qadar al-ghuraf al-muqbiḍah, Cairo, 1982.
Qāsim, Muḥammad Khalīl *Al-shamandūrah*, Cairo, 1968.
Al-Quᶜayyid (Al-Qaᶜīd), Muḥammad Yūsuf *Al-Ḥidād*, Cairo, 1969.
Akhbār ᶜizbat al-Manīsī, Cairo, 1971.
Al-Bayāt al-shatawī, Cairo, 1974
Yaḥduth fī Miṣr al-ān, Cairo, 1977.
Al-Ḥarb fī barr Miṣr, Beirut, 1978.
Al-Sharqāwī, ᶜAbd al-Raḥmān *Al-Arḍ*, Cairo, 1954; revised edition, 1968.
Qulūb khāliyah, Cairo, 1957.
Al-Shawāriᶜ al-khalfiyyah, Cairo, 1958.
Al-Fallāḥ, Cairo, 1968.
Taymūr, Maḥmud *Nidāʾ al-majhūl*, Cairo, 1940.
Kilyūbāṭrā fi Khān al-Khalīlī, Cairo, 1946.
Salwā fī mahabb al-rīḥ, Cairo, 1947.
Ilā 'l-liqāʾ ayyuhā 'l-ḥubb, Cairo, 1959.
Taymūr, Muḥammad *Al-Shabāb al-ḍāʾiᶜ*, Cairo, 1922 (in *Wamīḍ al-rūḥ*).
Al-Zayyāt, Laṭīfah *Al-Bāb al-maftūḥ*, Cairo, 1960.

B. *Arabic secondary sources*

Al-Ādāb, 28th year, nos 2 and 3, Feb.–March 1980, and nos 4 and 5, April–May 1980; numbers devoted to the Fez conference on the new Arabic novel.

Al-ᶜĀlim, Maḥmūd Amīn *Taᵓammulāt fī ᶜālam Najīb Maḥfūẓ*, Cairo, 1970.
ᶜAyyād. Muḥammad Shukrī 'Al-riwāyah al-ᶜarabiyyah al-muᶜāṣirah wa-azmat al-ḍamīr al-ᶜarabī', *ᶜĀlam al-fikr* III, 3 (Oct.–Dec. 1972), pp. 619–648.
Badr, ᶜAbd al-Muḥsin Ṭāhā *Taṭawwur al-riwāyah al-ᶜarabiyyah fī Miṣr, 1870-1938*, Cairo, 1963.
Al-riwāᵓī wa'l-arḍ, Cairo, 1971.
Dawwārah, Fuᵓād *Fī 'l-riwāyah al-miṣriyyah*, Cairo, n.d.
Al-Kharrāṭ, Idwār 'ᶜAlā sabīl al-taqdīm', *Al-Karmil* (Cyprus) 14 (1984), pp. 5–14 (Special number on contemporary Egyptian literature).
Mārbākh, ᶜAmīkām 'Riwāyat Zaynab min al wijhah al-fanniyyah', *Al-Karmil* (Haifa) 7 (1986), pp. 185–202.
Mūsā, Fāṭimah *Fī 'l-riwāyah al-ᶜarabiyyah al-muᶜāṣirah*, Cairo, 1972.
Al-Nassāj, Sayyid Ḥamīd *Panorama al-riwāyah al-ᶜarabiyyah al-ḥadīthah*, 2nd edn, Cairo, 1985.
Al-Quṭṭ, ᶜAbd al-Ḥamīd ᶜAbd al-ᶜAẓīm *Yūsuf Idrīs wa'l-fann al-qaṣaṣī*, Cairo, 1980.
Bināᵓ al-riwāyah fī 'l-adab al-miṣrī al-ḥadīth, Cairo, 1982.
Al-Rāᶜī, ᶜAlī *Dirāsāt fī 'l-riwāyah al-miṣriyyah*, Cairo, 1964.
Sālim, Jūrj *Al-mughāmarah al-riwāᵓiyyah. Dirāsāt fī 'l-riwāyah al-ᶜarabiyyah*, Damascus, 1973.
Al-Sayyid, Shafīᶜ *Ittijāhāt al-riwāyah al-miṣriyyah mundhu al-ḥarb al-ᶜālamiyyah al-thāniyah ilā sanat 1967*, Cairo, 1978.
Al-Shārūnī, Yūsuf 'Āthār al-taṭawwur al-ijtimāᶜī ᶜalā taṭawwur al-ashkāl al-fanniyyaḥ fī 'l-qiṣṣah al-miṣriyyah al-ḥadīthah', *Awrāq* 2 (1979), pp. 51–73.
Shukrī, Ghālī *Al-muntamī, Dirāsah fī adab Najīb Maḥfūẓ*, 2nd edn, Cairo, 1970.
Sūmīkh, Sāsūn *Lughat al-qiṣṣah fī adab Yūsuf Idrīs*, Acre, 1984.
Surūr, Ḥasan and Ṭāhā Wādī 'Bibliyūgrāfiyyā ᶜan al-riwāyah al-miṣriyyah min al-bidāyah wa-ḥattā 1987, *Al-Qāhirah* 88 (15 October 1988), pp. 58–66.
Ṭarābīshī, Jūrj *Sharq wa-gharb. Rujūlah wa-unūthah*, Beirut, 1977.
Wādī, Ṭāhā *Madkhal ilā taᵓrīkh al-riwāyah al-miṣriyyah 1905–1952*, Cairo, 1972.
Ṣūrat al-marᵓah fī 'l-riwāyah al-muᶜāṣirah, 3rd edn, Cairo, 1984.

C. Secondary sources in other languages

Allen, Roger 'Some recent works of Najīb Maḥfūẓ: A critical analysis', *Journal of the American Research Center in Egypt* XVI (1977), pp. 101–10.
The Arabic novel: an historical and critical introduction, Manchester, 1982.
Amo, Mercedes del 'Aproximación a la novela egipcia de entreguerras', *Miscelanea de Estudios Árabes y Hebráicos* (Granada) XXXII–XXXIII, 1 (1984–1985), pp. 7–36.
'Una panorámica de la novela egipcia desde la Segunda Guerra Mundial a la Revolución de 1952' in *Homenaje al Prof. Darío Cabanelas Rodríguez O.F.M. con motivo de su LXX aniversario*, Granada, 1987, vol. II, pp. 9–27.
'Bibliografía sobre la narrativa egipcia moderna (1975–1985)', *JAL* XVIII (1987), pp. 133–41.

Badawi, M. M. *Modern Arabic literature and the west*, London, 1985.

Draz, Céza Kassem 'In quest of new narrative forms. Irony in the works of four Egyptian writers', *JAL* XII (1981), pp. 137–59.

Fontaine, Jean 'Le nouveau roman égyptien 1975–1985', *IBLA* 49 no. 158 (1986), pp. 215–62.

Francis, Raymond *Taha Hussein romancier*, Cairo, n.d.

Gabalawy, Saad el- *Three pioneering Egyptian novels*, Fredericton, New Brunswick, 1986.

Hafez, Sabry 'The Egyptian novel in the sixties', *JAL* VII (1976), pp. 68–84.

Hoek, Albert-Jan van 'al-Ḥarām: Drie Verkenningen' (al-Ḥarām: Three explorations), unpublished doctoraalscriptie, Nijmegen, 1988.

Jad, Ali B. *Form and technique in the Egyptian novel 1912–1971*, London, 1983.

Kilpatrick, Hilary *The modern Egyptian novel*, London, 1974.

'Egyptian novels and Arabic literary tradition', *Proceedings of the 14th Congress of the Union Européenne des Arabisants et Islamisants, Budapest, 1988* (forthcoming)

Kirpichenko, V. N. *Sovremennaya egipetskaya proza 60–70e gody* (Contemporary Egyptian prose of the '60s and '70s), Moscow, 1986.

Mehrez, Samia 'Al-Zayni Barakāt: Narrative as Strategy', *Arab Studies Quarterly* 8, 2 (Spring 1986), pp. 120–42.

Moussa-Mahmoud, Fatma *The Arabic novel in Egypt, 1914–1970*, Cairo, 1973.

Peled, Mattityahu *Religion, my own. The literary works of Najīb Maḥfūẓ*, New Brunswick and London, 1983.

Sakkūt, Ḥamdī *The Egyptian novel and its main trends from 1913 to 1952*, Cairo, 1971.

Somekh, Sasson *The changing rhythm. A study of Najīb Maḥfūẓ's novels*, Leiden, 1973.

Tomiche, Nada 'Le roman égyptien après 1973 . . . Sa place dans le monde arabe et l'image qu'en reçoit l'Occident', *Annales Islamologiques* XV (1979). pp. 399–419.

Histoire de la littérature romanesque de l'Egypte moderne, Paris, 1981.

Vial, Charles 'Contribution à l'étude du roman et de la nouvelle en Egypte des origines à 1960'. *Revue de l'Occident musulman et de la Mediterranée* 4 (1967), pp. 133–74.

'Reflets d'une société: 1. La littérature' in M.C. Aulas *et al.* (eds) *L'Egypte d'aujourd'hui. Permanence et changements 1805–1976*, Paris, 1977, pp. 305–330.

Le personnage de la femme dans le roman et la nouvelle en Egypte de 1914 à 1960, Damascus, 1979.

Walther, W. 'Literatur als Zeitdokument – ᶜAbd ar-Raḥmān aš-Šarqāwīs Roman *al-Fallāḥ*' in Fritz Gruner (ed.), *Literaturen Asiens und Afrikas. Theoretische Probleme*, Berlin, 1981, pp. 297–303.

Wielandt, Rotraud *Das Bild der Europäer in der modernen arabischen Erzähl-und Theaterliteratur*, Beirut, 1980.

Das erzählerische Frühwerk Maḥmūd Taymūrs. Beitrag zu einen Archiv der modernen arabischen Literatur, Beirut, 1983.

8: MODERN ARABIC SHORT STORIES

A. Collections of short stories

The authors are listed alphabetically and their collections of short stories chronologically. An asterisk (*) is inserted in front of the first name of female writers, for it is not always easy to identify them from their first names alone. The year of birth and of death, if known, is inserted after the author's name, followed by the abbreviation [A (Saudi Arabia), B (Bahrain), D (Sudan),. E (Egypt), G (Algeria), I (Iraq), J (Jordan), K (Kuwait), L (Lebanon), Li (Libya), M (Morocco), O (Oman), P (Palestine), Q (Qatar), U (UAE), S (Syria), T (Tunisia), Y (Yemen)], to indicate his or her country of origin. One date following the author's name denotes date of birth. When the date of publication of a collection is not known the standard n.d. (no date) will be inserted followed by the suggested date in square brackets [...] in which a question mark (?) will appear after the suggested date if the researcher is in doubt about that date.

ʿAbbās, Nazār (1936, I) *Zuqāq al-fiʾrān*, Baghdad, 1972.

ʿAbbūd, Mārūn, (L) *Wujūh waḥikāyāt*, Beirut, 1945; *Aqzām jabbārah*, Beirut, 1948; *Aḥādīth al-qaryah*, Beirut, 1956.

ʿAbd al-ʿAzīz, *Malak (1921, E) *Al-Jawrab al-maqṭūʿ*, Cairo, 1962.

ʿAbd al-ʾAmīr, Khuḍayr (1934, I) *Ḥammām al-Saʿādah*, Baghdad, 1964; *Al-Raḥīl*, Baghdad, 1968; *ʿAwdat al-rajul al-mahzūz*, Baghdad, 1970; *Khaymah li'l-ʿAmm Ḥasan*, Baghdad, 1974; *Kānat hunāk ḥikāyah*, Beirut, 1974; *Al-Farrārah*, Baghdad, 1979; *Riyāḥ shitāʾiyyah dāfiʾah*, Baghdad, 1981; *Nujūm fi Samāʾ al-Nahār*, Baghdad, 1985; *ʿĀshiqān min Baghdād*, Cairo, 1987.

ʿAbd al-Majīd, Amīn (1934, A) *Al-ʾAʿzab al-faqīr*, Jiddah, 1969.

ʿAbd al-Majīd, Muḥammad (1943, I) *Mawt al-mughannī al-ladhī dhakkaranā bi-rāʾiḥat al-banafsaj*, Baghdad, 1974; *Ḥikāyāt al-suhūb al-baʿīdah*, Baghdad, 1985.

ʿAbd al-Malik,. Muḥammad (B) *Mawt ṣāḥib al-ʿarabah*, Bahrain, 1972; *Naḥn nuḥibb al-shams*, Bahrain, 1975; *Thuqūb fī riʾat al-madīnah*, Bahrain, 1979; *Al-Siyāj*, Bahrain, 1982.

ʿAbd al-Quddūs, Iḥsān (1919–90, E) *Ṣāniʿ al-ḥubb*, Cairo, 1949; *Bāʾiʿ al-ḥubb*, Cairo, 1950; *Sayyidat ṣālūn*, Cairo, 1952; *Al-Nazzārah al-sawdāʾ*, Cairo, 1952; *Ayn ʿumrī*, Cairo, 1954; *Al-Wisādah al-khāliyah*, Cairo, 1955; *Muntahā al-ḥubb*, Cairo, 1957; *Al-Banāt wa'l-ṣayf*, Beirut, 1957; *ʿAqlī wa qalbī*, Cairo, 1959; *Shafatāh*, Cairo, n. d. [1961]; *Lā laysjasaduk*, Beirut, 1962; *Bint al-sulṭān*, Cairo, 1963; *Biʾr al-ḥirmān*, Cairo, 1963; *ʿUlbah min al-ṣafīḥ al-ṣadiʾ*,Cairo, 1967; *Al-Nisāʾ lahun asnān bayḍāʾ*, Cairo, 1969; *Al-Raṣāṣah lā tazāl fi jaybī*, Cairo, 1973; *al-Hazīmah kān ismuhā Fāṭimah*, Cairo, 1975; *Al-ʿAdhrāʾ wa'l-shaʿr al-ʾabyaḍ*, Cairo, 1977; *Sayyidah fī khidmatik*, Cairo, 1979; *Lā Astaṭīʿ an ufakkir wa ʾanā arqus*, Cairo, 198?;*Dammī wa dumūʿī wa ʾibtisāmātī*, Cairo, 198?

ʿAbd al-Razzāq, ʿAbd al-ʾIlāh (1939, I) *Al-Safar dākhil al-ʾashyāʾ*, Baghdad, 1971; *Li-Ophelia jasad al-arḍ*, Baghdad, 1976.

ʿAbd al-Raḥmān, Mayfaʾ (Y) *Bakārat al-ʿarūs*, Aden, 1975.

ʿAbd al-Raḥmān, *ʿĀʾishah (E) see Bint al-Shāṭiʾ.

ʿAbd al-Ḥalīm, Ibrāhīm (1919–81, E) *Aẓmat kātib*, Cairo, 1965.

ʿAbd al-Walī, Muḥammad (Y) *Al-ʿArḍ yā Salmā*, Beirut, 1966; *Shayʿ ismuh al-ḥanīn*, Taʿz, 1972.

ʿAbd, ʿAbdullah (1940–73?, S) *Māt al-banafsaj*, Damascus, 1969; *Al-Sayrān wa luʿbat awlād Yaʿqūb*, Damascus, 1972.

ʿAbdullah, *Ṣūfī (1925, E) *Kulluhun ʿAyyūshah*, Cairo, 1956; *Thaman al-ḥubb*, Cairo, n.d. [1958]; *Baqāyā rajul*, Cairo, 1958; *Madrasat al-banāt*, Cairo, n.d. [1959]; *Niṣf Imraʾah*, Cairo, 1962; *Layāl lahā thaman*, Cairo, n.d. [1964]; *Muʿjizat al-Nīl*, Cairo, 1964; *Alf mabrūk*, Cairo, 1965; *ʿArūsah ʿalā al-raff*, Cairo, 1966; *Arbaʿat rijāl wa-fatah*, Cairo, 1973; *Al-Qafaṣ al-ʾaḥmar*, Cairo, 1975; *Shayʾ aqwā minhā*, Cairo, 1975; *Nabḍah taḥt al-jalīd*, Cairo, 1975.

ʿAbdullah, Muḥ. ʿAbd al-Ḥalīm, (1913–71, E) *Al-Nāfidhah al-gharbiyyah*, Cairo, n.d. [1953]; *Al-Māḍi lā yaʿūd*, Cairo, n.d. [1956]; *Alwān min al-saʿādah*, Cairo, n.d. [1958]; *Ashyāʾ li'l-dhikrā*, Cairo, 1958; *Al-Ḍafīrah al-sawdāʾ*, Cairo, n.d. [1963]; *Khuyūṭ al-Nūr*, Cairo, n.d. [1965]; *Ḥāfat al-jarīmah*, Cairo, n.d. [1966]; *Usṭūrah min kitāb al-ḥubb*, Cairo, n.d. [1967].

ʿAbdullah, Yaḥyā al-Ṭāhir (1940–81, E) *Thalāth shajarāt kabīrah tuthmir burtuqālan*, Cairo, 1970; *Al-Duff wa'l-ṣundūq*, Baghdad, 1972; *Anạ wa hiya wa zuhūr al-ʿālam*, Cairo, 1977; *Ḥikāyāt li'l-ʾamīr*, Cairo, 1978.

ʿAnqāwī, Fuʾād (1936, A) *Ayyām mubaʿtharah*, Riyadh, 1982.

ʿAqīl, ʿAbd al-Qādir (1949, B) *Istighāthāt fī 'l-ʿalam al-waḥshī*, Bahrain, 1979; *Masāʾ al-billawrāt*, Beirut, 1985; *Ruʾā al-jālis ʿalā ʿarsh*, Bahrain, 1987.

ʿArʿār, Muḥ. al-ʿĀlī (G) *al-Ḥālim*, Algiers, 1979.

ʿArūs, Al-ʿĪd Ibn (G) *Anā wa'l-shams*, Constantine, 1976.

ʿAtīq, ʿAbdullah al- (1959, A) *Ukdhūbat al-ṣamt wa'l-damār*, Riyadh, 1982.

ʿAwwād, Tawfīq Yūsuf (1910?–89, L) *Al-Ṣabiyy al-ʾaʿraj*, Beirut, 1936; *Qamīṣ al-ṣūf*, Beirut, 1937; *Al-ʿAdhārā*, Beirut, 1944.

ʿAyyād, Shukrī Muḥ. (1921, E) *Mīlād jadīd*, Cairo, n.d. [1958]; *Ṭarīq al-jāmiʿah*, Cairo, n.d. [1963]; *Zawjatī al-ʿazīzah al-jamīlah*, Cairo, 1977; *Rubāʿiyyāt*, Cairo, 1984; *Kahf al-ʾakhyār*, Cairo, 1985.

ʿAyyādī, Samīr al- (1947, T) *Ṣakhab al-ṣamt*, Tunis, 1970.

ʿAẓm, Yūsuf al- (J) *Yā ayyuhā 'l-ʾinsān*, Amman, 1960.

ʿAzzām, *Samīrah (1927–67, P) *Ashyāʾ ṣaghīrah*, Beirut, 1954; *Al-Ẓill al-kabīr*, Beirut, 1956; *Wa-Qiṣaṣ ukhrā*, Beirut, 1960; *Al-Sāʿah wa'l-ʾinsān*, Beirut, 1966; *Al-ʿĪd min al-nāfidhah al-gharbiyyah*, Beirut, 1971.

ʿAzzūz, *Hind (1926, T) *Al-Darb al-ṭawīl*, Tunis, n.d.

ʿĀdilī, Ismāʿīl al- (E) *Al-ʿĀm al-khāmis*, Cairo, 1982; *Ayyām al-maṭar*, Cairo, 1985.

ʿĀmirī, Muḥ. Adīb al- (1907, P) *Shuʿāʿ al-nūr*, Cairo, 1953.

Abāẓah, Tharwat (1926, E) *Al-ʾAyyām al-khaḍrāʾ*, Cairo, 1960; *Dhikrayāt baʿīdah*, Cairo, 1964; *Hadhih al-luʿbah*, Cairo, 1967; *Ḥīn yamīl al-mīzān*, Cairo, 1970; *Al-Sibāḥah fī 'l-rimāl*, Beirut, 1975.

Abū Ghanīmah, Ṣubḥī (S) *Aghāni al-layl*, Damascus, 1922.

Abū'l-Hayjāʾ, Nawwāf (1938, P) *Wa'l-Khaybah ayḍan*, Damascus, 1965; *Al-Ḍarb fī 'l-raʾs*, Damascus, 1966; *Mamarrāt muḍīʾah ilā aḥlām al-filisṭini*, Beirut, 1971; *In Kunt al-laylah waḥīdā*, Baghdad, 1978.

Abū'l-Najā, Muḥ. Abū'l-Maʿāṭī (1931, E) *Fatāh fī 'l-madīnah*, Beirut, 1960; *Al-ʾIbtisāmah al-ghāmiḍah*, Cairo, n.d. [1963]; *Al-Nās wa'l-ḥubb*, Beirut, 1966; *Al-Wahm wa'l-ḥaqīqah*, Cairo, 1974; *Al-Jamīʿ yarbaḥun al-jāʾizah*, Cairo, 1984.

Abū Rayyah, Yūsuf (1955, E) *Al-Ḍuḥā al-ʿālī*, Cairo, 1985.

Abū Shabakah, Ilyās (1903–47, L) *Ṭāqāt ẓuhūr*, Beirut, 1927.

Abū Shanab, ʿĀdil (1931, S) *ʿAlam wa lākinnah ṣaghīr*, Damascus, 1956; *Zahrah istiwāʾiyyah fī'l-quṭb*, Damascus, 1961; *Al-Thuwwār marrū bi baytinā*, Damascus, 1963; *Aḥlām sāʿat al-ṣifr*, Damascus, 1973; *Al-ʾĀs al-jamīl*, Damascus, 1979.

Abū Shāwir, Rashād (1942, P) *Dhikrā al-ayyām al-māḍiyah*, Beirut, 1970; *Bayt akhḍar dhū saqf qarmīdī*, Baghdad, 1974; *Al-Ashjār lā tanmū ʿalā 'l-dafātir*, Beirut, 1975; *Muhr al-barāri*, Beirut, 1977; *Pizza min ajl dhikrā Maryam*, Beirut, 1981.

Adhraʿ Al-Sharīf al- (G) *Mā qabl al-baʿd*, Algiers, 1978.

Al-Faramāwī, Wafīq (1954, E) *Al-Qatalah*, Cairo, 1985.

Al-Mudarris, Fātiḥ (1922, S) *ʿAwdat al-naʿnāʿ*, Damascus, 1981.

Aliksān, Jān (1933, S) *Nidāʾ al-ʿarḍ*, Qāmāshli, Syria, 1955; *Nahr min al-shamāl* Damascus, n.d. [1963]; *Al-Ḥudūd wa'l-ʾaswār*, Damascus, 1972; *Al-Muʿādah*, Baghdad, 1972; *Jidār fī qaryah amāmiyyah*, Damascus, 1978; *Al-Ḥūt wa'l-zawraq*, Damascus, 1981.

Amīr, *Dīzī al- (1935, I) *Al-Balad al-baʿīd al-ladhī nuḥibb*, Beirut, 1964; *Taʿūd al-mawjah*, Beirut, 1969; *Al-Bayt al-ʿarabī al-saʿīd* (Beirut, 1975; *Fī Dawwāmat al-ḥubb wa'l-karāhiyah*, Beirut, 1979; *Wuʿūd li'l-bayʿ*, Baghdad, 1981; *ʿAlā lāʾiḥat al-ʾintiẓār*, Baghdad, 1988.

Arnāʾūṭ, Maʿrūf al- (S) *Fāṭimah al-batūl*, Damascus, 1942.

Ashqar, Yūsuf Ḥabashī al- (L) *Ṭaʿm al-Ramād*, Beirut, 1953; *Layl al-shitāʾ*, Beirut, n.d.

Ayyūb, Maḥfūẓ (1934, S) *Muḥāwarāt al-masāʾ*, Damascus, 1971.

Ayyūb, Dhū'l-Nūn (1908–88, I) *Rusul al-thaqāfah*, Baghdad, 1937; *Al-Ḍaḥāyā*, Baghdad, n.d. [1938]; *Ṣadīqi*, Baghdad, 1938; *Waḥy al-fann*, Baghdad, 1938; *Burj Bābil*, Baghdad, 1939; *Al-Kādiḥūn*, Mosul, 1939; *Al-ʿAql fi miḥnah*, Mosul, 1940; *Ḥummiyyāt*, Baghdad, 1941; *Al-Kārithah al-shāmilah*, Baghdad, 1945; *ʿAẓamah fārighah*, Baghdad, n.d. [1948?]; *Qulūb ẓamʾā*, Baghdad, 1950; *Ṣuwar shattā*, Baghdad, 1954; *Al-Rasāʾil al-mansiyyah*, Baghdad, n.d. [1955]; *Qiṣaṣ min Vienna*, Baghdad, 1957; *ʿAlā 'l-ʾarḍ al-salām*, Baghdad, 1972.

Aḥmad, ʿAbd al-Ḥamīd (1943, U) *Al-Bīdār*, Beirut, 1987.

Aḥmadī, Kāẓim al- (1944, I) *Humūm shajarat al-bambar*, Baghdad, 1974; *Ṭāʾir al-khalīj*, Baghdad, 1976; *Ghināʾ al-Fawākhit*, Baghdad, 1980; *Shawāhid al-ʾazminah*, Baghdad, 1986.

Aṣlān, Ibrāhīm (1935, E) *Buḥayrat al-masāʾ*, Cairo, 1971; *Yūsuf wa'l-ridāʾ*, Cairo, 1987.

Baʿalbakī, *Laylā (1936, L) *Safīnat ḥanān ilā 'l-qamar*, Beirut, 1965.

Badawī, Maḥmūd al- (1908–86, E) *Al-Raḥīl*, Cairo, 1935; *Rajul*, Cairo, 1936; *Funduq al-Dānūb*, Cairo, 1941; *Al-Dhiʾāb al-jāʾiʿah* Cairo, 1944; *Al-ʿArabah al-ʾakhīrah*, Cairo, 1948; *Ḥadath dhāt laylah*, Cairo, 1953; *ʿAdhārā al-layl*, Cairo,

1956; *Al-ʾAʿraj fi al-mīnāʾ*, Cairo, 1958; *Al-Zallah al-ʾūlā*, Cairo, 1959; *Ghurfah ʿalā al-saṭḥ*, Cairo, 1960; *Laylah fī ʾl-ṭarīq*,Cairo, 1962; *Zawjat al-ṣayyād*, Cairo, n.d. [1962]; *Ḥāris al-bustān*, Cairo, n.d. [1963]; *ʿAdhrāʾ wa waḥsh*, Cairo, 1963; *Al-Jamāl al-ḥazīn*, Cairo, n.d. [1963]; *Masāʾ al-khamīs*, Cairo, 1966; *Ṣaqr al-layl*, Cairo, 1971; *Al-ʿAdhrāʾ wa'l-layl*, Cairo, 1975; *Al-Bāb al-ʾākhar*, Cairo, 1977.

Baghdādī, Shawqī (1928, S) *Ḥīnā yabṣuq daman*, Beirut, 1954; *Baytuhā fī safḥ al-jabal*, Damascus, 1978.

Bakhishwayn, ʿAbdullah (1953, A) *Al-Ḥaflah*, Jiddah, 1985.

Bakr, *Salwā (195?, E) *Zināt fī janāzat al-raʾīs*, Cairo, 1986; *Maqām ʿAṭiyyah*, Cairo, 1987; *ʿAn al-rūḥ allatī suriqat tadrījiyyan*, Cairo, 1989.

Balbūl, Yaʿqūb (1920, I) *Al-Jamrah al-ʾūlā*, Baghdad, 1938.

Bannānī, Aḥmad, (1918–78, M) *Fās fī sabʿ qiṣaṣ*, Rabat, 1968.

Baqṣamī, *Thurayyā al- (1944, K) *Al-ʿAraq al-ʾaswad*, Kuwait, 1977; *Al-Sidrah*, Kuwait, 1988.

Barakāt, Ḥalīm (1936, S) *Al-Ṣamt wa'l-maṭar*, Beirut, 1958.

Barrādah, Muḥammad (1938, M) *Salkh al-jild*, Beirut, 1979.

Baydas, Imīl Khalīl (P) *Qahqahat al-bāṭil*, Beirut, 1952; *Ḥattā al-thumālah*, Beirut, n.d.)

Baydas, Khalīl (1876–1949, P) *Masāriḥ al-ʾadhhān*, Cairo, 1924.

Baydas, Riyāḍ (P) *Al-Maslak*, Jerusalem, 1985; *Al-Rīḥ*, Nicusia, Cyprus, 1987.

Baḥrah, Naṣr-l-dīn al- (1934, S) *Hal tadmaʾ al-ʿuyūn*, Damascus, 1957; *Unshūdat al-murawwiḍ al-harim*, Damascus, 1972; *Ramy al-jimār*, Damascus, 1974.

Baṣrī, Mīr (1911, I) *Rijāl wa ẓilāl*, Baghdad, 1955; *Nufūs ẓāmiʾah*, Baghdad, 1966.

Bilʿāwī, Ḥakam (1946, P) *Mawwāl al-ʾArḍ*, Beirut, 1976; *Difāʿan ʿan al-shams*, Tunis, 1977.

Binʿabdullah, ʿAbd al-ʿAzīz (1920, M) *Shaqrāʾ al-Rīf*, Rabat, n.d.

Binjallūn, ʿAbd al-Majīd, (1919–81, M) *Wādi al-dimāʾ*, Rabat, n.d.; *Lawlā al-ʾinsān*, Rabat, 1972.

Binnūnah,* Khunāthah (1943, M) *Li Yasquṭ al-ṣāmt*, Casablanca, 1967; *Al-Nār wa'l-ikhtiyār*, Rabat, 1968; *Al-Ṣūrah wa'l-ṣawt*, Casablanca, 1975; *Al-ʿĀṣifah*, Baghdad, 1977; *Al-Ghad wa-l-ghaḍab* Casablanca, 1981.

*Bint al-Shāṭiʾ (1912, E) *Sirr al-Shāṭiʾ*, Cairo, 1952; *Imraʾah khāṭiʾah*, Cairo, 1958; *Ṣuwar min ḥayātihin*, Cairo, 1959.

Biqālī, Aḥmad ʿAbd al-Salām (1930, M) *Qiṣas min al-Maghrib*, Cairo, 1954; *Al-Fajr al-kādhib*, Beirut, 1964; *Yad al-maḥabbah*, Rabat, 1970?.

Biqṭāsh, Mirzāq (G) *Jarād al-baḥr*, Algiers, 1976.

Bisāṭī, Muḥammad al- (1938, E) *Al-Kibār wa'l-ṣighār*, Cairo, 1964; *Ḥadīth min al-ṭābiq al-thālith*, Cairo, 1970; *Aḥlām rijāl qiṣār al-ʿumr*, Cairo, 1979; *Hādha mā kān*, Cairo, 1988.

Bunnī, Waṣfī al (1915–83, S) *Fi qalb al-ghūṭah*, Beirut, 1954.

Burayk, *Samīrah (1935, S) *Aḥzān shajar al-laymūn*, Beirut, 1979.

Bustānī, Fuʾād Ifrām al- (L) *ʿAlā ʿahd al-ʾamīr*, Beirut, 1927.

Bādhīb, ʿAli (Y) *Mamnūʿ al-dukhūl*, Aden, n.d. [1968].

Bāwazīr, ʿAbdullah Sālim (Y) *Al-Rimāl al-dhahabiyyah*, Aden, 1965; *Thawrat al-burkān*, Aden, 1968.

Būʿallū, Muḥ. Ibrāhīm (1936, M) *Al-Saqf*, Casablanca, 1970; *Al-Fāris wa'l-ḥiṣan* Casablanca, 1975.

Būzfūr, Aḥmad (M) *Al-Naẓar fī 'l-wajh al-ʿazīz*, Casablanca, 1983.

Dabbāgh, Ghānim al- (1923, I) *Al-Māʾ al-ʿadhb*, Baghdad, 1969; *Sūnātah fī ḍawʾ al-qamar*, Baghdad, 1970.

Dakrūb, Muḥammad (1929, L) *Al-Shāriʿ al-ṭawīl*, Beirut, 1954; *Al-Turāb*, Beirut, n.d..

Dammāj, Zayd Muṭīʿ (Y) *Ṭāhish al-Ḥawbān*, Cairo, 1973.

Darwīsh, Shālūm (1913, I) *Aḥrār wa-ʿabīd*, Bagdad, 1941; *Baʿḍ al-nās*, Baghdad, 1948.

Dawālībī, *Dunyā (S) *Bint al-qamar*, Beirut, n.d.

Daḥḥān, Ṣāliḥ al- (Y) *Ant shuyūʿī*, Aden, 1956.

Duhnī, Ṣalāḥ (1925, S) *Ḥīn tamūt al-mudun*, Damascus, 1976.

Dulaymī, *Laṭīfah al- (1938, I) *Mamarr ilā aḥzān al-rijāl*, Baghdad, 1969; *Al-Bishārah*, Baghdad, 1975; *Al-Timthāl*, Baghdad, 1977; *Idhā kunt tuḥibb*, Baghdad, 1980.

Dāʿūq, ʿAdnān al- (1932, S) *15 Qiṣṣah sūriyyah*, Cairo, 1957; *Dhāt al-khāl*, Cairo, n.d. [1958]; *Satushriq al-shams zarqāʾ*, Cairo, 1960; *Al-Samakah wa'l-biḥār al-zurq*, Beirut, 1963; *Azhār al-burtuqāl*, Damascus, 1969; *Qārib al-raḥīl*, Tunis, 1976; *Ādam wa'l-jazzār*, Damascus 1979.

Dāwūd, Aḥmad (1942, S) *Raqṣat al-shams*, Damascus, 1973.

Dīrānī, Ilyān (1909, S) *Al-Sahm al-ʾakhḍar*, Damascus, 1976.

Dūdū, Abū al-ʿĪd (G) *Dār al-thalāthah*, Algiers, 1970.

Ḍamrah, Yūsuf (1952, P) *Al-ʿArabāt*, Damascus, 1979; *Najmah wa'l-ʾashjār*, Damascus, 1980; *Al-Makātīb lā taṣil ummī*, Amman, 1982; *Al-Yawm al-thālith li'l-ghiyāb*, Damascus, 1983.

Ḍūrānī, ʿAbd al-Wahāb al- (Y) *Al-Zinzānah*, Cairo, 1976.

Fahmī, *Zaynab (1940, M) See under her pen name Rafīqat al-Ṭabīʿah.

Faqīh, Aḥmad Ibrāhīm al- (1942, Li) *Al-Baḥr lā māʾ fīh*, Beirut, 1965; *Irbiṭū Aḥzimat al-Maqāʿid*, Tripoli, Libya, 1968; *Ikhtafat al-nujūm*, Tripoli, Libya, 1974; *Imraʾah min ḍawʾ*, Tripoli, Libya, 1985.

Faraj, *Maryam Jumʿah (U) *Fayrūz*, Sharjah, 1988.

Farḥān, Farḥān, al- (K) *Ālām ṣadīq*, Kuwait, 1948; *Sukhriyāt al-qadar*, Kuwait, n.d.

Fawwāl, *Minawwar (S) *Kibriyāʾ wa gharām*, Damascus, 1951; *Dumūʿ al-khāṭiʾah*, (Beirut, 1955; *Ghadan naltaqī*, Dasmascus, 1955.

Fayyāḍ, Sulaymān (1929, E) *ʿAṭshān yā Ṣabāyā*, Cairo, 1961; *Wa Baʿdanā al-ṭūfān*, Cairo, 1969; *Aḥzān Ḥuzayrān*, Beirut, 1969; *Al-ʿUyūn*, Beirut, 1972; *Zaman al-ṣamt wa'l-ḍabāb*, Beirut, 1974; *Al-Ṣūrah wa'l-ẓill*, Baghdad, 1976; *Wafāt ʿāmil maṭbaʿah*, Cairo, 1984?.

Fayyāḍ, Tawfīq (1939, P) *Al-Shāriʿ al-ʾaṣfar*, Beirut, 1968; *Al-Majmūʿah 778*, Beirut, 1974; *Ḥabībati Milīsha*, Beirut, 1976; *Al-Bahlūl*, Beirut, 1978.

Fazīʿ, Khalīl al- (1943, A) *Sūq al-Khamīs*, Riyadh, 197?; *Al-Sāʿah wa'l-nakhlah*, Riyadh, 197?.

Fāris, Bishr (L/E) *Sūʾ tafāhum*, Cairo, 1942.

Fārisī, Muṣṭafā al- (T) *Saraqt al-qamar*, Tunis, n.d.

Fāsī, ʿAbd al-Raḥman al- (1918, M) *ʿAmmi Būshnāq*, Rabat, 1972.

Fāḍil, ʿAbd al-Ḥaqq (1910, I) *Mizāḥ wa mā ashbah*, Mosul, 1940; *Ṭawāghīt*, Baghdad, 1958; *Ḥāʾirūn*, Baghdad, 1960?

Ghallāb, ʿAbd al-Karīm (1920, M) *Māt qarīr al-ʿayn*, Casablanca, 1965; *Al-ʾArḍ ḥabībatī*, Beirut, 1971; *Wa Akhrajahā min al-jannah*, Tunis, 1977.

Gharīb, *Rūz (L) *Khuṭūṭ wa ẓilāl*, Beirut, n.d.

Ghāmidī, *Maryam Muḥ. al- (A) *Uḥibbuk wa lakin*, Jiddah, 1987.

Ghānim, Fatḥī (1926, E) *Tajribat ḥubb*, Cairo, 1958; *Sūr ḥadīd mudabbab*, Cairo, 1964.

Ghīṭānī, Jamāl al- (1945, E) *Awrāq shāb ʿāsh mundh alf ʿām*, Cairo, 1969; *Arḍ. Arḍ*, Cairo, 1972; *Al-Zuwayl*, Baghdad, 1975; *Al-Ḥiṣār min thalāth jihāt*, Damascus, 1975; *Ḥikāyāt al-gharīb*, Cairo, 1976; *Dhikr mā jarā*, Cairo, 1978; *Itḥāf al-zamān bi ḥikāyat Jilbi al-Sulṭān*, Cairo, 1984; *Muntaṣaf layl al-ghurbah*, Cairo, 1984; *Aḥrāsh al-madīnah*, Cairo, 1985.

Haddūqah, ʿAbd al-Ḥamīd Ibn (1935, G) *Ẓilāl jazāʾiriyyah*, Beirut, n.d.; *Al-ʾAshiʿʿah al-sabʿah*, Algiers, 1962.

Hadhdhāl, ʿĀshiq (A) *Al-Kalb wa'l-ḥaḍārah*, Jiddah, 1984.

Halasā Ghālib (1939–89, J) *Wadīʿ wa'l-qiddīsah Mīlādah waʾĀkharūn*, Cairo, 1968; *Zunūj wa badw wa fallāḥūn*, Baghdad, 1977.

Harrādī, Muḥammad al- (1948, M) *Al-Lawz al-murr*, Damascus, 1980.

Hilāl, ʿAbd al-ʿAzīz (1933, S) *Imraʾatān fīʾl-ziḥām*, Damascus, 1970; *Al-Rajul al-ʾatharī*, Damascus, 1971.

Hindāwī, Khalīl (1905–76, L) *Al-Badāʾiʿ* Dayr al-Zawr, Syria, 1936; *Al-Ḥubb al-ʾawwal*, Aleppo, n.d. [1950]; *Damʿat Ṣalāḥ al-Dīn*, Beirut, 1958.

Hāshim, *Labībah (1880–1947, L) *Ka's min al-dumūʿ*, Cairo, 1941.

Hāshimī, Bashīr al- (Li) *Aḥzān ʿAmmi al-Dūkāli*, Tripoli, Libya, 1965; *Al-Nās wa 'l-dunyā*, Tripoli, Libya, 1966; *Al-ʾAṣābiʿ al-ṣaghīrah*, Tripoli, Libya, 1972.

Hūnī, Muḥ. Bilqāsim al- (Li) *Sharkh fī 'l-mirʾāh*, Tripoli, Libya, 1978; *Al-Jasad al-Ṣaghīr*, Tripoli, Libya, 1979.

Ḥabībī, Imīl (1922, P) *Sudāsiyyat al-ʾayyām al-sittah*, Jerusalem, 1968.

Ḥabābī, Muḥ. ʿAzīz al- (1923, M) *Al-ʿAḍḍ ʿalā al-ḥadīd*, Tunis, 1969.

Ḥaddād, ʿAbd al-Masīḥ (1881–1950, S) *Ḥikāyāt muhājir*, New York, 1921.

Ḥakīm, ʿAbd al-Jabbār al- (1937, I) *Al-Muwajahah wa ʾaḥlām al-ṣighār*, Baghdad, 1974.

Ḥakīm, Tawfīq al- (1898–1987, E) *Ahl al-fann*, Cairo, 1934; *ʿAhd al-shayṭān*, Cairo, 1937; *Qiṣaṣ Tawfīq al-Ḥakīm*, 5 vols., Cairo, 1939–49; *Laylat al-zifāf*,Cairo, n.d.; *Shajarat al-ḥukm* Cairo, 1953; *Arinī Allāh*, Cairo, n.d. [1954]; *ʿAwālim al-faraḥ*, Cairo, 1958; *Anā wa'l-qānūn wa'l-fann*, Cairo, 1973.

Ḥallāq, 'Abdullah Yūrkī (1911, S) *Al-Zafarāt*, Aleppo, 1933.

Ḥaqqī, Badīʿ (1922, S) *Al-Turāb al-ḥazīn*, Damascus, 1961; *Ḥīn tatamazzaq al-ẓilāl*, Damascus, n.d.

Ḥaqqī, Yaḥyā (1905, E) *Qindīl umm Hāshim*, Cairo, 1944; *Dimāʾ wa ṭīn*, Cairo, 1955; *Umm al-ʿawājiz*, Cairo, 1955; *ʿAntar wa Juliet*, Cairo, n.d. [1961]; *Sāriq al-kuḥl*, Cairo, 1984; *Al-Firāsh al-shāghir*, Cairo, 1986.

Ḥarbī, Muḥ. Ḥasan al- (U) *Ḥikāyāt qabīlah mātat*, Beirut, 1987.

Ḥassūn, ʿAli Muḥ. (1951, A) *Ḥiṣṣat zaman*, Riyadh, 1976; *Ḥiwār taḥt al-maṭar*, Riyadh, 1982.

Ḥassūnah, Muḥ. Amīn (1908–58?, E) *Al-Ward al-ʾabyaḍ*, Cairo, 1933.

Ḥaydar, Muḥammad (1929, S) *Al-ʿĀlam al-mashḥūr*, Damascus, 1962.

Ḥaydar, Ḥaydar (S) *Ḥakāyā al-nawras al-muhājir*, Damascus 1973; *Al-Wamḍ*, Damascus, 1976.

Ḥaydarah, Muḥ. Ṣāliḥ (Y) *Hāʾimah min al-Yaman*, Cairo, 1974.

Ḥaydarī, Yūsuf al- (1934, I) *Ḥīn yajiff al-baḥr*, Baghdad, 1967; *Rajul Takrahuh al-madīnah*, Baghdad, 1969; *Lughat al-mazāmīr*, Baghdad, 1986.

Ḥijjāwī, Zakariyyā al- (1914–76, E) *Nahr al-banafsaj*, Cairo, 1956.

Ḥinnāwī, *Fāṭimah (1949, A) *A ʿmāq bilād baḥḥār*, Jiddah, 1975?; *Al-Rajul al-Ẓill*, Jiddah, 1983?.

Ḥusayn Ṭāhā (1889–1973, E) *Al-Muʿadhdhabūn fī 'l-arḍ*, Cairo, 1949.

Ḥusayn, Ḥusayn ʿAlī (1950, A) *Al-Raḥil*, Riyadh, 1978; *Tarnīmat al-rajul al-muṭārad*, Riyadh, 1983; *Ṭābūr al-miyāh al-ḥadīdiyyah*, Riyadh, 1985; *Kabīr al-maqām*, Cairo, 1987.

Ḥātim, *Dalāl (1931, S) *Al-Dukhūl min al-bāb al-ḍayyiq*, Damascus, n.d.

Ḥāzimī, Ḥijāb al- (1945, A) *Wujūh min al-Rīf*, Riyadh, 1981.

Ḥūrānyiyyah, Saʿīd (1929, S) *Wa fī 'l-nās al-masarrah*, Damascus, 1954; *Shitāʾ qās ākhar*, Beirut, 1962; *Sanatān, wa taḥtariq al-ghābah*, Beirut, 1964.

Ḥūḥū, Aḥmad Riḍā (G) *Ṣāḥibat al-waḥy*, Constantine, 1954; *Namādhij bashariyyah*. Tunis, 1955.

ʿIbādī. Ghāzi al- (1935, I) *Ḥikāyāt min riḥlat al-Sindibād*, Baghdad, 1969; *Ibtisāmāt li'l-nās wa'l-rīḥ*, Baghdad, 1970; *Finjān qahwah li zāʾir al-Ṣabāh*, Beirut, 1973; *Min al-hudūʾ ilā al-ṣamt*, Baghdad, 1977; *Al-Maṭāf*, Baghdad, 1980; *Al-Sayyidah wa'l-masāʾ*, Beirut, 1981; *Īqāʿāt muntaṣaf al-layl*, Baghdad, 1982; *Wajbah sākhinah*, Baghdad, 1985.

ʿInānī, Aḥmad (P) *Ḥabbat al-burtuqāl*, Cairo, 1962.

Īrānī, Maḥmūd Sayf al-Dīn al- (1914–74, P) *Awwal al-shawṭ*, Jaffa, 1937; *Maʿ al-nās*, Amman, 1956; *Mā aqall al-thaman*, Amman, 1962; *Qiṭār al-layl*, Beirut, 1973; *Matā yantahī al-layl*, Amman, 1965.

ʿĪsā, ʿAbdulla (Q) *Al-Zawj al-muntaẓar*, Duha, 1987.

Idlibī, *Ulfat ʿUmar al- (1912, S) *Wadāʿan yā Dimashq* Damascus, 1952; *Qiṣas shāmiyyah*, Damascus, 1954; *Qiṣās ʿArabiyyah*, Damascus, 1956; *Wa Yaḍḥak al-shayṭān*, Damascus, 1970; *ʿAṣiyy al-damʿ* Damascus, 1976.

Idrīs, Suhayl (1924, L) *Ashwāq*, Beirut, 1947; *Nīrān wa thulūj*, Beirut, 1948; *Kulluhun nisāʾ*, Beirut, 1949; *Al-Damʿ al-murr* Beirut, 1956.

Idrīs, Yūsuf (1927–91, E) *Arkhaṣ layālī*, Cairo, 1954; *Jumhūriyyat Faraḥāt*, Cairo, 1956; *Al-Baṭal*, Cairo, 1957; *Alays kadhālik*, Cairo, 1957; *Ḥādithat sharaf*, Beirut, 1958; *Ākhir al-dunyā*, Cairo, 1961; *Al-ʿAskarī al-ʾaswad*, Cairo, 1962; *Lughat al-ʾāyʾ āy* Cairo, 1965; *Al-Naddāhah*, Cairo, 1969; *Bayt min laḥm*, Cairo, 1971; *Anā Sulṭān qānūn al-Wujūd*, Cairo, 1980; *Uqtulhā*, Cairo, 1982; *Al-ʿAtab ʿAlā al-naẓar*, Cairo, 1987.

Ikhlāṣī, Walīd (1935, S) *Qiṣaṣ*, Beirut, 1963; *Shitāʾ al-baḥr al-yābis*, Beirut, 1965; *Dimāʾ fī 'l-ṣubḥ al-ʾaghbar*, Beirut, 1968; *Zaman al-hijirāt al-qaṣīrah*, Damascus, 1970; *Al-Ṭīn*, Beirut, 1971; *Al-Dahshah fī 'l-ʿuyūn al-qāsiyah*, Damascus, 1972; *Al-Taqrīr*, Damascus, 1974; *Al-Aʿshāb al-sawdāʾ*, Damascus, 1980; *Yā Shajarah yā*, Tripoli, Libya, 1981; *Khān al-ward*, Damascus, 1983.

Ismāʿīl, Ismāʿīl Fahd (1940, K) *Al-Buqʿah al-dākinah*, Beirut, 1965; *Al-Aqfāṣ wa'l-lughah al-mushtarakah*, Beirut, 1974.

Ismāʿīl, Ṣidqi (1924–72, S) *Allah wa'l-faqr*, Damascus, 1970.

Isḥāq, *Malīḥah (1925, I) *ʿAqlī dalīlī*, Beirut, 1948; *Layālī milāh*, Cairo, 1950; *Rāʾiʿah*, Cairo, 1952.

Jabbūr, Zuhayr (1948, S) *Al-Ḥulm*, Damascus 1978; *Al-Ward al-ʾān wa'l-sikkīn*, Damascus, 1979; *Al-Waqt*, Damascus, 1981; *Ḥiṣār al-zaman al-ʾakhīr* Damascus, 1984.

Jabrā, Jabrā Ibrāhim (1919, P) *ʿAraq wa-qiṣaṣ ukhrā*, Beirut, 1956.

Jafrī, ʿAbdullah (1938, A) *Ḥayāh jāʾiʿah*, Riyadh, 1963; *Al-Jidār al-ʾākhar*, Riyadh, 1971; *Al-Ẓamaʾ*, Riyadh, 1980.

Jamʿān, ʿAbdullah (1938, A) *Bint al-wādi*, Riyadh, 1970; *Rajul ʿalā al-raṣīf*, Riyadh, 1977.

Jibrān, Jibrān Khalīl (1883–1931, L) *ʿArāʾis al-murūj*, Beirut, 1906; *Al-ʾArwāḥ al-mutamrridah*, Beirut, 1908.

Jindārī, Maḥmūd (1939, I) *A ʿwām al-zamaʾ*, Baghdad, 1969; *Al-Ḥiṣār*, Baghdad, 1978; *Ḥālāt*, Baghdad, 1984.

Jubayr, ʿAbduh (1950, E) *Fāris ʿalā ḥiṣān min al-khashab*, Cairo, 1976; *Al-Wadāʿ tāj min al-ʿushb*, Cairo, 1985.

Jundī, Anʿām al- (L) *Al-Shaʿb huwa al-qāʾid*, Sidon, 1954.

Jundī, Saʿīd al- (S) *Marrah fī 'l-ʿumr*, Amman, 1955; *Al-Lāh wa'l-shayṭān*, Damascus, n.d.; *Abū-Ḥannūn*, Damascus, 1959.

Jābirī, Muḥ. Ṣāliḥ (T) *Al-Rukhkh yajūl fī'l-ruqʿah*, Tunis, 1978; *Kayf lā uḥibb al-nahār*, Tunis, 1979.

Jād al-Ḥaqq, Yūsuf (1930, P) *Ashraqat al-shams*, Cairo, 1960; *Al-Nāfidhah al-mughlaqah*, Damascus, 1964; *Sanaltaqī dhāt yawm*, Cairo, 1969.

Kanafāni, Ghassān (1936–72, P) *Mawt sarīr raqm 12*, Beirut, 1962; *Arḍ al-burtuqāl al-ḥazīn*, Beirut, 1963; *ʿĀlam lays lanā*, Beirut, 1965; *ʿAn al-Rijāl wa'l-banādiq*, Beirut, 1968?.

Karam, Karam Malḥam (L) *Ashbāḥ al-qaryah*, Beirut, 1938; *Aṭyāf min Lubnān*, Beirut, 1952.

Kaylānī, *Qamar (1928, S) *ʿĀlam bilā ḥudūd*, Baghdad, 1972; *Al-Ṣayyādūn wa luʿbat al-mawt* Damascus, 1978; *Iʿtirāfāt imraʾah ṣaghīrah*, Damascus, 1980; *Imraʿah min khazaf*, Damaascus, 1981.

Kayyālī, Mawāhib al- (1922, S) *Darb ilā al-qimmah*, Beirut, 1951; *Al-Manādīl al-bīḍ*, Beirut, 1952.

Kayyālī, Ḥasīb al- (1924, S) *Maʿ al-nās*, Beirut, 1952; *Akhbār min al-balad*, Beirut, 1954; *Riḥlah jidāriyyah*, Damascus, 1971; *Ḥikāyah basīṭah*, Damascus, 1972; *Tilk al-ʾayyām*, Damascus, 1977; *Al-Ḥuḍūr fi akthar min makān*, Damascus, 1979; *Al-Muṭārad*, Damascus, 1982.

Khalaf, Aḥmad (1945, I) *Nuzhah fī shawāriʿ mahjūrah*, Baghdad, 1974; *Manzil al-ʿarāʾis*, Baghdad, 1978; *Al-Ḥadd al-fāṣil*, Baghdad, 1981; *Al-Qādim al-baʿīd*, Baghdad, 1988.

Khalaf, Bashīr (G) *Akhādīd ʿalā sharīṭ al-zaman*, Algiers, 1977.

Khalaf, Khalaf Aḥmad (B) *Al-Hulm wujūh ukhrā*, Bahrain, 1975.

Khalqī, ʿAlī (1911–84, S) *Rabīʿ wa kharīf*, Damascus, 1931.

Khalīfah, ʿAlī ʿAbdullah (B) *Laḥn al-shitāʾ*, Bahrain, 1975; *Al-Raml wa'l-yāsamīn*, Bahrain, 1979.

Khalīlī, Jaʿfar al- (1908?, I) *Al-Tuʿasāʾ*, Al-Najaf, Iraq, 1931?; *Ḥadīth al-suʿlā*, Al-Najaf, n.d. [1934]; *Khayāl al-ẓill*, Al-Najaf, n.d. [1934?]; *Yawmiyyāt*, 2 vols., Al-Najaf, 1935; *Al-Sajīn al-muṭlaq*, Al-Najaf, n.d. [1936?]; *Iʿtirāfāt*, Al-Najaf, 1937; *Majmaʿ al-mutanāqiḍāt*, Al-Najaf, n.d. [1938]; *Ḥadith al-quwwah*, Al-Najaf, n.d. [1942]; *Min fawq al-rābiyah*, Baghdad, 1949; *Awlād al-Khalīli*, Baghdad, 1955; *Haʾulāʾ al-nās*, Baghdad, 1956.

Khamīs, *Ẓabyah (U) *ʿUrūq al-jīr wa'l-ḥinnah*, Beirut, 1985.

Khamīsī, ʿAbd al-Raḥmān al- (1919–87, E) *Al-ʾAʿmāq*,Cairo, 1950; *Ṣayḥāt al-shaʿb*, Cairo, 1952; *Qumṣān al-damm*, Cairo, 1953; *Lan Namūt*, Cairo, 1953; *Riyāḥ al-nīrān*, Cairo, 1954; *Dimāʾlā tajiff*, Cairo, 1956; *Al-Bahlawān al-mudhish Aḥmad Kishkish*, Cairo, 1961; *Amīnah*, Cairo, n.d. [1962].

Kharrāṭ, Idwār al- (1926, E) *Ḥiṭān ʿĀliyah*, Cairo, n.d. [1958]; *Sāʿāt al-Kibriyāʾ* Beirut, 1972; *Maḥaṭṭat al-sikkah al-ḥadīd*, Cairo, 1985; *Turābuhā Zaʿfarān*, Cairo, 1986; *Yā Banāt Iskindiriyyah*, Beirut, 1990.

Khayyūn, ʿAlī (1951, I) *Qirāʾah fī awrāq al-fajr*, Baghdad, 1978; *Riḥlat al-layl al-ʾakhīrah*, Baghdad, 1980; *Al-Ḥidād la yalīq bi'l-shuhadāʾ* Baghdad, 1981; *Ḥudūd al-nār*, Baghdad, 1983; *Zāʾir ākhar*, Baghdad, 1984; *Ayyām fī 'l-dhākirah*, Baghdad, 1987.

Khaṭīb, Anwar al- (U) *Khāzūq*, Sharjah, n.d.; *Muzāyadāt*, Sharjah, 1985; *Al-ʾArwāḥ taskun al-madīnah*, Sharjah, 1988.

Khiṣbāk, ʿĀʾid (1945, I) *Al-Mawqiʿah*, Baghdad, 1970; *Al-Kūmīdyā al-ʿudwāniyyah*, Baghdad, 1983; *Al-Ṭāʾir wa'l-nahr*, Baghdad, 1986; *Ṣabāḥ al-malāʾikah*, Baghdad, 1987.

Khulayfī, Sulaymān al- (K) *Haddāmah*, Kuwait, 1974; *Al-Majmūʿah al-thāniyah*, Kuwait, 1978.

Khuḍayyir, Muḥammad (1940, I) *Al-Mamlakah al-sawsāʾ*, Baghdad, 1972; *Fī Darajat 45 miʾawī*, Baghdad, 1978.

Khāl, ʿAbduh (A) *Ḥiwār ʿala bawābat al-ʾarḍ*, Riyadh, 1987.

Khūrī, *Kūlīt al- (1936, S) *Anā wa'l-madā*, Beirut, 1962; *Kayān*, Beirut, 1966; *Dimashq baytī al-kabīr*, Damascus, 1969; *Al-Marḥalah al-murrah*, Damascus, 1970; *Al-Kalimah al-ʾunthā*, Damascus, 1971; *Qiṣṣatān*, Damascus, 1975.

Khūrī, Idrīs (1939, M) *Ḥuzn fī 'l-raʾs wa fī 'l-qalb*, Rabat, 1973; *Ẓilāl*, Casablanca, 1977; *Al-Bidāyāt*, Casablanca, 1980; *Al-ʾAyyām wa'l-layālī*, Rabat, 1984?.

Khūrī, Ilyās (194?, L) *Al-Mubtdaʾ wa'l-khabar*, Beirut, 1984.

Khūrī, Raʾīf (L) *Ḥabbat al-rummān*, Beirut, 1935.

Khūst, *Nadyā (1935, S) *Uḥibb al-shām*, Damascus, 1967; *Fī'l-Qalb shayʾ ākhar* Damascus, 1979; *Fī Sijn ʿAkkā*, Damascus, 1984.

Kirīdī, Mūsā (1940, I) *Aṣwāt fī 'l-madīnah*, Baghdad, 1968; *Khuṭwāt al-musāfir naḥw al-mawt*, Baghdad, 1970; *Ghuraf niṣf muḍāʾah*, Baghdad, 1979; *Faḍāʾ āt al-Rūḥ*, Baghdad, 1986.

Kuzbarī, * Salmā al-Ḥaffār al- (1922, S) *Ḥirmān*, Damascus, 1952; *Zawāyā*, Cairo, 1952; *Al-Garībah*, Beirut, 1966.

Kāmil, Maḥmūd (1906, E) *Al-Mutamarridūn*, Cairo, 1931; *Fī 'l-Bayt wa'l-shāriʿ*, Cairo, 1933; *8 Yūlyū*, Cairo, 1934; *Bāʾiʿ al-ʾaḥlām*, Cairo, 1935; *Awwal Yanāyir*, Cairo, 1936; *Thalāthūn qiṣṣah*, Cairo, 1936; *Ant wa ʾanā*, Cairo, 1937; *Al-Majnūnah*, Cairo, 1938; *Al-Rabīʿ al-ʾāthim*, Cairo, 1939; *Zawbaʿah taḥt jumjumah*, Cairo, 1941; *ʿUyūn maʿṣūbah*, Cairo, 1941; *Al-Rijāl munāfiqūn*, Cairo, 1942; *Ḥutām imraʾah*, Cairo, 1942; *Lāʿibāt bi'l-nār*, Cairo, 1943; *Fatayāt mansiyyāt*, Cairo, 1944; *Al-Qāfilah al-Ḍāllah* Cairo, 1946; *Ābār fī 'l-Ṣaḥrāʾ*, Cairo, 1948; *Al-Hāribūn min al-Māḍi*, Cairo, 1949; *Lawḥāt wa-ẓilāl*, Cairo, 1960; *Arwāḥ Bayn al-suḥub*, Cairo, 1962.

Kūnī, Ibrāhīm al- (Li) *Al-Ṣalāh khārij niṭāq al-ʾawqāt al-khams*, Tripoli, Libya, 1974.

Lāshīn Maḥmūd Ṭāhir (1894–1954, E) *Sukhriyat al-nāy*, Cairo, n.d. [1926]; *Yuḥkā ann*, Cairo n.d. [1929]; *Al-Niqāb al-ṭāʾir*, Cairo, 1940.

Lūqā, Iskandar (1929, S) *Ḥubb fī kanīsah*, Damascus, 1952; *Wa fī laylah qamrāʾ*, Damascus, 1953; *Al-ʿĀlam al-majhūl*, Damascus, 1954; *Anṣāf makhlūqāt*, Damascus, 1956; *Nāfidhah ʿalā 'l-ḥayah*, Damascus, 1958; *Ra's samakah*, Damascus, 1961; *Al-Nafaq wa'l-ʾarqām*, Damascus, 1963; *Min Malaffāt al-qaḍā'* Damascus, 1964; *Al-Walīmah*, Damascus, 1971; *Sirr al-ʿulbah al-mayyitah*, Damascus, 1972.

Mabrūk, Muḥ. Ibrāhīm (1942, E) *ʿAṭashī li māʾ al-baḥr*, Cairo, 1983.

Madanī, ʿIzz al-Din al- (1938, T) *Khurāfāt*, Tunis, 197?; *Al-ʾInsān al-ṣifr*, Tunis, 197?; *Al-ʿAdwā*, Tunis, 1980; *Min Ḥikāyāt hādhā 'l-ẓamạn*, Tunis, 1982.

Madfaʿī (Midfaʿī), Walīd (1932, S) *Ghurūb fī'l-fajr*, Damascus, 1961.

Makhzanjī. Muḥammad al- (195?, E) *al-ʾĀti*, Cairo, 1983; *Rashq al-sikkīn*, Cairo, 1984; *Al-Mawt yaḍḥak*, Cairo, 1988; *Al-Safar*, Cairo, 1989.

Makkāwī, Saʿd (1916–85, E) *Nisāʾ min khazaf*, Cairo, 1948; *Fi Qahwat al-majādhīb*, Cairo, 1955; *Rāhibah min al-Zamālik*, Cairo, 1955; *Makhālib wa ʾanyāb*, Cairo, 1956; *Al-Māʾ al-ʿakir*, Cairo, n.d. [1957]; *Shahīrah*, Cairo, 1959; *Majmaʿ al-shayāṭīn*, Cairo, 1959; *Al-Zaman al-waghd*, Cairo, 1962; *Abwāb al-layl*, Cairo, 1964; *Al-Qamar al-mashwī*, Cairo, 1967; *Rajul min ṭin*, Cairo, 1970; *Al-Raqṣ ʿalā 'l-ʿushb al-ʾakhḍar*, Cairo, 1973?; *Al-Fajr yazūr al-ḥadīqah*, Cairo, 1975.

Mannāʿ, ʿAbdullah (1938, A) *Lamasāt*, Riyadh, 1960; *Anīn al-ḥayārā*, Riyadh, 1968.

Maqhūr, Kāmil Ḥasan al- (Li) *Al-ʾAms al-mashnūq*, Tripoli, Libya, 1968; *14 Qiṣṣah min madīnatī*, Tripoli, Libya, 1978.

Maslātī, Muḥammad al- (Li) *Al-Ḍajīj*, Tunis, 1977.

Maḥfūẓ, Najīb (1911, E) *Hans al-junūn*, Cairo, 1938; *Dunyā al-Lah*, Cairo, n.d. [1963]; *Bayt sayyiʾ al-sumʿah*, Cairo, n.d. [1965]; *Khammārat al-qiṭṭ al-ʾaswad*, Cairo, 1968; *Taḥt al-miẓallah*, Cairo, n.d. [1969]; *Ḥikāyah bilā bidāyah walā nihāyah*, Cairo, 1971; *Shahr al-ʿasal*, Cairo, n.d. [1971]; *Al-Jarīmah*, Cairo, n.d. [1973]; *Al-Ḥubb fawq haḍabat al-Haram*, Cairo, 1979; *Al-Shayṭān yaʿiẓ*, Cairo, 1980; *Raʾayt fīmā yarā al-nāʾim*, Cairo, 1982; *Al-Tanẓīm al-sirrī*, Cairo, 1984; *Ṣabāḥ al-ward*, Cairo, 1987; *Al-Fajr al-kādhib*, Cairo, 1989.

Maḥmūd, Yūsuf Aḥmad al- (1932, S) *Al-Mufsidūn fī'l-arḍ*, Damascus, 1958; *Salāmāt ayyuhā al-suʿadāʾ*, Damascus, 1978; *Muftaraq al-maṭar*, Damascus, 1983.

Middīnī, Aḥmad al- (1948, M) *Al- ʿunf fī'l-dimāgh*, Casablanca, 1971; *Sifr al-ʾinshāʾ wa'l-tadmīr*, Casablanca, 1978; *Al-Muẓāharah*, Casablanca, 1986.

Milḥis, Amīn Fāris (P) *Min waḥy al-wāqiʿ*, Jerusalem, 1952.

Milḥis, *Thurayyā (P) *Al-ʿUqdah al-sābiʿah*, Beirut, 1961.

Mishrī, ʿAbd al-ʿAzīz (1955, A) *Mawt ʿalā 'l-māʾ*, Riyadh, 1979; *Asfār al-Sarawī*, Riyadh, 1986; *Bawḥ al-sanābil*, Riyadh, 1987; *Al-Zuhūr tabḥath ʿan āniyah*, Riyadh, 1987.

Misnāwī, Muṣṭafā (1953, M) *Ṭāriq al-ladhī lam yaftaḥ al-ʾAndalus*, Beirut, 1979.

Miṣarrātī, ʿAli Muṣṭafā al- (Li) *Mirsāl*, Beirut, 1962; *Al-Shirāʿ al-mumazzaq*, Cairo, 1963; *Ḥifnah min ramād*, Beirut, 1964.

Miṣrī, Ibrāhīm al- (1909–81?, E) *Al-ʾAdab al-ḥayy*, Cairo, 1930; *Al-ʾAdab al-ḥadith*, Cairo, 1932; *Kharīf Imraʾ ah*, Cairo, 1944; *Qulūb al-nās* (Cairo, n.d. [1947]; *Kaʾs al-ḥayāh*, Cairo, 1947; *Nufūs ʿāriyah*, Cairo, 1951; *Al-ʾUnthā al-khālidah*, Cairo, 1957; *Al-ʾInsān wa'l-qadar*, Cairo, 1959; *Ṣirāʿ al-rūḥ wa'l-jasad*, Cairo, 1961; *Qalb ʿadhrāʾ*, Cairo, 1962; *ʿĀlam al-gharāiz wa'l-ʾaḥlām*, Cairo, 1962; *Al-Bāb al-dhahabī*, Cairo, n.d. [1963], *Ṣuwar min al-ʾinsān*, Cairo, 1965; *Ṣirāʿ maʿ al-māḍī*, Cairo, 1967; *Al-Wajh wa'l-qināʿ*, Cairo, 1971?.

Munajjid, Ṣalāḥ al-Din al- (P) *Fi Quṣūr al-khulafāʾ*, Beirut, 1944.

Murtaḍī, ʿAbd al-Karīm al- (Y) *Al-Gharīb*, Sanʿa, 1972.

Muthannā, Muḥammad (Y) *Fi Jawf al-layl*, Cairo, n.d. [1976].

Muṣṭafā, Khalifah Ḥusayn (1948?, Li) *Ṣakhab al-mawtā*, Tunis, 1975; *Tawqīʿāt ʿalā 'l-laḥm*, Tripoli, Libya, 1978; *Ḥikāyāt Shāriʿ al-Gharbi*, Tripoli, Libya, 1979.

Muṭṭalibī, ʿAbd al-Razzāq al- (1943, I) *Shajar al-masāfāt*, Baghdad, 1979; *Kāʾināt layliyyah*, Baghdad, 1983.

Muẓaffar, Saʿūd al- (O) *Yawm Qabl Shurūq al-Shams*, Muscat, 1987; *Wa Ashraqat al-shams*, Muscat, 1988.

Mājid, Muḥammad al- (B) *Maqāṭiʿ min simfūniyyah ḥazīnah*, Kuwait, n,d.; *Al-Raḥīl ilā mudun al-faraḥ*, Bahrain, 1977; *Sīrat al-jūʿ wa'l-ṣamt*, Bahrain, 1981.

Mālik, Nayrūz (1943, S) *Al-Ṣadafah wa'l-baḥr*, Damascus, 1977; *Ḥarb ṣaghīrah*, Damascus, 1979; *Kūb min al-shāy al-bārid*, Damascus, 1981; *Kitāb al-waṭan*, Damascus, 1982; *Aḥwāl al-balad*, Damascus, 1983.

Mālikī, Ḥusayn Naṣīb al- (Li) *Maqbūlah*, Tripoli, Libya, 1979.

Māzinī, Ibrāhim ʿAbd al-Qādir al- (1890–1949, E) *Ṣundūq al-dunyā*, Cairo, 1929; *Khuyūṭ al-ʿankabūt*, Cairo, 1935; *Fī 'l-Ṭarīq* , Cairo, 1937; *ʿA'l-Māshī*, Cairo, 1937; *Min al-Nāfidhah*, Cairo, 1949; *Min al-Nāfidhah wa ṣuwar min al-ḥayāh*, Cairo, 1960.

Mīnah, Ḥannā (1924, S) *Al-Abnūsah al-bayḍāʾ*, Damascus, 1976; *Man yadhkur tilk al-ʾayyām*, with N. Al-ʿAṭṭār, Damascus, 1974.

Mūsā, Ṣabri (1932, E) *Al-Qamīṣ*, Cairo, 1958; *Ḥādith al-niṣf mitr*, Cairo, 1962; *Ḥikāyāt Ṣabri Mūsā*, Cairo, 1963; *Wajhā li Ẓahr*, Cairo, 1966; *Mashrūʿ qatl jārah*, Cairo, 1970.

Naʿʿās, *Marḍiyyah al- (Li) *Ghazālah*, Tripoli, Libya, n.d.

Nadīm, Muḥammad (1942, S) *Al-Ṭifl wa'l-mughāmarah*, Qamashli, Syria, 1979; *ʿĀm jadīd*, Damascus, 1980; *Abṭāl majhūlūn*, Damascus, 1981; *ʿĀlam khāṣ*, Damascus, 1982.

Najjār, Muḥammad al- (S) *Fī Quṣūr Dimashq*, Damascus, 1937.

Najm, Walīd (1943, S) *Al-Wilādah min al-zahr*, Damascus, 1977.

Nashʾat, Badr (1927, E) *Masāʾ al-khayr yā jidʿān*, Cairo, 1956; *Ḥilm laylat taʿab*, Cairo, 1962.

Naḥawī, Adīb (1924, S) *Kaʾs wa miṣbāḥ*, Aleppo, 1948; *Min Damm qalbi*, Aleppo, 1949; *Ḥattā yabqā al-ʿushb akhḍar*, Beirut, 1965; *Ḥikāyāt li'l-ḥuzn*, Beirut, 1967; *Qad Yakūn al-ḥubb*, Damascus, 1972; *Maqṣid al-ʿĀṣî*, Damascus, 1982.

Naṣr, ʿAbd al-Qādir bin al-Ḥāj (T) *Ṣalʿāʾ yā ḥabībatī*, Tunis, 1970.

Nimr, Nasīb (1925, L) *Maʿāwil*, Beirut, 1948.

Nuʿaymah, Mīkhāʾīl (1889–1988, L) *Kān mā Kān*, Beirut, 1937; *Akābir*, Beirut, 1956; *Abū-Baṭṭah*, Beirut, 1959.

Nāʿūrī, ʿĪsā al- (J) *Ṭarīq al-Shawk*, Amman, 1955; *Khalli al-sayf yaqūl*, Jerusalem, 1956; *ʿĀʾid ilā 'l-maydān*, Aleppo, 1961.

Nājī, Ibrāhīm (1898–1953, E) *Madīnat al-ʾAḥlām*, Cairo, 1938; *Adriknī yā duktūr*, Cairo, 1950.

Nāṣir, ʿAbd al-Sattār (1947, I) *Al-Raghbah fī waqt mutaʾakhkhir*, Baghdad, 1968; *Ṭāʾir al-ḥaqīqah, Nāṣir*, Baghdad, 1971; *Mūjaz ḥayāt Sharīf Nādir*, Damascus, 1975; *Lā Tasriq al-wardah rajāʾ*, Damascus, 1978; *Marrah wāḥidah wa ʾilā 'l-ʾabad*, Baghdad, 1979; *Al-Ḥubb ramyan bi'l-raṣāṣ*, Cairo, 1985; *Al-Shams ʿirāqiyyah*, Baghdad, 1986; *Maṭar taḥt al-shams*, Cairo, 1986; *Lā ʿAshāʾ baʿd al-laylah*, Cairo, 1987; *Nisāʾ min maṭar*, Baghdad, 1987; *Al-Safar ilā 'l-ḥubb*, Baghdad, 1988; *Ṭaʿm al-ṣibā*, Rabat, 1989.

Nāṣir, Ibrāhīm al- (1932, A) *Ummahātunā wa'l-niḍāl*, Cairo, 1961; *Arḍ bilā maṭar*, Riyadh, 1967; *Ghadīr al-banāt*, Riyadh, 1977.

Qaʿīd, Muḥ. Yūsuf al- (1944, E) *Ṭarḥ al-baḥr*, Cairo, 1976; *Tajfīf al-dumūʿ*, Cairo, 1982; *Ḥikāyāt al-zaman al-jarīh*, Cairo, 1982; *Qiṣaṣ min bilād al-fuqarāʾ*, Damascus, 1983; *Man yadhkur Miṣr al-ān*, Cairo, 1984; *Lam Yaʿud al-ḍaḥik mumkinan*, Cairo, 1987.

Qabāʾilī, *Luṭfiyyah al- (Li) *Amāni muʿallabah*, Tripoli, Libya, 1977.

Qalʿajī, *Anṣaf (J) *Li'l-Ḥuzn baqāyā faraḥ*, Amman, 1987.

Qalʿajī, Qadrī (P) *Qulūb muʿadhdhabah*, Cairo, 1955.

Qalamāwī *Sahīr (Suhayr) al- (1911, E) *Al-Shayāṭīn talhū*, Cairo, 1964.

Qammūdī, Muḥ, Ṣāliḥ al- (Li) *Iskimbīl bi-sittah*, Tripoli, Libya, 1973.

Qaysī, Jalīl al- (1937, I) *Ṣahīl al-mārah ḥawl al-ʿālam*, Beirut, 1968; *Zulaykhah, al-buʿd yaqtarib*, Baghdad, 1974; *Fi Zawraq wāḥid*, Baghdad, 1985.

Qiʿwār, *Najwā (J) *ʿĀbirū al-sabīl*, Amman, n.d.

Qiʿwār, Fakhrī (1945, J) *Li-Mādhā bakat Sūzi*, Amman, n.d.; *Mamnūʿ laʿib al-shaṭaranj*, Amman, n.d.

Qindīl, Muḥ al-Mansī (E) *Man qatal maryam al-Ṣāfī*, Cairo, 1985; *Iḥtiḍār qiṭṭ ʿajūz*, Cairo, 1986; *Bayʿ nafs bashariyyah*, Cairo, 1987.

Qurashī, Ḥasan ʿAbdullah (1930, A) *Annāt al-sāqiyah*, Cairo, 1956; *Ḥubb fī 'l-ẓalām*, Riyadh, 196?.

Quwayrī, ʿAbdullah al- (Li) *Ḥayātuhum*, Tripoli, Libya, 1960; *Al-ʿĪd fī 'l-ʾArḍ*, Tripoli, Libya, 1963; *Qaṣʿah min al-khubz*, Tripoli, Libya, 1965; *Al-Furṣah wa'l-qannāṣ*, Tripoli, Libya, 1965; *Al-Zayt wa'l-tamr*, Tunis, 1967; *Khayṭ lam yansijh al-ʿankabūt*, Tripoli, Libya, 1973; *Sittūn qiṣṣah*, Tunis, 1975.

Qāsim, ʿAbd al-Ḥakīm (1935–90, E) *Al-ʾUkht li-ʾabb*, Beirut, 1982; *Al-ʾAshwāq wa'l-ʾasā*, Cairo, 1984; *Suṭūr min daftar al-ʾaḥwāl*, Beirut, 1985; *Al-Ẓunūn wa'l-ruʾā*, Cairo, 1986; *Al-Ḥijrah ilā ghayr al-Maʾlūf*, Cairo, 1987.

Rabbāh, Walīd (1940, P) *Awrāq min mufakkirat munāḍil*, Amman, 1970; *Nuqūsh ʿalā judrān zinzānah*, Beirut, 1974.

Rabīʿ, Mubārak (1935, M) *Sayyidunā Qadar*, Tripoli, Libya, 1968; *Damm wa-dukhān*, Tunis, 1970; *Riḥlat al-Ḥubb wa'l-ḥaṣād*, Beirut, 1983.

Rajab, Muḥ. Ḥāfiẓ (1933, E) *Al-Kurah wa raʾs al-rajul*, Cairo, 1967; *Ghurabāʾ*, Cairo, 1968; *Makhlūqāt barrād al-shāy al-maghli*, Cairo, 1979.

Rashīd, *Fawziyyah (B) *Marāyā al-ẓill wa'l-faraḥ*, Beirut, 1983.

Raysūnī, Muḥ. Al-Khaḍr al- (1929, M) *Afrāḥ wa dumūʿ*, Tiṭwān, 1951; *Rabīʿ al-ḥayāh*, Tiṭwān, 1957.

Rifʿat, *Alīfah (1930, E) *Ḥawwāʾ taʿūd bi ʾĀdam*, Cairo, 1975.

Rifāʿiyah, Yāsīn (1934, S) *Al-Ḥuzn fī kull makān*, Damascus, 1960; *Al-ʿĀlam yaghraq*, Damascus, 1963; *Al-ʿAṣāfīr*, Beirut, 1974; *Al-Rijāl al-khaṭirūn*, Beirut, 1979; *Nahr ḥanān*, Beirut, 1983.

Rubayʿī, ʿAbd al-Raḥmān Majīd al- (1939, I) *Al-Sayf wa'l-safīnah*, Baghdad, 1966; *Al-Ẓill fī'l-raʾs*, Beirut, 1968; *Wujūh min riḥlat al-taʿab*, Baghdad, 1969; *Al-Mawāsim al-ʾukhrā*, Beirut, 1970; *ʿUyūn fī'l-ḥulm*, Damascus, 1974; *Dhākirat al-madīnah*, Baghdad, 1975; *Al-Khuyūl*, Tunis, 1977; *Al-Afwāh*, Beirut, 1979.

Rujayb, Walīd al- (1958, K) *Taʿlaq nuqṭah, tasquṭ ṭaq*, Beirut, 1983.

Rāhib, Hānī al- (1939, S) *Al-Madīnah al-fāḍilah*, Damascus, 1969; *Jarāʾim Don Quixote*, Damascus, 1978.

Rīmāwī, Maḥmūd al- (1946, P) *Al-ʿUry fī ṣaḥrāʾ layliyyah*, Baghdad, 1974.

Saʿdanī, Maḥmūd al- (1927, E) *Al-Samāʾ al-sawdāʾ*, Cairo, n.d. [1955]; *Jannat Raḍwān*, Cairo, 1956; *Bint madāris*, Cairo, 1960; *Al-ʾAfrīki*, Cairo, 1965.

Saʿdāwī, *Nawāl al- (1930, E) *Taʿallamt al-ḥubb*, Cairo, 1959; *Ḥanān qalīl*, Cairo, 1964; *Laḥẓat ṣidq*, Cairo, 1966; *Al-Khayṭ wa'l-jidār*, Cairo, 1972.

Saʿīd, Maḥmūd ʿAli al- (1943, S) *Al-Raṣaṣah*, Damascus, 1978; *Al-Midfaʾah*, Damascus, 1980; *Al-Qaṣabah*, Damascus, 1982; *Al-Minqal*, Aleppo, 1982.

Sakākīnī, *Widād (192?, S) *Marāyā a-nās*, Cairo, n.d.; *Bayn al-Nīl wa'l-nakhīl*, Cairo, n.d.; *Al-Sitār al-Marfūʿ*, Cairo, 1955; *Nufūs tatakallam*, Cairo, 1962.

Salmān, *Suhaylah Dāwūd (194?, I) *Intifāḍat qalb*, Beirut, 1965; *Wa-Fajʾah abdaʾ bi'l-ṣurākh*, Beirut, 1975; *Kān ismuh Ḍārī* Baghdad, 1979.

Sammān *Ghādah al- (1942, S) *ʿAynāk qadarī*, Beirut, 1962; *Lā Baḥr fī Beirut*, Beirut, 1963; *Raḥīl al-Marāfiʾ al-Qadīmah*, Beirut, 1970; *Layl al-ghurabāʾ*, Beirut, 1973.

Saqqāf, *Khayriyyah al- (1951, A) *An Tubḥir naḥw al-ʾabʿād*, Riyadh, 1982.

Sawāḥirī, Khalīl al- (1940, J) *Thalāthat aṣwāt*, with others, Amman, 1972; *Maqhā al-Bāshūrah*, Damascus, 1975; *17 Qiṣṣah qaṣīrah*, with others, Amman, 1976; *Zāʾir al-masāʾ*, Amman, 1985.

Sayf, *Salmā Maṭar (U) *ʿUshbah*, Beirut, 1988.

Sayyid, Maḥmūd Aḥmad al- (1901–37, I) *Al-Nakabāt*, Baghdad, 1922; *Al-Ṭalāʾiʿ*, Baghdad, 1929; *Fī Sāʿ min al-zaman*, Baghdad, 1935.

Sayyār, ʿAli (B) *Al-Sayyid*, Bahrain, 1976.

Shabīb, *Ruqayyah Ḥammūd (1957, A) *Ḥulm* Riyadh, 1985?; *Al-Ḥuzn al-ramādī*, Riyadh, 1987.

Shaghmūm, al-Milūdi (1947, M) *Ashyāʾ tataḥarrak*, Rabat, 1972; *Sifr al-ṭāʿah*, Casablanca, 1982.

Shaqḥāʾ, Muh, Manṣūr al- (1947, A) *Al-Baḥth ʿan ibtisāmah*, Riyadh, 1976;- *Ḥikāyat ḥubb sādhijah*, Riyadh, 1979; *Masāʾ yawm fī Ādhār*, Riyadh, 1981; *Intiẓār al-riḥlah al-mulghāh*, Riyadh, 1983.

Sharqāwī, ʿAbd al-Raḥmān al- (1920–87, E) *Arḍ al-maʿrakah*, Cairo, 1954; *Aḥlām ṣaghīrah*, Cairo, 1956.

Sharīf, Yūsuf al- (Li) *Al-Jidār*, Tripoli, Libya, 1965; *Al-ʾAqdām al-ʿāriyah*, Tripoli, Libya, 1975.

Sharīf, Ṣamīm al- (1927, S) *Anīn al-ʾarḍ*, Damascus, n.d. [1953]; *ʿIndamā yajūʿ al-ʾaṭfāl*, Damascus, 1961.

Shaykh, *Ḥanān al (1945, L) *Wardat al-Ṣaḥrāʾ*, Beirut, 1982.

Shaṭṭī, Sulaymān al- (194?, K) *Rijāl min al-Raff al-ʿĀli*, Kuwait, 1982.

Shukrī, Muḥammad (1935, M) *Majnūn al-ward*, Beirut, 1979; *Al-Khaymah*, Casablanca, 1985.

Shuraym, Akram (1943, P) *Lam Namut baʿd*, Cairo, 1967; *Al-Sujanāʾ lā yuḥāribūn*, Damascus, 1973.

Shurayqī, Zakariyyā (1940, S) *Ghubār al-ʾasmant*, Damascus, 1977; *Al-Ḍawʾ min al-bāb*, Damascus, 1978; *Ākhir akhbār qaryat al-ʿUlayq*, Damascus, 1979; *Qul yā baḥr*, Damascus, 1981; *Al-Yāfāwi*, Damascus, 1983.

Shurūrū, Yūsuf (1940, P) *Zawraq min damm*, Beirut, 1967; *ʿAyn fī 'l-nahār*, Beirut, 1974.

Shudwayhidī, Muḥ. al- (Li) *Aḥzān al-yawm al-wāḥid*, Benghazi, 1973; *Aqwāl shāhid ʿayān*, Tripoli, Libya, 1976.

Shāʾūl, Anwar (1904, I) *Al-Ḥaṣād al-ʾawwal*, Baghdad, 1930; *Fī Ziḥām al-madīnah*, Baghdad, 1955.

Shāhīn, Maḥmūd (1946, P) *Nār al-barāʾah*, Beirut, 1979.

Shārūnī, Yūsuf al- (1924, E) *Al-ʿUshshāq al-khamsah*, Cairo, 1954; *Risālah ilā imraʾah*, Cairo, 1960; *Al-Ziḥām*, Beirut, 1969; *Al-ʾUmm wa'l-waḥsh*, Cairo,1982?

Shāyib, Fuʾād al- (1910–70, S) *Tārīkh jurḥ*, Beirut, 1944.

Sibāʿī, Fāḍil, al- (1929, S) *Al-Shawq wa'l-liqāʾ*, Aleppo, 1958; *Ḍayf min al-sharq*, Beirut, 1959; *Ḥayāh jadīdah*, Aleppo, 1959; *Muwāṭin amām al-qaḍāʾ*, Cairo, 1959; *Al-Laylah al-ʾakhīrah*, Cairo, 1961; *Nujūm lā tuḥṣā*, Beirut, 1962; *Ḥuzn ḥattā al-mawt*, Beirut, 1975; *Riḥlat ḥanān*, Cairo, 1975.

Sibāʿī, Murād al- (1914, S) *Kastīja*, Homs, 1948; *Al-Dars al-mashʾūm*, Homs, 1949; *Hadhā mā kān*, Cairo, 1952; *Al-Sharārah al-ʾūlā*, Damascus, 1962; *Taḥt al-nāfidhah*, Damascus, 1974; *Asʾilah tuṭraḥ waʾaṣdāʾ tujīb*, Damascus, 1979.

Sibāʿī, Yūsuf al- (1917–78, E) *Nāʾib ʿIẓrāʾīl*, Cairo, n.d. [1947]; *Aṭyāf*, Cairo, n.d. [1947]; *Ithnatā ʿashrat imraʾah*, Cairo, n.d. [1948]; *Yā Ummah ḍaḥikat*, Cairo, n.d. [1948]; *Fī Mawkib al-hawā*, Cairo, n.d. [1949]; *Khabāyā al-ṣudūr*, Cairo, n.d. [1949]; *Min al-ʿālam al-majhūl*, Cairo, n.d. [1949]; *Ithnā ʿashar rajulā*, Cairo, n.d. [1949]; *Mabkā al-ʿushshāq*, Cairo, n.d. [1950]; *Hādhih al-nufūs*, Cairo, n.d. [1950]; *Ḥādhā ḥuwa al-ḥubb*, Cairo, n.d. [1951]; *Ughniyāt*, Cairo, n.d. [1951]; *Bayn Abu'l-Rīsh wa Junaynat Nāmīsh*, Cairo, n.d. [1951]; *Ṣuwar ṭibq al-ʾaṣl*, Cairo, n.d. [1951]; *Summār al-layālī*, Cairo, n.d. [1952]; *Sitt nisāʾ wa sittat rijāl*,

Cairo, n.d. [1952]; *Al-Shaykh Zuʿrub wa ʾākharūn*, Cairo, n.d. [1952]; *Nafḥah min al-ʾīmān*, Cairo, n.d. [1952]; *Ḥamsah ghābirah*, Cairo, 1953; *Laylat khamr*, Cairo, 1954; *Layālī wa dumūʿ*, Cairo, n.d. [1956]; *Al-Wiswās al-khannās*, Cairo, 1956.

Suhayl, *Kūlīt (S) see under Khūri, Kūlīt.

Suhayl, Ibrāhīm (1918, I) *Ilayhą*, Baghdad, 1941; *Anā*, Baghdad, 1945.

Sulṭān, Muẓaffar (1911, S) *Ḍamīr al-dhiʾb*, Beirut, 1960; *Fī Intiẓār al-maṣīr*, Damascus, 1976.

Surayyiʿ, ʿAbd al-ʿAziz al- (K) *Dumūʿ rajul tāfih*, Kuwait, 1985.

Suḥaymī, ʿAbd al-Jabbār al- (1939, M) *Al-Mumkin min al-mustaḥīl*, Cairo, 1969.

Sālim, *Laṭīfah Ibrāhīm al- (1951, A) *Al-Zaḥf al-ʾabyad*, Riyadh, 1982.

Sālim, Jūrj (1933–76, S) *Fuqarāʾ al-nās*, Damascus, n.d.; *Al-Raḥīl*, Damascus, 1970; *Ḥiwār al-ṣumm*, Damascus, 1973; *Ḥikāyat al-ẓamaʾ al-qadīm*, Damascus, 1976; *ʿAzf munfarid ʿalā ʾl-kamān*, Damascus, 1976.

Sālim, Wārid Badr al- (1956, I) *Dhalik al-bukāʾ al-jamīl*, Baghdad, 1983; *Aṣābiʿ al-ṣafṣāf*, Baghdad, 1987; *Judhūʿ fī ʾl-ʿArāʾ*, Baghdad, 1988.

Ṣabbāgh, Muḥammad al- (1929, M) *ʿUnqūd nadyy*, Casablanca, 1964; *Shumūʿ ʿalā ʾl-ṭarīq*, Tunis, 1968; *Nuqṭat niẓām*, Rabat, 1970; *Shajarat al-maḥār*, Rabat, 1972; *Tiṭwān taḥkī*, Casablanca, 1979.

Ṣabrī, Idmūn (1921–75, I) *Ḥaṣād al-dumūʿ*, Baghdad, 1953; *Al-Maʾmūr al-ʿajūz*, Baghdad, 1954; *Qāfilat al-ʾaḥyāʾ*, Baghdad, 1955; *Kātib wāridah*, Baghdad, 1955; *Khaybat amal*, Baghdad, 1956; *Shijār Saʿīd Afandi*, Baghdad, 1957; *Al-Khālah ʿAtiyyah*, Baghdad, 1958; *Fī Khiḍamm al-maṣāʾib*, Baghdad, 1959; *Hārib min al-ẓulm*, Baghdad, 1960; *Laylah muzʿijah*, Baghdad, 1960; *Khubz al-ḥukūmah*, Baghdad, 1961; *Zawjat al-marḥūm*, Baghdad, 1962; *ʿIndamā takūn al-ḥayāh rakhīṣah*, Baghdad, 1968; *Ḥikāyāt ʿan al-salāṭīn*, Baghdad, 1969; *Aqāṣīṣ min al-ḥayāh*, Baghdad, 1970.

Ṣafadī, Muṭāʿ (1930?, S) *Ashbāḥ abṭāl*, Beirut, 1959.

Ṣaqr, Mahdi ʿĪsā al- (1927, I) *Mujrimūn ṭayyibūn*, Baghdad, 1954; *Ghaḍab al-madīnah*, Baghdad, 1960; *Ḥayrat sayyidah ʿajūz*, Baghdad, 1986.

Ṣidqī, *Jādhibiyyah (1927, E) *Rabīb al-ṭuyūr*, Cairo, 1951; *Mamlakat Allāh*, Cairo, 1954; *Innah al-ḥubb*, Cairo, 1955; *Sattār yā layl*, Cairo, 1956; *Wa-Bakā qalbī*, Cairo, 1957; *Taʿalā*, Cairo, 1957; *Al-Bint min Baḥarī*, Cairo, 1958; *Shayʾ ḥarām*, Cairo, 1959; *Laylah bayḍā*, Cairo, 1960; *Al-Layl ṭawīl*, Cairo, 1961; *Ant qās*, Cairo, 1966; *Dabīb al-naml*, Cairo, 1968; *Al-Dunyā wa ʾanā*, Cairo, 1972; *Bawwābat al-Mutawallī*, Cairo, 1975; *Al-Baladī yuʾkal*, Cairo, 1976.

Ṣidqī, Muḥammad (1927, E) *Al-ʾAnfār*, Cairo, 1956; *Al-ʾAydī al-khashinah*, Cairo, 1958; *Sharkh fī jidār al-khawf*, Cairo, 1967; *Liqāʾ maʿ rajul majhūl*, Cairo, 1969.

Ṣidqī, Najātī (1905, P) *Al-ʾAkhawāt al-ḥazīnāt*, Cairo, 1953; *Al-Shuyūʿī al-milyūnayr*, Beirut, 1963.

Ṣāliḥ, Al-Ṭayyib (D) *Dawmat wad Ḥāmid*, Beirut, 1976.

Ṣāliḥ, Amīn (1950, B) *Hunā al-wardah hunā narquṣ*, Beirut, 1973; *Al-Farāshāt*, Bahrain, 1977; *Al-Ṣayd al-Malakī*, Beirut, 1982; *Al-Ṭarāʾid*, Beirut, 1983; *Nudamāʾ al-marfaʾ, nudamāʾ al-rīḥ*, Bahrain, 1987; *Al-ʿAnāṣir*, Bahrain, 1989.

Ṣāliḥ, Aḥmad Rushdī (1920–82, E) *Al-Zawjah al-thāniyah*, Cairo, 1955.

Takarlī, Fu'ād al- (1927, I) *Al-Wajh al-'ākhar*, Baghdad, 1960, and 1982.

Taqiyy al-Dīn, Khalīl (L) *ʿAshar qiṣaṣ*, Beirut, 1937; *Al-'Iʿdām*, Beirut, 1940; *Khawāṭir sādhaj*, Beirut, n.d.

Taqiyy al-Dīn, Saʿīd (L) *Al-Thalj al-'Aswad*, Beirut, 1946; *Mawjat nār*, Beirut, 1948; *Ghābat al-Kāfūr*, Beirut, 1951.

Tawfīq, Ḥabīb (1909–74, E) *Al-Rabīʿ*, Cairo, 1934; *Madīḥah*, Cairo, n.d. [1936]; *Fī Dunyā al-ʿadam*, Cairo, 1945; *Atyāf al-fann*, Cairo, 1948.

Tawfīq, *Saḥar (E) *An Tanḥadir al-shams*, Cairo, 1985

Taymūr, Maḥmūd (1894–1973, E) *Al-Shaykh Jumʿah*, Cairo, 1925; *ʿAmm Mitwallī*, Cairo, 1925; *Al-Shaykh Sayyid al-ʿAbīṭ*, Cairo, 1926; *Rajab Afandī*, Cairo, 1928; *Al-Ḥajj Shalabī*, Cairo, 1930; *Abū-ʿAlī ʿāmil artist*, Cairo, 1934; *Al-Shaykh ʿAfallah*, Cairo, 1936; *Al-Wathbah al-'ūlā*, Cairo, 1937; *Qalb ghāniyah*, Cairo, 1937; *Firʿawn al-ṣaghīr*, Cairo, 1939; *Maktūb ʿalā 'l-jabīn*, Cairo, 1941; *Bint al-Shayṭān*, Cairo, 1944; *Shafāh ghalīẓah*, Cairo, 1946; *Khalf al-lithām*, Cairo, 1948; *Iḥsān li'l-Lāh*, Cairo, 1949; *Kull ʿām wa 'antum bi khayr*, Cairo, 1950; *Shabāb wa ghāniyāt*,Cairo, 1951; *Abū'l-Shawārib*, Cairo, 1953; *Zāmir al-Ḥayy*, Cairo, 1953; *'Abū-ʿAli al-fannān*, Cairo, 1954; *Thā'irūn*, Cairo, 1955; *Dunyā jadīdah*, Cairo, 1957; *Nabbūt al-ghafīr*, Cairo, 1958; *Tamr Ḥinnah ʿajab*, Cairo, 1958; *Anā al-qātil*, Cairo, 1962; *Intiṣār al-ḥayāh*, Cairo, 1963; *Al-Bārūnah Umm Aḥmad*, Cairo, 1967; *Ḥikāyāt Abū ʿŪf*, Cairo, 1969; *Bint al-yawm*, Cairo, 1971.

Taymūr, Muḥammad (1892–1921, E) *Wamīḍ al-rūḥ*, Cairo, 1922.

Tikbālī, Khalīfah al- (Li) *Al-'Aʿmāl al-kāmilah*, Tunis, 1976.

Tāmir, Zakariyyā (1931, S) *Ṣahīl al-jawād al-'abyaḍ*, Beirut, 1960; *Rabīʿ fī'l-ramād*, Damascus, 1963; *Al-Raʿd*, Damascus, 1970; *Dimashq al-ḥarā'iq*, Damascus, 1973; *Al-Nimūr fī'l-yawm al-ʿāshir*, Damascus, 1978.

Tāzī, Muḥ. ʿIzz al-Dīn al- (1948, M) *Awṣāl al-shajar al-maqṭūʿah*, Rabat, 1975; *Abrāj al-madīnah*, Baghdad, 1978; *Al-Nidā' bi'l-'asmā'*, Beirut, 1981.

Tūnjī, Muḥammad al- (S) *ʿAdhārā wa mūmisāt* Aleppo, 1954; *Taʿālā narquṣ*, Damascus, 1958.

Ṭabīʿah, *Rafīqat al- (1940, M) *Rajul wa imra'ah*, Casablanca, 1969; *Taḥt al-qanṭarah*, Casablanca, 1976; *Rīḥ al-sumūm*, Casablanca, 1979.

Ṭāhir, Bahā' (1935, E) *Al-Khuṭūbah*, Cairo, 1972; *Bi'l-'Ams ḥalamt bik*, Cairo, 1984; *Anā al-Malik ji't*, Cairo, 1985.

Ṭanṭāwī, ʿAli al- (S) *Qiṣas min al-ḥayāh*, Damascus, 1939; *Qiṣaṣ min al-tārīkh*, Damascus, n.d.

ʿUbayd, ʿĪsā (189?–1922 S/E) *Iḥsān Hānim*,Cairo, 1921; *Thurayyā*, Cairo, 1922.

ʿUbayd, Shiḥātah (189?–1961, S/E) *Dars mu'lim*, Cairo, 1922.

ʿUjaylī, ʿAbd al-Salām (1919, S) *Bint al-sāḥirah*, Beirut, 1948; *Sāʿat al-mulāẓim*, Beirut, 1951; *Ḥikāyāt min al-raḥalāt*, Beirut, 1954; *Qanādīl Ashbīliyyah*, Beirut, 1956; *Al-Ḥubb wa'l-nafs*, Beirut, 1959; *Al-Khā'in*, Beirut, 1960; *Al-Khayl wa'l-nisā'*, Beirut, 1965; *Fāris madīnat al-Qunayṭirah*, Beirut, 1971; *Ḥikāyat majānīn*, Beirut, 1972.

ʿUlwān, Muḥammad (1948, A) *Al-Khubẓ wa'l-ṣamt*, Cairo, 1977; *Al-Ḥikāyah tabda' hākadha*, Riyadh, 1983.

ʿUmar, Aḥmad Maḥfūẓ (Y) *Al-'Indhār al-mumaẓẓaq*, Aden, 1960; *Al-'Ajrās al-*

ṣāmitah, Beirut, 1974.

ʿUthmān, *Iʿtidāl (E) *Yūnis wa'l-baḥr*, Cairo, 1987.

ʿUthmān, *Laylā al- (194?, K) *Imraʾah fīināʾ*, Kuwait, 1976; *Al-Raḥīl*, Beirut, 1979; *Fī 'l-Layl taʾtī al-ʿuyūn*, Beirut, 1980; *Al-Ḥubb lah ṣuwar*, Beirut, 1982.

ʿUthmān, Sibāʿī (D) *Al-Ṣamt wa'l-judrān*, Cairo, 1970; *Dawāʾir fī daftar al-zaman*, Khartoum, 1972.

Wanīsī, Zuhūr (G) *ʿAlā al-Shāṭiʾ al-ākhar*, Algiers, n.d.

Waṭṭār, al-Ṭāhir (1936, G) *Dukhān min qalbī*, Tunis, n.d.; *Al-Ṭaʿanāt*, Algiers, n.d. [1972?]; *Al-Shuhadāʾ yaʿūdūn hadhā 'l-ʾusbūʿ*, Baghdad, 1974.

Wirdānī, Ibrāhim al- (1919, E) *Al-Madīnah al-majnūnah*, Cairo, 1950; *Al-Layl*, Cairo, 1953; *Al-Madīnah*, Cairo, n.d. [1956]; *Al-Muʾallif wa'l-nisāʾ*, Cairo, 1965.

Wirdānī, Maḥmūd al- (195?, E) *Arbaʿ qiṣaṣ qaṣīrah*, Cairo, 1982; *Al-Sayr fī 'l-ḥadīqah laylan*, Cairo, 1984.

Yakhluf, Yaḥyā (1944, P) *Al-Muhrah*, Baghdad, 1972: *Nurmā wa rajul al-thalj*, Beirut, 1977; *Tilk al-Marʾah al-wardah*, Beirut, 1980.

Yaḥyā, Ḥasab-Allah (1944, I) *Al-Ghaḍab*, Mosul, 1967; *Ḍamīr al-Māʾ*, Beirut, 1972; *Al-Qayd hawl al-ʿunuq*, Baghdad, 1974; *Al-Ḥaṭab*, Baghdad, 1974; *Hiya Imraʾah ʿirāqiyyah*, Beirut, 1982; *Al-ʾAshwāq*, Baghdad, 1986; *Kitmān*, Baghdad, 1988.

Yāsīn, ʿAbd al-Ḥamīd (1908–75, P) *Aqāṣīṣ*, Jaffa, 1946; *Aqāṣīṣ wa ṣuwar*, Amman, 1959.

Yāsīn, Najmān (1952, I) *Iḥtirāq*, Baghdad, 197?; *Dhalik al-nahr al-gharīb*, Baghdad, 197?; *Ḥikāyāt al-ḥarb*, Baghdad, 1986.

Yūsuf, Khālid Aḥmad al- (1959, A) *Al-Jamājim tunkhar min al-dākhil*, Riyadh, 1984.

Zarqah, Muḥammad (Y) *Kabid al-faras*, Cairo, 1976.

Zarrūq, al-Ṭayyib (1935, D) *Qiṣaṣ sūdāniyyah*, Cairo, 1957; *Al-ʾArḍ al-ṣafrāʾ*, Cairo, 1961; *Al-Shayʾ al-ladhī taḥt*, Cairo, 1970; *Al-Rajul dhū 'l-wajh al-maʾlūf*, Khartoum, n.d.

Zarzūr, Fāris (1930, S) *Ḥattā al-qaṭrah al-ʾakhīrah*, Damascus, 1960; *42 rākiban wa niṣf*, Damascus, 1969; *Lā Huwa kamā huwa*, Tunis, 1975; *Abānā al-ladhī fī'l-ʾarḍ*, Damascus, 1983.

Zayyāt, *Laṭīfah al- (1925, E) *Al-Shaykhūkhah*, Cairo, 1986.

Zifzāf, Muḥammad (1945, M) *Ḥiwār fī layl mutʾakhkhir*, Damascus, 1970; *Buyūt wāṭiʾah*, Casablanca, 1977; *Qubūr fī 'l-māʾ*, Tunis, 1978; *Al-ʾAqwā*, Casablanca, 1980; *Al-Shajarah al-muqaddasah*, Casablanca, 1984?; *Al-Malāk al-ʾabyaḍ*, Cairo, 1988.

Zinaybar, Muḥammad (1925, M) *Al-Hawāʾ al-jadīd*, Casablanca, 1971.

Zūqarī, *Shafīqah Aḥmad (Y) *Nabaḍāt qalb*, Beirut, 1970.

B. Critical studies in Arabic

ʿAbbūd, Mārūn *Ruwwād al-nahḍah al-adabiyyah al-ḥadīthah*, Beirut, 1952.

ʿAbdullah, Muḥammad Ḥasan *Al-Ḥarakah al-adabiyyah wa'l-fikriyyah fī'l-Kuwayt*, Kuwait, 1973.

ᶜAbṭah, Maḥmūd al- *Al-Adab al-Maghribī al-muᶜāṣir*, Cairo, 1985.

ᶜAfīfī, Muḥammad al-Ṣādiq *Al-Fann al-qaṣaṣī wa'l-masraḥī fī'l-Maghrib al-ᶜArabī*, Beirut, 1971.

Al-Qiṣṣah al-maghribiyyah al-ḥadīthah, Casablanca, n.d.

ᶜAyyād, Shukrī Muḥammad *Al-Qiṣṣah al-qaṣīrah fī Miṣr; dirāsah fī taʾṣīl fann adabī*, Cairo, 1968.

ᶜĀmirī, Muḥammad al- Hādī al- *Al-Qiṣṣah al-tūnisiyyah al-qaṣīrah*, Tunis, n.d.

Abū-ᶜŪf, ᶜAbd al-Raḥman *Al-Baḥth ᶜan ṭariq jadīd li'l-qiṣṣah al-qaṣīrah al-miṣriyyah*, Cairo, 1971.

Aḥmad, ᶜAbd al-Ilāh *Nashʾat al-qiṣṣah wa-taṭawwuruhā fī'l-ᶜIrāq*, Baghdad, 1969.

Fihrist al-qiṣṣah al-ᶜirāqiyyah, Baghdad, 1973.

Al-Adab al-qaṣaṣi fī'l-ᶜIrāq mundh al-ḥarb al-ᶜalamiyyah al-thāniyah, 2 vols, Baghdad, 1976.

Asad, Naṣir al-Dīn al- *Khalīl Baydas: Rāᶜid al-qiṣṣah al-ᶜarabiyyah fī Filisṭīn*, Cairo, 1963.

Badr, ᶜAbd al-Muḥsin Ṭāhā *Taṭawwur al-riwāyah al-ᶜArabiyyah al-ḥadīthah fī Miṣr 1870–1938*, Cairo, 1963.

Ḥammūdī, Bāsim ᶜAbd al-Ḥamīd *Fī'l-Qiṣṣah al-ᶜirāqiyyah*, Baghdad, 1961.

Ḥaqqī, Yaḥyā *Fajr al-qiṣṣah al-miṣriyyah*, Cairo, 1960.

Khuṭuwāt fī'l-naqd, Cairo, 1962.

Ḥasan, Muḥammad Rushdī *Athar al-maqāmah fī nashʾat al-qiṣṣah al-Miṣriyyah al-ḥadīthah*, Cairo, 1974.

Haykal, Aḥmad *Al-Adab al-qaṣaṣī wa'l-masraḥī fī Miṣr*, Cairo, 1970.

Ḥusayn, Ṭāhā *Min Adabinā al-muᶜāṣir*, Cairo, 1959.

Ibn-ᶜAshūr, Muḥammad al-Fāḍil *Al-Ḥarakah al-adabiyyah wa'l-fikriyyah fī Tūnis*, Cairo, 1956.

Arkān al-nahḍah al-adabiyyah fī Tūnis, Tunis, 1965.

Ibn-Dhurayl, ᶜAdnān *Adab al-qiṣṣah fī Sūriyyah*, Damascus, n.d.

Ibrāhīm, ᶜAbd al-Ḥamīd *Al-Qiṣṣah al-miṣriyyah wa ṣūrat al-mujtamaᶜ al-ḥadīth*, Cairo, 1973.

Al-Qiṣṣah al-yamaniyyah al-muᶜāṣirah, Beirut, 1977.

Idrīs, Suhayl *Muḥāḍarāt ᶜan al-qiṣṣah fī Lubnān*, Cairo, 1957.

Ismāᶜīl, Fahd Ismāᶜīl *Al-Qiṣṣah al-ᶜarabiyyah fī'l-Kuwayt*, Beirut, 1980.

Jābrī, Muḥammad Ṣāliḥ al- *Al-Qiṣṣah al-tūnisiyyah; nashʾatuhā wa ruwwāduhā*, Tunis, 1975.

Kannūn, ᶜAbdullah *Aḥādīth ᶜan al-adab al-maghribī al-ḥadīth*, Cairo, 1964.

Khalīlī, Jaᶜfar al- *Al-Qiṣṣah al-ᶜIrāqiyyah qadīman wa ḥadīthan*, Beirut, 1962.

Khaḍr, ᶜAbbās *Al-Qiṣṣah al-qaṣīrah fī Miṣr*, Cairo, 1966.

Muḥammad Taymūr: ḥayātuh wa-adabuh, Cairo, 1966.

Khaṭīb, Ḥusām al- *Subul al-muʾaththirāt al-ajnabiyyah wa-ashkāluhā fī'l-qiṣṣah al-sūriyyah*, Cairo, 1973.

Kushayk, Muḥammad *ᶜAlāmāt al-taḥdīth fī'l-qiṣṣah al-miṣriyyah al-qasīrah*, Baghdad, 1988.

Maṣāyif, Muḥammad *Al-Qiṣṣah al-qaṣīrah al-ᶜarabiyyah al-jazāʾiriyyah fī ᶜahd al-*

ʾistiqlāl, Algiers, 1982.

Miʿaddāwī, Anwar al- *Kalimāt fī'l-adab*, Beirut, 1967.

Middīnī, Aḥmad al- *Fann al-qiṣṣah al-qaṣīrah bi'l-Maghrib*, Beirut, 1980.

Fī'l-Adab al-maghribī al-muʿāṣir, Rabat, 1985.

Mikkī, Al-Ṭāhir Aḥmad *Al-Qiṣṣah al-qaṣīrah*, Cairo, 1977.

Muṣṭafā, Shākir *Muḥāḍarāt ʿan al-qiṣṣah fī Sūriyyah*, Cairo, 1957.

Najm, Muḥammad Yūsuf *Al-Qiṣṣah fī'l-adab al-ʿarabī al-ḥadīth*, Cairo, 1952.

Nassāj, Sayyid Ḥāmid al- *Taṭawwur fann al-qiṣṣah al-qaṣīrah fī Miṣr*, Cairo, 1968.

Dalīl al-qiṣṣah al-miṣriyyah al-qaṣīrah, Cairo, 1972.

Qīnah, ʿUmar Bin *Ashkāl al-taʿbīr fī'l-qiṣṣah al-lībiyyah al-qaṣīrah*, Algiers, 1986.

Dirāsāt fī'l-qiṣṣah al-jazāʾiriyyah al-qaṣīrah wa'l-ṭawīlah, Algiers, 1986.

Rikaybī, ʿAbdullah Khalīfah *Al-Qiṣṣah al-qaṣīrah fil'l-adab al-jazāʾirī al-ḥadīth*, Cairo, 1969.

Saʿāfīn, Ibrāhīm al- *Taṭawwur al-riwāyah al-ʿarabiyyah fī bilād al-Shām*, Baghdad, 1980.

Sawāfirī, Kāmil al- *Al-Adab al-ʿarabī al muʿāṣir fī Filisṭīn*, Cairo, 1979.

Shawkat, Maḥmūd Ḥāmid *Al-Fann al-qaṣaṣi fī'l-adab al-ʿarabī al-ḥadīth*, Cairo, 1963.

Shārūnī, Yūsuf al- *Al-Qiṣṣah al-qaṣīrah naẓariyyan wa taṭbīqiyyan*, Cairo, 1977.

Sulaymān, Nabil and Yāsīn, Bū-ʿAlī *Al-Adab wa'l-aydūlūjyā fi Sūriyyah*, Beirut, 1979.

Taymūr, Maḥmūd *Nushūʾ al-qiṣṣah wa taṭawwuruhā*, Cairo, 1936.

Ṭāhir, ʿAli Jawād al- *Fī'l-Qaṣaṣ al-ʿirāqī al-muʿāṣir*, Beirut, 1967.

Maḥmūd Aḥmad al-Sayyid: rāʾid al-qiṣṣah al-ḥadīthah fī'l-ʿIrāq, Beirut, 1969.

ʿŪfī Najīb, al-*Muqārabat al-wāqiʿ fī'l-qiṣṣah al-qaṣīrah al-maghribiyyah: min al-taʾsīs ilā 'l tajnīs*, Beirut, 1987.

Yāfī, Naʿīm al- *Al-Taṭawwur al-fanni li-shakl al-qiṣṣah al-qaṣīrah fī'l-adab al-shāmī al-ḥadīth*, Damascus, 1982.

Yāghī, Hāshim *Al-Qiṣṣah al-qaṣīrah fī Filisṭīn wa'l-ʿUrdun*, Beirut, 1981.

Yūnis, ʿAbd al-Ḥamīd *Fann al-qiṣṣah al-qaṣīrah fī adabinā al-ḥadīth*, Cairo, 1973.

Zayd, Khālid Suʿūd al- *Shaykh al-qaṣṣāṣīn al-kuwaytiyyīn: Fahd al-Duwayrī*, Kuwait, 1984.

C. Critical studies in English and French

Abdel-Meguid, Abdel-Aziz *The modern Arabic short story: its emergence, development and form*, Cairo, n.d.

Allen, Walter *Some aspects of the American short story*, Oxford, 1973.

The short story in English, Oxford, 1981.

Allen, Roger *In the eye of the beholder: tales from the writings of Yusuf Idris*, Minneapolis & Chicago, 1978.

Artin, Yaʿkūb Pasha *Contes populaires inédits de la Vallée du Nil*, Paris, 1895.

Auerbach, Erich *Mimesis: the representation of reality in western literature*, tr. Willard Trask, Princeton, New Jersey, 1953.

Aycock, Wendell M., ed. *The teller and the tale: aspects of the short story*, Lubbock, Texas, 1982.

Bates, H. E., *The modern short story; a critical survey*, London, 1941.
Beachcroft, T. O. *The English short story*, 2 vols, London, 1967.
The modest art: a survey of the short story in English, Oxford, 1968.
Beyerl, Jan *The style of the modern Arabic short story*, Prague, 1971.
Blanchard, Marc Eli *Description, sign, self, desire*, The Hague, 1980.
Bonheim, Helmut *The narrative modes: techniques of the short story*, Cambridge, 1982.
Booth, Wayne *The rhetoric of fiction*, Chicago, 1961.
Brooks, Cleanth and Warren, Robert Penn *Understanding fiction*, New York, 1944.
Burke, Kenneth *Counter-statement*, Berkeley, 1968.
The philosophy of literary form, Berkeley, 1973.
Calderwood, James and Toliver, Harold E. *Perspectives on fiction*, Oxford, 1968.
Canby, Henry and Dashiell, Alfred *A study of the short story*, New York, 1935.
Chambers, Ross *Story and situation: narrative seduction and the power of fiction*, Manchester, 1984.
Chatman, Seymour *Story and discourse: narrative structure in fiction and film*, Ithaca, N.Y., 1978.
Cobham, Catherine 'The Importance of Yūsuf Idrīs' Short Story in the Development of an Indigenous Egyptian Literary Tradition', unpublished M.Phil. Thesis at the University of Manchester, 1974.
Cooke, Miriam *The anatomy of an Egyptian intellectual: Yahya Haqqi*, Washington, 1984.
Current-Garcia, Eugene and Patrick, Walton *What is the short story?*, New York, 1974.
Ferguson, John De Lancey *et al. Themes and variations in the short story?*, New York, 1972.
Grenier, Jean *Lettres d'Egypte*, Paris, 1959.
Hildick, Wallace *Thirteen types of narrative*, London, 1968.
Ingram, Forrest L. *Representative short story cycles of the twentieth century*, The Hague, 1971.
Kempton, Kenneth Payson *The short story*, Cambridge, Mass., 1947.
Kurpershoek, M. *The short stories of Yūsuf Idrīs*, Leiden, 1981.
Leavis, Q. D. *Fiction and the reading public*, London, 1965.
Lodge, David *Language of fiction*, London, 1966.
Lukács, Georg *Writer and critic*, tr. A. Khan, London, 1971.
The theory of the novel, tr. Anna Bostock, London, 1971.
Macherey, Pierre *A theory of literary production*, tr. Geoffrey Wall, London, 1978.
Makarius, Raoul and Laura Makarius *Anthologie de la litterature arabe contemporaine*, Paris, 1964.
Manzalaoui, Mahmoud, ed. *Arabic writing today, the short story*, Cairo, 1968.
Martin, Wallace *Recent theories of narrative*, Ithaca, N.Y., 1986.
May, Charles E. *Short story theories*, Ohio, 1976.
Mirrielees, E. R., *The story writer*, Boston, 1939.
O'Connor, Frank *The lonely voice: a study of the short story*, London, 1963.
O'Faolain, Sean *The short story*, London, 1948.

Pérès, Henri 'Le roman, le conte et la nouvelle dans la littérature Arabe moderne', published in *Annales de l'Institut des Etudes Orientales*, vol. 3 (1937), pp. 266–337.
Perkins, George *Realistic American short fiction*, Illinois, 1972.
Prince, Gerald *A grammar of stories*, The Hague, 1973.
Narratology: the form and function of narrative, The Hague, 1982.
Reid, Ian *The short story*, London, 1977.
Rimmon-Kenan, Shlomith *Narrative fiction*, London, 1983.
Scholes, Robert and Kellog, Robert *The nature of narrative*, Oxford, 1966.
Scott, Virgil *Studies in the short story*, New York, 1968.
Shaheen, Muḥammad *The modern Arabic short story*, London, 1989.
Smith, A. J. and Mason, W. H. *Short story study*, London, 1971.
Summers, Hollis, ed. *Discussions of the short story*, Boston, 1963.
Tomiche, Nada *Histoire de la littérature romanesque de l'Egypte moderne*, Paris, 1981.
Trask, Georginne and Burkhart, Charles, eds *Storytellers and their art*, New York, 1963.
Williams, William Carlos *A beginning on the short story*, Yonkers, 1950.

9: ARABIC DRAMA: EARLY DEVELOPMENTS

A. Texts

The date in brackets refers to the writing or first performance of a play, and is therefore the most relevant to this discussion. The fact that no other date is given is not an indication that the play was never published.

Anṭūn, Faraḥ *Miṣr al-jadīdah wa Miṣr al-qadīmah*, n.p., 1913.
Mukhtārāt min Faraḥ Anṭūn, Silsilat Manāhil al-adab al-'Arabī, 29, Beirut, 1950.
al-Sulṭān Ṣalāḥ al-Dīn wa mamlakat Urshalīm, n.p., 1914.
Najm, Muḥammad Yūsuf, ed. *al-Masraḥ al-ʿArabī dirāsāt wa nuṣūṣ, Mārūn al-Naqqāsh*, Beirut, 1964.
Muḥammad ʿUthmān Jalāl, Beirut, n.d. (1964?).
Salīm al-Naqqāsh, Beirut, 1964.
Al-Shaykh Aḥmad Abū Khalīl al-Qabbānī, Beirut, 1963.
Yaʿqūb Ṣannūʿ (Abū Naḍḍārah), Beirut, 1963.
Nuʿaymah, Mikhāʾīl *al-Ābāʾ wa'l-banūn*, (1917), Beirut.
Ramzī, Ibrāhīm *Abṭāl al-Manṣūrah*, (1915) Cairo, n.d.
Dukhūl al-ḥammām mish zayy khurūguh (1915–16) (reprinted in the periodical *al-Hilāl*, Cairo, July 1971).
Taqiyy al-Dīn, Saʿīd *Lawlā 'l-muḥāmī*, (1924) Beirut.
Taymūr, Muḥammad *Muʾallafāt*, 3 vols, Cairo, 1971–73.
Yazbak, Anṭūn *al-Dhabāʾiḥ: maʾsāh ʿaṣriyyah fī arbaʿat fuṣūl*, (1925), Cairo, n.d.

B. Arabic secondary sources

Abū Sayf, Laylā *Masraḥ Najīb al-Rīḥānī*, Cairo, 197?
Abū Shanab, ʿĀdil *Bawākīr al-taʾlīf al-masraḥī fi Sūriya*, Damascus, 1978.
Amer, Attia *Lughāt al-masraḥ al-ʿArabī*, Stockholm, 1967.
ʿAwaḍ, Ramsīs *al-Tārīkh al-sirrī li'l-masraḥ qabl thawrat 1919*, Cairo, 1972.
Ittijāhāt siyāsiyyah fi'l-masraḥ qabl thawrat 1919, Cairo, 1979.
Dardīrī, Ibrāhīm *Adab Ibrāhīm Ramzī*, Cairo, 1971.
Ghunaym, ʿAbd al-Ḥamīd *Ṣannūʿ rāʾid al-masraḥ al-ʿArabī*, Cairo, n.d.
ʿĪd, al-Sayyid Ḥasan *Taṭawwur al-naqd al-masraḥī fī Miṣr*, Cairo, 1965.
Ibn Dhurayl, ʿAdnān *al-Masraḥ al-Sūrī min al-Qabbānī ila'l-yawm*, Damascus, 1971.
Mandūr, Muḥammad *al-Masraḥ al-nathrī*, Cairo, 1959.
Nashāṭī, Fattūḥ *Khamsūn ʿām fī khidmat al-masraḥ*, 2 vols, Cairo, 1973–74.
al-Rāʿī, ʿAlī *Funūn al-kūmidiyā min Khayāl al-ẓill ilā Najīb al-Rīḥānī*, Cairo, 1971.
Masraḥ al-dam wa 'l-dumūʿ, Cairo, 1973.
Ṣāliḥ, Aḥmad Rushdī *al-Masraḥ al-ʿArabī*, Cairo, 1972.
Waḥīd, ʿAlāʾ al-Dīn *Masraḥ Muḥammad Taymūr*, Cairo, 1975.

C. Non-Arabic secondary sources

Abou Saif, L. 'Najīb al-Rīḥānī: from buffoonery to social comedy', *Journal of Arabic Literature*, 4 (1973), pp. 1–17.
Abul Naga, Atia *Les sources francaises du théâtre Egyptien (1870–1939)*, Algiers, 1972.
Badawi, M. M. *Early Arabic drama*, Cambridge, 1988.
Modern Arabic literature and the west, London, 1985.
Barbour, Nevill 'The Arabic theatre in Egypt', *Bulletin of the School of Oriental Studies*, 7 (1935–7), pp. 173–87.
Gendzier, Irene L. *The practical visions of Yaʿqub Sanuʿ*, Cambridge, Mass., 1966.
al-Khozai, Mohamed A. *The development of early Arabic drama (1847–1900)*, London, 1984.
Landau, Jacob M. *Studies in the Arab theater and cinema*, Philadelphia, 1958.
Moosa, Matti *The origins of modern Arabic fiction*, Washington, 1983.
Reid, D. M. *The odyssey of Faraḥ Antūn*, Minneapolis, 1975.
Tomiche, Nada *Histoire de la littérature romanesque de l'Egypt moderne*, Paris, 1981.

10: ARABIC DRAMA SINCE THE THIRTIES

A. Dramatists and plays discussed

ʿAbd al-Ṣabūr, Ṣalāḥ [Eg.] *Maʾsāt al-Ḥallāj* (1965) tr. by K. I. Samaan as *Murder in Baghdad*, Leiden, 1972.
Laylā wa 'l-majnūn (1970) ('Layla and the mad lover').
al-Amīrah tantaẓir (1971), tr. by S. Megally as *The princess waits*, Cairo, 1975.
Baʿd an yamūt al-malik (1973) ('After the king is dead').

Abū Qurayn, al-Mahdī [Lib.] *Zarīʿat al-shayāṭīn* (1973) ('The devils' farm').

Abū Rīshah, ʿUmar [Syr.] *Rāyāt Dhī 'l-Qār* (1936) ('The banners of Dhi'l-Qar').

al-ʿĀnī, Yūsuf [Irq.] *Ana ummuk yā Shākir* (1955) ('I am your mother, Shakir').

al-Miftāḥ (1967) ('The key').

al-Kharābah (1970) ('The waste land').

al-Khān (1976) ('The Khan').

al-Ashqar, Niḍāl [Leb.] *Iḍrāb al-ḥaramiyyah* (1971) ('The thieves on strike').

ʿĀshūr, Nuʿmān [Eg.] *ʿĀʾilat al-Dughrī* (1962) ('The Dughri family').

al-Barādiʿī, Khālid Muhyildīn [Syr.] *al-Salām yuḥāṣir Qarṭājannah* (1979) ('Peace besieges Carthage').

Basīsū, Muʿīn [Pal.] *Maʾsāt Guevara* (1969) ('The tragedy of Guevara').

Thawrat al-Zanj (1970) ('The revolution of the Zanj').

Shamshūn wa Dalīlah (1971) ('Samson and Delilah').

al-Dannāʿ, ʿAbd al-Karīm [Lib.] *Saʿdūn* (1974).

Diyāb, Maḥmūd [Eg.] *al-Zawbaʿah* (1976), tr. by Wadida Wassef as *The storm* in M. A. Manzalaoui, *Arabic writing today: the drama*, Cairo, 1977.

Layāli al-ḥiṣād (1967) ('Harvest nights').

Bāb al-Futūḥ (1971) ('The gateway to success').

Farag (Faraj), Alfred [Eg.] *Hallāq Baghdād* (1963) ('The barber of Baghdad').

Sulaymān al-Ḥalabī (1964).

ʿAskar wa ḥaramiyyah (1966) ('Cops and robbers')

al-Zīr Sālim (1967) ('Prince Salim').

ʿAlī Janāḥ al-Tabrīzī (1968).

al-Nār wa 'l-zaytūn (1970) ('Fire and olives').

Zawāj ʿalā waraqat ṭalāq (1973).

al-Ḥakīm, Tawfīq [Eg.] *al-Marʾah al-jadīdah* (1923).

al-ʿArīs (1924).

Khātim Sulaymān (1924).

ʿAlī Bābā (1926).

Raṣaṣāh fiʾl-qalb (1939) ('A bullet in the heart').

Ahl al-Kahf (1933) ('The men of the cave').

Shahrazād (1934), tr. by W. M. Hutchins (1981) in *Plays, prefaces and postscripts of Tawfiq al-Hakim*, Washington, 2 vols, 1981–84.

Praxa (1939; enlarged 1954).

Pygmalion (1942).

Sulaymān al-ḥakīm (1943) ('Solomon the wise'). Tr. by W. M. Hutchins in *Plays* as *The Wisdom of Solomon*, 1981.

al-Malik Ūdīb (1949), tr. as *King Oedipus* by W. M. Hutchins, *Plays*, 1981.

ʿImārat al-Muʿallim Kandūz (published, together with the next two items, in *Masraḥ al-Mujtamaʿ* (1950) ('*Mr. Kanduz's Property*')

Aʿmāl ḥurrah (1950) ('Private enterprise').

Law ʿaraf al-shabāb (1950) ('If youth only knew').

al-Aydī al-nāʿimah (1954) ('Soft hands'). Tr. by W. M. Hutchins in *Plays* as *Tender hands*, 1984.

Īzīs (1955) ('Isis').
al-Ṣafqah (1956) ('The deal').
al-Sulṭān al-ḥāʾir (1960), tr. as *The Sultan's Dilemma* both by Denys Johnson Davies, London, 1973, and M. M. Badawi, Cairo, 1977.
Yaṭāliʿ al-shajarah (1962), tr. by D. Johnson-Davies as *The tree climber*, Oxford 1966.
Shams al-nahār (1965), tr. by W. M. Hutchins in *Plays* as *Princess Sunshine*, 1981.
Kull shayʾ fī maḥallih (1966), tr. by D. Johnson-Davies as *Not a thing out of place*, published together with the next item, 1973.
Maṣīr Ṣarṣār (1966), tr. by D. Johnson-Davies as *Fate of a Cockroach* in *Fate of a Cockroach and other plays*, London, 1973.
Bank al-qalaq (1967) ('Anxiety Bank').
Īdrīs, Yūsuf [Eg.] *al-Farāfīr* (1964), tr. by Trevor Le Gassick as *Flipflap and his master* (in Manzalaoui, *Arabic writing today*), Cairo, 1977.
al-ʿIlj, Aḥmad al-Ṭayyib [Mor.] *Waliyy Allāh* (197?).
Madanī, ʿIzz al-Dīn [Tun.] *Thawrat ṣāḥib al-ḥimār* (1970) ('Revolution of the donkey-rider').
Dīwān al-Zanj (1972).
Riḥlat al-Ḥallāj (1973) ('Al-Hallaj's progress').
Mawlāy al-Sulṭān Ḥasan al-Ḥafṣī (1977).
Mardam, ʿAdnān [Syr.] *al-Hallāj* (1971).
Filāsṭīn al-thāʾirah (1974) ('Palestine in revolution').
al-Qāsim, Samīḥ [Pal.] *Qaraqāsh* (1970).
al-Qunaydī, Muḥammad ʿAbd al-Jalil [Lib.] *al-Aqniʿah* (197?) ('Masks').
al-Rashūd, Ṣaqr [Kuw.] *al-Ṭīn* (1965) ('Mud').
Rūmān, Mikhāʾīl [Eg.] *al-Dukhkhān* (1962) ('Smoke').
al-Wāfid (1965), tr. by M. Shaheen as *The Newcomer* (in Manzalaoui, *Arabic writing today*), Cairo, 1977.
Sālim, ʿAlī [Eg.] *Inta illi qatalt al-waḥsh* (1970) ('You killed the monster').
Sālim, Sulṭān [Bahraini] *al-ʿAnīd* (1977) ('Steadfast').
al-Sharqāwī, ʿAbd al-Raḥmān [Eg.] *Maʾsāt Jamīlah* (1962) ('The tragedy of Jamilah').
al-Husayn thāʾiran wa shahīdan (1969) ('al-Husayn, a revolutionary and martyr').
Shawqī, Aḥmad [Eg.] *Maṣraʿ Kilyūbaṭrah* (1929) ('The death of Cleopatra').
Majnūn Laylā (1931), tr. by A. J. Arberry as *Majun Layla, a poetical drama in five acts*, Cairo, 1933.
Qambīz (1931) ('Cambyses').
ʿAlī Bey al-Kabīr (1932).
Amīrat al-Andalus (1932) ('The princess of Andalusia').
al-Sitt Hudā (pub. posthumously).
al-Bakhīlah (incomplete).
al-Ṣiddīqī, al-Ṭayyib [Mor.] *Dīwān sīdī ʿAbd al-Rahmān al-Majdhūb* (1966).
Maqamāt Badīʿ al-Zamān al-Hamadhānī (1971).
Surayyiʿ, ʿAbd al-ʿAzīz [Kuw.] *Fulūs wa nufūs* (1969) ('Money and souls').

Surūr, Najīb [Eg.] *Yāsīn wa Bahiyyah* (1964).

Min ayn ajīb nās (1976) ('O would that I had listeners').

Wahbah, Saᶜd al-Dīn [Eg.] *Bīr al-Sillim* (1966) ('The stairwell').

Wannūs, Saᶜdallah [Syr.] *Ḥaflat samar min ajl khamsah Ḥuzayrān* (1968) ('A party to celebrate the 5th of June').

Mughāmarat raʾs al-mamlūk Jābir (1969) ('The adventures of the head of Mamluk Jabir').

Sahrah maᶜa Abī Khalīl al-Qabbānī (1972) ('An evening with Abu Khalil al-Qabbani').

al-Malik huwaʾl-malik (1977) ('The king is the king').

Yāsīn, Kātib [Alg.] *al-Juththah al-muḥāṣarah* (1968): an Arabic tr. of *The encircled corpse*.

Muḥammad Khudh ḥaqībatak (197?) ('Take your suitcase, Muhammad').

B. Critical studies

General: (i) In Arabic

al-Rāᶜī, ᶜAlī *al-Masraḥ fi'l-waṭan al-ᶜarabī*, Kuwait, 1980.

General: (ii) In European languages

Aziza, Mohamed *Regards sur le théâtre Arabe contemporain*, Tunis, 1970.

Ben Halima, Hamadi *Les principaux thèmes du théâtre Arabe contemporain, (de 1914 à 1960)*, Tunis, 1969.

Landau, Jacob M. *Studies in the Arab theatre and cinema*. Philadelphia, 1958.

Manzalaoui, Mahmoud, ed. *Arabic writing today: drama*, Cairo, 1977.

Egypt: (i) In Arabic

ᶜAbd al-Qādir, Fārūq *Izdihār wa suqūṭ al-masraḥ al-miṣrī*, Cairo, 1979.

Misāḥah fī'l ḍawʾ wa misāḥah li'l-ẓilāl: aᶜmāl fi'l-naqd al-masraḥī 67–77, Cairo, 1986.

Abyaḍ, Suᶜād *Jūrj Abyaḍ: Miʾat ᶜām min al-masraḥ al-miṣrī*, Cairo, 1970.

al-ᶜĀlim, Maḥmūd Amīn *al-Wajh waʾl-qināᶜ fī masraḥinā al-ᶜarabī al-muāṣir*, Beirut, 1973.

ᶜĀmir, Sāmī Munīr *al-Masraḥ al-miṣrī baᶜd al-ḥarb al-ᶜālamiyyah al-thāniyah 1945–1970*, 2 vols, Cairo, 1979.

ᶜĀwaḍ, Luwīs *Dirāsāt fi adabinā al-ḥadīth*, Cairo, 1961.

Dirāsāt fi 'l-naqd wa'l-adab, Cairo, 1964.

al-ᶜAyyūṭī, Amīn *Dirāsāt fī 'l-masraḥ*, Cairo, 1986.

Dawwārah, Fuʾād *Fī 'l-naqd al-masraḥī*, Cairo, 1965.

Masraḥ Tawfīq al-Ḥakīm, 2 vols, Cairo, 1985, 1986.

Masraḥ 85, Cairo, 1986.

Farag (Faraj), Alfred *Dalīl al-matufarrij al-dhakiyy ilā 'l-masraḥ*, Cairo, 1966.

Fahmī, Māhir Ḥasan *Aḥmad Shawqī*, Cairo, 1975.

al-Ḥajjājī, Shams al-Dīn *al-Usṭūrah fī 'l-masraḥ al-miṣrī al-muᶜāṣir*, 2 vols, Cairo, 1975.

Mandūr, Muḥammad *al-Masraḥ al-nathrī*, Cairo, 1959.
Masraḥ Tawfīq al-Ḥakīm, Cairo, 1960.
Masraḥiyyāt Shawqī, Cairo, 1954.
Masraḥiyyāt ᶜĀzīz Abāẓah, Cairo, 1958.
al-Masraḥ magazine, no. 3 (*al-Masraḥ al-miṣrī min 1952 ila 1962*), Cairo, 1966.
Nashāṭī, Fattūḥ *Khamsūn ᶜām fī khidmat al-masraḥ*, 2 vols, Cairo, 1973, 1974.
al-Rāᶜī, ᶜAlī *al-Kūmīdiyā al-murtajalah ᶜalā 'l-masraḥ al-Miṣrī*, Cairo, 1968.
Tawfīq al-Ḥakīm fannān al-furjah wa fannān al-fikr, Cairo, 1969.
Masraḥ al-dam wa ᵓl-dumūᶜ, Cairo, 1973.
Masraḥiyyāt wa masraḥiyyūn, Cairo, 1970.
Rushdī, Fāṭimāh *Kifāḥī fī 'l-masraḥ wa 'l-sīnimā*, Cairo, 1970.
Shawkat, Maḥmūd Ḥamīd *al-Fann al-masraḥī fī 'l-adab al-ᶜArabī al-ḥadīth*, Cairo, 1963.
Tāhir, Bahāᵓ *ᶜAshr masraḥiyyāt miṣriyyah*, Cairo, 1985.
al-Yūsuf, Fāṭimah *Dhikrayāt*, Cairo, n.d.

Egypt: (ii) In European languages

Abdel Wahab, Farouk, ed. *Modern Egyptian drama: an anthology*, Minneapolis and Chicago, 1974.
Badawi, M. M. *Modern Arabic drama in Egypt*, Cambridge, 1987.
Fontaine, Jean *Mort-resurrection: une lecture de Tawfiq al-Ḥakīm*, Tunis, 1978.
Ismail, Abd el Monem *Drama and society in contemporary Egypt*, Cairo, 1967.
Long, Richard *Tawfiq al-Hakim, playwright of Egypt*, London, 1979.
Somekh, Sasson *Two versions of dialogue in Mahmud Taymur's drama*, Princeton, 1975.
Starkey, Paul *From the ivory tower: a critical study of Tawfiq al-Ḥakīm*, London, 1987.

Syria and Lebanon: (i) In Arabic

Abū Hayf, ᶜAbd allah *al-Taᵓsīs Abḥāth fī 'l-masraḥ al-sūrī*, Damascus, 1979.
Abū Shanab, ᶜĀdil *Bawākīr al-ta'līf al-masraḥī fī Suriyā*, Damascus, 1978.
Balbūl, Farḥān *al-Masraḥ al-ᶜarabī al-muᶜāṣir*, Damascus, 1984.
Ibn Dhurayl, 'Adnān *al-Masraḥ al-Sūrī min al-Qabbānī ila ᵓl-yawm*, Damascus, 1971.
Qaṭṭāyah, Sulaymān *al-Masraḥ al-ᶜarabī min ayn wa ilā ayn*, Damascus, 1972.

Syria and Lebanon: (ii) In French

Salamé, Ghassane, *Le théâtre politique au Liban (1968–1973)*, Beirut, 1974.

Iraq

al-ᶜĀnī, Yūsuf *al-Tajribah al-masraḥiyya*, Beirut, 1979.
al-Ṭālib, ᶜAlī *al-Masraḥiyyah al-ᶜarabiyyyah fī 'l-ᶜIrāq*, Cairo, 1976.

Kuwait and Bahrain

ᶜAbd Allah, Muḥammad Ḥasan *al-Masraḥ fī 'l-Kuwayt*, Kuwait, 1977.
al-Masraḥ al-Kuwaytī bayn al-khashabah wa 'l-rajāᵓ, Kuwait, 1978.
Ghalūm, Ibrāhīm ᵓAbd Allah *Ẓawāhir al-tajribah al-masraḥiyyah fī 'l-Baḥrayn*, Kuwait, 1982.

al-Masraḥ wa 'l-taghyīr al-ijtimāʿī fī 'l-Khalīj al-ʿArabī, Kuwait, 1986.
Ḥaddād, Qāsim *al-Masraḥ al-baḥraynī: al-tajribah wa 'l-ufuq*, Bahrayn, 1981.
al-Khalīfī, Sulaymān *Ṣaqr al-Rashūd wa 'l-masraḥ fī 'l-Kuwayt*, Kuwait, 1980.
Abū Bakr, Walīd *al-Qaḍiyyah al-ijtimāʿiyyah fī 'l-masraḥ al-kuwaytī*, Kuwait, 1985.

Tunisia, Algeria and Morocco
al-Mahmah, Muḥammad Muṣṭafā Sallām *al-Mujtamaʿ al-aṣīlī wa 'l-masraḥ*, Rabat, 1975.
al-Māniʿī, Ḥasan *Abḥāth fī 'l-masraḥ al-maghribī*, Miknas, 1974.
al-Maṣāyif, Muḥammad *Fuṣūl fī 'l-naqd al-adabī al-jazāʾirī al-ḥadīth*, Algiers 1972.
al-Salawī, Adīb *al-Masraḥ al-maghribī*, Damascus, 1975.
Sharaf al-Dīn, al-Munṣif *Tārīkh al-masraḥ al-tūnisī mundh nashʾatih ilā nihāyat al-ḥarb al-ʿālamiyyah al-ʾūlā*, Tunis, 1972.
Zaydān, ʿAbd al-Raḥmān Ibn *Min qaḍāyā al-masraḥ al-maghribī*, Miknas, 1978.

11: THE PROSE STYLISTS

12: THE CRITICS

A. Books in Arabic

(A selection of books containing substantial information on literary theory and the development of criticism in various parts of the modern Arab world)

ʿAbd al-Ḥamīd, Bū Zuwaynah *Ẓāhirat al-taṭawwur al-adabī bayn al-naẓariyyah wa 'l-taṭbīq*, Algiers, 1979.
ʿAbd al-Muṭṭalib, Muḥammad *al-Balāghah wa 'l-uslūbiyyah*, Cairo, 1984.
Amīn, Aḥmad *al-Naqd al-adabī*, Cairo, 1963.
Amīn, ʿIzz al-Dīn al- *Nashʾat al-naqd al-adabī al-ḥadīth fī Miṣr*, Cairo, 1962.
ʿAyyād, Shukrī *al-Ruʾyā 'l-muqayyadah: dirāsāt fī 'l-tafsīr al-ḥaḍārī li ʾl-adab*, Cairo, 1978.
Bakkār, Yūsuf Ḥusayn *Bināʾ al-qaṣīdah fī 'l-naqd al-ʿArabī al-qadīm fī ḍawʾ al-naqd al-ḥadīth*, Beirut, 1983.
Balbaʿ, ʿAbd al-Ḥalīm *Ḥarakat al-tajdīd fī 'l-Mahjar bayn al-naẓariyyah wa 'l-taṭbīq*, Cairo, 1974.
Disūqī, ʿAbd al-ʿAzīz al- *Taṭawwur al-naqd al-adabī al-ḥadīth fī Miṣr*, Cairo, 1977.
Faḍl, Ṣalāḥ *Naẓariyyat al-bināʾiyyah fī 'l-naqd al-adabī*, Cairo, 1978.
ʿIlm al-uslūb: mabādiʾuh wa ijrāʾātuh, Beirut, 1985.
Ḥawī, Ibrāhīm al- *Ḥarakat al-naqd al-ḥadīth wa ʾl-muʿāṣir fī ʾl-shiʿr al-ʿArabi*, Beirut, 1984.
Hilāl, Muḥammad Ghunaymī *Dirāsāt wa manāhij fī madhāhib al-shiʿr wa naqdih*, Cairo, 1976.
Dawr al-adab al-muqāran fī tawjīh dirāsat al-adab al-ʿArabī al-muʿāṣir, Cairo, 1974.
al-Naqd al-adabī al-ḥadīth, Cairo, 1963.
Ismāʿīl, ʿIzz al-Dīn *al-Tafsīr al-nafsī li 'l-adab*, Cairo, 1963.

Jindī, Anwar al- *Khaṣā'iṣ al-adab al-ʿArabī fī muwājahat naẓariyyat al-naqd al-adabī al-ḥadīth*, Beirut, n.d.

Kāfūd. Muḥammad ʿAbd al-Raḥīm *al-Naqd al-adabī al-ḥadīth fī 'l-Khalīj al-ʿArabī*, al-Dawḥah, 1982.

Khafājī, Muḥammad ʿAbd al-Munʿim *Uṣūl al-naqd*, Cairo, 1975.

Khūrī, Ra'īf *al-Naqd wa 'l-dirāsah al-adabiyyah*, Beirut, 1939.

Kilītū, ʿAbd al-Fattāḥ *al-Adab wa 'l-gharābah: dirāsah binyawiyyah fī 'l-adab al-ʿArabī*, Beirut, 1982.

Maḥmūd, Zakī Najīb *Fī falsafat al-naqd*, Beirut, 1979.

Mandūr, Muḥammad *al-Naqd wa 'l-nuqqād al-muʿāṣirūn*, Cairo, n.d.

Marzūq, Ḥilmī ʿAlī *al-Naqd wa 'l-dirāsāt al-adabiyyah*, Beirut, 1982.

Maṣāyif Muhammad *al-Naqd al-adabī al-ḥadīth fī 'l-Maghrib al-ʿArabī*, Algiers, 1979.

Miftāh, Muḥammad *Fī Sīmyā' al-shiʿr al-qadīm*, Casablanca, 1982.

Muhammad, Ibrāhīm ʿAbd al-Raḥmān *al-Naẓariyyah wa 'l-taṭbīq fī 'l-adab al-muqāran*, Beirut, 1982.

Muḥammad, al-Ṣādiq ʿAfīfī *al-Naqd al-adabī al-ḥadīth fī 'l-Maghrib al-ʿArabī*, Beirut, 1971.

Najm, Muḥammad Yūsuf *Naẓariyyat al-naqd wa 'l-funūn wa 'l-madhābib al-adabiyyah fī 'l-adab al-ʿArabī al-ḥadīth; Muqaddimah wa Dalīl*, Beirut, 1985.

Nuwayhī, Muḥammad al- *Thaqāfat al-nāqid al-adabī*, Beirut, 1969.

Quṭb, Sayyid *al-Naqd al-adabī: uṣūluh wa manāhijuh*, Cairo, n.d.

Saḥartī, Muṣṭafā ʿAbd al-Laṭīf al- *al-Naqd al-adabī min khilāl tajāribī*, Maʿhad al-Dirāsāt al-ʿArabiyyah, 1962.

Ṣalībā, Jamīl *Ittijāhāt al-naqd al-ḥadīth fī Sūriyyā* (Damascus?), 1969.

Sallām, Muḥammad Zaghlūl *al-Naqd al-ʿArabī al-ḥadīth*, Cairo, 1964.

Shamʿah, Khaldūn al- *al-Naqd wa 'l-ḥurriyyah*, Damascus, 1977.

Shukrī, Ghālī *al-Mārksiyyah wa 'l-adab*, Beirut, 1979.

Sulaymān, Nabīl *As'ilat al-wāqiʿiyyah wa 'l-iltizām*, Latakia, 1985.

Ṭabānah, Badawī *al-Tayyārāt al-muʿāṣirah fī 'l-naqd al-adabī*, Cairo, 1963.

Ṭāhir, ʿAlī Jawād al- *Muqaddimah fī 'l-naqd al-adabī*, Beirut, 1979.

ʿUthmān, ʿAbd al-Raḥmān *Madhāhib al-naqd wa qaḍāyāh*, Cairo, 1975.

Wādī, Ṭāhā *Jamāliyyāt al-qaṣīdah al-muʿāṣirah*, Cairo, 1982.

Yāghī, ʿAbd al-Raḥmān *Fī 'l-Naqd al-naẓarī*, Amman, 1984.

Yāghī, Hāshim *al-Naqd al-adabī al-ḥadīth fī Lubnān*, 2 vols, Cairo, 1968.

Yāsīn, Bū ʿAlī and Nabīl Sulaymān *al-Adab wa 'l-idiyūlūjiyā fī Sūriyyah 1967–1973*, Latakia, 1985.

Yūnis, ʿAlī *al-Naqd al-adabī wa qaḍāyā 'l-shakl al-musīqī fī 'l-shiʿr al-jadīd*, Cairo, 1985.

al-Zaydī, Tawfīq *Athar al-lisāniyyāt fī 'l-naqd al-ʿArabī al-ḥadīth*, Tunis, 1984.

B. Books in European languages

Allen, Roger, comp. and ed. *A library of literary criticism: modern Arabic literature*, New York, 1987.

Badawi, M. M. *Modern Arabic literature and the west*, London, 1985.

Boullata, Issa, ed. *Critical perspectives on modern Arabic literature*, Washington, D.C., 1980.
Brugman, J. *An introduction to the history of modern Arabic literature in Egypt*, Leiden, 1984.
Cachia, Pierre *Ṭāhā Ḥusayn: his place in the Egyptian literary renaissance*, London, 1956.
Green, A. H., ed. *In quest of an Islamic humanism: studies in memory of Muḥammad al-Nowaihi*, Cairo, 1984.
Mazyad, A. M. H. *Aḥmad Amīn (Cairo 1886–1954), advocate of social and literary reform in Egypt*, Leiden, 1963.
Ostle, Robin, ed. *Studies in modern Arabic literature*, Warminster, 1975.
Semah, David *Four Egyptian literary critics*, Leiden, 1974.
Tahar, Meftah *Taha Husain: sa critique littéraire et ses sources françaises*, Tunis, 1976.

13: ARAB WOMEN WRITERS

A. Texts

ʿAbdallāh, Ṣūfī *Laʿnat al-jasad* ('The curse of the body') Cairo, 1957.
Nifirtītī, Cairo, 1952.
Nisāʾ muḥāribāt ('Fighting women'), Cairo, 1951.
ʿAbd al-Raḥmān, ʿĀʾishah (Bint al-Shāṭiʾ) *ʿAlā 'l-jisr* ('On the bridge'), Cairo, 1967.
Banāt al-nabiy ('The daughters of the Prophet'), Cairo, 1956.
Baṭalat Karbalāʾ. Zaynab Bint al-Zahrāʾ ('The heroine of Karbala. Zaynab Bint al-Zahra'), Cairo, n.d.
Al-Khansāʾ ('Al-Khansā'), Cairo, 1957.
Imraʾah khāṭiʾah ('A fallen woman'), Cairo, 1958.
Sayyid al-ʿizbah ('The landlord'), Cairo, 1944.
Sirr al-shāṭiʾ ('The secret of the coast'), Cairo, 1952.
Ṣuwar min ḥayātihinna ('Images from women's lives'), Cairo, 1959.
'*Thamānī ʿuyūnʾ* ('Eight eyes'), Cairo, 1975.
Abū Khālid, Fawziyyah *Ilā matā yakhtaṭifūnaki laylat al-ʿurs* ('How long will they keep raping you on your wedding night?'), Riyad, 1973.
Abū Zayd, Laylā *ʿĀm al-fīl* ('The year of the elephant'), Casablanca, 1983.
Amīn, Qāsim *Taḥrīr al-marʾah* ('Liberation of women'), Cairo, 1899.
al-Amīr, Daisy (Dīzī) *Fī dawwāmat al-ḥubb wa 'l-karāhīyah* ('In the vortex of love and hate'), Beirut, 1979.
Wuʿūd li 'l-bayʿ ('Promises for sale'), Beirut, 1981.
al-ʿAssāl, Najībah *Bayt al-ṭāʿah* ('House of obedience'), Cairo, 1962.
ʿAwdah, Rajāʾ Muḥammad *Innahu qadarī* ('It is my destiny'), Beirut, 1982.
Baʿalbakī, Laylā *Anā aḥyā* ('I live'), Beirut, 1958.
'*Safīnat ḥanān ilā 'l-qamar*' ('Spaceship of tenderness to the moon'), Beirut, 1964.
Bāḥithat al-Bādīyah *Nisāʾiyyāt* ('Feminist pieces'), Cairo, 1910.
Bannūnah, Khannātah *Al-Ṣūrah wa 'l-ṣawt* ('The image and the voice'), Casablanca, 1975.

al-Bikr, Fawziyyah *Al-Ṣibāḥah fī buḥayrat al-ᶜadam* 'Swimming in the lake of nothingness'), Jedda, 1979.

Bint al-Shāṭiʾ see ᶜAʾishah ᶜAbd al-Raḥmān.

Fawwāz, Zaynab *Al-Durr al-manthūr fī ṭabaqāt rabbāt al-khudūr* ('Scattered pearls on the classes of women'), Cairo, 1895.

Al-hawā wa 'l-wafāʾ ('Passion and loyalty'), Cairo, 1901.

Ḥusn al-ᶜawāqib aw al-ghādah al-ẓāhirah (Good outcomes, or, The shining maiden'), Cairo, 1899.

Al-malik Qurūsh ('King Qurush'), Cairo, 1892.

Ghurayyib, Rose *Nasamāt wa aᶜāṣīr fī 'l-shiᶜr al-nisāʾī al-ᶜarabī al-muᶜāṣir* ('Breezes and storms in contemporary Arabic feminist poetry), Beirut, 1980.

al-Ḥakīm, Tawfīq *Ughniyyat al-mawt* (Song of death), Cairo, 1950.

al-Idlibī, ʾUlfah *Dimashq ibtisām al-ḥuẓn* ('Damascus the smile of sadness'), Damascus, 1980.

Jabar, Kulthūm *Anta wa ghābat al-ṣamt wa' l-taraddud* ('You and the jungle of silence and hesitation'), Beirut, 1978.

al-Jayyūsī, Salmā al-Khaḍrāʾ al- *ᶜAwdah min al-nabᶜ al-ḥālim* ('Return from the dreaming source'), Beirut, 1960.

Kanafānī, Ghassān *Rijāl fī 'l-shams*, Beirut, 1963 (tr. into English as *Men in the sun*, London, 1978).

Khalīfah, Saḥar *ᶜAbbād al-shams* ('Sunflower'), Beirut, 1980.

Lam naᶜud jawāriya lakum ('We are no longer your slaves'), Beirut, 1974.

Mudhakkirāt imraʾah ghayr wāqiᶜiyyah ('Memoirs of an unrealistic woman'), Beirut, 1986.

Al-ṣubār ('Wild thorns'), Beirut, 1976.

Khayyāṭ, Najāʾ *Makhāḍ al-ṣamt* ('Labour pains of silence'), Jeddah, 1966.

al-Malāʾikah, Nāzik *Maʾsāt al-ḥayāh* ('Life's tragedy'), Baghdad, 1945.

Al-shaẓāyā wa 'l-ramād ('Splinters and ashes'), Beirut, 1949.

Marrāsh, Marianna *Bint Fikr* ('Daughter of thought'), Beirut, 1893.

Naṣrallah, Emily *Al-Iqlāᶜ ᶜaks al-ẓaman*, Beirut, 1981 (tr. into English as *Flight against time*, Montreal, 1987).

Nisāʾ rāʾidāt ('Pioneering women'), Beirut, 1986.

Tilka 'l-dhikrayāt ('Those memories'), Beirut, 1980.

Ṭuyūr Aylūl ('September birds'), Beirut, 1962.

Qābil, Thurayyā *Awẓān bākiyah* ('Weeping metres'), Beirut, 1972.

Qalamāwī, Suhayr *Aḥādīth jaddatī* ('My grandmother's tales'), Cairo, 1935.

Alf laylah wa laylah ('One thousand and one nights'), Cairo, 1943.

Qurrāᶜah, Saniyyah *Umm al-mulūk. Hind Bint ᶜUtba* ('The mother of kings. Hind Bint Utba'), Cairo, 1956.

ᶜArūs al-ẓuhd. Rabīᶜah al-ᶜAdawiyyah ('The bride of austerity: Rabiᶜa al-ᶜAdawiyyah'), Cairo, 1960.

Rifᶜat, Alīfah *Ḥawwāʾ taᶜūd bi Ādam ilā 'l-jannah* ('Eve takes Adam back to paradise'), Cairo, 1975.

Distant view of a minaret, London, 1984.

Man yakūn al-rajul? ('Who will be the man?'), Cairo, 1981.

al-Saʿdāwī, Nawāl *Imraʾah ʿind nuqṭat al-ṣifr*, Cairo, 1975 (tr. into English as *Woman at point zero*, London 1983; tr. into French as *Ferdaous: une voix à l'enfer*, 1981).

Imraʾatān fī imraʾah, 1975 (tr. into English as *Two women in one*, London, 1985).

Mawt al-rajul al-waḥīd ʿalā 'l-arḍ ('The death of the only man on earth', 1974; tr. into English as *God dies by the Nile*, London, 1985).

Mudhakkirātī fī sijn al-nisāʾ 1983 (tr. into English as *Memoirs from the women's prison*, London, 1986).

Suqūṭ al-imām, Cairo, 1988 (tr. into English as *The fall of the Imam*, London, 1989).

al-Ṣaḥrāʾ, Rīm *Zahrat al-ḥanān* ('The flower of tenderness'), 1979.

Samārah, Nuhā *Al-Ṭāwilāt ʿāshat akthar min Amīn* ('The tables lived longer than Amin'), Beirut, 1981.

Samīrah, Bint al-Jazīrah al-ʿArabiyyah *Barīq ʿaynayk* ('The gleam of your eyes'), Jeddah, 1963.

al-Sammān, Ghādah *ʿAynāk qadarī* ('Your eyes are my destiny'), Beirut, 1962.

Kawābīs Bayrūt ('Beirut nightmares'), Beirut, 1980.

Layl al-ghurabāʾ ('Night of the strangers'), Beirut, 1966.

Al-Sibāḥah fī buḥayrat al-shayṭan ('Swimming in the lake of the devil'), 1974.

al-Saqqāf, Khayriyyah *An tubḥir naḥwa 'l-abʿād* ('Let her take off into the blue'), Beirut, 1982.

'Qiṣṣat al-wāqiʿ' ('A true story'), Riyadh, 1979.

al-Shaykh, Ḥanān *Ḥikāyat Zahrah*, 1980 (tr. into English as *The story of Zahra*, London, 1986; tr. into French as *L'histoire de Zahra*, Paris, 1985).

Misk al-ghazāl, Beirut, 1988 (tr. into English as *Women of sand and myrrh*, London, 1989).

Wardat al-ṣaḥrāʾ, ('Desert rose'), Beirut, 1982.

Shākir, ʿAzzah Fuʾād *Ashriʿat al-layl* ('The sails of night'), Beirut, 1978.

Ṣidqī, Jāẓibiyyah *Wa bakā qalbī* ('My heart wept'), Cairo, 1957.

al-Sudīrī, Sulṭānah *ʿAynāya fidāk* ('My eyes are your ransom'), Beirut, 1963.

al-Taymūriyyah, ʿĀʾishah *Mirʾāt al-taʿammul fī 'l-umūr* ('The mirror of contemplation'), Cairo, 1892?

Natāʾij al-aḥwāl fī 'l-aqwāl wa 'l-afʿāl ('The results of circumstances in words and deeds'), 1888.

Ḥilyat al-ṭirāz (Embroidered ornaments'), 1909.

Ṭūqān, Fadwā *Amām al-bāb al-mughlaq* ('Before the locked gate'), 1967.

Aʿṭinā ḥubban ('Give us love'), 1960.

Al-Fidāʾī wa 'l-arḍ ('The freedom fighter and the land'), 1968.

Kābūs al-layl wa 'l-nahār ('The nightmare of night and day'), 1974.

Wajadtuhā ('I found her'), 1957.

Waḥdī maʿa 'l-ayyām ('Alone with the days'), 1955.

ʿUsayrān, Laylā *Qalʿat al-usṭa* ('Usta's citadel'), Beirut 1979.

al-Yāzijī, Wardah *Ḥadīqat al-ward* ('Rose garden'), 1867.

al-Zayd, Mūzah 'Ṭawāhā 'l-nisyānʾ ('She was forgotten'), in *Al-Waṭan*, Bahrain, 1955.

al-Zayyāt, Laṭīfah *Al-bāb al-maftūḥ* ('The open door'), Cairo, 1960.
Ziyādah, Mayy *ᶜĀʾishat Taymūr: shāᶜirat al-ṭalīᶜah* ('Aisha al-Taymur: the poet of the vanguard'), Cairo, 1926.

B. Arabic secondary sources

al-ᶜĀssimi, Malikah 'Al-Hikāyāt al-shaᶜbiyyah: ḥikāyāt al-nisāʾ', unpublished thesis for Doctorat du 3eme. Cycle at Muhammad V University, Rabat, 1987.
Ibrāhīm, Emily Fāris *Adībāt lubnāniyyāt*, Beirut, n.d.
al-Jayyūsī, Salmā al-Khaḍrā 'Al-marʾah wa ṣūrat al-marʾah ᶜinda Nāzik al-Malāʾikah' in *Nāzik al-Malāʾikah. Dirāsāt fīʾl-shᶜir wa 'l-shāᶜirah*, Kuwait, 1986.
Muḥammad, Fatḥiyyah *Balāghat al-nisāʾ fī 'l-qarn al-ᶜishrīn* ('Women's eloquence in the twentieth century'), Cairo, 1920.
Ṣalīḥ, Laylā *Adab al-marʾah fī 'l-Kuwayt*, Kuwait, 1978.
Adab al-marʾah fī 'l-jazīrah al-ᶜarabiyyah wa 'l-khalīj, Kuwait, 1982.
al-Shārūnī, Yūsuf *Al-laylah al-thāniyah baᶜda 'l-alf* ('The one thousand and second night'), Cairo, 1975.
Somekh, Sasson 'Al-ᶜilāqāt al-naṣṣiyyah fī 'l-niẓām al-adabī al-wāḥidʾ, *Al-Karmil*, Haifa, 7, 1986.

C. Secondary sources in European languages

Abu-Lughod, Lila *Veiled sentiments: honor and poetry in a Bedouin society*, Berkeley, 1986.
Badran, Margot and Cooke, Miriam *Opening the gates. A century of Arab feminist writing*, London/Bloomington, 1990.
Booth, Marilyn 'Mayy Ziyadah and the feminist perspective in Egypt 1908–1931', unpublished B.A.Hons. Thesis, Harvard University, 1974.
Cooke, Miriam *War's other voices: women writers on the Lebanese civil war*, Cambridge, 1988.
Eagleton, Mary, *Feminist literary theory. A reader*, Oxford/NY, 1986.
Gilbert, Sandra M. 'Soldier's heart: literary men, literary women, and the Great War', *Signs: Journal of Culture and Society*, Spring, 1983.
Gilman, Charlotte Perkins 'The yellow wallpaper' in *New England Magazine*, 1892.
Kilpatrick, Hilary 'Women and literature in the Arab world' in Mineke Schlipper, ed. *Unheard words. Women and literature in Africa, the Arab world, Asia, the Caribbean and Latin America*, London, 1985.
Mikhail, Mona N. *Images of Arab women*, Washington, 1979.
Moers, Ellen *Literary women. The great writers*, New York, 1976.
el-Rabie, Mahmoud Bikheet, 'Women writers and critics in modern Egypt 1888–1963', unpublished PhD thesis, School of Oriental and African Studies, London University, 1965.

Showalter, Elaine *A literature of their own: British novelists from Brontë to Lessing*, Princeton, 1979.
Suleyman, Michael 'Changing attitudes to women in Egypt. The role of fiction in women's magazines', *Middle Eastern Studies*, 14 (1981).

14: POETRY IN THE VERNACULAR

A. Texts

ʿAbd al-Bāqī, Samīr *al-Nashīd al-faqīr ʿan Bāblū Nīrūdā*, Cairo, 1976.
ʿAbd al-Jalīl, Fāyiq *Dīwān*, vol. I, Kuwait, 1982.
ʿAbdallāh, ʿAllām *Sakkay al-ʿaṭash*, Bahrain, 1981.
al-Abnūdī, ʿAbd al-Raḥmān *Aḥmad Ismāʿīn*, Cairo, 1972.
al-Arḍ wa'l-ʿiyāl, Cairo, 1964.
Baʿda 'l-taḥiyyah wa'l-salām, Cairo, 1975.
Fuṣūl, Cairo, 1975.
Jawābāt Ḥurājī al-quṭṭ al-ʿāmil fī'l-sadd al-ʿālī ilā zawjatihi Fāṭinah Aḥmad ʿAbd al-Ghaffār fī Jabalāyat al-Fār, Cairo, 1969.
Ṣamt al-jaras, Cairo, 1975.
al-Zaḥmah, Cairo, 1967.
Abū'l-Ṣādiq *Thawriyyāt: shiʿr al-muqāwamah al-shaʿbī al-filasṭīnī*, Beirut, n.d.
ʿAql, Saʿīd *Yāra*, Beirut, 1961.
ʿAwaḍ, Lūwīs *Balūtūlānd [Plutoland] wa qaṣā'id ukhrā*, Cairo, 1947.
al-ʿAwnī, Muḥammad ʿAbdallāh *Min al-shiʿr al-Najdī: Dīwān al-shāʿir Muḥammad ʿAbdallāh al-ʿAwnī*, ed. ʿAbdallāh b. Khālid al-Ḥātam, Kuwait, 1984.
al-ʿAzab, Yusrī *Taghrībat ʿAbrazāq al-Hilālī*, Cairo, 1984.
al-Dawīsh, ʿAbdallāh ʿAbd al-ʿAzīz, ed. *Dīwān al-Zuhayrī: majmūʿah min al-mawāwīl al-mashhūrah*, Kuwait, n.d.
al-Dawsirī, Musaffir *Li-ʿuyūnik aqūl*, Kuwait, 1982.
al-Ghāmidī, ʿAbd al-Raḥmān *Ḥamasāt jarīḥ*, Jedda, 1983, 3rd pr., 1986.
al-Layl wa'l-ḥirmān, Jedda, 1984, 1987.
Ghuṣayn, Jūzīf *Nawwār*, Beirut, 1962.
Ḥaddād, Fu'ād *Aḥrār warā' al-quḍbān*, Cairo, 1952.
Bi quwwat al-fallāḥīn wa bi quwwat al-ʿummāl, Cairo, 1967.
al-Ḥaḍrah al-zakiyyah, Cairo, 1985.
Min nūr al-khayāl wa ṣunʿ al-ajyāl fī tārīkh al-Qāhirah, Cairo, 1982.
al-Shāṭir Ḥasan, Cairo, 1984.
Ḥajjāj, Fu'ād *Yawmiyyāt ʿAbd al-ʿĀl*, Cairo, 1984.
al-Ḥamūd, Nawwār ʿAbd al-Qādir *Naqsh al-ḥannah*, Kuwait, n.d.
al-Ḥārdallū, Sayyid Aḥmad *ʿArḍaḥāl min jumlat ahālī al-sāfil yuwṣal: masraḥiyyah shiʿriyyah bi'l-ʿāmmiyyah al-sūdāniyyah*, Khartoum, 1980.
Ghadan naltaqī, Cairo, 1960.
Misdār . . . ʿashān baladī, Khartoum, 1978.
Muqaddimāt, Beirut, 1970.
Niḥnā, Khartoum, 1978.
Sindabād fī bilād al-sajam wa'l-rumād, Khartoum, 1978.

al-Ḥarshānī, Shanūf Jāsim *Dīwān*, Kuwait, 1985.

al-Ḥātam, ʿAbdallāh b. Khālid, ed. *Khiyār mā yultaqaṭ min shiʿr al-nabaṭ*, 2 vols, Kuwait, 3rd pr., 1981.

Ibn Subayyil, ʿAbdallāh b. Ḥamūd *Min al-shiʿr al-Najdī: Dīwān al-shāʿir ʿAbdallāh b. Ḥamūd b. Subayyil*, ed. ʿAbdallāh b. Khālid al-Ḥātam, Kuwait, 1984.

Ibn Sulṭān, al-Sharīf Manṣūr *Anīn wa ḥanīn*, Jedda, n.d.

al-Iryānī, Muṭahhar *Fawqa al-jabal*, Cairo, n.d.

Jāhīn, Ṣalāḥ *ʿAn al-qamar wa'l-ṭīn*, Cairo, 1961.

Anghām Siptimbiriyyah, Cairo, 1984.

Dawāwīn Ṣalāḥ Jāhīn, Cairo, 1977.

Kalimat salām, Cairo, 1955.

Mawwāl ʿashān al-qanāl, Cairo, 1956.

Qaṣāqīṣ waraq, Cairo, 2nd pr., 1967.

Rubāʿiyyāt, Cairo, 1962.

Jalāl, Muḥammad ʿUthmān *al-Arbaʿ riwāyāt min nakhb al-tiyātrāt*, Cairo, 1307 AH [1889/90].

Khalīfah, ʿAlī ʿAbdallāh *ʿAṭash al-nakhīl: mawāwīl*, 2nd pr., n.p., 1974.

al-Khayyāt, Muḥsin *Ḥikāyat Bahiyyah*, Cairo, 1986.

al-Lumayyiʿ, Sālim *Nujūm al-thurayyā*, Kuwait, n.d.

al-Najjār, Muḥammad *Majmūʿat al-azjāl*, Cairo, 1318 AH [1900/01].

Najm, Aḥmad Fuʾād *Baladī wa ḥabībatī: qaṣāʾid min al-muʿtaqal*, Beirut, 3rd pr., 1981.

ʿĪshī yā Miṣr, Beirut, 1979.

Ṣuwar min al-ḥayāh waʾl-sijn, Cairo, 1964.

Ṭaharān, Beirut, 1979.

Yaʿīsh ahl baladī: ashʿār miṣriyyah, Beirut, 5th pr., 1981.

Nakhlah, Rashīd *Dīwān Rashīd Nakhlah fīʾl-zajal*, ed. Amīn Nakhlah, Beirut, 1964.

al-Nawwāb, Muẓaffar *Lil-rāyil wa Ḥamid*, Beirut, n.d. [1969].

Qāʿūd, Fuʾād *al-Mawāwīl: shiʿr*, Cairo, 1978.

al-Rabīʿ, ʿAbd al-Raḥmān *Dīwān al-shiʿr al-shaʿbī*, Kuwait, n.d.

al-Riyāshī, Manṣūr *Nafaḥāt min Lubnān*, Beirut, 1973.

Sābā, Asʿad *Darb al-hawā*, Beirut, 1957.

al-Saʿīd, Ṭalāl ʿUthmān *Dumūʿ tabtasim*, Kuwait, 4th pr., 1983.

Ṣāliḥ, al-Jīlī Muḥammad *Dīwān Aḥājī ʾl-khirtīt*, Khartoum, n.d.

al-Samarrāʾī, ʿĀmir Rashīd, ed. *Mawwālāt Baghdādiyyah*, Baghdad, 1974.

al-Samāwī, ʿAzīz *Lawn al-thalj wa'l-ward bi'l-layl*, Beirut, 1980.

al-Samāwī, Shākir *al-ʿIshq wa'l-mawt wa binādam*, Damascus, 1984.

Sharaf al-Dīn, Aḥmad Ḥusayn, ed. *al-Ṭarāʾif al-mukhtārah min shiʿr al-Khafanjī waʾl-Qārah*, n.p., 1970.

Shawqī, Aḥmad *al-Shawqiyyāt al-majhūlah*, ed. M. Ṣabrī, 2 vols, 2nd edn, Beirut, 1979.

Ṣiddīq, Hāshim *Jawāb musajjal l'il-balad: ashʿār sūdāniyyah 1976–1985*, Khartoum, n.d.

Nabtā ḥabībatī: masraḥiyyah shiʿriyyah, Beirut, 1986.

al-Zaman wa'l-riḥlah, Khartoum, n.d.

Surūr, Najīb *Ā yā layl yā qamar: maʾsāh shiʿriyyah fī thalāthat fuṣūl*, Cairo, 1968.

Minayn ajīb al-nās, Cairo, 2nd pr., 1984.
Qūlū li-ᶜayn al-shams, Cairo, 1970.
Yāsīn wa Bahiyyah: riwāyah shiᶜriyyah, Cairo, 1965.
Ṭrād, Mīshāl *ᶜArabiyyī mukhallaᶜā*, Beirut, 1986.
Dūlāb, Beirut, 1957.
al-Ghurāb al-aᶜwar, Beirut, 1986.
Julnār, Beirut, 1951.
Kās ᶜaʾ shafāf al-dinī, Beirut, 1972.
Laysh, Beirut, 1964.
al-Tūnisī, Maḥmūd Bayram *al-Aᶜmāl al-kāmilah li Bayram al-Tūnisī*, ed. Rushdī Ṣāliḥ, I–X, Cairo, 1975–86.
Muntakhabāt al-Shabāb, ed. ᶜAbd al-ᶜAziz al-Ṣadr, II, Cairo, 1923.
ᶜUways, Sulaymān *Mawāwīl rāfiḍah*, Beirut, n.d. [1980].
al-Zaᶜannī, ᶜUmar *ᶜUmar al-Zaᶜannī: Mūliyīr al-sharq*, ed. al-Zaᶜannī al-Ṣaghīr, Beirut, 1980.

B. Arabic secondary sources

ᶜAbbūd, Mārūn *al-Shiᶜr al-ᶜāmmī*, Beirut, 1968.
ᶜAbduh, Ibrāhīm *Abū Naẓẓārah: Imām al-ṣaḥāfah al-fukāhiyyah al-muṣawwarah wa-ẓaᶜīm al-masraḥ fī Miṣr 1839–1912*, Cairo, 1953.
ᶜĀbidīn, ᶜAbd al-Majīd 'al-Ḥārdallū: Amīr al-shiᶜr al-shaᶜbī fī'l-Sūdān', *al-Majallah* 70 (Nov. 1962), pp. 40–5.
al-Ahwānī, ᶜAbd al-ᶜAzīz *al-Zajal fī'l-Andalus*, Cairo, 1957.
al-ᶜAllāf, ᶜAbd al-Karīm, ed. *al-Mawwāl al-Baghdādī*, Baghdad, 1963.
Āmāl/Promesses, Special Issue on *al-Shiᶜr al-malḥūn*, Algiers, 1970.
al-ᶜAqrab, ᶜAlī and al-Sanūsī Bilāl, eds *al-Shiᶜr al-shaᶜbī fī maᶜrakat al-inqādh*, Chicago, 1986.
ᶜAwlaqī, Saᶜīd 'Ḥadīth maᶜa ᶜAbdallāh Salām Nājī', *al-Ḥikmah* (Sanaa) VI no. 49 (April 1976), pp. 82–90.
al-Baghdādī, Muḥammad 'Lā Uḥibb an akūn al-shāᶜir al-Ṣaᶜīdī' (interview with ᶜAbd al-Raḥmān al-Abnūdī), *Ṣabāḥ al-Khayr* 1581 (24 April 1986), pp. 42–45, 62.
al-Bardūnī, ᶜAbdallāh *Funūn al-adab al-shaᶜbī fī'l-Yaman*, Beirut, 2nd pr., 1988.
Riḥlah fī'l-shiᶜr al-Yamanī qadīman wa-ḥadīthan, Beirut, 3rd pr., 1978.
Bilfaqīh, ᶜAbdallāh ᶜUmar 'Al-Miḥḍār yubashshirunā bi'l-jadīd', *al-Ḥikmah* (Sanaa) VI no. 50 (May 1976), pp. 77–81.
al-Ghunayy, ᶜAbd Rabbih *Dirāsāt fī'l-adab al-shaᶜbī*, pts 1–3, Benghazi, Beirut, 1968.
al-Ḥibshī, ᶜAbdallāh Muḥammad *al-Adab al-Yamanī ᶜaṣr khurūj al-atrāk al-awwal min al-Yaman*, Beirut, 1986.
Ibn Khaldūn, ᶜAbd al-Raḥmān *Muqaddimat al-ᶜallāmah Ibn Khaldūn*, Beirut, 5th pr., 1982.
Ibn Khamīs, ᶜAbdallāh b. Muḥammad *Rāshid al-Khalawī*, 2nd. pr., n.p., 1982.

Ibn al-Shaykh, al-Tallī *Dawr al-shiʿr al-shaʿbī al-Jazāʾirī fī'l-thawrah 1830–1945*, Algiers, 1983.
Ismāʿīl ʿIzz al-Dīn *al-Shiʿr al-qawmī fī'l-Sūdān*, Beirut, 1968.
al-Jabbūrī, Jamīl *Ḥabaẓ Būẓ fī tārīkh ṣaḥāfat al-hazl wa'l-kārīkatūr fī'l-ʿIrāq*, Baghdad, 1986.
al-Jammāl, Aḥmad Ṣādiq *al-Adab al-ʿāmmī fī Miṣr fī'l-ʿaṣr al-Mamlūkī*, Cairo, 1966.
al-Khāqānī, ʿAlī *Funūn al-adab al-shaʿbī*, pts 1–3, Baghdad, 1962.
al-Maqāliḥ, ʿAbd al-ʿAzīz *Shiʿr al-ʿāmmiyyah fī'l-Yaman*, Beirut, 1978.
Shuʿarāʾ min al-Yaman, Beirut, 1983.
al-Marzūqī, Muḥammad *al-Shiʿr al-shaʿbī wa'l-intifāḍāt al-taḥarruriyah*, Tunis, 1971.
al-Naqqāsh, Farīdah 'Ẓāhirat al-shāʿir wa'l-shaykh', in A. F. Najm, *Baladī wa-ḥabībatī: qaṣāʾid min al-muʿtaqal*, Beirut, 3rd pr., 1981, pp. 3–25.
al-Quṣūṣ, Jiryis 'al-Ḥayāh al-adabiyyah fī sharq al-Urdun, *al-Risālah* 151 (25 May 1936), pp. 865–7.
al-Rabīʿān, Yaḥyā, ed. *Ibn Liʿbūn: ḥayātuhu wa-shiʿruhu*, Kuwait, 1982.
Riyāḍ, Ḥusayn Maẓlūm and Muṣṭafā Muḥammad al-Ṣabāḥī *Tārīkh adab al-shaʿb: nashʾatuh, taṭawwuruh, aʿlāmuh*, Cairo, 1936.
Ṣaʿb, Wilyam 'al-Adab fī'l-zajal', *al-Adīb* II no 1 (Jan. 1943), pp. 41–4.
al-Shamarī, Rabīʿ *al-ʿArūḍ fī'l-shiʿr al-shaʿbī al-ʿIrāqī*, Baghdad, 1987.
Shukrī, Ghālī *Shiʿrunā al-ḥadīth: ilā ayn?*, Cairo, 1968.
Wuhaybah, Munīr Ilyās (al-Khāzinī al-Ghassānī) *al-Zajal: tārīkhuh, adabuh, aʿlāmuh qadīman wa-ḥadīthan*, Ḥarīṣā, 1952.

C. Secondary sources in European languages

Badawi, M. M. *A Critical introduction to modern Arabic poetry*, Cambridge, 1975.
Booth, Marilyn *Bayram al-Tunisi's Egypt: social criticism and narrative strategies*, Exeter, 1990.
'Colloquial Arabic Poetry, Politics, and the Press in Modern Egypt', *International Journal of Middle East Studies*, 24 No. 3 (August 1992).
'Writing to be heard: colloquial Arabic verse and the press in Egypt, (1877–1930), *ARCE Newsletter* 140 (Winter 1987/1988), pp. 1–6.
Cachia, Pierre 'The Egyptian *Mawwāl*: its ancestry, its development, and its present forms', *JAL* VIII (1977), pp. 77–103.
Cour, A. 'Constantine en 1802 dʾaprés une chanson populaire du Cheikh Belqasem Er-Rahmouni El-Haddad', *Revue africaine* 60 no. 299 (2nd trim. 1919), pp. 224–40.
'La poésie populaire politique au temps de l'ḿir 'Abdelqader', *Revue africaine* 59 nos. 296–297 (3rd and 4th trim. 1918), pp. 458–93.
Desparmet, J. 'La chanson d'Alger pendant la Grande Guerre', *Revue africaine* 73 nos. 350–351 (1st and 2nd trim. 1932), pp. 54–83.
'L'entrée des français à Alger par le Cheikh Abdelkadir, *Revue africaine* 71 nos. 344–45 (3rd and 4th trim. 1930), pp. 225–56.

Gliouiz, Azaiez 'La presse humoristique tunisienne de ses origines jusquʾen 1923', diss. 3rd cycle, University of Paris III, 1978.
Grotzfeld, Heinz 'L'expérience de Saʿīd ʿAql: l'arabe libanais employé comme langue littéraire', *Orientalia Suecana* (Uppsala) 22 (1973), pp. 37–51.
Haydar, Adnan 'The development of Lebanese zajal: genre, meter and verbal duel', ms. courtesy of the author.
Jayyusi, Salma Khadra *Trends and movements in modern Arabic poetry*, 2 vols, Leiden, 1977.
Kheir Beik, Kamal *Le mouvement moderniste de la poésie arabe contemporaine*, Paris, 1978.
Lecerf, Jean 'Littérature dialectale et renaissance Arabe moderne', *Bulletin d'études orientales* II (1932), pp. 179–258, and III (1933), pp. 44–171.
Lyons, M. C. and Maalouf, E. *The poetic vocabulary of Michel Trad*, Beirut, 1969.
Serjeant, R. B. *South Arabian poetry I: Poetry and prose from Hadramawt*, London, 1951.
Sowayan, Saad Abdullah *Nabaṭi poetry: The oral poetry of Arabia*, Berkeley, 1985.
Stern, Samuel, *Hispano-Arabic strophic poetry*, Oxford, 1974.

INDEX

CPSIA information can be obtained at www.ICGtesting.com
Printed in the USA
LVOW080345250513

335351LV00002B/19/A